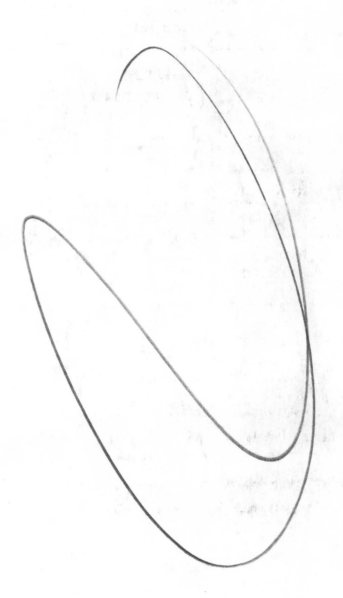

Glencoe

SCIENCE INTERACTIONS

Course 3

With Features by:
NATIONAL
GEOGRAPHIC
SOCIETY

GLENCOE
McGraw-Hill

New York, New York   Columbus, Ohio   Woodland Hills, California   Peoria, Illinois

Science Interactions

Student Edition

Teacher Wraparound Edition

Science Discovery Activities

Teacher Classroom Resources

Laboratory Manual

Study Guide

Section Focus Transparencies

Teaching Transparencies

Performance Assessment

Performance Assessment in the Science Classroom

Computer Test Bank: IBM and Macintosh Versions

Spanish Resources

English/Spanish Audiocassettes

Science and Technology Videodisc Series

Integrated Science Videodisc Program

MindJogger Videoquizzes

Glencoe/McGraw-Hill

*A Division of The **McGraw·Hill** Companies*

Series Design: DECODE, Inc.

Send all inquiries to:
Glencoe/McGraw-Hill
936 Eastwind Drive
Westerville, OH 43081

ISBN 0-02-827435-0

Printed in the United States of America.

3 4 5 6 7 8 9 10 071/043 06 05 04 03 02 01 00 99 98

With Features by:

NATIONAL
GEOGRAPHIC
SOCIETY

Bill Aldridge, M.S.
Director—Division of Science Education Solutions
Airborne Research and Services, Inc.
Fredericksburg, Virginia

Russell Aiuto, Ph.D.
Educational Consultant
Frederick, Maryland

Albert Kaskel, M.Ed.
Biology Teacher, Emeritus
Evanston Township High School
Evanston, Illinois

Jack Ballinger, Ed.D.
Professor of Chemistry
St. Louis Community College at Florissant Valley
St. Louis, Missouri

Craig Kramer, M.A.
Physics Teacher
Bexley High School
Bexley, Ohio

Anne Barefoot, A.G.C.
Physics and Chemistry Teacher, Emeritus
Whiteville High School
Whiteville, North Carolina

Edward Ortleb, A.G.C.
Science Consultant
St. Louis Board of Education
St. Louis, Missouri

Linda Crow, Ed.D.
Associate Professor
University of Houston—Downtown
Houston, Texas

Susan Snyder, M.S.
Earth Science Teacher
Jones Middle School
Upper Arlington, Ohio

Ralph M. Feather, Jr., M.Ed.
Science Department Chair
Derry Area School District
Derry, Pennsylvania

Paul W. Zitzewitz, Ph.D.
Professor of Physics
University of Michigan-Dearborn
Dearborn, Michigan

With Features by:

NATIONAL GEOGRAPHIC SOCIETY

The National Geographic Society, founded in 1888 for the increase and diffusion of geographic knowledge, is the world's largest nonprofit scientific and educational organization. Since its earliest days, the Society has used sophisticated communication technologies, from color photography to holography, to convey geographic knowledge to a worldwide membership. The Education Products Division supports the Society's mission by developing innovative educational programs—ranging from traditional print materials to multimedia programs including CD-ROMS, videodiscs, and software.

Consultants

Chemistry

Richard J. Merrill
Director,
Project Physical Science
Associate Director, Institute
for Chemical Education
University of California
Berkeley, California

Robert W. Parry, Ph.D.
Dist. Professor of Chemistry
University of Utah
Salt Lake City, Utah

Earth Science

Allan A. Ekdale, Ph.D.
Professor of Geology
University of Utah
Salt Lake City, Utah

Janifer Mayden
Aerospace Education Specialist
NASA
Washington, DC

James B. Phipps, Ph.D.
Professor of Geology
and Oceanography
Gray's Harbor College
Aberdeen, Washington

Life Science

David M. Armstrong, Ph.D.
Professor of Environmental,
Population and
Organismic Biology
University of
Colorado-Boulder
Boulder, Colorado

Mary D. Coyne, Ph.D.
Professor of Biological Sciences
Wellesley College
Wellesley, Massachusetts

David Futch, Ph.D.
Professor of Biology
San Diego State University
San Diego, California

Richard D. Storey, Ph.D.
Associate Professor of Biology
Colorado College
Colorado Springs, Colorado

Physics

David Haaes, Ph.D.
Professor of Physics
North Carolina State University
North Carolina

Patrick Hamill, Ph.D.
Professor of Physics
San Jose State University
San Jose, California

Middle School Science

Garland E. Johnson
Science and Education
Consultant
Fresno, California

Multicultural

Thomas Custer
Coordinator of Science
Anne Arundel County Schools
Annapolis, Maryland

Francisco Hernandez
Science Department Chair
John B. Hood Middle School
Dallas, Texas

Carol T. Mitchell
Instructor
Elementary Science Methods
College of Teacher Education
University of Omaha at Omaha
Omaha, Nebraska

Karen Muir, Ph.D.
Lead Instructor
Department of Social and
Behavioral Sciences
Columbus State
Community College
Columbus, Ohio

Reading

Elizabeth Gray, Ph.D.
Reading Specialist
Heath City Schools
Heath, Ohio
Adjunct Professor
Otterbein College
Westerville, Ohio

Timothy Heron, Ph.D.
Professor, Department
of Educational
Services & Research
The Ohio State University
Columbus, Ohio

Barbara Pettegrew, Ph.D.
Director of Reading
Study Center
Assistant Professor
of Education
Otterbein College
Westerville, Ohio

LEP

Ross M. Arnold
Magnet School Coordinator
Van Nuys Junior High
Van Nuys, California

Linda E. Heckenberg
Director
Eisenhower Program
Van Nuys, California

**Harold Frederick
Robertson, Jr.**
Science Resource Teacher
LAUSD Science Materials Center
Van Nuys, California

Safety

Robert Tatz, Ph.D.
Instructional Lab Supervisor
Department of Chemistry
The Ohio State University
Columbus, Ohio

Reviewers

Lillian Valeria Jordan Alston
Science Consultant
Institute of Government
University of North Carolina
Chapel Hill, North Carolina

Jamye Barnes
Science Teacher
Prescott Middle School
Prescott, Arkansas

Betty Bordelon
Science Teacher
Haynes Middle School
Metairie, Louisiana

James Carbaugh
Science Teacher
Greencastle Middle School
Greencastle, Pennsylvania

Elberta Casey
8th Grade Earth Science Teacher
Crawford Middle School
Lexington, Kentucky

Linda Culpeper
Science Department Chairperson
Piedmont Open Middle School
Charlotte, North Carolina

Nancy Donohue
General Science Teacher
Emerson Junior High School
Yonkers, New York

Susan Duhaime
5th/6th Grade Science Teacher
Assistant Principal
St. Anthony School
Manchester, New Hampshire

Melville Fuller
Professor of Science Education
Department of Teacher Education
University of Arkansas
at Little Rock
Little Rock, Arkansas

Janet Grush
7th Grade Science/Math Teacher
Wirth Middle School
Cahokia, Illinois

Joanne Hardy
7th Grade Science/Social
Studies/Language Arts Teacher
Memorial Middle School
Conyers, Georgia

Nancy J. Hopkins
Gifted/Talented Coordinating
Teacher for Middle School Science
Morrill Elementary
San Antonio, Texas

Amy Jacobs
7th Grade Life Science Teacher
Morton Middle School
Lexington, Kentucky

Rebecca King
Chemistry Teacher
New Hanover High School
Wilmington, North Carolina

Kenneth Krause
Science Teacher
Harriet Tubman Middle School
Portland, Oregon

Martha Scully Lai
Science Teacher
Department Chairperson
Highland High School
Medina, Ohio

William Lavinghousez, Jr.
MAGNET Program Director
Ronald McNair MAGNET School
Cocoa, Florida

Fred J. Mayberry
Earth/Life Science Teacher
Department Chairperson
Vernon Junior High School
Harlingen, Texas

Susan Middlebrooks
7th Grade Science Teacher
Pulaski Heights Jr. High
Little Rock, Arkansas

Judy Nielsen
Middle School Science Teacher
Nyssa Middle School
Nyssa, Oregon

Chuck Porrazzo
Science Department Chairperson
Bronx Career Technical
Assistance Center
Junior High 145
New York, New York

Bonnie Keith Temple
8th Grade Science Teacher
Zebulon Middle School
Zebulon, North Carolina

James Todd
7th/8th Grade Science Teacher
East Hardin Middle School
Glendale, Kentucky

Deborah Tully
8th Grade Earth Science Teacher
Department Chairperson
Winburn Middle School
Lexington, Kentucky

Patsy Wagoner
6th Grade Science Teacher
Erwin Middle School
Salisbury, North Carolina

Marianne Wilson
Science-Health-Drug Coordinator
Pulaski County Special Schools
Sherwood, Arkansas

Ronald Wolfe
8th Grade Science Teacher
Project Discovery Teacher Leader
Beachwood Middle School
Beachwood, Ohio

Maurice Yaggi
Instructional Leader for Science
Wilton Public Schools
Wilton, Connecticut

SCIENCE INTERACTIONS
CONTENTS OVERVIEW
Course 3

UNIT
5

Observing the World Around You   564

Think big! With our busy lives on Earth, it's hard to
remember that there is an even larger world of planets,
stars, and galaxies, of which we are but one part.

UNIT 1

ELECTRICITY AND MAGNETISM 18

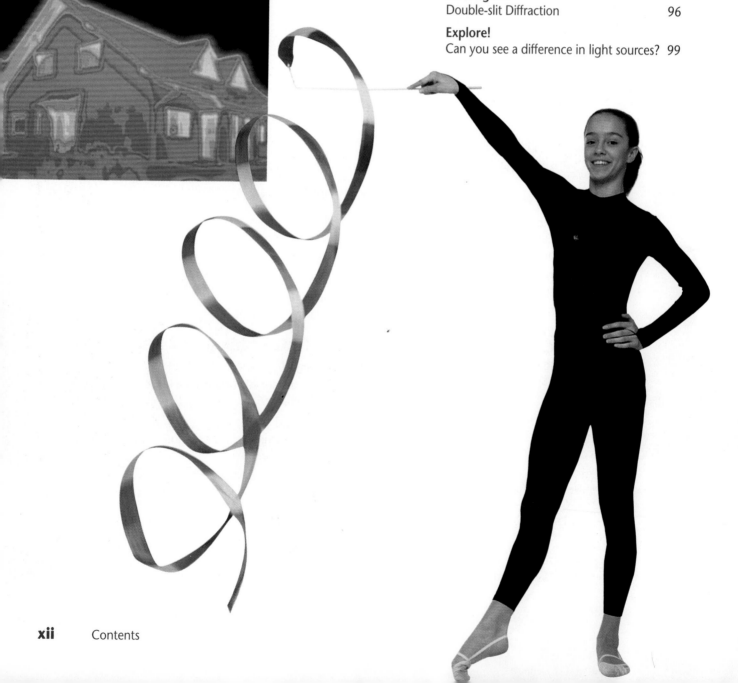

UNIT 2

ATOMS AND MOLECULES

108

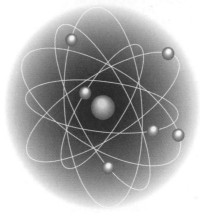

Chapter 8   Weather   240

Chapter 16   Geologic Time   502

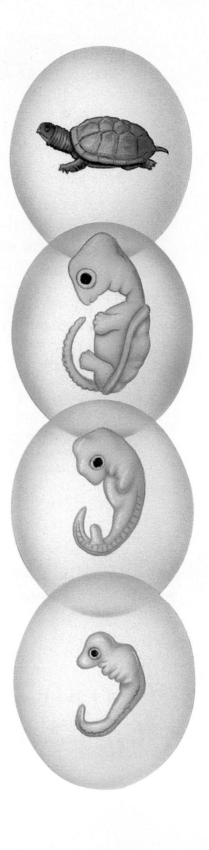

Chapter 17 Evolution of Life   534

observing THE WORLD around you

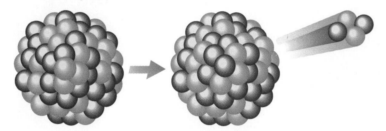

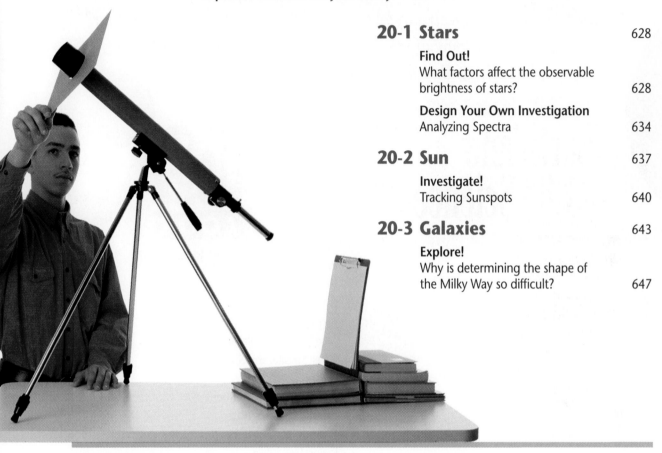

SCIENCE CONNECTIONS

Have you ever noticed that you really can't talk about eels without mentioning electricity? How is one science related to another? Expand your view of science through A CLOSER LOOK and Science Connections features in each chapter.

Earth and Life Science

Physics and Chemistry

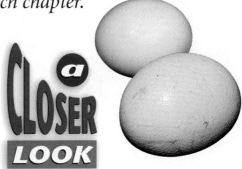

A CLOSER LOOK

Science is something that refuses to stay locked away in a laboratory. In both the Science and Society and the Technology features, you'll learn how science impacts the world you live in today. You may also be asked to think about science-related questions that will affect your life fifty years from now.

Science and Society

Technology Connection

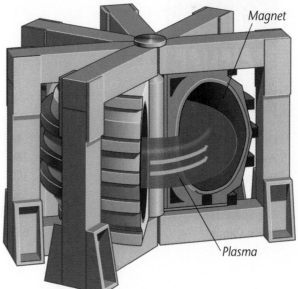

Magnet

Plasma

CROSS-CURRICULUM CONNECTIONS

With the EXPAND YOUR VIEW features at the end of each chapter, you'll quickly become aware that science is an important part of every subject you'll ever encounter in school. Read these features to learn how science has affected history, health, and even leisure time.

NATIONAL GEOGRAPHIC CONNECTIONS

As you begin each unit of Science Interactions, start by envisioning the big picture with the help of an exciting National Geographic Society illustration. Then look for the National Geographic SciFacts article in each unit to enrich and extend your understanding of science in the real world.

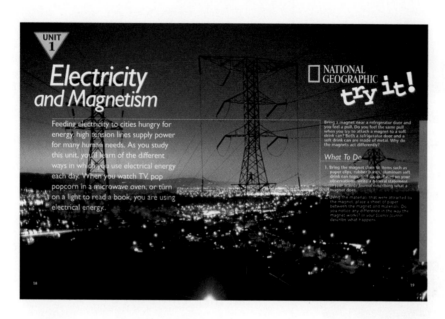

NATIONAL GEOGRAPHIC SOCIETY

Contents   **1**

SCIENCE: A Tool for Solving Problems

What is "scientific thinking"? Does it always require beakers, magnets, or graph paper? How is scientific thinking the same as other thinking? How is it different? Do you ever use scientific thinking when you're not at school?

Follow Lee, Erin, and the rest of their science class as they prepare for a competition called Science Challenge and learn more about scientific thinking. As they prepare for the Science Challenge, the class discovers that scientific thinking can help them not only in this competition, but throughout their entire lives.

Using What You Already Know

"I've been learning the periodic table for the Science Challenge," Lee told Ms. Borga and the rest of his science class. "I've memorized nearly all the elements!"

"That kind of knowledge helped this class win the school Science Challenge," Ms. Borga told him, "but you'll need more than that when we go to the regional Science Challenge in two weeks. The judges there will give you problems to solve, and you won't be able to rely on just pulling the answers out of your memory. To solve these problems, you'll need to know how to use what you've learned and how to think scientifically."

"Now we're in trouble!" Erin said. "How do you think scientifically?"

"Well, first tell me what science is," Ms. Borga asked. "Who remembers how we defined science?"

For a minute or two, everyone stared at the floor or out the window. Then Andy tentatively raised his hand. "You know, I think I remember. Science is a way of learning about things that happen in the natural world. When we understand how something works, we can use what we know to invent things or make things run more smoothly."

Ms. Borga said, "Can you think of an example?"

"Well, when you know how an engine works, you can design one that will use fuel more efficiently," Andy said.

Kisha raised her hand. "I remember an example. As scientists learn more about how our bodies work, they can make new medicines and devise new surgery techniques. They know more about what we should eat and how much exercise we should get, too."

Ms. Borga nodded. "That's basically it. Science is a way of learning about natural things and coming to appreciate them. The more we know and learn, the more we can enjoy the natural world. One way we learn is by using what we already know and applying it to new situations. Let's do an experiment to see how this works.

Find Out! ACTIVITY

Using What You Know to Find Out What You Don't.

In this activity, you'll work with a partner to test how flour, powdered sugar, and baking soda each react with water and with vinegar. Then you'll use what you learned about these reactions to identify an unknown powder. **CAUTION:** *Never taste any powder or substance in a scientific investigation. It could be poisonous.*

What To Do

1. *In your journal,* make a chart like the one below.

2. Pour flour into a shallow dish. Use a dropper to place a drop or two of water on the flour. Record what happens to the water when it hits the flour.

3. Use another dropper to drop vinegar on a different area of the flour. Record what happens.

4. Repeat Steps 2 and 3 using powdered sugar and then baking soda in place of the flour. Record your observations.

5. When you've completed all of your observations, ask your teacher for the final sample, the "unknown".

6. Examine the unknown sample and form a hypothesis about what it is. Record your hypothesis *in your Journal.*

7. Observe the reaction of the unknown with water and with vinegar. Record your observations and your conclusion about what the unknown sample is.

Conclude and Apply

1. Compare and contrast the reactions of each solid with water and vinegar.

2. Explain how you used the "known" to find out the "unknown."

Data and Observations		
	Reaction with Water	Reaction with Vinegar
Flour		
Powdered Sugar		
Baking Soda		

4   Science: A Tool for Solving Problems

■ Solving a Problem—Scientifically

"Now I see what you meant." Kisha said. "After we experimented to find out how the three powders reacted, we could look at the information we had gathered and figure out what the unknown sample was."

Lee nodded. "So science is a way of using what we know to find out things we don't know. That means we can use science to add to what we already know." He looked worried. "Will the judges at the Science Challenge expect us to use science to solve problems? Is that what you meant by 'thinking scientifically'?"

"Yes, but as you've already seen, it isn't that difficult," Ms. Borga reassured him. "Let's talk about different ways to solve problems scientifically. You've already done an experiment to solve a problem, using what you know to find out more."

One of Frederick McKinley Jones's refrigerated Trucks

Cool Science

Thanks to a self-taught engineer who was able to apply what he knew to solve a challenging problem, we have air conditioning to cool our cars and refrigerated trucks to ship our food.

In 1937 Frederick McKinley Jones, an African American who began his career as an auto mechanic, was tired of driving around in the Minneapolis summer heat. He thought there must be a way to put the air conditioning used to cool buildings into cars.

About the same time, Joseph Numero, the owner of a Minneapolis trucking company, had become frustrated with having truckloads of food spoil in the heat. A friend who knew both Jones and Numero got them together. Jones used his knowledge of shock-proof and vibration-proof gadgets to build a sturdy, light-weight air conditioning unit for Numero's trucks. The two men formed a very successful refrigeration company.

"Now suppose we're aeronautical engineers. We've designed a new shape for an airplane wing. Here's our question: 'Will this design increase the airflow over the wing?' We expect the answer to be 'yes.' That's our hypothesis, that the design will improve airflow. How could we test our hypothesis?"

"We could build a model of our new design," Erin suggested, "and see if it works better than the wing we're using now."

Ms. Borga nodded. "That's a scientific way to test our hypothesis:" make a model and see how it works. It's too difficult and too dangerous to put our new design on a real airplane and test it, so we make a model of the wing. Then we can test it under controlled conditions in an air tunnel."

■ Making a Model

"Will we need to make a model at the Science Challenge?" Andy asked. "Maybe we ought to, you know, practice."

Ms. Borga smiled. "Okay, here's a question you can answer using a model: 'What is the phase of the moon during a solar eclipse?' Remember that a solar eclipse occurs when the moon is in a position to block sunlight from reaching certain parts of Earth."

Model Aircraft

Orville and Wilbur Wright ran a bicycle shop in Dayton, Ohio. They studied everything that was known about flight and then applied it to their airplane designs. These amateur scientists created 200 models of airplane wings, tested each one in a wind tunnel, and recorded their results on a graph. The first airplane they built, in 1903, included the wing design that had performed best in their tests up to that point.

Each new wing design they created and each flight they attempted built on what they had learned from previous trials. The brothers persevered and were able to lengthen their flights from 12 seconds to 38 minutes, after which they had to land because they had run out of fuel!

What is the phase of the moon during a solar eclipse?

You can use models to gather information when an event or a process is too big, too small, or too difficult to study directly.

What To Do

1. Obtain a medium-sized ball (Earth), a small ball (moon), and a flashlight (sun).

2. Shine the flashlight on Earth. Then move the moon slowly around Earth to represent the moon's orbit.

3. When the sun, moon, and Earth are in a relationship that would result in a solar eclipse, observe and record the moon's phase. Record all of your observations and the answers to the questions that follow *in your Journal.*

Conclude and Apply

1. What is the phase of the moon during a solar eclipse?

2. What are at least two other questions you could answer using this model?

3. What questions did constructing this model bring up?

4. Why is a model the best way to answer this question?

■ Learning by Observing

"That wasn't so hard!" Andy admitted. "The model made it easier to see what was happening."

"Right! Models can be used to help you experimental. Now here's another problem to solve scientifically," Ms. Borga said. "'Is the hole in the ozone layer getting bigger?' What could our hypothesis be in this case?"

"The hole is getting bigger," Kisha said. "That would be my hypothesis."

"But we can't do an experiment or make a model of the ozone layer to test that hypothesis," Lee said. "Maybe there's an instrument you could use to measure the hole in the ozone layer. If there were such an instrument, we could measure the hole again in a few months to see if it changed. Maybe we could use the space shuttle or a satellite to photograph the ozone layer."

"That's another good example of scientific thinking." Ms. Borga told the class. "Observation is a key way to gather information and test a hypothesis. We can also use observation to form a hypothesis." She held up a chunk of rock. "For example, we could use observation and previous knowledge to form a hypothesis about where this rock came from."

Explore! ACTIVITY

What's the origin of the rock?

You can form a hypothesis about where a rock formed by carefully observing its physical characteristics.

What To Do

1. Study the chart of the characteristics that indicate an igneous rock's origin, found below. This is your "previous knowledge."

2. Use a magnifying glass to examine a chunk of rock. Record your observations.

3. Form a hypothesis about the origin of the rock.

4. Explain how you could use further observation to test your hypothesis.

Characteristics and Origin of Igneous Rocks			
		Color	
		Dark	Light
Mineral	Large	Oceanic Intrusive	Continental Intrusive
Size	Small	Oceanic Extrusive	Continental Extrusive

■ Different Kinds of Observations

"So you solve problems scientifically by asking a question, thinking of the answer you expect—that's your hypothesis—and then testing your hypothesis in as many ways as possible to see if you're right. You might use an experiment or a model or observations," Erin summarized.

"That's right," Ms. Borga agreed. "In scientific problem solving, you're using the experiment, model, or observation to gather information to see whether your hypothesis is correct. Sometimes you may need to alter your hypothesis, and sometimes you discover that the initial hypothesis is wrong. That's not failure. It's progress, because now you can make a new hypothesis and test it.

"Solving problems in fields outside of science is similar, but sometimes you gather information in different ways. Let's compare solving problems in science to, say, solving problems in history. What's a good history problem?"

Andy smiled. "Here's a problem Mr. Morrow asked us to solve by next week: 'What was the real cause of the Civil War?' We sure can't do experiments or design models or make observations to find out. I'm going to have to spend forever in the library doing research."

"You probably won't be there forever, but you'll have to read a lot of different accounts to see where they agree," Ms. Borga said. "You'll be reviewing other people's observations of what happened. However, you may find that these observations include some bias because they're written from one person's point of view. That makes them different from scientific observations, which are ideally based on fact."

Lee nodded. "Someone from the South might describe the causes of the Civil War differently than someone from the North."

"That's probably true," Ms. Borga agreed. "So you'll have to read accounts written by people from both sides of the war and gather as much other information as possible so you can decide objectively what caused the war."

Kisha had been thinking. "Solving problems in history is also different because we can't observe the Civil War directly, the way we observed the powder samples or those rocks."

"But remember that you still have to interpret your observations," Ms. Borga said. "When you read science articles, you are reading interpretations of data along with the data."

■ Planning an Approach

"Thinking in science isn't that different from thinking in other fields." Ms. Borga posted a chart labeled FLEX Your Brain. "Here's a basic approach you can use."

- Review what you know about a topic.
- Ask a question about something you want to or need to know.
- Suggest a possible the answer (your hypothesis).
- Think of ways to gather information and check your answer.
- Gather the information.
- Analyze what you found out.
- Draw conclusions about whether your hypothesis was correct.
- Clearly explain what you learned to others.

Ms. Borga looked around the room. "Can you do it? Are you ready for the regional Science Challenge?"

Erin bit her lip. "Maybe we need just a little more practice!"

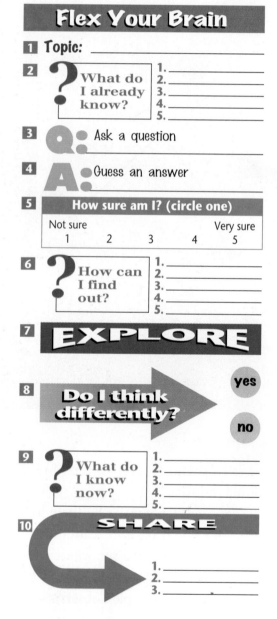

Can you think scientifically?

1. Think of a topic that is related to the natural world that interests you. You might choose air pollution, vegetarian diets, hurricanes, or another topic.

2. Use Steps 1 through 6 of the FLEX Your Brain approach to outline how you would ask and answer a question about that topic.

3. Share your question and your approach to answering it with the class.

"Now you're ready for a practice Challenge," Ms. Borga told the class. First, she divided the students into teams of four. Then she put a large, clear container of water on a table where everyone could see it. Next, she lowered two cans of the same brand of soft drink into the water. The can of diet soft drink floated in the water, while the can of regular soft drink sank to the bottom.

Ms. Borga looked at the class. "Teams, here's your Challenge. Something unexpected happened here. It's up to you to explain why this happened."

Can you solve this problem?

Use the FLEX Your Brain strategy to investigate and explain why the two cans behaved differently when they were placed in water.

Problem

(You will make up your own problem statement.)

Materials

1 can of diet soft drink

1 can of regular soft drink

a container of water large enough to hold two soft drink cans

(Your team might also decide to use other materials.)

What To Do

1 Follow the FLEX Your Brain steps. You may think of several hypotheses to explain what happened. Start by choosing the one that seems to be the most likely explanation. Then design a way to test it. Make sure the method(s) you choose to test the hypothesis actually do test that hypothesis.

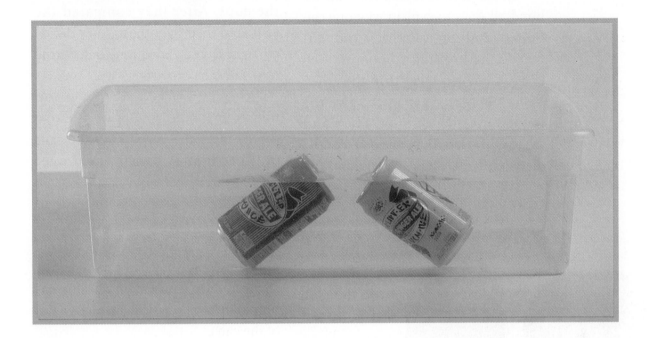

2 After you have designed your plan, get your teacher to approve it.

3 You may need to test several hypotheses before you find one that explains why the cans reacted differently.

Analyzing

1. Which hypothesis was supported by the information you gathered?

2. Which hypotheses did you reject after reviewing the information you gathered?

3. For which hypotheses was the information you gathered inconclusive? How can you explain this? What else could you do to support or rule out these hypotheses?

4. Which methods of gathering information seemed to be most effective in testing these particular hypotheses?

Concluding and Applying

5. How did you handle inconsistent test results?

6. How did the FLEX Your Brain strategy help or hinder your investigation?

7. **Going further** Suppose you have 12 cans of diet and 12 cans of regular soft drink. *Predict* how many cans of each would float and how many would sink, based on your investigation.

■ Testing Hypotheses

Erin's group seemed to have a hundred ways to explain why one can floated and one sank. Lee thought maybe the bottling company filled one kind of can fuller than the other. Kisha thought sugar might give the regular soft drink more mass and make it heavier. Andy guessed that the diet soft drink might have more carbonation than the regular one, causing the diet can to float.

First, the group decided to see whether sugar gave the soft drink more mass. They poured exactly the same amount of each kind of soft drink into separate small cups and weighed the cups. After they compared the results to their hypothesis, they decided to test Lee's idea and determine how full each can was.

As they worked, Erin's group noticed that other groups were testing more cans of the same brand and cans of other brands to see which ones floated and which sank.

Finally, the groups were ready to share their results. They didn't all agree on the reasons the cans reacted differently, but they had used scientific methods to gather a lot of information about the physical characteristics of the cans.

■ Using Science Every Day

Toward the end of the discussion, Andy said, "You know, I just realized I already know how to think scientifically. When I shoot baskets, I keep experimenting with different ways to hold the ball to see which one works best."

we'll need to know the elements before we can figure out something we don't know. The Science Challenge might be something like figuring out what that unknown sample was."

Erin nodded. "I guess that's what science is—both knowledge and a way of finding out more." Then she grinned. "But I don't know the periodic table, so I want to be on Lee's team!"

These ways of thinking scientifically will come in handy as you continue to study in the chapters ahead. You may want to look back at this chapter as you are trying to solve problems in class. But remember, scientific thinking and problem solving are not just useful in science class, they can be useful in your daily life.

"And at this club I belong to," Kisha added, "we made different types of doormats and tried them out at home. Then we picked the best one to make and sell. That's sort of like using a model." She smiled and looked around the class. "Anyone want to buy a doormat?" Everyone laughed.

"Bird-watching is my hobby, but it's also scientific observation," Erin said. "Did I tell you I saw a great blue heron last week in the creek by the park? It was something else!"

Ms. Borga nodded. "Those are all good examples of scientific thinking and information gathering. So, do you think you're ready for the Science Challenge?"

"I think so," said Lee. "And maybe my memorizing the periodic table will come in handy. When you think scientifically, the first thing to do is review what you know, right? Maybe

REVIEWING MAIN IDEAS

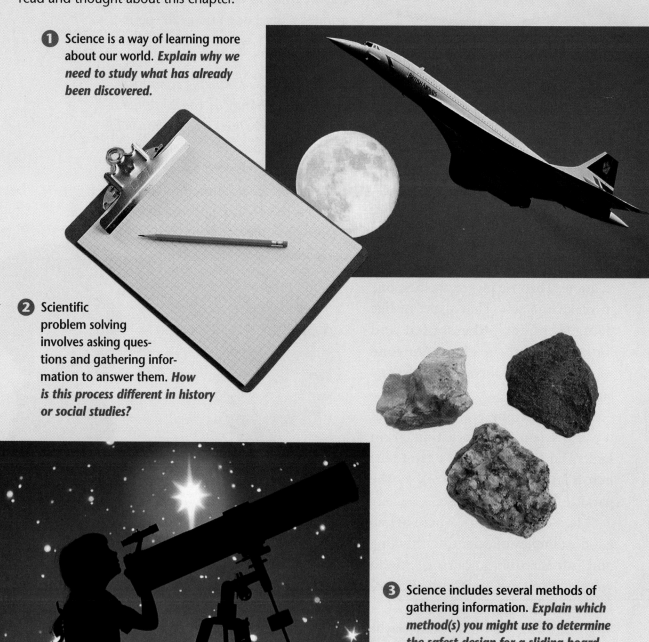

Science Journal

Review the statements below about the big ideas presented in this chapter, and answer the questions. Then write *in your Science Journal* one or two new things you learned about science as you read and thought about this chapter.

1 Science is a way of learning more about our world. *Explain why we need to study what has already been discovered.*

2 Scientific problem solving involves asking questions and gathering information to answer them. *How is this process different in history or social studies?*

3 Science includes several methods of gathering information. *Explain which method(s) you might use to determine the safest design for a sliding board, to choose the best fertilizer for a garden, and to determine any changes in the weather patterns in your area.*

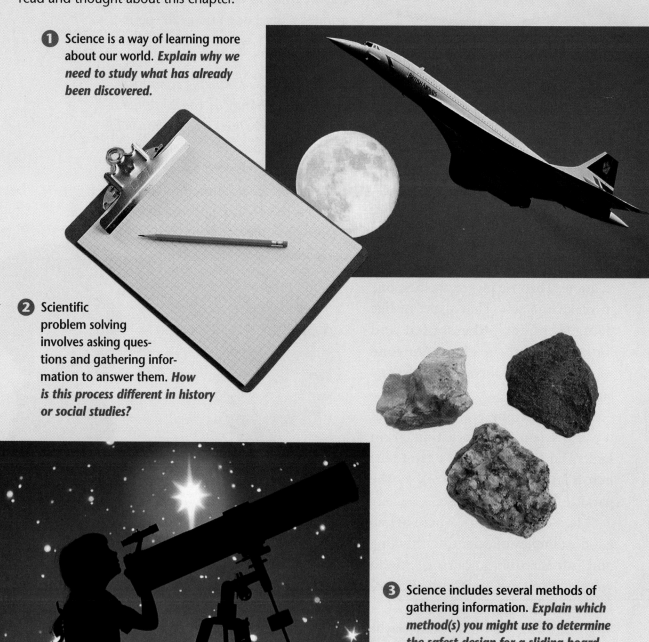

16 Science: A Tool for Solving Problems

Understanding Ideas

1. Is it possible to do an experiment with models? Explain.
2. Compare and contrast making models and observing.
3. Outline the steps you would take when designing a way to investigate a problem.

Critical Thinking

In your journal, *answer each of the following questions.*

1. Why is someone who knows nothing about electricity unlikely to make a discovery that will add to our knowledge of electricity?
2. The people in one town cannot agree about what to build on several undeveloped acres of land. What are some questions that science could answer relating to this problem? What are some questions that depend on people's opinions?
3. What are at least two ways you do or could use scientific thinking to answer questions in your own life?

Problem Solving

Read the following problem and discuss your answers in a brief paragraph.

It's winter and some young people in a Chicago neighborhood are eager to start playing ice hockey. However, no one is sure when the ice on the park pond will be frozen solid enough for a game. How could they solve this problem scientifically?

1. List at least three things the team probably already knows about this topic.
2. Write the question they need to answer. (Be specific.)
3. Form a hypothesis.
4. Think of ways they could test this hypothesis safely.
5. After the team determines whether its hypothesis was correct, what additional information will they have available next fall?

Electricity and Magnetism

Feeding electricity to cities hungry for energy, high tension lines supply power for many human needs. As you study this unit, you'll learn of the different ways in which you use electrical energy each day. When you watch TV, pop popcorn in a microwave oven, or turn on a light to read a book, you are using electrical energy..

Bring a magnet near a refrigerator door and you feel a pull. Do you feel the same pull when you try to attach a magnet to a soft drink can? Both a refrigerator door and a soft drink can are made of metal. Why do the magnets act differently?

What To Do

1. Bring the magnet close to items such as paper clips, rubber bands, aluminum soft drink can tops, and paper. Based on your observations, write a general statement *in your Science Journal* describing what a magnet does.

2. Using the materials that were attracted by the magnet, place a sheet of paper between the magnet and materials. Do you notice any difference in the way the magnet works? *In your Science Journal,* describe what happens.

CHAPTER 1

ELECTRICITY

Did you ever wonder...

✓ **What static cling is?**

✓ **What makes electric eels electric?**

✓ **Where is the safest place to be during an electrical storm?**

Science Journal

Before you study electricity, think about these questions and answer them *in your Science Journal*. When you finish the chapter, compare your journal write-up with what you have learned.

A bright light and the crash of thunder awaken you one night. You watch through your window as an electrical storm moves across the sky. Bright white bolts of lightning flash and then streak outward like cracks in breaking glass. What draws this energy from the sky to Earth? Is this the same form of energy that lights lamps and heats toasters? In this chapter, you will learn about a form of energy that we take very much for granted. Without this form of energy, every aspect of our lives would be very different.

▶ *Less than a hundred years ago, this energy — electricity—was a new and mysterious novelty. In the activity on the next page, explore one of the first electrical phenomena examined.*

Explore! ACTIVITY

Can a comb pick up paper?

What To Do

1. Take a small plastic comb and hold it over several tiny scraps of paper. What happens?

2. Now hold a piece of dry, wool cloth in one hand and brush the comb along it several times with the other hand.

3. Then hold the comb over the scraps of paper. What happens?

4. How can the comb produce a force that can overcome gravity? Why does the paper jump to the comb after brushing with wool? What did the rubbing of the wool do to the comb? *In your Journal,* explain how you think these things happen.

1-1

Forces and Electrical Charges

Section Objectives
- Observe the force caused by electrical charges.
- Demonstrate the two kinds of electrical charges.

Key Terms
electrical charge
unlike charges
like charges

Static Electricity

After you rubbed the comb on the cloth in the Explore activity, the comb attracted the tiny scraps of paper. In doing so, you repeated an experiment done by Thales about 600 B.C.E. and Gilbert in 1570. They both saw an effect of static electricity. Perhaps you've gotten a shock from touching a doorknob after walking on a carpet.

You might even have seen a spark jump. These activities result from static electricity. Lightning is a more spectacular result of static electricity.

You can explore another property of static electricity by doing the activity below.

Figure 1-1

Ⓐ Everything contains electrical charges—people, trees, cats, and minerals. Thales, a Greek who lived around 600 B.C.E., was one of the first to describe a phenomenon related to electricity. He described what happened when amber was rubbed with a bit of wool.

Thales

Ⓑ This photo shows Thales's results. In 1570, English scientist William Gilbert repeated and expanded on the experiment. He named the effects *electricity* after the Greek word for amber, *elektron*.

Find Out! ACTIVITY

Do electric charges interact?

Electricity is so common, we're not used to examining its properties. In this activity, you can find out one of these properties by using transparent tape.

What To Do

1. Fold over about 5 mm on the end of the tape for a handle. Then tear off a strip 8 to 10 cm long. Stick the strip on a dry, smooth surface, such as your desktop. Make a second strip and stick it on top of the first.

2. Quickly pull both pieces off the desk and pull them apart. Then bring the tapes close together. Observe what happens.

3. Now make two new strips of tape, but this time press each one onto the desk. Then pull them off and bring the two strips close together. What happens?

Conclude and Apply

1. What happened when you brought the first pair of tapes close together? What happened when you brought the second pair together?

2. What did you do that might have caused the two different reactions?

When you pulled the strips of tape from the desk, you caused them to have an electrical charge. An **electrical charge** is a concentration of electricity. By sticking one strip on top of the other, you treated the two strips differently. Each strip had an excess of different charges. **Unlike charges** attract one another. When you prepared the strips the same way, they received like charges. **Like charges** repel one another.

You can learn more about different types of charge produced by various materials in the Investigate activity on the next page.

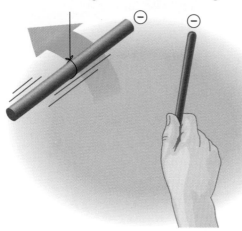

Like charges on rods

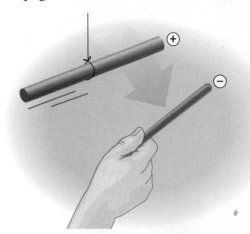

Unlike charges on rods

Figure 1-2

The two effects you saw in the Find Out activity showed you that there must be at least two different kinds of charge. Like the tape strips you prepared, the rods with like charges repel one another and those with unlike charges attract one another.

INVESTIGATION

Charging Up

You are probably familiar with the static cling clothes have when they come out of the clothes dryer. That attraction comes from fabrics rubbing together. The clothes gain an electrical charge. Other objects can also become charged when they rub against fabric. A cellophane tape charge detector can be used to help you determine whether an object is electrically charged.

Preparation

Problem

How can charged objects and fabrics be detected and identified?

Hypothesis

As a group, form a hypothesis about the kinds of materials that can become electrically charged and how that charge can be detected and identified.

Objectives

- Design a procedure that will test the hypothesis.
- Predict the differences in charges among objects and fabrics.
- Identify the kinds of charges produced.

Materials

cellophane tape charge detectors
objects made of plastic, glass, and ceramic
fabrics such as wool, silk, cotton, and fake fur

Safety

Take care with glass and other breakable objects.

Plan the Experiment

1 Prepare a data table *in your Science Journal* or in a database on the computer for the objects and fabrics you will test.

2 Will you test more than one kind of object? Will you use more than one fabric?

Check the Plan

1 How will you make the cellophane tape charge detectors? How will you distinguish between the two detectors?

2 How will you charge the objects?

How will you use the tape detector to check for charge? Will you use both pieces of tape?

3 Watch for the strength of the attraction. Does one combination of fabric and object make a stronger charge? Are the detectors attracted to the objects or fabrics if they are not rubbed together?

4 Write out your plan and check it with your teacher. Make any suggested changes and carry out your experiment.

Analyze and Conclude

1. **Analyze** How many different kinds of charge did you differentiate?

2. **Compare** Compare the charges on the object and the fabric. Are they alike or different? Explain. Was your hypothesis accurate?

3. **Identify** Was there any material that did not become charged? If so, identify the material. Why was it not charged?

4. **Conclude** When an electrical charge is produced by rubbing, are the charges always opposite?

Going Further

A plastic comb is rubbed with a piece of wool and is suspended from a string. What will happen if a glass object that has been rubbed with silk is brought near the comb?

Figure 1-3

Photocopier
Copying machines use static electricity to operate in a process called electrostatic copying.

In the Investigate activity you saw the interaction of charges on several materials. The two kinds of charge you observed are more commonly called positive (+) and negative (-).

As Thales and Gilbert discovered, electricity is everywhere. You often see its effects when you comb your hair, when you walk across a carpet, and in the sky during a thunderstorm. Static charges have some interesting uses as the following illustration shows.

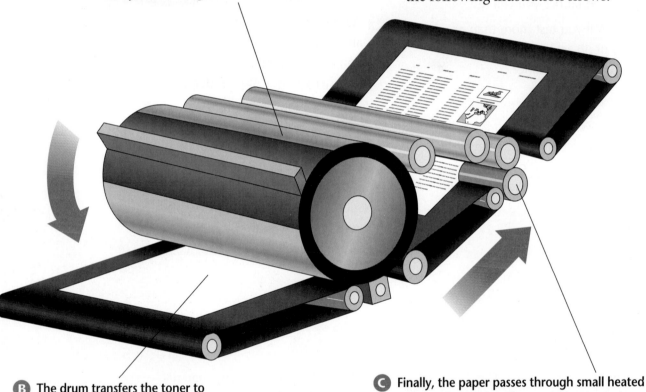

A Light reflected from an original image produces an invisible copy image of positive charges on the large drum. A fine black powder called toner, containing carbon particles and plastic beads, is attracted to the drum, producing a dusty, visible image there.

B The drum transfers the toner to negatively charged paper.

C Finally, the paper passes through small heated rollers which melt and set the image permanently. What properties of electricity does this process demonstrate?

check your UNDERSTANDING

1. As you move two charged cellophane tapes closer together, do the forces between them become greater or smaller? Explain your answer using your observations.

2. If you rub hard rubber with a piece of wool, what charge is on the piece of rubber?

3. **Apply** Explain why your comb sometimes attracts your hair after use.

Electrical Charge Carriers

Electrical Charges

In the last section, you observed that electrical charges may be positive (+) or negative (-). What type of material moves charges from one place to another? Do all materials move charges in the same way? Do electrical charges stay put on some materials? You can answer this question by combining and expanding two activities from Section 1-1.

Find Out! ACTIVITY

Do electrical charges stay put?

As you've observed, electrical charges move to and from objects. What controls that movement?

What To Do

1. Charge a plastic comb by rubbing one end of it with a piece of wool while holding it by the other end. Bring it close to a tape charge detector.

2. Now, with your finger, touch the comb on the end you charged. Bring the comb near the charge detector again.

Conclude and Apply

1. *In your Journal*, describe what happened the first time you brought the comb near the charge detector.

2. What happened the second time you brought the comb to the charge detector?

3. What happened to the electrical charge?

In the Find Out activity above, you observed that the comb held a charge until you touched the charged end. Electrical charges don't move freely from one place to another through some materials such as plastic. If the charges had been able to move in the comb, you wouldn't have had to touch its other end to remove the charges. A material in which electrical charges do not move freely from place to place is called an **insulator**.

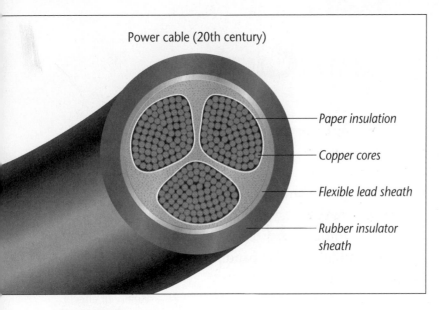

Power cable (20th century)

— Paper insulation

— Copper cores

— Flexible lead sheath

— Rubber insulator
sheath

Figure 1-4

Insulators include paper, plastic, rubber, wood, and glass.
Conductors include most metals such as copper, aluminum, gold,
and silver. The copper conductor and rubber insulator of this
power cable combine to safely transmit electricity.

In other materials, electrical charges can move anywhere. A material in which electrical charges can move freely from place to place is called a **conductor**. Your body is a conductor, which is why the charge left the comb after you touched it. Because your body is a conductor, electricity can be dangerous. Power cables are insulated to protect you. **Figure 1-4** shows the conductor and insulator in a power cable. The electrical cords in your home are like it—conductors wrapped in an insulating material. In the activity on the next page, you can explore an example of charges moving through a conductor.

Stunning Eels

Many scientists have tried to find out why electric eels do not electrocute themselves. One hypothesis is that the brain and heart of electric eels are packed in a fatty tissue that protects and insulates these two vital organs from the strong electrical impulses. The other organs of their body apparently are able to withstand the impulses without a fatty layer.

The Eel Circuit

The electric eel is positively charged at the head and negatively charged at the tail. The tail, which makes up four-fifths of the 8-foot-long fish, has

three pairs of electric organs made of thousands of plates arranged like the cells in a storage battery. While the electric charge can be released in a fraction of a second, an eel may need nearly an hour to recharge its batteries. By the way, an electric eel is not an eel at all. It's a freshwater fish related to carp and minnows.

Eel Power In Use

Does it seem strange that a fish like the electric eel has electricity? All animals—even you—have electrical activity in your body. For example, your muscles move because of electrical stimulus. Electric eels use the

Do conductors hold a charge?

What To Do

1. Hold a balloon that has been given a negative charge by being rubbed with wool over a few small (less than 1 cm x 1 cm) scraps of aluminum foil. Is the foil attracted to the negatively charged balloon?

2. Hold the positively charged wool over the foil. Is the result the same? Can you explain why?

3. Now, try the same experiment with a charged shiny metallic balloon like the one shown. What happens? *In your Journal, draw what you think happened and write a brief explanation.*

The Explore activity showed that conductors are attracted to both positive and negative charges. The shiny balloon didn't hold a static charge because the thin layer of aluminum on the balloon is a conductor. The charge flowed around the balloon and through you to the ground.

impulse to stun their prey, fend off predators, and detect underwater objects.

The shock of an electric eel is large enough to kill an animal as large as a horse. When an animal is stunned by an electric shock, it stops breathing and drowns. Usually the electricity from electric eels stuns small prey, such as fish or frogs.

What Do You Think?

Besides the electric eel, other animals that live in water—the electric ray, for example—use electric impulses to stun their prey and protect themselves.

1. Why do you think water animals use electricity in this way, while animals that live on land do not?

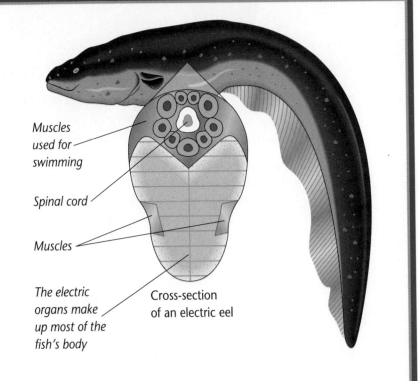

Muscles used for swimming

Spinal cord

Muscles

The electric organs make up most of the fish's body

Cross-section of an electric eel

2. Why might it matter where the electrical impulses enter the body of an electric eel's prey?

Like the foil, uncharged objects are attracted to charged objects. That's why you can stick a charged balloon to an uncharged wall. The charges on the balloon repel the like charges on the wall's surface. The remaining unlike charges are attracted to the charges on the balloon. The force of attraction isn't as strong as between two charged objects, but it's enough to hold up a lightweight balloon.

Lightning is a more impressive example of the spark that jumps from your finger to a doorknob after you've built up a static charge. Such small static charges can be useful as you saw on page 26. Photocopiers and electric spray painters make use of the forces between electric charges.

SKILLBUILDER

Recognizing Cause and Effect

You have two balloons, each with an equal positive charge. You bring the first one up to cellophane tape charge detectors and the pieces of tape repel. Why? Hold the charge detectors between both balloons and the tapes repel even further. Why? If you need help, refer to the **Skill Handbook** on page 684.

Figure 1-5

Lightning can travel up to 14 kilometers to reach the ground. Between clouds, it can travel up to nine times farther.

As you'll see in the next section, using conductors to control the movement of electrical charges is also enormously useful.

check your UNDERSTANDING

1. If a charged object touches the end of an insulator, what happens to the charge? What happens on a conductor?
2. Why does a negative charge in clouds produce a positive charge at ground level?
3. List three examples of how static charges are built up and describe the visible effects of the charges.
4. **Apply** Why is it safe to be inside a metal enclosure during an electrical storm?

1-3 Making Electricity Flow

Moving Electrical Charges

During a thunderstorm, the charge jumping from cloud to cloud or striking Earth produces a flash of light. Could you light a lamp this way? Probably not. The spark occurs for only an instant. A lamp needs energy from a continuous flow of charge to stay lit.

It takes energy to separate positive and negative charges. Till now, you've provided that energy either by rubbing or pulling tape away from a desk top. There are more convenient ways to store that energy for use later. After you study the diagrams below, try making charges flow by doing the activity on the next page.

Section Objectives

- State the function of a battery in a circuit.
- Light a bulb using a battery.
- Explain the effect of resistance on the current in a circuit.

Key Terms

potential difference
circuit
current
resistance

Figure 1-6

Water Wheel

A continuous flow of electrical charge can be maintained in the same way that water in the diagram below is made to flow.

A The water pump works against gravity, lifting water into the reservoir. The potential energy added by the pump does work as the water escapes and turns the water wheel.

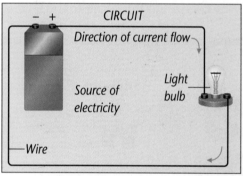

B Electrical charges can be made to flow and do work in much the same way as water. A chemical reaction in a battery adds potential energy as it separates charges. Charges move along a conducting wire. The potential energy does work as it lights a light bulb. What forms of energy do we use electricity to produce?

Find Out! ACTIVITY

How does charge flow from a battery through a light bulb?

Every electrical circuit has some basic parts. Do this activity to find out some simple ways those parts go together.

What To Do

1. Try to connect a battery, bulb, and a wire to light the bulb.
CAUTION: *If a connecting wire gets hot, immediately disconnect one end of the wire from the battery and try another connection.*

Conclude and Apply

1. Draw a picture of the battery, bulb, and wire. Trace the flow of charges in your drawing.

2. *In your Journal,* explain how electric current flows along this path by comparing the circuit to the flow of water.

What Causes Lightning?

When you see city lights, you are seeing electrical energy under control. When you see lightning shatter the sky, you see electricity that is out of control. The electricity in lightning has a potential of 100 million volts, causing a temperature that ranges from 15 000 to 33 000°C—hotter than the surface of the sun!

What causes the violent discharge of electrical energy in lightning? It starts very simply with the particles in a rain cloud. Lighter particles of water in the cloud collide with heavy particles, such as hail. During the collision, the heavy particles gain negative charges from the lighter particles and become negatively charged. Since the lighter particles lose negative charges, they become positively charged. The heavier, negative particles fall to the bottom of the cloud. The lighter, positive particles drift up to the top of the cloud.

Because the bottom of the cloud is negatively charged, it repels negative charges on the ground beneath it. Because the ground is a conductor, the negative charges can flow away. This leaves a large concentration of positive charges in the ground under the clouds overhead. The number of charges makes the electrical potential energy enormous.

When you made the battery light the bulb, you created a complete path through which charge flowed. Such a complete, or closed, path is called a **circuit**.

The rate at which charges flow through the lamp and wires is called electric current. **Current** is how much electric charge flows past a point in a circuit during a given time. It's measured in amperes (A).

The electric potential energy is the total stored energy of all the charges. The change in potential energy divided by the total charge is called the electric potential difference, or **potential difference**. The potential differ-

Figure 1-7

A You can use an instrument called an ammeter to measure the rate of current flowing through this three-way bulb. When the switch is at the lowest setting, the current is small.

B At the medium setting, an ammeter shows that the current is greater. How can you tell?

C The current is greatest at the highest setting. What does this tell you about the effect of the switch on the current?

When Lightning Strikes

Lightning begins with a weak, downward discharge in which large numbers of negative charges flow toward the ground. This is followed immediately by a bright flash, or return stroke, from the ground to the cloud along the same path.

The shorter the distance from the ground to the cloud, the easier it is for the electrical discharge to take place. It's not a good idea to run under a tree during an electrical storm. The lightning seeks the shortest path to the ground, and the tree provides that path.

People can sometimes have a warning of a nearby lightning strike. They feel their skin tingling and their hair standing on end. A person in this situation should fall to the ground to reduce the chance of being struck by a lightning bolt.

What Do You Think?

Buildings, particularly farm buildings in open areas, have lightning rods atop their roofs. How are these rods used? How can these rods help avoid a fire due to lightning?

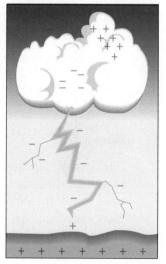

ence is measured in volts (V) and, therefore, is also called voltage.

When charges move through a bulb, their electrical potential energy is converted into thermal energy and light. Chemical action in the battery maintains the potential difference needed to keep the charges flowing.

Resistance is a property of materials that indicates how much energy changes to thermal energy and light as an electrical charge flows through the material. Even very good conductors such as gold offer some resistance to the flow of charges. Electrical wiring has very low resistance so that very little energy is lost to heat and light. Tungsten light bulb filaments and heating elements like those in a toaster are designed to have very high resistance because the light and heat are useful. The illustration shows how resistances are used in electrical circuits. Try the activity on the next page to find out the relationship between resistance and electrical current.

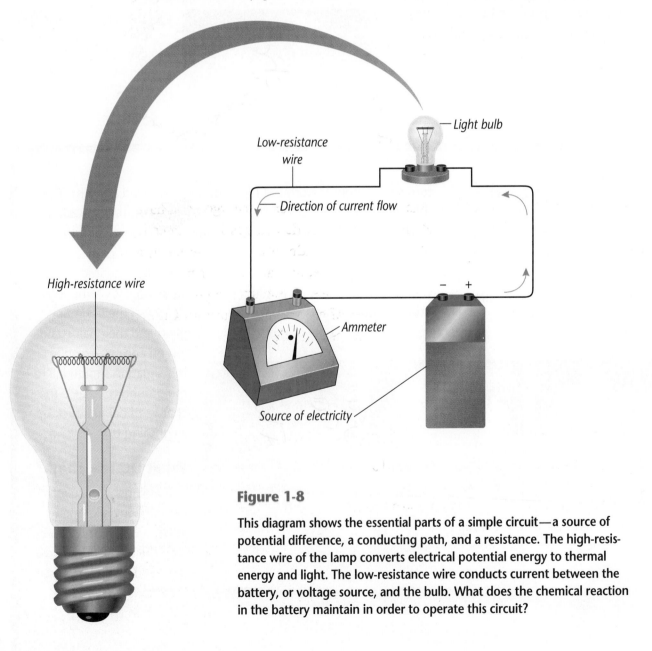

High-resistance wire

Low-resistance wire

Light bulb

Direction of current flow

Ammeter

Source of electricity

Figure 1-8

This diagram shows the essential parts of a simple circuit—a source of potential difference, a conducting path, and a resistance. The high-resistance wire of the lamp converts electrical potential energy to thermal energy and light. The low-resistance wire conducts current between the battery, or voltage source, and the bulb. What does the chemical reaction in the battery maintain in order to operate this circuit?

How does electric current depend on the resistance in a circuit?

Examining changes in a simple working circuit will help you understand how resistance and current are related.

What To Do

1. Make a complete circuit containing a battery and a single bulb. Observe how brightly the bulb glows.
2. Next, add a second bulb as shown in the photograph. Note the brightness of the bulbs.
3. Finally, add another bulb to the circuit as shown. Observe the brightness of the bulbs.

Conclude and Apply

1. What happened when you added the second bulb to the circuit? When you added the third?
2. *In your Journal,* explain what you observed.

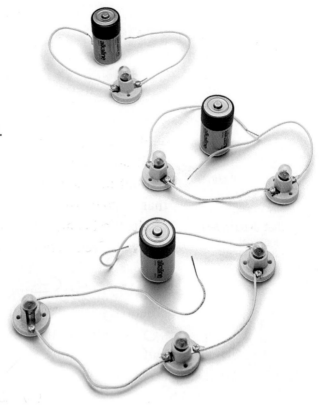

Each added bulb, or added resistance, decreased the brightness of all the bulbs. You could infer that less bright means less current was flowing. When the voltage remains the same, the current decreases as the resistance increases.

Instead of static charges, you have seen dynamic charges in an electric circuit made of a complete path, a resistance, and a source of potential difference. These simple circuits are part of electric appliances and tools you use every day.

check your UNDERSTANDING

1. Draw a circuit using a 6-V battery and a bulb that would cause the bulb to glow.
2. What keeps the charges flowing in a circuit? What happens to the potential energy when the charges pass through the bulb?
3. **Apply** Suppose you replaced the bulb in the circuit you drew in Question 1 with one of higher resistance. Describe the change in the current through the bulb. How would the new bulb's brightness compare with that of the bulb you replaced?

Resistance, Current, and Voltage

1-4

Section Objectives
- Control the amount of current in a circuit.
- List the variables that determine electrical resistance.

Connect to...

Chemistry

The reactions in most chemical electrical cells produce only slightly more than one volt. How do you think larger voltages are produced?

Potential Difference and Current

As you saw on page 31, a battery in a circuit acts something like a pump in a water system. It increases the potential energy of electrical charges. The larger the battery's voltage, the greater the difference in potential across its terminals.

Consider a circuit containing a battery and bulb. A chemical reaction causes an increase in potential across the battery. There is an equal decrease in potential across the bulb. As **Figure 1-9** below shows, there is also a loss in potential energy of water flowing over a waterfall to a lower level. Water flowing over Niagara Falls has more potential energy than water flowing over a beaver's dam. Do the activity on the next page to see how potential difference and electrical current are related.

Figure 1-9

These two dams hold back water with different amounts of potential energy. As the water gates are opened, the water falls and changes potential energy to kinetic energy. The water which falls farther is flowing fastest when it reaches the bottom. What does this suggest about the effect of different potential differences, or voltages, on electric current?

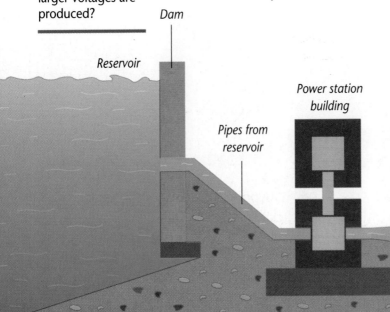

Reservoir

Dam

Pipes from reservoir

Power station building

How does increasing voltage affect current?

Why do some flashlights have more D-cells than others? To find out, you'll need two D-cells, wire, and two bulbs.

What To Do

1. Make a complete circuit with the two bulbs and one D-cell as shown. Observe the brightness of the bulbs.

2. Disconnect the circuit and add a second D-cell as shown. Be sure the D-cell connections match the photo before connecting the bulbs. Again, observe the brightness of the bulbs.

Conclude and Apply

In your Journal, write to explain how the brightness in the first circuit compares with the brightness in the second circuit. Explain any differences.

If a pump lifts water to an even higher level, the water will have to fall back a larger distance. Similarly, if a battery with a higher voltage is used, the potential drop across the bulb will be greater. How will this affect the current? We can investigate this with another water model.

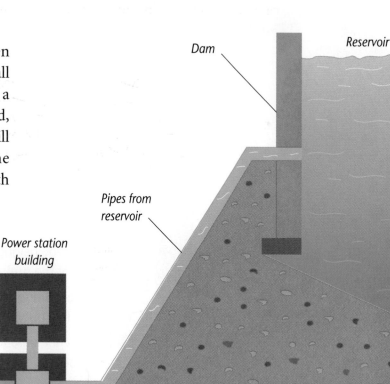

Dam

Reservoir

Pipes from reservoir

Power station building

Potential Difference and Current

Water currents aren't exactly like electric currents. However, the two are similar enough that water can be used in models of electric circuits. Investigate how a water current is affected by changes in potential and resistance.

Problem

How does changing the potential difference and resistance affect the current for a water system?

Materials

plastic funnel
1-m lengths of rubber tubing of different diameters

stopwatch or clock
ring stand with ring
meterstick
2 500-mL beakers

Safety Precautions

What To Do

1 Assemble the *model* apparatus as shown in the photo on the left.

2 *Measure* the height from the top of the funnel to the outlet end of the rubber tubing (photo ***A***). Record your data.

3 Practice pouring water into the funnel fast enough to keep it full, but not overflowing (photo ***B***).

4 *Measure* the time for 100 mL of water to flow into the lower beaker.

A

B

C

5 *Design an experiment* to explore the effect of higher and lower potential differences, and the effect of larger and smaller resistance on the flow of water. Show your design to your teacher. If you are advised to revise your design, be sure to check with your teacher again before you begin.

Analyzing

 1. Organize your data in a table.

 2. *Calculate* the rate of flow of 100 mL of water at each height of the funnel.

 3. *Make a graph* to compare funnel height and the rate of water flow.

4. At what height is the rate of flow the greatest? What effect does the diameter of the tube have on the rate of water flow?

Concluding and Applying

5. If the water in this model is similar to electrical charges in a circuit, which trial corresponds to the circuit with the highest voltage? What electrical property does the hose diameter represent?

6. *Going Further* If the smaller diameter hose corresponds to a greater electrical resistance, what do you think will happen to the electric current if resistance is increased while the voltage remains constant? If the resistance in a circuit remains constant, what happens to the current when the voltage is increased?

The Investigate you just completed illustrates a basic principle of electricity. With a constant voltage, increasing the resistance will decrease the current. As you observed in Section 1-3, using a model is an important tool for drawing conclusions about various properties. In the activity below, you can find out another property of resistance.

Find Out! ACTIVITY

How does the length of a conductor affect its resistance?

It takes a special tool to measure resistance precisely, but you can see how length and resistance are related using simple equipment.

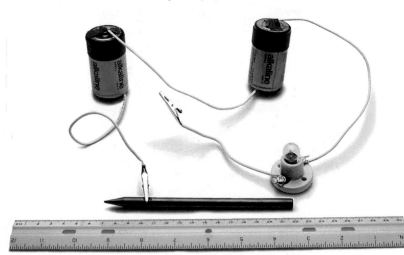

What To Do

1. Connect two D-cells to a light and clips as shown in the photo. Attach one clip to the end of a thick pencil lead farthest from the lamp.

2. Then, touch the second clip to the opposite end of the pencil lead. *In your Journal*, describe what happens.

3. Slowly slide the clip up the pencil lead toward the other clip. Note any changes *in your Journal*.

Conclude and Apply

1. What happened when you slid the clip up the pencil lead? What does that imply about the current in the circuit? How could you test your guess?

2. What conclusions can you draw about the resistance of the pencil lead?

As you've just seen, resistance of a conductor depends on length. When you increase the length of the conductor, you increase the resistance. Thickness also affects resistance.

Figure 1-10

This hand-held control determines the speed of the toy electric car to which it's connected. Squeezing the triggers varies the resistance. As the resistance is lowered, the car speeds up. What does this demonstrate about the relationship between current and resistance?

Ohm's Law

The relationship among current, resistance, and potential difference can be made quantitative by using measurements. We can say that current is equal to the potential difference divided by the resistance. The relationship can be expressed mathematically: V/R=I.

Figure 1-11

A These two batteries produce a potential difference of 18V. How would increasing the voltage affect the current in the circuit?

Batteries

Multimeter

B The multimeter, resistor, and light bulb all add together to produce a resistance of 36Ω. How would increasing the resistance affect the current in the circuit?

Bulb

Resistor

C Using the mathematical expression, V/R=I, the current in the circuit is 18V/36Ω, or 0.5A. Try calculating the current using two or three different values for voltage and resistance.

Units and Symbols used in Ohm's Law			
	V ÷	**R** =	**I**
	potential difference	resistence	current
Unit	volt	ohms	ampere
Symbol	V	Ω	A

check your UNDERSTANDING

1. Two flashlight bulbs are powered by separate, identical 9-volt batteries. One bulb is dimmer. What does that imply about the resistance of the bulbs? How do the currents in the two circuits compare?

2. A piece of carbon, resistance 18Ω, is connected to a 12-V battery. Find the current in the carbon. What would be the current if a 6-V battery were used?

3. **Apply** A length of wire is cut in half, forming two shorter wires. How does the resistance of each half compare to that of the original wire? If the two short wires are placed side by side and twisted together, how does the resistance of the combination compare to the resistance of one short wire? How could you test your answers to these questions?

Science *and* Society

Recycling Batteries

What is as small as a button and very dangerous to the environment? The answer is the kind of battery you find in watches, hearing aids, and cameras. They make up 25 percent of the hazardous wastes from households. Tiny button batteries may have as much as 1.1 grams of mercury, a metal that can cause birth defects and brain and kidney damage. Even one battery in six tons of garbage is more mercury per ton than allowed by government standards.

What Can Be Done?

If people used rechargeable batteries, fewer toxic metals would be discharged into the environment. Rechargeables cost three times more than ordinary batteries but last 40 times longer, so they are more economical. Recycling is also a partial solution. Jewelry stores usually accept button bat-

teries and turn them in at recycling centers. However, only 23 states now require stores to accept old batteries for recycling.

What Other Countries Do

In 1983, the citizens of Tokyo discovered that one incinerator was emitting 30 times more mercury than the amount declared safe by the World Health Organization. They insisted that local facilities remove batteries from garbage before incineration.

In Austria, some recycling plants use an experimental process to remove the mercury and zinc from old batteries. These metals and the rest of the battery can be reused.

In Denmark, there is a refund surcharge on batteries. Consumers who return used batteries get the money back.

Science Journal

In your Science Journal, list what you and your family can do to reduce the amount of mercury in the environment. What sources of mercury are in your home? How can the people in your community dispose of hazardous household substances?

Technology Connection

Latimer's Light

Ever since Thomas Edison patented the light bulb, people have been trying to improve it.

One of the first to improve the light bulb was Lewis Howard Latimer. Latimer, a self-taught draftsman, worked for Alexander Graham Bell in the 1870s. Latimer's ability

to draw detailed diagrams of complex electrical devices was invaluable. He drew the plans for Bell that resulted in the 1876 patent of the telephone.

Latimer first became associated with Thomas Edison when Edison patented the first incandescent bulb in 1879. Latimer set about making it better. His improved method for securing the carbon filament to metal wires inside the vacuum bulb was patented in 1881. Latimer continued to work on the incandescent bulb and in 1882 received what he considered his most important patent. He improved the process for producing the carbon filaments used in light bulbs.

Latimer was the only African American invited to join the Edison Pioneers, a group of scientists and inventors who worked for Edison. He was asked to supervise the instal-lation of electrical streetlights in New York City, Philadelphia, and London.

Making Better Light Bulbs

The part of a modern light bulb that lights up is the thin tungsten wire, the filament, in the center. When an electric current passes through it, it glows. Unfortunately, some of the tungsten molecules get so hot that they vaporize, leaving the wire and adhering to the glass bulb. When enough tungsten has left the filament, the light bulb dies.

In newer bulbs, krypton gas may be used. A light bulb full of krypton gas stays relatively cool, so less tungsten gets hot enough to leave the filament. This makes the light bulb last longer at the same brightness.

If brightness is more important than long life, the krypton-filled bulb can be operated at higher filament temperatures to give a brighter light more efficiently than non-krypton-filled bulbs. Brighter krypton bulbs are used in slide and movie projectors.

One vital use for krypton light bulbs is illuminating airport runways at night. Electric-arc lights filled with krypton pierce fog for 300 meters (1000 feet) or more.

What Do You Think?

Think of several other places on Earth or in the solar system where krypton bulbs' greater brightness or longer life might be useful.

Teens in SCIENCE

Overcoming Obstacles

Nineteen-year-old Sieu Ngo was able to overcome much difficulty in his life and went on to complete an award-winning science project in electrochemistry.

Sieu Ngo is of Chinese origin. Most of his family lives in Vietnam. He immigrated to America when he was just seven years old. It was not an easy journey. Sieu was held in a refugee camp in Malaysia for more than nine months. The overcrowded camp was even more uncomfortable for Sieu because he had chicken pox!

Sacrifices...

Finally settling in Oklahoma, Sieu began working and attending high school.

"I worked in a gas station from 11 p.m. to 7 a.m." With school beginning at 8 a.m., Sieu was exhausted most mornings. Sometimes he became discouraged.

Once Sieu even thought about giving up his science interests. "One night I was cleaning the refreshment stand. I was thinking about the kids I would be competing against. As I cleaned, I imagined them at home working on their computers or studying. What chance did I have? I almost quit."

...and Rewards

But Sieu Ngo's hard work and dedication had not gone unnoticed. His science teacher believed in the young man. In fact, he invited Sieu to live with his family until Sieu's project was complete.

This was just the break that Sieu needed. With more time and energy to devote, he made great strides on the project. "I spent a lot of nights in the computer lab. I was still working all night, but this time for myself, for something I believed in."

It was a race right up to the deadline. In fact, Sieu's classmates helped him finish mounting his displays on the bus ride to the competition.

Despite many obstacles, Sieu Ngo's project has earned him a good deal of respect. He also won a full scholarship to the University of Oklahoma where he studies chemical engineering. "To me, life is one big mathematical equation. The amount of hardship in a person's life is equal to the amount of personal good. I am optimistic that life is fair."

What Do You Think?

Sieu Ngo describes life as a mathematical equation. What do you think he means?

Science Journal

Review the statements below about the big ideas presented in this chapter, and answer the questions. Then, reread your answers to the Did You Ever Wonder questions at the beginning of the chapter.

In your Science Journal, write a paragraph about how your understanding of the big ideas in the chapter has changed.

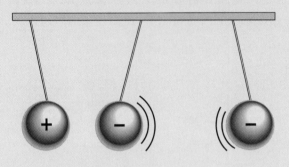

1 There are two kinds of electrical charges, positive and negative. *How could you tell if a charge was positive or negative?*

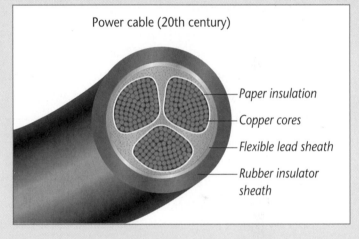

Power cable (20th century)

Paper insulation
Copper cores
Flexible lead sheath
Rubber insulator sheath

2 Electric charges can move easily through conductors, but not through insulators. *How could you tell if an object is an insulator or a conductor?*

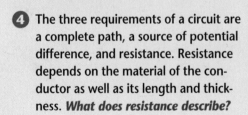

3 Electrical charges flow through a circuit and do work by changing potential energy into other forms of energy. *What role does a battery play in an electrical circuit?*

4 The three requirements of a circuit are a complete path, a source of potential difference, and resistance. Resistance depends on the material of the conductor as well as its length and thickness. *What does resistance describe?*

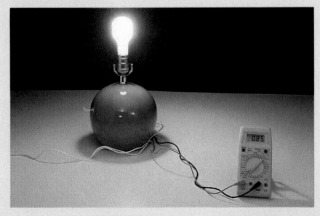

Using Key Science Terms

circuit   like charges
conductor   potential difference
current   resistance
electrical charge   unlike charges
insulator

Explain the differences between the terms in each of the following sets.

1. circuit, current
2. conductor, insulator
3. electrical charge, like charges, unlike charges
4. potential difference, resistance

Understanding Ideas

Answer the following questions in your Journal *using complete sentences.*

1. What are the names for the two types of electrical charge?
2. You observe that a very large voltage produces only a small current in a circuit. What do you conclude about the resistance in the circuit?
3. Would you connect a battery to a bulb with a thick or thin copper wire if you did not want the wire to become hot? Explain your answer.
4. Should a long extension cord needed to carry high currents be made of thick or thin copper wires? Why?
5. What type of charge would you use to attract a positive charge?
6. Why can separated positive and negative charges be used to do work?

Developing Skills

Use your understanding of the concepts developed in this chapter to answer each of the following questions.

1. **Concept Mapping** Complete the concept map of electricity.

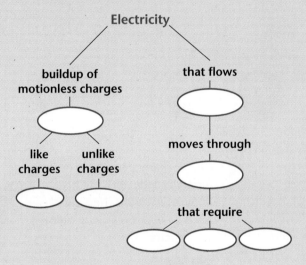

2. **Observing and Inferring** Repeat the Explore activity on page 29 using two identical balloons. Attach string to one balloon and hang it from the desk. Charge both balloons by rubbing them with the cloth. Bring the second balloon toward the hanging balloon. What happens? Bring the cloth near the hanging balloon. What happens? Remove the charge from one of the balloons and bring the other balloon toward it. Explain what happens.

3. **Interpreting Data** Review the Find Out activity on page 40 on resistance and give examples of where resistors are used. What current flows through a conductor having a resistance of 84 ohms connected across a 12-volt battery?

Critical Thinking

In your Journal, *answer each of the following questions.*

1. A bird can sit on a single power line wire without harm. Why? What would happen if the bird was to touch another wire of lower potential at the same time?

2. Signs often say "Danger - High Voltage." Why don't they say "Danger - High Current"?

3. Electrical cords attached to a household appliance are constructed as shown in the diagram. Explain the materials used in this construction.

 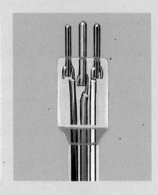

4. How does turning a dimmer light switch adjust current flow?

5. If a circuit containing 1 meter of wire and three light bulbs was changed to 0.75 meter of wire and two light bulbs, what would happen to the current if the power supply was kept the same?

Problem Solving

Read the following problem and discuss your answers in a brief paragraph.

You are playing with your friends in a field. Suddenly, there is a bright flash of light. You know that a thunderstorm is coming and you had better take shelter. Nearby there is a metal building, a car, and a tree.

Which would be safe places to wait out the storm? Why? Which would be the most hazardous? Why?

CONNECTING IDEAS

Discuss each of the following in a brief paragraph.

1. **Theme—Energy** After you receive a shock from a doorknob, touching it right away a second time probably will not produce a second shock. Why? What could you do to give yourself a shock a second time?

2. **Theme—Systems and Interactions** Many times a car will not start if one of its battery terminals is covered with corrosion. Why won't the car start? How could it be fixed? What electrical property of the corrosion causes this problem?

3. **A Closer Look** Describe the role negatively charged particles play in producing lightning.

4. **Science and Society** What are two actions that you can take to decrease the hazard caused by discarded batteries?

MAGNETISM

Did you ever wonder...

✓ **How a magnet attracts or repels another magnet nearby?**

✓ **Why paper clips sometimes act like magnets?**

✓ **How a stereo loudspeaker changes electric current into sound?**

Science Journal

Before you begin to study about magnetism, think about these questions and answer them *in your Science Journal*. When you finish the chapter, compare your journal write-up with what you have learned.

Remember playing with toy magnets as a child? There was something magical about a piece of iron suddenly leaping off the floor and flying into the air. How did they work? And what about the mysterious behavior of a compass? A needle, jiggling on a pin to find its balance, swings back and forth a dozen times. Every time it stops moving, it's aligned north and south. Why? What causes it to turn? Why does it always point the same direction when it stops? The actions of the toys and the compass seem mysterious. They don't match our ideas of the way things work. We can't see what's happening, what's making the objects move. Since we can't see magnetism, we can figure out how it works only by observing its effects. You can observe these effects while doing the activities in this chapter. You may find that magnets play an important role in your daily life.

▶ *Do the activity on the next page and explore some everyday uses of magnets.*

48

Explore! ACTIVITY

How are magnets used in your home and at school?

Some magnets in your home may keep doors closed. Others may keep game pieces on a board. Look for examples of magnets at home and at school. Make a list of their uses. Then, with a group of classmates brainstorm a list of ten other uses.

Forces and Fields

Section Objectives

- Describe the forces magnets produce.
- Identify the north and south poles of a magnet.
- Explain the role of magnetic fields.

Key Terms

magnetic poles
magnetic field

Forces at Work

Besides being fun and intriguing toys, magnets play many useful roles in everyday life. Some uses are obvious. But for other uses, magnets are hidden in places you might not suspect. There are magnets as fine as powder that store images and sounds on videotape and information on computer disks. There are magnets in telephones, television sets, and radios. Some of these magnets change electric currents into sounds. Some hold doors closed or make motors turn. Magnets are all around you. You can begin to understand how magnets work by making some simple observations in the activity below.

Explore! ACTIVITY

Can you make your own compass?

What To Do

1. Hang a bar magnet by a thread, as shown. When the magnet stops swinging, record the direction of the bar.

2. Turn the magnet slightly and then let it turn by itself. What happens?

3. Hang the magnet in another place. When it stops moving, in what direction does it point?

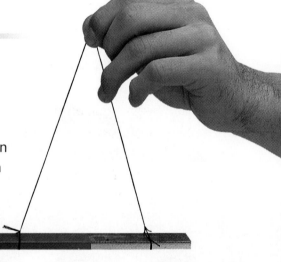

Figure 2-1

A More than 2000 years ago, the Greeks discovered that a certain kind of rock was attracted toward materials that contained iron. This rock was named magnetite because it was found in a region of the world that was then called Magnesia.

Magnetite

B This early compass contained lodestone, or *leading stone,* another name for magnetite. When the compass was suspended by a string, the fish's head turned to point at the lodestar. What do we call the lodestar now?

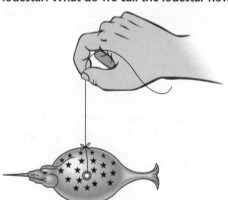

← **N**

■ Magnetic Poles

One end of your suspended bar magnet always pointed north while the other end always pointed south. When a magnet is allowed to turn freely, the two ends of the magnet that point north-south are called the **magnetic poles**. The end pointing north is called the north-seeking pole or just the north pole. Remember that by just looking at a magnet we might not be able to directly observe any differences between the north and south poles. Try the activity below to find out how magnetic poles interact.

Find Out! ACTIVITY

How do magnetic poles interact?

What happens when two magnets interact?

What To Do

1. From your teacher obtain two magnets, tape, and string.

2. Suspend one magnet with string. After it stops moving, place a piece of tape or a dot of paint on the pole of your magnet that points north.

3. Hang a second magnet more than 50 cm away from the first magnet. Mark it as in Step 2. Then, observe what happens as you bring each possible combination of poles (N-N, N-S, S-S) together. *In your Journal*, describe

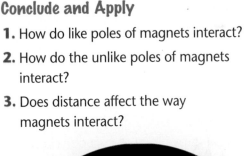

what happens as you move one magnet away from the other.

Conclude and Apply

1. How do like poles of magnets interact?

2. How do the unlike poles of magnets interact?

3. Does distance affect the way magnets interact?

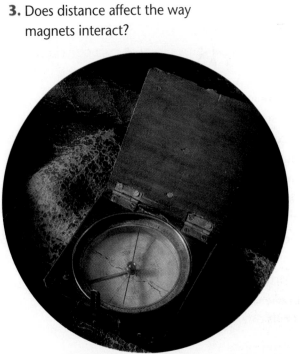

C These dial compasses were among the first ever developed. For what might very early dial compasses have been used?

As you can see, the poles of a magnet act differently from each other. Two north poles repel each other. Two south poles also repel each other. But a north pole and a south pole attract each other. The distance between the magnets also affects how they react to each other. As the poles are moved closer together, the force between them becomes greater. The behavior of magnetic poles should remind you of the behavior of electric charges you studied earlier.

Can a magnet have a single pole? If you break a bar magnet in half, what happens? You get two complete magnets, each with its own north and south poles. As **Figure 2-2** shows, no matter how many times you break a magnet, you are left with more complete magnets, each with two poles.

Figure 2-3 below shows Earth's magnetic poles and how they interact with other magnetic poles.

Figure 2-2

Each piece of the original magnet is a new magnet with two poles. How many smaller magnets do you suppose could be made from one large magnet?

Figure 2-3

Compass needles are magnets. Just like two suspended bar magnets turn to point at one another's poles, these compass needles turn to point north and south. This is because Earth has magnetic poles much like a bar magnet. Scientists think Earth's magnetism is produced by materials deep in its core.

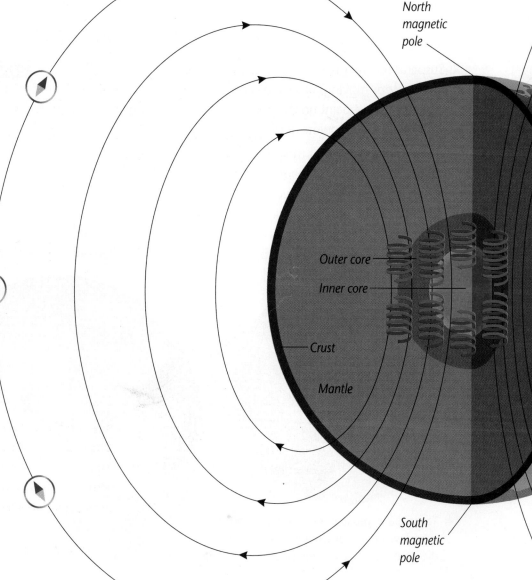

North magnetic pole

Outer core

Inner core

Crust

Mantle

South magnetic pole

Revealing Magnetic Forces

You know that a force acts between magnetic poles. But you've seen only its effects on other magnets—attraction or repulsion. What is the effect of a magnet on the region around it? Do the Explore activity below and find out.

Connect to...
Earth Science

Earth's magnetic and geographic poles aren't in the same place. Navigators must adjust compasses to find true north. Do you think this adjustment is the same worldwide? Why or why not?

Explore! ACTIVITY

Can you map a magnet's force?

What To Do

1. Obtain two bar magnets and iron filings from your teacher.
2. Place a bar magnet on a table and cover it with a piece of white paper as shown.
3. Sprinkle iron filings onto the paper and gently tap it. Observe the pattern that results and sketch it *in your Journal*. Label the location of the magnet's poles. How far from the magnet does the pattern extend?
4. Use the paper, both magnets, and iron filings to make sketches *in your Journal* of the pattern formed by two like poles about 2 cm apart and two unlike poles about 2 cm apart. How do the patterns differ? How are they similar?

 Compass needle

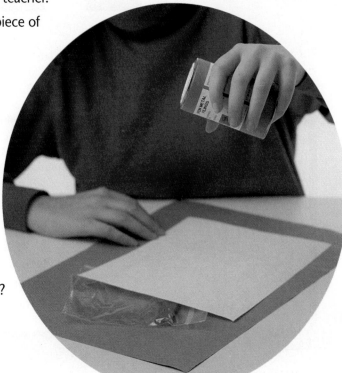

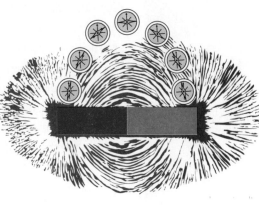

Figure 2-4

The iron filings around this bar magnet clump together where the force of the magnet is strongest. The compass needles also point along the lines formed by the iron filings. The force acting on the needles must also be causing the iron filings to align.

The patterns of filings form lines around the magnet. The region around a magnet where the magnetic force acts is called a **magnetic field**.

When you bring like poles together, the field lines from each of these poles bend away from the pole of the other magnet. When you bring unlike poles near each other, the filings line up to reveal that the magnetic field links the two poles.

Figure 2-5

The magnetic lines of force in a magnetic field are not always the same distance apart. Where are magnetic field lines most numerous and closest together? Where is a magnetic field the strongest?

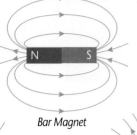

Bar Magnet

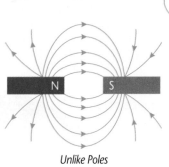

Unlike Poles

Like Poles

Earth Science CONNECTION

Van Allen Belts

You make use of Earth's magnetic field every time you find direction with a compass. You can see in the drawing how Earth's huge magnetic field extends far out in space.

The field acts as an umbrella that protects us from the shower of high-energy, charged particles from space. These particles could cause cancer and genetic damage in living things.

When the first artificial satellites were launched into space, scientists discovered a previously unknown region of charged particles in space near Earth. Dr. James Van Allen of the University of Iowa suggested that the particles the satellite detected come from the solar wind, the stream of charged

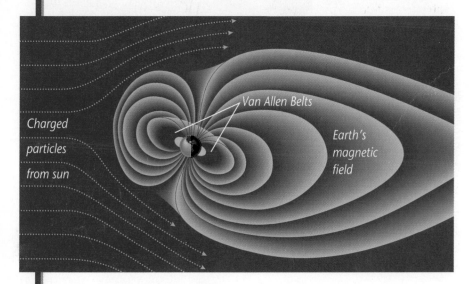

Charged particles from sun

Van Allen Belts

Earth's magnetic field

Van Allen radiation belts extend from approximately 1000 to 25 000 km above the surface of the Earth.

Figure 2-6

The paper and iron filings showed you only part of a bar magnet's field. The magnetic field isn't flat like paper, it's three-dimensional. The field extends around the magnet on all sides. The iron filings in this tank of mineral oil have clumped and aligned on all sides of the two cylindrical magnets inside.

particles emitted by the sun. He hypothesized that charged particles from the sun interact with Earth's magnetic field. Van Allen said that the force due to Earth's magnetic field makes the particles move in circles around the field lines. The drawing shows how the particles are trapped in regions above Earth's equator. These regions are now called Van Allen Belts in honor of the scientist who first explained them.

Occasionally, the sun emits larger than usual numbers of particles. The excess particles are pushed along Earth's magnetic field lines toward the north and south magnetic poles. There the particles interact with gases high in the atmosphere, creating spectacular displays known as the northern and southern lights, as shown in the photo to the right.

You Try It!

Intense solar flares can disrupt the Van Allen Belts. Solar flares can lead to changes on Earth, such as interference with radio reception, surges in electric power lines, and more visible northern and southern lights. Write a newspaper story explaining such happenings as if they occurred in your area. Mention Dr. Van Allen.

Northern and southern lights may be visible any time of the year, but they occur more frequently during periods of concentrated sunspot and other solar activity.

Figure 2-7

Ⓐ Much geologic activity occurs under the sea near the boundaries of huge, rocky plates on Earth's crust. Liquid rock from Earth's core pushes up. This liquid rock may be magnetized by Earth's magnetic field. When the rock cools and becomes solid, the magnetic field is "frozen" in. Geologists have used these rocks to study how Earth's magnetic field has changed over time.

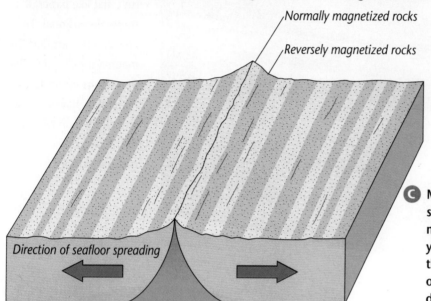

Normally magnetized rocks

Reversely magnetized rocks

Direction of seafloor spreading

Ⓒ Magnetic fields surround doughnut magnets. What can you observe about the magnetic poles of this stack of doughnut magnets?

Ⓑ Earth's magnetic field has flip-flopped, north and south, at least 171 times. One way scientists know this is by the direction of magnetized rock on the sea floor.

Your experience with magnetic toys, refrigerator magnets, and magnetic compasses showed you that magnets acted differently from other materials. Now you've started to understand the behavior of magnets. You've seen that every magnet has two kinds of poles—north and south. Like poles repel each other and unlike poles attract each other. You've seen that the poles are the part of the magnet where its force is strongest. You've mapped the region around the magnet, where the magnetic forces act, and identified it as the magnetic field of the magnet. The strength of the field can be found from the magnetic field lines. Earth has a magnetic field that resembles the field of a gigantic bar magnet.

check your UNDERSTANDING

1. Figure 2-7 shows the field around a doughnut-shaped magnet. Where are this magnet's poles? How would you identify the magnet's north and south poles?

2. Figure 2-7 also shows five doughnut-shaped magnets on a pencil. Suppose the lower pole on the bottom magnet is the north pole. Identify both poles on each of the four magnets.

3. What is the relationship between the magnetic force and the magnetic field?

4. **Apply** If a magnetic compass needle points north, what is the actual polarity of Earth's northern pole? Explain.

2-2 Magnets

Magnetic Attraction

In the previous section, you observed that there are magnetic fields around Earth and around bar magnets. And you know that if you break a magnet, you get two smaller magnets. But, what is a magnet? Does making a magnet require special materials? Can you make a magnet from something nonmagnetic? Do the Explore activity and find out.

Explore! ACTIVITY

Can you magnetize a nail?

What To Do

1. Place an iron nail near one end of a bar magnet. Sprinkle some iron filings on the nail. What happens?

2. Remove the bar magnet and tap the nail. *In your Journal,* describe what happens to the iron filings.

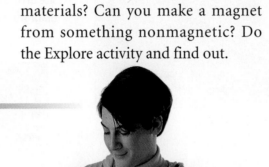

■ What Makes Magnets

The iron nail you magnetized is only a temporary magnet. Its magnetism was caused by the presence of a strong magnetic field. Magnetism that occurs only in the presence of a magnetic field is called **induced magnetism**. The iron nail developed magnetic poles while it was near the magnet. When you removed the nail from the magnetic field, the nail's poles soon disappeared. Why was it possible to make a magnet? Would a piece of plastic or an aluminum nail act this way? Try it!

From the Explore activity you might hypothesize that the magnetism of materials depends on the kind of atom of which they are made. For materials attracted to the bar magnet, our hypothesis would suggest that their atoms have tiny net magnetic fields. Therefore, the atoms can act like magnets.

Section Objectives

- Explain the effects of magnetic fields on various materials.
- Make magnets out of nonmagnetic materials.
- Make an electromagnet and demonstrate its magnetic effects.
- Use magnetic domain to describe how objects can be magnetized or demagnetized.

Key Terms

induced magnetism
electromagnet

DID YOU KNOW?

Lightning can magnetize objects so strongly that they are capable of lifting objects as much as three times their own weight.

2-2 Magnets **57**

One atom produces a very weak magnetic field. Many atoms with N and S poles aligned produce a much stronger field. Groups of atoms in which magnetic fields are aligned are called domains. Each polygon in the figures below represents a domain containing millions of atoms. Each arrow indicates the direction of that domain's magnetic field.

Figure 2-8

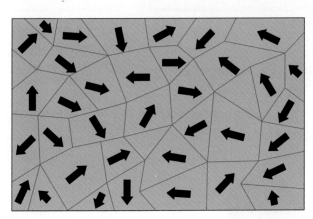

Non-magnetic

Ⓐ In substances that are not magnetized, all of the magnetic fields of the domains are not oriented in the same direction. If you look carefully, each arrow has an opposite arrow, which cancels its effect. Select an arrow in the diagram; can you find its opposite arrow?

Ⓑ A horseshoe magnet is one example of a magnetized substance.

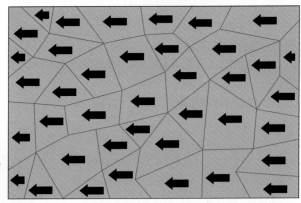

Magnetic

Ⓒ In substances that are magnetized, most of the magnetic fields are oriented in the same direction.

You've already made a temporary magnet, one that works only in the presence of a magnetic field. From what you know about magnetic domains, do you think you can make a permanent magnet? Try the activity on the next page to find out.

How Do We Know?

Is there any observable evidence that magnetic domains exist?

Yes. A fine powder of iron oxide, also known as rust, is spread over a smooth surface of a magnetized metal. It's a little like placing iron filings around a bar magnet. The powder collects along the boundaries between neighboring clusters of magnetic atoms. These clusters are called domains. The boundaries are visible under a microscope and can be photographed. These outlines allow us to observe the way magnetic atoms interact with each other.

Find Out! ACTIVITY

Can you make a permanent magnet?

You've used magnets many times, but how are they created?

What To Do

1. Obtain from your teacher a sewing needle, bar magnet, paper clips, small plastic bottle, Bunsen burner, and tongs or pliers.

2. Stroke the needle along the length of a bar magnet about 50 times.

3. Now, see how many paper clips the needle can pick up. *In your Journal*, use the theory of magnetic domains to explain how this magnet was created.

4. Put the needle into the plastic bottle and shake it hard for 30 seconds. Test the needle's magnetism again. Has it changed?

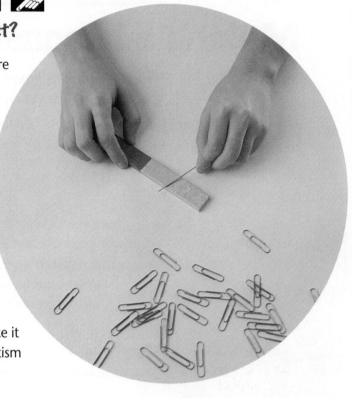

Conclude and Apply

1. Use the theory of magnetic domains to explain how the steel needle lost its magnetism.

2. Make another steel needle magnet. Then, heat it red hot using the Bunsen burner and tongs. After it's cooled, test its magnetism again. Did the needle change? If so, why?

■ Permanent Magnets

Some materials are noticeably influenced by magnetic fields—they become magnets themselves. Materials that can be made into permanent magnets are most useful. One such material is an alloy of aluminum, nickel, and cobalt. ALNICO (ALuminum, NIckel, and CObalt) magnets retain their magnetism for a long time.

The temporary and permanent magnets you've observed have been made of magnetic materials. Can a magnetic field exist without a magnetic material? Do the Investigation on the next pages to find an answer.

SKILLBUILDER

Observing and Inferring

A group of students must identify the poles of three magnets. Each end of each magnet is a different color. The students suspend one magnet. It rotates until its red end points north and its silver end points south. For the second magnet, they find that the green end repels the red end, but the yellow end attracts the red. Then the students place a blue/pink magnet next to the red/silver magnet. Both the blue end and the pink end attract the red end. How should the students label the green/yellow magnet? What can they conclude about the blue/pink magnet? If you need help, refer to the **Skill Handbook** on page 683.

DESIGN YOUR OWN
INVESTIGATION

Making a Magnet

In this chapter, you've studied magnets made of magnetic material. Electromagnets are made from nonmagnetic materials. When an electric current flows through a wire, it produces a magnetic field. A compass needle will be deflected by this field. Electromagnets are used in many devices from an electromagnetic crane to a door bell.

Preparation

Problem
What determines the strength of an electromagnet?

Form a Hypothesis
After your group examines the materials and the photos on these pages, write down factors that you think would affect the strength of an electromagnet. Form a hypothesis about how to make the strongest electromagnet.

Objectives
- Make electromagnets.
- Design an experiment to test the strength of each electromagnet.
- Determine the factors that make an electromagnet strong.

Materials
1 m of 22-gauge insulated wire
large iron nail
craft stick
3 D-cell batteries
metal paper clips
magnetic compass
scissors

Safety

Plan the Experiment

1 Before you build a strong electromagnet, start an electric current flowing through a wire, then hold a compass near it. Notice what happens. Is this an electromagnet?

2 As a group, discuss factors that may influence the strength of an electromagnet.

3 Design electromagnets on paper, changing one factor in each design. How will you test the strength of each electromagnet you make from the designs?

4 Design a data table in your Science Journal to record your test results.

Check the Plan

1 You should design at least five different electromagnets.

2 Make certain you use all the materials provided in one electromagnetic design or another.

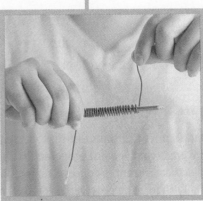

3 Before you proceed with your investigation, make sure your teacher approves your plan.

4 Carry out your investigation and record your data *in your Science Journal.*

Analyze and Conclude

1. Analyze How does the number of batteries affect the strength of the magnet?

2. Compare Which number of turns of wire produced the strongest effect?

3. Compare Is the electromagnet stronger or weaker without a core? Does the material used as a core to wrap the wire affect the strength of the magnet?

4. Infer How does the strength of the current affect the strength of the magnetic field? The number of turns of wire?

5. Conclude Which electromagnet design produced the strongest magnet? What materials did it use? What factors were important in its construction? Did this result support your hypothesis?

Going Further

Design a system using an electromagnet to ring a bell.

You have seen that it's possible to make a magnet out of nothing more than a current-carrying wire. Such a magnet is called an **electromagnet**. The photo below shows an example of the first evidence of electromagnetism.

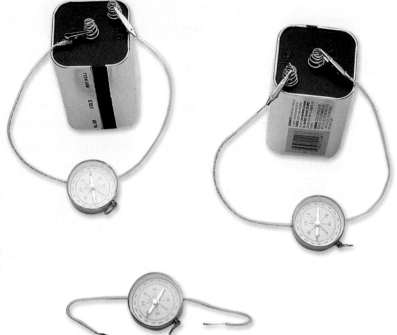

Figure 2-9

A Danish physicist, Hans Christian Oersted, discovered what you just observed first-hand: an electrical current produces a magnetic field. By chance, he observed a compass needle move when he turned on a switch. Notice how the lone compass points north while the two compasses on top of current-carrying wires point at right angles to the wires.

How Can You Make a Transformer?

Similar in appearance to an electromagnet, a transformer is made using an iron core and wire coils. The magnetic field produced in the iron core links two coils in a special way. Alternating current is transmitted to the second coil and its voltage is changed based on how many loops of wire are in each coil.

Insert a large nail in a soda straw that has been cut to the same length as the nail. Wrap 30 turns of 32-gauge wire in a tight compact coil at one end of the straw. Make a coil at the other end that has 120 turns. Use sandpaper to remove the insulating coating from the ends of the wire.

Connect the ends of the 30-turn coil to a low-voltage AC power supply. This will be the source of the voltage your transformer will change. Connect the ends of the 120-turn wire to the light bulb, the

An electric power station

Electromagnets at Work

You use wires and magnets whenever you listen to a tape recording, talk on a telephone, ring an electric doorbell, or dry your hair with an electric dryer. Electromagnets are useful because their magnetism

Figure 2-10

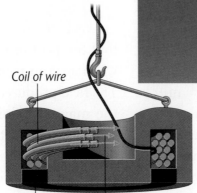

A In a crane electromagnet, a magnetic field occurs when electric current flows through the coil of wire.

Coil of wire

Soft iron core   Flow of charges

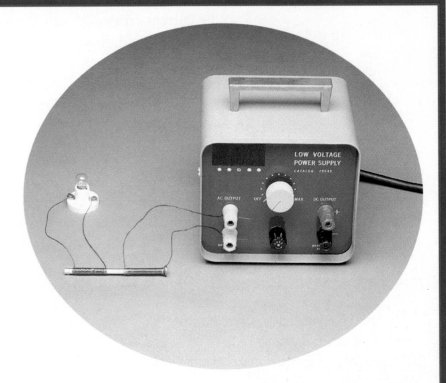

B How does a crane operator release an object that is held by an electromagnet?

user to which your transformer will transmit electricity. Observe how brightly the light bulb glows. Now reverse the position of the coils—connect the 120-turn coil to the power supply and the 30-turn coil to the light bulb. How brightly does the bulb glow in this arrangement?

Transformers are generally called step-up transformers or step-down transformers. Use your observations to determine which time your coil-wrapped straw acted like a step-up transformer. Explain your choice.

What Do You Think?

Repeat the activity you just completed without placing the iron nail inside the straw. Record your observations. Then place several other items, such as a paper clip, a pencil lead, and a string, inside the straw. What happens? Use your knowledge of magnetism, magnetic fields, and electric fields to explain your observations.

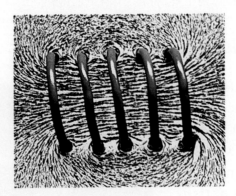

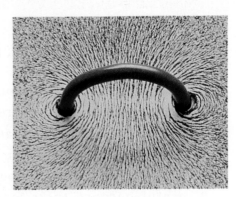

Making Models and Observing and Inferring

The right-hand rule is useful for determining the direction of the magnetic field around a current-carrying wire when the direction of the current is shown. You think of grasping the wire in your right hand, as shown below. When your thumb extends in the direction of the current, as your fingers curl, they travel around the wire in the direction of the magnetic field. The photographs to the right show coils and iron filings. What direction is the magnetic field inside the coils? If you need help, refer to the **Skill Handbook** on pages 692 and 683.

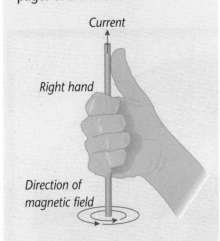

Current

Right hand

Direction of magnetic field

can be turned on and off and because they can produce magnetic fields much stronger than any permanent magnets.

When you allowed current to flow through the wire of your electromagnet the current created a magnetic field. You increased the strength of the magnet by increasing the number of batteries and by increasing the number of turns of wire. You also found that the field of the coil was stronger when an iron nail was inside the coil. The field produced by the coil realigns the magnetic domains in the iron. This adds strength to the field produced by the current in the wire coil.

In this section, you've discovered that a magnet is a collection of domains, most of which are lined up in the same direction. You've made magnets that lasted for a short time and magnets that were more permanent. And, you produced a magnetic field without using a permanent magnet. Next, you'll learn how magnets and electric currents interact.

check your UNDERSTANDING

1. Why are certain materials affected by magnets while others are not?
2. Describe how you would make a permanent magnet out of a paper clip.
3. Compare and contrast an electromagnet with a permanent magnet.
4. Using magnetic domains, explain how and why a permanent magnet can lose its magnetism.
5. **Apply** You leave a box of paper clips on top of your TV. When you go to use them, you find they are stuck together. What might you infer about the TV?

2-3 ◆ Effects of Magnetic Fields

Magnetism and Electric Currents

Section Objectives
■ Demonstrate the effects of magnetic fields on wires carrying electric currents.
■ Explain how loudspeakers and electric motors work.

Key Terms
loudspeaker
electric motor

In the last chapter, you saw that an electric current can create a magnetic field. But what about the reverse situation? What effect does a magnetic field have on a static electric charge or on a current? You can combine what you learned from Chapter 1 and your new experiences with magnets to test the two parts of this question. Do the activity below to answer the first part.

Explore! ACTIVITY

Does a magnetic field exert force on a charge?

What To Do

1. Obtain from your teacher transparent tape and a bar magnet.

2. Make two oppositely charged pieces of tape as in the Find Out activity in Chapter 1 on pages 22 and 23.

3. Bring one pole of a bar magnet near one tape, then near the other. *In your Journal*, describe what happens. (Remember that an uncharged conductor, such as your finger, will attract both tapes. So, if both tapes move, make sure you are not observing this effect.)

Now, remember what you know about circuits and currents and do the activity on the next page to answer the second part of the question.

Find Out! ACTIVITY

Does a magnetic field exert force on a current?

Magnets seem to have no effect on static charges. What do they do to moving charges?

What To Do

1. Obtain from your teacher a D-cell, 50 cm of 22-gauge wire, and a bar magnet.

2. Connect one end of the wire to the D-cell. Then, form a large, loose loop of wire and put one pole of the magnet about 2 cm away. Touch the free end of the wire to the other terminal of the D-cell. What happens?

3. Try Step 2 with as many different arrangements of magnet poles and wire connections as possible. Do the results differ? Why?

Conclude and Apply

How did the magnetic field affect the wire?

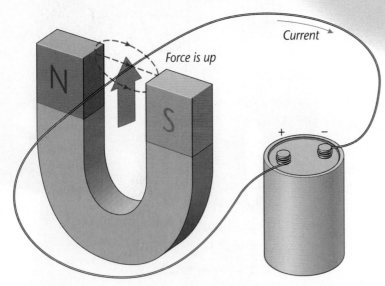

Figure 2-11

While current flows through the wire, the magnet exerts a force on the wire. The force is at right angles to the lines of the magnetic field and to the direction of the current. In this case, the force is up.

A magnetic field has no effect on a static charge. However, you can see that a magnetic field does exert force on a wire in which current is flowing. When you placed the current-carrying wire near the magnet, the magnet pushed the wire one way or the other. The direction depended on which end of the magnet you brought near the wire. The poles of the magnetic field in the loop of wire could also be reversed—by reversing the current direction. The diagram to the left shows the direction of the current and of the force on the wire.

Changing Current Into Sound

Here's one use of magnets many people enjoy every day: radios or stereos. They run on electricity, but what comes out are voices and music, not current. The following activity will help explain how radios and speakers transform electric current into entertaining or informative sounds.

Find Out! ACTIVITY

How does electricity turn into sound?

Many appliances produce sound for your pleasure. What makes them work?

What To Do

1. Strip 1 cm of insulation from each end of a 2 m wire. Make a coil of 10, 1-cm in diameter turns in the middle of the wire and glue the coil securely to the bottom of a paper cup.

2. Attach one stripped end to each wire of an earphone plug from a portable radio.

3. Turn on the radio, tune in a local station, and insert the plug into the earphone jack. Then, hold the magnet very close to the coil as shown in the figure.

Conclude and Apply

1. What happens?
2. Why do you think this happens?

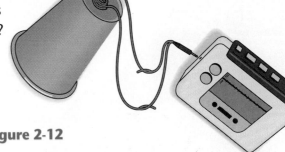

Figure 2-12

Your portable stereo turns electric current into sound.

The radio sends a constantly changing current through the wire. When you bring the magnet near the coil, the coil's changing magnetic field interacts with the magnet. The motion of the coil causes the cup to vibrate, creating sound waves. What you've observed is electric energy being changed into sound energy. You've built a loudspeaker. A **loudspeaker** changes variations in electric current into sound waves. Currents and magnetic fields can work in other ways. Do the Investigate activity on the next pages to see how.

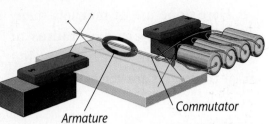

Armature

Commutator

INVESTIGATE!

Make an Electric Motor

When you made the paper cup loudspeaker, you changed electric energy into sound. In this activity, you'll change electric energy into mechanical energy.

Problem

How can you change electric energy into motion?

Materials

2 m 22-gauge insulated wire	masking tape
steel knitting needle or thin steel rod	fine sandpaper
	wooden board (approximately 14 x 16 cm)
4 nails	
2 bar magnets	2 wooden blocks
16-gauge insulated wire	6-V battery
	scissors or wire cutters

Safety Precautions

What To Do

1. Strip the insulation from 4 cm of each end of the 22-gauge wire.

2. Leaving about 4 cm free at each end, form a coil of at least 30 turns by winding the 22-gauge wire around a cylinder, such as a battery. Slide the coil off the cylinder and tape the turns of wire together.

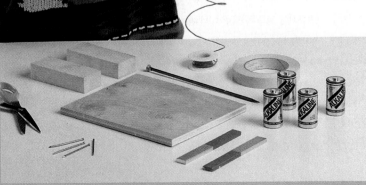

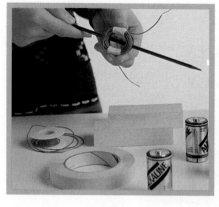

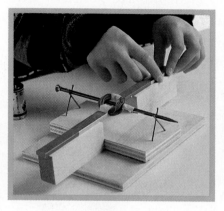

A   **B**   **C**

3 Insert the knitting needle through the coil. Try to have an equal number of turns on each side of the needle (see Photo **A**). The coil is the armature. Tape each of the wire's bare ends to one side of the needle. This part of the motor is the commutator.

4 Mount the needle on the crossed nails as shown in the diagram.

5 Tape a magnet to each block and place them on each side of the coil-needle assembly as shown (see Photo **B**). Be sure the poles are placed as indicated.

6 Take two 30 cm lengths of 16-gauge wire. Strip both ends and attach one length to each terminal of the battery (see Photo **C**). Holding only the insulated part of each wire, hold one wire gently against each bare wire of the commutator. Observe what happens to the armature.

Analyzing

1. Observe that the armature is designed so that the current through it changes direction as the armature rotates. How could you test it to see if it is working?

2. Is there any position of the coil that makes it easier to start it spinning? Why would you hypothesize that this is true?

Concluding and Applying

3. The electric motor operates on three basic principles. What are they?

4. Going Further Would the motor work if you replaced the armature with a permanent magnet? Explain.

In making the motor, you see a practical application of the interaction between magnetism and electricity. Air conditioners, vacuum cleaners, and washing machines use electric motors. An **electric motor** uses an electromagnet to change electric energy into mechanical energy, which can be used to do work. This illustration of a vacuum cleaner shows how such motors work.

Figure 2-13

A An electric motor that is powered by a battery contains a wire loop that spins on a shaft, a permanent magnet, a commutator, and brushes.

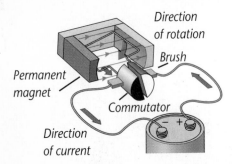

B As electricity is applied to the brushes that touch the commutator, a current creates a force on the sides of the wire loop.

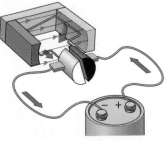

Figure 2-14

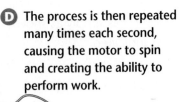

This vacuum cleaner is driven by an electric motor which uses 120V household current. It is similar to the simpler, low voltage motors in the illustrations to the left.

Fan

Motor

Dustbag

C When that side of the wire loop moves past the magnet, the commutator changes the direction of the current, and the forces are reversed so the rotation continues.

D The process is then repeated many times each second, causing the motor to spin and creating the ability to perform work.

In this section, you've seen that magnetic fields can affect the direction of electric current. This interaction can be used in devices such as loudspeakers and electric motors. In the next section, you'll find out about still other useful roles that magnets play in day-to-day life.

check your UNDERSTANDING

1. How must a loudspeaker coil and magnet be arranged to make the coil vibrate?
2. Why do most electric motors contain both a permanent magnet and an electromagnet?
3. **Apply** In what direction—with respect to a magnetic field—would you run a wire carrying a current, so that the force on it due to the field is zero?

2-4 ▸ Producing Electric Currents

Magnetism and Electric Current

Section Objectives
- Demonstrate the ability of a changing magnetic field to produce an electric current.
- Describe the working principles behind electric generators.
- Explain the operation of transformers.

Key Terms
induced current
electric generator
transformer

When you made the electromagnet in the last section, you found evidence that an electric current could produce magnetism. Once again, think about the reverse situation. Can magnetism produce electricity? An American scientist and a British scientist independently discovered that it could be done. You can find out how below.

Find Out! ACTIVITY

Does a moving magnet produce a current?

Electric current in conductors can make magnets. What effect do magnets have on conductors?

What To Do

1. Leaving enough free wire to connect to the galvanometer, form a coil just large enough to accept the magnet.

2. Connect the wire ends to the galvanometer terminals.

3. Observe the galvanometer as you **a.** insert the magnet into the coil; **b.** hold the magnet inside the coil; **c.** pull the magnet out; **d.** hold the magnet just outside the coil; and **e.** move the magnet back and forth inside the coil. *In your Journal,* record your observations.

Conclude and Apply

1. Did the magnet produce a current? How do you know?

2. When the direction of the magnetic field changed, what happened?

When you move the magnet into the coil, the galvanometer pointer moves to the left of zero, indicating a small current. When you remove the magnet, the pointer swings the opposite direction, indicating a small current in the opposite direction. If you kept moving the magnet back and forth, you would create a current that kept changing direction.

Moving either the coil or the magnet will produce a current. It's the motion of one in relation to the other that matters. Any time a conductor, such as the coil, experiences a changing magnetic field, an electric current is induced in the conductor. An electric current produced by using a magnet is an **induced current**.

■ Generating Current

Induced current has made it possible for every home and business to receive electric energy from a central source. The current commonly used is produced by electric generators. An **electric generator** like those shown in **Figures 2-15** and **2-16** changes kinetic energy of rotation into electric energy.

Figure 2-15

Ⓐ One simple generator converts mechanical energy from cranking into electrical energy. It consists of a loop of wire that rotates in a horseshoe magnet. As the loop turns, it moves through the magnetic field and produces an induced current.

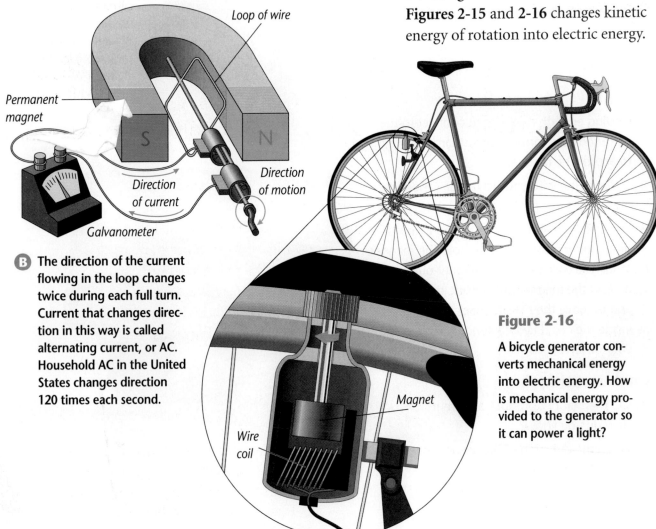

Loop of wire

Permanent magnet

S   N

Direction of current

Direction of motion

Galvanometer

Ⓑ The direction of the current flowing in the loop changes twice during each full turn. Current that changes direction in this way is called alternating current, or AC. Household AC in the United States changes direction 120 times each second.

Magnet

Wire coil

Figure 2-16

A bicycle generator converts mechanical energy into electric energy. How is mechanical energy provided to the generator so it can power a light?

Changing Currents

Power companies use transformers to ensure the proper voltage for the circuits of lights, home appliances, and other electric equipment in your home. Transformers also enable power companies to transmit alternating current to their users easily and efficiently. A **transformer** can raise or lower the voltage. Look at **Figure 2-17** below.

Step-up Transformer

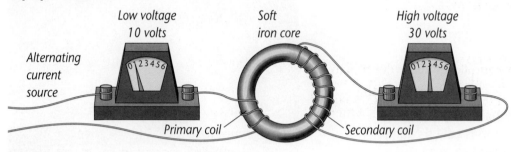

Low voltage 10 volts • Soft iron core • High voltage 30 volts • Alternating current source • Primary coil • Secondary coil

Step-Down Transformer

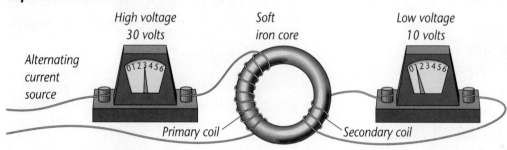

High voltage 30 volts • Soft iron core • Low voltage 10 volts • Alternating current source • Primary coil • Secondary coil

Figure 2-17

When an alternating current passes through the primary coil of a step-up or step-down transformer, a changing magnetic field is created, inducing a current to flow in the secondary coil. What determines the exact voltage increase or decrease in these transformers?

Step-up transformers raise the voltage to a level that allows the electrical energy to travel long distances with little loss. When the energy reaches the area where it will be used, step-down transformers there lower the voltage to the level needed. Like generators, transformers work by inducing currents.

In this section, you've learned that a current is induced in a coil when a magnetic field is changed. The field can be changed by moving either the magnet or the coil. Electric generators induce current by rotating a coil in a magnetic field. You're unlikely to own a generator, but you probably use electricity from one daily.

check your UNDERSTANDING

1. Describe three ways in which a current can be induced in a circuit.
2. How is a generator like a motor? How is it different?
3. **Apply** Generators are used in some electric cars to transform energy from braking to electricity to recharge the car's batteries. Describe how this might work.

Science *and* Society

High-Tech Health Care

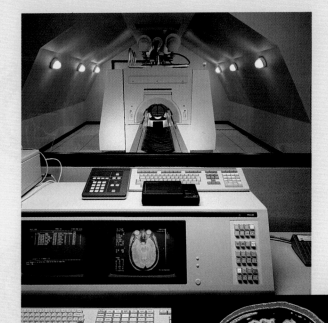

Several new technologies allow doctors to produce images of what is inside the human body without using X rays. One of the most common is called Magnetic Resonance Imaging (MRI). The machine consists of a large coil that creates a strong magnetic field. MRI works because the positively charged particles at the center of each atom making up the body act like tiny bar magnets. These bar magnets aren't usually lined up in any orderly fashion, but when put in a strong magnetic field, the magnets line up like soldiers on parade.

An electromagnetic wave is created in the region of the organ being studied. If the wave has exactly the correct frequency, it can cause the tiny magnets to flip over. The flipping requires energy—the more magnets flipped, the more energy required.

CAREER connection

MRI technicians must be able to operate imaging equipment. They also need to use probes to measure the magnetic field strength. A period of specialized training is required. MRI technicians work in hospitals and medical schools.

Medical Uses

The frequency needed to flip the magnets depends on the tissue in which they are located. Therefore, as the frequency of the wave is varied, first one type of tissue absorbs energy, then another type. A computer creates a three-dimensional image based on energy absorption patterns.

Being able to distinguish between diseased and normal tissue while it is still inside a patient's body, without surgery, is a great breakthrough. With MRI, doctors can watch the swelling caused by arthritis shrink when medicine is applied to a swollen knee.

Operating Costs

As wonderful as these advances in medical science are, they do not come cheaply. An MRI machine is expensive and hard to maintain. The machine must be shielded from magnetic materials in the surrounding area. Even a lawn mower being run outside the hospital could affect test results. The powerful magnets could also affect other equipment in the hospital, causing it to malfunction. The cost of running MRI machinery is high. To supply and operate a machine costs about $100 000 a year.

Some people say hospitals shouldn't purchase costly equipment because such purchases make the bill for ordinary medical care much higher than it should be. They think MRI machines should be limited to only a few hospitals. What do you think? Would your opinion change if someone in your family needed to be diagnosed with MRI?

You Try It!

Call or visit a hospital in your area that offers MRI services. Find out how much the machine costs to purchase and how much it costs to maintain. Inquire about the source of the funds for these expenses.

 **Granville T. Woods**

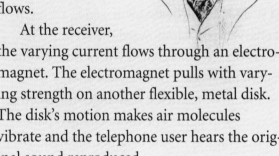

The communications industry owes much to Granville T. Woods. In 1884, the young African-American inventor patented one of the most important applications of electromagnets in recent history—a new telephone transmitter system. It produced a much more distinct sound and was able to carry a voice signal over a much greater length of wire than previous transmitter systems.

In the transmitter, a metal disk presses on a box filled with tiny grains of carbon. The disk moves back and forth in response to sound waves. When the carbon grains are compressed they have lower resistance and more current flows through the box of carbon grains to the receiver. When the disk flexes the other way, the grains have higher resistance and less current flows.

At the receiver, the varying current flows through an electromagnet. The electromagnet pulls with varying strength on another flexible, metal disk. The disk's motion makes air molecules vibrate and the telephone user hears the original sound reproduced.

 **Science Journal**

In your Science Journal compare Woods' telephone transmitter with a modern one. How are they similar? How are they different?

HOW IT WORKS

Television Picture Tube

Suppose you are watching an exciting movie on TV. When you see the action, you wonder how your favorite actors appear on your television screen. Part of the answer lies in the magnetic and electric fields produced in the picture tube of your set.

Look at the illustration. At one end of the picture tube is the rectangular glass screen where you can watch the movie. Inside the television set, video or picture signals are received. These signals are sent through the air on radio waves from the broadcasting station.

A wire in the tube heats up when you turn on your TV. The heated wire sends a stream of charged particles toward the screen. The television screen is coated with a fluorescent material that absorbs electrical energy from the stream of particles. It changes the electrical energy to light. The more charged particles that hit a spot, the brighter the light. In this way, a picture of what is happening at a distance is "painted" on your screen with varying colors and intensities.

When your TV is tuned in, the signals from the TV station are processed in the TV set, and vary the stream of particles. The

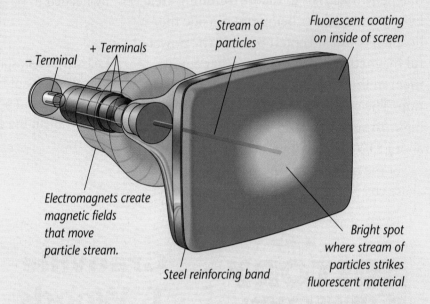

− Terminal

+ Terminals

Stream of particles

Fluorescent coating on inside of screen

Electromagnets create magnetic fields that move particle stream.

Steel reinforcing band

Bright spot where stream of particles strikes fluorescent material

number of particles then corresponds to the picture that is being broadcast.

The particles are moved across the television screen by two varying magnetic fields. One field moves the stream of particles up and down. The other field moves the stream left and right. This movement allows the stream of charged particles to sweep across the entire screen. In one-thirtieth of a second, a total of 535 lines of light resulting from the particles cover the glass tube. A full, smoothly moving picture results.

You Try It!

Closed-circuit television lets you watch what is happening in another part of the building. Find out how this works. From what you have learned about television, write an article that explains how closed-circuit TV works at your school or in a building lobby.

Science Journal

Review the statements below about the big ideas presented in this chapter, and answer the questions. Then, reread your answers to the Did You Ever Wonder questions at the beginning of the chapter. *In your Science Journal*, write a paragraph about how your understanding of the big ideas in the chapter has changed.

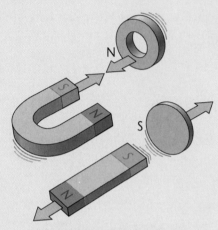

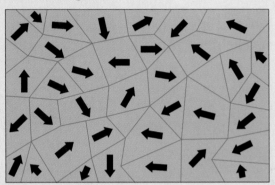

1 Magnets have two poles, the places where the magnetic field is strongest. Like poles repel each other; unlike poles attract each other. *How could you locate the poles on an unusually shaped magnet?*

2 Atoms themselves have tiny magnetic fields. In an unmagnetized substance, the atomic magnets point in random directions, but in a magnetized substance, they line up. *How can you make groups of atomic magnets line up?*

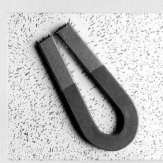

3 A magnetic field is a region where magnetic forces act. *How could you identify the shape of a magnetic field around an object?*

4 An electric current creates a magnetic field, making electromagnets and electric motors possible. *Why do electric motors turn?*

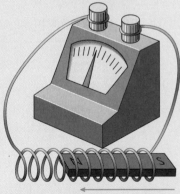

(1)   (2)

5 In an electric generator, a changing magnetic field induces an electric current. Transformers step up or step down a voltage. *How is the magnetic field changed in a generator?*

chapter 2
CHAPTER REVIEW

Using Key Science Terms

electric generator	loudspeaker
electric motor	magnetic field
electromagnet	magnetic poles
induced current	transformer
induced magnetism	

Distinguish between the terms in each of the following pairs.

1. magnetic field, magnetic poles
2. permanent magnet, electromagnet
3. induced current, induced magnetism
4. electric generator, electric motor

Understanding Ideas

Answer the following questions in your Journal using complete sentences.

1. What is one method of revealing a magnet's field?
2. What does a galvanometer detect?
3. What happens when a coil of wire cuts through a magnetic field?
4. What device is used to raise or lower voltage?
5. What does a loudspeaker do?
6. Name the three elements from which most magnets are made.

7. What is the purpose of the commutator in an electric motor?
8. You can induce a current in a coil by passing a magnet through the coil. What are three ways of increasing the strength of the induced current? How can you change the direction of the induced current?

Developing Skills

Use your understanding of the concepts developed in this chapter to answer each of the following questions.

1. **Predicting** Refer to the Investigation on pages 60-61. Suppose you had made a magnet with 4 batteries and 60 turns of wire. Compare the number of paper clips this magnet could pick up to the number picked up by a magnet with 2 batteries and 30 turns of wire.

2. **Interpreting Scientific Illustrations** Refer to the illustration accompanying the Skillbuilder on page 64. Use this illustration to describe the magnetic field produced by 1) a wire carrying current toward you, and 2) a wire carrying current away from you.

3. **Observing and Inferring** Look at the magnetic field lines in Figure 2-5 and in the illustration accompanying the Skillbuilder on page 64. What is similar about the field lines in the two pictures?

4. **Recognizing Cause and Effect** Using the principles you've learned in this chapter, describe how a windmill-driven generator works.

Critical Thinking

Use your understanding of the concepts developed in the chapter to answer each of the following questions.

1. If a coil of wire were placed between these magnets, and a current passed through the wire, would the coil move? Explain.

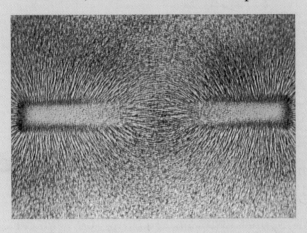

2. Is the magnetic pole in Earth's northern hemisphere like the north or south pole of a bar magnet? How do you know?

3. Explain how you could use Earth's magnetic field to help you magnetize a piece of iron.
4. Why will a magnet attract a nail to either of its poles but attract another magnet to only one of its poles?
5. What would you expect the current to be in a wire coil wrapped around a horseshoe magnet? Explain your answer.

Problem Solving

Read the following problem and discuss your answer in a brief paragraph.

Abdul has a small motor that requires 12 V of electricity. He is building a transformer to change the 120 V from the wall outlet to 12 V. If the input coil has 800 turns, how many turns will the output coil have?

CONNECTING IDEAS

Discuss each of the following in a brief paragraph.

1. **Scale and Structure** How are magnetic poles like electric charges? How are they different?
2. **Systems and Interactions** A wire carrying an electric current has a magnetic field, but a metal sphere that has a static electric charge doesn't produce a magnetic field. What do these facts suggest about the relationship between magnetism and electricity?
3. **A Closer Look** How would you build a transformer to change 12 V power to 60 V? What type of transformer is this?
4. **Earth Science Connection** How are the Van Allen radiation belts produced?
5. **Science and Society** Describe the role of the electromagnet in an MRI machine. How does this magnet allow doctors to see different body tissues?

CHAPTER 3

ELECTROMAGNETIC waves

Did you ever wonder...

✓ How walkie talkies send signals through the air?

✓ Why people in warm climates wear white clothing?

✓ Why you see colors on a black oil slick in the street?

Science Journal

Before you begin to study about electromagnetic waves, think about these questions and answer them *in your Science Journal.* When you finish the chapter, compare your journal write-up with what you have learned.

Waves carrying energy surround you every day. Some waves can be seen, the presence of others felt, but most can't be observed directly with your senses.

Have you ever listened to music on a portable radio, warmed your hands in front of a fire, or had your teeth checked for cavities at a dentist's office? You've heard about radio waves, microwaves, and X rays. But what are they? Are they very different, or related in some way?

▶ *This chapter will help you find answers to these questions. In the activity on the next page, explore one of the characteristics of electromagnetic waves.*

Explore! ACTIVITY

Do electrical appliances create disturbances?

What To Do

1. Tune a small, battery-powered AM radio between two stations so that you hear only noise.

2. Carry the radio around your house. Listen closely to the noise coming from the radio as you turn on and off a lamp, the television or vacuum cleaner, or a fluorescent light. Use any electrical appliances that are handy.

3. In Chapter 1, you learned that these appliances depend on moving electrical charges or the effects of magnetic fields. *In your Journal,* explain how you think electricity or magnetism is related to what you heard on the radio.

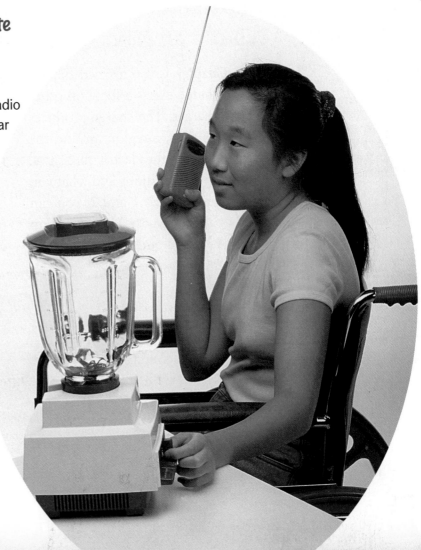

3-1 The Electromagnetic Spectrum

Section Objectives

■ Describe the nature of electromagnetic waves.

■ Compare and contrast the characteristics of waves in various parts of the electromagnetic spectrum.

■ Recognize the uses of energy carried by electromagnetic waves.

Key Terms

electromagnetic wave

electromagnetic spectrum

radiation

What's an Electromagnetic Wave?

In Chapter 1, you learned that an electric charge exerts a force on other electric charges. The charge produces an electric field, a region around the charge in which the electric force acts. From your observations and what you learned in Chapters 1 and 2, you can see that there may be a connection between electric and magnetic fields.

When you made an electromagnet, you used an electric current to produce a magnetic field. You also learned that magnetic fields exert a force on moving electric charges.

Figure 3-1 shows how an oscillating electric charge makes a combination of electric and magnetic fields called an **electromagnetic wave**.

Figure 3-1

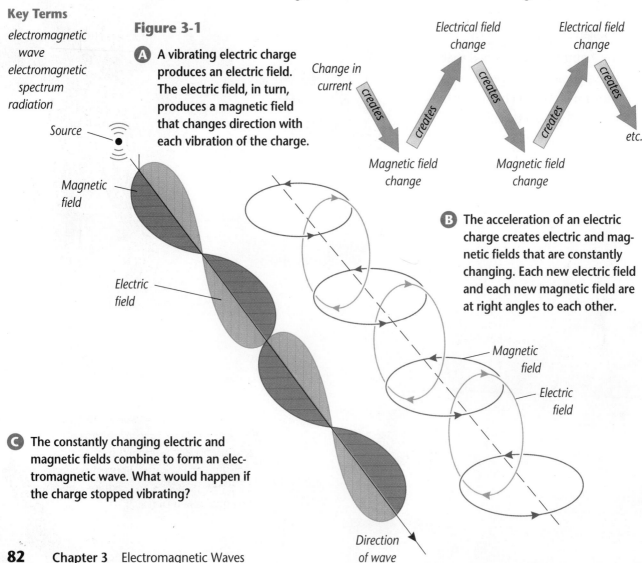

Ⓐ A vibrating electric charge produces an electric field. The electric field, in turn, produces a magnetic field that changes direction with each vibration of the charge.

Source

Magnetic field

Electric field

Change in current

creates

Magnetic field change

creates

Electrical field change

creates

Magnetic field change

creates

Electrical field change

creates

etc.

Ⓑ The acceleration of an electric charge creates electric and magnetic fields that are constantly changing. Each new electric field and each new magnetic field are at right angles to each other.

Magnetic field

Electric field

Ⓒ The constantly changing electric and magnetic fields combine to form an electromagnetic wave. What would happen if the charge stopped vibrating?

Direction of wave

Characteristics of Electromagnetic Waves

In the opening Explore activity with the portable radio, you detected electromagnetic waves coming from a variety of appliances as you changed the electrical and magnetic fields in the appliances. More elaborate experiments show that electromagnetic waves have properties of transverse waves and do not need a medium through which to travel. **Figure 3-2** below contrasts transverse and longitudinal waves.

Figure 3-2

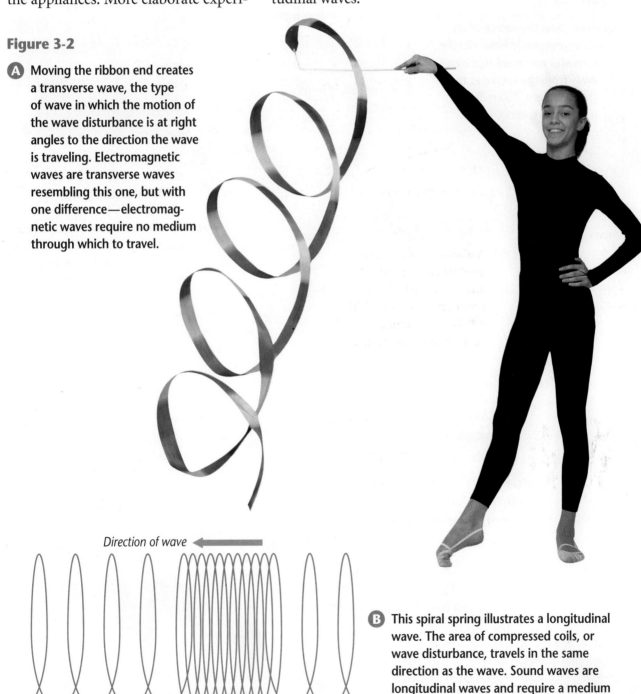

Ⓐ Moving the ribbon end creates a transverse wave, the type of wave in which the motion of the wave disturbance is at right angles to the direction the wave is traveling. Electromagnetic waves are transverse waves resembling this one, but with one difference—electromagnetic waves require no medium through which to travel.

Direction of wave ⟵

Ⓑ This spiral spring illustrates a longitudinal wave. The area of compressed coils, or wave disturbance, travels in the same direction as the wave. Sound waves are longitudinal waves and require a medium through which to travel.

Like all waves, electromagnetic waves can be described by their frequency, their wavelength, and speed as **Figure 3-3** shows.

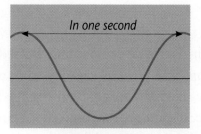

Low-frequency

In one second

High-frequency

In one second

B The distance from a point on one wave to the corresponding point on the next wave is called the wavelength.

Figure 3-3

A Every time the source of an electromagnetic wave vibrates, it creates one wave that moves away from the source at the speed of light, 300 million meters per second.

One wavelength

Source

C The more times per second an electric charge vibrates, the higher the frequency of the resulting electromagnetic wave. Because an electromagnetic wave moves out at a constant speed, its wavelength is inversely proportional to its frequency. If the frequency of a wave increases, does its wavelength get longer or shorter?

We can check the relationship between these three by using the units in which each is measured. Speed is distance divided by time—meters/second. Wavelength is the length, in meters, of one wave. We could express this as meters/wave. Finally, frequency is in hertz, or the number of waves per second. What mathematical relationship can we uncover by examining these units?

$$\frac{\text{meters}}{\text{second}} = \frac{\text{meters}}{\text{wave}} \times \frac{\text{waves}}{\text{second}}$$

$$\text{speed} = \text{wavelength} \times \text{frequency}$$

You can then solve this equation for any of the terms you wish to find. What is the frequency of an electromagnetic wave which has a wavelength of 100 m?

$$\text{speed} = \text{wavelength} \times \text{frequency}$$

Dividing both sides by wavelength, we get

$$\text{frequency} = \text{speed/wavelength}$$

The speed of light is a constant.

$$= \frac{300\ 000\ 000\ \text{m/s}}{100\ \text{m/wave}}$$

$$= 3\ 000\ 000\ \frac{\text{waves}}{\text{second}}$$

$$= 3\ 000\ 000\ \text{Hz}$$

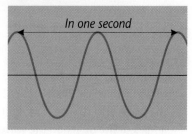

Electromagnetic waves come in a wide range of wavelengths and frequencies. Each wavelength is useful in a different way. We've mentioned electricity, light, and radio. At the beginning of the chapter, we also talked about X rays and microwaves. Do the Find Out activity below to see how the frequencies and wavelengths of these waves compare.

Find Out! ACTIVITY

How do frequencies of electromagnetic waves compare?

What To Do

Use the equation you've just learned to find the frequency of the electromagnetic waves listed to the right.

Conclude and Apply

1. Which wave has the lowest frequency? The highest?

2. What is the relationship between wavelength and frequency?

Wavelength vs. Frequency		
Wave source	Wavelength	Frequency
AM radio	500 m	
VHF TV	5.0 m	
FM radio	3.33 m	
UHF TV	1.0 m	
Radar	0.03 m	
Visible light	0.000 000 5 m	
X rays	0.000 000 009 m	

In the Find Out activity, you discovered that there is an inverse relationship between the frequency and wavelength of electromagnetic waves. In other words, as long as the speed of the wave is constant, the longer the wavelength, the lower its frequency and the shorter the wavelength, the higher its frequency.

Use of Electromagnetic Waves

In the Find Out activity you calculated frequencies for different types of waves. The entire range of electromagnetic waves, from extremely low to extremely high frequencies, is called the **electromagnetic spectrum**. Parts of the spectrum have been given names. A diagram of the electromagnetic spectrum is shown in **Figure 3-4** below.

A A cellular phone uses radio waves to enable people to talk to each other.

Note: Wave not to scale

Radiowaves						Microwaves		Infrared radiation			

10^3	10^4	10^5	10^6	10^7	10^8	10^9	10^{10}	10^{11}	10^{12}	10^{13}	10^{14}
10^5	10^4	10^3	10^2	10	1	10^{-1}	10^{-2}	10^{-3}	10^{-4}	10^{-5}	10^{-6}

Figure 3-4

B A microwave oven cooks food using microwaves.

Life Science CONNECTION

Sunscreens

As summer approaches, the lure of summer sports brings you outdoors. If you are health conscious, however, you apply a good sunscreen to protect yourself from the sun's radiation. The greatest danger lies in the solar radiation you cannot see—ultraviolet (UV) rays.

UV rays have wavelengths about half as long as light. A wave of 0.00000028 meters wavelength (or 280 x 10⁻⁹ m) would be UV radiation.

In recent years, scientists have vigorously studied the effect of UV radiation. Sunscreens have been developed to block ultraviolet B (UVB). UVB is the name given to shorter-wavelength ultraviolet waves. UVB causes sunburn and can cause cancer in people with a history of sunburn. Now, scientists warn that a longer wavelength of UV—UVA—penetrates the skin even more deeply than UVB. UVA causes wrinkling and aging of the skin and increases the chances that UVB will cause skin cancer.

■ Protecting Yourself

Whether or not your skin is harmed by UV depends on your type of skin. Darker skin has more melanin, the pigment that protects the skin against UV. Fair skin has less melanin. Fair skin burns quickly and

Unlike the mechanical waves that you learned about previously, electromagnetic waves need no medium through which to travel. The energy is transferred from one point to another without matter carrying it. The transfer of energy by electromagnetic waves is called **radiation**.

The amount of energy transferred by radiation is affected by many things. The Investigation on the next pages examines some of those factors.

C A lamp lights up a room by radiating electromagnetic waves in the visible part of the spectrum.

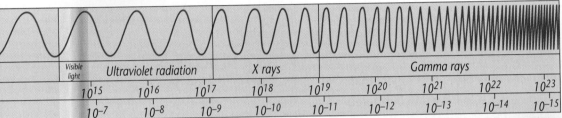

Electromagnetic spectrum
Frequency (f) in hertz
Wavelength (λ) in meters

Visible light   Ultraviolet radiation   X rays   Gamma rays

10^{15} 10^{16} 10^{17} 10^{18} 10^{19} 10^{20} 10^{21} 10^{22} 10^{23}

10^{-7} 10^{-8} 10^{-9} 10^{-10} 10^{-11} 10^{-12} 10^{-13} 10^{-14} 10^{-15}

D In an infrared photograph, portions of an object that radiate at slightly different frequencies show up as different colors.

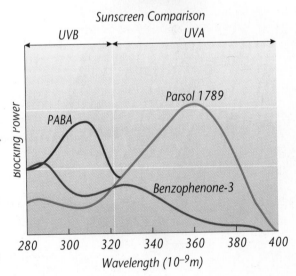

painfully, then peels. Light brown skin burns little and tans easily. Dark brown skin doesn't burn unless exposed to the sun for a long period.

To choose the right sunscreen, you have to understand how the sunscreen works and how your skin reacts to it. Think about the shortest exposure needed to cause your skin to become slightly red 24 hours later. This time varies according to skin type, geographic location, and time of the year. For example, suppose you burn after 10 minutes in the sun. If you use a sunscreen with Sun Protection Factor (SPF) 15, you could stay in the sun for 150 minutes before burning.

You Try It!

In order to absorb UVA rays, a sunscreen must contain a chemical called Parsol 1789. Another chemical, Benzophenone-3, absorbs some UVA. PABA, an active ingredient in sunscreens, absorbs no UVA. The graph to the right compares these three chemicals. Study the sunscreens available in your area. List those containing Parsol 1789, PABA, and Benzophenone-3. Also list the SPF of the sunscreens. Which sunscreen would you buy for maximum protection?

Sunscreen Comparison

UVB   UVA

Blocking Power

Parsol 1789

PABA

Benzophenone-3

280   300   320   340   360   380   400
Wavelength (10^{-9}m)

Infrared Radiation

You probably know that some people buy light-colored cars hoping that when the car sits in the sun it won't heat up inside as much as darker colored automobiles. How much of a difference does the color of an object make in its capacity to absorb and release infrared radiation?

Preparation

Problem

Does the color of an object make a difference in how much infrared radiation it absorbs or releases?

Form a Hypothesis

As a group, decide on a hypothesis that predicts the effect of color on both heating and cooling of an object.

Objectives

- Design an experiment that tests the absorption and release of infrared radiation.
- Measure the results of the experiment and graph the data.

Materials

3 aluminum cans of equal size: one black inside and out, one white inside and out, one shiny
water
3 thermometers
stopwatch
heat lamp

Safety Precautions

Avoid burning yourself when using the heat lamp. Keep water away from the lamp and cord.

DESIGN YOUR OWN
INVESTIGATION

Plan the Experiment

1 Use the materials to design an experiment to measure how well the three different colors of cans absorb and release infrared radiation.

2 Make certain that all conditions are kept the same except for the variable.

3 How often will you need to make and record observations during your experiment? For what period of time will you carry out the observations?

4 Prepare a data table *in your Science Journal* or in a database on the computer. Make certain that you plan your observations so that the data recorded can be graphed in a meaningful way.

Check the Plan

1 In your experiment, what are you measuring? How is the measuring to be done? Observation intervals should be the same length.

2 Do you provide identical conditions for the variables in the experiment? Is your equipment safely set up?

3 Before you carry out your investigation, make certain that your teacher approves your experiment.

4 Carry out your experiment and record your observations either *in your Science Journal* or in a database.

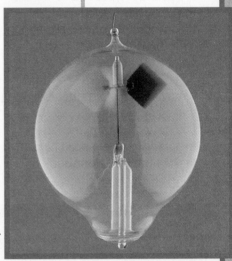

A radiometer converts radiant energy into mechanical energy as light waves from the sun heat the vanes and make them spin.

Analyze and Conclude

1. Make and use graphs Make a graph of your data. Use a different color pencil for each can.

2. Compare Which can became warm at the fastest rate? Cooled at the fastest rate?

3. Analyze Did the temperature of any can increase or decrease by the same amount during each data collection interval?

4. Infer Use your graphs to decide if your hypothesis was supported. What color absorbs the most infrared radiation?

5. Apply If you wanted the roof of your home to absorb solar radiation to help heat the house, would you install black shingles or white shingles? What color would you buy for keeping the house cool in a sunny, warm climate?

Going Further

Builders often use insulation covered with shiny aluminum foil. Infer how this would help keep a house warm or cool.

Using Observations to Form a Hypothesis

Formulate a hypothesis to explain the observations you made in the Investigate activity. Use your hypothesis to predict at what point the temperature of an object would become constant. It may help you to remember that all objects radiate energy. The hotter they are, the faster they radiate. If you need help, refer to the **Skill Handbook** on page 687.

You may have noticed in the Investigate activity that as the cans warmed up, their rate of warming slowed. That is, when they were cool their temperature increased rapidly. But, after they were warm, it took much longer for

their temperature to increase the same amount. In the Skillbuilder you can use what you know about radiation to explain this observation.

Infrared radiation is one of the common and useful parts of the electromagnetic spectrum. There are several other forms of electromagnetic waves that are less common, but all are transverse waves that travel at the speed of light. These waves have a wide range of frequencies and wavelengths, and they transfer energy from one place to another by radiation.

Without light, you wouldn't be reading this page right now. In the next section, you'll find out why scientists theorize that light is a form of electromagnetic energy.

New York City

Figure 3-5

This infrared photograph shows areas of different temperature.

check your UNDERSTANDING

1. How is an electromagnetic wave created by a vibrating electrical charge?
2. Arrange the following electromagnetic waves in order of frequency, from lowest to highest: X rays, radio waves, ultraviolet waves, infrared radiation, microwaves. Will these waves then be in the order of wavelength? Explain.
3. Keep a record of the different kinds of electromagnetic energy you use in one day. You may need to refer to Figure 3-4. Which form(s) did you use most often?
4. **Apply** People with swimming pools often cover them to use the sun to help heat the water. What color cover would work best—white, shiny aluminum, or black?

3-2 The Wave Model of Light

The Properties of Light

Light travels in straight lines and can be reflected off surfaces. Light's straight-line path can be bent when light passes from air into substances like water or glass. As you have probably seen after a summer thunderstorm, white light can be separated into a rainbow of colors when it goes through droplets of water. What further evidence will we need to build a model of light that explains all these phenomena? The observations you make in the Find Out activity below will give you your first clue.

Find Out! ACTIVITY

How is a light beam changed when it passes through a thin slit?

You'll need a very sharp knife, an index card, red and blue filters, and a lamp that your teacher will provide.

What To Do

1. Use a razor blade or craft knife to cut a slit about 5 cm long in the middle of an index card.

2. With all other lights off, close one eye and hold the card in front of the other eye.

3. Sight the lamp through the slit in your card. Using one hand on each side of the card, gently pull the sides of the card apart so that the slit opens slightly.

4. After your teacher covers the lamp with two color filters, repeat Step 3. *In your Journal*, make a sketch to record your observations.

Conclude and Apply

1. As you made the slit wider, what happened to the image of the lamp filament?

2. Did the filters change anything besides the color of the lamp image?

Section Objectives

- Explain how diffraction through thin slits supports a wave model of light.
- Describe how various observations of color and light can be explained by the wave model.

Key Terms

diffraction

Diffraction

In the Find Out activity, if the light traveled straight through the opening, you would see just the filament. Because you saw something next to the filament, the light must have spread out in some way. It must have bent as it passed through the slit. The bending of light around a barrier is called **diffraction**.

Does the wave model in **Figure 3-6** explain our other observations with a thin slit? You expect to see a straight column of waves after they've passed through the gap. Instead, waves spread out in a semi-circular pattern. As you saw in the Find Out, this effect increases with increasing wavelength.

Figure 3-6

The bending of waves around barriers is called diffraction. This photograph shows how the waves bend as they pass through a narrow gap. This is also what you observed in the Find Out activity. The image of the filament appeared blurred because the light waves from it were diffracted, or spread out, when they passed through the slit in the index card. Diffraction also happens when waves pass around a barrier. What property of shadows does this kind of diffraction explain?

Interference

You may have seen shimmering colors when some oil or gasoline has been spilled in water. **Figure 3-7** provides an example of this. You can see colors in the same way in soap bubbles. Both sets of bright colors are produced by light interacting with thin films. Let's explore how light behaves when it interacts with the thin film of a soap bubble.

Explore! ACTIVITY

What colors are made by soap bubbles?

You'll need bubble solution, a large wire loop, and a cookie sheet.

What To Do

1. Make a big bubble and catch it gently on the cookie sheet.

2. Watch the bubble carefully. What patterns of color and light do you see? *In your Journal*, make a sketch of the patterns and label the colors.

3. Observe several bubbles. How do the patterns of each bubble change over time? Look down at each bubble. What color is the top center of each bubble just before it breaks?

Figure 3-7

The different colors seen in a film of oil on water are a result of the interference of light waves reflected from the two different surfaces.

Thin Films

In the Explore activity, you looked at light as it was reflected from a soap bubble. You saw alternate bands of color. The top of the bubble looked black. Why did this happen? Look at the reflection of a pencil in a pair of eyeglasses or a piece of window glass. You see two images, one reflected from the front surface of the glass, the other from the back. In a soap bubble the two surfaces are very close together. Thin layers that produce a rainbow effect when light strikes them are called thin films. As **Figure 3-8** shows, the wave model of light can help explain why a soap bubble separates the light into colors rather than simply reflecting it.

The film of a soap bubble isn't all the same thickness. Gravity makes the bubble thinner on top. As the thickness varies, the interference alternates between constructive and destructive.

A soap film forms colored bands because each color has a different wavelength. In the Explore activity, you saw the color bands move down the bubble. Red light needs a greater thickness of film to produce constructive interference than purple light.

Figure 3-8

Ⓐ The cross marks represent wave crests. When the crests of one wave line up with the crests of another, constructive interference occurs. The waves add together and the result is a new wave with greater amplitude.

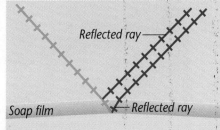

Constructive interference

Reflected ray

Soap film — Reflected ray

— Result

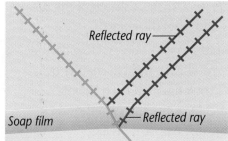

Destructive interference

Reflected ray

Soap film — Reflected ray

Result wave is flat line

Ⓑ When crests of one wave align with troughs of another wave, destructive interference occurs. The waves subtract from one another and the result is a wave with 0 amplitude. How thick does the soap film have to be for a given wavelength to produce constructive interference? Destructive interference?

Ⓒ Light reflecting from the inside surface of a soap bubble interferes with light reflecting from the outside surface. The thickness of the bubble varies from top to bottom. Because each color of light has a different wavelength, the bubble produces rainbow bands of constructive interference.

Diffraction Gratings

A morpho butterfly's colors aren't the result of thin films. The wings of this butterfly contain hundreds of ridges. Each ridge reflects some light and produces colors. We can find out how by looking at a more familiar object, a compact disc, or CD. **Figure 3-9** shows what the surface of a CD looks like. Now we'll see how a CD resembles a butterfly's wing.

Figure 3-9

The surface of a CD contains thousands of microscopic pits.

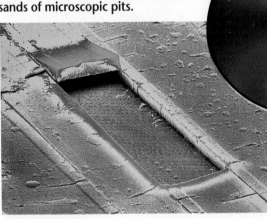

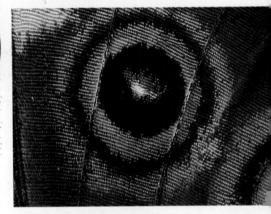

Ⓐ Each pit in a CD diffracts light, and the diffracted light comes together to form a rainbow.

Ⓑ Like a CD, each of the hundreds of ridges on a morpho butterfly's wings reflects light and produces colors.

Explore! ACTIVITY

What happens when light strikes a CD?

You'll need either a whole or broken CD and a lamp.

What To Do

1. Sit with a lamp in front of you. Hold the CD, label side down, at waist level. Tilt the CD so you see the direct reflection of the lamp.

2. Now, very slowly move your head back. *In your Journal*, describe in detail what you see.

3. Keep moving your head back slowly. Is there a pattern in what you see? If so, describe it *in your Journal*.

When light is reflected from a single CD pit, it is spread out, or diffracted, as if it were going through a slit. On the CD, there are many pits, all equally spaced. Each reflects light that comes together to produce a rainbow of color. Let's build a model to help you understand this property of light.

Double-slit Diffraction

The interactions of light waves can be difficult to observe. Sometimes, a model can make those interactions easier to understand.

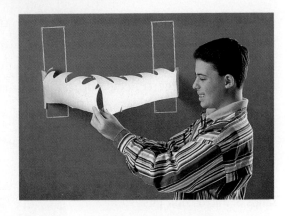

Problem
How does a CD produce a spectrum?

Materials
2 strips of shelf or butcher's paper, each about 30 cm wide by 2 m long	scissors masking tape

Safety Precautions

Be careful when cutting with scissors.

What To Do

1 Draw a wave pattern along the center of one strip that matches the example provided by your teacher. On the second strip of paper, draw a similar pattern with a wavelength about 3/4 that of the first.

2 Cut along the line, separating the paper into a pair of long strips (see Photo **A**).

3 Draw two 40 cm high x 10 cm wide boxes, 40 cm apart on the board (see Photo **B**). Leave space below for another set of boxes.

A

B

C

4 Fold and adjust the strips so each begins at the board with the top of a wave. Then, attach one strip to the outside center of each box with the waves pointing up.

5 Stand directly in front of the board holding the two strips together about 1/3 in from the end. This represents the light waves from the two slits combining at an observer's eye when standing the same distance from each slit. The waves' crests should line up.

6 Put a small piece of tape on the floor to mark your position (see Photo **C**).

7 Keep the same distance from the board and move to the left or the right, letting the paper slip through your fingers. Stop at the first point where the troughs of one wave line up with the crests of the other. Put another tape mark on the floor.

8 Move farther. When the crests again line up, put a tape mark on the floor.

9 Repeat Steps 6 through 8 moving in the opposite direction as before.

10 Repeat Steps 3 through 9 with the second pair of paper strips. Put the second set of boxes on the board directly below the first. Label the tape marks to indicate the second wavelength.

Analyzing

1. At the points where troughs line up with crests, what would you *predict* to happen? If it were light, what would you see?

2. At which points on the floor did the model show destructive interference? Constructive interference?

Concluding and Applying

3. Would you *predict* that both red and blue light would be bright directly in front of the two slits?

4. Going Further Yellow light has a wavelength between that of blue and red. *Predict* where you would see a bright band of yellow off-center from the slits.

Figure 3-11

A In a neon sign, electricity is applied to different gases to produce light. The red light in a neon sign is produced from the gas neon.

B The neon emission spectrum—the spectrum of light emitted by neon—contains a unique pattern of lines.

hot steel to find out the elements used to make the particular alloy. An astronomer uses the spectrum to find out which elements are in a star. Almost any source of light can be analyzed using this method.

All the properties of light we have described are well explained by a wave model. For that reason, scientists say that light is an electromagnetic wave. Light is only a tiny part of the electromagnetic spectrum. Your model of light helped you to understand some of the characteristics of light. It may have helped you understand how important models are to science.

Even though the CD isn't a very precise scientific instrument, you could use it to identify an unknown light source once you had observed the spectra formed by different sources. A chemist uses a spectrometer to identify the elements. A metallurgist looks at the light of glowing

check your UNDERSTANDING

1. How does the behavior of light as it passes through a thin slit support the wave model of light?
2. If you see shimmering colors from oil spilled on water, where do the reflections occur that create the interference?
3. **Apply** You can see a rainbow-like spectrum with a phonograph record. What causes this?

Science and Society

How Roomy Is the Spectrum?

Y ou've probably been frustrated by trying to tune in a radio station when another station was interfering with the signal. The Federal Communications Commission (FCC) tries to regulate assignment of frequencies to prevent overlaps, but the number of available frequencies is limited, so the radio range of the electromagnetic spectrum is becoming crowded.

Users of the Spectrum

Spectrum crowding is a bigger problem than you may realize. Think of communication tools that are wireless today: all radios, satellite cable-TV broadcasts, personal pagers, cellular telephones, cordless telephones, and more. And the numbers are exploding. In 1984, cellular telephone subscribers didn't exist; by 1992, there were more than 10 million U.S. subscribers. By the year 2000, there may be 251 million worldwide. Are there frequencies for them all?

For now, cellular service suppliers are increasing capacity by using new transmission technology. However, such technology also has its limits. Once a range of frequencies is fully used, a supplier has three choices: take no new customers, crowd frequencies so much that signals overlap, or convince the FCC to grant them more space.

Demands of New Technology

The FCC is already allocating room for the next generation of wireless communication tools: Personal Communication Systems (PCS). Under PCS, users may have one phone, indoors or out, at home or around the world. The phone will be a wristwatch or ring, or perhaps a miniature transmitter under your skin. You'll be able to contact anyone else who has a PCS. With PCS and a computer, you'll be able to access and transmit data over networks.

Science Journal

If the FCC finds room for PCS, there's still a problem: who gets the room? Cable TV and telephone companies and cellular suppliers all want to sell this new technology. How should the FCC handle disputes among people who want to use radio frequencies? Who do you think should get to use a piece of the spectrum to exploit new communication tools?

NATIONAL GEOGRAPHIC
SciFacts

What is the Ultraviolet Index?

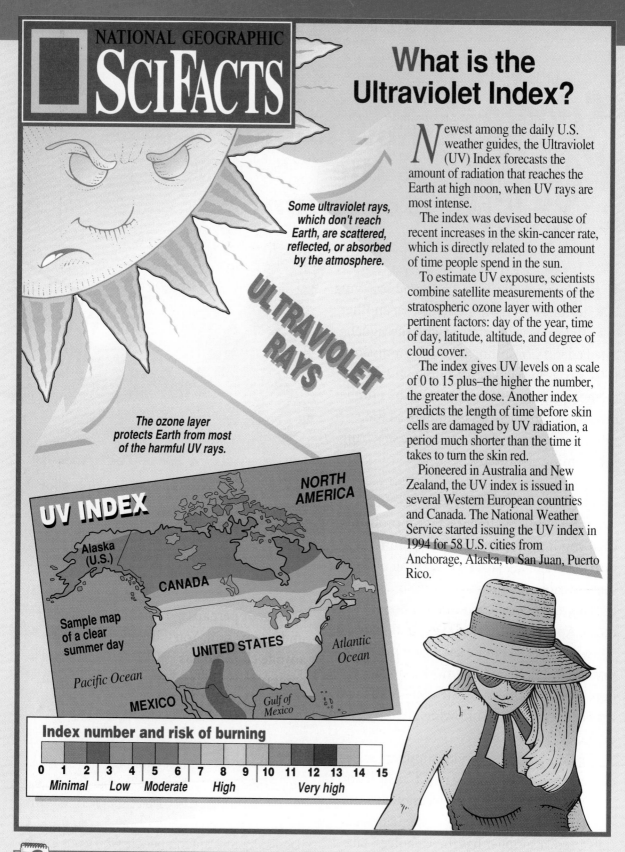

Some ultraviolet rays, which don't reach Earth, are scattered, reflected, or absorbed by the atmosphere.

ULTRAVIOLET RAYS

The ozone layer protects Earth from most of the harmful UV rays.

UV INDEX

NORTH AMERICA

Alaska (U.S.)

CANADA

Sample map of a clear summer day

UNITED STATES

Pacific Ocean

MEXICO

Atlantic Ocean

Gulf of Mexico

Index number and risk of burning

0	1	2	3	4	5	6	7	8	9	10	11	12	13	14	15

Minimal   *Low*   *Moderate*   *High*   *Very high*

Newest among the daily U.S. weather guides, the Ultraviolet (UV) Index forecasts the amount of radiation that reaches the Earth at high noon, when UV rays are most intense.

The index was devised because of recent increases in the skin-cancer rate, which is directly related to the amount of time people spend in the sun.

To estimate UV exposure, scientists combine satellite measurements of the stratospheric ozone layer with other pertinent factors: day of the year, time of day, latitude, altitude, and degree of cloud cover.

The index gives UV levels on a scale of 0 to 15 plus–the higher the number, the greater the dose. Another index predicts the length of time before skin cells are damaged by UV radiation, a period much shorter than the time it takes to turn the skin red.

Pioneered in Australia and New Zealand, the UV index is issued in several Western European countries and Canada. The National Weather Service started issuing the UV index in 1994 for 58 U.S. cities from Anchorage, Alaska, to San Juan, Puerto Rico.

Science Journal

In your Science Journal, describe what precautions you might have to take if your area had a UV index level of 8.

HOW IT WORKS

Detecting Weapons with X Rays

People who travel on airplanes are routinely delayed by some kind of security check. Most travelers think it is worth the time spent if guns, rifles, and bombs are kept off their plane.

Guns and other weapons are often easier to detect than bombs. Weapons usually show up in an ordinary X-ray baggage check, such as the one shown below on the left.

The kinds of bombs that have caused several airline crashes would not be detected by the usual airport X-ray machine. These bombs are made using plastic explosive, a putty-like material that can be formed into any shape to fool the inspectors. The explosive is made of the lighter elements carbon, oxygen, and nitrogen. In an ordinary X ray, it appears to be a dense, nonmetallic material.

New Detection Systems

Several new types of X-ray machines and other high-tech detectors are being tested to respond to this new kind of threat to air travelers' safety.

One kind of X-ray detector sends two different frequencies of X rays through a piece of luggage. A computer analyzes the characteristics of the objects in the bag based on the two X-ray images. One X ray passes through the objects in the luggage, and the other is reflected from objects that have a certain chemical makeup. Nitrogen is one of the substances that reflects low-frequency X rays. The same luggage is shown again below on the right. This time plastic explosive is revealed by the bright white image.

You Try It!

Find out what kind of X-ray machine is used to examine luggage at an airport near you.

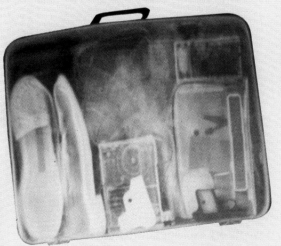

At airports, X rays are used to detect objects such as weapons that are hidden inside luggage.

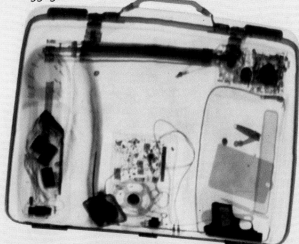

Combining images from X rays of two different frequencies can detect dangerous materials, such as plastic explosives, that would not show up on a single X-ray image.

Science Journal

Review the statements below about the big ideas presented in this chapter, and answer the questions. Then, re-read your answers to the Did You Ever Wonder questions at the beginning of the chapter. *In your Science Journal, write a paragraph about how your understanding of the big ideas in the chapter has changed.*

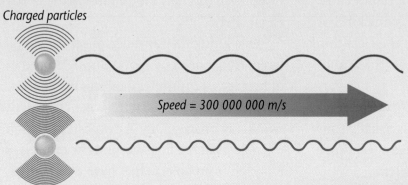

Charged particles

Speed = 300 000 000 m/s

1 Electromagnetic waves are transverse waves produced by an oscillating electric charge. One complete oscillation creates one wave. The frequency times the wavelength of every electromagnetic wave equals the speed of light, about 3.0×10^8 meters/second. *What is the frequency of light with wavelength 6.0×10^{-7} m?*

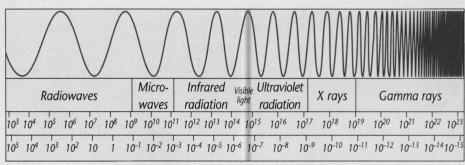

Radiowaves	Micro-waves	Infrared radiation	Visible light	Ultraviolet radiation	X rays	Gamma rays	Electromagnetic spectrum

Frequency (f) in hertz: 10^3 10^4 10^5 10^6 10^7 10^8 10^9 10^{10} 10^{11} 10^{12} 10^{13} 10^{14} 10^{15} 10^{16} 10^{17} 10^{18} 10^{19} 10^{20} 10^{21} 10^{22} 10^{23}

Wavelength (λ) in meters: 10^5 10^4 10^3 10^2 10 1 10^{-1} 10^{-2} 10^{-3} 10^{-4} 10^{-5} 10^{-6} 10^{-7} 10^{-8} 10^{-9} 10^{-10} 10^{-11} 10^{-12} 10^{-13} 10^{-14} 10^{-15}

2 Electromagnetic waves include: radio, microwave, infrared, visible light, ultraviolet, X rays, and gamma rays. Radio waves have the longest wavelength and lowest frequency. *How do the wavelengths of infrared and gamma rays compare?*

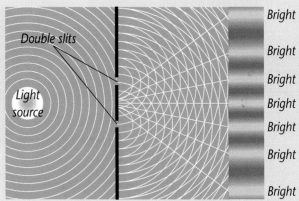

Double slits

Light source

Bright
Bright
Bright
Bright
Bright
Bright
Bright

3 Light exhibits properties of waves. The wave theory explains how diffracted light produces interference patterns. *If the white lines indicate wave crests, where are the areas of constructive interference on the image?*

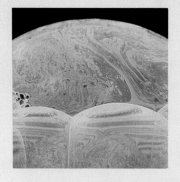

4 Interference patterns made by thin films depend on the thickness of the film, wavelength of light, angle of viewing, and other properties of the object producing the patterns. *Would you expect a thicker or thinner film to produce a constructive interference pattern of blue light?*

Using Key Science Terms

diffraction
electromagnetic spectrum
electromagnetic wave
radiation

Using the list above, replace the underlined words with the correct key science term.

1. The bending of light around a barrier is evidence that light travels in waves.
2. X rays, microwaves, and visible light are examples of energy that travels in waves with oscillating electrical and magnetic fields.
3. Radio waves, infrared waves, and X rays are part of the range of electromagnetic waves.

Understanding Ideas

Answer the following questions in your Journal using complete sentences.

1. How does a thin film produce colors?
2. As the wavelength of an electromagnetic wave increases, what happens to the frequency?
3. How do we know that light is bent as it goes through a narrow opening?
4. What is the frequency of electromagnetic radiation with a wavelength of 300 m?
5. Name a type of electromagnetic energy that your body gives off.
6. What instrument uses a diffraction grating to separate light into different wavelengths?

7. What is the electromagnetic wave type with the next longest wavelength to visible light?
8. If you know a wave's frequency and wavelength, how can you use them to determine its speed?
9. Give three examples of thin-film interference in which light is separated into colors.
10. What determines the frequency of electromagnetic waves?
11. What are three scientific uses of a spectrometer?

Developing Skills

Use your understanding of the concepts developed in this chapter to answer each of the following questions.

1. **Sequencing** Electromagnetic wave X has a wavelength of 0.062 km while electromagnetic wave Y has a wavelength of 5790 cm. Which wave has a higher frequency? Explain.
2. **Recognizing Cause and Effect** Imagine that you make a soap film while orbiting Earth in the space shuttle. Would you expect the film to contain the same set of colored lines as you observed in the Explore activity on page 93? Explain.
3. **Observing and Inferring** You are told that an electromagnetic wave has a wavelength of 20 m and a frequency of 6 million Hz. What can you conclude about this information?
4. **Compare and contrast** surface water waves and electromagnetic waves.

Critical Thinking

In your Journal, *answer each of the following questions.*

1. How does a vibrating charge create an electromagnetic wave?

2. How would you use a diffraction grating to identify the source of a light?

3. Describe the appearance of a wave after passing through a narrow slit and after passing through a much wider slit. What pattern would result if a wave passed through two narrow, side by side slits?

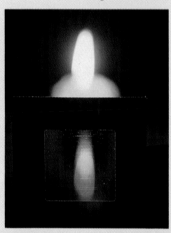

4. The color blue is seen in the top portion of a thin film and the color red in the bottom of the same film. Which portion of the film is thicker?

Problem Solving

Read the following problem and discuss your answers in a brief paragraph.

You are going camping with a friend and expect it to get quite cold during the night. You are taking with you a foam sleeping pad that is silver on one side to put under your sleeping bag. You are also taking a "space blanket"—a very thin, shiny silver plastic blanket.

1. Which side of the sleeping pad should face up when you put it on the ground? Why?

2. Why will wrapping yourself in the plastic blanket before climbing into your sleeping bag keep you warmer than the sleeping bag alone?

3. Should you take light or dark colored clothing for your trip, or does it matter? Explain.

CONNECTING IDEAS

Discuss each of the following in a brief paragraph.

1. **Theme—Energy** Discuss two ways in which electromagnetic waves differ from the electricity discussed in Chapters 1 and 2.

2. **Theme—Systems and Interactions** Do you think radio waves would produce interference patterns? Explain your answer.

3. **A Closer Look** How do astrophysicists know a star's composition?

4. **Life Science Connection** How would you decide which SPF value of sunscreen to select?

5. **Science and Society** Explain why the spectrum is becoming crowded.

ELECTRICITY AND MAGNETISM

In Unit 1, you worked with electricity and magnetism. You discovered that electrical energy is used in many appliances around the home. You found out that an electric current produces a magnetic field and a changing magnetic field produces an electric current. You also learned how electromagnetic waves are created. You explored the different ways that electromagnetic waves carry information and energy for our use and enjoyment.

Try the exercises and activity that follow— they will challenge you to use and apply some of the ideas you learned in this unit.

CONNECTING IDEAS

1. Do you think that pushing the button of an electric doorbell completes a circuit or opens one? If you were designing a doorbell button, would you use an electrical conductor, an insulator, or both? Explain your answer. Describe the purpose of the coil of copper wire found inside an electric doorbell.

2. **Analyzing Data:** Suppose your electric bill rose by twenty dollars the month after your family bought an air conditioner. If the electric company charges 10 cents for each kilowatt-hour of energy, how many extra kilowatt-hours are used by the air conditioner in one month?

Exploring Further ACTIVITY

Design a circuit with a bulb, an electromagnet, a switch, and a D-cell.

Connect the circuit elements so that changing the position of the switch turns on the electromagnet and turns off the bulb. Then, draw a diagram of your circuit design.

Atoms and Molecules

Take a journey to a universe too small to see—the realm of the atom. The painting shows neutrons crashing into the nuclei of several atoms during a nuclear reaction. Each nucleus contains protons (yellow balls) and neutrons (red balls). Smaller electrons whirl around the nuclei. In Unit 2, you'll discover how physical properties of matter determine how substances react with one another.

NATIONAL GEOGRAPHIC
try it!

In the atomic world, the size of particles and the distances between them are small indeed. Yet size and distance are relative. To an ant, a bread crumb is a full meal and a heavy load to carry back to the nest. To you, it's so small that it drops unnoticed from your sandwich to the floor. You may not know much about atoms yet, but you may know that each has a nucleus at its center. How large do you suppose the nucleus of an atom is relative to the whole atom? If the nucleus of an atom were as large as an ant, how large would the atom be?

What To Do

1. Draw an ant in the center of a page *in your Science Journal.*

2. Next to the ant, draw a circle as large as you think an atom would be.

3. After you've learned more about atoms, try this activity again to see if your ideas about atomic structure change.

structure OF THE atom

When you look at a globe, you know you're not looking at Earth itself. The globe is a model, a small and very useful representation of a much larger and more complicated object— Earth. A globe is an actual physical model that you can see and touch. You can also make mental pictures of things you want to understand—mental models. In this chapter, you'll follow the story of how scientists have developed the model of the atom.

▶ *In the activity on the next page, explore how you can determine the shape of an object without seeing it.*

Did you ever wonder...

✓ Why bones can be seen on X rays?
✓ Where radiation comes from?
✓ What an atom looks like?

Science Journal

Before you begin to study about the structure of the atom, think about these questions and answer them *in your Science Journal*. When you finish the chapter, compare your journal write-up with what you have learned.

Explore! ACTIVITY

How can you determine the shape of an object you cannot see?

What To Do

1. Place a paper clip, a pencil, a brick, or a small bag of sand on the floor. Hold a large piece of cardboard about six inches above the object.

2. Without looking under the cardboard, take turns rolling a marble under the cardboard.

3. Compare the direction the marble rolled toward the object with the direction the marble rolled after it hit the object.

4. Roll the marble into the object from several different directions. Record and diagram your observations *in your Journal.* Can you determine which object is under the cardboard, based on your observations?

4-1 Early Discoveries

Discovering Atoms

More than 2400 years ago, Greek philosophers discussed the idea of atoms. The Greeks imagined what might happen if a material were cut repeatedly. Eventually, the piece of material would be so small it could not be cut again and still have the properties of the material. The Greeks called this basic part of matter an *atom*, meaning "indivisible."

■ The Atomic Theory

According to the atomic theory, atoms are the building blocks of matter. Acceptance of this theory of matter was slow, and understandably so. How can you prove the existence of something you can't see? You know from the Explore activity how difficult it is to determine the shape of something invisible. It was the mid-1800s before most scientists accepted the existence of atoms. The atomic theory offered a simple and useful explanation for the behavior of gases. It was also useful in explaining chemical compounds and the products of chemical reactions. In all, the atomic theory accounted for observations about matter better than any earlier theory had. Yet, scientists wondered if the atoms involved in chemistry could be further divided. The answer came from an unlikely experiment.

■ Discovery of the Electron

William Crookes was a British physicist. In the late 1800s, he was interested in the vacuum tube. A vacuum tube is a sealed glass tube with the air removed from it. **Figures 4-1** and **4-2** demonstrate some of his vacuum tube experiments.

Figure 4-1

The vacuum tube William Crookes used in his experiments had a positive terminal at one end and a negative terminal at the other end. When the terminals were connected to a battery, a greenish glow formed at the negative end of the tube and then gradually moved toward the positive end of the tube.

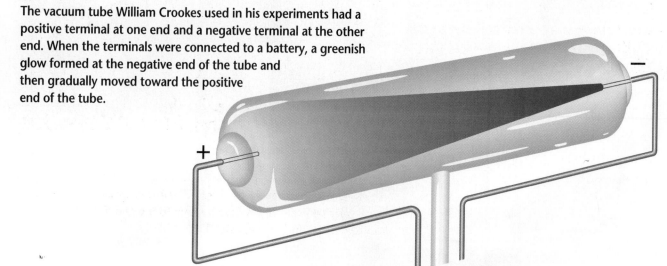

Figure 4-2

In another experiment, an object placed in the path of the green glow cast a shadow. Crookes knew that shadows are cast by waves or particles that travel in straight lines. Knowing that, what could Crookes conclude about the green glow?

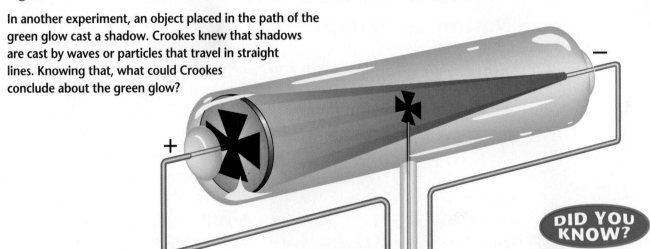

Nearly 20 years after Crookes' work, the British physicist J. J. Thomson repeated the experiment with Crookes' vacuum tube, which was now called a cathode-ray tube. Thomson observed that the waves, or beam of particles, formed inside the tube were bent when they passed through an electric field. Similar observations were made with magnetic fields, as shown in **Figure 4-3**.

In addition to showing that the beam was made up of charged particles, Thomson showed that the particles had much less mass than any atoms have. Thomson also found that the kind of material used for the tube's metal plates did not seem to affect how many charged particles were produced or how they behaved. Thomson had shown that particles even smaller than atoms existed. The particle was given the name **electron**. In 1906, Thomson received the Nobel Prize in physics for his discovery of the electron.

■ Radiation

The electrons Crookes and Thomson observed are a form of radiation. The term radiation is commonly used to describe any form of energy—heat, light, or even beams of small particles—given off by an object. What caused the negative terminal in the vacuum tube to radiate these particles? Does radiation only occur when there is a voltage present? Is there any type of radiation that occurs naturally?

DID YOU KNOW?

The tube Crookes used was the ancestor of the television tube and the computer screen. Each of these modern devices relies on a vacuum tube with positive and negative metal plates. The inside of each tube is coated with materials that glow when they are struck by electrons, making the beam easy to see.

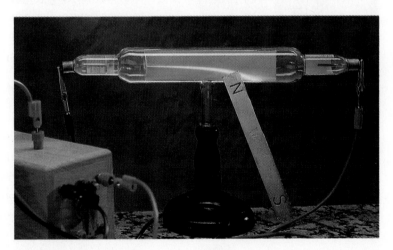

Figure 4-3

In this experiment, a cathode-ray tube was placed in a magnetic field. The magnetic field caused the beam of particles inside the tube to bend. What do you think would happen to the rays if the tube were removed from the magnetic field?

Natural Radiation

Perhaps you've had a broken arm x-rayed. Maybe you've seen an X-ray photograph of a person's lungs or

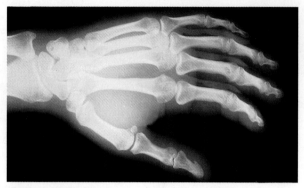

Figure 4-4

X rays pass through soft tissues such as skin and muscle but are stopped by hard tissue, thereby revealing the bones underneath.

hand. X rays can even show cracks or breaks in steel bridges and building supports. The material to be tested is placed between the X-ray source and a sheet of film. Wherever the X rays pass through the material, the film clouds as though it has been exposed to light.

There are other forms of radiation that can affect film. Nearly a hundred years ago, a French physicist, Henri Becquerel, accidentally left a small sample of a uranium compound on top of a photographic plate. The plate was in a drawer, wrapped tightly in

Radon Testing

In the past few years, many people began to worry that their homes might be hazardous to their health. Reports in the newspapers warned people that their homes might contain dangerous levels of radon.

What is Radon?

Radon is a radioactive gas that is produced from uranium and thorium. Radon produces charged particles that are attracted to dust. When inhaled, these particles can produce a higher risk of cancer than normal. Some homes built over rocks containing uranium and thorium have been found to have high levels of radon gas.

Sources of Radon

The problem of radon gas in homes was discovered by accident. A construction worker helping to build a nuclear power plant in Pennsylvania kept setting off the radiation alarms at the plant. After it was found that he was not being exposed to radiation at work, investigators checked out his home. They found that his house was built on radioactive rocks that were filling the air in his home with radon gas.

There are other sources of radon gas. Some modern lightning rods contain radon gas that can leak into the attics of homes.

light-colored paper. Yet, when Becquerel went to use the plate, he found it fogged. It seemed as if the compound were giving off radiation that could go through paper. Becquerel began to study the radiation further. The radiation penetrated matter just as X rays did, and it was given off in all directions by the compound. The radiation could even be deflected by a magnetic field. Becquerel inferred that the radiation had to be—at least partly—made up of tiny, charged particles. Eventually, he concluded that the negatively charged part of the radiation was due to negatively charged particles. Becquerel further concluded that these particles were

Figure 4-5

Henri Becquerel discovered that atoms of uranium give off negatively charged particles, which provided evidence that atoms are made up of smaller particles.

identical to those in Thomson's experiment. They were electrons. Where were the electrons coming from? The only possible source was the uranium compound, or rather the atoms of the uranium compound. Here was more evidence that the atom must have smaller parts. Furthermore, one of those parts must be a light, negatively charged particle—an electron.

Testing for Radon

Kits are now available to test for high radon levels. Most kits contain activated charcoal, which attracts radon particles. The kit is then sent to a laboratory for an interpretation of the results.

What To Do

People who find that their homes contain high amounts of radon gas are advised to make modifications in their homes. In some cases, added ventilation solves the problem. In other cases, walls, ceilings, or floors must be sealed against the gas.

You Try It!

Get a radon testing kit either from your state or local health department. Check your home or school for radon gas. Usually, buildings that are well insulated collect gases more than those that are built off the ground or are not so tightly built. Compare the results of a test on a new building with those of a test on an old building.

Radon-testing kits may be purchased and include easy-to-follow instructions.

More Atomic Particles

Radiation can be given off by metal plates in a vacuum tube or by elements such as uranium. Uranium is said to be an unstable element—it breaks apart on its own. Such elements are radioactive. The release of high-energy particles by radioactive elements is called **radioactivity**.

The study of radioactivity contributed a lot to our current ideas about the atom. Following Becquerel, Ernest Rutherford used uranium and thorium, two radioactive elements, to make some important observations. **Figure 4-6** shows the results of his experiments using magnetic fields.

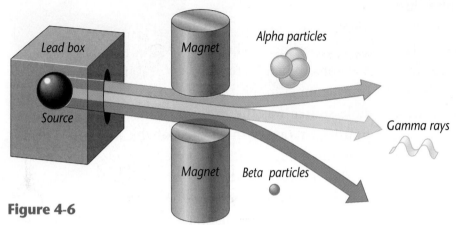

Figure 4-6

When radioactive rays pass through a magnetic field, alpha particles are bent slightly in one direction, beta particles are bent to a greater degree in the opposite direction, and gamma rays are not bent at all.

How Do We Know?

How can we detect radiation?

One method of measuring radiation uses a Geiger counter. A Geiger counter, shown at right, is a device that produces an electric current whenever radiation is present.

The tube is filled with gas at a low pressure and a positively charged wire runs through the center of a negatively charged copper cylinder. The wire and the cylinder are connected to a voltage source. Radiation enters the tube at one end and strips the electrons from the gaseous atoms. The electrons are attracted to the positive wire. As they move to the wire, they knock more electrons off the atoms in the gas. An "electron avalanche" is produced, and a large number of electrons reach the wire. This produces a short, intense current in the wire. This current is amplified to produce a clicking sound or flashing light. The intensity of radiation present is determined by the number of clicks in each second.

Geiger counters can be made very small and portable. They are often used to test the radioactivity at job sites where workers can be exposed to radioactive materials, such as workers in a hospital radiation lab or at a nuclear power plant.

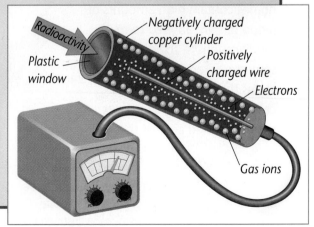

Figure 4-7

This diagram shows the different strengths of alpha, beta, and gamma rays. Alpha particles will be stopped by a sheet of paper. Beta particles will pass through paper, but will be stopped by a sheet of aluminum. Gamma rays will pass through both paper and aluminum, but will be stopped by a sheet of lead. Would X rays be able to pass through the sheet of lead?

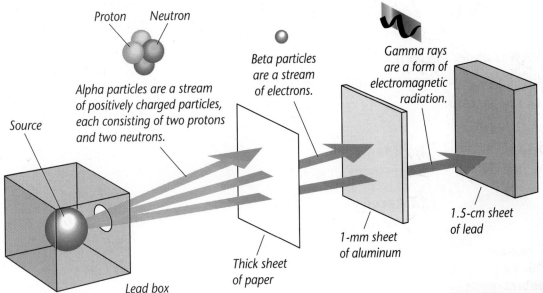

Proton *Neutron*

Alpha particles are a stream of positively charged particles, each consisting of two protons and two neutrons.

Beta particles are a stream of electrons.

Gamma rays are a form of electromagnetic radiation.

Source

Lead box

Thick sheet of paper

1-mm sheet of aluminum

1.5-cm sheet of lead

■ Alpha Particles, Beta Particles, and Gamma Rays

Rutherford gave the three parts of the radiation he observed three names taken from the first letters of the Greek alphabet: alpha, beta, and gamma. Additional observations that he made are illustrated in **Figure 4-7**. Because beta radiation behaved like the particles in Crookes' and Thomson's experiments, Rutherford inferred that beta radiation must contain negatively charged particles. Later experiments supported this inference. Beta radiation is now known as beta particles. A high-speed electron given off by a radioactive substance is a **beta particle.**

The alpha radiation was affected by the magnetic field, but the alpha particles didn't bend as much as the beta particles had. Rutherford also observed that alpha and beta particles bent in opposite directions. These observations led Rutherford to conclude that **alpha particles** are positively charged particles given off by radioactive substances and have more mass than beta particles. The gamma radiation was not deflected by a magnetic field and was more penetrating than X rays were. Rutherford's laboratory proved that **gamma rays** were electromagnetic radiation.

These observations led to other questions. One of the most puzzling was: How are the parts of an atom arranged? In the following Investigate, you will explore, through modeling, what is inside an atom.

INVESTIGATE!

Parts of an Atom

Think back to the Explore activity you did at the beginning of this chapter. Suppose you were absolutely certain the brick was under the cardboard, but the marble seemed to roll as if nothing were under the cardboard. What would you think?

Problem

What's inside an atom?

Materials

regular-size aluminum pie pan	12-mm steel ball
	4 steel marbles
4 glass marbles	grooved ruler

What To Do

1 Gently press the 4 glass marbles into the pie pan so that they make small indentations near the center of the pan (see photo **A**).

2 Roll the 12-mm steel ball down the grooved ruler, (see photo **B**). Try to hit the marbles.

3 *Observe* and record what happens to the steel ball. Does it ever change its path? Does the steel ball ever bounce back?

A

B

C

4 Place the ruler at different slopes (see photo **C**). Record any effect this has on your observations.

5 Now put steel marbles into the indentations in the pie pan.

6 Repeat Steps 2, 3, and 4 rolling a glass marble down the grooved ruler.

Analyzing

1. *Compare* and *contrast* the results in Step 6 with the previous observations.

2. Why were the results different?

3. What effect did the slope of the ruler have on the way the rolling ball or marble behaved? What *hypothesis* can there be for your observation?

Concluding and Applying

4. Which has a greater effect on the way the rolling ball acts after a collision, the mass of the rolling ball or the mass of the ball in the indentation?

5. **Going Further** How would your observations change if the marbles and the rolling steel ball were all positively charged?

Alpha Particle Experiments

Connect to...

Physics

Visible light, radio waves, infrared light, ultraviolet rays, X rays, and gamma rays are all types of electromagnetic radiation. Make a diagram of the electromagnetic spectrum that includes the frequency and wavelength for each of these types of electromagnetic radiation.

In this Investigate, you learned that the way objects interact is affected by their mass, their velocity, and whether or not they are charged. Rutherford used a similar experiment to study the way alpha particles interacted with matter.

Rutherford and his colleagues wanted to learn more about alpha particles. They designed an experiment to study the ability of alpha particles to pass through different metals. The setup is shown in **Figure 4-8**.

Rutherford, talking about his gold foil experiment some years later, was quoted: "It was about as believable as if you had fired a 15-inch shell at a piece of tissue paper, and it came back and hit you."

Rutherford's team set out to learn more about alpha particles. Instead, they made one of history's most important observations about atoms. Look at **Figure 4-9**.

Rutherford's team concluded from their gold foil experiments that somewhere in the gold atom was a very massive charged object that would repel the positively charged alpha particles. After they made these observations, other scientists became very interested in just what an atom looked like and how the parts of an atom were arranged. The problem was that they had no tools to directly observe the atom. Instead, they had to rely on mental pictures of the atom.

Figure 4-8

In his experiment, Rutherford fired a beam of positively charged alpha particles at a very thin sheet of gold foil. He expected the particles to pass straight through the foil. The alpha particles appeared as tiny flashes of light on the fluorescent screen. However, the boundary of the circle formed by the flashes was fuzzy, which meant that some of the particles had been deflected. A few alpha particles even bounced back from the foil. Observing this, Rutherford concluded that an atom is mostly empty space, with a dense, positively charged center.

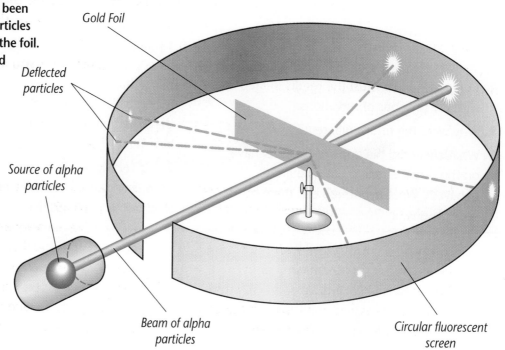

Gold Foil

Deflected particles

Source of alpha particles

Beam of alpha particles

Circular fluorescent screen

Figure 4-9

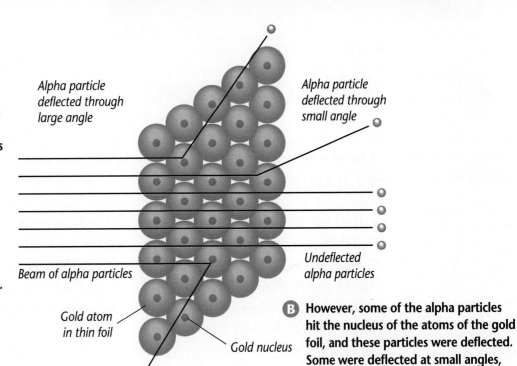

A This diagram shows the path of the alpha particles as they passed through the atoms of the gold foil. Most of the alpha particles passed straight through the empty space of the atoms and appeared on the fluorescent screen.

Alpha particle deflected through large angle

Alpha particle deflected through small angle

Beam of alpha particles

Undeflected alpha particles

Gold atom in thin foil

Gold nucleus

B However, some of the alpha particles hit the nucleus of the atoms of the gold foil, and these particles were deflected. Some were deflected at small angles, and a few were deflected back at very large angles. Why were the particles deflected by the nucleus?

■ Atomic Research: Hard Work and Good Luck

The development of the current idea of an atom is an example of how hard work and luck contribute to scientific discoveries. Crookes and Thomson performed experiments to explore the possibilities of atomic structure. Meanwhile, Becquerel's accidental discovery of the radiation given off by radioactive elements offered new information about the structure of atoms. In addition, Rutherford's work with alpha, beta, and gamma rays led to more information about the atom and even more questions and problems to solve.

In the next section, you will use all the observations made during these experiments to build a model of the atom. A model is an idea, system, or structure that represents what you are trying to explain.

check your UNDERSTANDING

1. What do you do when you want to find out what is inside a wrapped present but can't open it? How is that like what Crookes, Thomson, Becquerel, and Rutherford did to find out the composition of an atom?

2. What is the connection between the green glow in Crookes' vacuum tube and the beta particle that Rutherford discovered?

3. How would you tell a beta particle from an alpha particle?

4. **Apply** Draw a diagram to show what observations would be made if zeta rays were very light positively charged particles and theta rays were very heavy negatively charged particles, and they passed through a magnetic field.

A Model Atom

4-2

Section Objectives
- Trace the development of the model of the atom.
- Distinguish among electrons, protons, and neutrons.

Key Terms

nucleus
proton
neutron

Modeling Atoms

You are probably familiar with several types of models, such as model trains, globes, and the ones shown in **Figure 4-10**. A model helps you understand how an object is built or how it works. A good model of an object can explain all your observations of that object. Sometimes, rather than an object you can touch, a model is a mental picture. The following activity will give some experience in forming a mental picture.

Find Out! ACTIVITY

How can you make a mental picture of an atom?

What To Do

1. Your teacher will give you some bolts, nuts, and/or washers. Each group in the class will get different amounts of hardware.

2. Bury your hardware in a piece of modeling clay.

3. Form the clay into a ball so that you cannot see the hardware or determine its shape.

4. Trade clay balls with another group.

5. Try to find out what is inside the clay ball. The only observations you may make are with toothpicks. To make your observations, stick toothpicks one at a time into the clay ball.

6. Try to find out how many and which hardware pieces are hidden in the clay. Do not pull apart the clay! Record your observations *in your Journal*.

Conclude and Apply

1. What inference can you make about the contents of the clay?

2. Evaluate the procedure for making a mental picture or a model. Why are models necessary?

Figure 4-10

Architects build models to show how a building will be made and what it will look like when it's done.

As you did the Find Out activity, you probably tried to form a mental picture of what was inside the clay ball. You made a model of the clay ball and its contents.

As scientists study matter, they try to form a mental picture of what an atom might look like. Like any model, a good model of the atom must explain the information that is known about matter and atoms. As more data are collected, a model may need to be changed. The model of the atom we use today is the result of the work of many scientists over many years.

■ **Early Models of Atoms**

In 1802, John Dalton, a British chemist, developed the first model of the atom, illustrated in **Figure 4-11A**. Dalton observed that the gases of the air could be compressed only so far. He concluded that air and all other matter was made up of particles too tiny to be seen. However, these particles were solid and indestructible, like tiny billiard balls.

Think back to Crookes and Thomson. Does Dalton's billiard ball

model of the atom give any clue about the electrons Crookes and Thomson observed? Based on their work, electrons had to come from atoms. To accommodate this observation, Thomson claimed the atom was a solid mass with electrons scattered through it, rather like the blueberries in a blueberry muffin shown in **Figure 4-11B**.

■ **Discovery of the Nucleus**

Does Thomson's model explain the observations Rutherford made? What about the great amounts of empty space inside the atom? Rutherford's first change to the model was to give the atom a dense center. The beam of positive alpha particles was sometimes greatly deflected from the center of gold atoms, as shown in **Figure 4-8** on page 120. Therefore, the center must have a positive charge. The dense, positively charged center of an atom is called the **nucleus**.

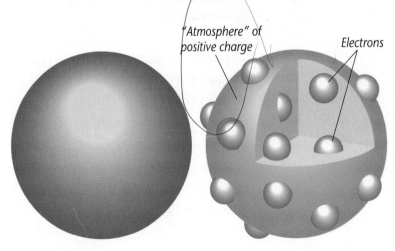

"Atmosphere" of positive charge

Electrons

Figure 4-11

Ⓐ In Dalton's model, the atom was a solid, indivisible particle.

Ⓑ Thomson's blueberry muffin model pictured the atom as a solid, puddinglike material with electrons scattered throughout it.

Figure 4-12

A Based on his experiments, Rutherford devised a model of the atom that was mostly empty space. In Bohr's model of the atom, the electrons moved in fixed orbits around the nucleus. The orbits of the electrons are located at specific distances from the nucleus.

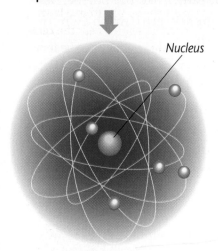

Nucleus

B This model of the atom pictured the electrons moving around the nucleus in a region called the electron cloud. The electron cloud represents the various locations within an atom where the electrons are likely to be found.

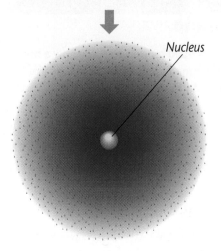

Nucleus

■ Discovery of the Proton

Rutherford then reasoned that the positively charged alpha particles emitted by the radioactive source must have come from the nucleus of the atom. Therefore, the nucleus must contain positively charged particles. Rutherford named the positively charged particle in the nucleus of an atom a **proton.**

Remember that Thomson, Becquerel, and Rutherford all observed negatively charged particles of relatively small mass—electrons. To account for the large angle deflection in his gold foil experiment, Rutherford suggested that electrons are scattered in the empty space around a tiny, dense nucleus. It took Rutherford ten years to fully understand all of his observations. He tried many different ideas and tested them before

making his final inferences.

Rutherford's model of the atom had a major impact on science. The model shown in **Figure 4-12A** was later proposed by Niels Bohr in 1913. Bohr's theory helped explain the arrangement of the electrons.

■ The Electron Cloud Model

In 1926, scientists changed the model of the atom again. A diagram of this model appears in **Figure 4-12B**. Because the electron's mass is so small, it is impossible to describe exactly where it is as it moves in the atom. The electron cloud represents the probable locations of electrons within an atom. You can compare the electron cloud to the spray of water drops from a lawn sprinkler. Each drop represents a probable location of an electron in the cloud. As you can see in

Figure 4-13, most of the drops are concentrated near the center of the spray. In an atom, the most probable location of electrons is in the electron cloud, distributed about the nucleus.

The diameter of the nucleus is about 1/100 000 the diameter of the electron cloud. **Figure 4-14** illustrates the vast differences in size through modeling.

The electron cloud model of the atom answers questions about electrons and their relationship with an atom's nucleus. However, there are observations of the nucleus that have not yet been included in our model. In the early 1900s, Rutherford compared the charge and mass of several particles he had observed. He knew that of all the elements, hydrogen had the least mass. Therefore, he assigned the hydrogen

nucleus a mass of one atomic mass unit. From the model, the nucleus would have one positively charged particle, a proton. There would be

Figure 4-13

The currently accepted model of an electron cloud can be compared to the spray of water drops from a lawn sprinkler. Most of the water drops are concentrated near the center of the spray. In an atom, electrons are most likely to be found in the electron cloud, distributed around the nucleus. In this photograph, what represents the nucleus?

Figure 4-14

Ⓐ Imagine a model of an atom with an electron cloud as wide as this football field.

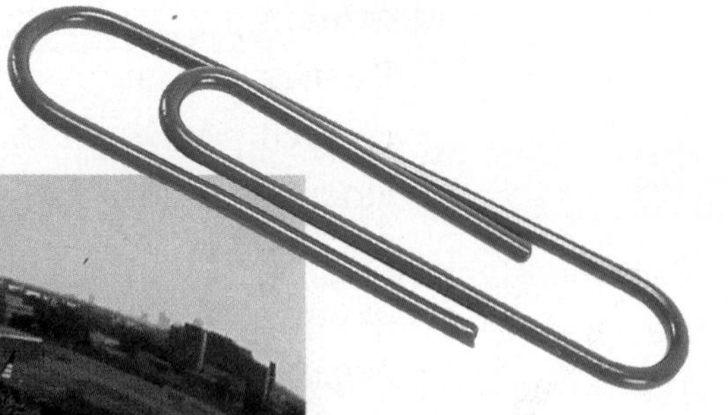

Ⓑ In this model, the nucleus of the atom would be about as thick as the wire in a paper clip.

one electron, of very little mass, associated with this nucleus to make a hydrogen atom.

Rutherford compared this information with data he gathered about alpha particles. One alpha particle had a positive charge of two. According to the model it should have had two protons and a mass of two. Yet, when Rutherford measured the mass of an alpha particle he found it was four times as heavy as a hydrogen atom instead of twice as heavy. There were two extra units of mass and no additional charge! What could have caused the extra mass?

Figure 4-15

Ⓐ This stamp was printed to honor Ernest Rutherford and his contributions to our knowledge of atomic structure.

Ⓑ This stamp pays tribute to Niels Bohr and his achievements in science.

■ Discovery of the Neutron

In 1932, James Chadwick, a student of Rutherford's, answered that question. Chadwick had heard of a new type of very penetrating particle radiation obtained from beryllium that had been bombarded with alpha particles. The path of this radiation did not change when it was surrounded by an electric field. Therefore, researchers could conclude that this radiation had no charge.

Chadwick used this new radiation to bombard paraffin wax. As a result, the hydrogen atoms in the wax emitted high-speed protons. Chadwick studied the speed of the protons and proposed that the uncharged radiation was made up of particles with a mass about equal to the mass of the proton. Chadwick called the particle a neutron.

How Do We Know?

What does an atom look like?

Many models of the atom have been presented. How do we know which one is closest to the real thing? Seeing an actual atom would answer that question once and for all. Modern techniques permit the photographing of individual atoms that are only 30 billionths of a centimeter across. The microscope works by moving a fine metal point across the object being examined. This discovery may lead to building molecules one atom at a time. The point traces the shape of the surface of the object just as your finger detects rough spots when moved across your desk. When a desired position is reached, an atom can be deposited. The picture shown here was taken using a scanning tunneling microscope. Each hill is a single xenon atom, and the atoms have been arranged to form a pattern.

Figure 4-16

The nucleus of an atom contains both protons (green) and neutrons (orange), which are about equal in mass.

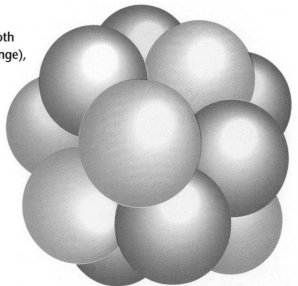

A **neutron** is a particle with no charge and with a mass about equal to that of a proton, and it is found in the nucleus of an atom. The name was chosen because the particle has no electric charge. It is neutral. This uncharged particle suited the theory nicely. It explained the extra mass of the alpha particle and did not upset the balance of charges. Thus, Chadwick's discovery of the neutron answered many questions about the structure and behavior of atoms.

With the discovery of the neutron, the model of the atom was modified to include a nucleus made up of protons and neutrons. The proton-neutron model of the nucleus is still accepted today.

Table 4-1 summarizes information about the three basic particles of atomic structure. Does it seem like a lot was learned from all these years of work? What are these findings really telling us about all matter on Earth? Researchers set to work to see how this atomic model could be used to explain the differences between one element and another. They also used the model to explain how different elements interact with one another.

DID YOU KNOW?

Protons and neutrons can be split into smaller particles called quarks. The names of the six known types of quarks are up, down, charm, strange, top, and bottom!

Table 4-1

Atomic particles			
	Relative Mass	Charge	Location in the Atom
Proton	1	1+	Part of nucleus
Neutron	1	none	Part of nucleus
Electron	0.0005	1−	Moves around nucleus

This table lists the three basic particles of atoms, showing for each its mass, electric charge, and location in the atom.

Energy Levels of Electrons

Although all the electrons in an atom are contained in the electron cloud, within the cloud itself the electrons are at different distances from the nucleus. One way scientists know that electrons are different distances from the nucleus is that it takes different amounts of energy to pry an electron away from its spot around a nucleus.

In the following Explore activity, you will make a model of an atom. The magnet will represent the positive nucleus of the atom, while the ball bearings will represent the negative electrons. How much energy is needed to pull the bearings away from the magnet?

Physics CONNECTION

Quirk, Quork, Quark!

Scientists found that the atom was made up of neutrons, protons, and electrons. For some time afterward, they were happily convinced that they had discovered the smallest units of matter in the universe. As experimentation continued, however, scientists found that even smaller particles make up neutrons and protons. These particles are called quarks. Quarks have electric charges that are fractions of the

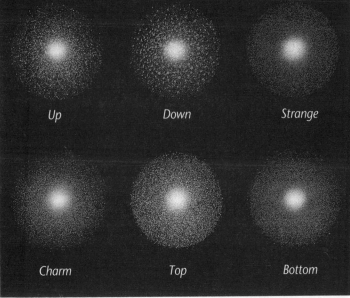

Up   Down   Strange

Charm   Top   Bottom

This diagram shows the six different types of quarks that make up protons and neutrons.

Does a magnet hold everything with the same strength?

What To Do

1. Place a horseshoe magnet in a bowl of ball bearings or tacks. When you pull the magnet from the bearings, several layers of bearings will be attached to the magnet.

2. One at a time, pull the bearings away from the magnet. Which bearings are easier to remove from the magnet, the ones closest to or farthest from the magnet? Record your answer *in your Journal.* Do you need more energy to pull the bearings that are farther from the magnet's poles or those closest to the magnet's poles?

elementary charge of an electron. For example, the charge may be 1/3, -1/3, or 2/3 the charge of an electron.

Discovering Quarks

The first quarks discovered were known as up, down, and strange. By 1985, three other types of quarks had been identified: charm, top, and bottom. All six names are used only for identification and tell nothing about the quark. Scientists lightheartedly refer to these six types as the flavors of quarks. Scientists continue to study atoms and may yet find still more quarks, or particles even smaller than quarks, as technology improves.

...Quirks and Quarks

Murray Gell-Mann, one of the discoverers of quarks, called them "quorks," a nonsense word by which he meant "those funny little things." Other scientists, noting their behavior, called them "quirks." Finally, Gell-Mann found a passage in James Joyce's book *Finnegan's Wake* that referred to "Three quarks for Master Mark!" He borrowed the spelling of quark, and that is the name used now.

When the idea of quarks was introduced in 1964, many scientists thought it an unlikely theory. Experiments much like those that led to the discovery of the nucleus proved that quarks did, indeed, exist. Today's mod-

els of quarks indicate that quarks have electrical charge, spin, and a type of strong charge called *color charge.* Scientists have now decided that quarks come in six flavors, each of which can have one of three colors.

It is thought that quarks never appear alone in nature—they are always found in groups of two or more.

What Do You Think?

Think about an onion. Look at it from the outside. It looks solid. Peel off a layer, and you find another layer underneath. Layer after layer is revealed as one is peeled away. How does this compare with the atom model?

It takes more energy to remove electrons that are closest to the nucleus. Electrons farther from the nucleus require less energy to be separated from the nucleus. Do you think the green glow in Crookes' tube was caused by electrons that had been close to or far from the nucleus of an atom?

The arrangement of electrons around a nucleus is shown in **Figure** 4-17. Remember that average locations of the electrons in each level form spherical clouds.

You can represent the energy differences of electrons by picturing them on a flight of stairs. If the floor is the nucleus, then an electron on step 3 has more energy than an electron on step 1. The difference in heights between the steps is the difference in energy between the electrons. The atom differs from the model because the actual electron levels are not all of equal distance apart.

Figure 4-17

Ⓐ This diagram illustrates the various energy levels of electrons around the nucleus. The first, or innermost, energy level can hold 2 electrons. The second level can hold 8 electrons; the third level, 18 electrons; and the fourth level, 32 electrons.

Energy level in atom	Maximum number of electrons
4	32
3	18
2	8
1	2

ENERGY INCREASES

Ⓑ The closer an electron is to the nucleus, the more energy it takes to separate the electron from the nucleus. Would it be easier to remove an electron from the second level or the third level?

Because the electron cloud is spherical, the farther away the energy level is from the nucleus, the larger the energy level is and the more electrons that level can hold. **Figure 4-17** shows the maximum number of electrons that each of the first four energy levels can hold.

Because the mass of an electron is so small, the mass of a single atom is about equal to the number of particles in its nucleus. If a carbon atom has 6 protons and its mass is 12, where will you find the remaining mass? What particle is responsible for the mass? The neutron. If an atom's mass is 12 and the number of protons is 6, then 6 neutrons provide the remaining mass. The mass of an oxygen atom is 16—its nucleus has 8 protons. How many neutrons does it have? Right, 8. In the next chapter, you'll use this idea to find out more about atoms.

Atoms and Elements

One of the really useful characteristics of our model of the atom is that it gives us a way to explain the wide variety of elements we can observe. Every atom of the same element has the same number of protons. It is the number of protons in an element's nucleus that distinguishes one element from another. Atoms of different elements have different numbers of protons. For example, look at **Table 4-2**. Every carbon atom has 6 protons. Furthermore, the model tells us that if an atom has 6 protons, it must have 6 electrons because there must be an equal number of positive and negative charges. This is because an atom is always neutral. It has no net charge. An oxygen atom has 8 protons. How many electrons does it have? What do you know about an atom that has 8 protons in its nucleus?

Table 4-2

This table lists selected elements, showing the number of protons in each element and its mass number, which is the combined number of protons and neutrons in an atom of the element.

Elements		
Element	Number of Protons	Mass Number
Hydrogen	1	1
Helium	2	4
Lithium	3	7
Beryllium	4	9
Boron	5	11
Carbon	6	12
Nitrogen	7	14
Oxygen	8	16
Fluorine	9	19
Neon	10	20
Sodium	11	23
Magnesium	12	24
Aluminum	13	27

Figure 4-18

Ⓐ Helium is used to inflate these balloons and keep them afloat.

Ⓑ All of these objects are made of aluminum or copper, which are very useful metals.

Ⓒ Matches burn by using sulfur, while many coins are made out of the metal nickel.

INVESTIGATION

Models of Atomic Structure

Over the years, scientists have developed models of the atom. Making a model and evaluating models made by others will help you learn how protons, neutrons, and electrons are arranged in an atom.

Preparation

Problem

How can you make a model that demonstrates the structure of an atom and that can be used to predict similarities in atomic structures?

Form a Hypothesis

Write a hypothesis that explains how your group can use a model to identify an element.

Objectives

*   Make a model of an element.
*   Identify the elements represented by the models made by others.

Materials

magnetic board	marker
rubber magnetic strips	bingo chips
	grapes
paper	coins

Safety

Never eat any food used in a laboratory experiment. Dispose of all food after your experiment.

Plan the Experiment

1 Choose an element from the periodic table to model. How do you know the number of protons, neutrons, and electrons in an atom of an element?

2 Use what you know about the structure of the atom to plan which objects will represent electrons in your model. Can you represent the nucleus of the atom? How will you indicate the protons and neutrons?

3 How will you arrange the electrons around the nucleus? What assumptions are you making about the charge of the atom? Can an element be identified by knowing only the number of protons?

Check the Plan

1 Before you begin, make sure your teacher approves your plan.

2 Once your model has been completed, write down any observations and include a sketch *in your Science Journal.*

3 Construct a model for a different element.

4 Observe the models made by your classmates. Identify the elements their models represent.

Analyze and Conclude

1. **Interpreting Data** What elements were you able to identify using your hypothesis? Explain.

2. **Conclude** In a neutral atom, identify which particles are always present in equal numbers.

3. **Predict** Predict what would happen to the charge of an atom if one of the electrons were removed. What happens to an atom if one proton and one electron are removed?

4. **Compare and Contrast** Compare your model with the electron cloud model of the atom.

Going Further

Why are some models more helpful than others? What other scientific ideas might a model help you understand?

In the Investigate, you used an atomic model to predict similarities in atomic structure and to identify an element by the number of protons in its nucleus. In the chapters to come, you will use similar models to explain the physical and chemical properties of elements, as well as the characteristics of solids, liquids, and gases.

■ Model Development

This chapter presented the development of a model of the atom as if all the events came together in an orderly manner. You might get the impression that developing the atomic model was similar to several people working at the same time on a jigsaw puzzle. But the model of the atom did not come together that easily. Everyone was not working in the same room. Everyone did not know that he or she had a puzzle piece. The atomic puzzle pieces were in laboratories scattered throughout the world. Sometimes the results of an experiment—or accident—were not even recognized as part of the atomic puzzle. Remember Becquerel's film? At first, it did not seem at all related to Rutherford's or Thomson's work. However, newly reported results often lead researchers to re-examine their data and observations. As researchers reported their observations, the atomic model was revised and refined.

Remember, the model of the atom has been revised since the first theory was proposed by ancient Greeks. And while the model is based on previous observations, it must fit observations yet to come. It is possible that you may make observations during your lifetime that will help further refine the atomic model.

Figure 4-19

Scientists around the world worked simultaneously to produce a model of the atom in much the same way as these kids are working on individual portions of a puzzle.

check your UNDERSTANDING

1. Suppose you held a proton, a neutron, and an electron in your hand. How could you tell them apart?
2. How did Rutherford model the atom after his famous gold foil experiment was completed?
3. Describe the structure of the present model of an atom.
4. **Apply** What kinds of experiments do you think have been done to discover the smaller particles that make up a proton or neutron?

Science and Society

Can You Give Me a Float to School?

For centuries, people have dreamed of levitation—floating suspended in air. With the discovery of superconductivity, levitation may no longer be a fantasy.

What is Superconductivity?

Superconductivity is the conduction of electricity without the slightest power loss. Once electrons begin moving, they no longer have the problems associated with friction, resistance, and loss of power over distances—they can move forever.

Scientists have known about superconductive material for a long time. But in order to be superconductive, materials must be chilled to a few degrees above absolute zero when the movement of atoms slows almost to a standstill.

In 1986, however, a new era of superconducting science and technology began,
when scientists started developing materials that are superconductive at higher temperatures.

One of the characteristics of superconductors allows a magnet to hover just above the material. The current moving through the superconductor produces a magnetic field, which repels the magnet, as shown in the photograph.

Possibilities?

When superconductors are developed that work at air temperature, the possibilities are limitless. Until then, the cooling process is extremely
expensive. Superconductors may make electric cars more practical, and high-speed ground transportation and faster computers possible. The time may come soon when we can just rise up in the air and float wherever we need to go.

USING MATH

Absolute zero forms the basis of a temperature scale known as the Kelvin scale. Absolute zero equals −273°C. Express classroom temperature of 27°C in kelvins. If your body temperature is 310 K, do you have a fever?

Literature Connection

Wisdom in Many Forms

*O*ur textbook said that 'atoms are the smallest particle in the universe.' And yet I knew from my tradition that 'There is nothing that is so small but that there is something smaller. There is nothing so large but that there is something larger'...When I asked my teacher, he answered, 'You'd better give the answer in the book unless you want to be graded for error...Then down at the bottom of the page you can say anything you want to say...anything at all.'"

Three Strands in the Braid
by Paula Underwood

Superstition, Tradition, and Science

Sometimes we think of anything that cannot be easily proven as superstition. In some cases, however, after much study we learn that the so-called superstition was right in the first place.

Scientists work to discover the secrets of the world. Sometimes they study atoms, sometimes rocks, sometimes human tissue. In every case, they are attempting to learn how things work and explain things we don't yet understand. Every scientist relies on the work of those who have gone before and builds on that information. Scientists rely on experimentation, intuition, lucky accidents, and education to develop new ideas and new products. Usually it is a combination of all those things that brings about important discoveries in science. In some cultures, however, tradition is a very important influence on what people believe about the world.

Three Strands in the Braid

In her book, Paula Underwood tells of tribal ancestors who created Learning Stories. Each ancient story traditionally ended with the question of what may be learned from it. Listeners would be encouraged to exercise three ways of understanding the story—the way of the Mind, the Body, and the Spirit—

to gain a deep and complete understanding. The three strands in the braid symbolized three ways of understanding, woven into a greater whole. Native American beliefs about the world and the universe were handed down through the telling of stories.

In some Native American cultures, there is a belief that nothing is so small that something else can't be smaller. When Paula Underwood was in school, scientists hypoth-esized that the atom was the smallest unit of matter. Her own tradition, however, had taught her that although atoms were small, there were always smaller things.

What Do You Think?

Given what you have learned about quarks, what do you think of the Native American belief? How can you learn from many different kinds of wisdom?

Health CONNECTION

Nuclear Medicine

In its short history, nuclear energy has presented some terrible instances of death and destruction. On the other hand, millions of people owe their lives to the applications of nuclear energy in the diagnosis and treatment of a wide variety of diseases and disorders. Some of the simplest applications involve radioactive tracers.

Radioactive Isotopes

Radioactive isotopes are used as tracers. In addition to its ability to emit radiation, a tracer must be nontoxic. That is, it must be a substance that can be introduced into the body without causing a dangerous reaction. The substance should be only a weak source of radiation. A stronger source could cause radiation sickness or destruction of healthy tissue.

Uses of Isotopes

The isotope can be introduced into the patient's digestive, circulatory, or nervous system. Once introduced, the tracer emits radiation as it travels through the body. Physicians follow the path of the radiation to determine the location of any problems or abnormalities.

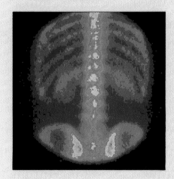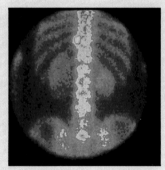

What Do You Think?

Do the benefits of nuclear energy to the field of medicine outweigh its negative, destructive uses? What would you think if you were in need of one of the applications of nuclear medicine?

Leisure Connection

Your Nose Knows

Have you ever had Mylar® balloons for your birthday? Coming in a variety of shapes and colors, these shiny balloons certainly add a festive flair to any occasion. Mylar® balloons filled with helium stay inflated for a long time. How small are those helium gas particles that stay trapped inside these balloons?

Finding Particle Sizes

Scientists use sophisticated equipment and complicated mathematical formulas to find out the size of particles. This is necessary when investigating atoms and tiny molecules, but we can find out some things about particle sizes with just a sniff.

Consider bleach bottles or hamburger wrappers. What if the particles that make up the bleach or the hamburger are smaller than the spaces between the particles of the plastic or the paper that holds them? You would know what's inside the container by just sniffing. That's true with paper hamburger wrappers. Particles of chemicals in onions and meat can easily pass through the paper wrapper, so you can smell the hamburger before you unwrap it.

Some Experiments to Try

There are experiments you can conduct to determine the relative size of particles. Place five to ten drops of vanilla extract into a balloon. Blow up the balloon and tie the end closed. You'll find that you can smell that vanilla through the inflated balloon. Because you can smell it, you know that the particles of the vanilla extract are smaller than the spaces between balloon particles.

Choosing the Right Container

The different sizes of particles are important in choosing containers for different materials. While you might enjoy the smell of a hamburger or vanilla, you wouldn't want the whole house to smell like bleach just because you want to do laundry.

What Do You Think?

Why do you think Mylar® balloons are most often used to hold helium? Have you ever had a rubber balloon filled with helium? How did it change over a few days? What can you conclude about the particle size of helium, compared to the spaces between the particles of Mylar® or rubber?

Science Journal

Review the statements below about the big ideas presented in this chapter, and answer the questions. Then, reread your answers to the Did You Ever Wonder questions at the beginning of the chapter. *In your Science Journal*, write a paragraph about how your understanding of the big ideas in the chapter has changed.

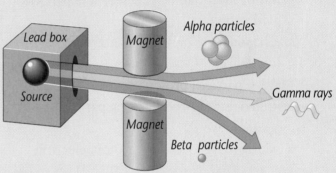

1 Using cathode-ray tubes, Thomson demonstrated the existence of a negatively charged particle he called the electron. *How did he arrive at this conclusion?*

Lead box   Magnet   *Alpha particles*

Source   *Gamma rays*

Magnet   *Beta particles*

2 Rutherford observed the existence of alpha particles, beta particles, and gamma rays. *How do these particles and rays compare?*

Electron   Nucleus

3 Our model of the structure of the atom has been changed as new experiments provided more information. *What model do we generally refer to now?*

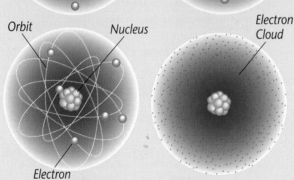

Orbit   Nucleus   Electron Cloud

Electron

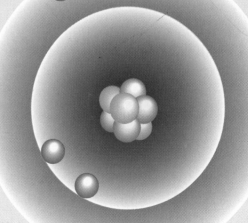

4 The atom consists of a nucleus containing protons and neutrons surrounded by electrons in energy levels within their electron cloud. *Draw a model of a helium atom.*

Using Key Science Terms

alpha particle   neutron

beta particle   nucleus

electron   proton

gamma ray   radioactivity

For each set of terms below, choose the one term that does not belong and explain why it does not belong.

1. radioactivity, alpha particle, beta particle, gamma ray
2. electron, beta particle, gamma ray, negative charge
3. alpha particle, proton, neutron, electron
4. radioactivity, proton, alpha particle, gamma ray
5. neutron, radioactivity, proton, electron

Understanding Ideas

Answer the following questions in your Journal using complete sentences.

1. If an atom has 4 protons and 5 neutrons, how many electrons does it have? Explain.
2. What is the maximum number of electrons that can be found in an atom's second energy level?
3. Who formulated:
   a. the billiard ball model of the atom?
   b. the blueberry muffin model of the atom?
4. What did the gold foil experiment reveal about gold atoms?
5. What is a model?
6. Which requires more energy to remove from an atom, an electron in the first energy level or an electron in the third energy level? Explain.

Developing Skills

Use your understanding of the concepts developed in this chapter to answer each of the following questions.

1. **Observing and Inferring** In the gold foil experiment, most of the alpha particles went through the foil. Suppose that, instead, only a few particles had gone through the foil. How would Rutherford's conclusion have been different?
2. **Predicting** Imagine an omega particle that has the same mass as an alpha particle and a positive charge of three. If an alpha particle and an omega particle pass through a magnetic field, how will their paths differ?
3. **Concept Mapping** Create a spider concept map that depicts the atom through a description of its component particles.

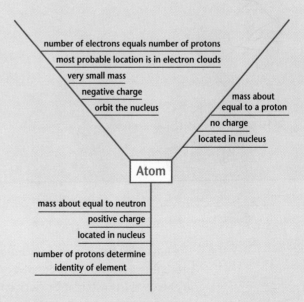

number of electrons equals number of protons

most probable location is in electron clouds

very small mass

negative charge

orbit the nucleus

mass about equal to a proton

no charge

located in nucleus

Atom

mass about equal to neutron

positive charge

located in nucleus

number of protons determine identity of element

Critical Thinking

In your Journal, *answer each of the following questions.*

1. Three particles are fired into a box that is positively charged on one side and negatively charged on the other. The result is shown in the picture. Which particle is the proton? Which particle is the electron? Which particle is the neutron? Explain.

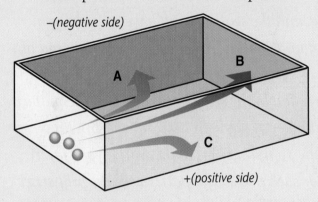

–(negative side)

A

B

C

+(positive side)

2. If you wanted to repeat an experiment to test a hypothesis you didn't believe, what is most important for you to find out and do?

Problem Solving

Read the following problem and discuss your answers in a brief paragraph.

Carbon-14 (14 particles in the nucleus) atoms are unstable. Carbon-14 is a radioactive form of carbon. Normal carbon atoms are carbon-12 (12 particles in the nucleus). It takes 5700 years for half the atoms in a sample of carbon-14 to release their extra energy and particles and become stable. In another 5700 years, half of the remaining atoms in the sample would become stable, and so on every 5700 years.

All living things have carbon atoms in them. Living organisms absorb some carbon-14 from the atmosphere. When the organisms die, no new atoms are taken in. The carbon-14 atoms present begin to break down into stable atoms.

How could these facts be used to determine the age of a mummy found in a newly discovered ancient Egyptian tomb?

CONNECTING IDEAS

Discuss each of the following in a brief paragraph.

1. **Theme—Systems and Interactions** What would happen to beta particles in an electric field? Explain.

2. **Theme—Scale and Structure** Figure 4-12B on page 124 shows a model of an atom. Is the size of the nucleus accurate in relation to the size of the electron cloud? Explain.

3. **Literature Connection** "This can't be true because science has never proven it." Describe how you might respond to such a statement.

4. **A Closer Look** What steps can be taken to reduce the level of radon in a home?

CHAPTER 5

THE periodic TABLE

Did you ever wonder...

✓ How the pioneers made soap?

✓ Why racing bicycles are so light?

✓ What is used to mark the white lines on baseball diamonds and football fields?

Science Journal

Before you study the periodic table, think about these questions and answer them *in your Science Journal*. When you finish the chapter, compare your answers with what you have learned.

The movement of a metronome, a playground swing, and the seasons—all have something in common. What do you think it is? What kind of patterns exist in the examples above? In the swing, it is the height and direction of the seat. In the seasons, the pattern could be the number of daylight hours or the growth of trees and plants. To make sense of the world, your brain always looks for such patterns—patterns in the properties of things.

In this chapter, you will discover some similarities and patterns among elements. You'll also see how the elements can be placed in a pattern based on their characteristics.

▶ *In the activity on the next page, explore different ways of organizing your classmates.*

Explore! ACTIVITY

Can you organize your classmates?

What To Do

1. Work in groups to identify the different characteristics of your classmates. In addition to physical appearance, don't forget things like birth month or date, or telephone number. Be creative. Record these characteristics *in your Journal.*

2. Use your list to arrange your classmates in some pattern.

3. Compare your group's arrangement to that of others.

Structure of the Periodic Table

5-1

Section Objectives

- Describe the arrangement of the elements in the periodic table.
- Find the number of protons and electrons in an atom using the periodic table.
- Explain atomic number.
- Identify mass number and calculate atomic mass.

Key Terms

periodic table
atomic number
mass number
isotopes
atomic mass

Decisions, Decisions

You've been asked to design a new product for a very successful company. You find out that the material must be lightweight, strong, flexible, and resistant to heat and weather. How do you decide what to use? One way would be to obtain a list of all the thousands of available substances and start checking out their properties. Wow! What a job! Perhaps if you started with the elements in these substances, you could at least narrow the list down to a hundred or so.

You may remember from learning about elements that metals have many of the desired properties, but that still leaves a lot of work. Wouldn't it be nice if someone arranged those elements so that you could quickly find the one you want? Properties such as

Figure 5-1

In making new products, different materials are selected based on the usefulness of their properties.

flexibility, resistance to heat, strength, and ability to combine with other elements need to be considered. These elements need to be arranged based on such properties and repeating patterns in these properties. In such an arrangement, you'd be able to predict which elements would have the properties you want to make your revolutionary new product.

■ The Birth of the Periodic Table

In the late 1800s, as more and more elements were discovered, the need arose to arrange them into a pattern that would simplify their study. Dmitri Mendeleev, a Russian chemist, searched for a meaningful way to organize the elements. He decided to put them in order of increasing masses.

Figure 5-2

The Russian chemist Dmitri Mendeleev arranged the elements in order of increasing mass, forming one of the first periodic tables.

When Mendeleev put the elements in order by mass, he found that other properties, such as density, malleability, and the ability to react with other elements, seemed to repeat over and over. This repeating pattern is called periodic, and he called his table the **periodic table** of the elements.

In the following Investigate, try to develop a good strategy for arranging and identifying characteristics of elements by arranging something more common instead.

INVESTIGATION

Recognizing Patterns

People can have similar traits, such as height, hair or skin color, or athletic ability. Objects can also share similarities. In the first periodic table of elements, Mendeleev arranged the elements by mass. He found that properties of the elements then formed repeating patterns. From this organization, Mendeleev was able to predict the properties of undiscovered elements.

Preparation

Problem
Can 20 different balls be arranged in a table by similar characteristics?

Form a Hypothesis
As a group, form a hypothesis about how the balls can be arranged into a table by similarities to predict the properties of other "undiscovered" balls.

Objectives
- Classify objects by properties.
- Predict the properties of an object by use of a periodic table.

Materials
20 balls of various colors and sizes; colors can be duplicated but no two balls should be exactly alike.
paper squares—5 cm × 5 cm

Plan the Experiment

1 On what properties of the balls will you design your table?

2 How many rows and columns are necessary to make a table?

3 Will your arrangement have gaps like Mendeleev's periodic table of the elements? How will you hold those places open for the "undiscovered" balls?

Check the Plan

1 Make certain that the balls are arranged to share properties down the columns and that the arrangment across the rows is in an orderly sequence.

2 Before you proceed, check your plan with your teacher.

3 Carry out your investigation. Record your table *in your Science Journal.*

Analyze and Conclude

1. Observe How many columns did you have? How many rows? Why did you have more of one than the other?

2. Analyze What properties did you use to arrange the balls? What properties did they have in common down the columns? What properties repeated periodically?

3. Conclude For each paper square holding a spot in your table, what are the properties of the "undiscovered" balls? Was your hypothesis supported?

Going Further

Try making a similar table with 20 objects selected randomly. Is it always possible to find patterns and classify objects by their properties?.

Arrangement of the Periodic Table

Mendeleev arranged the elements by increasing mass. When he did this, some of the elements' properties didn't match with what was expected in the pattern of periods. The periodic table we now use today takes care of that problem.

Remember that atoms are composed of protons, neutrons, and electrons. In the periodic table each element has one more proton in its nucleus than the one before it. The number of protons in an atom of an element is called the **atomic number** of the element. Since atoms are electrically neutral, there must be the same number of electrons (negative charges) in the atom as there are protons (positive charges). The atomic number tells you both the number of protons and the number of electrons. The modern periodic table shown on pages 164-165 is arranged in order of increasing atomic number.

Look at the information given in one box of the periodic table, shown in **Figure 5-3**.

This box represents the element boron. The box contains the atomic number (5), the chemical symbol (B), the name, and the atomic mass (10.811) of the element. What do we mean by atomic mass?

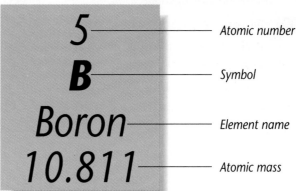

5 —— Atomic number

B —— Symbol

Boron —— Element name

10.811 —— Atomic mass

Figure 5-3

This is how the element boron is listed in the periodic table, showing its atomic number, its symbol, the name of the element, and its atomic mass.

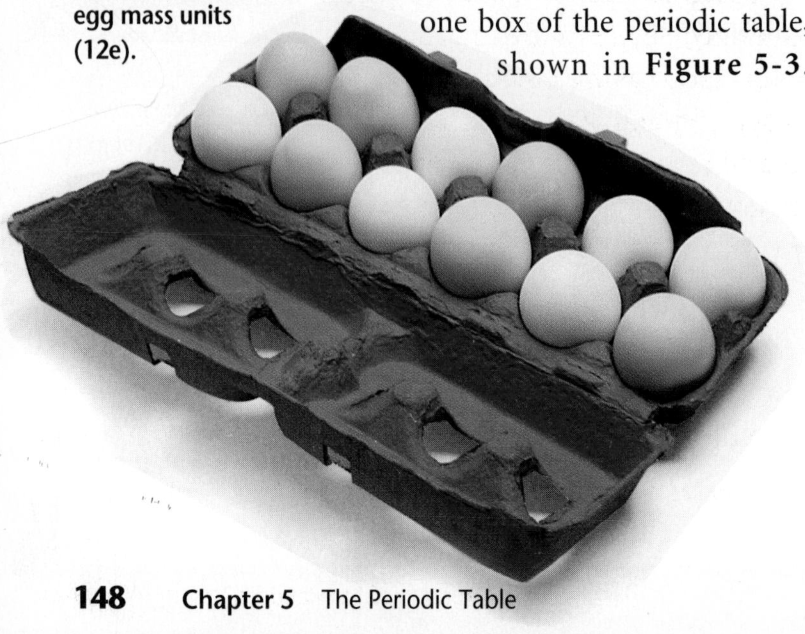

■ Atomic Mass

Imagine you are asked the mass of a carton of eggs that contains six white eggs and six brown eggs, as shown in **Figure 5-4**. You decide that each egg has about the same mass and the carton is very light by comparison, so you decide to measure the mass of the eggs in terms of the number of eggs. That is, you define the mass of an egg as one egg mass unit (e). You tell the person that the mass of the carton of eggs is twelve! Twelve egg mass units—12 e!

Since atoms are so small, the easiest way to describe their mass is by describing the total number of protons and neutrons in the nucleus—the

Figure 5-4

Since each of these eggs has about the same mass, the "mass" of a carton of eggs could be defined as twelve egg mass units (12e).

Figure 5-5

An atom of carbon-12 has 6 protons and 6 neutrons, so the mass of the atom is 12 atomic mass units.

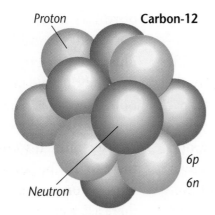

Proton   Carbon-12

Neutron

6p
6n

mass number. Protons and neutrons are like the brown and white eggs. They have different properties, but just about the same mass. If there are 6 protons and 6 neutrons in the nucleus, you say that the mass of the atom is 12 atomic mass units (u). Why aren't the electrons included? Even if we counted all the electrons in the biggest atom, their total mass would be only a fraction of the mass of a proton.

If an atom has a mass number of 23 and contains 12 neutrons, how many protons does it have? In other words, what is its atomic number, and what element is it? Remember that the mass number, 23, is the total number of protons and neutrons in the nucleus. If 12 of them are neutrons, how many are protons? (23-12=11 protons.) That is the atomic number. Find that number on the periodic table on pages 164-165. The element is Na—sodium.

Try this. An atom has 9 protons and 10 neutrons. Look at the periodic table and figure out what element it is. Use the number of protons—the atomic number. What element has an atomic number of 9? Fluorine!

What is the mass number of this fluorine atom? That's right—19.

What if you looked for the mass number on the table? Oops! There is no element with a mass number of 19. Fluorine is listed at 18.998. And 18.998 is called the atomic mass, not the mass number. Are atomic mass and mass number the same? If so, why is the atomic mass not a whole number when you are counting protons and neutrons? Are there pieces of protons and neutrons?

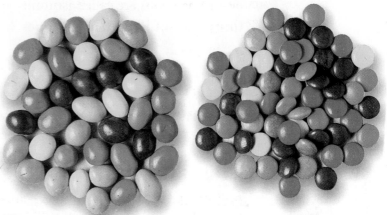

Figure 5-6

The combined number of individual chocolates and peanuts in this pile of candy would determine the candy's "mass number."

■ Isotopes

Imagine that you have 100 pieces of candy; 60 are candy-coated chocolates, each having a mass of 1 candy mass unit, and 40 of them are candy-coated peanuts, each with a mass of 2 candy mass units (c). First, what is the total mass of the 100 pieces of candy?

$$
\begin{aligned}
60 \times 1\,c &= 60\,c \\
40 \times 2\,c &= 80\,c \\
\hline
100 \text{ pieces} &= 140\,c
\end{aligned}
$$

The average mass of one piece is:
140 c / 100 pieces = 1.4 c/piece

Atoms of the same element always have the same number of protons—their atomic number. This identifies them as the element they are. But all atoms of the same element don't necessarily have the same number of neutrons. For example, boron is a dark, gray solid. All boron atoms have 5 protons. Four-fifths of them have 6 neutrons. What is their mass number? The other one-fifth of all boron atoms found in nature have 5 neutrons. What is their mass number? Atoms of the same element with different numbers of neutrons are called **isotopes** of that element. The two isotopes of boron as discussed are referred to as boron-11 and boron-10 and are illustrated in **Figure 5-7**. The numbers indicate the mass number of that isotope.

What is the average mass of 100 boron atoms? It would be closer to 11 than to 10, because there are more boron atoms with a mass of 11 than there are with a mass of 10.

$$
\begin{aligned}
4/5 \times 100 \text{ atoms} &= 80 \text{ atoms} \\
1/5 \times 100 \text{ atoms} &= 20 \text{ atoms} \\
80 \text{ atoms} \times 11 \text{ u/atom} &= 880 \text{ u} \\
20 \text{ atoms} \times 10 \text{ u/atom} &= 200 \text{ u} \\
\hline
100 \text{ atoms} &= 1080 \text{ u} \\
1080 \text{ u/100 atoms} &= 10.8 \text{ u/atom}
\end{aligned}
$$

CLOSER a LOOK

Medical Uses of Radiation

Although people are concerned about the possible health risks due to radiation, doctors sometimes choose to expose their patients to radiation. The earliest and best-known medical use of radiation involves X rays. X rays travel easily through most body tissue but are stopped by bone. X rays help locate breaks in the bones.

Detecting Abnormalities

Radioactive isotopes release radiation that can be measured. The measurements can then be interpreted by a computer and a picture of soft tissue such as the brain, kidneys, and lungs is produced. In this way doctors can determine the extent of a tumor or other abnormality.

Here, a radioisotope reveals that the patient's bone is diseased.

Note boron's atomic mass shown on the periodic table. The **atomic mass** is the average mass of the isotopes of an element found in nature which explains why they are not whole numbers. Let's investigate more about the way isotopes and atomic mass are related.

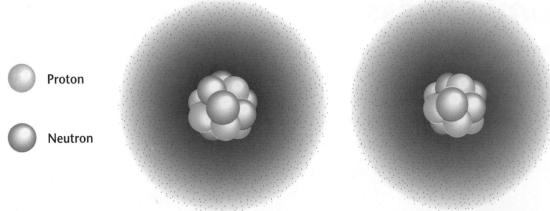

- ○ Proton
- ○ Neutron

Figure 5-7

The most common isotope of boron has six neutrons, but some boron atoms have five neutrons, making them a different isotope.

Detecting Viruses, Hormones, and Drugs

Radioactive isotopes can also be used to determine—very precisely—how much of a virus, hormone, or drug is in a patient's body. The technique, radioimmunoassay (RIA), was pioneered in the 1950s by Rosalyn Yalow and Solomon Berson. Yalow was awarded a Nobel prize for her work. In an RIA test, the patient is given a precise amount of a radioactive compound. Compounds used in the test are chosen for their ability to take the place of the virus, hormone, or drug normally present in the body's fluids. Then a precise measurement of the radioactivity given off by the patient's blood or

In this photograph, a radioisotope shows that the patient's bone is healthy.

urine is made. By comparing the measurements, physicians can determine the amount of the substance under study present in a patient's body. For example, it was widely believed that diabetes was a condition that resulted from a total lack of insulin in the patient's blood. RIA showed that diabetes can occur even if insulin is present.

RIA has been used successfully to treat diabetes, reduce the risk of transmitting hepatitis in transfused blood, and in identifying infectious diseases such as tuberculosis.

*inter*NET CONNECTION

Visit the Nuclear Medicine Research Council on the World Wide Web. Prepare a presentation about an isotope and its medical uses.

INVESTIGATE!

Isotopes and Atomic Mass

In this Investigate, you'll use a model of isotopes to help you understand the concept of atomic mass.

Problem
How do isotopes affect average atomic mass?

Materials
4 red and 3 green candy-coated peanuts
2 red and 3 green candy-coated chocolates

What To Do

1 Copy the data table *into your Journal*.

2 Make a pile of four red candy-coated peanuts and two red candy-coated chocolates (see photo **A**). The two different kinds of candy represent two isotopes of the same element.

3 Assume that a red peanut has a mass of 2 candy units, and a red chocolate has a mass of 1 candy unit. *Calculate* the average mass of the red candy as follows:

    a. Multiply the number of red peanuts by the mass in candy units.

Data and Observations

	Peanut (candy x candy unit)	Chocolate (candy x candy unit)	Average (total mass) (total candies)
Red			
Green			

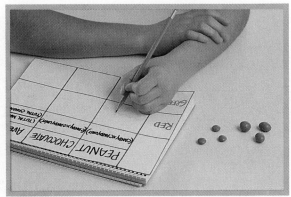

A

B

b. Multiply the number of red chocolates by the mass in candy units.

c. Add the masses and divide by the total number of candies.

4 Repeat Steps 2 and 3, but use three green peanuts and three green chocolates. Assume a green peanut has a mass of 4 units, and a green chocolate has a mass of 3 units.

5 Record your calculations *in your Journal* (see photo **B**).

Analyzing

1. There were six red and six green candies. Why were their calculated average masses not the same?

2. If a sample of element Z contains 100 atoms of Z-12 and 10 atoms of Z-14, *calculate* the average mass of Z.

Concluding and Applying

3. An element needed for most nuclear reactors is uranium. Its two major isotopes are U-235 and U-238. Look up the mass of uranium on the periodic table. *Infer* which isotope is the most common. Explain.

4. *Compare* and *contrast* mass number and atomic mass.

5. **Going Further** Hydrogen has three isotopes. The most common one, protium, has no neutrons. Deuterium, the second isotope, has one neutron. Tritium has two neutrons. Using this information, *calculate* the mass number of these isotopes.

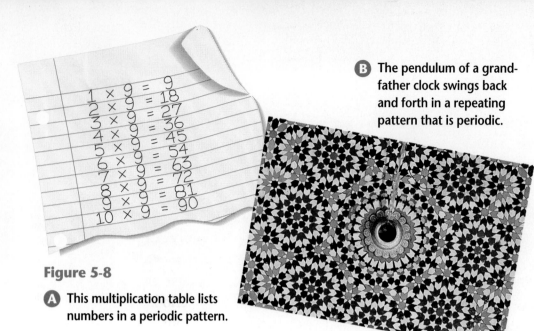

B The pendulum of a grand-father clock swings back and forth in a repeating pattern that is periodic.

Figure 5-8

A This multiplication table lists numbers in a periodic pattern.

You just used a candy mass unit as a model for atomic mass. The calculations you used to find the average candy mass are similar to the calculations you used to find the atomic mass of an element. Some elements may have only identical atoms, while several elements have as many as 6 or 7 isotopes. The atomic mass is found by calculating the average mass of a sample of atoms. Carbon has 6 isotopes, with mass numbers ranging from 10 to 15. However, almost 99 percent of carbon atoms have 6 protons and 6 neutrons—mass number 12. This is referred to as carbon-12.

C These tiles are arranged in a repeating pattern much like the elements are arranged in the periodic table.

Tile arrangements, the pendulum of a clock, and the multiplication table, shown in **Figure 5-8**, all occur in repeating patterns that are periodic. Elements can also be organized into a table that shows repeating patterns of properties. In the next section, you'll take a closer look at the organization of the periodic table and how it is used.

check your UNDERSTANDING

1. How does the arrangement of the modern periodic table differ from Mendeleev's table?
2. Use the periodic table to find the name, atomic number, and atomic mass of the following elements: O, N, Ca, Ba, and Br.
3. Name three pieces of information that you can learn from an atomic number.

4. **Apply** Complete the following table.

Symbol	Atomic No.	Mass No.	No. of Neutrons
N	7		7
F		19	10
K	19	39	
Co	27		32

 **Families of Elements**

Organizing the Elements

Section Objectives
- Identify a family of elements.
- Recognize the alkali family.
- Describe the alkaline earth family.

Key Terms

family of elements
alkali metals
alkaline earth metals

We began this chapter by using properties to organize elements in a way that would allow us to quickly locate them and to predict other properties. These might be density, strength, or any other chemical or physical characteristic of the element. What else do the elements have in common? You'll examine the periodic table in the next activity to find out.

Find Out! ACTIVITY

How are elements alike and different?

What To Do

1. Select two elements from the list provided by your teacher.

2. For each of your chosen elements, prepare an index card. In the upper left-hand corner of the card, place a box like the one on the periodic table. This should show the atomic number, symbol, name, and atomic mass of the element.

3. Do some research on the element and write a few sentences about its properties and uses.

4. Attach either an object or a picture to the card that shows its properties. For example, for iron, you could attach a nail. For helium, you might have a picture of a floating balloon.

5. Make a large periodic table using your cards and those of your classmates.

Conclude and Apply

1. *In your Journal,* record what you notice about the properties of elements on the left side of your table.

2. What about the right side?

Columns of the Periodic Table

On the periodic table, elements in the same column are called a **family of elements**. Do you recognize the three elements in Family 11 on the periodic table? Copper, silver, and gold, shown in **Figure 5-9,** are called the coinage metals. Although they are different colors, they have similar physical and chemical properties. They are all malleable, shiny, and resistant to change.

Noble gases—such as helium and neon—are called noble because, like royalty refusing to associate with common people, these elements rarely combine with other elements. What other elements would you expect to behave in the same way? On the other hand, members of Family 17, the halogens, are very reactive and often combine with other elements.

Why do elements in the same family have similar properties? Electrons in an atom are arranged in energy levels around the nucleus, as shown in **Figure 5-10**. The number of electrons in the outer energy level of an atom determines if and how an element will combine with other elements. These outer electrons are so important that a special system is used to represent them.

Figure 5-9

 The Navajo turquoise and silver jewelry are among the treasures found at a Shiprock, New Mexico trading post. Bogota's gold museum displays fine art and jewelry made by Indian goldsmiths.

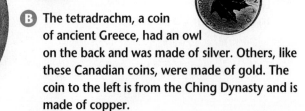 The tetradrachm, a coin of ancient Greece, had an owl on the back and was made of silver. Others, like these Canadian coins, were made of gold. The coin to the left is from the Ching Dynasty and is made of copper.

Figure 5-10

These diagrams of lithium, boron, sodium, and chlorine show the different arrangements of electrons in the energy levels around the nucleus of the atom.

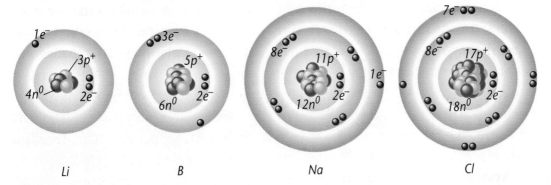

Li   B   Na   Cl

■ Dot Diagrams

A dot diagram is simply the symbol for an element surrounded by as many dots as there are electrons in the outer energy level. How can you tell how many electrons there will be? If you skip the elements in Families 3 through 12 on your periodic table, the other columns have a very simple pattern. There will be one electron in the outer level of column 1, two in column 2, three in column 13, and so on until you reach column 18, which has eight electrons in the outer level, except for helium which has two electrons in its one energy level. The pattern of outer electrons is simply one through eight. How many electrons are in the last energy level of the halogens? They are in Family 17, so it's seven. **Figure 5-11** shows examples of dot diagrams.

How would you write dot diagrams for the element sulfur? First, write the symbol for the element—S. Then look at its position on the periodic table. What column is it in? Family 16. How many electrons does it have in its outer energy level? Using the pattern mentioned above, we see that it has six. **Figure 5-11** shows how dot diagrams are drawn.

Figure 5-11

A These are dot diagrams of potassium and aluminum. Potassium is represented by the symbol K and has one electron in its outer energy level. Aluminum is represented by the symbol Al. How many electrons are in the outer energy level of an atom of aluminum?

B Sulfur is in Family 16 of the periodic table, so it has six electrons in its outer energy level. These are shown as six dots around the symbol for sulfur, S. There are five dots around the symbol for phosphorus, P. What family of the periodic table is phosphorus in?

Notice that, with the exception of helium, all of the noble gases have eight electrons in their outer energy level. Once eight is reached, the next element adds an energy level and begins again with one electron. It would seem that the presence of eight electrons makes the energy level full, or complete. You know that noble gases do not combine easily with other elements. They seem very stable—that is, they resist change.

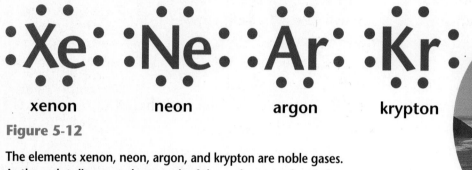

xenon　　　neon　　　argon　　　krypton

Figure 5-12

The elements xenon, neon, argon, and krypton are noble gases. As these dot diagrams show, each of these elements already has eight electrons in its outer energy level. As a result, these gases do not combine easily with other elements.

Figure 5-13

Xenon and other noble gases are often used in electric lamps. Many lighthouses use xenon arc lamps, which produce an intense blue-white light.

■ Combining Atoms

By observation, we find that when other elements combine, they tend to do so in a way that will give them eight electrons in their outer energy level. Let's look at one example. **Figure 5-14** shows dot diagrams of an atom of sodium and an atom of chlorine. If the sodium gives its electron to chlorine, how many electrons will chlorine have in its outer level? How many will sodium have after it loses that electron?

There is an exception to this rule of having eight electrons in the outer level. Hydrogen and helium are so small that they only have electrons in the first energy level. In this first energy level, there is only room for two electrons. Therefore, the noble gas helium is complete with two electrons in its outer energy level. When elements such as lithium (Li) and beryllium (Be) lose their outer electrons, their outer levels become like helium, and they are stable.

Figure 5-14

This diagram shows one atom of sodium combining with one atom of chlorine to form sodium chloride. The sodium atom gives up one electron to the chlorine atom. The chlorine atom then has eight electrons in its outer energy level, making it complete, while the sodium atom is left with eight electrons in its outer energy level. Do you think sodium chloride is a stable compound?

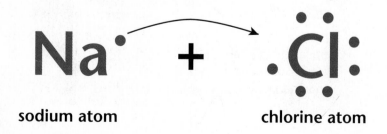

sodium atom　　　　　　　　chlorine atom

Some Important Families

DID YOU KNOW?

■ Alkali Metals

Since each Family 1 element has one outer electron to lose, they will all behave like sodium and combine with chlorine. What other elements, in addition to sodium, would you expect to react with chlorine?

The column 1 elements belong to a family known as the **alkali metals**. They differ from typical metals because they are so soft they can be cut with a knife. They have a metallic luster, conduct heat and electricity, and are malleable.

In nature, alkali metal atoms immediately react with air, water, or other substances in the environment as shown in **Figure 5-15B**. Pure alkali metals must therefore be stored in kerosene or some other liquid that doesn't react with them.

Compounds of sodium are used in the manufacture of detergents and soaps. Pioneers made soap by collecting water that ran through ashes and cooking it with grease. The water contained mainly potassium hydroxide. Alkali means to roast ashes in a pan.

Figure 5-15

A The orange-yellow glow of a street lamp is produced when electricity passes through the sodium vapor inside the lamp.

B The atoms of the alkali metals, such as the sodium shown here, react immediately with water or other substances in the environment.

■ Alkaline Earth Metals

The second vertical column of elements is the **alkaline earth metals**. In what ways do their properties seem different from those of the alkali metals? **Figure 5-16** shows a reaction between magnesium nitrate and a solution of baking soda. What do you expect would happen if strontium nitrate were added to a baking soda solution? What other nitrates should behave in the same way?

Figure 5-16

The alkaline earth metals, which include magnesium, are not quite as reactive as the alkali metals. This photograph shows what happens when a solution of baking soda is added to magnesium nitrate.

Figure 5-17

A The bright colors you see in a fireworks display are produced mainly by alkaline earth metals. Magnesium is used in some fireworks to produce a brilliant white light. Strontium is used to produce a crimson light, and barium is used to produce green light. Would other alkaline earth metals produce different colors?

B Magnesium is often mixed with aluminum in alloys. These alloys are used in products such as tennis rackets and bicycle frames because they are strong but lightweight. Why do you think alkali metals such as sodium are not used in these products?

Connect to...

Life Science

Some coral polyps secrete calcium carbonate skeletons. These are called hard corals. Make a diagram of three different types of hard corals.

Calcium compounds, found in dairy products, are an essential building block for strong bones and teeth. Calcium hydroxide is a white powder used to make baseball diamond and football field lines. It is also used to neutralize acidity in soil. Calcium chloride is used in winter to keep ice from forming on roads and walks. Uses of magnesium, another alkaline earth metal, are discussed in **Figure 5-17**.

Because members of a chemical family have the same number of outer electrons, they also have similar abilities to form compounds with other elements. Rather than having to test each individual element, you can simply look at the periodic table and identify the family to which an element belongs. Then you can predict how it will behave and how it might be used.

check your UNDERSTANDING

1. List four of the elements in Family 16 of the periodic table. Draw dot diagrams for them.
2. Compare and contrast the properties of alkali metals and alkaline earth metals.
3. **Apply** An element is shiny, but easily cut with a knife. When dropped in water, it reacts immediately, giving off a flash of light. It is placed in a container with another element that is a gas. Nothing happens. What families would you guess these two elements are in? Explain your answer using the periodic table on pages 164-165.

Periods of Elements

5-3

What's the Period in the Periodic Table?

You know that the elements in a column of the periodic table are related as members of the same family. What about the rows of the periodic table? What information can you infer about the elements in a particular row? Do they share similar properties as well? Do this next activity to see how you can use a familiar table to infer information.

Section Objectives

- Describe a period on the periodic table.
- Identify where metals, non-metals, and metalloids are located on the periodic table.
- Use the periodic table to classify an element.

Key Terms
period

Find Out! ACTIVITY

How can you use a table of repeating events to predict or explain?

What To Do

1. The figure shows a familiar table of repeating properties. What is it? Of course, it's a calendar, but one with a difference. This calendar has some missing information.

2. Determine what is missing by examining the information surrounding the spot where the missing information goes. This periodic table is made up of families of days, Sunday through Saturday, and by horizontal periods called weeks.

Conclude and Apply

1. Two of the days in Families 3 and 4 are marked with an @ and a #. What dates should go in these positions? Explain your reasons *in your Journal.*

2. Family 5 doesn't have a name. What is the correct name for this family?

3. What dates are included in the third period of the table?

4. Assuming that the previous month had 30 days, what day would the 28th of that month have been? What period of this table would it appear in?

SUN	MON	TUE	WED		FRI	SAT
			1		2	3
4	5	6	7	8	9	10
11	12	@	#	15	16	17
18	19	20	21	22	23	24
25	26	27	28	29	30	31

The calendar is just one example of a table of periodic events. One repeat of a pattern is called a **period**. On the periodic table of elements, shown on pages 164-165, each row begins as the pattern of physical and chemical properties of elements begins to repeat itself. When arranged in this manner, the 100+ known elements form 7 horizontal rows, or periods, because of the periodic repetition of properties as you move from left to right. Breaking the sequence of elements into periods created 18 columns called families. This is similar to the calendar in the Find Out activity.

On the periodic table, locate the stair-step line toward the right side that divides the table. The elements to the left of this line are metals, except hydrogen. Notice that the box containing hydrogen is slightly above the rest of the table. Although hydrogen has one electron in its outer energy level, you might also say that it has one less than it needs to become non-reactive like helium. In that case, it would be placed at the top of the halogen family. As you know, hydrogen is a gas and has properties of a nonmetal. It is placed in Family 1 because the formulas for its compounds are similar to those formed by Family 1 elements.

You've learned that most metals are solid at room temperature, shiny,

Life Science CONNECTION

The Chernobyl Disaster

History's worst accident at a nuclear power plant occurred on April 26, 1986, in Chernobyl in the Soviet Union.

This reactor used graphite to regulate the nuclear reaction, and water to carry the thermal energy to the turbine, which then produced electrical energy. On that day, the water flow past the core (where the nuclear reaction occurs) was stopped. Part of the reactor got so hot that the graphite caught fire and caused an explosion that ripped apart the reactor and released large amounts of radioactive material into the

The explosion at the Chernobyl nuclear reactor caused considerable damage and released large amounts of harmful radioactive material into the atmosphere.

and good conductors of heat and electricity. In your index card periodic table, locate examples of metals you are familiar with, such as iron, zinc, copper, and silver. Elements in Families 3 through 12 are called transition elements. They include many of the metals found in everyday objects.

The elements to the right of the stair-step line are the nonmetals. Many of them are gases. The solids, such as carbon and sulfur, are easily crushed and do not shine.

The properties of elements change gradually as they move from left to right. On either side of the stair-step line is a special group of elements called metalloids, elements that have some properties of both metals and nonmetals. They are dull in color, not malleable or ductile, but they do conduct a current. Because metalloids, such as silicon and germanium, do not conduct as well as a metal, they are called semiconductors. These elements are used to make transistors, integrated circuits, and other critical parts of electronic devices, such as computers and video games.

Figure 5-18

A Like most of the transition elements, titanium is hard and has a high melting point.

B Vanadium, another of the transition elements, is often used to form alloys such as vanadium steel.

---

atmosphere. At least 31 people died from radiation sickness or burns. Many more may die in the coming years as a result of this accident.

Strontium-90

People who lived in the Soviet Union were not the only ones affected by the Chernobyl disaster. Some radioactive material was carried by wind into northern and central Europe. Health experts in Europe were particularly concerned about strontium-90, an isotope of the element strontium that has a half-life of 28 years.

If you look at the periodic table, you will notice that strontium is just beneath calcium. Elements that belong to the same group in the periodic table have many similar characteristics. Strontium, therefore, can take the place of calcium in many chemical reactions.

Effects on the Human Body

Our bones are made up almost entirely of calcium compounds. If strontium-90 enters the human body, it replaces some of that calcium and exposes the bones to radiation. Constant exposure to this type of radiation can seriously damage bone marrow, causing diseases such as leukemia.

Strontium-90 enters our bodies the same way that calcium enters our bodies. When grass grows, it absorbs calcium from the soil. Cows eat the grass and produce milk. When we drink milk or eat milk products, such as butter and cheese, our bodies absorb the calcium.

That's why, in the aftermath of the Chernobyl explosion, European health officials carefully monitored the level of strontium-90 in milk. Some milk had to be thrown away because it contained too much of the radioactive material.

What Do You Think?

Many people were evacuated from the vicinity of the Chernobyl nuclear power plant when it caught fire in 1986. From what you've learned about strontium-90, do you think they have been allowed to return?

Figure 5-19

In the periodic table, all of the known elements are arranged in rows and columns according to their properties. Elements arranged in the same column make up a family of elements. One of the elements in Family 11 is gold, which has the symbol Au. What is the atomic number of gold?

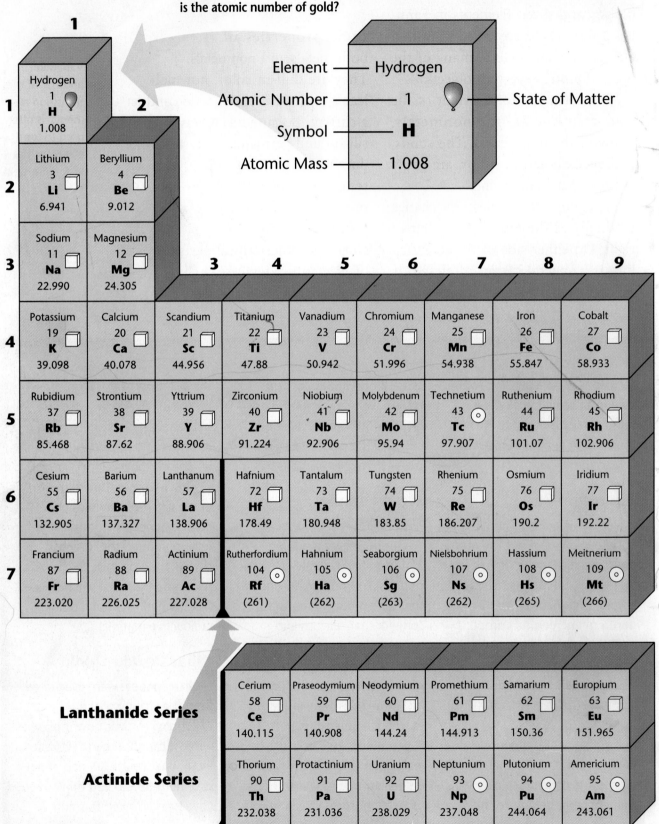

Element	Hydrogen
Atomic Number	1
Symbol	**H**
Atomic Mass	1.008

State of Matter

Lanthanide Series

Actinide Series

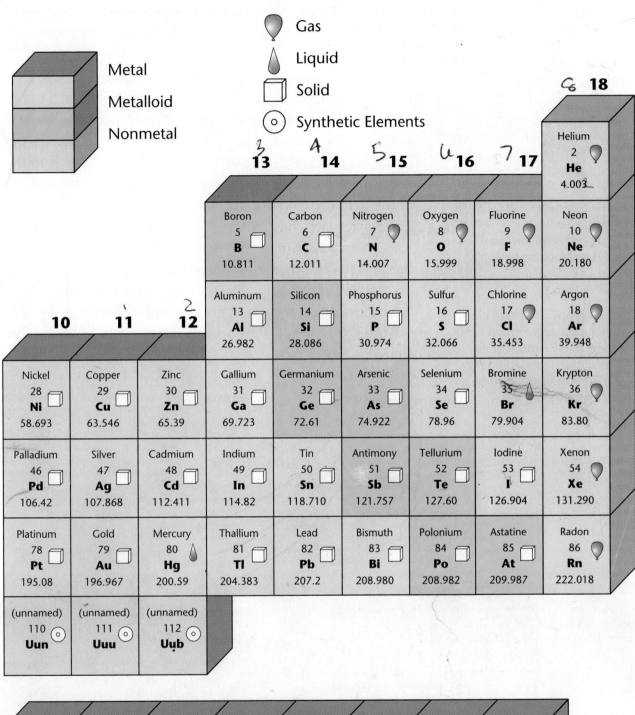

Metal
Metalloid
Nonmetal

Gas
Liquid
Solid
Synthetic Elements

			13	14	15	16	17	Cₑ 18
			3	4	5	6	7	Helium 2 He 4.003
			Boron 5 B 10.811	Carbon 6 C 12.011	Nitrogen 7 N 14.007	Oxygen 8 O 15.999	Fluorine 9 F 18.998	Neon 10 Ne 20.180
			Aluminum 13 Al 26.982	Silicon 14 Si 28.086	Phosphorus 15 P 30.974	Sulfur 16 S 32.066	Chlorine 17 Cl 35.453	Argon 18 Ar 39.948
10	11¹	12²	Gallium 31 Ga 69.723	Germanium 32 Ge 72.61	Arsenic 33 As 74.922	Selenium 34 Se 78.96	Bromine 35 Br 79.904	Krypton 36 Kr 83.80
Nickel 28 Ni 58.693	Copper 29 Cu 63.546	Zinc 30 Zn 65.39	Indium 49 In 114.82	Tin 50 Sn 118.710	Antimony 51 Sb 121.757	Tellurium 52 Te 127.60	Iodine 53 I 126.904	Xenon 54 Xe 131.290
Palladium 46 Pd 106.42	Silver 47 Ag 107.868	Cadmium 48 Cd 112.411	Thallium 81 Tl 204.383	Lead 82 Pb 207.2	Bismuth 83 Bi 208.980	Polonium 84 Po 208.982	Astatine 85 At 209.987	Radon 86 Rn 222.018
Platinum 78 Pt 195.08	Gold 79 Au 196.967	Mercury 80 Hg 200.59						
(unnamed) 110 Uun	(unnamed) 111 Uuu	(unnamed) 112 Uub						

Gadolinium 64 Gd 157.25	Terbium 65 Tb 158.925	Dysprosium 66 Dy 162.50	Holmium 67 Ho 164.930	Erbium 68 Er 167.26	Thulium 69 Tm 168.934	Ytterbium 70 Yb 173.04	Lutetium 71 Lu 174.967
Curium 96 Cm 247.070	Berkelium 97 Bk 247.070	Californium 98 Cf 251.080	Einsteinium 99 Es 252.083	Fermium 100 Fm 257.095	Mendelevium 101 Md 258.099	Nobelium 102 No 259.101	Lawrencium 103 Lr 260.105

■ Reactivity of Elements

You learned that the metals in Family 1, or alkali metals are so reactive that they are never found uncombined in nature. Of the alkali metals, those nearest the bottom are the most active. The most active metals are in the lower left corner of the periodic table. Their outer electrons are so far away from the nucleus that the attraction between the electrons and the protons is much weaker. Therefore, these elements easily lose electrons.

The opposite is true of the nonmetals. If you don't count the noble gases, Family 18, the most active nonmetals are found in the upper right corner. Recall that nonmetals gain electrons from other elements, rather than losing them. Since the nucleus is positive and will attract electrons, the closer the outer energy level is to the nucleus, the easier it is for the atom to attract electrons. In the case of fluorine, the outer energy level is closer to the nucleus than any of the larger atoms in Family 17. Therefore, fluorine is the most active nonmetal.

You've taken a short trip through the periodic table. If you had the task of designing the new product mentioned at the beginning of the chapter, you can see how it would be simplified by using the table.

Classifying

Use the periodic table on pages 164-165 to name and classify the following elements into families: If you need help, refer to the **Skill Handbook** on page 677.
K Cu Cr C Sn Li
As F Na Pb Ag I

1. How many families of elements are represented here?
2. How many periods of elements are represented here?
3. What is the atomic number of carbon?

Figure 5-20

Like the other nonmetals in Family 17 of the periodic table, chlorine is very active. If one of these train cars had been a chlorine tanker, a spill would be very hazardous.

You may have noticed that there's one section we haven't discussed. What are those two rows doing down at the bottom of the table? The atomic numbers would indicate they should be placed between Families 2 and 3 in periods 6 and 7. Why aren't they there? Simple—the table wouldn't fit on the page! The table is made more compact and useful by placing them at the bottom.

As you continue your education, you'll find that organizing information according to systematic patterns can help you study, learn, and recall important facts more easily. Lists and tables are one way to do this. You're sure to discover other methods of organization that will also work well for you. Even now, you can probably recall the names of families of elements that appear in columns one, two, and eighteen of the periodic table. Working with an organized system can make studying fun. **Figure 5-21** illustrates

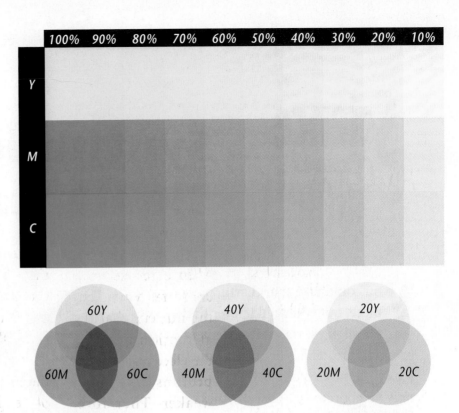

Figure 5-21

Pigments are coloring materials used to make paints. The three primary pigments are yellow; magenta, which is a reddish color; and cyan, which is a bluish color. The figure shows that each pigment family—cyan, magenta, and yellow—is made up of several shades of the pigment. By mixing different percentages of these three pigments, different colors can be produced. Note the color patterns created.

another such system. You may want to experiment with a system something like this in some of your other classes.

check your UNDERSTANDING

1. What happens to atomic numbers as you follow a period across the periodic table? Why is it called a period?
2. Locate the positions on the periodic table for metals, nonmetals, and metalloids. Sequence these three categories from the one containing the largest number of elements to the smallest.
3. Give the period and family in which each of the following elements is found: nitrogen, sodium, iodine, and mercury. Tell whether the element is a metal, nonmetal, or metalloid.
4. **Apply** Which element is more reactive?
   a. potassium or magnesium
   b. phosphorus or chlorine

Science *and* Society

Synthetic Elements

Y ou could take apart Earth, piece by piece, but you would never find even the slightest trace of an element called promethium. That's because promethium is a synthetic element, one that is produced only in laboratories. Like all other synthetic elements, promethium is radioactive. It has been used as a miniature electric power source for pacemakers and artificial hearts like the one shown.

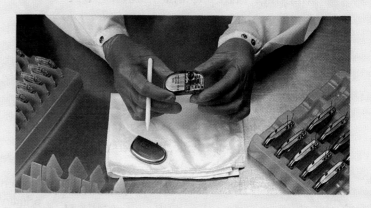

Lanthanides and Actinides

Promethium belongs to a part of the periodic table known as the lanthanide series, a group of elements with atomic numbers from 57 through 71. These elements share similar chemical properties. The same is true of elements belonging to the actinide series, which includes atomic numbers from 89 through 103. Most synthetic elements are found in the actinide series, and most are known as transuranium elements. Transuranium literally means "beyond uranium." A transuranium element has an atomic number greater than uranium's atomic number, 92.

In 1940, physicists created a transuranium element by bombarding uranium with slow neutrons. The element was named neptunium because uranium was named after the planet Uranus, and Neptune is the next

planet in the solar system. Another transuranium element, discovered later that year, was named plutonium after the planet Pluto.

The Plutonium Problem

Plutonium is perhaps the best known of all the synthetic elements. It has been used in nuclear warheads. Small amounts of plutonium powered the Voyager spacecrafts to the outer planets and beyond.

Nearly 40 metric tons of plutonium are produced each year. Most of it is in the form of nuclear waste. Finding ways to dispose of plutonium is one of society's most challenging problems. Plutonium is one of the most toxic substances on Earth—a lump the size of an orange could poison an entire city and it remains radioactive for more than 24 000 years.

Methods of Disposal

How, then, do you dispose of plutonium? One suggestion would be to load it up on rockets and launch it into space. But what if the rocket explodes or crashes shortly after lift off? Another idea is to bury containers filled with nuclear waste beneath the polar ice caps. But what if the radioactive heat melts the polar ice caps and causes worldwide flooding?

Many experts believe that the safest way to dispose of plutonium would be to bury it deep underground. The United States government is considering a place to bury highly radioactive nuclear waste beneath the Yucca Mountain in Nevada shown in the photo.

Before the plutonium is buried, it has to be sealed in specially constructed stainless steel canisters. These canisters have been dropped from a height of 600 meters, crashed into a concrete wall at 128 kilometers per hour, and submerged in burning fuel. Despite all of this punishment, none of the containers ever sprang a leak. Even so, no one can be certain what would have happened if the containers had been filled with plutonium when they were tested.

The canisters may be placed in tunnels dug more than 300 meters beneath the Yucca Mountain. Most of the mountain is composed of volcanic rock, which will carry heat away from the canisters as they cool down.

After 60 years, the canisters would be inspected. If there are no leaks, the tunnels would be permanently sealed. In all, the dump site would contain more than 187 kilometers of tunnels, enough to hold nearly 70 000 metric tons of radioactive waste.

Worries

Some people who live in Nevada are worried about the dump site. What would happen if there were ever a volcanic eruption? Or an earthquake? What if the canisters ever came in contact with underground water?

Science Journal

Energy creates pollution. When you burn fossil fuels—such as natural gas, coal, and oil—you release toxic chemicals into the air. Nuclear power, by comparison, is a very clean source of energy. But nuclear waste, such as plutonium, is a potential threat to the environment. Some people feel that no more nuclear power plants should be constructed until scientists develop a foolproof way to store nuclear wastes. *In your Science Journal* explain how you feel about the use of nuclear power.

HISTORY CONNECTION

Experimental Disproof

Dr. Chien-Shiung Wu was born in China near Shanghai. In 1936, she immigrated to the United States to study at the University of California at Berkeley. There, Wu worked on nuclear research for her doctoral thesis. Her research project on radioactive decay was completed in 1940. Her work was not published until after World War II, but copies of it were sent to the Los Alamos Laboratories to help with their work on atomic energy. Dr. Wu began teaching physics at Smith College in Massachusetts after receiving her doctorate. After one year at Smith, she was asked to teach physics at Princeton University. Then in 1944, after a few months at Princeton, Dr. Wu accepted an offer to work on the Manhattan Project at Columbia University. Dr. Wu saw this as an opportunity to contribute to the war effort because the Manhattan Project was a project to develop an atomic bomb. While on the Manhattan Project, she worked extensively on improving methods for detecting radiation and helped to perfect the Geiger counter.

Right-Handed or Left-Handed?

After the war, Dr. Wu became a Research Associate at Columbia and continued working in physics. She is well-known for experimentally disproving one of the foundations of physics: the law of atomic parity. The law of atomic parity states that like particles always act alike, and the behavior of an object and that of its mirror image are identical. Wu's experiment showed that, in fact, atomic particles are either "right-handed" or "left-handed," and each has different patterns of behavior.

Dr. Wu has recently worked in the field of biophysics in an effort to find a cure for sickle-cell anemia, a disease common in African and African American populations.

You Try It!

The law of parity states that an object and its mirror image will behave the same way. Stand in front of a mirror and unscrew a bottle lid using a counterclockwise motion. The lid comes off. The motion you see in the mirror image will be clockwise, not counterclockwise, but the lid still comes off. What happens if you try to use a clockwise motion to unscrew the lid? Does the lid come off? If it does, it demonstrates parity because the object and the image behave in the same way. If the lid does not come off, the object behaved differently from its mirror image and shows a lack of parity.

Science Journal

Review the statements below about the big ideas presented in this chapter, and answer the questions. Then, reread your answers to the Did You Ever Wonder questions at the beginning of the chapter. *In your Science Journal,* write a paragraph about how your understanding of the big ideas in the chapter has changed.

SUN	MON	TUE	WED	THUR	FRI	SAT
	1	2	3 Birthday	4	5	6
7	8 New moon	9	10	11	12	13
14	15 Taxes due	16	17 Photo club	18	19	20
21	22	23	24 School starts	25	26	27
28	29	30	31			

1 Your life is full of events that repeat and thus are periodic. *What types of properties are represented by the periodic table?*

2 A period is made up of a series of elements with increasing atomic numbers. *When must a new period begin?*

37 Rb 85.468	38 Sr 87.62	39 Y 88.906	40 Zr 91.224	41 Nb 92.906	42 Mo 95.94	43 Tc 97.91	44 Ru 101.07	45 Rh 102.91	46 Pd 106.42	47 Ag 107.87	48 Cd 112.41	49 In 114.82	50 Sn 118.71	51 Sb 121.75	52 Te 127.60	53 I 126.90	54 Xe 131.29

3 Elements with like properties are placed in columns. *What are columns called?*

4 Be 9.0122
12 Mg 24.305
20 Ca 40.078
38 Sr 87.62
56 Ba 137.33
88 Ra (226)

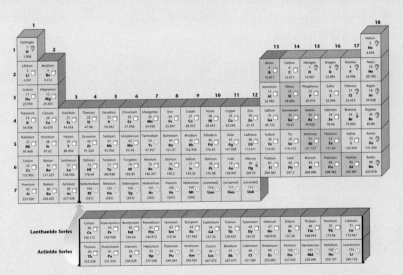

4 An approximate diagonal from the top of Family 13 in the periodic table to the lower right corner roughly separates the metal elements from the nonmetals. *Where are metalloids located on the periodic table? What are the properties of metalloids?*

Using Key Science Terms

alkali metals	isotopes
alkaline earth metals	mass number
atomic mass	period
atomic number	periodic table
family of elements	

The sentences below include terms that have been used incorrectly. Change the incorrect terms so that the sentence reads correctly. Underline your change.

1. The atomic mass of an element represents the total mass of all its isotopes.
2. Family 1 on the periodic table is called the alkaline earth metals.
3. A horizontal row in the periodic table is called a family of elements.
4. The halogens are a very reactive period in the periodic table.
5. The atomic number of an element is the number of neutrons in its nucleus.
6. Magnesium and calcium are alkali metals.

Understanding Ideas

Answer the following questions in your Journal using complete sentences. Use the periodic table on pages 164-165 as needed.

1. Name three elements in each of the following families of elements.
   a. alkali metals
   b. noble gases
   c. alkaline earth metals
2. An element has an atomic number of 11. What is the atomic number of the next heaviest element with similar properties?

3. What are the atomic numbers of the elements in period four?
4. Name three metalloids.
5. An element has an atomic number of 7 and a mass number of 14. How many neutrons are in the nucleus? What is the element?
6. How many electrons do the halogens have in their outer energy level?
7. What do all of the transition elements have in common?
8. Why do elements in the same family have similar properties?
9. How many electrons are in each of the energy levels of a phosphorus atom?

Developing Skills

Use your understanding of the concepts developed in this chapter to answer each of the following questions.

1. **Concept Mapping** Using the word list, complete the following concept map: *metals, metalloids, nonmetals*

metals, metalloids, nonmetals
Elements

2. **Making and Using Graphs** Suppose a sample of 200 atoms of an element contains the isotopes listed in the following table. List the isotopes and make a pie graph representing this data.

Isotope Sampling	
Mass Number of Isotopes	Number of Atoms
34	72
35	46
36	82

3. Recognizing Cause and Effect A helium atom has only two electrons. Why does helium behave as a noble gas?

Critical Thinking

In your Journal, *answer each of the following questions.*

1. A silver sample contains 52 atoms, each having 60 neutrons, and 48 atoms, each having 62 neutrons. What is the sample's average atomic mass?

2. According to the periodic table, what is the most active metal? The most active nonmetal? What would you expect if these two elements were brought together?

3. What are the family numbers of the elements diagrammed below?

Problem Solving

Read the following problem and discuss your answers in a brief paragraph.

You are a public official in a town that has been isolated by a natural disaster. A major factory in your town uses cadmium in a process that is vital to the town's survival. All sources of cadmium have been cut off.

1. Suggest two elements that might replace cadmium in the factory's process. Explain your suggestions.

2. The town workers must handle this element in the manufacturing process. Explain which of your two choices from Question 1 you would recommend.

CONNECTING IDEAS

Discuss each of the following in a brief paragraph.

1. **Theme—Stability and Change** When an atom of element X emits an alpha particle, one product is Pb-214. What are the atomic number and mass number of element X? What element is it?

2. **Theme—Scale and Structure** Atoms in a family of elements increase in size as you move downward in the periodic table. Explain why this is so.

3. **Life Science Connection** What radioactive element could easily replace the calcium in human bones?

4. **Science and Society** List four benefits and four risks associated with synthetic elements. Do you think the benefits outweigh the risks? Explain.

combining Atoms

Did you ever dream of being a fire fighter? Today's fire fighters do more than just pour water on fires. If a tanker truck full of chemicals has an accident, the fire department may spray a special foam over the truck. If there is a gas leak, fire fighters decide what precautions to use until the leak is stopped. Perhaps they should be renamed "chemical reaction technicians."

Fire is a very rapid chemical reaction that releases heat and produces new compounds. Putting out a fire may also involve chemical reactions. In this chapter, you'll learn more about the language scientists use to describe such reactions.

▶ *In the activity on the next page, explore an example of how atoms combine.*

Did you ever wonder...

✓ Why water puts out fire?
✓ Why water is called H_2O?
✓ How a detergent gets your clothes clean?

Science Journal
Before you study combining atoms, think about these questions and answer them *in your Science Journal*. When you finish the chapter, compare your journal write-up with what you have learned.

Explore! ACTIVITY

How can a fire be extinguished?

Modern fire extinguishers do not contain these specific chemicals, but you can use this activity to see how a fire can be put out by a chemical reaction.

What To Do

1. Put 20 grams of baking soda into a small test tube.

2. Pour 50 mL of vinegar into a 500-mL flask.

3. Carefully lower the test tube into the flask, making sure the baking soda does not contact the vinegar.

4. Put a one-hole stopper containing a piece of tubing into the mouth of the flask.

5. While pointing the tubing into the sink, tilt the flask so that the vinegar wets the baking soda. Record your observations *in your Journal*. **CAUTION:** *If the contents react too fast, the stopper can blow out.*

Kinds of Chemical Bonds

6-1

Section Objectives

- Describe ionic and covalent bonds.
- Identify particles produced by ionic and covalent bonding.
- Distinguish between a nonpolar covalent and a polar covalent bond.

Key Terms

ion
ionic bond
molecule
covalent bond
polar molecule
nonpolar molecule

Atomic Glue

Three different products were formed when you mixed ordinary vinegar, also called acetic acid, with baking soda, also called sodium hydrogen carbonate, in the Explore activity. These products were water, carbon dioxide, and sodium acetate, a salt. Each of these products can put out a fire. The salt cuts off the oxygen supply and suffocates the fire. Water lowers the temperature of the burning materials below their ignition point and reduces the oxygen supply to the fire. Carbon dioxide is more dense than air, so it forms a blanket over the flames and cuts off the supply of oxygen. Some fire extinguishers work just like the one you made.

■ Why Atoms Combine

How and why do the atoms in these chemicals join together in the first place? Is there some atomic glue that keeps them together? And why do some elements form compounds much more easily than others do?

Figure 6-1

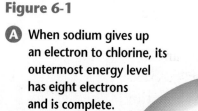

A When sodium gives up an electron to chlorine, its outermost energy level has eight electrons and is complete.

B When chlorine takes on an electron from sodium, its outermost energy level has eight electrons, and it then is complete.

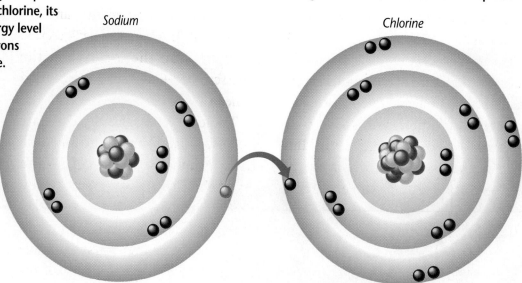

Sodium

Chlorine

C This makes the resulting charged sodium and chlorine atoms very stable. What is the common name for sodium chloride?

176   **Chapter 6**   Combining Atoms

Recall from Chapter 5 that having a complete outer energy level makes an atom very stable. **Figure 6-1** shows how this stability is achieved when sodium chloride, common table salt, is formed during a reaction between atoms of sodium and chlorine. When sodium gives its outer level electron to chlorine, both will have filled outer electron levels. **Figure 6-2** shows what happens when a small amount of the metal sodium is placed in a beaker of chlorine gas.

Recall from Chapter 4 that atoms are neutral—that is, they have equal numbers of positive and negative charges. Sodium has 11 protons (11+) and 11 electrons (11-). When it loses one of those electrons, what happens to the overall charge? It now has only 10 electrons (10-) and thus has an overall charge of 1+. (11+) + (10-) = 1+. This charged atom is called an **ion**. In this case the ion is positively charged because it has one fewer electron than proton. It is written Na^+.

In the meantime, what has happened to the chlorine atom with its 7 outer level electrons? When chlorine gains one electron from sodium, it has 8 electrons in its outermost energy level. Sodium and chlorine now both have full outer energy levels. But chlorine has 17 protons with a charge of 17+ and 18 electrons with a charge of 18-. If you add the charges, you can see that (17+) + (18-) = 1-. Chlorine is a negative ion because it contains one more electron than proton. Scientists call it a chloride ion and write it as Cl^-.

Figure 6-2

Sodium is a metal, and chlorine is a gas. When a small amount of sodium is placed in a beaker of chlorine, the metal bursts into a bright yellow flame and a white powder, which is sodium chloride, is formed.

■ Formulas for Ions

Notice that when we write the shorthand for the ions Na^+ and Cl^-, the sign is slightly above the symbol. This is called a superscript, *super-* meaning above. You'll see superscripts, such as those in Al^{3+} and O^{2-} throughout the chapter. They describe the charge on the ion. When the superscript is + or -, it is understood to mean 1+ or 1-.

The charges of the two ions are opposite. Therefore, they attract each other to make up the compound NaCl. NaCl is the white smoke you see as the reaction in **Figure 6-2** takes place. Because the positive charge of the sodium ion is equal, but opposite in sign, to the negative charge of the chloride ion, the compound NaCl, sodium chloride, is neutral.

Ionic Bonding

There are many compounds that form in a way similar to the way sodium chloride is formed. When atoms gain or lose electrons, they become ions. Because some of these ions are positively charged and some are negatively charged, they attract one another. This attraction of positive ions for negative ions is called an **ionic bond**.

Figure 6-3

This salt crystal is an example of an ionic compound.

■ Ionic Compounds

Compounds that are made up of ions are ionic compounds. Although there are exceptions, most ionic compounds have certain properties. Ionic compounds will conduct an electric current when the compounds are melted or dissolved in water. Most of them are solid crystals with high melting points. Is NaCl, as is shown in **Figure 6-3**, an ionic compound? Yes, it is, because it is made up of ions, and the bonds that hold it together are ionic bonds—not atomic glue!

Silver Streaks and Speeding Electrons

The properties of aluminum are determined by the action of its electrons. The atoms in every element contain a specific number of electrons around the nucleus of the atom. An atom of aluminum has 13 electrons. The electrons nearest the nucleus are relatively stable and closely bound to the nucleus. Those in the outer energy levels, however, are farther from the nucleus and they are more loosely held. They easily move away from their own atom to bond with other atoms.

Roving Electrons

The electrons in the outer energy levels of aluminum and many other metals actually move freely among all the millions of atoms that make up a

In metallic bonding, the electrons in the outer energy levels of an atom of aluminum move away from the nucleus easily and freely bond with other atoms that make up the piece of aluminum.

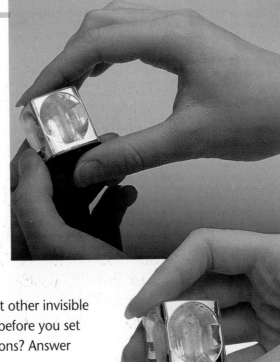

Explore! ACTIVITY

Can you see an ionic reaction?

Examine a camera flashbulb.

What To Do

1. List the properties of the substance(s) inside the bulb.

2. Without looking directly at the bulb, set it off. After it has cooled, examine it again.

3. How have the properties changed? What other invisible substance do you think was in the bulb before you set it off? Have you seen other similar reactions? Answer these questions *in your Journal*.

piece of aluminum. In fact, they form a kind of sea of electrons that makes aluminum lustrous,

The chemical reaction that takes place here can remove tarnish from silver.

as well as a good conductor of heat and electricity.

The ability of these roving electrons to combine with other elements, however, allows metals such as silver to become easily tarnished. Silver atoms bond readily with sulfur in the air to create silver sulfide. Silver polishes remove the silver sulfide, but every time you polish silver, you take a little of the silver away.

You Try It!

Can you take the tarnish off silver

without losing the silver? Line a glass bowl with aluminum foil. Place a tarnished silver spoon or fork into the bowl. Dissolve several tablespoons of baking soda in enough boiling water to cover the silver. Pour the water over the silver. With a wooden or plastic spoon, press the ends of the aluminum foil loosely over the silver. It only has to touch the silver in a few places.

After fifteen minutes, pour out the water and rinse off the silver. How do the silver and aluminum foil look? Write down "in the presence of baking soda" and the word equation for the reaction that you think might have occurred here. What is the black substance on the aluminum?

The fine wire you saw in the flash-bulb before setting it off was the element magnesium. You know that a chemical reaction must have taken place because energy was given off in the form of light, and a new substance was formed. The magnesium reacted with oxygen gas, which was also present in the flashbulb.

Magnesium has 2 electrons in its outermost energy level. Oxygen has 6 outer electrons. When magnesium reacts with oxygen, a magnesium atom loses 2 electrons and becomes a positively charged ion, Mg^{2+}. At the same time, the oxygen atom gains the 2 electrons and becomes a negatively charged oxide ion, O^{2-}. The compound as a whole is neutral because the sum of the charges of the ions is zero.

Figure 6-4

While magnesium loses two electrons in a chemical reaction, chlorine needs only one electron to complete its outermost energy level. So for magnesium and chlorine to combine, there must be two atoms of chlorine for each atom of magnesium. A magnesium atom gives one electron to each chlorine atom. The result is one Mg^{2+} ion and two Cl^- ions. What is the name of the compound formed in this reaction?

■ Another Ionic Compound

Predict what ions would form when magnesium reacts with chlorine. This reaction is shown in **Figure 6-4**, which shows how the product $MgCl_2$ is formed.

The small 2 after Cl in the formula is called a subscript. *Sub-* means below. The subscript indicates the number of atoms of the element in the compound. When there is no subscript, as in Mg, the number of atoms is understood to be 1. The compound is neutral because $(1 \times 2+) + (2 \times 1-) = 0$.

Most stable atoms have 8 electrons in their outer energy level. As you remember from Chapter 5, only the noble gases occur naturally with 8. They not only have a complete outer energy level, but they are also neutral. As you've seen, some atoms without 8 electrons may get a complete outer energy level by gaining or losing electrons, but when they do they become charged. The more electrons an atom gains or loses, the higher its charge. As charges increase, the ionic bond becomes less stable. But there is a path to stability other than forming charged ions.

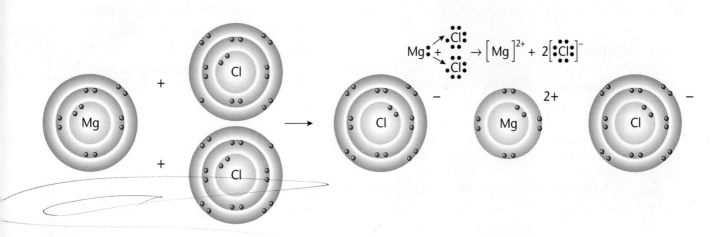

$$Mg\!:\; + \begin{array}{c} \cdot\ddot{Cl}\!: \\ \cdot\ddot{Cl}\!: \end{array} \rightarrow \left[Mg \right]^{2+} + 2\left[:\!\ddot{Cl}\!: \right]^-$$

Molecules and Covalent Bonds

Some atoms become more chemically stable by sharing electrons, rather than by losing or gaining electrons. In such bonds, electrons spend time in the outer energy levels of each atom, allowing each atom to, at some time, have a full outer energy level. The neutral particles formed as a result of atoms sharing electrons are called **molecules**. The bond that forms between atoms when they share electrons is called a **covalent bond**. Examples of covalent bonds are shown in **Figure 6-5**. Notice that covalent molecules aren't charged. Because no electrons have been gained or lost, only shared, both the atoms and molecule remain neutral.

You can better understand how atoms gain, lose, or share electrons by working with models of electron energy levels in the following Investigate.

Figure 6-5

In covalent bonding, atoms combine by sharing electrons.

A When two atoms of hydrogen combine, the pair of electrons will be shared by both hydrogen atoms, making both energy levels complete.

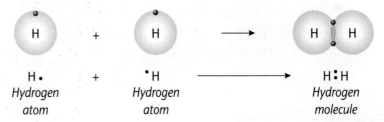

B The same is true when two atoms of chlorine combine—as the two atoms share a pair of electrons, each atom, at one time or another, has its outer energy level complete.

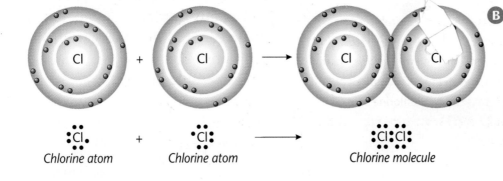

C In a water molecule, two pairs of electrons are shared by two hydrogen atoms and an oxygen atom, making each atom in the molecule stable. What is the electric charge of a water molecule?

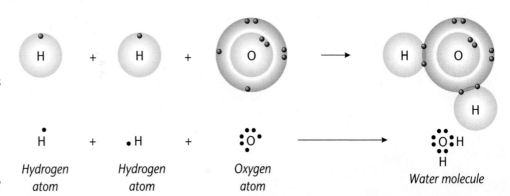

DESIGN YOUR OWN
INVESTIGATION

Models of Combining Atoms

Recall that having a complete outer energy level makes an atom stable. There are compounds that form by gaining and losing electrons to achieve stability. Some atoms become more stable by sharing electrons with other atoms. In this experiment you will model the filling of an outer energy level and the formation of compounds.

Preparation

Problem
How can a model show the way atoms gain, lose, or share electrons?

Hypothesis
With your group, hypothesize how an element from the second row of the periodic table will combine with other second-row elements.

Objectives
- Demonstrate how atoms combine by gaining, losing, and sharing electrons.
- Determine which compounds can be made by elements from the second row of the periodic table.

Possible Materials
modified egg carton
marbles
dried beans
buttons
candy

Safety

Never eat food used in a laboratory experiment. Dispose of food items after your experiment.

Plan the Experiment

1 What will you use to represent the atom's energy levels? The electrons?

2 Choose an element from the second row of the periodic table. How many electrons do you need to make up this element? How many electrons will go in the first energy level? The second?

3 When you look at your classmates' models, how will you know which ones will be able to combine with yours to make a full outer energy level? Will it take more than one model to combine with yours?

Check the Plan

1 How will you keep track of the combinations you were able to make?

2 Can more than two different elements be represented in your compound? Can two or more of the same element combine?

3 Have your teacher check your plan and then proceed with your experiment.

Analyze and Conclude

1. Infer Would you infer that your model is a metal or a nonmetal? Did it combine with a metal or a nonmetal? How do you know?

2. Identify Identify the combinations that you made as having ionic or covalent bonds. How did you decide?

3. Predict What combinations of boron and fluorine do you predict will give you complete energy levels?

Going Further

How would you have to change your model to show how sodium (Na) combines?

Polar and Nonpolar Molecules

In the Investigate, you could see how atoms can lose, gain, or share electrons to become stable.

Do atoms always share electrons equally? You know that an atom such as oxygen has more protons than an atom such as hydrogen. For this reason, an oxygen atom will have a greater attraction for electrons than will hydrogen. As is shown in **Figure 6-6**, electrons are not shared equally when hydrogen and oxygen form water. This makes the oxygen end a little more negative and the hydrogen end a little more positive than if the electrons were shared equally. We call this type of bond a polar bond. Polar means having two opposite ends or poles. A polar bond may result in a **polar molecule**, which has a slightly positive end and a slightly negative end. Molecules that do not have these unbalanced charges are called **nonpolar molecules**.

In the next section, you will find out more about the scientific shorthand used to describe compounds.

SKILLBUILDER

Comparing and Contrasting

Compare and contrast ionic, polar covalent, and nonpolar covalent bonds. If you need help, refer to the **Skill Handbook** on page 683.

Figure 6-6

A Because an atom of oxygen has more protons than does an atom of hydrogen, an oxygen atom will have a stronger attraction for electrons. As a result, the oxygen end of a water molecule has a slight negative charge, while the hydrogen end has a slight positive charge. This makes a water molecule a polar molecule. Which do electrons spend more time with in a water molecule, hydrogen or oxygen?

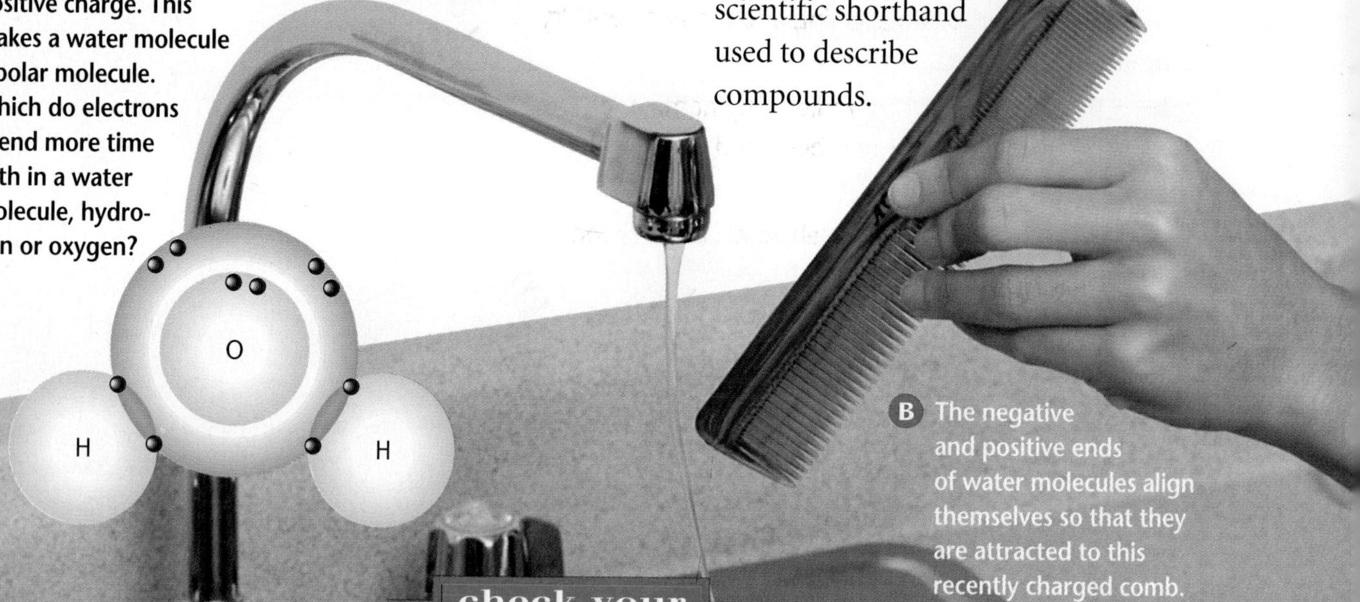

B The negative and positive ends of water molecules align themselves so that they are attracted to this recently charged comb.

check your UNDERSTANDING

1. What is the smallest unit in each of the following bonds: **a.** ionic; **b.** polar covalent; **c.** nonpolar covalent?
2. Sodium reacts in air to form a white compound. Write a formula for this compound.
3. **Apply** Most laundry detergents work because one end of their molecule is soluble in grease and the other in water. What is the most probable type of molecule in these detergents?

Chemical Shorthand

The World of Alphabet Soup

If you take a close look at many of the containers around your home and school, you'll find enough combinations of letters and numbers to fill a can of alphabet soup. Let's explore several possibilities.

Section Objectives
- Explain how to determine oxidation numbers.
- Give formulas for compounds from their names.
- Name compounds from their formulas.

Key Terms
oxidation number
binary compound
polyatomic ion

Explore! ACTIVITY

What's it made of?

What To Do

1. Study the chemical content on a bag of lawn fertilizer, dog or cat food, a can of paint, and a box of laundry detergent or bleach.

2. *In your Journal*, list the ingredients by name and include any symbols or numbers used to describe the ingredients.

3. Do these products have any elements in common?

Was it easy for you to know what made up each ingredient that was listed on each label? How could the lists of chemicals you saw on the packages have been written in a shorter form so that everyone would still understand them? You have learned that all matter is made up of elements and that each element can be represented by a symbol. Let's see how we can combine symbols to describe how elements form compounds.

Figure 6-7

Ⓐ Alchemists practiced a form of "chemistry" in the Middle Ages. In fact, alchemists were the ancestors of modern chemists.

Ⓑ Like the alchemist, the modern chemist investigates the structure of matter. But chemistry has come a long way since the days of the ancient alchemist.

	Sulfur	Iron	Zinc	Silver	Mercury	Lead
Ancient						
Dalton's						
Modern	S	Fe	Zn	Ag	Hg	Pb

Figure 6-8

Symbols have been used to represent the elements since the times of the alchemists. John Dalton, who helped develop the atomic theory, came up with his own symbols. Modern chemists use symbols that can be understood by scientists around the world.

■ Chemical Shorthand

The two people in **Figure 6-7** seem to have little in common. Yet, in a sense, the medieval alchemist is the ancestor of the modern chemist. Both are shown at work investigating matter. Notice how each would write symbols for the elements silver and sulfur. If the alchemist knew the composition of tarnish, how might he write its formula? The modern chemist does know its composition. She would write it Ag_2S. Being able to use this kind of shorthand can enable you to write a great deal of information in just a short time.

When you write Ag_2S, chemists around the world know exactly what you mean. Chemical formulas allow scientists to communicate and share research. Where do formulas come from, and what do they mean?

■ Chemical Formulas

Recall the fire extinguisher you made at the beginning of this chapter. A scientist would write the reaction like this:

acetic acid + sodium hydrogen carbonate →
sodium acetate + water + carbon dioxide
$$HC_2H_3O_2 + NaHCO_3 \rightarrow$$
$$NaC_2H_3O_2 + H_2O + CO_2$$

The words you've used before to name compounds have been replaced by a kind of chemical shorthand called a formula. The formula of a compound tells a chemist how much of each element is present. For example, in the formula, H_2O, the subscript 2 shows 2 atoms of the element hydrogen. Because there is no subscript on the O, 1 atom is present. How are these numbers determined?

Oxidation Number

Recall that you can tell how many electrons an element has in its outermost energy level from its family number on the periodic table. Most atoms will tend to lose, gain, or share these electrons to become stable.

The number of electrons that an atom gains, loses, or shares when bonding with another atom is called its **oxidation number**. For example, when sodium forms an ion, it loses an electron and has a charge of 1+, so the oxidation number of sodium is 1+. When chlorine forms an ion, it gains an electron and has a charge of 1-, so its oxidation number is 1-.

The red numbers printed on the periodic table shown in **Figure 6-10** are the oxidation numbers for many elements that form binary compounds. The prefix *bi*–means two. Thus, a **binary compound** is one that is composed of two elements. The oxidation numbers of the transition elements may change from compound to compound.

Some elements have more than one oxidation number, as shown in **Figure 6-9**. When an element can have more than one oxidation number, a Roman numeral is used in the name of the compound to indicate the oxidation number.

Figure 6-9

As shown, some elements have more than one oxidation number. How many electrons does lead lose when it bonds with another atom?

copper(I)	Cu^+
copper(II)	Cu^{2+}
iron(II)	Fe^{2+}
iron(III)	Fe^{3+}
chromium(II)	Cr^{2+}
chromium(III)	Cr^{3+}
lead(II)	Pb^{2+}
lead(IV)	Pb^{4+}

1+ 1 H	2+ 2					3+ 13	4+,4− 14	3− 15	2− 16	1− 17	0 18 2 He
3 Li	4 Be					5 B	6 C	7 N	8 O	9 F	10 Ne
11 Na	12 Mg					13 Al	14 Si	15 P	16 S	17 Cl	18 Ar
19 K	20 Ca		Families 3–12 not shown			31 Ga	32 Ge	33 As	34 Se	35 Br	36 Kr
37 Rb	38 Sr					49 In	50 Sn	51 Sb	52 Te	53 I	54 Xe
55 Cs	56 Ba					81 Tl	82 Pb	83 Bi	84 Po	85 At	86 Rn
87 Fr	88 Ra										

Metallic properties → Nonmetallic properties

Figure 6-10

In the periodic table, all the elements are arranged in rows and columns according to their properties. The elements with metallic properties are listed on the left side of the table, and the elements with nonmetallic properties are listed on the right side. Based on the table, is magnesium classified as a metal or a nonmetal?

Formulas and Names for Binary Compounds

Once you know how to find the oxidation numbers of elements when they are in binary compounds, you can write the formulas for these compounds by using the rules that are shown below in **Table 6-1**.

Table 6-1

How to Write Formulas for Binary Compounds	
1. Write the symbol of the element with the positive oxidation number. Hydrogen and all metals have positive oxidation numbers.	Ca
2. Then write the symbol of the element with the negative oxidation number.	F
3. Look up the oxidation numbers on the periodic table and write them above the symbols.	$Ca^{2+}F^-$
4. In the completed formula, there must be an equal number of positive and negative charges. The charge is calculated by multiplying the number of atoms of the element by its oxidation number. When Ca^{2+} and F^- combine, we see that one Ca atom will combine with two F atoms. We know this because one atom of Ca times a charge of 2+ equals 2+. Two atoms of F times a charge of 1– equals 2–. The sum of 2+ and 2– is zero, and the compound is neutral.	$Ca^{2+} + 2\,F^-$
5. The last step is to put subscripts in so that the sum of the charges in the formula is zero.	CaF_2

You can also name a binary compound from its formula by using these rules.

1. Write the name of the first element.
2. Write the root of the name of the second element.
3. Add the suffix -*ide* to the root.

To name the compounds of elements having two oxidation numbers, you must first figure out the oxidation numbers of each of the elements. For example, suppose you wanted to name CrO. Because Cr can have more than one oxidation number, you would first look up the oxidation number of the negative element. The oxidation number of oxygen is 2-. Next, figure out the oxidation number of the positive element. That number added to 2- will give a total charge of zero. (2+) + (2-) = 0. Finally, write the name of the compound, using a Roman numeral for the positive oxidation number. In this case the positive oxidation number is 2 and the compound is chromium(II) oxide.

Compounds with Polyatomic Ions

Have you ever used baking soda in cooking, as a medicine, or to brush your teeth? You'll remember that baking soda was one of the ingredients in our homemade fire extinguisher. Some compounds, including baking soda, contain polyatomic ions. The prefix *poly-* means many, so polyatomic means having many atoms. A **polyatomic ion** is a group of positively or negatively charged covalently bonded atoms. In the case of baking soda, Na^+ is the positive ion, and HCO_3^- is the negative, polyatomic ion.

■ Naming

Table 6-2 lists several polyatomic ions. To name a compound that contains one or more of these ions, use the name of the polyatomic ion. Other than that, use the same rules used for a binary compound. For example K_2SO_4 is potassium sulfate. What are the names of $Sr(OH)_2$ and NH_4Cl?

■ Writing Formulas

To write formulas for compounds containing polyatomic ions, follow the rules for writing formulas for binary compounds, with one addition. Use parentheses around the group representing the polyatomic ion when more than one of that ion is needed, such as $Mg(OH)_2$. Without the parentheses, it appears as though there are two hydrogen atoms, rather than two hydroxide ions.

Example Problem:
Writing a Formula with Polyatomic Ions
Problem Statement:
What is the formula for calcium nitrate?
Problem-Solving Steps:
1. Write symbols and oxidation numbers for calcium and the nitrate ion.
$$2+ \quad 1-$$
$$Ca \quad NO_3$$
2. Write in subscripts so that the sum of the oxidation numbers is zero. Enclose the NO_3 in parentheses.
$$2+ \quad 1-$$
$$Ca \quad (NO_3)_2$$
Solution:
Final Formula: $Ca(NO_3)_2$

Table 6-2

Common Polyatomic Ions		
Charge	Name	Formula
1+	Ammonium	NH_4^+
1–	Acetate	$CH_3CO_2^-$
1–	Chlorate	ClO_3^-
1–	Hydroxide	OH^-
1–	Nitrate	NO_3^-
2–	Carbonate	CO_3^{2-}
2–	Sulfate	SO_4^{2-}
3–	Phosphate	PO_4^{3-}

This table lists eight polyatomic ions, showing each ion's formula and charge.

Names of Compounds

Why do we need standards and rules for naming compounds? Early in the history of chemistry, the discoverer of a new compound would name it. Often the discoverer would choose a name that described some chemical or physical property of the new compound. For example, a common name for potassium carbonate, K_2CO_3, is potash because the compound could be produced by boiling wood ash in iron pots. Laughing gas was named for the effect it has on humans when it is inhaled. Sodium hydrogen carbonate, written $NaHCO_3$, is commonly called baking soda. It's one of the compounds that helps baked goods rise. Sulfuric acid was once called oil of vitriol. Lye and plaster of paris are other common names of compounds. While these names may be very descriptive, they tell us nothing about the chemical composition of the compound.

Life Science CONNECTION

This photograph of algae was taken using a microscope.

Pond Scum Be Gone!

If your pond is green and scummy, just throw in a few bales of rotting straw. Scientists in England have discovered that rotting straw may initiate a reaction that destroys pond scum.

What Is Pond Scum?

Algae are simple organisms that live in oceans, lakes, rivers, ponds, and moist soil. Algae flourish in water that is high in phosphates, compounds that contain the phosphate ion. Phosphates run into water from many sources. They are found in detergents. They come from fertilizers that are spread on crops in the country and on lawns and golf courses in the city. Phosphates are present in the manure of farm animals and in sewage that has been treated by city treatment plants.

Phosphates act as fertilizer for the algae and encourage the algae population to grow with incredible speed. Soon the entire surface of the water is covered with green pond scum. This speedy growth upsets the natural balance of life in the water. Bacteria use huge quantities of oxygen from the water in the decay process. As the large amounts of algae die, oxygen levels in the water fall, causing fish and other life-forms to die out.

The Need for a System

As the number of known compounds grew, it became necessary to establish a system for naming, part of which you have learned. For example, there are 217 different known compounds that have the simple formula C_6H_6. Each of them has a unique name based on a system accepted by chemists worldwide. Because hundreds of thousands of new compounds are made each year, it's clear that a systematic naming system is necessary.

SKILLBUILDER

Making and Using Tables
Name the following compounds: Li_2S, MgF_2, FeO, $CuCl$. Strategy Hint: For names of elements with more than one oxidation number, remember to include the Roman numeral. If you need help, refer to the **Skill Handbook** on page 680.

check your UNDERSTANDING

1. Name the following compounds: NaI, FeI_3, NH_4Br.
2. Write formulas for compounds composed of (a) lithium and sulfur, (b) calcium and the acetate ion, and (c) barium and oxygen.
3. Assign an oxidation number to each element in the following: Al_2O_3; $ZnCl_2$; $FeBr_2$.
4. **Apply** The label on a package of plant food lists potassium nitrate as one ingredient. What is the formula for potassium nitrate?

Getting Rid of Pond Scum

Scientists followed up on a lead from a farmer who accidentally dropped rotten bales of straw into his lake and was amazed to see the green scum disappear. They thought a chemical that stops algae growth may have been produced by the rotting straw. Fish and plants do not appear to be affected by this unknown chemical. Researchers are still studying this solution to pond scum but recommend throwing straw into ponds twice a year, once in the fall, and again in the spring.

What Do You Think?

Bodies of water support a delicate balance of life processes. Algae trap sunlight and provide oxygen and food through

Phosphorus in water causes algae to grow extremely fast, until the entire surface of the water is covered with green pond scum.

photosynthesis. Microscopic zooplankton eat the algae, and fish eat the zooplankton. Bacteria break down organic matter and release nutrients. When the cycle is in balance, each life cycle supports the others. Pollution of the water upsets this balance. Although scientists think the straw releases a chemical that kills the excess algae, there may be other explanations. How do you think the bales of straw help bring the ponds back into balance?

 **Balancing Chemical Equations**

Section Objectives

- Explain what is meant by a balanced chemical equation.
- Demonstrate how to write a balanced chemical equation.

Key Terms

balanced chemical equation

Checking for Balance

If you were to write an equation for making applesauce, you might say that 10 apples + 1 pound of sugar = 3 cups of applesauce. The apples and sugar represent reactants. When heated together, they make applesauce, the product. Another example is shown in **Figure 6-11**, where several ingredients, representing reactants, produce one cake, representing the product. The numbers in front of each item are called coefficients. They describe how many units of that substance are involved in the recipe. Let's learn more about this type of equation in the following activity.

Explore! ACTIVITY

Must the sum of the reactant and product coefficients be equal?

What To Do

1. Obtain a marked card from your teacher.

2. With others in your class, assemble all the cards to represent a basketball team. When you write this as an equation, you have something like this: 2 guards + 2 forwards + 1 center = 1 team.

3. Why aren't the sums of the coefficients on each side of the equation equal?

4. What other examples like this can you think of?

Figure 6-11

Combining several different ingredients—milk, eggs, and cake mix—results in one new product, a cake.

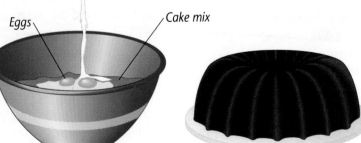

Milk

Eggs

Cake mix

Let's see how the coefficients for the reactants and products in a chemical reaction compare to the Explore activity. Have you ever seen silver polish in the supermarket? It's used to remove tarnish from silver. Tarnish can make silver appear almost black. Where does tarnish come from? It forms when sulfur-containing compounds in air or food react with silver to form silver sulfide, the black tarnish.

■ Matter is Conserved

Let's write the chemical equation for tarnishing:

$Ag + H_2S \rightarrow Ag_2S + H_2$.

Look at the equation closely. Remember that matter is never created or destroyed in an ordinary chemical reaction. Notice that one silver atom appears in the reactants, $Ag + H_2S$. However, two silver atoms appear in the product, $Ag_2S + H_2$. As you know, one silver atom can't just become two. The equation must be balanced so that it shows a true picture of what takes place in the reaction. A **balanced chemical equation** has the same number of atoms of each element on both sides of the equation. In the Explore activity, even though there were 2 guards, 2 forwards, and 1 center on one side and 1 team on the other, no players had been lost. The player "equation" was balanced. To find out if the equation for tarnishing is balanced, make a chart like that shown in **Table 6-3**.

Table 6-3

Atoms in an Unbalanced Equation		
Kind of Atom	Number of Atoms $Ag + H_2S = Ag_2S + H_2$	
Ag	1	2
H	2	2
S	1	1

This table shows an unbalanced equation, in which the number of atoms of each element on one side of the equation is not equal to the number of atoms of that element on the other side of the equation.

Figure 6-12

This diagram shows the unbalanced equation from Table 6-3. There are two atoms of silver on the right side, but only one on the left.

Using Coefficients

The number of hydrogen and sulfur atoms is balanced, as shown in **Table 6-3**. However, there were two silver atoms on the right side of the equation and only one on the left side. We cannot change the subscripts of a correct formula in order to balance an equation. Instead, we place whole-number coefficients to the left of the formulas of the reactants and products so that there are equal numbers of silver atoms on both sides of the equation. If the coefficient is one, no coefficient is written. How do we choose which coefficients to use to balance this or any other equation?

■ Choosing Coefficients

The decision for choosing coefficients is often a trial-and-error process. With practice, however, the process becomes simple to perform.

In the chemical equation for tarnishing, you found that both the sulfur atoms and the hydrogen atoms were already balanced. So look at the formulas containing silver atoms: Ag and Ag_2S. There are two atoms of silver on the right side and only one silver atom on the left side. If you put a coefficient of 2 before Ag, the equation is balanced, as shown in **Table 6-4** and **Figure 6-13**.

This table depicts a balanced equation, the coefficients showing that the kinds of atoms and the number of each kind are equal on both sides of the equation.

Table 6-4

Atoms in a Balanced Equation		
Kind of Atom	Number of Atoms $2Ag + H_2S = Ag_2S + H_2$	
Ag	2	2
H	2	2
S	1	1

Figure 6-13

This diagram shows the balanced equation from Table 6-4. There are two atoms of silver, two atoms of hydrogen, and one atom of sulfur on each side.

Writing Balanced Equations

Figure 6-14 shows that when a silver nitrate solution is mixed with a sodium chloride solution, a white, insoluble solid, silver chloride, is formed. This silver chloride solid falls to the bottom of the container. The sodium nitrate formed remains in solution. Here are some guidelines to follow if you are to write a balanced equation for this reaction.

1. Describe the reaction in words. Silver nitrate plus sodium chloride produces silver chloride plus sodium nitrate.

2. Write a chemical equation for the reaction using formulas and symbols for each term. Review Section 6-2 on how to write formulas for compounds. The formulas for elements are generally just their symbols.

$$AgNO_3 + NaCl \rightarrow AgCl + NaNO_3$$

3. Check the equation for balance. Set up a chart similar to **Table 6-5** to help you. Notice that there are already equal numbers of atoms of each element on both sides of the equation. This equation is balanced.

4. Determine coefficients. This equation is balanced, so no coefficients need to be changed.

In the next section, you will take a closer look at a number of familiar and unfamiliar types of chemical equations and how they are classified.

Figure 6-14

Silver and chloride ions combine to form a solid. The sodium and nitrate ions remain in the solution.

Table 6-5

| Kind of Atom | Number of Atoms | | | |
	$AgNO_3$ +	NaCl $\rightarrow$	AgCl +	$NaNO_3$
Ag	1		1	
N	1			1
O	3			3
Na		1		1
Cl		1	1	

Atoms in a Balanced Equation

This table depicts the balanced equation describing the reaction that takes place when silver nitrate is mixed with sodium chloride.

check your UNDERSTANDING

1. Write balanced chemical equations for the following reactions: (a) copper plus sulfur produces copper(I) sulfide, (b) sodium plus water produces sodium hydroxide plus hydrogen gas.

2. Rust, iron(III) oxide, can be formed when iron is exposed to oxygen in the air. Write a balanced equation for this reaction.

3. **Apply** When charcoal burns, it appears that the ashes have less mass and take up less space than the charcoal did. How can this be explained in terms of a balanced equation?

Chemical Reactions

Classifying Chemical Reactions

Section Objectives

- Describe four types of chemical reactions, using their general formulas.
- Classify various chemical reactions by type.

Scientists have developed a system of classification for chemical reactions. It is based on the way that atoms rearrange themselves in the reaction. Most reactions can be placed in one of four groups: synthesis, decomposition, single displacement, or double displacement reactions.

You've worked with three of these in word equations. Now you'll be able to write balanced chemical equations for these reactions.

In the following Find Out activity, you'll discover how chemical reactions enable a space shuttle to be launched.

Find Out! ACTIVITY

How does a chemical reaction enable a space shuttle to be launched?

What To Do

Read the following information.
A space shuttle is powered by a chemical reaction between pure liquid hydrogen and pure liquid oxygen. Liquid hydrogen actually serves as the fuel. The fuel tank contains 1 464 000 liters of H_2. The oxidizer tank contains 544 734 liters of O_2. The reaction between H_2 and O_2 is a synthesis reaction that produces large amounts of energy. In a synthesis reaction two or more reactants produce a single product.

Conclude and Apply

1. What do you predict the product of H_2 and O_2 will be?

2. Write a balanced equation for the reaction.

■ Synthesis Reactions

The easiest reaction to recognize is a synthesis reaction, where two or more substances combine, forming another substance. Typically, synthesis reactions give off energy in the form of heat and light. The general formula for a synthesis reaction is: A + B → AB.

Figure 6-15

Ⓐ The corrosion on this wheel is a product of a synthesis reaction.

Ⓑ This equation describes the synthesis reaction in which aluminum and oxygen combine to form aluminum oxide.

$$4Al + 3O_2 \rightarrow 2Al_2O_3$$

■ Decomposition Reactions

In a decomposition reaction, one substance breaks down into simpler substances. The general formula for this type of reaction is: AB → A + B. Most decomposition reactions require the addition of energy.

Figure 6-16

Ⓐ This equation describes the decomposition reaction in which carbonic acid breaks down to form water and carbon dioxide, causing bubbles in the soda.

$$H_2CO_3 \rightarrow H_2O + CO_2$$

Ⓑ The bubbles in this soda are a product of a decomposition reaction.

■ Single Displacement Reactions

A single displacement reaction occurs when one element replaces another in a compound, such as

A + BC → AC + B or

D + BC → BD + C.

In the first case the positive ion is replaced, and in the second case the negative ion is replaced.

The following Investigate shows yet another type of reaction.

Figure 6-17

Ⓐ The tarnish that has formed on this silver is an example of a single displacement reaction.

$$2Al + 3Ag_2S \rightarrow Al_2S_3 + 6Ag$$

Ⓑ This equation describes the single displacement reaction in which aluminum and silver sulfide react to form aluminum sulfide and silver.

Double Displacement Reactions

One other type of reaction is called double displacement. Let's investigate one way you can tell when this type of reaction occurs.

Problem

How does a water softener work?

Materials

5 test tubes and rack
small beaker
saturated solutions
   of calcium sulfate,
   CaSO₄, and
   magnesium
   sulfate, MgSO₄
distilled water
soap solution—1%

sodium carbonate,
   Na₂CO₃
25-mL graduated
   cylinder
filter paper
funnel
stoppers
dropper
stirring rod

Safety Precautions

What To Do

1 The CaSO₄ and MgSO₄ solutions represent hard water. Place 10 mL of distilled water and 10 mL of each of the hard water solutions in separate test tubes.

2 Place 2 mL (about 40 drops) of soap solution in each tube. Stopper each tube and shake. Observe the amount of suds formed.

A   B   C

3 Place 15 mL of one of the hard water samples in a small beaker. Add 5 mL of sodium carbonate solution. Stir thoroughly. Record your observations.

4 Filter the solution, collecting the clear liquid in a test tube. Add 2 mL of soap solution and shake. Compare the suds formed with the suds formed before the reaction in Step 3.

5 Repeat Steps 3 and 4 with the other hard water solution.

Analyzing

1. What evidence of a chemical reaction did you **observe** in Step 3?

2. **Compare** the suds formed in the hard water solutions before the reaction with sodium carbonate with the suds formed after the reaction.

3. How would you account for the fact that more suds formed after the reaction in Step 3?

Concluding and Applying

4. Write a word equation for the reaction in Step 3. Based on your knowledge of single displacement reactions, what would you **infer** the products to be in this double displacement reaction? Write a balanced equation for what you see.

5. **Going Further** In terms of cleanliness and cost, what are the advantages of having a water softener?

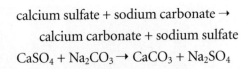

Double Displacement Reactions

In a double displacement reaction, the positive ion of one compound replaces the positive ion of the other compound, forming two new compounds. The general formula for this type of reaction is:

$$AB + CD \rightarrow AD + CB.$$

The two reactions in the Investigate are both double displacement.

calcium sulfate + sodium carbonate →

calcium carbonate + sodium sulfate

$$CaSO_4 + Na_2CO_3 \rightarrow CaCO_3 + Na_2SO_4$$

The reaction with magnesium is identical except that Mg is used instead of Ca.

Life could not exist without chemical reactions. You get up in the morning, wash your face, and brush your teeth. Toothpaste and soap are both made with chemicals. Eating involves more chemical reactions occurring within your body.

Chemistry is all around you. Understanding how chemical reactions occur can help you understand your world.

Figure 6-18

(A) Most acid-base reactions are double displacement reactions. Drinking some antacids results in a reaction that involves the antacid (base) and stomach acid.

(B) This equation describes the double displacement reaction in which the magnesium hydroxide in the antacid combines with hydrochloric acid in the stomach to form magnesium chloride and water.

$$Mg(OH)_2 + 2HCl \rightarrow MgCl_2 + 2H_2O$$

check your UNDERSTANDING

1. Which type of reaction is each general formula?
   a. $XY \rightarrow X + Y$
   b. $XY + Z \rightarrow XZ + Y$
   c. $X + Z \rightarrow XZ$
   d. $WZ + XY \rightarrow WY + XZ$

2. Classify the following reactions by type:

   a. $2KClO_3 \rightarrow 2KCl + 3O_2$
   b. $CaBr_2 + Na_2CO_3 \rightarrow CaCO_3 + 2NaBr$

3. **Apply** The copper bottoms of some cooking pans turn black after being used. The copper reacts with oxygen forming black copper(II) oxide. Write a balanced chemical equation for this reaction.

Science and Society

Chemical Detectives

In recent times science, particularly chemistry, has provided law enforcement agencies with a powerful tool. This tool, known as forensic chemistry, not only helps police to understand more about the crime itself, but often leads to identification of the criminal.

Who does the blood found at the scene of the crime belong to? Was the fire an accident or was it deliberately set? Is the piece of art or the letter from Abraham Lincoln real or a forgery? The forensic chemist can answer those questions.

Collecting and Using Evidence

Law enforcement agencies are becoming more and more systematic and careful about collecting and preserving evidence at the scene of a crime. Police now often call in evidence technicians to collect the evidence rather than do it themselves.

Forensic chemists work with the tiniest bits of hair, skin, and fibers from clothing or rugs, blood, or other materials that the untrained eye might overlook. Evidence is sent to one of several hundred crime labs around the United States and Canada. These labs are fully equipped with the latest computerized testing equipment, such as the electron microscope shown in the photo, and staffed with highly trained personnel who examine evidence from crime scenes.

Other laboratories work solely on evidence in cases concerning violations of federal or state laws. These may involve identifying pollutants, testing imported materials or products sold to the public, or verifying that a particular substance is an illegal drug.

Types of Evidence

In crime labs, body fluids and internal organs are commonly analyzed for poisons, drugs, and alcohol. Even knowing what the victim ate at his or her last meal can provide information as to where he or she might have been before the crime. Blood, saliva, and hair can be classified as to type. While once it was only possible to identify a couple of different blood types, it is now possible to compare 30 or more characteristics of a tissue sample.

Evidence can be divided into several categories. For example, the paint from a car can be identified as to the car manufacturer who uses it and possibly the years in which it was used. This type of qualitative testing identifies that the evidence comes from a certain class of substances. It cannot, however, show that the sample came from a specific car. The sample could come from any car from that manufacturer produced during those years.

What if the car has been repainted on several occasions? If the sequence of paint colors in the sample matches that of the suspect car, there is a much greater probability that they are from the same car.

The composition of the water in the lungs of a drowning victim could, if not identify where the victim drowned, at least rule out bodies of water that did not possess the same composition.

Forensic chemists can restore charred documents and analyze debris from a fire scene. This residue may be an indication of arson.

In the Future

While the present techniques are excellent, new forensic chemistry equipment is constantly being developed. It's possible to identify a substance if it is present in

A career in forensic chemistry, the study of evidence connected with criminal activity, requires a degree in chemistry. Forensic chemists need to be good problem solvers to be able to explain complex procedures in simple terms.

amounts of only a few parts per million. That's like finding one specific person in a city with a population of a million people.

When forensic chemists testify in court, they testify to what their tests have shown and under what circumstances one could expect to observe the same findings.

Science Journal

Imagine that you are a forensic chemist. You have tested some fibers found at the scene of a murder and fibers from the jacket of the person arrested. The fibers match. Write *in your Science Journal* what you would say when you testify in court.

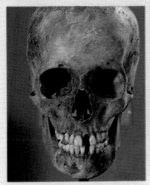

By analyzing this skeleton, forensic chemists determined that it is the remains of an eight-year-old girl who was murdered.

Using the data gathered, artists reconstructed a likeness of the person with precision.

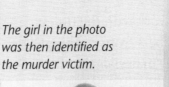

The girl in the photo was then identified as the murder victim.

Such a test could determine whether Abraham Lincoln had a disease called Marfan's syndrome, which used to be called gigantism.

Healthful Structures

When you eat healthful foods or take a daily vitamin supplement, each vitamin taken into your body has a necessary job to do. How can scientists identify a vitamin and know what each vitamin does to keep us healthy? Dorothy Crowfoot Hodgkin, an English chemist, worked to answer such questions.

Finding the Structure

If scientists know what elements are present in a substance and how the atoms are arranged, they can predict how that substance will react with other materials in the body. Vitamin B_{12}, for example, has a complicated structure. Dr. Hodgkin used X rays to determine what atoms vitamin B_{12} contains and how they are arranged.

Pernicious Anemia

The body uses this vitamin to build red blood cells and to prevent the disease pernicious anemia. When people have this disease, they have severe problems with digesting food and may have numbness or paralysis in their hands or legs. After Dr. Hodgkin discovered the structure of vitamin B_{12}, its reactions could be predicted and it was used in prevention of and treatment for pernicious anemia. Before the use of vitamin B_{12}, people who suffered from this disease frequently died.

Other Work

Dr. Hodgkin did not limit her X-ray studies to vitamin B_{12}. She also used this technique to determine the structure of many other complicated molecules that could be used to treat disease.

One of the molecular structures Dr. Hodgkin discovered was that of penicillin, a common antibiotic. She also discovered the structure of insulin, the hormone that regulates blood sugar level. Not only did all these discoveries help scientists learn how chemical changes take place in the body, they also helped chemists make (synthesize) these medications in the laboratory. These synthetic medications are usually more plentiful and cost less than medications produced from living organisms.

For her accomplishment in determining the structure of vitamin B_{12}, Dr. Hodgkin was awarded the Nobel Prize for Chemistry in 1964.

economics connection

Using It Up

A s our knowledge of chemistry and chemical reactions has improved, we have found many ways of using these reactions to produce the products we all use. As the technology of such production improves and spreads throughout the world's countries, there is increased competition for raw materials. In many countries, these raw materials are found as minerals in Earth. But the supply of these minerals is limited.

The graph shows three different possible outcomes for how soon the raw materials from which metals are produced might be used up in the United States. Line A shows what will happen if, in the future, we continue to use raw materials at the present rate. What would produce the lines shown in B and C?

You Try It!

Your teacher will divide the class into small groups and will assign each group a certain course of action. Discuss this action with your group and answer the following questions.

1. Which of the lines on the graph would indicate the results of the action you take?
2. What are the advantages and disadvantages of this action in terms of the country's economy? In terms of the environment?
3. How would this action affect your own personal lifestyle?

After discussing your action, share your results with the class. Since most of these actions would probably require government action, what groups might oppose the passage of each of the laws? Working with your team, think of several other actions that will move our use of metal-containing resources toward line C on the graph.

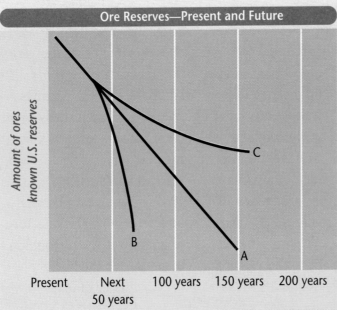

Ore Reserves—Present and Future

Amount of ores known U.S. reserves

Present | Next 50 years | 100 years | 150 years | 200 years

Science Journal

Review the statements below about the big ideas presented in this chapter, and answer the questions. Then, reread your answers to the Did You Ever Wonder questions at the beginning of the chapter. *In your Science Journal*, write a paragraph about how your understanding of the big ideas in the chapter has changed.

1 Ions and covalent molecules are found in all living things. *Which of the symbols shown represent ions, and which represent molecules?*

Na^+
K^+
Fe^{2+}
O_2
H_2O
CO_2

Na^+
K^+
Fe^{2+}
O_2
H_2O
CO_2

AgAgHHS AgAgHHS

2 The total number of atoms of each element in the reactants equals the total number of atoms in the products. All chemical reactions must be balanced. *Why must a chemical reaction be balanced?*

3 Four major types of reactions are synthesis (a), decomposition (b), single displacement (c), and double displacement (d). All can be expressed as balanced chemical equations. *Which type of reaction is the opposite of synthesis?*

Using Key Science Terms

balanced chemical
  equation

binary compound

covalent bond

ion

ionic bond

molecule

nonpolar molecule

oxidation number

polar molecule

polyatomic ion

Use what you know about the above terms to answer the following questions.

1. How does a polar molecule differ from a nonpolar molecule? Give an example of each.

2. How do you know whether a chemical equation is balanced?

3. Can sodium and chlorine combine to form a molecule of sodium chloride? Explain.

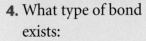

4. What type of bond exists:
   a. in calcium chloride?
   b. in chlorine gas?

5. Your friend says that water is not a binary compound because a water molecule contains three atoms. Is she right? Explain.

6. Name three elements that have more than one oxidation number.

7. Name a compound formed by combining two polyatomic ions.

Understanding Ideas

Answer the following questions in your Journal using complete sentences.

1. In a chemical equation, explain the difference between a subscript and a coefficient.

2. What is the formula for iron(III) chlorate?

3. Could a nitrate ion and a sulfate ion combine to form a compound? Explain.

4. What is the oxidation number of Fe in Fe_2S_3?

5. $Mg + O_2 \rightarrow MgO$.
   What coefficients would balance this equation?

6. $H_2 + S \rightarrow H_2S$ is an example of which type of reaction?

7. A chemical reaction yields two elements as products. What type of reaction has probably occurred? Explain.

8. When a benzene molecule, C_6H_6, burns, how many carbon dioxide molecules are formed?

Developing Skills

Use your understanding of the concepts developed in the chapter to answer each of the following questions.

1. **Classifying** Classify the following reactions by reaction type.
   a. $Zn + CuSO_4 \rightarrow Cu + ZnSO_4$
   b. $NaOH + HCl \rightarrow NaCl + H_2O$
   c. $CaO + H_2O \rightarrow Ca(OH)_2$
   d. $2H_2O_2 \rightarrow 2H_2O + O_2$

2. **Making Models** Draw a picture of a methane (CH_4) molecule, showing how electrons are shared by the atoms.

3. **Predicting** Suppose that equal masses of copper(I) chloride and copper(II) chloride are decomposed into their component elements, copper and chlorine. Predict which compound will yield more copper. Explain your answer.

4. **Sequencing** Sequence the following compounds in order of increasing oxidation number of the metal in the compound. $Fe_2(SO_4)_3$, $Cu(CH_3CO_2)_2$, $SnCl_4$, Hg_2O

Critical Thinking

In your Journal, *answer each of the following questions.*

1. The diagram shows the reactants in a chemical reaction. Write a balanced equation for this reaction.

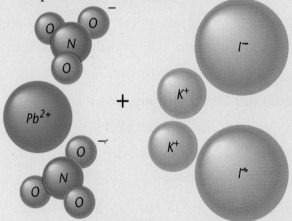

2. Element X has oxidation numbers of 3+ and 5+. Element Z has oxidation numbers of 2- and 3-. Write formulas for the four different compounds of X and Z.

3. Balance the following equation:
$$Fe_3O_4 + H_2 \rightarrow Fe + H_2O$$

Problem Solving

Read the following problem and discuss your answers in a brief paragraph.

You are living on the shore of a body of water and you get 250 days of sunshine a year. The problems of storing and transporting hydrogen have been solved.

Suggest how you would use the electricity from solar cells to produce a clean, nonpolluting fuel. What use(s) could you make of any other products of this reaction?

CONNECTING IDEAS

Answer each of the following.

1. **Theme—Stability and Change** In nature, tin is found in ore as tin(IV) oxide. When the tin(IV) oxide is heated with carbon, the products are tin and carbon dioxide. Write a balanced equation for this reaction. What type of reaction is this?

2. **Theme—Systems and Interactions** The unbalanced reaction involved in photosynthesis is CO_2 + $H_2O \rightarrow C_6H_{12}O_6$ (sugar) + O_2. This takes place in the presence of light energy and chlorophyll. What set of coefficients will balance this equation?

3. **Science and Society** What's the difference between forensic and other laboratories?

4. **Life Science Connection** Why do phosphates cause ponds to be overrun with plant growth?

5. **A Closer Look** How does the behavior of silver's outer electrons contribute to the properties of silver?

CHAPTER 7

MOLECULES in MOTION

Did you ever wonder...

✓ **Why you feel cooler if you splash yourself with water?**

✓ **Why water pours faster than catsup or syrup?**

✓ **Why the tar squeezes out of street cracks in warm weather?**

Science Journal

Before you begin to study about how moving molecules affect you, think about these questions and answer them *in your Science Journal.* When you finish the chapter, compare your journal write-up with what you have learned.

It's a warm, clear, sunny day, and you and your friends are on the way home from the beach. You had arrived early enough in the day to get a choice spot on the beach and put on a sunscreen. Then you waded knee deep into the water to test the temperature. Perfect!

After lying in the sun for 20 minutes, you were so warm that you began to sweat. You decided it would be a good time for a swim. You dove into the surf, but started shivering when you got out of the water. Why?

Now, walking home, you are starting to get hot again. You and your friends decide to buy ice cream cones. But you must finish the cones fast before they melt all over your hands.

▶ *What causes all these changes? You'll find out in this chapter with the help of the kinetic-molecular theory. You can begin your discoveries with this Explore activity.*

Explore! ACTIVITY

Do hot things move?

What To Do

1. Place 75 mL of ice water into one beaker, 75 mL of tap water into a second beaker, and 75 mL of hot water into a third.

2. Measure and record the temperature in each beaker.

3. Drop a piece of brightly colored hard candy into each beaker. Observe the beakers. Is there a pattern to what you observed?

4. *In your Journal*, record your observations. What can you infer to explain your observations?

7-1 Solids and Liquids

Section Objectives

■ Describe the molecular structure of solids.

■ Explain how solids and liquids expand when heated.

■ Discuss melting in terms of kinetic theory.

■ Explain evaporation, condensation, and sublimation.

Key Terms

kinetic-molecular theory
thermal expansion
viscosity
evaporation
boiling
sublimation
condensation

The Kinetic-Molecular Theory

In the 1800s, a scientist named James P. Joule discovered that the increase in thermal energy produced by a given amount of mechanical work was always the same. The experiment shown in **Figure 7-1** below demonstrates that work can be changed into thermal energy.

Joule used the idea that all matter is made up of atoms and molecules in motion to explain what happened. In his experiment, the movement of the paddle wheel caused the water molecules to move faster.

The explanation of thermal energy as the random movement of atoms or molecules is part of what is called the **kinetic-molecular theory**.

In this section, you'll see how the kinetic-molecular theory explains the properties and behavior of matter with which you're familiar.

Figure 7-1

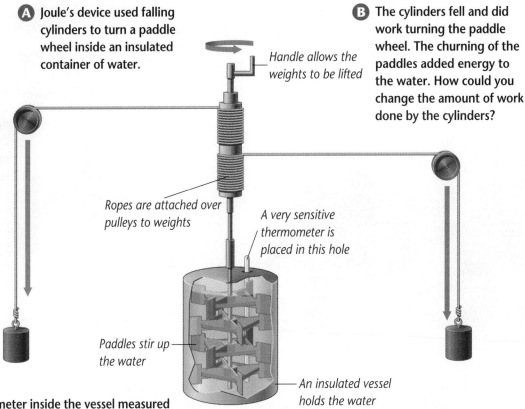

A Joule's device used falling cylinders to turn a paddle wheel inside an insulated container of water.

Handle allows the weights to be lifted

B The cylinders fell and did work turning the paddle wheel. The churning of the paddles added energy to the water. How could you change the amount of work done by the cylinders?

Ropes are attached over pulleys to weights

A very sensitive thermometer is placed in this hole

Paddles stir up the water

An insulated vessel holds the water

C The thermometer inside the vessel measured an increase in temperature that corresponded to the work done by the falling cylinders.

What Makes a Solid Solid?

During your day at the beach, you might buy a soft drink to cool off. The paper cup, ice, and coins you get as change are examples of solids. A solid has a definite shape and fills a definite amount of space. Because solids are rigid, there must be forces of attraction that hold their particles in a definite shape. Although solids appear rigid and unmoving, the kinetic-molecular theory says that the ions, atoms, or molecules in solid matter are in constant motion. **Figure 7-2** below shows how this apparent contradiction is resolved.

What effect does this internal motion have on a solid when its temperature rises? You can investigate this question on the next pages using common drinking straws.

Figure 7-2

A This diagram shows a model of a solid. In this model, the particles of the solid are represented by small balls, and forces between the particles are represented by springs.

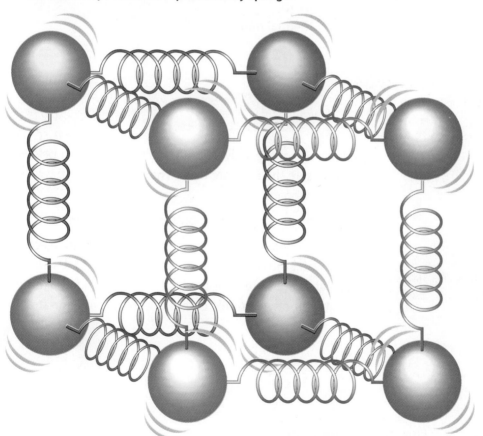

B Springs hold the balls in position. If you push or pull on any ball, the springs resist the motion. When you release the ball, it vibrates around its rest position. This shows how particles in a solid can move while the solid retains its shape and volume.

C An increase in temperature is represented by greater vibration of the particles in the framework. The particles vibrate faster and move further from their rest positions.

INVESTIGATE!

High Temperature Straws

An increase in temperature of a solid indicates an increase in the kinetic energy of the particles in the solid. What are some effects of this increased motion?

Problem

What happens to a solid as its temperature rises?

Materials

2 plastic drinking straws	very hot water
cardboard sheet	cooking syringe
2 drinking cups	pencil
tape	thermal mitt

Safety Precautions

Be careful with the hot water to avoid being burned. Use the syringe carefully to avoid injury.

What To Do

1 Tape two of the straws tightly together as shown below. Make sure the ends are even. Then, tape these straws to the cardboard.

2 Mark the positions of the bottoms of the straws.

3 Use the cooking syringe and the thermal mitt to inject the hot water into one of the straws (see Photo **A**). Use a cup to catch the water as it runs out the other end. Make sure that the hot water only comes in contact with one straw.

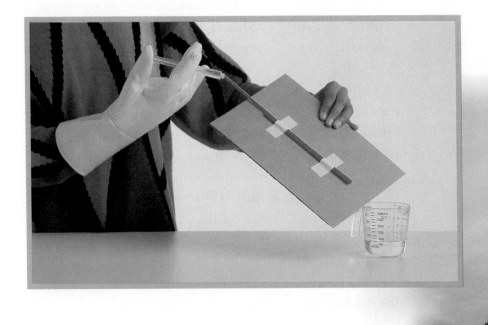

4 Observe what happens to the two straws. Record your observations *in your Journal.*

Heat causes the particles in solids to vibrate faster, which explains why the Eiffel Tower in Paris grows 7.5 centimeters (about 3 inches) every summer.

Analyzing

1. Describe the motion of the two-straw combination when one straw was heated.

2. Make a drawing that shows the two straws after the hot water was injected. Indicate which straw was heated and which straw was not.

Concluding and Applying

3. Did the heated straw get larger or smaller? Use the kinetic-molecular theory to *hypothesize* why this happened.

4. *Predict* two ways to make the straws return to their normal shape.

5. **Going Further** You have a metal storm door that opens and closes easily in the winter, but sticks in the summer. Explain why this happens.

Of course, you normally would have no reason to consider how drinking straws change when heated. When the temperature increases, a solid tends to expand. The expansion of the straw you observed was small, but it is important to the design of structures such as highways, railroads, and bridges as **Figure 7-3** shows.

The expansion that occurs as a solid is heated is called **thermal expansion**. As the temperature of a solid increases, its atoms or molecules vibrate with greater speed and amplitude. The atoms move a little farther from their home position. In terms of the ball-and-spring model, the balls vibrate faster and with greater amplitude. The average length of the springs increases.

Figure 7-3

This railroad track wasn't designed to handle record-breaking summer temperatures. The expanding rails pushed one another out of line.

Life Science
CONNECTION

Sounds Fishy to Me

Imagine fish living in the frigid Arctic waters near the North Pole. How do they survive without being frozen solid?

Unlike humans, fish aren't able to increase or maintain a constant body temperature by breaking down foods. The reason many fish survive in freezing waters is because they have what scientists call a natural antifreeze.

Antifreeze in a car's radiator does not warm up the car. Instead, it keeps cars running in frigid weather by lowering the freezing temperature of water.

Water freezes at 0°C. If water turned to ice inside a car, it would expand and crack the radiator. If a fish's blood froze inside its body, the sharp ice crystals would break cell membranes and do all sorts of dam-

The Alaskan blackfish can survive in freezing waters because it has a natural antifreeze that lowers the freezing point of its body fluids.

The Nature of Liquids

Early in your science studies, you probably learned that a liquid has a definite volume and tends to be hard to compress. A liquid also expands as its temperature rises. Kinetic theory explains this expansion in the same way that it explains the expansion of solids. The thermal expansion of some liquids like mercury and alcohol is regular over a wide temperature range. This regularity allows the liquids to be used in thermometers.

Figure 7-4

Either mercury or alcohol is used in thermometers like this one because each expands nearly the same amount for the change from -21°C to -20°C as for the change from 40°C to 41°C.

age. A fish's natural antifreeze works by lowering the freezing point of its blood and other body fluids.

Some fish, like the Alaskan blackfish pictured, live near the bottom of freshwater lakes that are almost completely frozen.

The super-cooled lake bottom waters remain unfrozen—even at temperatures below 0°C—because flowing water currents prevent ice crystals from forming. Most fish avoid the higher waters where ice is forming to keep ice crystals from forming in their bodies. But fish with natural antifreeze can swim almost anywhere.

An active ingredient in car antifreeze is a substance called ethylene glycol. Scientists have discovered that an active ingredient in fish's natural antifreeze is a substance called glyco-protein. It's also been found that fish that live closer to the frozen surface, where ice crystals form, have more glyco-protein than fish that stay near the bottom, where ice crystals don't form.

The antifreeze in this car's radiator keeps the car running during the cold winter.

Antifreeze contains ethylene glycol, which lowers the freezing temperature of the water in the radiator.

What Do You Think?

The Alaskan blackfish is one type of fish that lives in frigid waters. Read about other fish that live in frigid waters and share that information with your classmates.

Figure 7-5

Unlike a solid, the molecules in a drop of water are constantly touching and sliding over and around one another.

Attractive forces must exist between a liquid's molecules, or else the liquid would not stay together at all. As in solids, the molecules resist being squeezed together. In a liquid, however, the attractive forces between the molecules are too weak to maintain a particular shape.

Is this force between molecules the same for all liquids? Do the activity below and see for yourself.

Find Out! ACTIVITY

How do the molecular forces within liquids compare?

You can't directly observe the forces between a liquid's molecules, but you can make inferences from properties of the liquid.

What To Do

1. Obtain from your teacher three clear glasses, three large plates, and liquid samples.

2. Put about 25 mL of water in one glass. Try to coat the inside of the glass with water.

3. Slowly turn the glass upside down and pour the water into one of the pie plates. Observe how long it takes all the water to pour out. What happens as the water reaches the pie plate?

4. Repeat Steps 2-3 for two or three other liquids.

Conclude and Apply

1. Make a list of liquids you tested, sequencing from fastest to slowest pouring.

2. Use your results to form a hypothesis about the attractive forces between the molecules in the liquids you tested.

As you discovered in the Find Out activity, one liquid may change shape less readily than another. A liquid's resistance to changing shape is called its **viscosity**. As **Figure 7-6** shows, a liquid with high viscosity, such as syrup, pours more slowly than a liquid with low viscosity, such as water. Viscosity depends on the attractive forces between a liquid's molecules. The stronger the force, the more viscous the liquid. The temperature of the liquid affects the strength of this force. This is because when a liquid is cold, its molecules have less kinetic energy and are closer together. The force holding the molecules together depends on distance.

■ Freezing and Melting

If you heat almost any solid, it will melt into a liquid. You have to add energy to a solid to melt it. If you drop an ice cube into water, the ener-gy that melts the ice comes from the water. The water temperature drops as a result.

After you've examined **Figure 7-7**, turn the page and do the Explore activity to discover a unique property of one liquid.

Figure 7-6

Different liquids have different viscosities. Liquids such as water or juice have a low viscosity, and run down the board quickly. Paint and motor oil have higher viscosities, so they run down the board more slowly. Honey has a much higher viscosity, so it runs down the board very slowly. Which of these four liquids has the strongest attractive force between its molecules?

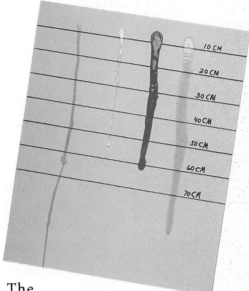

Figure 7-7

(A) This chocolate was just heated. Some of the bonds holding the solid in a regular shape have been broken. The corners of the block are rounding and smoothing as the molecules in the chocolate start to move around one another.

(B) This candle has just been blown out. The liquid wax at the top of the candle is cooling. As its temperature drops, its molecules move more slowly. Eventually, they clump together and the liquid changes to a solid.

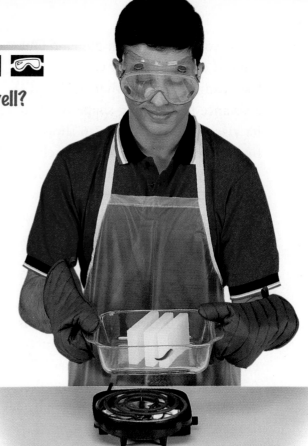

Explore! ACTIVITY

Do cooling liquids shrink or swell?

What To Do

1. Pour water into a tray or square cake pan until the tray is two-thirds full. Mark the level of the water on one side of the tray, then place the tray in the freezer.

2. Observe the tray after the water has completely frozen. Record your observations *in your Journal.*

3. Next, warm paraffin in a small, clear container over a hot plate. Let the wax cool to room temperature. How did the wax change when it cooled?

4. *In your Journal,* compare your observations of solidifying water and wax.

Knowing how a drop in temperature affects the interaction of molecules, you might have accurately predicted the behavior of the wax. Generally, the solid phase of a substance occupies a smaller volume than the liquid phase does. Molecules do, on the whole, move more slowly and stay closer together as a substance freezes or solidifies. Water turns out to be the chief exception to this. As water cools its volume decreases, but only until the temperature reaches 4°C. Below that temperature, water does something unusual—it expands. It expands even more when it freezes. Can you explain why icebergs float?

Because water expands when it freezes, ice floats. Rivers and streams freeze from the top down. Many forms of life survive under the ice instead of being trapped on the surface. Scientists hypothesize that planets too cold to ever have had liquid water aren't likely to develop life. Liquids on such planets would all freeze from the bottom up. The floor of a non-water ocean would be a harsh place for developing life.

■ Evaporation

You've seen what happens when solids gain and lose energy. What happens to liquids as energy is added? If your T-shirt gets wet at the beach, it eventually dries out in the sun. Where does the water go? Why do you and the shirt feel cool? Try this Explore activity to experience and observe a similar change.

Do you need sunlight to make a liquid change state?

What To Do

1. Using a dropper, place five drops of rubbing alcohol on the back of one hand.

2. Wait two minutes. *In your Journal*, describe what you saw and felt.

3. Has energy entered or left your hand? How do you know?

Figure 7-8

A You feel cool when you come out of the water because your body is losing thermal energy to the water on your skin. You pass more thermal energy to the water on your skin than you usually do to surrounding air molecules.

■ Evaporation and Condensation

As energy moves from your skin to the alcohol, the alcohol molecules move faster. The fastest ones soon gain enough energy to break free into the open air as an invisible gas. The process of a liquid changing to a gas is called **evaporation**. Similarly, as **Figure 7-8** shows, water evaporates from your skin when you come out of the water at the beach and you also feel cool.

B Evaporating sweat cools your body. During evaporation, the highest energy molecules escape from the surface first. This lowers the average energy of the molecules remaining in the liquid.

■ Boiling

Water evaporates faster from your warm skin than it does from a container at room temperature. If you warm the water on a stove, it evaporates even faster. If you heat the water further, bubbles form throughout it and rise to the surface. The water is **boiling** because the pressure of escaping water vapor equals air pressure.

Figure 7-9

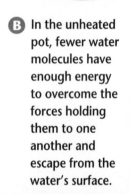

A The water in the heated pot evaporates faster than the water in the unheated pot. More molecules in the heated pot have enough energy to escape from the water's surface.

B In the unheated pot, fewer water molecules have enough energy to overcome the forces holding them to one another and escape from the water's surface.

C In this pot, the water is boiling and many molecules are escaping the water's surface as invisible water vapor. The water vapor molecules are moving much faster and are much farther apart than water molecules.

■ Sublimation

Solids can undergo a process similar to evaporation. If you leave a tray of ice cubes in the freezer for several months, you find that the once-full tray now has only small cubes of ice in it. The temperature was below freezing, so the cubes couldn't have melted, and then evaporated in the normal way. Instead, the water changed directly from solid to gas. In this process, called **sublimation**, a solid changes into a gas without first becoming a liquid.

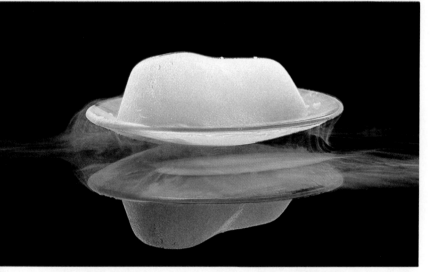

Figure 7-10

Solid carbon dioxide is usually called dry ice because it doesn't become a liquid before it becomes a gas. In other words, it sublimates. Dry ice is much colder than regular ice, so a fog of condensed water vapor forms as air surrounding it cools. This result is often used for special effects onstage.

▪ Condensation

If you've had a cold glass of water on a hot day, you've probably noticed that water collects on the outside of the glass. Experiments have proved that since the water didn't move through the glass, it must have come from the surrounding air. Molecules of water vapor in the air must have changed into liquid. The process of a gas becoming a liquid is called **condensation**. **Figure 7-11** gives two examples of condensation.

Figure 7-11

Ⓐ The water drops on this window pane form as water vapor molecules transfer energy to the cold glass and condense.

Ⓑ The space shuttle's main fuel tank is so cold that even during a blazing hot day, water condenses and then freezes on it.

The kinetic-molecular theory can explain the properties of solids and liquids in terms of moving molecules and the forces between them. In solids, strong bonds between particles restrict their movement to vibrations about fixed points.

Heating a solid causes its particles to vibrate increasingly faster. Solids melt when the vibrations exert larger forces than those holding the particles together. Forces between molecules of a liquid are strong enough to give it a definite volume but are too weak to give it a particular shape. If you boil a liquid, its particles gain enough kinetic energy to break away from the surface and become a gas.

check your UNDERSTANDING

1. Compare and contrast the way the particles in a solid and liquid are arranged.
2. Suppose you have filled a gasoline can to the brim on a cool morning. You come back to it in the hot afternoon to find that some gasoline leaked from the can. The can isn't damaged. How can you explain it?
3. Explain melting and evaporation in terms of the kinetic-molecular theory.

 4. **Apply** Experiments have shown that it takes more than five times as much energy to change 1 g of water at 100°C to water vapor at 100°C, as it does to heat that gram of water from 0°C to 100°C. In terms of energy transfer, why do you get a more severe burn from steam than you do from boiling water?

Kinetic Theory of Gases

Section Objectives

- Describe pressure in terms of kinetic-molecular theory.
- Explain the meaning of temperature in gases.
- Discuss what absolute zero means.

Key Terms

absolute zero

Pressure

Consider how air behaves when you blow up a party balloon. You take a deep breath, put the balloon to your lips, and try to force air into the balloon. The balloon pushes the air back, and you feel it pushing against your cheeks. Finally, the rubber begins to stretch. The more air you can keep inside the balloon after each breath, the more readily the balloon expands. Try this activity to see how something like air, made up of tiny moving particles with relatively large spaces between them, exerts pressure.

Find Out! ACTIVITY

How do collisions produce pressure?

You can feel air move when the wind blows, but what keeps a balloon inflated?

What To Do

1. Tape the bottoms of two identical cardboard boxes together and place them on a smooth floor so both open tops are exposed.

2. Have two groups stand about two meters away from each opening of the box and toss tennis balls into the box facing them. Find out what has to happen for the boxes to move toward a group and what has to happen for the boxes to remain centered between the groups.

Conclude and Apply

1. How does the motion of the boxes change when the number of balls hitting the boxes increases?

2. Compare the effect of the fast balls and the slow balls on the boxes' motion.

3. If the tennis balls are air molecules, what might the boxes represent?

You've seen that the force exerted on the boxes depended on the speed and number of balls thrown. In the same way, the force that molecules in the air exert is related to their kinetic energy, which depends on their mass and velocity. Although the motion of the box may have been uneven, moving only when a ball hit it, imagine billions of balls hitting both sides of the boxes at the same time. Your body is constantly experiencing those billions of collisions. Because the collisions are the same on all sides you don't feel any movement or impact. **Figure 7-12** below shows how this applies to a balloon. After you've studied the photos, do the activity on the next pages to see how temperature affects balloons.

Connect to...
Earth Science
When the elastic limit of a balloon is exceeded, it bursts. Research what happens when the elastic limit of rocks on a fault is exceeded.

Figure 7-12

A When you try to inflate a balloon, the rubber of the balloon exerts a force against the air you're trying to blow inside. If you don't blow enough air into the balloon to overcome the force, the balloon will not inflate.

B When a balloon is fully inflated, the molecules of air inside exert enough force to keep the rubber stretched. They exert more force than the air outside because there are more of them per cm³. The air inside is slightly denser than the air outside.

C You know that if too much air is added to a balloon, the rubber tears and the balloon bursts. What happens to the air molecules inside when a balloon bursts?

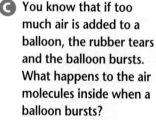

DESIGN YOUR OWN
INVESTIGATION

Gases and Temperature

You have learned that temperature affects the volume of solids and liquids. Does temperature also affect the volume of gas? How do hot air balloons rise and fall? In this investigation, you will find out how temperature affects gases.

Preparation

Problem
How does an increase or decrease in temperature affect the gas inside a balloon?

Hypothesis
As a group agree on a statement about what you think happens to a gas when its temperature changes.

Objectives
- Observe what happens to a gas-filled balloon.
- Measure volume.
- Interpret your data and conclude what happens to the volume of gas when temperature changes.

Materials
2 medium-sized, round balloons
—uninflated
string
permanent marker
meterstick
small bucket
tongs
thermometer
water
ice
hot plate

Safety

Be careful if you use hot or boiling water.

Data and Observations for Balloon 1			
Trial	Temperature	Circumference	Volume
1			
2			
3			

Plan the Experiment

1 You have two round balloons to fill with air, a mixture of gases. As a group, look at the other materials provided. How can you test your hypothesis?

2 In the experiment, what will you be comparing? What will be the control? What is the variable?

3 Measurement is important in this experiment because you need to know if the volume changes. Calculate the volume of each balloon by using this formula for finding the volume of a sphere: Volume = (circumference)^3/59. Make certain that you record your volume measurements in a data table *in your Science Journal*.

4 It is also important to measure and record temperature. How will you do that?

5 Write a step-by-step procedure to test your hypothesis.

Check the Plan

1 How may trials will you do?

What are you changing in each trial of the experiment? When you change a factor, what do you expect to happen?

2 Will more than one person check each measurement to assure accuracy?

3 Make certain your teacher approves your plan before you proceed.

4 Carry out the experiment, make observations, and record data.

Analyze and Conclude

1. Interpret Data Using the data from your experiment, make a line graph that shows the relationship between temperature change and gas volume.

2. Interpret Scientific Illustrations Interpret the line graph and state the relationship between temperature and the volume of gas.

3. Conclude Using the kinetic theory, explain how the movement of air molecules inside the balloons caused gas volume to change.

Going Further

Would you expect the tires on an automobile to have greater pressure after sitting overnight or after a long road trip? Why? How do a tire and a balloon differ?

In this section, we've discussed the behavior of gases in kinetic-molecular terms. But, scientists established the laws that describe this behavior before they were even sure that atoms and molecules existed. In fact, the laws relating the temperature, pressure, and volume of gases provided strong evidence for the existence of these particles.

We now picture a gas as a group of widely separated atoms or molecules in constant, random motion—always colliding with each other and, when contained, colliding with the walls of their container. These collisions produce pressure. More collisions result in more pressure.

Figure 7-17

Molecules in a solid exert large forces on one another, so a solid has a definite shape and volume. In a liquid, the forces between the molecules are smaller, so a liquid doesn't have a definite shape, but it does have a definite volume. The molecules in a gas are very far apart, so a gas does not have a definite shape or a definite volume.

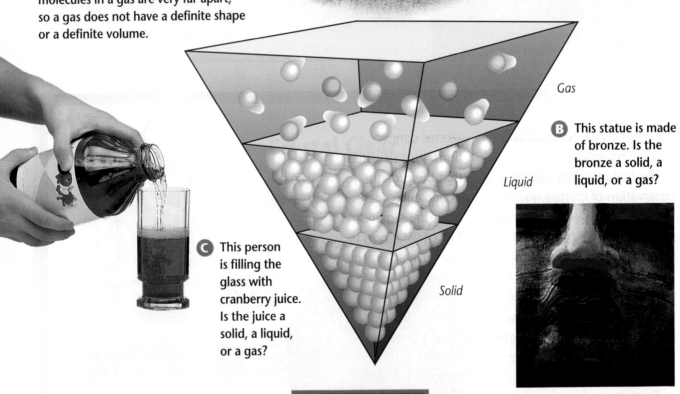

A This train is powered by steam. Is steam a solid, a liquid, or a gas?

Gas

B This statue is made of bronze. Is the bronze a solid, a liquid, or a gas?

Liquid

C This person is filling the glass with cranberry juice. Is the juice a solid, a liquid, or a gas?

Solid

check your UNDERSTANDING

1. Explain how air exerts pressure on the top of your desk.
2. Define the temperature of a gas in terms of kinetic-molecular theory.
3. Explain why no gas can be cooled to a temperature of absolute zero (0 K).
4. **Apply** When you are eating hot soup, why does blowing on a spoonful make it cool off faster?

Science and Society

Keeping Your Cool

No matter how hot and sweaty you are, walking inside a cool, air-conditioned building on a hot day can refresh you immediately.

Air-conditioning technology began in the 1920s, but home air conditioning was too expensive for most people until the 1960s. The common use of air conditioning helped turn Southern cities like Houston, Texas, and Atlanta, Georgia, into major business centers.

About 95 percent of all cars built in the United States now also have air conditioning. In the summer, millions of people drive from their air-conditioned homes in air-conditioned cars to go to work in air-conditioned office buildings.

Cool Problems

With modern air-conditioning technology, people can work in comfort year round. In some buildings air is recirculated over and over again. Cigarette smoke, food odors, bacteria, viruses, and chemical fumes from office machines can circulate through air vents. Under these conditions, some workers get frequent colds. In places where this happens a lot, the office is said to have sick building syndrome.

Using air conditioning also means using more energy—especially on extremely hot days. Most often, this electrical energy is produced at coal-, oil-, or nuclear-powered plants. Coal- and oil-powered electric plants create air pollution. Radioactive waste from nuclear power plants is also a problem.

Many air conditioners contain a coolant that uses a compound made with chlorine and fluorine atoms. When coolants are released into the air as chlorofluorocarbon gases, commonly called CFCs, they damage the atmosphere's ozone layer. This layer filters and protects us from the full intensity of the sun's ultraviolet rays.

Because of the growing use of air conditioning, scientists and others are working to find solutions to some of the problems associated with it, for example, working to replace CFCs with HFCs, or hydrofluorocarbons. HFCs don't have ozone-damaging chlorine atoms. People are also working to make air conditioners more energy efficient.

USING MATH

A large room air conditioner uses about 0.9 kWh (kilowatt hour) of electricity in an hour. 0.14 kg of coal generates 1 kWh of electricity. In a city with 100 000 room air conditioners, how much coal would be burned in one day?

SciFacts

Why are astronomers excited about mercury?

HOW IT WORKS

*I*t's mercury the liquid metal, not Mercury the planet closest to the sun, that has astronomers excited. The excitement comes from applying an idea that dates back more than a century. Astronomers have long proposed that the curved, aluminized-glass mirrors at the base of most reflecting telescopes could be replaced with spinning dishes of liquid mercury. These mercury mirrors provide higher quality reflecting surfaces, which produce better images.

Mercury is highly reflective. Scientists hypothesized that spinning a large dish of the metal at a constant speed could produce the exacting parabolic mirror shape that gives these telescopes their vision into the cosmos.

Until recently, such dishes were extremely susceptible to vibration. Now prototypes of spinning-mercury mirrors use air bearings instead of traditional mechanical ones to smooth out the bumps. The toxic mercury vapor that rises from the metal is contained once a thin layer of mercury oxide forms, insuring astronomers' safety. And, spinning- mercury mirrors cost only one percent as much as traditional aluminized-glass mirrors.

Prototype mercury mirrors
Scientists report that the image quality from mercury mirrors rivals that of the glass mirror used in the Hubble Space Telescope.

❶
As the base is rotated, it spins a ball of mercury in the middle.

❷
The spinning mercury is pushed out and up towards the edge.

❸
The mercury forms into a perfect parabolic-shaped mirror.

● **Fairbanks, Alaska**
2.6-meter-diameter mirror

CANADA

● **Vancouver, British Columbia**
2.65-meter-diameter mirror

London, Ontario
2.7-meter-diameter mirror

UNITED STATES

● **Sunspot, New Mexico**
2.9-meter-diameter mirror

Atlantic Ocean

MEXICO

Gulf of Mexico

Pacific Ocean

Science Journal

In your Science Journal, speculate why telescopes using mercury mirrors can only point straight up. Your answer should include something about a physical property of mercury.

Technology
Connection

Sweet Evaporation

What tastes sweet, sprinkles easily, and comes from beets or sugar cane? Chances are you know the answer—sugar. But do you know how sugar is made?

Thousands of years ago, people found that if they removed some of the water from maple tree sap or sugar cane juice, the result would be sweeter than the original.

In the eighteenth and nineteenth centuries, the process of getting concentrated sweetness from sugar cane was slow and costly. Sugar refining was accomplished by pouring boiling sugar cane juice from one open steaming kettle to another. In the last and smallest kettle, the juice was heated to crystallization. There was no way to control the kettles' temperature, so the sugar from this process was caramelized, dark, crude, and occasionally looked like molasses.

Innovations Under Pressure

By 1840, engineers had applied some physical principles to sugar refining. They knew that a liquid can be made to boil at a lower temperature if the atmospheric pressure is reduced. If sugar cane were boiled in a partial vacuum, the boiling temperature could be kept lower than the caramelization temperature. Vacuum pans and evaporating coils were used to evaporate water from sugar cane juice at a relatively low temperature. Norbert Rillieux, however, took the process one step further.

Rillieux, an African-American engineer, designed a process that started with the same vacuum pans and coils, but added a second evaporation chamber at a lower pressure than the first.

The vapor from the first condensing chamber heated the juice in the second chamber. The temperature could be controlled and kept below the caramelization temperature. Best of all—no additional heat source was needed! Rillieux patented his process—which produced a better sugar and used only half the fuel—in 1843 and in 1846. White crystal sugar moved from a luxury to an everyday commodity.

His improved process for sugar cane and sugar beets was patented in 1881. Today, his process is the foundation for processing products as varied as condensed milk, soap, gelatin, and glue. Those with a sweet tooth, will always remember Rillieux for his contribution to the sugar industry.

You Try It!

List the steps, in order, that occur in the Rillieux process. Indicate which stages have higher and which have lower temperatures, and higher and lower pressures.

water. How do your results differ? What results would you expect from a liquid with a lower boiling point than rubbing alcohol?

Critical Thinking

In your Journal, *answer each of the following questions.*

1. Citrus growers often put buckets of water underneath their orange and grapefruit trees to protect the fruit from overnight freezes. Explain why this technique works.
2. How would you use temperature to remove a tight gold ring from a finger?
3. What happens on the molecular level that causes a bottle of soft drink placed in the freezer to break?
4. What happens to an inflated balloon if you take it outside on a cold day? Explain your answer.

Problem Solving

Read the following problem and discuss your answers in a brief paragraph.

You've been asked to prepare the tires on a car for a vacation trip. The car has just been dropped off to you after being driven for several miles.

1. You want to know if the tires have been inflated to the manufacturer's recommendations. Would you check the pressure now or would you wait? Explain.
2. The owner of the car is taking a trip into an area that is experiencing very cold temperatures. Would you recommend that more or less air than normal be put into the tires? Explain.

CONNECTING IDEAS

Discuss each of the following in a brief paragraph.

1. **Systems and Interactions** Why is there generally more snowfall near a large body of water than 50 or 60 kilometers away?
2. **Stability and Change** Use the kinetic theory to explain the cracks that

appear in rocks during the process of weathering.
3. **Energy** How do you think a steam engine uses the change from water to water vapor to produce motion?
4. **Life Science Connection** Describe how some arctic fish keep from freezing.

5. **Science and Society** List some advantages and disadvantages of air conditioning.
6. **Technology Connection** What relationship between temperature and pressure was used to improve sugar refining?

ATOMS AND MOLECULES

In this unit, you investigated the development of atomic models from concise drawings as attempts to show the true nature of an atom. You have learned that the number of electrons located in the outer energy shell of an atom determines how it reacts in the presence of other atoms. The periodic table of elements is based on atomic mass and structure and helps you predict how one element will react with another.

Try the exercises and activity that follow—they will challenge you to apply some of the ideas you learned in this unit.

CONNECTING IDEAS

1. Particles experiencing elastic collisions do not lose kinetic energy when they collide. What do you think would happen if the collisions between particles of matter were not perfectly elastic? Explain your answer in a brief paragraph.

2. Using the periodic table, select three elements—a solid, a liquid, and a gas—in the natural state. Prepare a chart showing how the kinetic-molecular theory explains their states. Give at least one use of each element that depends on its state.

Exploring Further   ACTIVITY

How does air freshener spread?

Some air fresheners are heated. Some are plugged into an electrical outlet. Using the concept of sublimation, explain why this is so. Design an experiment to time how long it takes to smell the air freshener at a certain place in the room for three different temperatures. How might the usefulness of air fresheners be affected if they were made from elements having very large masses?

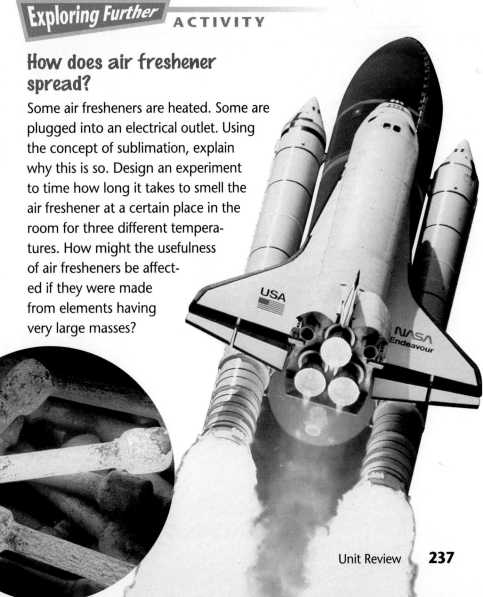

Our Fluid Environment

Skipping and twisting with explosive force, a tornado roars across the Texas plains. Whirling molecules of air and dust give the twister its distinctive shape and propel it on its destructive path. In fact, molecules in motion cause all forms of weather. Moving molecules also let streams babble and blood circulate in your body. As you'll discover, the world would be a very different place if molecules stood still.

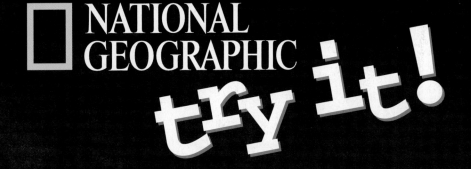

Even though molecules are on the move all around us, it's impossible to see the motion of individual molecules without the help of special equipment. You can, however, observe the motion of groups of them.

What To Do

1. Make a loop in one end of a paper clip. Use the other end of the paper clip as a handle.

2. Dip the loop into liquid soap. Lift the loop and gently blow on the film inside the loop. A bubble will float into the air.

3. *In your Science Journal*, record the motion of the bubble throughout the room. In what direction were molecules moving around the bubble? How do you know? Repeat the activity several times in various places around the room.

weather

Did you ever wonder...

✓ **What fog is?**
✓ **What causes clouds?**
✓ **Why weather changes?**

Science Journal

Before you begin to study about the weather, think about these questions and answer them *in your Science Journal*. When you finish this chapter, compare your journal write-up with what you have learned.

You look out the window at the beautiful, sunny day, daydreaming about your after-school plans. By three o'clock, the wind has blown huge storm clouds overhead, and the rain is coming down in sheets. Your plans for going to the park or playing basketball with your friends have to be canceled.

Your first thought in the morning might be, "What's the weather going to be like today?" You'd want to know whether you needed to take an umbrella to school or whether you might need sweatpants for track practice afterward. Sometimes you might think you know what the weather will be like, but it changes!

▶ *In the following activity explore how weather maps help us in predicting the weather.*

Explore! ACTIVITY

What kind of data can you find on a weather map?

Weather maps can tell us many things, such as whether it will be rainy or sunny or both. During this activity you'll discover how weather maps use symbols to show the weather for the day.

What To Do

1. Look at the weather map in a newspaper on three consecutive days.

2. *In your Journal*, write down the symbols and other graphics you observed on the maps during the three-day period.

3. How did the symbols on the maps relate to the weather for the day?

4. How accurate of a prediction can you make for tomorrow based on today's weather map? Make a prediction and record it *in your Journal*. Check the next day to see if you were correct.

8-1 What Is Weather?

Section Objectives

- Explain the role of water vapor in the atmosphere and how it affects weather.
- Relate relative humidity to weather.
- Explain how clouds form.

Key Terms

relative humidity
saturated
dew point

Water and Weather

Several factors determine what kind of weather you see outside the window each day. Some of these factors are plainly visible, such as cloud cover and the wind blowing the leaves on trees. Other factors can be felt, such as the temperature from the thermal energy of the sun or the amount of moisture in the air.

Weather is also greatly affected by one of Earth's most abundant substances: water. How do you think water affects weather?

You talk about weather all the time because it affects you every day. Can you explain what weather is? Try this next activity and find out.

Explore! ACTIVITY

What things make up the weather?

What To Do

1. Look out the window and *in your Journal* write down everything you can about today's weather.

2. Observe the sky. Are there clouds? If so, what do they look like? Are they moving?

3. Observe objects near the ground. Is the ground wet? Are the leaves on the trees blowing?

4. Some of the things you should be describing are the presence and strength of the wind, the air temperature, the amount and type of cloud cover, and whether it is raining, snowing, or clear.

5. What are some of the things you think of when you think of weather?

In the activity you probably mentioned clouds, rain, snow, wind and sunshine. Much of what you observed is related to how water moves. How much do you know about the water cycle? Water on Earth's surface does not stay in one place for long. Some water sinks into the ground. Other water runs off the surface into rivers and then into lakes and oceans. A great deal of water evaporates into the air.

The sun provides the energy to evaporate water from the oceans and other bodies of water. Then, as the water vapor cools in the upper atmosphere, it condenses and forms clouds. The water eventually falls back to Earth as precipitation such as rain or snow. This water cycle forms the basis of Earth's weather.

Water vapor is a large component of the water cycle. The amount of water vapor in the air is called humidity. You've probably heard this term used before. People sometimes comment about how humid it is on hot summer days.

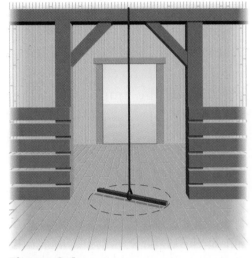

Figure 8-1

A hayloft hygrometer is a homemade instrument used to help forecast the weather. When the moisture content of the air increases, the rope absorbs moisture and lengthens, and the stick gradually moves and points in a different direction.

■ Humidity

Think of air as a sponge. A sponge has holes that allow it to hold water. The holes can be completely or partially full of water. Air doesn't exactly have holes, but there are spaces between the molecules that make up air. Water vapor molecules are distributed within those spaces.

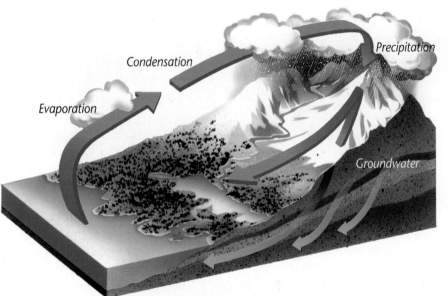

Evaporation
Condensation
Precipitation
Groundwater

Figure 8-2

The water cycle supplies living things with fresh water. Examine this diagram of the water cycle carefully. Is the water cycle a continuous chain of events? Explain.

■ Relative Humidity

No doubt you've also heard a weather forecaster mention relative humidity. **Relative humidity** is a measure of the amount of water vapor in the air at a particular temperature compared with the total amount of water vapor air can hold at that temperature.

For example if the relative humidity is 50 percent, the air contains only half of the water vapor possible at its current temperature. Weather forecasters have developed a simple instrument for measuring relative humidity.

The maximum amount of water vapor possible depends on the temperature of the air. Recall from Chapter 7 that the molecules in matter move more rapidly as matter is heated. In warm air, water vapor molecules are moving rapidly. It is more difficult for water vapor molecules to join and condense in warm air than in cold air, where molecules are moving more slowly. Because water vapor condenses more easily out of cold air, the maximum amount of water vapor possible in cold air is less than the maximum amount of water vapor possible in warm air. This can be seen in **Figure 8-3.**

For example, a cubic meter of air can contain a maximum of 22 grams of water vapor at 25°C. On the other hand, the same air cooled to 15°C can contain only about 13 grams of water vapor. In the next Investigate, you will see more clearly how water vapor in the air is related to changes we see in temperature.

Recognizing Cause and Effect

Suppose the relative humidity of the air in a room is 50 percent. If the thermostat is turned up, will the relative humidity change? Explain your answer. If you need help, refer to the **Skill Handbook** on page 684.

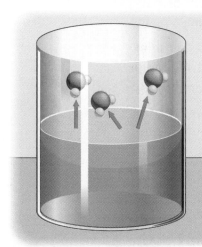
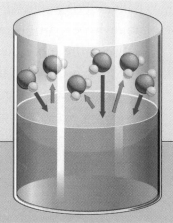

Figure 8-3

Ⓐ Even though the air and the water in this container have the same temperature, the speed of the water molecules is great enough to allow some of them to escape into the air and become water vapor.

Ⓑ The air in this container is saturated—it cannot contain any additional water vapor. If one water molecule moves from the air into the water, what will another water molecule do?

Ⓒ The water and the air are growing warmer. Would you expect there to be a greater or smaller number of water molecules in the air? Explain.

What happens to air that is cooled to the point where it cannot hold any more water?

What To Do

1. Partially fill a shiny metal container, such as a cup or can, with water at room temperature.

2. Slowly stir the water with a stirring rod and carefully add small amounts of ice.

3. Watch the outside of the container. *In your journal* note the temperature at which a thin film of moisture first begins to form.

4. Repeat the procedure two more times, making sure that you start with water at room temperature and with the outside of the container dry. Calculate the average of the three temperatures.

Conclude and Apply

1. Where did the water on the container come from?

2. What do you think happened to the air surrounding the container as you added ice to the water?

3. Why did the water on the outside of the container appear?

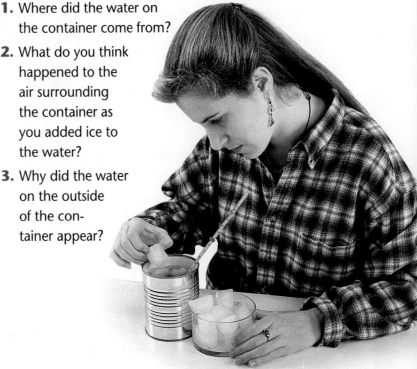

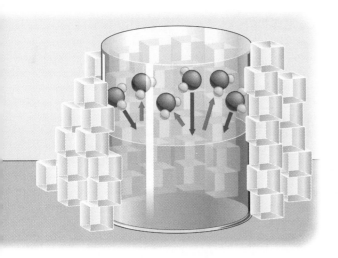

D If the air and the water in the container are allowed to cool, the water molecules and the air molecules will move more slowly.

When the relative humidity of air reaches 100 percent, the air contains all the moisture it possibly can at that temperature. When this happens, the air is **saturated**. As you saw in the Find Out activity, when the temperature of the air around the container was cooled to the point of saturation, water vapor in the air condensed on the container's outside surface. Dew forms on grass in the same way. When air near the ground is cooled to a point where the air is saturated with water, water vapor condenses and forms droplets on the grass. The temperature at which air is saturated and condensation takes place is called the **dew point**.

Relative Humidity

Does the air feel humid today or does it feel dry? You may be able to tell by examining your hair. When relative humidity is high, curly hair tends to be more curly. You can more accurately determine relative humidity by using a psychrometer, a device with two thermometers—one wet and one dry.

Preparation

Problem
Where is the relative humidity highest–in your science classroom, in the school hallway, or on the walkway outside the school?

Form a Hypothesis
Recall what you have learned about relative humidity. Decide whether the conditions in the three locations mentioned above lend themselves to high or low relative humidity.

Objectives
- Design an experiment to find the relative humidity in selected locations.
- Make a psychrometer to determine relative humidity.

Materials
identical alcohol Celsius thermometers (2)
piece of gauze, 2 cm^2
tape
string
cardboard
beakers of water at air temperature

Safety

Be careful when you handle glass thermometers.

DESIGN YOUR OWN
INVESTIGATION

Plan the Experiment

1 A psychrometer is an instrument with two thermometers, one wet and one dry. As moisture from the wet thermometer evaporates, it takes heat energy from its environment, and the environment immediately around it becomes cooler. The wet thermometer records a lower temperature. Relative humidity reflects the temperature difference between the wet bulb and the dry bulb thermometers.

2 List the steps needed to measure the relative humidity of the three test locations. Include how you will saturate each wet bulb thermometer. How will you protect the psychrometers from wind?

3 How will you obtain accurate temperature readings? Should you put the thermometer in direct sunlight? Should all the temperature readings be taken at the same time?

4 Determine relative humidity from the relative humidity table shown here.

Relative Humidity

Dry Bulb Temp.	Dry Bulb Temperature Minus Wet Bulb Temperature, °C									
	1	2	3	4	5	6	7	8	9	10
10°C	88	77	66	55	44	34	24	15	6	
12°C	89	78	68	58	48	39	29	21	12	
14°C	90	79	70	60	51	42	34	26	18	10
16°C	90	81	71	63	54	46	38	30	23	15
18°C	91	82	73	65	57	49	41	34	27	20
20°C	91	83	74	67	59	53	46	39	32	26
22°C	92	83	76	68	61	54	47	40	34	28
24°C	92	84	77	69	62	56	49	43	37	31
26°C	92	85	78	71	64	58	51	46	40	34
28°C	93	85	78	72	65	59	53	48	42	37
30°C	93	86	79	73	67	61	55	50	44	39

Check the Plan

1 Make certain that you understand what is being measured in the tests.

2 Design a data table *in your Science Journal* for your data.

3 Before you proceed, have your teacher approve your plan.

4 Carry out the investigation. Record your data and figure out the relative humidity.

Analyze and Conclude

1. Infer From your data, infer why the molecules of water on the gauze of the wet bulb thermometer react differently in dry air and in saturated air.

2. Compare How did the wet bulb temperature compare with the dry bulb temperature at each site? Which area had the highest relative humidity? Which had the lowest?

3. Conclude Why might the relative humidity have varied at your three test sites?

4. Predict Predict the relative humidity if the wet bulb and dry bulb thermometers record the same temperature.

Going Further

Use the table above to determine whether two areas with the same relative humidity also have the same temperature. Is the same amount of water vapor present in the air at both areas? Explain.

Clouds and Precipitation

When you think of a cloud, what kind of cloud do you imagine? Some people think of fluffy, white clouds, while others think of dark storm clouds. There are many different types of clouds. They vary in shape and in the altitude at which they form.

In the atmosphere, clouds form as humid air is cooled to its dew point. The water vapor in the air condenses. The condensing water vapor forms tiny drops of water around dust particles in the atmosphere. These tiny drops of water in the atmosphere are called cloud droplets.

Cloud droplets are so small that the slightest air movement keeps them from falling to the ground. When millions of these drops cluster together, a cloud forms.

Figure 8-4

Cirrus clouds
Clouds have different shapes and sizes. Cirrus clouds are usually found at very high altitudes. Cirrus clouds contain ice crystals. Describe the shapes of the cirrus clouds in the photograph below.

Figure 8-5

Stratus clouds
Stratus clouds typically form near the ground. They are layered, gray clouds associated with light precipitation and are the type of clouds from which fog forms.

Figure 8-6

Cumulus clouds
Cumulus clouds look like large, puffy balls of cotton. Although cumulus clouds sometimes develop into thunderstorms, they are often seen whenever the weather is fair. What kind of clouds are in the sky above you today?

Explore! ACTIVITY

How can you make a cloud?

Would you like to walk through a cloud? Then walk outside on a foggy day. Fog is simply a stratus cloud that has formed at Earth's surface. How do fog and other clouds form?

What To Do

1. Make a cloud using hot water, a bottle, and an ice cube.

2. Put about 25 mL of hot water in the bottom of a tall, slender bottle such as a soft drink bottle.

3. Then place an ice cube so that it rests on top of the bottle.

4. *In your Journal,* explain what happens.

In the last Explore activity, you made a cloud. Do you think you could also make rain? Actually, you did make rain. Did you notice that where the fog came in contact with the inside of the bottle, water droplets joined together and slid down the sides of the bottle? These large droplets were rain.

Water droplets in a cloud swirl around and bump into one another. When they collide, they merge into bigger droplets. When these water droplets reach a diameter of between 0.05 and 0.5 mm, they are too heavy to remain suspended in the atmosphere. As a result, the drops fall out of the clouds as precipitation. Precipitation refers to water that falls to Earth in the form of rain, snow, sleet, or hail.

DID YOU KNOW?

Arica, Chile, is the driest place on Earth. During one 14-year period, no rain fell at all. During a 59-year period, the average annual rainfall was 0.76 mm.

Figure 8-7

Fog is a cloud that forms close to Earth's surface. How does fog form?

Figure 8-8

When water vapor in the air collects on a nucleus to form water droplets, the type of precipitation that is received on the ground depends on the temperature of the air.

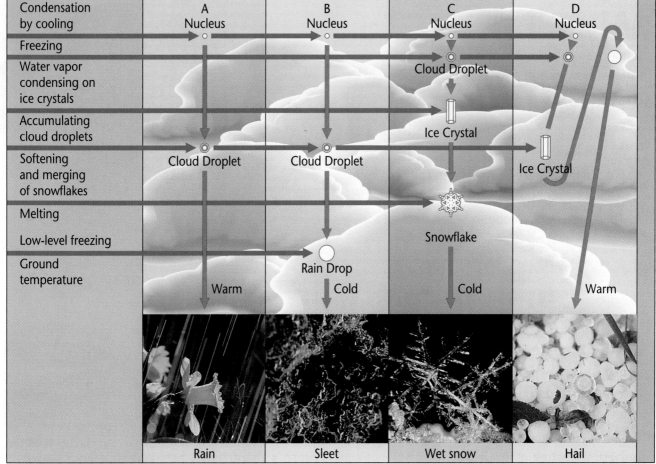

	Rain	Sleet	Wet snow	Hail

Ⓐ When water vapor collects and forms raindrops that fall to the ground, the temperature of the air near the ground is warm.

Ⓑ Sleet is made up of many small ice pellets that form when the temperature of the air near the ground is cold.

Ⓒ Water vapor forms snowflakes that fall to the ground when the temperature of the air is very cold.

Ⓓ Hailstones are pellets of ice made up of many layers. A water droplet in the air forms a hailstone by going through the cycle illustrated above several times.

check your UNDERSTANDING

1. How does air temperature affect the type of precipitation that falls?
2. What is the relative humidity when dew forms? Explain.
3. Explain why cold air can hold less moisture than warm air.

4. Use the terms evaporation and condensation to explain how clouds form.
5. **Apply** Two rooms of the same size have the same humidity. It is colder in room A than room B. Which room has the higher relative humidity?

Changes in Weather

Air Masses

Have you ever noticed that the weather you're having today may be gone tomorrow? That's because the air is moving. The changes in weather are caused by the development and movement of large air masses.

An **air mass** is a large body of air with properties determined by the part of Earth's surface over which it develops. For example, an air mass that develops over land is dry compared with one that develops over water. An air mass that develops near the equator is warmer than one that develops at a higher latitude. What characteristics might you expect of an air mass that forms over northern Canada compared to one that forms over Mexico?

Air masses move and swirl over the surface of Earth. Because they move in different directions and at different speeds, they often bump into each other. Rain, thunderstorms, snow, tornadoes—all of these weather-related events can result when air masses meet. When an air mass moves and collides with another air mass, a boundary forms between the two air masses. This boundary is called a **front**. The next activity will show you what happens at the boundary.

Section Objectives
- Describe the weather associated with different types of fronts.
- Explain why high pressure systems usually bring clear weather and low pressure systems bring cloudy weather.

Key Terms
air mass
front

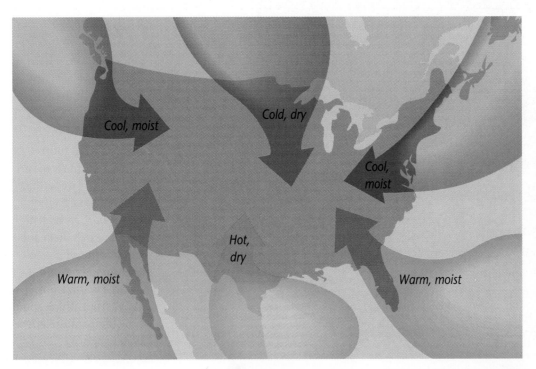

Cool, moist

Cold, dry

Cool, moist

Hot, dry

Warm, moist

Warm, moist

Figure 8-9

During the year, different air masses will dominate the weather. In the United States during winter, the cold, dry air masses meet with a warm, moist air mass to bring snow to the northern sections.

What happens when two air masses meet?

What To Do

1. For this activity, you will need an aquarium with a glass lid, a cold bag of sand or marbles, and a pan of very hot water.

2. Place the pan of water inside the aquarium next to the cold bag.

3. Cover the aquarium with the glass lid. Observe and record what happens *in your Journal.*

Conclude and Apply

1. What happened above the pan of hot water? Why do you think this occurred?

You created a model of a front in the Find Out activity. Although you couldn't see it, the front formed where the cool air and warm air met.

Much of what we think of as weather occurs along these fronts. The following diagrams show how weather is affected by the fronts that are formed.

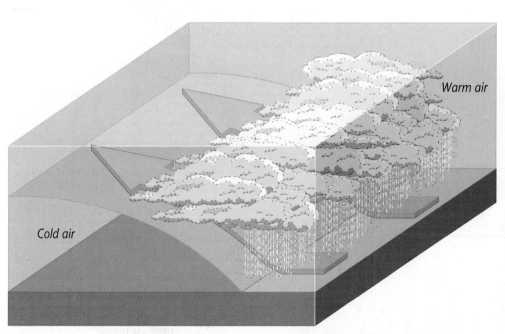

Cold air

Warm air

Figure 8-10

A warm front forms when a warm air mass slides over a departing cold air mass. As the warm air rises, its temperature falls. Rain and other forms of precipitation sometimes form along a warm front. Why? (Hint: Think about how temperature affects water vapor.)

Figure 8-11

When a cold air mass overtakes and moves underneath a warm air mass, warm air is forced quickly upward, and a cold front forms. The most violent storms often occur along cold fronts.

Warm air

Cold air

Figure 8-12

A stationary front occurs when a cold air mass meets a warm air mass, and neither mass moves. Precipitation sometimes forms along the front between these masses. If a stationary front is located near where you live, and it is raining, will it rain for a short time, or a long time? Why?

Warm air

Cold air

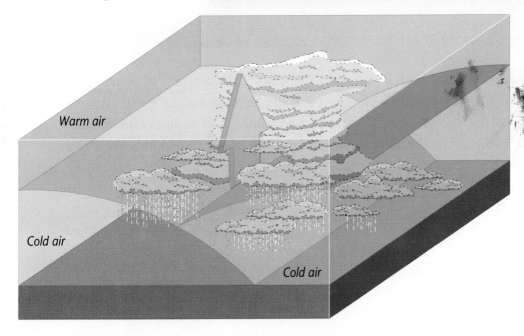

Figure 8-13

An occluded front forms when two cold air masses meet, and force a warm air mass between them to rise completely off the ground. Weather that forms along an occluded front is often difficult to predict because three air masses are involved.

Warm air

Cold air

Cold air

Pressure Systems

SKILLBUILDER

Making and Using Tables

Make a table that shows the four types of fronts and the weather associated with each. If you need help, refer to the **Skill Handbook** on page 680.

Differences in pressure have a great effect on the weather. High pressure usually means clear weather, and low pressure might bring cloudy, rainy weather.

As you learned in chapter 7, air has mass, and as air particles collide, they exert pressure on one another. When they are more densely packed, high pressure results. Air that is less densely packed exerts less pressure. Let's explore how such an air mass moves.

Explore! ACTIVITY

How do pressure systems move?

What To Do

1. Place an empty, capped thermos bottle in the freezer for several hours.

2. Remove the thermos from the freezer and take off the cap.

3. Hold the thermos upside down above your head. What are you feeling?

4. *In your Journal,* describe what is taking place.

Dense air sinks. You felt this for yourself in the Explore activity. The cold air in the thermos was more dense than the air in the room, so it flowed out and down onto your head.

This also happens in high pressure systems. As cool, dense air sinks toward Earth's surface, it starts to become warmer. As the air becomes warmer, it can hold more water vapor.

Although the amount of water vapor in the air remains the same, the relative humidity of warmer air decreases. Droplets of water in clouds evaporate. That is why high pressure usually means fair weather. Moisture in the air is evaporated, so few clouds form.

The reverse is true with low pressure systems. Because its density is low, warm air of a low pressure system is forced upward by surrounding, denser air. As it gains altitude, the air cools. As the air cools, its relative humidity increases. The air eventually reaches its dew point. Condensation takes place, and clouds form. You can see how low pressure often leads to rain, snow, sleet, or hail in the forecast.

Figure 8-14

Ⓐ Air pressure is not constant on Earth. It is different from one place to another. In a high pressure system, what prevents warm, moist air from being forced upward by denser surrounding air?

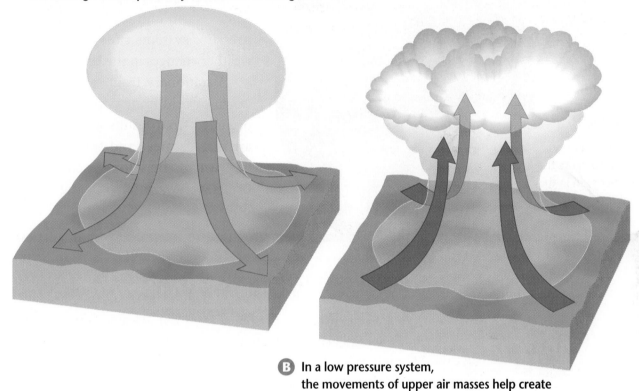

Ⓑ In a low pressure system, the movements of upper air masses help create low air pressure near the ground.

Because high and low pressure systems are constantly moving and shifting, the National Weather Service uses information gathered at many different locations. Each location communicates its data, and the Weather Service combines them to make weather maps used to forecast the weather. The information shown in symbols on the map is called a station model. A key to the symbols is shown in Appendix I. Symbols are used because if words were written on such maps, they would be too cluttered to read.

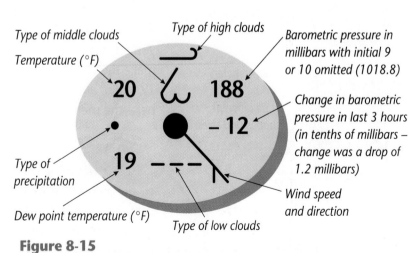

Figure 8-15

Symbols like these are used to describe and forecast the weather.

■ Moving Fronts

When you witness a change in the weather from one day to the next, it is due to the movement of air masses.

Figure 8-16

What pressure system could cause the weather seen in this photograph?

The movement and collision of air masses cause weather conditions to change. The boundary formed between moving air masses is a front.

A warm front develops when a warm air mass meets a cold air mass. A cold front forms when a cold air mass invades a warm air mass. Low pressure usually forms along fronts where warm and cold air meet. Low pressure systems cause most of the weather changes in the United States.

A stationary front results when a warm or cold front stops moving. An occluded front results when two cold air masses meet and trap warm air between them. Along each of these fronts, the warm air is being cooled.

Forecasting the Weather

You can tell what current weather conditions are by simply making observations. However, the weather is continually changing, so you can't always rely on your own observations to predict what the weather will be like later. Instead you rely on the people who make the weather forecasts on TV, radio, and in the newspaper—the meteorologists.

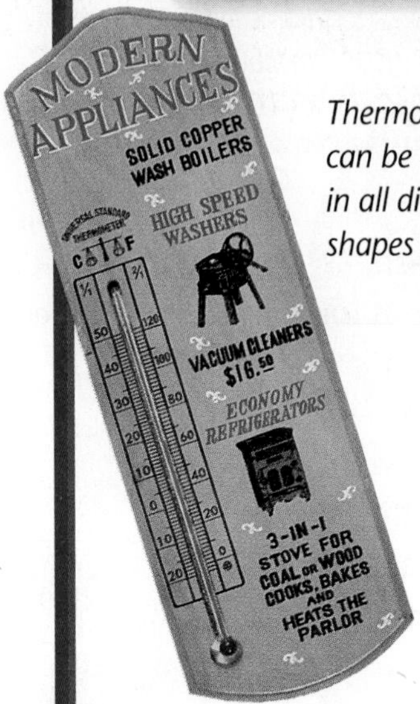

Thermometers can be found in all different shapes and sizes.

You've learned that thermometers measure temperature and that psychrometers measure relative humidity. In the How it Works section you'll learn how barometers measure atmospheric pressure. In addition to these instruments, meteorologists use satellites, radar, and computers to help them forecast the weather.

Uses of Satellites

Some satellites gather information on global weather patterns by recording information

Barometers are sensitive instruments that are used to measure atmospheric pressure.

When the air becomes saturated, precipitation falls.

You'll learn more about the severe weather associated with low pressure systems in the next section.

Figure 8-17

Sunny days are caused by what kind of pressure system?

check your UNDERSTANDING

1. Compare and contrast warm fronts and cold fronts.
2. Suppose a weather report states that a high pressure system will cover your area tomorrow. Why can you expect the skies to become clear?
3. What weather might you expect if cool, dry air from Canada meets warm, moist air from the Gulf of Mexico?
4. **Apply** Air that stays over the Gulf of Mexico for a period of time forms an air mass. Describe the humidity and temperature of that air mass in general terms.

on the temperature and moisture of the air at different heights. Stationary satellites remain at the same spot above the equator and record air currents and cloud formation. Information from these satellites is entered into computers and the data are shared with weather stations around the world. Radar, or radio wave pictures, is used by meteorologists to detect raindrops and ice particles up to 400 kilometers away, revealing what type of weather is approaching.

Once these data are gathered, meteorologists can make predictions, or forecasts, about the weather. To make short-range forecasts, meteorologists use a combination of computer analysis of data and human interpretation. Long-range forecasts are made by computers that compare current weather information with information from previous years.

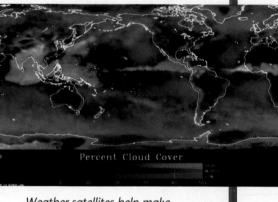

Weather satellites help make weather forecasts more accurate.

You Try It!

Make your own observations of the weather in your city. Observe such things as temperature, barometric pressure, clouds, rainfall, and wind direction and speed. Record your observations at the same time each day, over a period of several days or a week. Based on your data, forecast the weather for the next three days. Check your results against actual weather forecasts.

Reading a Weather Map

In this activity, you'll read and interpret the symbols on a weather map so that you can predict the weather.

Problem

How can you use symbols on a weather map to forecast the weather?

Materials

hand lens (optional, if needed)
Appendix I

What To Do

1 Use the information that is provided in the questions and Appendix I to read a weather map.

2 Find the station models on the map below for Tucson, Arizona, and Albuquerque, New Mexico (see photo **A**). Find the dew point, cloud coverage, pressure, and temperature at each location.

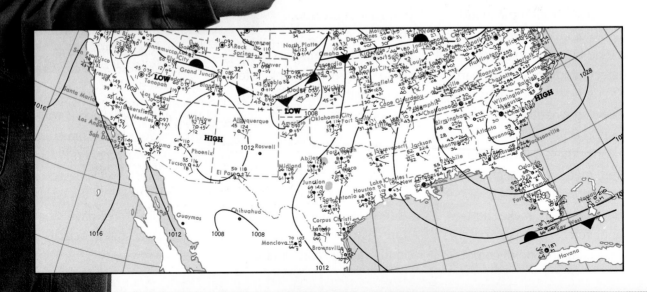

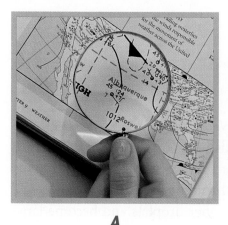

A   B   C

3 Fronts and pressure systems are indicated on the map by symbols, too. Find the front located near Key West, Florida.

4 The triangles or half circles on the weather front symbol are on the side of the line that indicates the direction the front is moving. Study the direction that the cold front located over Colorado and Kansas is moving.

Analyzing

1. *In your Journal,* record the dew point, cloud coverage, pressure, and temperature at each location.

2. What type of front is located near Key West, Florida?

3. In what direction is the cold front located over Colorado and Kansas moving?

Concluding and Applying

4. The prevailing westerlies are the winds responsible for the movement of weather across the United States and Canada. Based on this fact, would you *predict* that Charleston, South Carolina, will continue to have clear skies over the next several days? Explain your answer.

5. The line on the station model that indicates wind speed shows from which direction the wind is blowing, and the wind is named according to the direction from which the wind blows. What is the name of the wind at Jackson, Mississippi?

6. Going Further Locate the pressure system over Winslow, Arizona. *Infer* the effect this system would have on the weather of Wichita, Kansas, if it moved there.

8-3 Severe Weather

Section Objectives

- Describe what causes thunderstorms.
- Relate how tornadoes evolve from thunderstorms.
- Compare and contrast tornadoes and hurricanes.

Key Terms

tornado
hurricane

Thunderstorms

Thunderstorms are formed by the rapid upward movement of warm, moist air. They can occur within warm, moist air masses but often occur at cold fronts. As the warm, moist air is forced upward, it cools and its water vapor condenses, forming cumulus clouds that can reach heights of 10 kilometers. A thunderstorm can cause a great deal of damage.

Water droplets that form in the clouds begin falling the long distance toward Earth's surface. As the droplets fall through the clouds, they collide with other droplets and become larger. These falling droplets create a downward motion of air that spreads out at Earth's surface and causes some of the strong winds associated with thunderstorms.

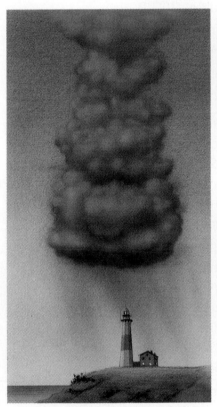
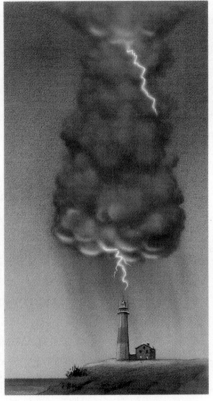
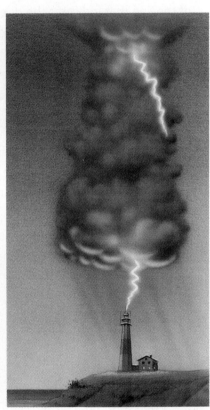

Figure 8-18

Ⓐ Lightning is a sudden, violent discharge of electricity.

Ⓑ Lightning occurs because an attraction exists between positive and negative electrical charges.

Ⓒ Lightning strikes taller objects such as trees and buildings.

■ Lightning

Lightning is also associated with thunderstorms. Lightning, which is nothing more than electricity, occurs when current flows between regions of opposite electrical charge. Bolts of lightning can leap from cloud to cloud, from a cloud to Earth's surface, or from Earth's surface to a cloud.

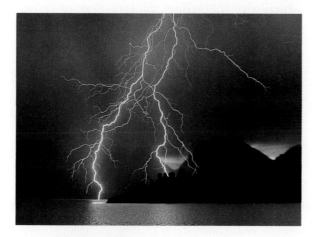

Figure 8-19

Lightning strikes Earth about 100 times each second.

If you've seen lightning, you've probably heard thunder, too. Thunder results from the rapid heating of the air around a lightning bolt. The air close by expands rapidly, forming a sound wave. It's hard to believe, but lightning can reach temperatures of about 28 000°C.

Heavy rains from thunderstorms sometimes cause flooding and mudslides. Lightning can strike trees and other objects, setting them on fire, and can electrocute people and animals. Strong winds can also cause damage.

If a thunderstorm has winds traveling faster than 89 kilometers per hour, weather forecasters classify it as a severe thunderstorm. These storms often contain large hailstones. Hail this size can dent cars and the siding on houses. It can also flatten and destroy a crop in a matter of minutes.

DID YOU KNOW?

There are an estimated 44 000 thunderstorms on Earth each day that produce over 8 million bolts of lightning!

Find Out! ACTIVITY

How does air in a tornado move?

What To Do

1. Obtain two 2-liter plastic bottles.
2. Fill one about three-quarters full of water and add one drop of dishwashing soap.
3. Tape the mouth of the empty bottle to the mouth of the bottle with water in it. Make sure the tape secures the bottles together so that they won't leak.
4. Now, flip the bottles so that the one with the water is on top.
5. Move the top bottle in a circular motion.

Conclude and Apply

1. *In your Journal,* record what you see forming in the bottle.
2. How is this model of a tornado similar to a real tornado?

Tornadoes

A **tornado** is a violent, funnel-shaped storm with whirling winds that move in a narrow path over land. Tornadoes form from severe thunderstorms. As with regular thunderstorms, tornado-producing thunderstorms involve the rapid upward movement of warm, moist air.

Scientists aren't exactly sure what causes this upward-moving air to rotate. They think the upward-moving air is twisted when it comes in contact with the cooler winds moving in a different direction at the top of the cloud. As the speed of the rotating air mass increases, even more warm air is drawn into the low pressure at the center. A funnel-shaped cloud then extends from the bottom of the storm cloud, sometimes touching the ground. The funnel cloud picks up dirt and debris from the ground, which give the funnel its dark gray or black color.

Although tornadoes average only 200 meters in diameter and usually last less than 10 minutes, they are one of the most destructive types of storms.

Physics
CONNECTION

A New Storm Detection Tool

When people are warned in time that tornadoes and severe thunderstorms are approaching, not as many people die. There are also fewer injuries and less property damage. That's reason enough for scientists to study tornadoes and hurricanes and try to develop better tools for predicting their paths. One such tool is a new kind of radar.

Doppler weather radar measures precipitation and wind speed and direction and allows meteorologists to predict and track storms.

Figure 8-20

Although tornadoes tend to occur more often during spring than during any other season of the year, they can occur anytime.

Doppler Weather Radar

Doppler radar uses the Doppler effect, named after Dr. Christian Johann Doppler. (Dr. Doppler discovered why a moving train whistle seems to change in pitch as it passes you.) If a source of sound is moving, the sound waves are bunched up ahead of it and stretched out behind it. As the source passes you, you hear the bunched-up sound waves as a higher pitch and the stretched-out sound waves as a lower pitch.

Doppler radar uses the Doppler effect to measure the speed and direction of water droplets and winds. Airplanes equipped with Doppler radar can study thunderstorms, tornados, and even hurricanes, and determine their speeds and directions. A storm may contain several different wind speeds and wind directions; the Doppler-radar screen shows them in different colors. It can also tell the difference between the small drops of rain that a normal cloud produces and the big drops that a thunderhead produces. It can even distinguish rain clouds from dust clouds and clouds of mosquitoes or birds.

When installed at airports, Doppler radar can detect wind shear regions and warn planes not to take off or land. Wind shear regions are places where the wind speed or direction changes greatly in a small area. Wind shear near Earth's surface is usually caused by strong downdrafts of air. When the downdraft strikes the surface, it blows out strongly in all directions across the surface, thus making a wind shear region. Wind shear near or on an airport runway can cause serious accidents, but with Doppler radar, wind shear can be detected and accidents prevented.

What Do You Think?

You know that the Doppler effect causes an outside listener to hear first high, then low pitches from the moving siren. What do you think the siren would sound like to a listener who was moving along with the siren?

Hurricanes

The largest storm that occurs on Earth is the hurricane. A **hurricane** is a very large, swirling, low pressure system that forms over tropical oceans. For a storm to be called a hurricane, it must have winds that blow at least 120 kilometers per hour. Hurricanes may be many kilometers in diameter. Because they form over large bodies of water and have a steady supply of energy, they may go on for many days, until they reach land.

Hurricanes form over warm, tropical oceans where two opposing winds meet and begin to swirl. A low pressure area forms in the middle of the swirl and begins rotating. Warm, moist air is forced up into the middle of the low pressure area. You already know what happens when warm, moist air is forced upward. It cools, and moisture starts to condense.

Just as in a tornado, the dropping air pressure inside the low pressure area pulls air toward the center, causing even greater winds and lower air pressure. Hurricanes weaken when they strike land because they no longer receive energy from the warm water.

Figure 8-21

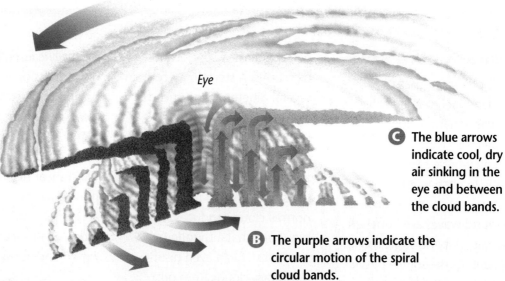

A In this hurricane cross-section, the red arrows indicate rising warm, moist air forming cumulus clouds in bands around the eye.

Eye

C The blue arrows indicate cool, dry air sinking in the eye and between the cloud bands.

B The purple arrows indicate the circular motion of the spiral cloud bands.

check your UNDERSTANDING

1. Describe how thunderstorms occur and why they cause the damage they do.
2. Explain how scientists think tornadoes evolve from thunderstorms.
3. How does a tornado differ from a hurricane? What are the similarities between the storms?
4. **Apply** Tornadoes sometimes form when hurricanes come onto land. Discuss how the tornadoes might form.

Science *and* Society

Is Cloud Seeding a Good Idea?

As you know, weather is extremely changeable and often difficult to predict. Human activities can cause weather changes. Cloud seeding is an example of how people intentionally try to change the weather.

The Seeding Process

The process of seeding clouds was pioneered in 1946. Dry ice, or frozen carbon dioxide, was first used to cause the moisture in supercooled clouds (temperatures below -5°C) to adhere to the dry ice crystals. The crystals get heavier and soon begin to fall as snow or rain. Silver iodide is now the most common chemical used for cloud seeding. Silver iodide's crystalline structure is like that of dry ice and causes silver iodide to act like dry ice. Ice crystals form, grow, absorb the moisture in the clouds, and eventually drop out of the clouds as rain.

Cloud-seeding aircraft, as shown here, feed smoke trails of silver iodide into the updrafts of clouds. In other cases, rockets filled with silver iodide are shot from the ground into clouds, where water droplets are collecting, to prevent the formation of large hailstones.

While the results seem positive, there are problems. Some cloud-seeding projects have led to court battles. Some communities accuse the seeders of "cloud rustling" because they take the water out of clouds that normally drop moisture on their towns.

What Do You Think?

You love to ski, but the ski resort nearest your home hasn't had enough snow this year to open. Should they seed the clouds?

HOW IT WORKS

Barometers

Atmospheric pressure influences weather patterns all around the world. These pressure systems help us predict what our weather will be. Barometers are instruments used to determine atmospheric pressure. How do barometers work?

One common type of barometer, pictured on the right, is an aneroid barometer. It works on the principle that a sealed metal chamber contracts and expands with changes in the atmospheric pressure. For example, if high pressure moves in, pressure outside the chamber is greater than pressure inside the chamber, and the chamber contracts. If low pressure moves in, pressure outside the chamber is less than pressure inside the chamber, and the chamber expands.

A small chain extends between the chamber to a pointer on a dial that is read on the face of the barometer.

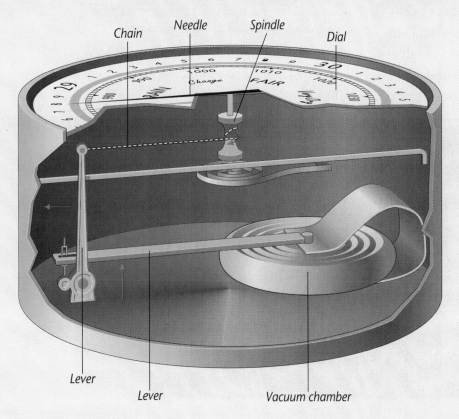

Chain   Needle   Spindle   Dial

Lever

Lever   Vacuum chamber

Using Computers

Take barometric pressure readings regularly each morning and evening for a week. Be sure it is about the same time each day. On your computer, make a graph to show the pressure readings. Based on what you know about high and low pressure systems, what can you predict using only the pressure data?

Literature Connection

Surviving an Everglades Hurricane

Nowadays many of us spend most of our time indoors. If we hear warnings of an approaching weather disaster such as a blizzard, tornado or hurricane, we rush around protecting our property. Then we move into the safest part of our homes and wait out the storm. But what if you were spending the summer camping out in the Florida Everglades and suddenly you learned that a hurricane was approaching? To make it even more interesting, what if you were camping out on your own?

Well, at least you wouldn't have to rush around closing garage doors or putting tape on your windowpanes. You'd have only yourself to worry about. What would you do?

For a hurricane in the Everglades, of course, one must plan for high water as well as high wind. One must find a place of refuge thirteen feet above sea level in order to be safe from the tidal wave associated with hurricanes there. That requirement makes your task even trickier.

If you're having trouble coming up with a hurricane safety plan for the Everglades, read *The Talking Earth* by Jean Craighead George (Harper & Row, 1983). In this novel Billie Wind, a thirteen-year-old Seminole, finds herself in the Everglades during both a fire and a hurricane. Somehow she keeps herself and her animal companions (an otter, a panther cub, a turtle, and others) alive.

What Do You Think?

Before you read *The Talking Earth*, list some things you would do to survive a hurricane in the Everglades. *In your Science Journal,* write down supplies you would need to help you survive. Then, after you have read *The Talking Earth*, go back to your list and evaluate it. What survival tips do you need to add to your list?

Teens in SCIENCE

Weather Watch

Christopher Maiorino's science teacher invited him to see the Lakeland High School's weather station three and a half years ago. "I thought, 'Why not?'" said Chris. "I never left. I'd like to do this as a career."

Chris and his teacher, Tim Maloy, arrive at the weather station every day at 6:30 A.M. Together they call weather stations from Salt Lake City to Connecticut, which are equipped with satellite weather maps as shown in the photo, for the daily weather data. The station has a fully equipped weather laboratory with a computer and modem, barometer, weather radio, and other equipment for

measuring temperature, air pressure, wind, and humidity. More members of the Weather Club come in later to discuss the predictions. Then Chris broadcasts the weather forecast in the morning and in the afternoon over the local radio station.

Maloy, Chris's teacher, took over the Lakeland High School Weather Club in 1976, and since that time has installed a lot of new equipment, including a satellite dish. "Weather prediction gets exciting," he says, "when there's a potential for a good storm."

Science Journal
Review the statements below about the big ideas presented in this chapter, and answer the questions. Then, re-read your answers to the Did You Ever Wonder questions at the beginning of the chapter. In your Science Journal, write a paragraph about how your understanding of the big ideas in the chapter has changed.

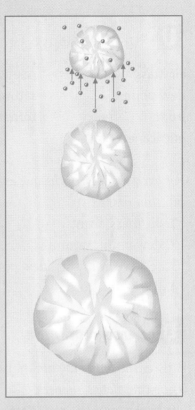

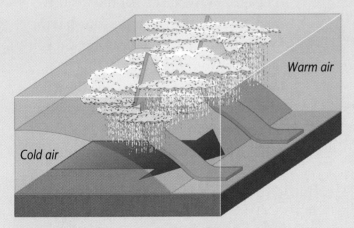

❶ Water evaporates into the atmosphere and condenses to form clouds. *How does air temperature affect how much water vapor is contained in the air?*

❷ Different processes control what form of precipitation falls. *Using Figure 8-8, compare the processes that form hail to the processes that form snow.*

Warm air

Cold air

❸ Weather at a front depends on the types of air masses that meet. *Compare weather along a cold front to the weather that occurs along a stationary front.*

❹ Hurricanes and tornadoes both form from low pressure systems. *How do hurricanes differ from tornadoes?*

Using Key Science Terms

air mass   relative humidity

dew point   saturated

front   tornado

hurricane

For each set of terms below, explain the relationship that exists.

1. air mass, front
2. dew point, saturated
3. relative humidity, dew point
4. hurricane, tornado

Understanding Ideas

Answer the following questions in your Journal using complete sentences.

1. If one cubic meter of air at 25°C can contain 15 g of water vapor, but it only contains 5 g, what is its relative humidity?
2. When does dew form?
3. If air masses stayed in their source areas, how would this affect weather conditions?
4. If you were given the task of predicting the weather for your area over the next few days, what information and instruments would you need to determine the upcoming weather conditions?
5. How does a tornado differ from a hurricane? How are they alike?
6. Why do hurricanes weaken as they move over land?

Developing Skills

Use your understanding of the concepts developed in this chapter to answer each of the following questions.

1. **Concept Mapping** Complete the concept map of clouds.

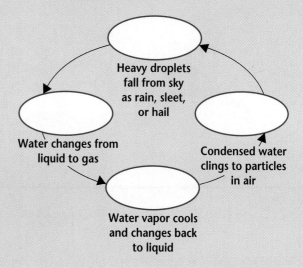

2. **Predicting** Using the information you collected from weather maps for three consecutive days in the Explore activity on page 241, predict what the weather map might look like on the fourth day. What trends of weather features did you include in your prediction?
3. **Interpreting Data** Reviewing the data you collected in the Investigate activity on relative humidity on page 246, how could the relative humidity in your classroom be lowered?

Critical Thinking

In your Journal, *answer each of the following questions.*

1. Why would an air mass formed off the coast of Oregon have different qualities after it moved across the western United States and crossed the Rockies?

2. Fred walks out of an air-conditioned building. His eyeglasses immediately fog up. Why?

3. You go into the basement of your school building. In the ceiling, you see two identical copper pipes. You know one carries cold water, the other hot water. The left pipe is moist on the outside. Without touching the pipes, how can you tell which pipe has the hot water?

4. The relative humidity of the air outside has remained 50 percent all day, despite an increase in temperature. Explain why this can happen.

5. Describe the weather conditions shown on the station model in the diagram. The initial 10 is omitted from the barometer reading.

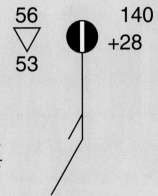

Problem Solving

Read the following problem and discuss your answers in a brief paragraph.

Jason and Kim were helping their father by fixing spaghetti for supper. They filled a pot two-thirds full of water and put it on the stove to heat. Then they went to watch television. When Jason went to check the pot a while later, it was only half full of water. On the wall above the stove were droplets of water. What had happened? What happened to the relative humidity of the room as the water boiled?

CONNECTING IDEAS

Discuss each of the following in a brief paragraph.

1. **Theme—Systems and Interactions** Explain how air masses are related to the formation of weather systems.

2. **Theme—Systems and Interactions** How is the water cycle related to the weather?

3. **Theme—Systems and Interactions** How are temperature and pressure related in air masses?

4. **A Closer Look** What are some of the weather factors that forecasters must collect data on in order to predict the weather?

5. **Science and Society** Explain how the process of cloud seeding works.

CHAPTER 9

OCEAN WATER AND LIFE

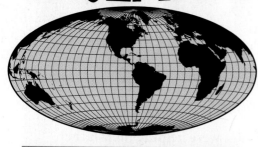

Did you ever wonder...

✓ How the oceans formed and where all that water came from?

✓ Why the water level at the seashore rises and falls each day?

✓ Why the oceans are salty?

Science Journal

Before you begin to study about the oceans, think about these questions and answer them *in your Science Journal.* When you finish the chapter, compare your journal write-up with what you have learned.

S urf's up! That's what you and your friend have been waiting all morning to hear. You grab your surfboards and start paddling out to the breaking waves.

You bravely stand on your board—feet apart, knees bent, arms out for balance—and, for the next few seconds, ride a wall of water nearly 8 feet tall.

But look—your friend has been snagged by the top of the wave! She loses her balance and tumbles into the water. After the wave passes, however, she surfaces and catches her breath. So do you.

Surfing is a lot of fun, but it can also be dangerous. If you've ever been knocked over by a wave, you know how much energy water in motion can have.

▶ *In the next activity, you'll explore how ocean water moves as you simulate a wave.*

Life in The Intertidal Zone

You may think that few organisms could live in an area that is pounded by waves and raked over by rocks and sand day after day.

However, a wide variety of plants and animals thrive in the **intertidal zone**, the area of a coastline between high and low tide. For the organisms that live in the intertidal zone, it's a dangerous way of life. They are threatened daily with the possibility of being dried up, eaten by birds and other animals, or washed out to sea. But the intertidal organisms have adapted to these conditions in some surprising ways.

Figure 9-8

Life in Different Tidal Zones

The intertidal zone is one of Earth's ecosystems. In this rocky intertidal zone, you can see the shoreline along which oysters, mussels, and barnacles grip the rocks so tightly that even storm waves can't pry them loose. What three things do you suppose these animals' hard shells protect them from? Since they don't move, how do you suppose they get food?

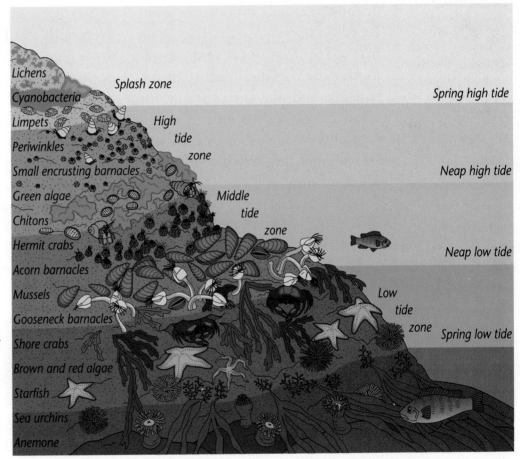

Lichens
Cyanobacteria
Limpets
Periwinkles
Small encrusting barnacles
Green algae
Chitons
Hermit crabs
Acorn barnacles
Mussels
Gooseneck barnacles
Shore crabs
Brown and red algae
Starfish
Sea urchins
Anemone

Splash zone
High tide zone
Middle tide zone
Low tide zone

Spring high tide
Neap high tide
Neap low tide
Spring low tide

check your UNDERSTANDING

1. How does wind affect water waves?
2. What effect does the moon have on Earth's oceans?
3. Describe the living conditions in the intertidal zone and name two characteristics that enable animals to survive there.
4. **Apply** When a wave passes, why do harbor markers bob up and down in the water?

9-2 The Origin and Composition of Oceans

Section Objectives

■ Describe the origin of ocean water.

■ Discuss the origin of ocean salts, and explain why the salinity of the ocean does not change.

■ Describe the benefits that organisms get from seawater.

Key Terms

salinity

The Origin of Ocean Water

Ocean water covers nearly three-quarters of Earth's surface. Where do you think all this water came from? Scientists can only hypothesize about the origin of ocean water. They think that in Earth's younger years, it was much more volcanically active than it is today, and that the water in our oceans came from volcanoes.

Not only do volcanoes spew lava and ash, but they also give off water vapor, as you can see in **Figure 9-9**. About 4 billion years ago, water vapor from volcanoes began to accumulate in Earth's atmosphere. The vapor eventually cooled enough to condense. Precipitation began to fall, and oceans formed over millions of years as this water filled low areas. Now, almost three-fourths of Earth's surface is covered by water. But why is ocean water so salty?

Figure 9-9

Origin of Ocean Water and Ocean Salt

Ⓐ As Earth's surface cooled about 4 billion years ago, it formed a thin crust. Water vapor and other gases from volcanic eruptions formed the early atmosphere. Cooling of Earth caused moisture to condense in the atmosphere, and rainstorms soaked the planet. It took tens of millions of years for these rains to gradually cease.

Ⓑ As the clouds thinned and the sun again shone on Earth, volcanic eruptions and Earth's shifting crust molded the ocean basins.

The Origin of Ocean Salts

If you've ever accidentally swallowed a mouthful of ocean water, you could tell immediately that it was different from the water you drink at home. Ocean water contains many dissolved materials, including sodium, chlorine, silicon, and calcium. Where do these materials come from? Look at **Figure 9-10** to find out.

■ Salinity

Salinity is a measure of the amount of solids—primarily salts—dissolved in ocean water. On average, every 1000 grams of ocean water contains about 35 grams of dissolved salts. Do the experiment on page 284 to compare the characteristics of different saltwater solutions.

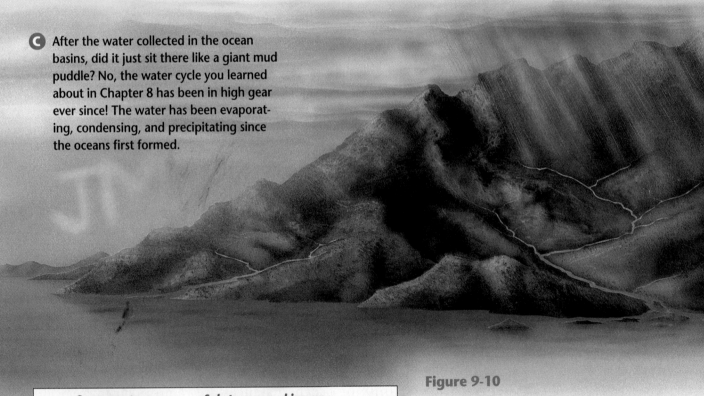

C After the water collected in the ocean basins, did it just sit there like a giant mud puddle? No, the water cycle you learned about in Chapter 8 has been in high gear ever since! The water has been evaporating, condensing, and precipitating since the oceans first formed.

Figure 9-10

The constant runoff of water gradually dissolved many elements and minerals, depositing them in the oceans. Other elements came from the atmosphere and volcanic eruptions. As they collected, the oceans became saltier until they reached their current salinity. The most abundant sea salts form from chlorine and sodium. They combine to form halite which you might know better as common table salt.

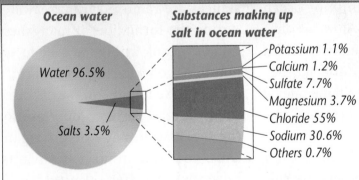

Ocean water

Water 96.5%

Salts 3.5%

Substances making up salt in ocean water

Potassium 1.1%
Calcium 1.2%
Sulfate 7.7%
Magnesium 3.7%
Chloride 55%
Sodium 30.6%
Others 0.7%

Find Out! ACTIVITY

How does salt affect the density of water?

What To Do

1. Carefully stick a thumbtack into the eraser end of a pencil.

2. Fill a tall, narrow glass to 1 cm from the top with water.

3. Place the pencil in the water, eraser end first. Mark the water level on the floating pencil with a grease pencil.

4. Add 1 tablespoon of salt to the water, and stir until the salt is completely dissolved. Predict *in your Journal* where the water level on the pencil will be. Place the pencil in the water and mark the new water level. How did your prediction compare with your observations? How can you explain the difference in water levels?

5. Add another tablespoon of salt and find out what the level will be.

Conclude and Apply

Is seawater more or less dense than fresh water?

As this experiment showed, the saltier the water, the higher the pencil floated. This is because the presence of salt in water causes the water to become denser, and objects float more easily in dense water.

Generally, the salinity of ocean water does not change. Although substances are added constantly by rivers, volcanoes, and the atmosphere, they are being removed at the same rate by plants and animals, or they are forming solids on the ocean bottom.

Some marine animals use calcium to form bones, while others use silicon or calcium to form shells. Because there are so many sea plants and animals, calcium, silicon and other minerals are constantly removed from seawater.

Other minerals and dissolved substances are removed from seawater during the formation of manganese nodules. Look at **Figure 9-11** to see how these golf ball-sized rocks form.

As you've found out, the dissolved solids in seawater are important for the survival of many ocean organisms. For land animals and plants, however, seawater salinity can be harmful. In order to drink the water in Earth's oceans, the salts and other solids must first be removed. In the next Investigate, you will explore one method of removing salt from salt water.

SKILLBUILDER

Recognizing Cause and Effect

Discuss what would happen to the composition of seawater if all organisms having bones or shells suddenly died. If you need help, refer to the **Skill Handbook** on page 684.

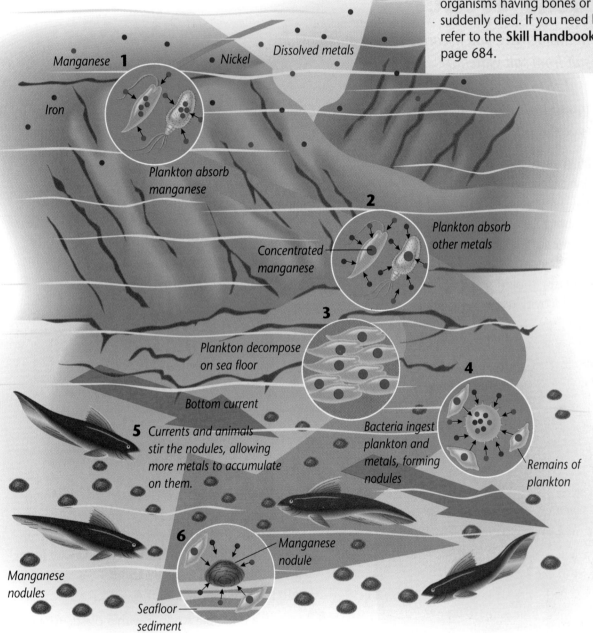

1 Manganese Nickel Dissolved metals Iron
Plankton absorb manganese

2 Concentrated manganese Plankton absorb other metals

3 Plankton decompose on sea floor

Bottom current

4 Bacteria ingest plankton and metals, forming nodules Remains of plankton

5 Currents and animals stir the nodules, allowing more metals to accumulate on them.

6 Manganese nodule Seafloor sediment

Manganese nodules

Figure 9-11

Manganese Nodules
What's at the heart of manganese nodules? Maybe a shark's tooth—or some plankton! How do they get there? Solids in seawater—mainly oxides of iron and manganese—precipitate out of their solution and fall to the ocean floor. But how the metals concentrate is still a mystery. One theory is shown above. These minerals then collect around a small object until they've formed a rounded rock the size of a golf or tennis ball.

INVESTIGATE!

Fresh Water From Salt Water

In this activity, you'll learn one way of removing salt from salt water.

Problem

How can you make drinking water from ocean water?

Materials

pan balance	table salt	water
1000-mL beakers (2)	1000-mL flask	1-hole rubber
rubber tubing	hot plate	stopper
cardboard	ice	shallow pan
polyethylene	glycerine	towel
plastic tubing	scissors	washers
conductivity tester		

Safety Precautions

Be careful when using the hot plate. It should be cool before moving glassware.

What To Do

1 Be sure the glassware is clean before beginning this experiment. *Measure* and dissolve 18 g of table salt into a beaker containing 500 mL of water. Test the solution with a conductivity tester. Record the results *in your Journal*. Pour the solution into the flask (see diagram A).

2 Obtain a one-hole stopper with a plastic tube inserted into it from your teacher.

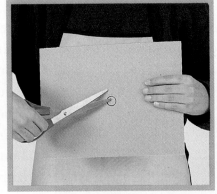

A   B   C

3 Insert the tube-stopper assembly into the flask. Make sure the plastic tubing is above the surface of the solution.

4 Cut a small hole in the cardboard (see diagram B). Insert the free end of the rubber tubing through the hole. Be sure to keep the tubing away from the hot plate.

5 Place the flask on a hot plate, but do not turn on the hot plate yet.

6 Place the cardboard over the clean beaker. Add several washers to the cardboard to hold it in place (see diagram C). Set the beaker in a shallow pan filled with ice.

7 Turn on the hot plate. Bring the solution to a boil. Observe the flask and the beaker. Continue boiling until the solution is almost boiled away. Turn off the hot plate, remove the flask, and let them cool.

8 Test the water in the beaker with the conductivity tester. Plain water does not conduct electricity as well as salt water. What kind of water can you *infer* is in the beaker?

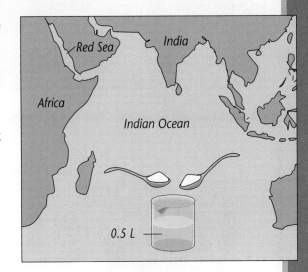

The Red Sea's salinity is equal to two teaspoons of salt dissolved in 0.5 L of water.

Analyzing

1. What happened to the water in the flask as you boiled the solution?

2. What happened inside the beaker? Explain.

3. What remains in the flask?

Concluding and Applying

4. Explain how evaporation can be used to obtain fresh water from salty water.

5. **Going Further** *Infer* how this process could be used to extract minerals from seawater.

Ocean Water Supports Life

You've already seen how marine organisms need the calcium and silicon dissolved in ocean water to survive. Oxygen and carbon dioxide, also necessary for life, are dissolved in ocean water too. Animals use oxygen to breathe. Protists, such as the green algae shown in **Figure 9-12B**, need carbon dioxide to photosynthesize.

In the next section, you will learn about how changes in the salinity and temperature of ocean water affect the way it moves.

Figure 9-12

Ⓐ A coral reef

A Long Drink of Water

You just discovered in the Investigate a method for removing salt from seawater to produce fresh water. Desalination plants use a similar method for producing fresh water. These plants are an important source of fresh water for people living in desert areas, near an ocean.

Although there are many different ways desalination can occur, the most efficient is a process called flash distillation. **Figure 9-13** is a diagram of a flash distillation plant. Follow the diagram as you read how it works. It all begins by heating sea water to around 80° Celsius (A). The hot water then enters a series of chambers (B) which have very little air pressure in them. The low air pressure causes some of the water to evaporate into water vapor. Just

A distillation plant

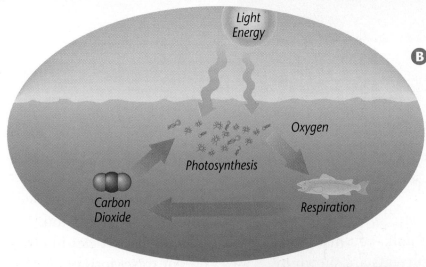

B Through photosynthesis, phytoplankton, such as green algae, take in dissolved carbon dioxide and release oxygen, using energy from sunlight. Other organisms then use this oxygen and release carbon dioxide in the process of respiration.

check your UNDERSTANDING

1. What role do scientists think volcanoes played in the formation of the oceans?

2. What makes ocean water salty, and where do these substances come from? Why doesn't the salinity of the ocean change?

3. Discuss how organisms benefit from ocean water and its dissolved substances.

4. **Apply** What might happen to sea animals if all the green algae in the ocean died? Explain.

---

as in the Investigate you just did, this water vapor doesn't contain the salts and other dissolved elements found in seawater. The vapor condenses on the cold coils (C) at the top of each chamber. The condensed fresh water drips into a collector (D) and is ready for drinking. As the seawater moves from chamber to chamber, it becomes a more concentrated brine.

What Do You Think?

Imagine you live in a desert region along the ocean. You are on the committee to investigate options for how to meet your community's increasing need for fresh water. You suggest a desalination plant would be a worthwhile investment. Before you present your plan to the city council, brainstorm some ways to improve the benefits of the desalination plant. How could you heat the water economically? What could you do with the brine that's produced? How would you protect the plant from pollution such as oil spills? Assemble your ideas in a report to city council.

Figure 9-13

Ocean Currents

Section Objectives
- Contrast surface currents and density currents.
- Discuss ways that ocean currents affect organisms.
- Describe the movement of water in an upwelling.

Key Terms

surface current
plankton
nekton
density current
upwelling

What Are Currents?

When you stir chocolate syrup into a glass of milk, you make currents. These currents are shown by the dark swirls of chocolate made by stirring with your spoon.

Oceans have currents too. You know that water particles in ocean waves do not travel forward. Rather, they move in a circle as the energy of the wave temporarily displaces them. In currents, however, water particles flow in one direction like giant rivers in the ocean.

Figure 9-14

Current Movement Around the World
Many factors influence the directions and temperatures of the ocean currents that travel about Earth. In the figure, examine the currents north and south of the equator. Which move clockwise? Counterclockwise?

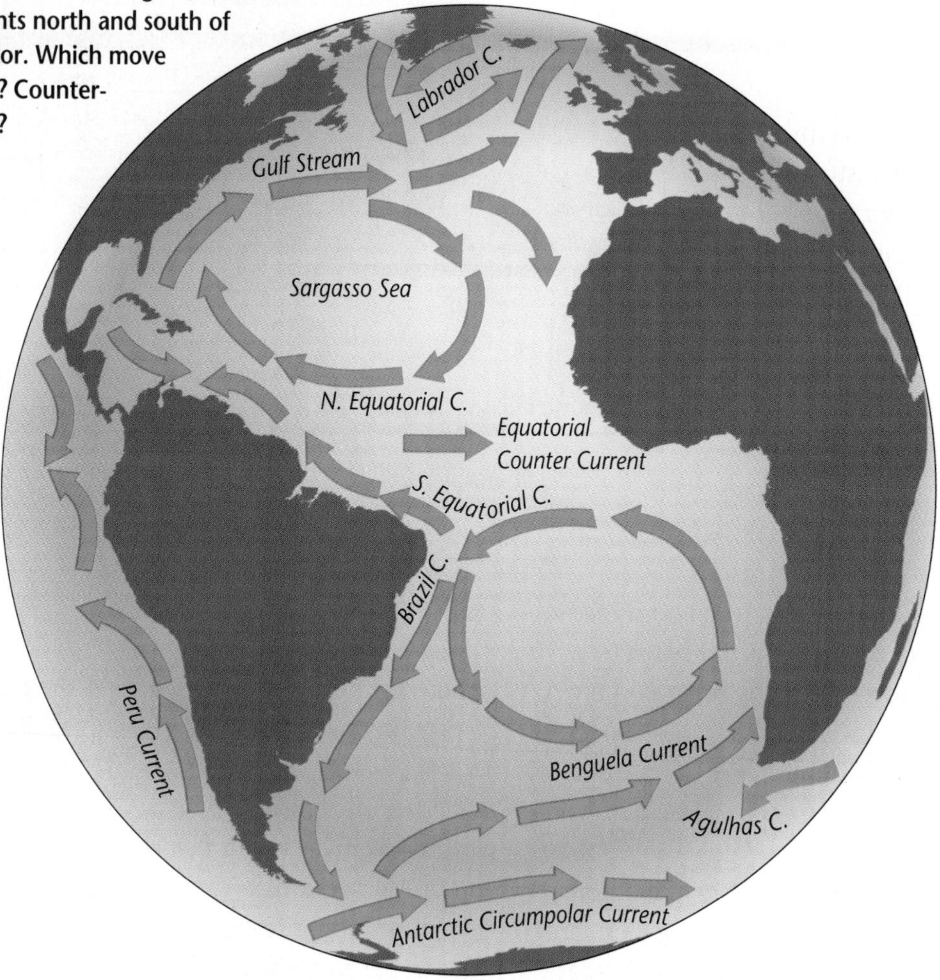

Labrador C.

Gulf Stream

Sargasso Sea

N. Equatorial C.

Equatorial Counter Current

S. Equatorial C.

Brazil C.

Peru Current

Benguela Current

Agulhas C.

Antarctic Circumpolar Current

A When a continent gets in the way of a current, the current is deflected. For example, in the Pacific Ocean, currents moving west are deflected northward by Asia.

Surface Currents

In the late 1760s, the American colonists noticed that it took their mail ships two weeks longer to travel from England to America than it took whaling ships to make the same trip. It was learned that the whalers knew of a place in the ocean where the water moved in a northeasterly direction. When they wanted to travel southwest from Europe to America, the whalers sailed outside this area.

The current was mapped so mail ship captains could avoid it on their way back to America. Because it seemed to flow out of the Gulf of Mexico, the current was named the Gulf Stream.

The Gulf Stream is one of several surface currents in Earth's oceans. A **surface current** is movement of water that affects only the upper few hundred meters of seawater. Most surface currents are caused by wind.

■ Surface Currents and Climates

If you live near a seacoast, how do you think the warm or cold currents off your coastline affect your climate? Do you know that currents can have an effect on you even if you don't live along the coast?

Iceland is located near the Arctic Circle, so you would expect it to have a very frigid climate. But the Gulf Stream flows past Iceland, carrying with it warm water from the Equator. The current's warm water heats the surrounding air, causing the entire country to have a surprisingly mild climate.

North Pacific Current

Kuroshio Current

California Current

N. Equatorial Current

Equatorial Counter Current

S. Equatorial Current

E. Australian Current

B Many surface currents on the western coasts of continents are cold because they generally originate in the cooler latitudes, far from the equator. What does this tell you about the probable temperature of currents on the eastern coasts?

The latitudes of San Diego, California, and Charleston, South Carolina, are exactly the same. However, the average yearly water temperature in the ocean off Charleston is much higher than the water temperature off San Diego. Use Figure 9-14 to help explain why. If you need help, refer to the **Skill Handbook** on page 691.

■ **Surface Currents and Marine Organisms**

Surface currents also greatly affect marine life. Most photosynthetic plants and protists live in the upper 140 meters of the ocean because this is about how far sunlight will penetrate ocean water. Most animals live where there are algae because of the food and oxygen the algae provide. Therefore, most marine organisms live where there are surface currents.

One way of classifying marine organisms is by how they move. Drifting organisms are called **plankton**. Most plankton are microscopic and depend largely on dissolved substances in the seawater for their survival. The currents carry nutrients to these organisms and carry the wastes away.

Nekton include all swimming forms of fish and other animals, from tiny herring to huge whales. Nekton are able to easily move from one depth to another. Their ability to move reduces the effects surface currents have on them. However, some animals use surface currents for migrating and searching for food.

Life Science CONNECTION

The Ocean's Skin

You've read that most marine life exists in the "sunlight zone," the upper 140 meters of the ocean, where some protists can photosynthesize and provide food for

The arrows in this diagram represent the flow of energy through an ocean ecosystem. Where does the energy originally come from?

Figure 9-15

Is there a pasture in the sea? Some people say there is—the huge masses of plankton on the ocean's surface. *Plankton* means "wandering"—why is this an appropriate name? *Nekton* means "swimming." Why is this name appropriate for the fishes and turtles in this drawing?

marine animals. A narrower, paper-thin habitat exists on the surface of the ocean that separates the water from the atmosphere. This microlayer or, "skin," is a rich ecological niche where thousands of insects, fish, crustacean larvae, protists, and monerans—most invisible to the naked eye—cluster near the water's surface.

A Marine Nursery

Because of its special ability to nurture life, the surface serves as a nursery for many fish species. Billions of fish eggs float to the surface where they attach themselves with fat globules to the film until they hatch. Shellfish larvae seek the surface to feed on the microscopic plankton. Bacteria adhere to the underside of the surface film. Other organisms use air bubbles to float on the film.

The Oceanic Buffet

This surface area is like a large dining room for multitudes of species. Tiny life-forms inhabiting the water's surface, invisible to the naked eye, are the base of an extensive food web. Small fish feed on these plankton, only to constitute a meal for larger and larger fish that swim upward to feed at the top. Seabirds feast by skimming food from the water's surface.

You Try It!

You can see for yourself that water that appears clear and empty can be full of life. Take a trip to an ocean, pond, lake, or stream and collect some water in a glass jar. If possible, get some samples from different water sources.

Look at your samples through magnifying glasses and microscopes, slowly increasing the magnification as you view the samples.

Take a drop of water from one of your samples with an eyedropper. Make a slide and look through a high-powered microscope. How many more organisms can you find?

Draw pictures of what you see. Try to identify the organisms from a field guide.

Density Currents

Water below a few hundred meters is too deep to be affected by winds, and yet it also has currents. These currents are called density currents. A **density current** is movement of water that occurs when dense seawater moves toward an area of less dense seawater. What do you think would cause differences in the density of seawater?

Explore! ACTIVITY

Can temperature affect water density?

What To Do

1. Fill a large glass jar with warm water. Gently add a drop of food coloring in the center.

2. Now carefully float an ice cube on top of the food coloring. Observe for one minute. What happens to the food coloring?

3. Add two drops of food coloring directly on the ice cube to help you see what is happening. Record your observations *in your Journal.*

In the Explore activity, you saw that temperature affects the movement of water. The molecules in cold water are less active and are closer together than molecules in warm water, making the cold water more dense. Dense water sinks, forming a vertical current.

In the ocean, cold air near the North and South poles cools the water, causing it to become more dense than water in nonpolar areas. Can you think of something else besides temperature that might affect the density of seawater?

Explore! ACTIVITY

How are density and salinity related?

1. Fill a large jar three-quarters full with water at room temperature.

2. Mix several teaspoons of table salt into a small glass of water of the same temperature as the water in the jar.

3. Add a few drops of food coloring to the salt water and pour the solution very slowly and gently into the jar of water. Describe what happens *in your Journal*.

As you can see from this activity, salinity affects the density of water. The colored salt solution sank to the bottom of the jar because it was more dense than the fresh water around it. What do you think causes salinity differences in the ocean?

Figure 9-16

Warm and Cold Currents

A This diagram demonstrates the effect of temperature on sea water. Compare this to air in a freezer. At what latitudes is the surface water the coldest? Why might it then move away from its original location, producing density currents?

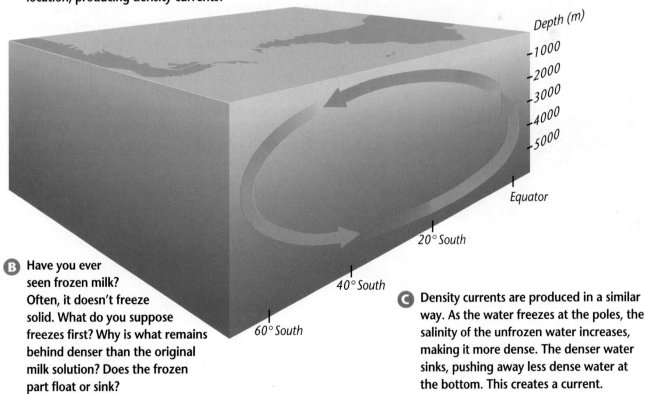

B Have you ever seen frozen milk? Often, it doesn't freeze solid. What do you suppose freezes first? Why is what remains behind denser than the original milk solution? Does the frozen part float or sink?

C Density currents are produced in a similar way. As the water freezes at the poles, the salinity of the unfrozen water increases, making it more dense. The denser water sinks, pushing away less dense water at the bottom. This creates a current.

Upwellings

In some regions of the world, the density current cycle is interrupted. This happens where strong, wind-driven surface currents carry warm surface water away from an area. In such an area, cold water from deep below rises to replace water at the surface. This upward movement of cold water is called an **upwelling**.

Whether your family makes its living from the ocean, or you occasionally visit the coast, or you have never even seen the ocean, the composition and movement of the ocean has a tremendous effect on your daily life. What would life on Earth be like without oceans?

Upwelling in Peru
When wind-driven coastal currents flow along a continent, as they do in Peru, they cause water to flow away from the continent. An upwelling of deeper water replaces the surface water that has been moved away. As a result, nutrients from the ocean floor are brought up, enriching the diet of the plankton in the surface water. How would this benefit the fishing industry?

Figure 9-17

If you mix up the water in a fish bowl, any food laying on the bottom will float back up. How does this phenomenon apply to the effect of the trade winds in this diagram? How does it differ?

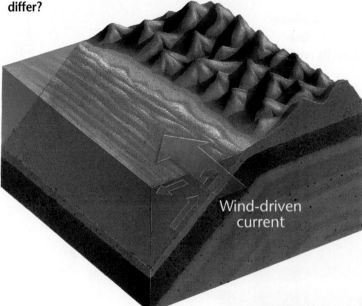

Wind-driven current

check your UNDERSTANDING

1. What is the difference between surface currents and density currents?
2. How do ocean currents affect organisms?
3. What causes an upwelling? Why might commercial fisheries be on the lookout for upwellings?
4. **Apply** How are density currents similar to convection currents?

Science and Society

Aquaculture

One of the most difficult problems facing the world of tomorrow is how to feed our growing population when food-producing areas on land remain the same size or get smaller. Where will we turn for new food sources?

A good place to find them is under water. Aquaculture is the controlled raising, or farming, of shellfish, fish, and plants that live in water. Aquaculture is done in both fresh water and seawater, and is done in both natural bodies of water and enclosures built on land. By controlling the environment—providing proper nutrients, providing protection from predators, and controlling breeding—farm-raised plants and animals often grow faster and larger than those in the wild.

In Japan's Inland Sea, oysters and mussels are cultivated on ropes hanging into the water from rafts. The Hanging Gardens of the Inland Sea are really very large undersea fields for growing bivalves. Hundreds of oysters are hung into the sea from floating rafts that give the animals a place on which to grow and mature. The oysters get their food in the form of algae and are ready to harvest in a few months to a couple of years, depending on the animal.

Besides shellfish, many types of fish are also raised as aquaculture crops. Fish farms in the United States raise mostly salmon, catfish and trout. Many other countries—including China, India, Chile, and Norway—also have fish farms.

Plants are also often cultivated through aquaculture. Seaweeds are raised most often. They are used as food or as other products, such as thickeners for foods and drugs.

Aquaculture is not a recent invention. It has been practiced in China for more than 3000 years. Its importance in providing food will continue to grow in the future.

Use the website of the American Tilapia Association to learn about tilapia, a type of food fish cultivated using aquaculture. What positive and negative effects does a controlled environment have on the fish?

Literature Connection

Two Views of the Ocean

Writers have written about water and the seas for thousands of years. The images they have presented have brought clear pictures, even to those who have never seen the ocean. Read the following excerpt from "The Rime of the Ancient Mariner" by Samuel Taylor Coleridge.

> Day after day, day after day,
> We stuck, nor breath nor motion;
> As idle as a painted ship
> Upon a painted ocean.
> Water, water, everywhere,
> And all the boards did shrink;
> Water, water, everywhere,
> Nor any drop to drink.

Rachel Carson (1907-1964) presented another view of the ocean. As a marine biologist who spent most of her life working for the United States Fish and Wildlife Service, the author was especially interested in the sea.

In her writing, Carson emphasized how all living things are interrelated. Read the chapter "A Changing Year" from Carson's book *The Sea Around Us.* "A Changing Year" describes life in the sea as the seasons change. It tells us that nothing is ever wasted in the sea. Instead, it is used and then passed on from one organism to another. The minerals in seawater are vital to the life of even the smallest of marine protists. Everything in the ocean is necessary for the survival of something else in the ocean.

Science Journal

Using information from Carson's book, write a poem *in your Science Journal* in the style of Samuel Taylor Coleridge.

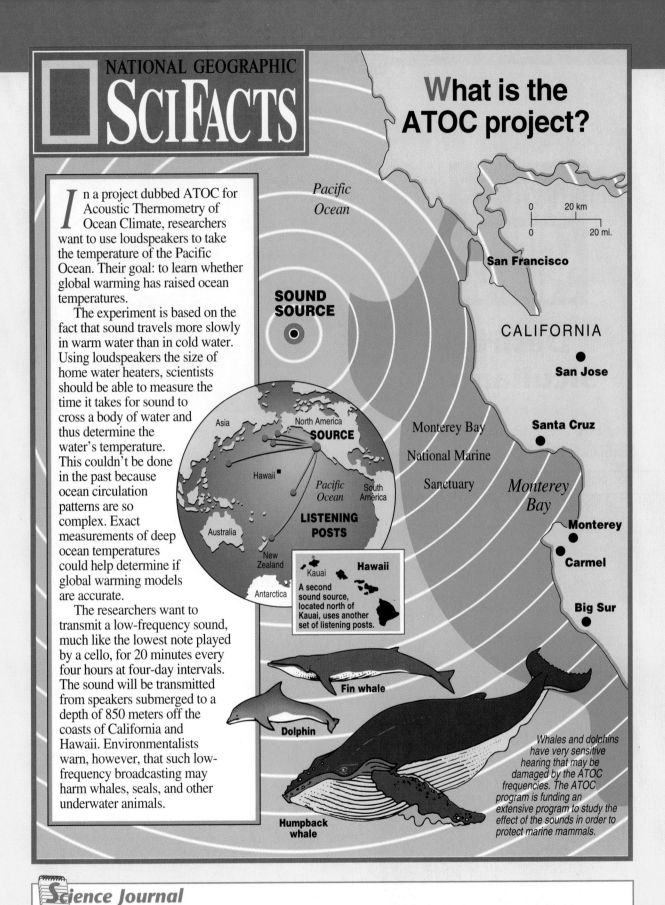

NATIONAL GEOGRAPHIC
SciFacts

What is the ATOC project?

In a project dubbed ATOC for Acoustic Thermometry of Ocean Climate, researchers want to use loudspeakers to take the temperature of the Pacific Ocean. Their goal: to learn whether global warming has raised ocean temperatures.

The experiment is based on the fact that sound travels more slowly in warm water than in cold water. Using loudspeakers the size of home water heaters, scientists should be able to measure the time it takes for sound to cross a body of water and thus determine the water's temperature. This couldn't be done in the past because ocean circulation patterns are so complex. Exact measurements of deep ocean temperatures could help determine if global warming models are accurate.

The researchers want to transmit a low-frequency sound, much like the lowest note played by a cello, for 20 minutes every four hours at four-day intervals. The sound will be transmitted from speakers submerged to a depth of 850 meters off the coasts of California and Hawaii. Environmentalists warn, however, that such low-frequency broadcasting may harm whales, seals, and other underwater animals.

Pacific Ocean

SOUND SOURCE

0   20 km
0   20 mi.

San Francisco

CALIFORNIA

San Jose

Monterey Bay National Marine Sanctuary

Santa Cruz

Monterey Bay

Monterey

Carmel

Big Sur

Asia
North America
SOURCE
Hawaii
Pacific Ocean
South America
LISTENING POSTS
Australia
New Zealand
Antarctica

Kauai   Hawaii
A second sound source, located north of Kauai, uses another set of listening posts.

Fin whale

Dolphin

Humpback whale

Whales and dolphins have very sensitive hearing that may be damaged by the ATOC frequencies. The ATOC program is funding an extensive program to study the effect of the sounds in order to protect marine mammals.

Science Journal

The data gathered from ATOC may help reduce global warming, yet if implemented, could harm marine animals. Explain *in your Science Journal* whether you think that the benefits of ATOC outweigh the costs.

Teens in SCIENCE

Desiree Siculiano

At the age of 12, Desiree Siculiano started as a volunteer guide in the New York City Aquarium. She worked at the touching tank, a large tank holding various aquatic animals, such as horseshoe crabs, that visitors are encouraged to touch. She was the youngest volunteer at the Aquarium when she started. How did she have the self-confidence to volunteer at such a young age? "My science teacher said it would be a good program for me for the summer. If he thought I could do it, so did I." Desiree convinced her brother to volunteer with her, and they worked as a team for four years.

Desiree is in the College Now program at John Dewey High School in Brooklyn. She takes college-level courses after the regular school day and plans to study marine biology in college. To help her reach this goal, she works in the culture room at the aquarium where she studies brown algae, which are used to feed small aquatic animals, and fry—baby fish—at the aquarium. Microscopic animals also eat algae. "This type of organism (algae) is at the very bottom of the food chain," says Desiree, whose task is purifying the water in which the algae grow.

Science Journal

Review the statements below about the big ideas presented in this chapter, and answer the questions. Then, reread your answers to the Did You Ever Wonder questions at the beginning of the chapter. *In your Science Journal,* write a paragraph about how your understanding of the big ideas in the chapter has changed.

1 In a water wave, water particles are temporarily displaced while the energy of the wave passes. The water itself does not move forward with the wave. *What is the shape water particles move in as a wave passes?*

2 Water waves are usually caused by wind, but tides are kinds of waves caused by the gravitational attraction among the moon, the sun, and Earth. *When during the month are tides the most extreme?*

3 Scientists think that oceans were formed when water vapor from volcanoes condensed and fell to Earth as precipitation. Ocean water contains dissolved solids such as salt and dissolved gases such as oxygen and carbon dioxide. *Where did many of the dissolved solids found in the ocean come from?*

4 Ocean currents are like rivers of water in the sea. Marine protists and animals depend on currents to bring them food, carry away waste, and provide them with transportation. *What are two types of ocean currents?*

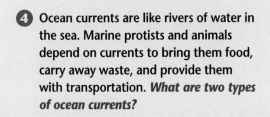

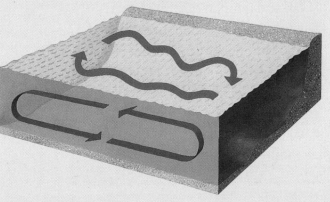

Using Key Science Terms

density current   intertidal zone

nekton   plankton

salinity   surface current

upwelling

Use the terms from the list to answer the following questions.

1. How does a density current differ from a surface current?
2. How do the movements of nekton and plankton differ?
3. What is salinity and how do manganese nodules affect the salinity of ocean water?
4. Why is fishing so successful in areas of upwellings?

Understanding Ideas

Answer the following questions in your Journal using complete sentences.

1. If the pull of gravity between Earth and the moon increased, how would it affect tides on Earth?
2. The Mediterranean Sea has high evaporation and low precipitation. How would its water density compare to ocean water from an area where there is a lot of rainfall and temperatures are lower?
3. How does the Gulf Stream affect the climate in England and Ireland?
4. If your drinking water ran out as you were sailing around the world, how could you get more?
5. What is the relationship between the salinity of water and its density?

Developing Skills

Use your understanding of the concepts developed in this chapter to answer each of the following questions.

1. **Concept Mapping** Complete the concept map of Ocean Water.

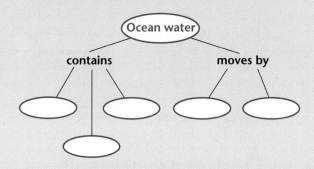

2. **Predicting** Repeat the density experiment on page 284 using an egg. Predict if more or less salt will be required to make the egg float in the water than it did to make the pencil float. Compare your results with your prediction.
3. **Predicting and Sequencing** Repeat the Explore activity on density and salinity on page 295 using three jars of water with different salinities and one jar with plain tap water. Make each jar of salt water a different color and leave the plain water clear. Using what you have learned about salinity and density, sequence the water samples from highest to lowest density. Using a clear straw, test your prediction and see if you can layer the colored water in the straw.

Critical Thinking

In your Journal, *answer each of the following questions.*

1. In which direction would you expect a surface current off the southern coast of Africa to flow?

2. *Thermo-* refers to temperature and *haline* to salinity. Why do you think density currents are sometimes called *thermohaline* currents?

3. Look at the map below. How are fishing grounds related to the location of surface currents, as shown in **Figure 9-14?**

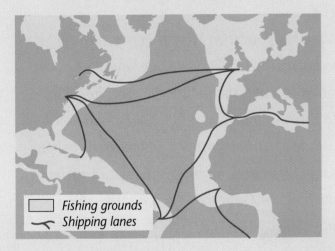

Fishing grounds
Shipping lanes

4. How are the shipping lanes shown on the map related to the location of surface currents?

5. Why do you think 80 percent of the kinds of seaweed found off the east coast of North America are also found off the west coast of Great Britain?

Problem Solving

Read the following problem and discuss your answers in a brief paragraph.

Suppose your local park district is running a contest to design a water amusement park for the city. After reading this chapter, you decide to enter the contest. Using what you know about the movement of water in currents and waves, describe in words and pictures three different water rides you would design.

1. Identify the source of energy for each ride.

2. Discuss how objects or people move in the ride.

3. Make diagrams of your rides.

CONNECTING IDEAS

Discuss each of the following in a brief paragraph.

1. **Theme - Energy** What do ocean waves and sound waves have in common? How are they different?

2. **Theme - Systems and Interactions** If the moon is full, what kind of tide would you expect? Why?

3. **A Closer Look** Why is the fresh water trapped in icebergs largely free from organic matter?

4. **Literature Connection** Read Rachel Carson's book, *The Sea Around Us.* How does Ms. Carson describe the chemistry of the sea?

CHAPTER 10

Organic
chemistry

✓ What gas is carried in that pipeline under your street?

✓ What causes the pain when you are bitten by an ant?

✓ What the difference is between a saturated and an unsaturated fat?

Science Journal

Before you begin to study about organic chemistry, think about these questions and answer them *in your Science Journal*. When you finish the chapter, compare your journal write-up with what you have learned.

Every day you wake up, get dressed, eat something, and head out the door. Maybe you listened to music on the radio. Do you ride a bus to school? Your nylon backpack holds your books, notebook paper, pens and pencils.

Is carbon a part of your life? Most things you come in contact with today involve carbon in some way. The clothes you wear, the food you eat, the fuel in the bus, the cassette tape you use to listen to music, even the basketball you play with are made of carbon compounds. Why is carbon found in so many different compounds? How can carbon be used to make fuels and foods? In this chapter you will learn about some carbon compounds and what they mean to you.

▶ *In the activity on the next page, explore one way that foods can be tested for carbon.*

Explore! ACTIVITY

How can you test for carbon?

Carbon is a part of many things including clothes, fuels, sporting equipment, and foods. Test some different foods for the presence of carbon.

What To Do

1. Take a small piece of marshmallow, tomato, bread, apple, and sugar.

2. Carefully heat each one separately in an open crucible, over a flame. The food will appear to change a couple of times. Keep heating until you do not see any more changes.

3. *In your Journal*, record what each substance looked like after it was heated.

10-1 Simple Organic Compounds

Section Objectives

- Describe structures of organic compounds and explain why carbon forms so many compounds.
- Distinguish between saturated and unsaturated hydrocarbons.
- Identify isomers of organic compounds.

Key Terms

organic compounds
hydrocarbon
isomers

Organic Compounds

Would you eat a piece of charcoal? If you have ever eaten a marshmallow, you might be surprised to learn that both marshmallows and charcoal contain the element carbon. Most substances that contain carbon are **organic compounds**. For years, scientists thought that living things were needed to make organic compounds. In 1828, a German scientist accidentally formed the organic compound urea from inorganic materials. This made other scientists realize that living organisms weren't always necessary to form organic compounds.

Today, the term organic is used to describe nearly all carbon-containing substances, whether or not they are found in living organisms. Most of the millions of different organic compounds that exist can be synthesized from carbon-containing raw materials such as wood, oil, natural gas, and coal.

You have already seen how you can turn simple substances, such as bread and apple, into carbon. How can you make other forms of carbon, such as charcoal?

  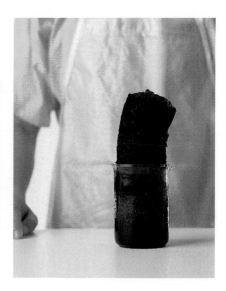

Figure 10-1

Ⓐ An interesting reaction occurs when concentrated sulfuric acid is poured into a beaker containing sugar, or sucrose.

Ⓑ How would you describe the reaction that is occurring?

Ⓒ Carbon is produced when sulfuric acid pulls the water out of sucrose. What happened to the water in this reaction?

How do you make charcoal from wood?

Although wood and charcoal appear different, they both contain carbon.

What To Do

1. Fill a clean, empty 1/4-pint varnish or paint can with sawdust from either a white pine or an oak.

2. Punch a small round hole (about 1/4" in diameter) through the center of the lid with a nail. Press the lid firmly in place and place the can on a hot plate.

3. Begin heating until white smoke comes out of the hole. Carefully light the smoke with a match until a yellow flame appears.

4. Continue heating until the flame disappears from the hole.

5. Turn off the hot plate and allow the can to cool overnight. Open the can the following day.

Conclude and Apply

1. What do you observe?

2. *In your Journal,* record what happened to the sawdust.

Carbon forms many different compounds because it has an atomic structure that allows it to combine with a tremendous number of different elements. A carbon atom has four electrons in its outer energy level. This electron arrangement means that the carbon atom can form four covalent bonds, as shown in **Figure 10-2**, with other carbon atoms or with atoms of other elements such as hydrogen and nitrogen.

In chapter 6 you learned that a covalent bond forms when two atoms share a pair of electrons. Carbon can form single, double, or triple covalent bonds with other atoms. Single covalent bonds contain one pair of shared electrons. Double bonds contain two shared electron pairs. Triple bonds contain three shared electron pairs.

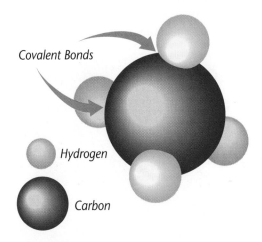

Covalent Bonds

Hydrogen

Carbon

Figure 10-2

This model of a carbon atom is bonded covalently with four hydrogen atoms. Is there a limit to the number of covalent bonds this carbon atom can form? Why or why not?

Hydrocarbons

Carbon atoms form an enormous number of compounds with hydrogen alone. A **hydrocarbon** is a compound that contains only carbon and hydrogen. Hydrocarbons form the basis for the structure and chemistry of a number of other organic compounds.

The shorter hydrocarbons are lighter molecules. In general, these compounds have low boiling points, and so they evaporate and burn more easily. This makes them useful as fuel gases. Longer hydrocarbons are heavy molecules that form solids or liquids at room temperature. They can be used as oils, waxes, or in asphalt.

Does the furnace, stove, or water heater in your home burn natural gas? This fuel, methane, is brought to homes through the pipeline underneath the street. Why do you suppose it's called natural gas?

Methane is the first and simplest member of the hydrocarbon family. Each line between atoms in a structural formula represents a single covalent bond. In methane, the carbon atom has four single covalent bonds to hydrogen atoms.

Other hydrocarbon molecules in this family are made by joining additional carbon and hydrogen atoms to methane. Every time another carbon atom is added, a new molecule is formed with its own set of properties.

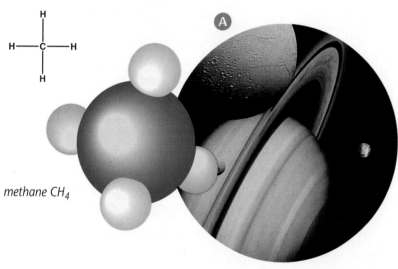

methane CH_4

Figure 10-3

Methane has been discovered on distant planets such as Saturn (A). On Earth, natural gas (B) is a fuel that is mostly methane, CH_4.

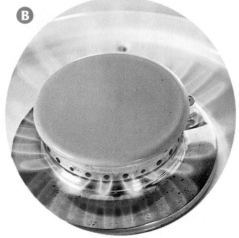

Figure 10-4

Ethane is formed by adding a -CH_2 group to methane. Compare the structural formulas of methane and ethane. In what ways are they similar?

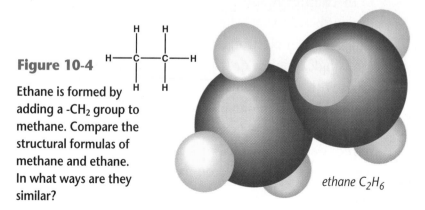

ethane C_2H_6

◼ Saturated Hydrocarbons

Methane, ethane, propane, and their cousins make up a family of molecules known as saturated hydrocarbons. A hydrocarbon that is saturated contains only single covalent bonds. What would be the chemical and structural formulas for the next members of the methane family? **Table 10-1** shows formulas for some saturated hydrocarbons.

Have you ever opened your refrigerator and wondered why some foods seem to spoil quickly? How can you find out how this process works?

Table 10-1

Hydrocarbon Series	
NAME	FORMULA
Methane	CH_4
Ethane	C_2H_6
Propane	C_3H_8
Butane	C_4H_{10}
Octane	C_8H_{18}

A saturated hydrocarbon can be described as one in which all carbon atoms are bonded to the maximum number of hydrogen atoms. Think about the structural formulas of these hydrocarbons. Are all of their carbon atoms bonded to the maximum number of hydrogen atoms?

Figure 10-5

Propane is another popular fuel that is often used to generate the heat that enables hot air balloons to rise. Propane is the third member of the methane family and has the chemical formula C_3H_8. How does propane differ from ethane?

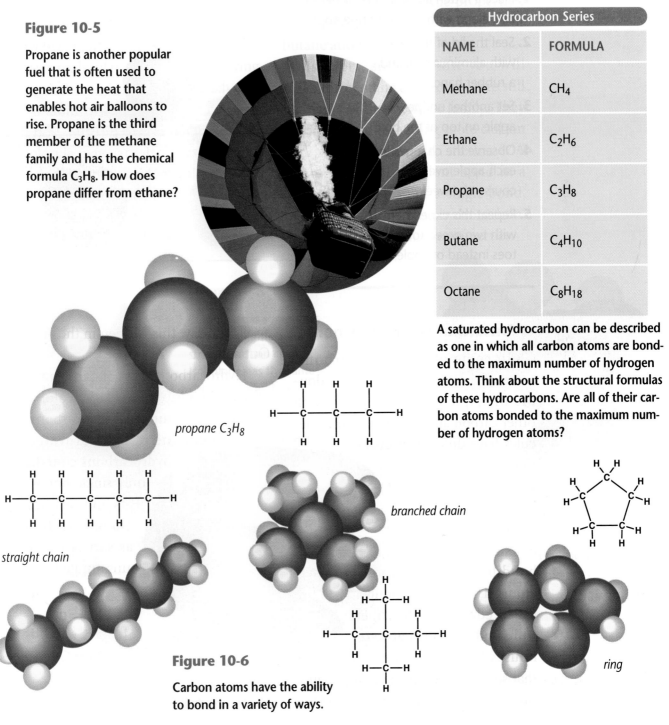

propane C_3H_8

straight chain

branched chain

ring

Figure 10-6

Carbon atoms have the ability to bond in a variety of ways.

Do pentane and hexane have isomers?

What To Do

1. Using gum drops for carbon atoms, raisins for hydrogen atoms, and toothpicks for covalent bonds, try to make a model of pentane, C_5H_{12}. Remember that each carbon atom must have four bonds, while each hydrogen atom can have only one bond.

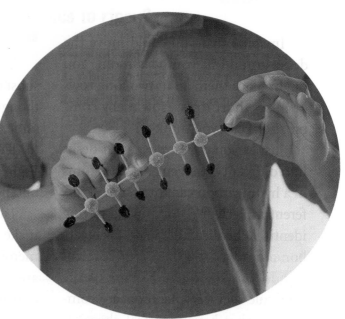

2. How many different models of pentane can you build?

3. Try to make a model of hexane, C_6H_{14}. Follow the same rules as for pentane.

4. How many different models can you build now?

Most hydrocarbons form isomers. Because the larger molecules have more carbon atoms they form more isomers. Octane, C_8H_{18}, the hydrocarbon used in gasoline, has 18 possible isomers. These isomers can have straight chains or branched chains.

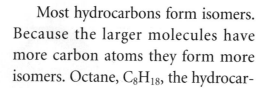

How Do We Know?

How are octane numbers assigned?

When fuel burns in an engine, small amounts of it will occasionally explode rather than burning evenly. These tiny explosions can be heard and are referred to as knocking. You might also notice that the car does not run as smoothly when knocking occurs. Fuels are rated on their ability to burn evenly, rather than explode. The rating is called the octane number.

Rating Fuels

Two compounds are used as standards in creating the scale for octane numbers. Isooctane, which resists knocking very well, is assigned an octane number of 100. Heptane, which knocks very badly, has an octane number of 0. The amount of knocking in a fuel is compared with a known mixture of these two compounds. For example, a sample of gasoline that knocks the same amount as a mixture of 90 percent isooctane and 10 percent heptane would have an octane number of 90. If a fuel knocks less than pure isooctane, it can have an octane number greater than 100. Gasoline pumps have an octane rating on them.

You may have heard of octane rating applied to gasoline. Octane rating does not measure the amount of octane in the fuel, but rather the tendency of fuel to knock. Knocking occurs when a fuel does not burn evenly.

Hydrocarbons directly affect you. The major source of energy in the world comes from chemicals made from organic compounds found in petroleum or natural gas. Over 90 percent of the energy used in homes, schools, industry, and transportation comes from methane and the other hydrocarbons. Products ranging from fertilizer to skateboards are manufactured from hydrocarbons. Can hydrocarbons be used to make more complicated molecules? In the next section, you will learn how three special types of organic compounds are synthesized from hydrocarbons.

SKILLBUILDER

Making and Using Graphs

Make a graph of the information in Table 10-1. For each compound, plot the number of carbon atoms on one axis and the number of hydrogen atoms on the other axis. Use this graph to predict the formula for the saturated hydrocarbon that has 11 carbon atoms. If you need help, refer to the **Skill Handbook** on page 681.

Figure 10-9

Each of the different kinds of gasoline is given an octane rating. You can see the octane ratings, 92, 87, and 89, in this photo.

check your UNDERSTANDING

1. Why can carbon form so many different organic compounds?
2. How is an unsaturated hydrocarbon different from a saturated hydrocarbon?
3. How many isomers can you make from heptane, C_7H_{16}?

4. **Apply** Cyclopropane is a saturated hydrocarbon containing three carbon atoms. In this compound, each carbon atom is bonded to two other carbon atoms. Draw its structural formula. Are cyclopropane and propane isomers? Explain.

10-2

Other Organic Compounds

Section Objectives

- Classify substituted hydrocarbons as belonging to the alcohol, carboxylic acid, or amine family.
- Describe the structure of an alcohol, a carboxylic acid, and an amine.
- Draw the structural formula for the simplest alcohol, carboxylic acid, and amine.

Key Terms

alcohol
carboxylic acid
amines

Substituted Hydrocarbons

Usually a cheeseburger is a hamburger covered with American cheese and served on a bun. However, you can make a cheeseburger with Swiss cheese and serve it on slices of rye bread. If you ate this cheeseburger, you would notice that the substitutions affected the taste.

Explore! ACTIVITY

Can you make new models from your hexane structures?

What To Do

1. Make a gumdrop/raisin/toothpick model for hexane.

2. Remove a hydrogen raisin and replace it with a mini marshmallow.

3. Then exchange the marshmallow with a raisin already on your model.

4. Replace another raisin with a gummy candy.

5. Make as many different models as you can.

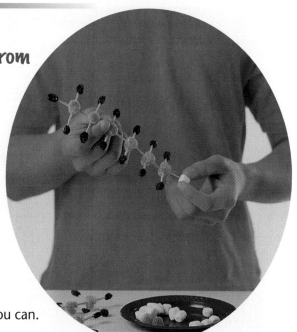

Chemists make similar changes to organic compounds. These changes produce compounds called substituted hydrocarbons. A substituted hydrocarbon has had one or more of its hydrogen atoms replaced by atoms or groups of atoms of other elements.

In the Explore activity, you substituted marshmallows and gummy candy for the raisin/hydrogen in the gumdrop/hexane model. Substituting even one new chemical group on a hydrocarbon forms an entirely new class of compounds with chemical properties different from those of the original compound. Sometimes two or more chemical groups can replace hydrogen atoms. You can imagine how complicated these new molecules can become. This is why millions of organic compounds exist in our world.

■ Alcohols

Ethanol, shown in **Figure 10-10A**, is an example of an alcohol. **Alcohol** is the name of a family of compounds formed when a hydroxyl (-OH) group replaces one or more hydrogen atoms in a hydrocarbon. Ethanol is produced naturally by sugar fermenting in corn, grains, and fruits. You will learn more about mixing ethanol with gasoline to fuel cars.

Table 10-2 lists some common alcohols and their uses.

Table 10-2

	METHANOL $$H \atop H-C-OH \atop H$$	ETHANOL $$H \quad H \atop H-C-C-OH \atop H \quad H$$	ISOPROPYL ALCOHOL $$H \quad OH \quad H \atop H-C-C-C-H \atop H \quad H \quad H$$
Some Common Alcohols			
Uses			
Fuel	√	√	
Cleaner	√	√	√
Disinfectant		√	√
Manufacturing chemicals	√		√

ethanol C₂H₅OH

Figure 10-10

A Alcohol is a compound that contains oxygen in the form of hydroxyl groups. Some alcohols contain more than one hydroxyl group. Is ethanol an alcohol that contains more than one hydroxyl group?

methanoic acid

■ Carboxylic Acid

If you have ever tasted salad dressing made with too much vinegar, you probably made a face because of the sour taste. Acetic acid in vinegar causes that sour taste.

A **carboxylic acid** is formed when a -CH₃ group is displaced by a carboxyl (-COOH) group. The simplest carboxylic acid is methanoic acid or

B Methanoic acid, also called formic acid, is an example of a carboxylic acid. The carbon has a double bond to the oxygen atom, a single bond to the hydroxyl (-OH) group, and a single bond to what remains of the original hydrocarbon molecule. Some ants have a gland that makes formic acid, which is connected to a powerful stinger at the end of their abdomen.

formic acid, as seen in **Figure 10-10B**. This acid is made by ants and is injected into your skin and causes pain when an ant bites you.

■ Amines

In another group of substituted hydrocarbons, nitrogen forms covalent bonds with the carbon and hydrogen in the molecule. When the amine group, $-NH_2$, replaces the hydrogen in a hydrocarbon, organic compounds called **amines** are formed.

Methylamine, CH_3NH_2, shown in **Figure 10-11**, is the simplest amine. Have you ever been given novocaine at a dentist's office? Do you take vitamins that include niacin? Does your soft drink contain caffeine? These are all hydrocarbons substituted with nitrogen.

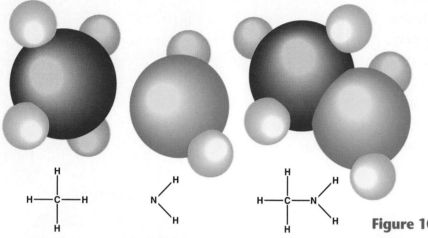

methane   amine group   methylamine

Figure 10-11

Methylamine, CH_3NH_2, is formed when an amine group ($-NH_2$) replaces a hydrogen in methane.

Organic Motor Fuels

Did you know that about 90 percent of the total United States energy needs are met by fossil fuels, such as oil and natural gas?

Oil, of course, is used for a variety of purposes, from plastics production to the food manufacturing industry. One of the most important uses of oil is as a fuel to power the engines of automobiles and other forms of transportation.

Fossil Fuels

As you know, fossil fuels are considered to be nonrenewable energy sources. In other words, once they have been used up, they're gone forever. Right now, we are using up fossil fuels much faster than can be replaced by Earth. What fuels will power the engines of the transportation vehicles of the future?

Since the energy crisis of the 1970s, scientists have been working on the development of new sources of energy, especially ones that can be used to power engines.

Gasohol

Did you ever see a sign like the one pictured here? Gasohol is a combination of the alcohol ethanol and gasoline. The gasohol used currently contains about 90 percent gasoline and

■ Amino Acids

As well as being in novocaine, niacin, and caffeine, amines occur in many other biological compounds. A special type of amine-substituted hydrocarbon forms when both the -NH₂ group and the -COOH group replace hydrogens on the same molecule. This type of compound is called an amino acid, which is a building block for the formation of proteins. You may have eaten an amino acid lately if you like gelatin desserts.

Many organic compounds are composed of different combinations of carbon, hydrogen, oxygen, and nitrogen atoms. You have already learned about alcohols, carboxylic acids, and amines. Can one of these types of hydrocarbons be converted into another?

Glycine

amine group   acid group

Figure 10-12

Gelatin desserts contain glycine, an amino acid. Amino acids are a key ingredient of proteins. Why are proteins important to you?

---

10 percent ethanol. As you recall, ethanol is the substituted hydrocarbon found in all alcoholic beverages.

Gasohol has many advantages over gasoline. Ethanol is produced commercially by the fermentation of potatoes, sugar cane, and grains, such as corn and wheat. Because it is produced from plant materials, ethanol is considered to be a renewable energy source.

Another advantage of using gasohol is that most car engines do not have to be modified to burn the gasohol manufactured today. In fact, car engines can be made to burn pure ethanol, and engineers are working hard to design engines that can use ethanol efficiently.

What Do You Think?

Clearly, we need to develop new sources of fuel for our transportation vehicles. Gasohol shows some promise as an alternative fuel, but there are some disadvantages to gasohol as well. Commercial production of ethanol results in numerous environmental problems. Among these are disruption of the ecosystem, fertilizer runoff, and erosion. Do you think gasohol is an answer to our fossil fuel problems? Explain your answers.

A New Compound from Alcohol

Natural substances, such as air or bacteria, can cause changes in alcohols. A bottle of wine containing ethanol can sometimes be spoiled by such a natural chemical process. This chemical conversion can be demonstrated in this activity.

Problem

What new compound can be formed from an alcohol?

Materials

test tube and stopper	3 drops of ethanol
1 mL potassium permanganate solution	goggles
	apron
	pH test paper
1 mL sodium hydroxide solution	graduated cylinder

Safety Precautions

Wear safety goggles and an apron when working with chemicals.

Be careful when working with potassium permanganate and sodium hydroxide.

Dispose of materials properly.

What To Do

1 *Measure* and pour 1 mL of potassium permanganate solution and 1 mL of sodium hydroxide solution into a test tube. **CAUTION:** *Handle both of these chemicals with care; immediately flush any spill with water and call your teacher.*

2 Test the sample with pH paper (see photo **A**). Record the result *in your Journal.*

3 Add three drops of ethanol to the test tube (see photo **B**).

A

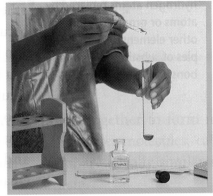

B

C

4 Stopper the test tube and gently shake it for one minute.

5 Observe what happens in the test tube. *In your Journal*, record any changes you notice for the next five minutes.

6 Test the sample with pH paper again. Record your observation.

7 Dispose of solutions as directed by the teacher.

Analyzing

1. What is the chemical formula for ethanol?

2. What part of a molecule identifies a compound as an alcohol?

3. What part of a molecule identifies a compound as a carboxylic acid?

Concluding and Applying

4. What would lead you to *infer* that a chemical change took place in the test tube?

5. In the presence of potassium permanganate, an alcohol may undergo a chemical change into an acid. If the alcohol used is ethanol, what would you *predict* to be the chemical formula of the acid produced?

6. Going Further The acid from ethanol is found in a common household product. What is the acid's name? In what common household product is the acid found? What happens to a bottle of wine that undergoes this change?

Lipids

What do butter, margarine, the oil part of salad dressings, and some vitamins have in common? They are all included in the third major type of biological compound called a lipid. **Lipids** are organic compounds that

Explore! ACTIVITY

How can you tell a fat from an oil?

What To Do

1. Obtain small samples of butter, soybean oil, margarine, olive oil, and solid shortening. Observe them at room temperature.

2. *In your Journal,* list which ones have similar properties.

Life Science CONNECTION

Poisonous Proteins

The next time you visit the zoo to learn about the exotic animals, you just might want to bring along a chemistry book! Why?

Biological Compounds

In this chapter, you learned that living organisms are made of the biological compounds—proteins, carbohydrates, and lipids. As you know, these compounds are important for the metabolic processes of cells. Cell structures are made primarily of proteins, and lipids and carbohydrates are important for the functioning of cells. Lipids and carbohydrates provide energy for cells.

Biotoxins

It's clear that if the cells of organisms did not manufacture proteins from amino acids, organisms couldn't stay alive. But would you believe that there are many animals and plants that produce proteins that can mean immediate death for other organisms? Such proteins are organic poisons that are known as biotoxins, and they are produced and used by animals, plants, fungi, and bacteria for defense against predators and for obtaining food.

The reptile house at the zoo is a great place to learn about animals that produce biotoxins. Many species of snakes, includ-

feel greasy and will not dissolve in water. Fats, oils, waxes, and related compounds make up this group of biological compounds.

Although lipids contain the same elements—carbon, hydrogen, and oxygen—that carbohydrates do, they are put together in different proportions. Lipids are a more concentrated source of energy for the body than carbohydrates. They provide twice as much energy per gram as carbohydrates.

Have you ever heard that eating too much saturated fat can be unhealthy? Fats and oils are classified as saturated or unsaturated according to the types of bonds in their carbon chains. Let's test for the presence of fats and starches in various foods.

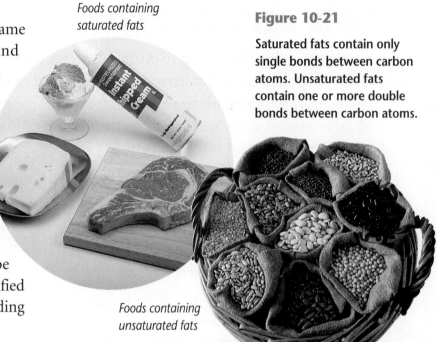

Foods containing saturated fats

Foods containing unsaturated fats

Figure 10-21

Saturated fats contain only single bonds between carbon atoms. Unsaturated fats contain one or more double bonds between carbon atoms.

---

ing North American snakes, produce a substance called venom. Some types, similar to the snake shown in the photo at the left, are more poisonous to humans than others.

Snake Venom

Scientists know more about the chemical makeup of snake venom than any other animal biotoxin. Proteins in snake venom are of a special group called enzymes. Enzymes are large and complex protein molecules that work by breaking down other organic molecules. The most common protein in snake venom is an enzyme called cholinesterase, which disrupts the functioning of the nervous system.

The most poisonous land snake in the world is the tiger snake from Australia, shown in the photo at the right. Tiger snake venom is extremely poisonous. It only takes about one-half a milligram of tiger snake venom to kill an adult human.

Science Journal

Besides snakes, many other species of animals, including insects, frogs, toads, and fish, produce biotoxins. More is known about snake venom for two reasons. First, scientists are able to obtain more venom from snakes than biotoxins from other animals.

More importantly, the enzymes in snake venom are important for the development of drugs to treat illness. *In your Science Journal,* describe how you suppose studying the proteins found in snake venom can help scientists develop new types of drugs.

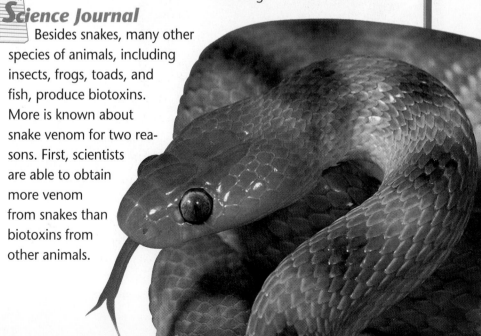

Fats and Starches

Simple tests can be performed to discover whether carbohydrates and fats are present in foods. Foods that contain starches turn dark blue when a drop of iodine solution is placed on them. When rubbed on brown paper, foods that contain fats leave a grease spot. Not all experiments require beakers and test tubes. Part of this experiment can be done using a paper grocery sack.

Preparation

Problem

Does a food contain starch? Does a food contain fat?

Form a Hypothesis

Work with your group to predict if a food item contains starch, fat, or both.

Objectives

- Predict which foods contain starch and which contain fat.
- Use lab techniques to test each food to determine the presence of starch and fat.

Materials

paper grocery sack	raw potato slice
iodine solution	cooked bacon
in dropper bottle	cheese
marker	cracker
scissors	cooked egg
liquid cooking oil	white
bread	potato chip

Safety

Be careful working with iodine; it is poisonous.

Never eat food used in a laboratory experiment. Dispose of all food after your experiment.

Plan the Experiment

1 Examine the food samples provided by your teacher.

2 How can you use information from the opening paragraph to help you plan your experiment?

3 Liquid cooking oil is a fat. Bread contains starch. Testing these foods will result in a positive test. Can they be used as comparisons?

4 Write the procedure that you will use to test your hypothesis.

Check the Plan

1 What is your control or test substance? Be sure you can recognize a positive test.

2 How will you compare your results to your predictions? Do you have a graph or data table ready?

3 Before you do your experiment, have your teacher check your plan.

Analyze and Conclude

1. Observe and Infer What evidence did you have that fat was present in the food? What evidence did you have that starch was present in the food?

2. Analyze Were your predictions accurate? How did your experiment confirm or deny your hypothesis?

 3. Use Computers Design a spreadsheet that could be used in place of the paper sack as the testing area. Would computer paper work as well for showing the grease spot?

Going Further

Obtain samples of cosmetics and test them for starches and fats.

■ Cholesterol

Besides saturated fats, animal foods contain another lipid called cholesterol. Do you know that even if you never eat foods containing cholesterol, your body will still make its own supply? Cholesterol is needed by your body to build cell membranes and is also found in bile, a fluid made by the liver and needed for digestion. Too much cholesterol is not good and can result in a buildup of cholesterol in arteries.

We have discussed three important classes of biological compounds: proteins, carbohydrates, and lipids. Many of these compounds are very long and complicated polymers. Carbohydrates and lipids are in foods that provide energy for the body. Proteins are present in every living substance and are needed in food for growth and to renew the body. Each of these compounds exists because of carbon's ability to form covalent bonds with other atoms such as oxygen or nitrogen.

Figure 10-22

Foods high in cholesterol (A) can contribute to a buildup of cholesterol in an artery (B). What dangers are posed when cholesterol builds up and clings to walls of the arteries?

check your UNDERSTANDING

1. How are polymers formed?
2. Name some examples of biological compounds. Where are they found?
3. What do proteins, carbohydrates, and lipids in the foods you eat provide for your body?

4. **Apply** Unlike animals, plants cannot digest the foods necessary to form biological compounds. Explain how plants make the biological compounds they need.

Technology Connection

The Discovery of DNA Structure

Almost everyone has heard of DNA today, but in the 1950s, DNA structure was a mystery. In fact, one of the major scientific events of the 20th century was the discovery of the structure of DNA. Much of the research that led to this discovery was based on the work of an English scientist, Rosalind Elsie Franklin.

X-ray Crystallography

From 1947 to 1950, Franklin studied the basics of a technique called X-ray crystallography. In X-ray crystallography, X rays are sent through a substance to find out how atoms are arranged. She used this technique to research changes in the arrangement of carbon atoms when coal is heated. Her work was invaluable to the coking and atomic technology industries.

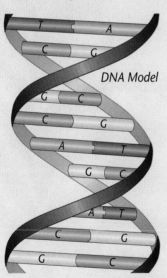

DNA Model

In 1951, Franklin applied X-ray crystallography techniques to the study of DNA. She is credited with discovering the density of DNA and its double-strand structure. She died of cancer at the age of 37.

DNA Structure

Using Franklin's invaluable discoveries, other scientists continued the study of DNA. They started their work knowing that DNA is a large molecule composed of a sugar and phosphate groups linked in long chains plus nitrogen-containing compounds called bases. They did not know, however, how all these components fit together.

With further use of X-ray crystallography, James D. Watson, Francis Crick, and Maurice Wilkins, discovered the exact structure of DNA. Watson, Crick, and Wilkins received the Nobel Prize for this discovery in 1962. Franklin's early discoveries paved the way for the work that continues to expand our knowledge of human genetic material.

What Do You Think?

Do you always work straight through a problem from beginning to end? Did you ever wake up in the middle of the night knowing just how to solve a problem? Can you draw any conclusions from these experiences about how the mind works?

Science *and* Society

Pile It On!

Do you have a compost pile in your backyard? Compost is one of the best fertilizers available to gardeners and is free for the making. In fact, compost has been produced for eons without any help from people. Before farmers and homeowners began moving things around, leaves and weeds fell on the ground, rotted there, and provided a constant source of food for growing plants. Without knowing it, landowners created an ideal environment for encouraging growth. When we rake leaves, plant grass, and pull weeds and throw them away, we break that natural cycle.

Some are higher in carbon, such as twigs, sawdust, dried leaves, and hay. Others are higher in nitrogen, such as green grass clippings, kitchen vegetable waste, and animal by-products. The ratio of carbon to nitrogen

Composting

Composting is the process of breaking down waste material and changing it into useful products. The main ingredients in compost are carbon and nitrogen. All plant materials contain both of these elements.

determines how quickly the waste will be turned into useful fertilizer. Most materials have more carbon than nitrogen, so adding nitrogen makes the process go faster. A pile of sawdust, which is mostly carbon, can take years to break down, but if you mix the sawdust with green grass and animal manure, it will turn into rich compost in a matter of several months.

Anaerobic and Aerobic Composting

The process of composting is done in two ways. Anaerobic composting (without air) is done in closed bins. By keeping the air out, you are able to prevent the loss of valuable nitrogen. Nitrogen is necessary for all plant growth and is the main ingredient in most fertilizers. With this kind of composting, methane gas is produced and can then be used as a fuel for heating or lighting. Many small farms use this free source of fuel gained from anaerobic composting.

Most composting, however, is done aerobically (with air). The materials are piled in bins or simply in piles and turned occasionally to let the air circulate through and speed up the decomposition process. Heat is produced from the chemical reaction that makes the compost.

Benefits

In either method of composting, the result is nitrogen-rich soil that will feed your plants and encourage them to grow. Addition of many different kinds of materials to your compost heap will also add beneficial minerals, such as calcium, phosphates, and potash.

Composting is also one of the easiest and most beneficial ways everyone can protect the environment. Many communities now have laws that prohibit yard waste from being put in landfills. It takes up space and is wasteful! Instead of throwing all these valuable resources away, you can easily return them to nature to help the trees, grass, flowers, and vegetables grow healthier and faster.

*inter*NET
CONNECTION

Visit the New Brunswick Community and Environmental Education website to find out more details about building and using a compost pile. What materials will you need to build and operate a compost pile? What compost materials should you avoid? How does a compost pile change over time?

Teens in SCIENCE

Cleaning up Earth

Teenagers may be more environmentally sensitive than their parents were at the same age. They know that the world they are inheriting needs cleaning up. Individuals and groups such as bands, scouts, and science clubs routinely gather up recyclable materials and raise money by taking them to recycling centers. Many others are going even farther to clean up the environment.

Testing River Water

Teenagers from Quincy High School in Illinois monitor the Mississippi River for pollutants. They use tests that show levels of dissolved oxygen. If there is a low level of oxygen, life in the river suffers. The students are working directly with The Illinois Rivers Project to make sure that the river is clean and that those who use the water do so responsibly.

Roland Ng

When eighteen years old, Roland Ng of Tracy, California, headed up a recycling project that collected throw-aways—cans, bottles, and paper all over town. Roland coaches a team of seven year olds at the Boys and Girls Club in Tracy, and uses the money earned from recycling to buy basketballs and other sports equipment for the children.

Using Computers

Contact the recycling centers in your area. Do they take aluminum, glass, plastic, and paper? Record your data on a computer spreadsheet. Start recycling materials from your own home.

CAREER connection

Environmental scientists have many options. They monitor bodies of water, air, and industry for possible pollutants. They research ways to control or eliminate pollutants. They work for government agencies, industry, or have their own consulting or research businesses.

CLEAN GLASS ONLY

Science Journal

Review the statements below about the big ideas presented in this chapter, and answer the questions. Then, reread your answers to the Did You Ever Wonder questions at the beginning of the chapter. *In your Science Journal*, write a paragraph about how your understanding of the big ideas in the chapter has changed.

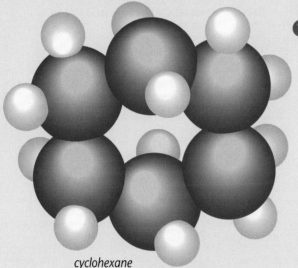

cyclohexane

1 Carbon's unique ability to form four covalent bonds with other atoms enables it to make a huge number of compounds. *How does the structure of a compound determine its properties?*

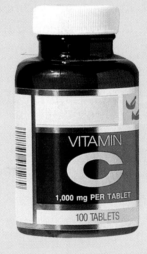

2 Hydrocarbons can be composed of hydrogen and carbon alone, or other chemical groups may be substituted for hydrogen on the molecule to form new compounds, as with vitamin C. *Compared and contrast the three types of substituted hydrocarbons.*

3 Biological compounds are complex compounds that make up living things. Your body needs the proteins, carbohydrates, and lipids that are found in food to provide energy and to repair or replace cells. *What are two examples of foods that provide protein? Carbohydrates? Lipids?*

Using Key Science Terms

alcohol   isomers
amines   lipids
carbohydrates   organic compound
carboxylic acid polymers
hydrocarbon   proteins

For each set of terms below, choose the one term that does not belong and explain why it does not belong.

1. alcohol, amines, carboxylic acid
2. hydrocarbon, alcohol, amines
3. polymers, alcohol, amines
4. proteins, lipids, isomers

Understanding Ideas

Answer the following questions in your Journal using complete sentences.

1. Name three types of substituted hydrocarbons.

2. If a carbohydrate has 16 oxygen atoms, how many hydrogen atoms does it have?
3. Do you expect hexane or butane to have a higher boiling point? Explain.

4. Monomers of which type make up a protein polymer?
5. A healthy diet includes lipids, proteins, and carbohydrates. What is the recommended percentage of calories in your diet from each of these three groups?

Developing Skills

Use your understanding of the concepts developed in this chapter to answer each of the following questions.

1. **Making and Using Graphs** - The boiling points of ethane, propane, butane, and hexane are as follows:
   ethane -89°C   butane -1°C
   propane -42°C   hexane 69°C
   Make a graph of the data. Plot the number of carbon atoms on the x-axis and the boiling point on the y-axis. Use your graph to estimate the boiling point of pentane.

2. **Classifying** - For each of the following tell whether the compound given is an alcohol, amine, or carboxylic acid:
   a. C_3H_7OH
   b. CH_3CH_2COOH
   c. $CH_3CH_2NH_2$
   d. CH_3OH
   e. $C_8H_{17}COOH$

3. **Comparing and Contrasting** - Repeat the test for protein in the Explore activity on page 322 using different foods. Use a piece of apple, a peanut, and a kidney bean. Compare the results of this activity with those made in the original activity.

Critical Thinking

In your Journal, *answer each of the following questions.*

1. Compare and contrast saturated and unsaturated fats.
2. Why do butane and isobutane have different properties?
3. How does an amino acid differ from a carboxylic acid?
4. Describe the substitution process in which butane changes to butyl alcohol.

Problem Solving

Read the following problem and discuss your answers in a brief paragraph.

Maria bought some green, unripe bananas at the store. She needs to make a banana cake tomorrow but the bananas are too green to mash. She wants to eat some bananas during the week.

1. What can she do to help the bananas for the cake ripen faster between now and tomorrow?
2. What can she do to keep the bananas she wants to eat from ripening too quickly?

CONNECTING IDEAS

Discuss each of the following in a brief paragraph.

1. **Theme—Scale and Structure** Octane number is used as a measure of a gasoline's ability to burn evenly. The higher the octane number for a gasoline, the less likely it is to cause an engine to knock or ping when driving. Look at the diagram. It shows three types of gasolines and their octane numbers. What do you think is the relationship between even burning and molecular structure?

a. Heptane 0

b. 2-methylheptane 23

c. 2,2,4-trimethylpentane 100

2. **Theme—Energy** One gram of a lipid yields about 9 calories in energy, while one gram of a carbohydrate only yields 4 calories. If lipids produce more energy than carbohydrates, why shouldn't they make up the larger part of a healthful diet?

3. **Life Science Connection** What are biotoxins, and of what organic molecules are many of them composed?

4. **Science and Society** Describe some of the benefits of composting.

FUELING the BODY

✓ **How long someone could live without food?**

✓ **Why your stomach makes noises when you're hungry?**

✓ **How large the area of your small intestine is?**

Science Journal

Before you begin to study about fueling the body, think about these questions and answer them *in your Science Journal*. When you finish the chapter, compare your journal write-up with what you have learned.

W elcome to Blanca Hidalgo's garden. Those red-ripe tomatoes soon will find their way into a spicy salsa. The carrots and zucchini will become part of a fresh vegetable salad. And those onions and peppers will add zip to tonight's tacos.

Animals benefit from Blanca's garden too. Pesky crows swoop down to sample the ripening corn. A rabbit nibbles at the lettuce and aphids suck juices from the tomato stems.

All living things—from the largest animal to the tiniest cell—require nourishment. In this chapter you will learn about the fuel your body needs and how your body processes that fuel to keep you healthy!

▶ ***In the Explore activity you will learn about different diets that people eat.***

How is your diet different from that of your classmates?

Not everyone eats the same kinds of food. You have favorite foods, foods you tolerate, and foods you do not care for at all.

What To Do

1. Make a list of the foods you eat most often at home. Be honest about your snacking habits, too.

2. Compare your list with your classmates'.

3. What foods are common to everyone's lists?

4. What foods are different?

5. What foods are on your classmates' lists that you would be willing to try?

Six Important Nutrients

In Chapter 10, you were introduced to the chemistry of organic compounds, including proteins and carbohydrates. These are just two of the six nutrients your body needs to function properly. The other nutrients are fats, vitamins, minerals, and water. Fats and vitamins are also organic compounds because they contain carbon atoms. Water and minerals are inorganic compounds. They contain no carbon atoms.

Look at the size and complexity of the diagrams of water, carbohydrate, and protein in **Figure 11-3**. What do you notice?

Carbohydrates, fats, and proteins in foods are usually in a form that must be broken down into simpler molecules before they can be absorbed and used by your body. In contrast, smaller molecules, such as water, vitamins, and minerals, are absorbed quickly.

Protein

Water

Carbohydrate

Figure 11-3

Organic molecules, such as protein and carbohydrate, are large and more complex than inorganic molecules, such as water.

Explore! ACTIVITY

How nutritious is one breakfast cereal?

What To Do

1. Look again at the list of nutrients on the cereal box label in Figure 11-1.

2. Which of the six nutrients does the cereal contain?

3. How much of each nutrient is present in the cereal? Nutrients are measured in grams and milligrams.

4. To get a better idea of just how much of each nutrient is present, measure out a gram of salt or sugar for comparison.

5. What vitamins are present? In what amounts?

6. What minerals are present?

7. Which of the nutrients will be absorbed most quickly by your body? Why?

■ Water

Water is a critical nutrient for life. Your body might function for weeks on limited amounts of food. But without water, your body would remain alive only for a few days.

Why is water so important? All of the cells of your body are mostly water. All chemical reactions and other cellular functions take place in the cell's cytoplasm, a substance that is primarily water.

Explore! ACTIVITY

How much of you is water?

Believe it or not, by weight, your body is nearly two-thirds water. Generally, when a person diets, the first pounds lost are actually pounds of water.

What To Do

1. To figure out how much of you is water, multiply your weight by 66 percent.

2. What figure do you get? Record your answer *in your Journal.*

Figure 11-4

Why do you drink liquid when you feel thirsty? Your body is trying to maintain a balanced internal condition. Exercise, perspiration, and urination deplete your body's supply of water. Messages are sent to your brain and you feel thirsty. After you replenish your water supply, more messages are sent to your brain and you no longer feel thirsty.

Figure 11-5

Your body cells all contain water. The amount of water in the cells depends on the type of tissue they make up.

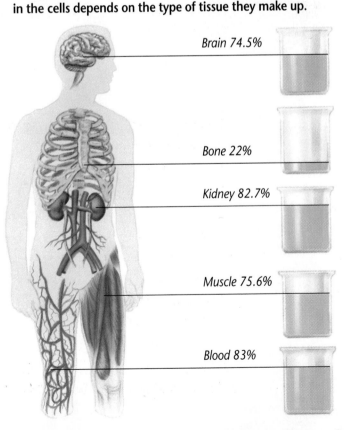

Brain 74.5%

Bone 22%

Kidney 82.7%

Muscle 75.6%

Blood 83%

■ Minerals

Like water, minerals are also important nutrients for your body. Salt is a mineral, and minerals come from Earth. **Minerals** are inorganic compounds that regulate many of the chemical reactions that take place in your body. But why is your body composed of molecules from Earth?

Some scientists hypothesize that all life on Earth began in the sea. The sea is rich in minerals, so it makes sense that organisms that began life in this "mineral soup" are mineral-rich themselves. In fact, the water in your body contains dissolved minerals that make it chemically similar to the water in the ocean.

Of all the elements listed in the periodic table, your body requires about 14 to regulate its chemical reactions. These include calcium, phosphorous, sodium, potassium, magnesium, and iron. They are required by your body in small amounts. A deficiency in any one mineral, however small, can result in disease such as osteoporosis or goiter.

Figure 11-6 shows some of the most important minerals your body needs, how they function in your body, and which foods contain them. Look back at the chart of foods you've been eating during the past week. Is your body being provided with the minerals it needs?

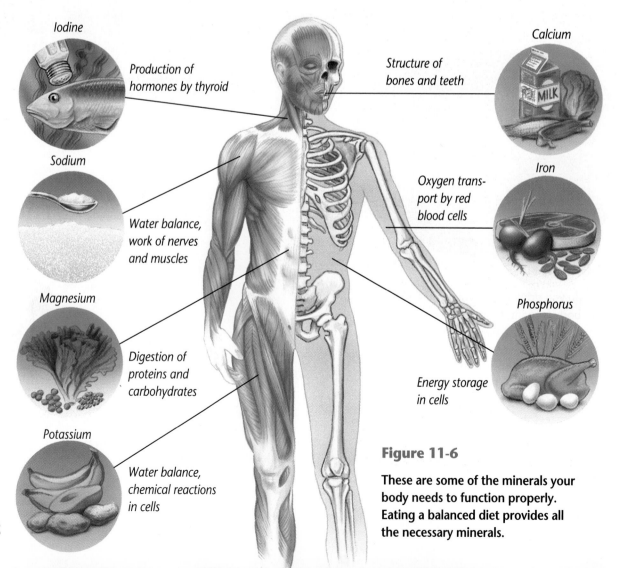

Iodine — Production of hormones by thyroid

Sodium — Water balance, work of nerves and muscles

Magnesium — Digestion of proteins and carbohydrates

Potassium — Water balance, chemical reactions in cells

Structure of bones and teeth — Calcium

Oxygen transport by red blood cells — Iron

Energy storage in cells — Phosphorus

Figure 11-6

These are some of the minerals your body needs to function properly. Eating a balanced diet provides all the necessary minerals.

342

■ Carbohydrates

The next time you come home from school feeling tired, do what the nutrition pros do for an energy boost. Eat a potato, a dish of three-bean salad, or a plate of spaghetti. All of these foods contain carbohydrates. Carbohydrates are organic compounds and are the main source of energy for most organisms.

Carbohydrates come in three forms: sugars, starches, and cellulose. Sugar is a simple carbohydrate. Sugar comes in many forms, including glucose, dextrose, fructose, corn syrup, and molasses. Energy that you use for all your body's activities is released from simple carbohydrates when they are broken down in your cells.

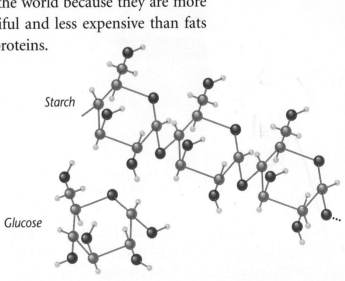

Explore! ACTIVITY

Which foods contain carbohydrates?

What To Do

1. Look at the nutrition labels on the packages of ten foods that you eat often, such as frozen pizza, pasta, orange juice, bread, and so on.
2. Which foods contain carbohydrates?
3. How many total grams of carbohydrates does a serving contain?

Starches, found in foods such as pasta, potatoes, and cassava root are complex carbohydrates. So is cellulose, the tough fiber that makes up the cell walls in plants. Complex carbohydrates are made up of large molecules that have to be broken down into smaller forms, simple carbohydrates, before they can be used by your body. Complex carbohydrates, especially grains, are important foods in diets all over the world because they are more plentiful and less expensive than fats and proteins.

Figure 11-7

Carbohydrates are the main source of energy for you and other animals. Sugars that are found in carbohydrates can be used almost immediately by your body and help to fulfill your short-term energy needs. How do the starches found in carbohydrates help fulfill your long-term energy needs?

Starch

Glucose

■ Fats

Fats are large organic molecules—some larger than carbohydrates. Like carbohydrates, fats are broken down to release energy to fuel your body. In fact, fats release more energy per molecule than carbohydrates do. Usually, however, you get your energy from carbohydrates because they make up the largest part of your diet. Only in an emergency, when your supply of carbohydrates is low, does your body turn to its fat reserves for energy.

The next time you're in your kitchen, open the refrigerator and see just how "fat" it is. Chances are you'll see some butter, margarine, or cheese in there. All of these foods contain fats. Solid vegetable shortening, corn oil, and olive oil are fats too. In addition, fats are present in meat, nuts, ice cream and cookies.

■ How Much Fat?

Just how much fat do you need? Most nutritionists thought that 30 percent of your calories should come from fats. Today, some think that figure should be 20 percent or lower. Your body does need some fat. Excess fat contributes to becoming overweight, and saturated fats—found in meat, dairy products, and some tropical oils—increase the risk of heart and artery disease. The result may be a narrowing of the arteries, preventing an adequate blood supply from reaching the heart muscle. Unsaturated fats, found in vegetable oils, are much more healthy.

Making and Using Tables

As you learn about the six nutrients needed by your body, organize this information into a table that lists each nutrient, its sources, and its nutritional value. If you need help, refer to the **Skill Handbook** on page 680.

Figure 11-8

More than 75% Calories from fat	40-50% Calories from fat	Less than 20% Calories from fat
1 medium avocado - 31 g	1/2 cup ice cream - 7g	1 medium white fish - 1g

An avocado contains unsaturated fat, while ice cream and white fish contain saturated fat. The percentage and type of fat in a food needs to be considered in determining how good it is for your body.

What percentage of the calories you consume comes from fat?

You can use a simple mathematical formula to calculate your fat intake from certain foods. You can find the information that you need to know on nutrition labels, such as the total number of Calories per serving and the total grams of fat per serving.

What To Do

1. Suppose that you're eating one serving of breakfast cereal. One serving has 65 Calories and 1 gram of fat.

2. To find out what percentage of your breakfast Calories comes from fat, multiply the grams of fat by 9. There are 9 Calories in each gram of fat. Then divide the result by the total Calories:

    $1 \times 9 = 9$

    $9 \div 65 = 0.1384$, or 14 percent

3. Is your breakfast a healthful one? What makes you think so?

Conclude and Apply

1. Suppose you ate cheesecake that has 300 Calories and 25 grams of fat. What percentage of the Calories comes from fat?

2. Is this a healthful food choice? Explain your answer?

■ Protein

How do you feel about insects? If you're like most people, the fewer insects you see, the better. In some cultures, however, insects play an important role in diet. You'd probably be surprised to learn that in parts of Africa, for example, termites are considered quite a delicacy. African termites are much larger than those found in the United States, and they are enjoyed both fresh and fried.

Why termites? Well, termites are an important source of protein. Termites are just about 50 percent protein. Protein is an organic compound containing nitrogen that is used throughout the body for growth and to replace and repair cells. Proteins are the building blocks of body tissue.

You learned in Chapter 10 that proteins are composed of long chains of molecules called amino acids. Your body requires twenty different kinds of amino acids. Twelve of these amino acids, called nonessential amino acids, can be made in the cells in your body. The other eight, called essential amino acids, have to be supplied by the food you eat.

Connect to...

Chemistry

When a leech feeds on an organism, it may take in and store enough blood to keep itself alive for four months. Research and explain to your class the function of an anticoagulant. Explain why an anticoagulent benefits the leech.

Complete and Incomplete Protein

The protein in meat, eggs, and dairy products contains the eight essential amino acids your body cannot produce. That's why the protein in these foods is called complete protein. The protein in plants is incomplete—that is, it contains some, but not all, of the eight essential amino acids. **Figure 11-9b** shows examples of vegetables that do not have all of the essential amino acids. By combining different types of plant proteins, however, you can get all eight essential amino acids in your diet. Beans, rice, and grains are all excellent sources of protein.

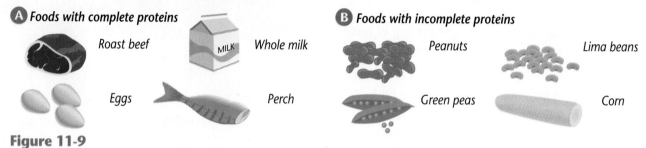

A Foods with complete proteins

Roast beef

Whole milk

Eggs

Perch

B Foods with incomplete proteins

Peanuts

Lima beans

Green peas

Corn

Figure 11-9

Complete proteins (A) such as roast beef, perch, eggs, and whole milk provide the eight essential amino acids that your body needs. Peanuts, green peas, lima beans and corn each have some, but not all, of the essential amino acids and are therefore incomplete proteins (B).

A CLOSER LOOK

Eating Like a Bird

The expression "eats like a bird" describes someone who eats very little. Birds, however, eat a lot of food because flying requires a lot of energy.

Hummingbirds beat their wings up to 90 times a second when they are hovering at a flower. This activity burns energy so quickly that hummingbirds need to eat 70 percent of their body weight each day.

Some large organisms eat large things, while others eat small things. What do you think this blue whale eats?

Amount and Type of Food

How much food an animal needs to eat depends on both the kind of animal and the kind of food. Animals that eat berries eat more than animals that eat nuts and seeds. Berries contain a lot of water but supply little energy. Nuts and seeds are mostly dry and are packed full of nutrients.

Whether an animal eats plants or other animals also affects how much food is consumed. In general, animals that feed on plants eat larger quantities of food to get the nutrients they need than meat-eating

■ Vitamins

If you're not getting the right vitamins, you might actually be suffering from malnutrition! **Vitamins** are organic nutrients necessary to your continued good health. Most vitamins are required in extremely small amounts. However, a deficiency in any one vitamin can sometimes cause serious health problems. Each vitamin is needed and contributes to the functioning of your body.

Vitamin D controls calcium & phosphorus levels

Vitamin A healthy skin & eyes, growth

Vitamin E reproduction, cell growth, wound healing

Vitamin B growth, healthy skin & mucous membrane

Vitamin K blood clotting

Vitamin C healing, maintains body cell connections

Figure 11-10

Vitamins are classified as fat-soluble A, D, E and K, and water-soluble B and C. Fat-soluble vitamins are stored in fat tissues. Water-soluble vitamins are not stored by the human body.

animals do. Plants are harder to digest than meat. Plant cells contain cellulose, a rigid substance that gives support to stems and leaves.

Time Spent Eating

A 6000-kilogram African bull elephant, for example, eats about 170 kilograms of plants a day. Consequently, elephants spend a lot of time grazing—17 to 19 hours a day. Cows, deer, horses, and other grazing animals also spend almost all of the time they are awake eating.

Meat eaters, on the other hand, spend much less time eating. An adult male lion weighing between 150 and 250 kilograms eats about 32.5 kilograms of food each day.

About 170 kg of plants provides a tasty, balanced diet for an elephant.

USING MATH

Keep a record of all the food you eat in one day. Estimate the number of kilograms you consume. Prepackaged foods list the amount on the label. If possible, use a balance to measure food servings. How much of your total body mass do you consume in food each day?

347

Vitamin C

Orange juice is a popular drink. Many people drink orange juice because they like it. Other people drink it because it is healthy and contains vitamin C. Orange juice comes in different forms. You can squeeze it fresh from oranges, mix it from frozen orange concentrate, or buy it bottled. Which form is best for obtaining vitamin C?

Preparation

Problem
How can you determine the amount of vitamin C in each type of orange juice?

Hypothesis
As a group, form a hypothesis about which form of orange juice contains the most vitamin C.

Objectives
- Demonstrate which form of orange juice has the most vitamin C.

Materials
test-tube rack with ten test tubes, each containing 15 mL indophenol solution
4 dropper bottles containing:
(a) refrigerated tap water;
(b) frozen orange concentrate mixed according to directions;
(c) bottled orange juice; and
(d) fresh squeezed orange juice
labels

Safety

Wear safety goggles and a protective apron during the entire experiment.
CAUTION: *Indophenol is a skin irritant and can stain skin and clothing. Notify your teacher if any is spilled.*

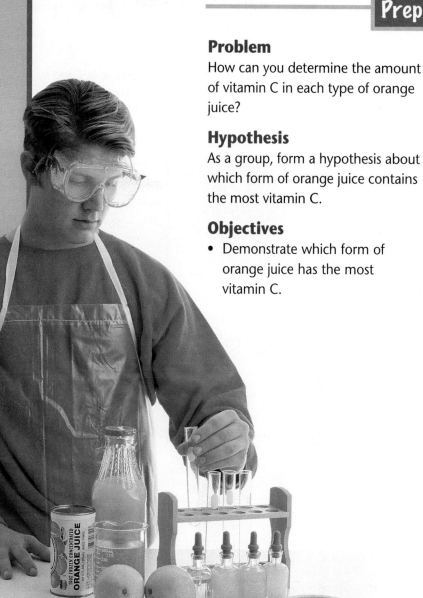

Plan the Experiment

1 Indophenol is an indicator that changes from blue to colorless when enough vitamin C is present.

2 Keep track of your materials by labelling them. Record what is in the bottles *in your Science Journal*.

3 Design a step-by-step procedure to test your hypothesis.

4 What will be your control? Add 20 drops of water from dropper bottle A to test tube 1. Swirl the mixture. The solution will stay blue. This is your control. Check the color of other solutions against it.

5 Decide how you will test the juice in each experiment. How many drops will you use?

6 Draw a data table *in your Science Journal*. Be certain to record how many drops go in each tube and what happens with each drop. For accuracy, you need to run more than one trial for each experiment.

Check the Plan

1 Keep an accurate count of the drops added to the indophenol solution.

2 Make certain your teacher has approved your plan before you proceed.

3 Carry out your investigation and record your observations *in your Science Journal*.

Analyze and Conclude

1. **Compare and Contrast** Compare the amount of vitamin C in the orange juices tested. Which orange juice contained the most vitamin C? Which contained the least? How do you know?

2. **Infer** Was your hypothesis supported? Use your data to explain.

3. **Infer** Why did you add the drops of orange juice one by one?

4. **Infer** Why did you test each juice more than once and average the results?

5. **Analyze** Why was water used as a control?

6. **Conclude** What can you conclude about the amount of vitamin C in the different forms of orange juice?

Going Further

If orange juice was not refrigerated for several days, what would happen to the vitamin C content? How would you test this?

In the Investigation, you tested the vitamin C content in various forms of orange juice. There are similar tests that can be done to test for the presence of other vitamins, minerals, and nutrients in foods. Tests such as these help provide accurate nutritional information that can then be listed on food labels.

■ Nutrient Content Change

The nutrient content of many foods can change greatly from the time they are harvested until they are consumed. Tests show that certain methods of storage and preparation can cause a significant decrease in the amount of useful nutrients in a food. Oxygen from the air and excessive cooking are two culprits that break certain nutrients down into less useful substances or remove them from the foods.

As you can see in **Figure 11-11**, all of the nutrients that we have discussed in this section are essential to your good health. The more scientists study the relationship between diet and health, the more convinced they are that what we eat has a direct effect on how we feel and how our bodies respond to daily stresses. In this sense, you really are what you eat! In the next section, you'll learn how the human digestive system breaks down the foods that you have eaten so your body can use the nutrients to maintain itself.

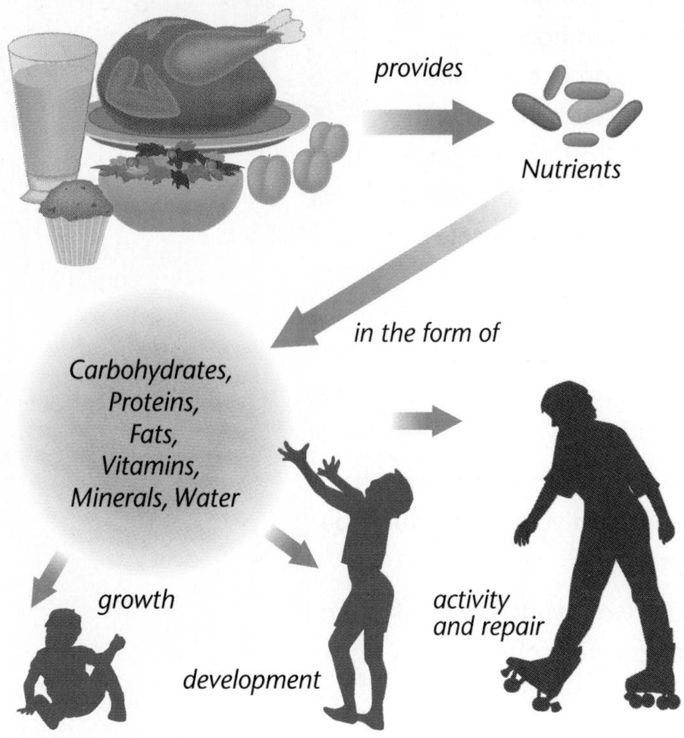

Figure 11-11

Eating a balanced diet provides necessary nutrients that result in growth and development. Nutrients also supply a healthy body with raw materials to effectively repair wounds, such as scrapes, cuts, or broken bones.

check your UNDERSTANDING

1. It has been said that we "cannot live by bread alone." Explain why this statement is true from a nutritional point of view.
2. Describe the six different types of nutrients and explain how your body uses each type.
3. **Apply** Using what you've learned about nutrients, plan a healthful meal for you and your classmates. Explain which nutrients are present in your meal and why you think it is healthful.

11-2 Digestion: A Disassembly Line

The Disassembly Line

Remember all the nutritious foods growing in Blanca Hidalgo's garden? All those fruits and vegetables were packed with all the nutrients your body needs to grow strong and healthy. But how does your body "get to" those nutrients so it can use them for energy, tissue growth and repair, and other important body functions? The answer is a remarkable process called digestion.

You've heard of assembly lines in factories where products are put together quickly and efficiently? Your digestive system, shown in **Figure 11-12**, works in reverse. Digestion is a disassembly line where foods you eat are taken apart. **Digestion** is the process that breaks down carbohydrates, fats, and proteins into smaller and simpler molecules that can be absorbed and used by the cells in your body. Later, your cells use these molecules as building blocks for growth and repair and as fuel from which energy is released. Any molecules that are not absorbed by your cells eventually pass out of your body as solid wastes.

Chemical digestion works on individual molecules, breaking down large molecules into smaller molecules using chemicals produced by your body. Chemical digestion is one process of metabolism, which includes all of the chemical changes that take place in your body—including the breakdown of food molecules for energy.

Section Objectives
- Describe the purpose of the mechanical breakdown of food in your digestive system.
- Explain the role of enzymes in chemical digestion.
- Describe what happens to food as it passes through each organ of the digestive system.

Key Terms

digestion, enzyme, peristalsis, villi

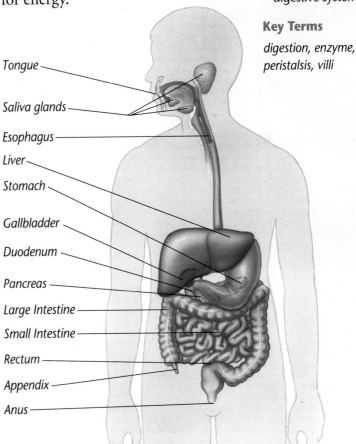

Tongue
Saliva glands
Esophagus
Liver
Stomach
Gallbladder
Duodenum
Pancreas
Large Intestine
Small Intestine
Rectum
Appendix
Anus

Figure 11-12

The human digestive system includes many organs that work to break down the food you eat.

The Mouth

You've just returned home from gymnastics practice, and you're ready for a snack. You pop two slices of pepperoni pizza in the microwave, and in a few minutes you're biting into a delicious treat. Let's follow that pizza as it moves through your digestive system, beginning in your mouth.

Digestion begins as teeth start to work on food. Teeth are adapted to the kinds of food an animal eats. Look at the illustration of human teeth in **Figure 11-15**. You'll use your incisors to take that first bite of pizza. Then you'll use your molars at the back of your mouth to grind the pizza into smaller bits. This is mechanical digestion. But that's not all that's going on in your mouth.

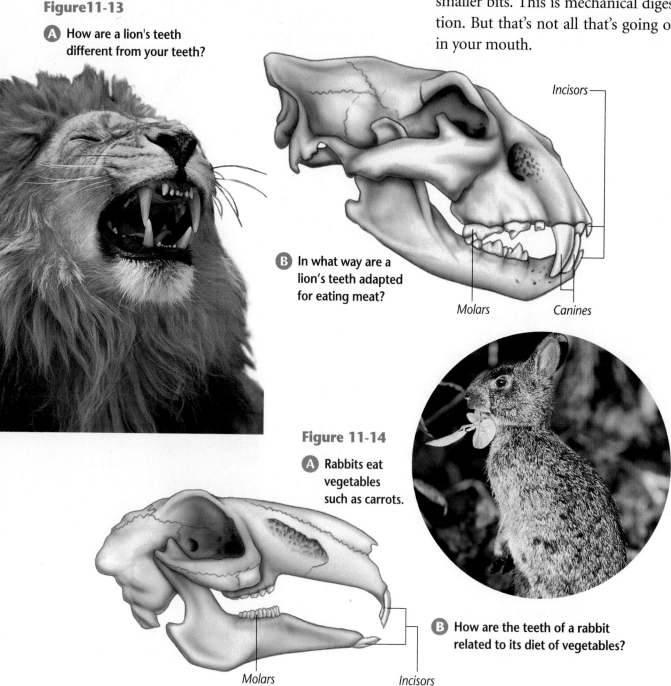

Figure11-13

A How are a lion's teeth different from your teeth?

B In what way are a lion's teeth adapted for eating meat?

Incisors

Molars   Canines

Figure 11-14

A Rabbits eat vegetables such as carrots.

B How are the teeth of a rabbit related to its diet of vegetables?

Molars   Incisors

Where does digestion begin?

You just learned that mechanical digestion starts in your mouth as you chew your food. Is that all that happens in your mouth?

What To Do

1. Chew a saltine cracker or large hard pretzel, but don't swallow it. It won't be too easy, but hold it in your mouth for about five minutes.

2. After five minutes, how does the cracker taste?

3. Why has the taste of the cracker changed?

The cracker you chewed was made from wheat flour or some other grain and contains complex carbohydrates. Remember, carbohydrates are broken down into smaller sugar molecules before they can be used as fuel for your body. What's going on in your mouth? Let's investigate.

Figure 11-15

When food is mechanically digested by your teeth, it is broken down into smaller pieces. In what way are your teeth like knives and forks?

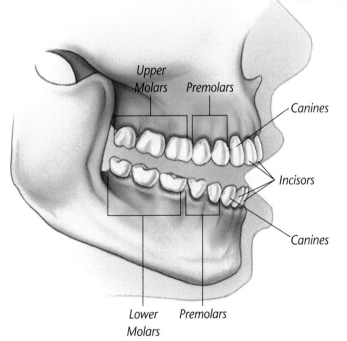

Figure 11-16

Organisms eat a great variety of foods. Analyze how teeth are suited for eating various foods.

Chemical Digestion

While eating you usually chew your food. This mechanical digestion breaks the food into smaller particles. In the Explore activity you kept a chewed cracker in your mouth for a few minutes. During that time the taste of the cracker changed.

Problem

How can you determine if chemical digestion begins in the mouth?

Materials

4 test tubes	glucose
test-tube rack	teaspoon
100-mL graduated cylinder	medicine dropper
10-mL graduated cylinder	iodine solution
	Benedict's solution
250-mL beaker	hot plate
tap water	safety goggles
non-instant oatmeal	test-tube clamp
diastase solution (saliva substitute)	apron

Safety Precautions

Be careful when handling hot objects and using electrical equipment.

Wear safety goggles.

Handle chemicals carefully.

Wear protective clothing to prevent stains.

What To Do

1. Make a data table *in your Journal*.

2. **CAUTION:** *Put on your safety glasses.* Label four test tubes 1 through 4.

3. Fill a beaker with 100 mL of water. Soak a handful of oatmeal in the water. Allow to stand for 10 minutes, stirring once or twice. Pour off the milky-white liquid. Use this as your starch solution.

4. *Measure* 10 mL starch solution into test tubes 1, 3, and 4.

5. Completely dissolve 1 teaspoon of glucose in 25 mL of water. *Measure* 10 mL sugar solution into test tube 2.

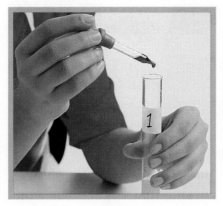

A

B

C

6 Wash the starch solution out of the beaker, fill it half full with hot tap water, and place it on a hot plate.

7 Add 4 drops of iodine solution to test tube 1. Iodine will turn blue-black in the presence of starch. Observe the test tube and record your observations by indicating a positive (starch present) or a negative (no starch present) result.

8 Add 4 drops of Benedict's solution to test tube 2 and heat it in the hot water in the beaker. Benedict's solution is an indicator. If sugar is present, it turns muddy green to yellow to rust to red. Record your observations in the data table.

9 Add 10 drops of enzyme (saliva substitute) to test tubes 3 and 4, and swirl carefully. Wait 5 minutes.

10 Add 4 drops of iodine solution to test tube 3. Record your observations.

11 Add 4 drops of Benedict's solution to test tube 4. Wait for the water bath to boil. Using a test-tube clamp, place test tube 4 in the water bath and leave it there for 5 minutes. Record your observations.

Analyzing

1. How did you test for the presence of starch?

2. How did you test for sugar?

Concluding and Applying

3. What can you *conclude* from your data? What process begins as you chew food?

4. Going Further *Infer* why chewing your food is an important part of the digestive process.

Figure 11-17

How are the actions of enzymes like putting together and taking apart a jigsaw puzzle?

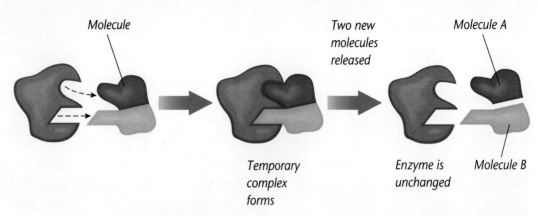

Molecule

Two new molecules released

Molecule A

Temporary complex forms

Enzyme is unchanged

Molecule B

The Investigate showed that digestion begins in your mouth. Saliva contains an enzyme that begins the process. An **enzyme** is a protein molecule that controls the rate of hundreds of different processes in your body. Enzymes are a vital part of chemical digestion. They work on nutrient molecules like a key in a lock. Each enzyme fits just one type of molecule, breaking the nutrient into smaller molecules, as in **Figure 11-17**.

You have over 700 different enzymes in your body, each with a unique function. When an enzyme in your saliva mixes with the starchy wheat crust of the pizza you're eating, chemical digestion begins and starch is broken down to sugar.

Is gravity responsible for getting food from your mouth to your stomach? Let's find out.

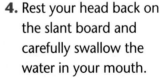

DID YOU KNOW?

One enzyme molecule can break down millions of starch molecules.

Find Out! ACTIVITY

Does gravity move food to your stomach?

You are usually sitting or standing when you eat or drink something. Is it possible to eat when you are lying down with your head lower than your stomach?

What To Do

1. Get a glass of water with a flexible straw.

2. Lie down on an exercise slant board with your head at the lower end.

3. Lift up your head and take a small mouthful of water through the straw. Don't swallow it yet!

4. Rest your head back on the slant board and carefully swallow the water in your mouth.

Conclude and Apply
What role does gravity play in digestion?

From Mouth to Stomach

Even though your head was tilted downward, you were still able to swallow the water. **Figure 11-18** illustrates the process of **peristalsis**. During peristalsis, the smooth muscles of the esophagus contract in waves, carrying

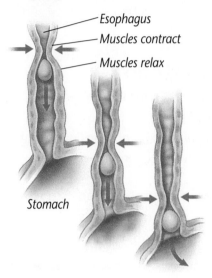

Esophagus
Muscles contract
Muscles relax
Stomach

Figure 11-18

Food is moved through the esophagus to the stomach by waves of contractions of the esophagus muscles. Are these contractions voluntary?

food to your stomach. This same muscle action moves food through your entire digestive system.

The muscle action of your esophagus slowly fills your stomach where mechanical and chemical digestion continues. Your stomach muscles churn and mix the partially digested pizza. Meanwhile, the cells in your stomach wall produce hydrochloric acid and enzymes that attack the pizza chemically.

Figure 11-19

The inner lining of an empty stomach has many wrinkles and folds. Do you think a full stomach is the same? Why or why not?

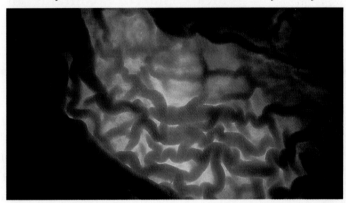

How Do We Know?

The Stomach Observed

Much of what we know about the actions of the stomach is based on an accident. In 1822, a young French Canadian fur trapper named Alexis St. Martin was shot in his left side. An army surgeon named William Beaumont successfully removed the bullet and saved Alexis's life. However, Dr. Beaumont could not close the wound completely, and Alexis was left

with a hole in his side leading straight into his stomach.

Observing and Analyzing

Dr. Beaumont was a scientist as well as a physician. For a number of years, he observed the activity in Alexis's stomach under various conditions. For instance, he tied different kinds of foods on strings and lowered them into Alexis's stomach to observe the effect of stomach fluids on the different foods.

Dr. Beaumont also removed samples of these fluids and had them analyzed. He identified hydrochloric acid in the fluid. More importantly, he discovered that although meats are chemically digested in the stomach, other types of food are not.

Dr. Beaumont published his observations in a book that is still referred to today. Alexis, by the way, lived to be 83.

Find Out! ACTIVITY

How do enzymes work?

You have already learned that enzymes convert starch to sugar. How can you tell if an enzyme is working?

What To Do

1. Obtain two beef samples. Moisten each with water. Sprinkle one sample generously with tenderizer. The other sample will not be treated. It is your control.

2. After one half hour, examine the two samples. Feel the texture of each one.

Conclude and Apply

1. Do you detect any differences in the samples?

2. As a result of your observations, what is the function of enzymes?

Meat tenderizer contains an enzyme that breaks down protein. Your stomach also contains enzymes to break down protein. Your stomach produces a coating of slimy mucus that protects it from digesting itself.

Physics CONNECTION

Do You Always Have a Temperature?

You might think that the only time you have a temperature is when you are sick. Even when you are healthy, your body has a temperature of about 37°C. Where does that warmth come from?

The process of cellular respiration releases energy. Only a small amount of this energy is captured in a form that is used by your body for daily activities. Most of the energy released from stored nutrients is thermal energy. Some of this energy maintains a constant body temperature.

For birds and mammals, a constant body temperature makes it possible to live and be active in a wide range of habitats, no matter what the temperature of the environment is. Birds and mammals can live in the Arctic, where winter temperatures are below freezing. Amphibians and reptiles, which depend on heat from the environment to regulate their body temperature, cannot live in such a cold habitat.

Amount of Energy Loss

Not all of the energy released by metabolism of food is used by an animal, however. Much is lost to the environment through the skin. Just how much energy is lost depends on an animal's size.

Traveling Through the Intestines

Your pizza will spend about four hours in your stomach being mechanically and chemically changed into a thin, watery liquid. Then, little by little, the muscles in your stomach push this liquid into your small intestine.

■ Small Intestine

Most chemical digestion takes place in your small intestine. Your liver, gallbladder, and pancreas supply different digestive juices needed for chemical digestion to your small intestine, shown in **Figure 11-20**.

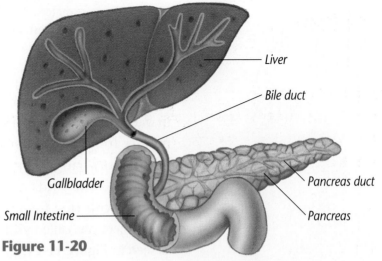

Figure 11-20

Bile is an important digestive juice that breaks up large fat particles found in foods. Bile is produced in the liver and stored in the gallbladder. When needed, bile moves through a duct into the small intestine. What is a duct?

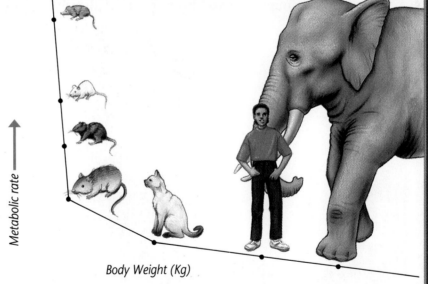

Small animals lose energy faster than larger ones do, because small animals have a large surface area-to-volume ratio. (Surface area is how much surface is exposed to the environment.) The larger the ratio, the more surface there is through which heat can be lost from the inside. Small animals that have a higher rate of metabolism than larger animals do lose heat more rapidly. The graph shows the relationship between body size and metabolism for several different species.

Rate of Metabolism

A higher rate of metabolism in turn requires more food consumption. So small animals also eat more, relative to body size.

For example, a mouse with a mass of 3 grams eats 30 times more food per gram of body mass than a 5000-kilogram elephant.

You Try It!

Freeze 1 L of water into a single block. Freeze another 1 L of water as small cubes. Place the large block in one pan and the small cubes in another pan. Allow all the ice to melt. Keep track of how long it takes. Which melts faster, the large block or the small cubes? Explain your answer in terms of surface area-to-volume ratio.

Figure 11-21

The many villi of your small intestine increase the surface area dramatically. The surface area of your small intestine is over 264 square meters. Why is this important for digestion?

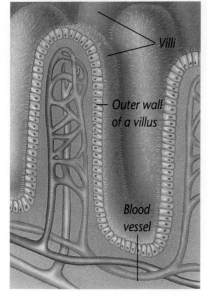

Villi

Outer wall of a villus

Blood vessel

Your small intestine is less than two centimeters in diameter but is over six meters long! It is lined with many ridges and folds, and the folds are covered with tiny finger-like projections called **villi** as seen in **Figure 11-21**.

Notice the many blood vessels in the villi. By the time your snack reaches your small intestine, its molecules have been broken down into a size small enough to pass through the walls of your villi and into your bloodstream. As the muscles of your small intestine move the liquid nutrient mixture along, the villi are completely bathed in the liquid, and nutrient molecules move from your digestive system into your circulatory system. From here, nutrients will be carried to cells throughout your body.

■ The End of the Line—Your Large Intestine

The last stage of digestion is about to take place. The thin, watery liquid that's been moving through your small intestine is now pushed into your large intestine. This digestive organ is almost two meters long and six to seven centimeters in diameter. Muscle contractions here are much slower than they were in your small intestine. The large intestine absorbs large amounts of water. The food that isn't absorbed is concentrated into a somewhat solid mass of undigested material.

The solidified wastes also contain large numbers of bacteria that are beneficial. They consume some of the last microscopic bits of food and produce vitamins—vitamin K and some of the B vitamins. Finally, the solidified wastes are eliminated from your body as feces.

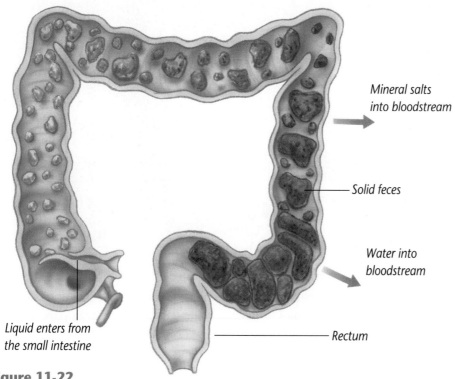

Mineral salts into bloodstream

Solid feces

Water into bloodstream

Liquid enters from the small intestine

Rectum

Figure 11-22

The words "small" and "large" are used to describe the two intestines of the human body. Do these words refer to the diameter or the length of the intestine they are used to describe?

The Nutritional Payoff

The pizza you snacked on provided your body with starch, protein, fat, vitamins, water and minerals. Once these nutrients have been distributed throughout your body by your circulatory system, how are they used?

Some of the nutrients you've taken in act as fuel for a variety of metabolic processes, including cell growth, development and repair. They provide your body with the energy it needs to function and maintain itself.

DID YOU KNOW?

Why does your stomach growl when you're hungry? Your stomach and intestines make noise constantly as food is pushed through your digestive system. However, when your stomach is empty and your digestive muscles contract, your stomach acts as an amplifier.

Find Out! ACTIVITY

How much energy do you need?

You can calculate the rate at which your body uses energy. First you need to know that a Calorie is a unit of measurement of the energy available in food. Males use about 1.0 Calories per kilogram of body mass per hour. Females use less—about 0.9.

What To Do

1. Convert your mass in pounds to kilograms by multiplying your weight by 0.453.

2. Then multiply your mass in kilograms by 1.0 if you're a male and 0.9 if you're a female.

3. The result is the energy in Calories you use per hour. Record this in your Journal.

Conclude and Apply

1. How many Calories of food energy do you use per day?

2. Compare the Calories needed per day by a 100 pound woman and a 150 pound man.

3. What factors would affect the calories you need on a given day?

These daily energy requirements are averages. If you're more active, you'll use more energy. If you take in more Calories of energy than you use in any given time period, the extra will be stored as fat. If you don't take in as many Calories as you require, your body will take them from your fat reserve, and you'll start to lose weight.

Calories and Calorie Use

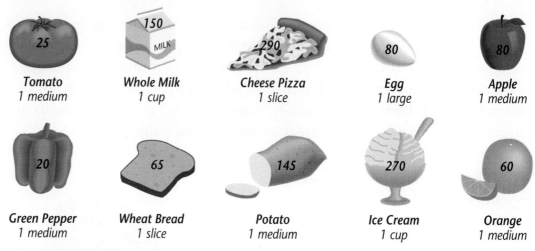

Tomato 1 medium (25)	**Whole Milk** 1 cup (150)	**Cheese Pizza** 1 slice (290)	**Egg** 1 large (80)	**Apple** 1 medium (80)
Green Pepper 1 medium (20)	**Wheat Bread** 1 slice (65)	**Potato** 1 medium (145)	**Ice Cream** 1 cup (270)	**Orange** 1 medium (60)

Figure 11-23

The foods you eat contain different numbers of Calories. How many apples would you need to eat to equal the Calories in one cup of ice cream?

A sample listing of some foods and their calories are given in **Figure 11-23**. **Figure 11-24** shows the Calories used up during some different physical activities.

Your digestive system is an incredible machine. It will process thousands of pounds of food for you during your lifetime. It will break down the nutrients you need and send them off across the villi into your bloodstream for transport throughout your body. What it can't use, it will efficiently eliminate. Supply it with useful nutrients, and your digestive system will help you remain healthy and strong.

Figure 11-24

Has there ever been a moment in your life when you did not use energy in the form of Calories? Using the table to the right and the Calories listed in Figure 11-23, how long would it take you to use the calories in one slice of cheese pizza if you were running? Sitting?

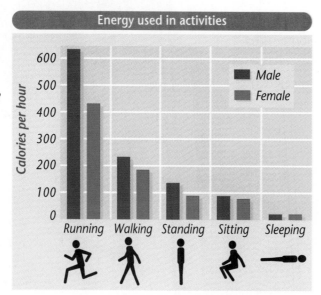

check your UNDERSTANDING

1. What is the difference between mechanical and chemical digestion?
2. How do enzymes work?
3. **Apply** Suppose you ate a cheeseburger with lettuce and tomato for lunch. Identify the various types of nutrients it contains and explain what is happening to them on the way from your mouth to your cells.

Health CONNECTION

Eating a Balanced Diet

A healthy body needs proteins, fats, carbohydrates, vitamins, and minerals. How much of each of these nutrients does your body need each day?

Specific Nutrients

Nutrition experts recommend that people pay more attention to the specific nutrients they eat. For example, no more than 30 percent of the calories in your daily food intake should be from fat. The average American diet has 48 percent of the calories from fat. Scientists have long known that too much fat in the diet can increase the risk of heart disease. A high level of dietary fat is also associated with breast and colon cancer.

Americans need to cut down on meat consumption as well. Current research now links too much protein from meat to heart disease and cancer. Just about 30 grams of protein are needed each day, but most people eat around 100 grams.

Healthful Diet

A healthful diet should be high in complex carbohydrates, fiber, vitamins, and minerals. To eat a healthful diet, there are certain guidelines you should follow. Think of your diet as a pyramid. At the bottom, which is the

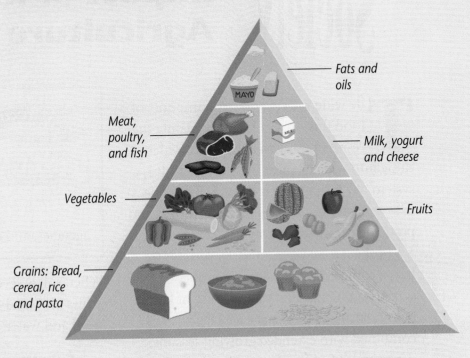

Fats and oils

Meat, poultry, and fish

Milk, yogurt and cheese

Vegetables

Fruits

Grains: Bread, cereal, rice and pasta

widest part, are grains. Grains include bread, cereal, rice, and pasta.

Your diet should also contain large amounts of fresh fruits and vegetables, the next layer in the pyramid. A much smaller portion of your diet should be dairy products and meat because these foods are high in fat. Even lean meat and chicken can contribute too much fat to your diet. The protein they provide can be obtained as easily by eating grains and beans instead. Grains and beans contain little fat.

You Try It!

Draw a diagram that shows the proportions of the different nutrients in your diet. How does your diet compare to what is recommended for a healthful diet?

Science and Society

Environmental Impact of Modern Agriculture

The wide variety and large amounts of food that are available are mainly the result of modern agriculture which came into wide use after World War II. It is a system of farming that relies heavily on the use of machinery and chemical fertilizers and pesticides to increase crop yields.

In the last 30 years, modern agriculture has become associated with a number of serious problems. For example, use of large heavy machines to manage vast fields, combined with extended growing seasons, depletes soil fertility. Eventually, the soil breaks down and can no longer be farmed.

An agronomist is an agricultural scientist. Agronomists study biology. They work for corporations, government agencies, and colleges and universities.

When soil is severely damaged, nothing grows in it, and often it is carried away by wind and water.

Fertilizers and Pesticides

The use of chemical fertilizers and pesticides is associated with environmental contamination and threats to human and animal health. In California's San Joaquin Valley, for example, about one million people have been exposed to the pesticide DBCP in their drinking water. This chemical, created to eliminate pests on the roots of farm crops, is known to cause cancer and sterility. Its use has been banned. Water from 1500 wells in the region cannot be used for drinking, bathing, or cooking because of contamination with other pesticides known to cause kidney and liver damage, cancer, sterility, and genetic damage. About half the states in the country have some contamination of water supplies from farm chemicals.

Sustainable Farms

Many techniques are available to make agriculture sustainable. A sustainable farm is one that produces good quality food at a profit while keeping the soil fertile and healthy. To save energy, reduce pollution, and cut costs, farm chemicals and fuels are replaced whenever possible by resources found on the farm.

For example, some farmers use solar or wind power to generate electricity. Chemical pesticides are replaced by biological pest controls, such as insect predators and microorganisms that infect insect pests. Animal and green manure are used instead of chemical fertilizers.

Crop Rotation and Diversity

Another important method in sustainable agriculture is crop rotation. Over the course of several growing seasons, a planned series of different crops is grown in a given field.

Diversity is another key characteristic of sustainable farms. Unlike standard farms, which grow huge fields of only one or a few kinds of crops, sustainable farms have livestock, trees, and a mixture of species and varieties of crops.

In case of a natural disaster or a sudden drop in prices for a single crop, farmers with more diverse crops are less likely to lose their entire yield for a season.

In 1980, there were between 20 000 and 30 000 farmers using sustainable agriculture methods, according to the U.S. Department of Agriculture. Farm experts estimate that today there may be two to three times that number. However, that is still just a tiny percent of the country's two million farmers.

Converting to Sustainable Methods

Converting from standard farming to sustainable methods is not easy or quick. The more damaged the soil is and the more dependent on chemicals the farm is, the longer it takes the soil to be returned to a productive condition without the use of applied fertilizers.

Government policies have also worked to discourage farmers from using sustainable methods. For example, the federal government purchases a handful of crops and sets prices for them. So farmers who want to be certain of a profit are, in a way, trapped by a system of federal price supports. Because so many farmers are heavily in debt, they are unable to switch to sustainable methods. To do so would mean risking economic loss.

Science Journal

Should the federal government help farmers convert to sustainable methods? Explain your answer. How might the government help with this change?

HOW IT WORKS

How Does a Microwave Oven Cook Food?

Suppose you want to have a snack. You find a frozen pizza and decide to cook it in the microwave oven. How does the microwave oven work?

Microwaves

A microwave oven produces microwaves. Microwaves are a kind of electromagnetic radiation, like visible light and radio waves. Like radio waves, microwaves cannot be seen. They can, however, be reflected off metal surfaces.

The door of the oven is covered with a metal grid. Inside the oven is shiny metal plating on the back wall as well. When you turn on the oven, microwave radiation is produced and bounces around inside the oven. The metal surfaces reflect the waves over and over again, causing them to build up to a density of many million for each cubic inch of space. Anything inside the oven gets zapped with microwave radiation.

Water

Only substances that contain water are affected by the microwave energy. That is why glass and ceramic containers stay cool in a microwave. They have no water molecules in them.

When the microwaves strike the food, however, they cause the water molecules in the food to vibrate very quickly. This causes the food to cook, and the water in the food actually boils. Thus, the food literally cooks from the inside out.

You Try It!

Prepare some prepackaged microwave popcorn according to the directions. Notice the steam that comes out when you carefully open the package. Where does the steam come from? Explain your answer in terms of how a microwave works.

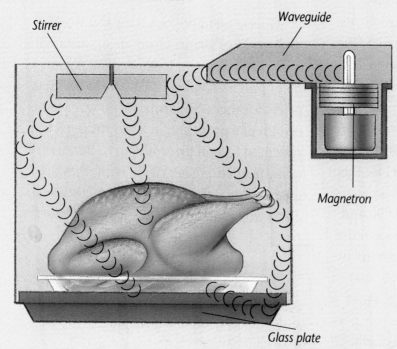

Stirrer

Waveguide

Magnetron

Glass plate

Science Journal

Review the statements below about the big ideas presented in this chapter, and answer the questions. Then, reread your answers to the Did You Ever Wonder questions at the beginning of the chapter. *In your Science Journal,* write a paragraph about how your understanding of the big ideas in the chapter has changed.

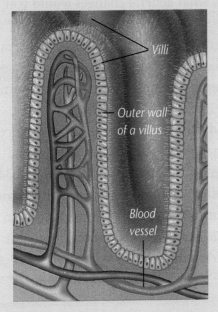

1 Nutrients are the chemical substances in foods that your body uses for growth and repair and as fuel to release energy. *What is the importance of each of the six nutrients for the body? What could result from an improper amount of a particular nutrient?*

2 Your digestive system is a long, complex tube in which nutrients are mechanically and chemically broken down. *What is the difference between chemical and mechanical digestion? Where does each occur?*

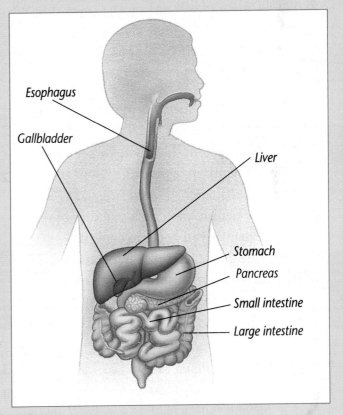

Esophagus

Gallbladder

Liver

Stomach

Pancreas

Small intestine

Large intestine

Villi

Outer wall of a villus

Blood vessel

3 Absorption is an important part of the digestive process. It is through the villi that nutrients pass into the bloodstream, to be delivered to individual cells throughout the body. *Where are the villi located and why is that area of the body suitable for absorption?*

BLOOD transport and protection

Science Journal
Before you begin to study about blood, think about the questions and answer them *in your Science Journal.* When you finish the chapter, compare your journal write-up with what you have learned.

Imagine you could shrink yourself to the size of the period at the end of this sentence and go sailing through some of your body's blood vessels. Riding down a water slide is similar to the twisting and turning travels of a blood cell inside a blood vessel. Right now, blood pumping through your blood vessels is behaving very much like the water that rapidly propels you through a narrow passageway in a waterslide. Just as rushing water surrounds and carries you along, solid particles move in a liquid through your arteries and veins propelled by the beating of your heart. In this chapter, you will learn about the liquid and solid parts that make up your blood. You will also come to understand how your blood acts as a natural defense system to protect your body from disease.

▶ *In the activity on the next page, explore how much blood is in your body.*

Explore! ACTIVITY

How much blood is in your body right now?

Generally, blood makes up about eight percent of your body's total mass.

What To Do

1. If possible, measure your total body mass on a scale with SI units. If such a scale is not available, figure out your total body mass by multiplying your weight in pounds by 0.45. This will give you your body mass in kilograms.

2. After you calculate your body mass, you will then have to find eight percent of that figure.

3. The answer will be your body's mass of blood in kilograms. Record your answer *in your Journal.*

Blood: Transporter of Life

Section Objectives

- Describe how blood transports substances within living organisms.
- Describe plasma, red and white blood cells, and hemoglobin in the blood and explain their functions.

Key Terms

plasma
red blood cells
hemoglobin
white blood cells

Blood

In the Explore activity, you may have discovered that the amount of blood in a person's body depends on the size of the individual. Although we have varying amounts of blood in our bodies, we all need it to survive and to maintain good health. In fact, blood composition is one of the most accurate indicators of your health. That is why a blood test is a vital part of a good physical exam. It tells your doctor much about the condition of your body and its systems.

Blood, shown magnified in **Figure 12-1A**, is a tissue consisting of cells, cell fragments, and liquid. Blood has many important functions and plays a part in every major activity of your body. It functions like the highway system that nurtures your community. Blood supplies and renews the community of cells that work together to make up your body.

■ Movement of Blood

Just as water in a waterslide is continuously pumped to transport you through its chutes, you have a heart that recirculates blood to keep it moving throughout your body. If the amount of water and the pressure in the slide decreases, you may stop moving. Similarly, your blood is moved into and out of your heart in a continuous fashion so that the materials your body needs for survival can be transported to all parts of the body. This is critical to your health. If the heart, brain, and other vital organs do not receive oxygen that is carried by blood, they can become permanently damaged.

Figure 12-1

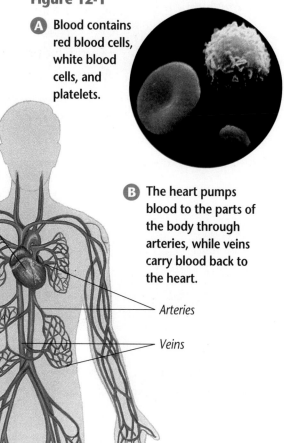

Ⓐ Blood contains red blood cells, white blood cells, and platelets.

Ⓑ The heart pumps blood to the parts of the body through arteries, while veins carry blood back to the heart.

Heart

Arteries

Veins

The Functions of Blood

You have learned that the cells of most organisms need nutrients and oxygen to release energy for work. One-celled organisms get nutrients and oxygen directly from their environment. Cytoplasm streams around inside of them so their bodies do not need an elaborate system to move nutrients and waste products. Certain many-celled organisms, such as jellyfish and sponges, do not have a circulatory system or blood either. In these animals, oxygen diffuses directly from their watery environment through the outer cells and into their inner body layers. The majority of many-celled organisms, however, contain a complex circulatory system with blood that performs many of the same jobs as human blood.

As you just learned, many simple animals get their food and oxygen directly from their environment, such as the ocean. Our blood on the other hand, provides us with an inner ocean. Let's take a close look at the components that make up this vital fluid tissue.

■ Plasma

Blood is a tissue made of red and white blood cells, platelets, and plasma. About 55 percent of your blood is made up of plasma. **Plasma** is the liquid part of blood and consists mostly of water. The following Explore will give you an idea of how this complex fluid is constructed.

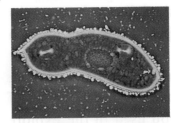

Figure 12-2

A One-celled organisms such as the euglena shown here, take in oxygen and nutrients directly from their environment.

B Jellyfish do not need blood because oxygen diffuses directly from the water through their outer cells and into their bodies.

Explore! ACTIVITY

What substances make up your blood?

You can make a model of blood using cooking oil, water, and red food coloring.

What To Do

1. In a test tube, pour 5 mL of cooking oil into 5 mL of water.
2. Add a drop of red food coloring. Put a stopper in the tube and shake it.
3. Allow the liquids to separate. How many layers do you see?

373

■ White Blood Cells

In contrast to red blood cells, there are only about five to ten thousand white blood cells in a cubic millimeter of blood. This means that for every 500 red cells in your blood, you will find only one white cell! That is quite a difference, isn't it? Is their function different from red blood cells?

White blood cells, like the one you see in **Figure 12-5**, fight bacteria, viruses, and other foreign substances that constantly try to invade your body. Your body responds to infections by increasing its number of white blood cells. In the next section, you will learn more about how white blood cells destroy bacteria, viruses, and other foreign substances that invade your body.

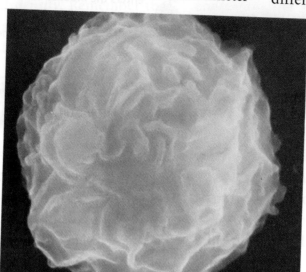

Figure 12-5

White blood cells are important in helping your body fight bacteria, viruses, and other foreign substances.

Physics CONNECTION

Oxygen and Carbon Dioxide Transport

The average red blood cell contains about 265 million hemoglobin molecules. Because each hemoglobin molecule can carry four oxygen atoms, each red blood cell can carry an enormous amount of oxygen. What makes hemoglobin such a good carrier of oxygen?

As you know, hemoglobin contains iron, which has a strong attraction for oxygen. Within hemoglobin, oxygen attaches to iron very loosely. Under certain conditions, these loosely attached oxygen molecules can be released from the iron.

Partial Pressure

Whether oxygen is held or released by hemoglobin depends on a property called

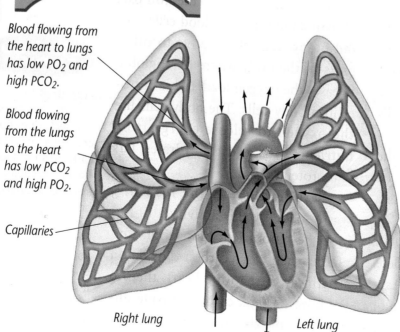

Blood flowing from the heart to lungs has low PO_2 and high PCO_2.

Blood flowing from the lungs to the heart has low PCO_2 and high PO_2.

Capillaries

Right lung

Left lung

■ Platelets

Figure 12-6 shows what blood looks like under a microscope. You can see in this photo that blood contains tiny, irregularly shaped cell fragments called platelets. While a red blood cell may live up to 120 days, the life span of a platelet is only about 5 to 9 days. Yet, in this short time, platelets play an important role in healing wounds to keep your body free from disease. You will learn more about how platelets accomplish this later in this chapter.

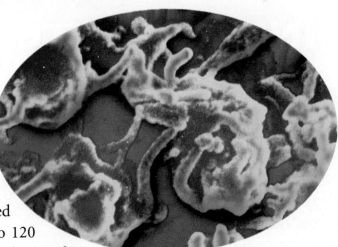

Figure 12-6

Platelets are tiny pieces of cells that do not have a nucleus. They are important in healing wounds.

In this section, you have learned that blood is made up of several different components. Do you think that blood from all vertebrates contains these same components? Investigate to find the answer to this question.

---

partial pressure. Partial pressure is the pressure caused by each gas within a mixture of gases.

The air you breathe is a mixture of gases that includes oxygen, nitrogen, and carbon dioxide. At sea level, air pressure is 760 millimeters of mercury.

Air is only 21 percent oxygen, so only 21 percent of the air pressure is caused by oxygen. This amount is the partial pressure of oxygen (PO_2). How does the partial pressure of oxygen affect oxygen transport by hemoglobin? Hemoglobin holds on to oxygen when the partial pressure of oxygen surrounding it is high and lets go of oxygen when it is low.

More oxygen molecules are in the lungs than anywhere else in the body, so the partial pressure of oxygen is highest there. Blood passing through lung tissue picks up oxygen easily. When the blood reaches other parts of the body, where there is much less oxygen, hemoglobin releases the oxygen molecules to the cells.

Carbon Dioxide

The transport of carbon dioxide works somewhat differently. Hemoglobin carries only 11 percent of the carbon dioxide in the blood. The rest is carried by blood plasma. Whether the blood is picking up or letting go of carbon dioxide also depends on partial pressure.

In active tissues, the partial pressure of carbon dioxide (PCO_2) is high. Thus, carbon dioxide moves easily and quickly into the blood. In the lungs, the partial pressure of carbon dioxide is much lower, so the carbon dioxide diffuses out of the blood and is exhaled from the lungs.

What Do You Think?

At very high altitudes, the air is thinner, and the air pressure is much lower than at sea level. The lower air pressure can be dangerous for mountain climbers. Experienced climbers usually ascend a high peak over several days to give their bodies time to adjust to the change in air pressure by producing more red blood cells. How does this help the body survive?

Are All Blood Cells Alike?

Textbooks often include illustrations of human blood cells when describing blood tissue. For this reason, we usually think that all blood cells look alike. In this activity, you will compare and contrast blood cells from several different vertebrates.

Problem
Do blood cells of vertebrates differ?

Materials
prepared microscope slides of
    human blood and
    blood of two other vertebrates
    (fish, frog, bird, reptile)
microscope

Safety Precautions

Be careful when using a microscope.

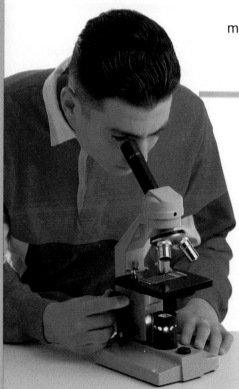

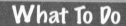

What To Do

1 Copy the data table *into your Journal*.

2 Under low power, observe the prepared slide of human blood.

3 Locate and examine the red blood cells under high power.

4 Draw, count, and describe the red blood cells.

5 Move the slide to another position. Find one or two white blood cells. The nuclei will be blue or purple due to the stain.

6 Record the information about white cells in your data table.

7 Still using high power, examine the slide for very small fragments that are blue. These are platelets.

8 Record the information about platelets in your data table.

9 Follows Steps 2 through 8 for each of the other two slides of vertebrate blood.

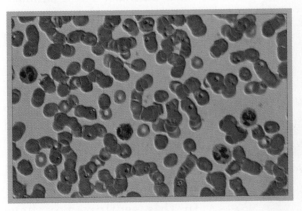

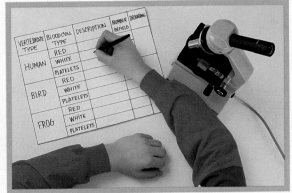

A

B

Data and Observations

Vertebrate Type	Blood Cell Type	Description	Number in Field	Drawing
Human	Red			
	White			
	Platelets			
Bird	Red			
	White			
	Platelets			
Frog	Red			
	White			
	Platelets			

Analyzing

1. Which type of blood cells are present in the greatest number in your samples?

2. *Compare and contrast* the red blood cells, white blood cells, and platelets of the other vertebrates to the human cells.

Concluding and Applying

3. *Interpret your data* to tell if each vertebrate has all three cell and cell fragment components.

4. **Going Further** What might you *infer* about the ability of different red blood cells to carry oxygen? Explain your answer.

Figure 12-7

The blood of a dolphin (A) a bald eagle (B), and a frog (C) contain the same basic components as human blood—red blood cells, white blood cells, and platelets. Blood in these animals serves the same functions as in humans — it supplies oxygen and fights disease.

was similar. What do you think this tells you about how these parts function in other animals? These similarities may show an evolutionary relationship or that all vertebrates have similar needs. Birds, frogs, and other animals require oxygen, face disease and infection, and get injured, like yourself.

In this section, you have learned that the different components of blood have different functions. Plasma transports nutrients, minerals, and oxygen to all the cells in your body. It delivers waste products produced by the cells to other organs, such as the lungs or kidneys, where they are eliminated. Red blood cells transport oxygen that cells throughout the body use for energy. They then deliver small amounts of carbon dioxide to the lungs where it is exhaled. White blood cells help the body fight disease and infection, while platelets help to heal wounds.

In the next section, you will further understand how these different parts of blood help your body fight infections and heal wounds.

You can see from the results of the Investigate that blood in different vertebrates is similar in that it contains certain basic components. All of the vertebrate blood you examined contained red blood cells, white blood cells, and platelets.

You probably also noticed that the shape of each type of cell or fragment

check your UNDERSTANDING

1. Describe the characteristics and functions of red blood cells and plasma.
2. Explain how white blood cells differ from red blood cells.

3. **Apply** Predict what would happen to your tissues if red blood cells and plasma did not pick up and eliminate carbon dioxide from your cells.

Blood: The Body's Defense

Sealing the Leaks

Your skin is your body's first line of defense against potentially harmful invading bacteria. Because of this, your body works quickly to plug up and seal off cuts in your skin. Think back to the last time you were cut. The wound stopped bleeding after a short time and a scab formed over the wound. How did this happen?

A cut stops bleeding due to the action of platelets in your blood. **Platelets** are cell fragments that stop the flow of blood from a broken blood vessel. When you cut yourself, you tear open numerous capillaries. Blood in these vessels begins to flow out through the opening in your skin, like water out of a leaking garden hose. But unlike a hose, you know from experience that the flow of blood usually stops fairly quickly. Platelets in your blood act to prevent serious bleeding. How do platelets stop the bleeding?

The process by which a broken blood vessel seals off is called **clotting**. The process of clotting is shown in **Figure 12-8**.

Section Objectives
- Describe the basic steps in blood clotting.
- Explain the natural defenses your body has against disease.
- Describe the differences between active and passive immunity.
- Explain the nature of communicable diseases.

Key Terms
platelets, clotting antigens, antibodies immunity, vaccine

Figure 12-8

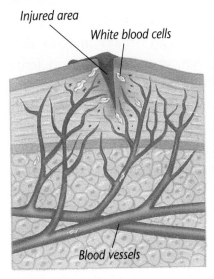

A As soon as skin is cut and a blood vessel breaks, platelets start sticking to the walls of the vessel and to each other.

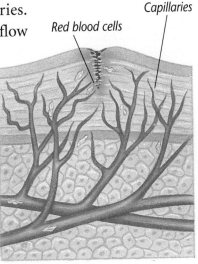

B Chemicals released by platelets react with substances in plasma. Sticky fibers are produced that trap blood cells.

Figure 12-9

Fibrin is a protein in blood that helps in the process of clotting.

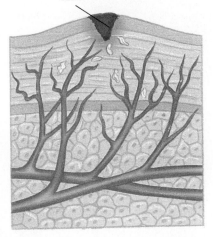

C A clot is formed that seals the break and hardens into a scab. The scab is pushed off by the growth of new cells under it.

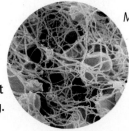

Magnification: x1830

Natural Defense

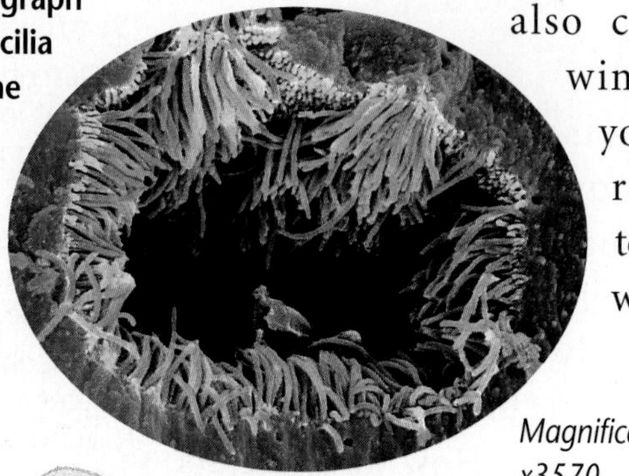

Figure 12-10

This photograph shows the cilia that line the trachea.

In addition to your skin and your blood, other body systems maintain your health. The trachea, also called the windpipe, in your respiratory system is lined with short,

Magnification: x3570

Tonsils: store white blood cells

Thymus gland: produces white blood cells in infants

Lymph nodes: store white blood cells

Spleen: stores red blood cells, gets rid of old red blood cells, and makes white blood cells

Lymph vessels and fluid: carry white blood cells throughout the body

Bone marrow: makes red and white blood cells

hairlike cilia and mucus that trap both harmful and harmless organisms. You expel bacteria that are trapped in the mucus when you cough to clear your throat. But sometimes, bacteria get swallowed. In that event, your digestive system contains chemicals that can destroy most disease-causing organisms that might enter through your mouth.

Your body is like a well-equipped fortress. Cells, blood, organs, and body systems all work together to fight bacteria. All of these structures are part of your immune system. The immune system, pictured in **Figure 12-11**, is a complex group of defenses that work to fight disease in your body.

Millions of helpful bacteria live on your skin and give you your first line of defense by killing many harmful types of bacteria. Nevertheless, disease-causing bacteria can enter your body through breaks in your skin. Even then, your body is not defenseless. Your body mobilizes a series of defenses against these disease-causing intruders.

Let's find out what kind of challenge your immune system meets every day in a location where you spend quite a bit of time.

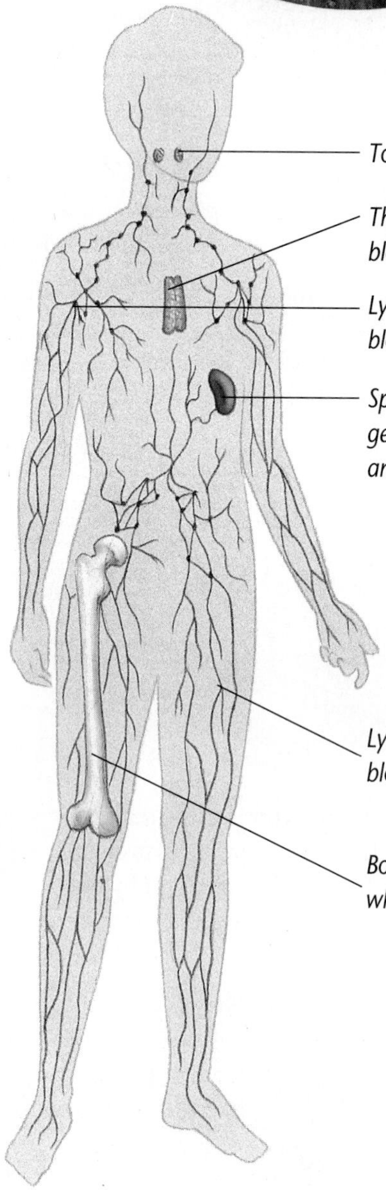

Figure 12-11

Besides white blood cells, the human immune system includes many other structures of the body. Which of the body structures shown in this diagram are commonly removed without harming the immune system?

What kinds of organisms live in your classroom?

You share your classroom with thousands of organisms, some of which are bacteria and fungi. You can collect some of these organisms.

What To Do

1. Place an open petri dish of agar in the classroom. After an hour, place a lid on the dish and tape it in place.

2. Have your teacher incubate it in a warm, dark place for two days.

3. Then, inspect the unopened dish. **CAUTION:** *Do not open the petri dish.*

Conclude and Apply

1. Did the contents of the dish change at all?

2. Use a magnifying glass to get a closer look at the contents of the dish. Describe what you see on the agar *in your Journal.*

Most of the organisms that grew in your petri dish are not harmful. The few bacteria that cause disease when they get inside your body are the focus of the immune system.

When disease-causing bacteria attack body cells, your immune system springs into action. Blood carries white blood cells to the site of the invading bacteria. White blood cells send out tendril-like extensions that surround and digest invading bacteria, as shown in **Figure 12-12**.

All of the functions of your immune system are general defenses to keep you disease-free. But they don't always work. Let's look at your body's other lines of defense.

Figure 12-12

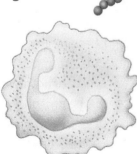 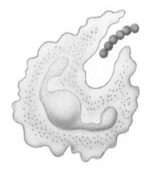  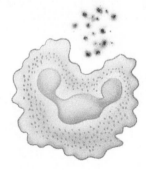

A A white blood cell approaches the bacteria.

B The white blood cell flows around the bacteria.

C Once inside the white blood cell, enzymes break down the bacteria.

D The white blood cell then flows away, leaving behind the undigested remains of the bacteria.

Specific Defenses

When your body fights disease, it is really battling proteins or chemicals that don't belong in your system. Proteins and chemicals that are foreign to your body are called **antigens**. A healthy immune system responds to an antigen by forming a specific substance to fight that antigen. The substance that forms to fight the antigen is called an antibody. **Antibodies** are substances produced in response to specific antigens. Antibodies are produced on the surface of certain kinds of white blood cells. Your blood carries these antibodies to the site of the antigens. **Figure 12-13** shows in a simplified way how each anti-

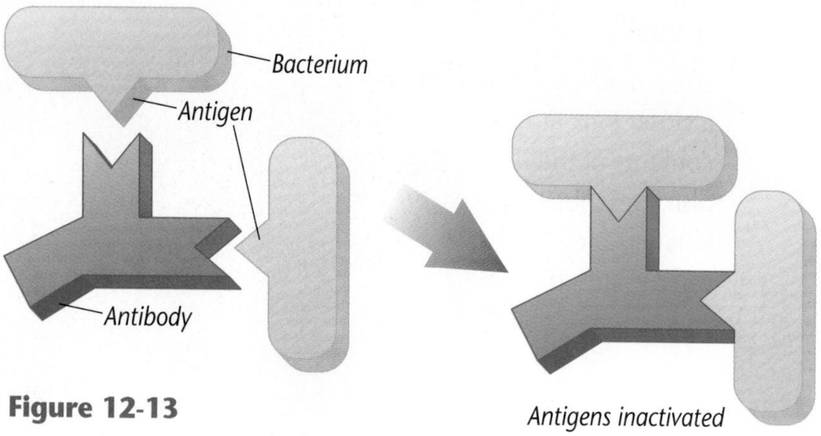

Figure 12-13

Bacterium

Antigen

Antibody

Antigens inactivated

An antibody conforms to the specific shape of an antigen and then binds with the antigen, rendering it harmless.

Producing Antibodies

Disease-causing viruses, bacteria, and parasites are all around you and would be deadly were it not for your immune system. Antibodies, a key part of your immune system, are a group of proteins that circulate in the blood. They are also found in mucus and saliva. White blood cells, shown in the photograph, produce antibodies.

Antigens

Antibodies are produced in response to antigens—*anti*body *gen*erators. Just about any large molecule, from protein to complex carbohydrate, can be an antigen. For example, protein molecules on the surface of viruses act as antigens. Molecules on the surface of bacteria and parasites also act as

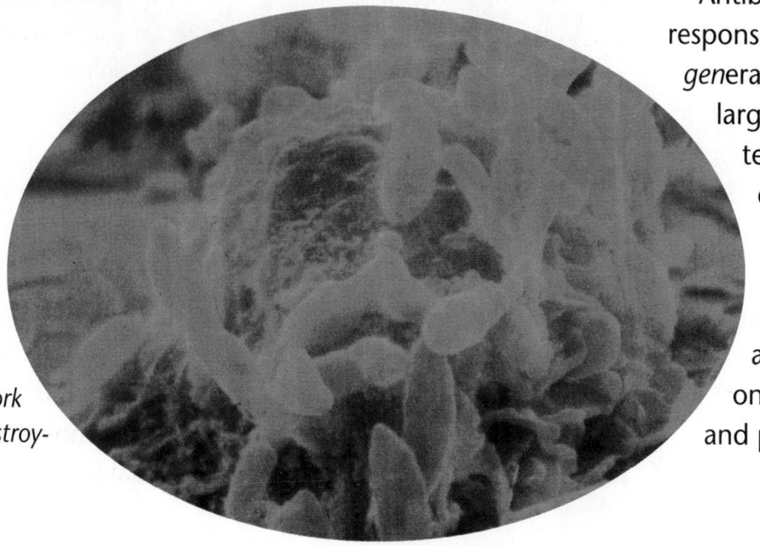

Here, a white blood cell is at work engulfing and destroying bacteria.

body binds with an antigen, making it harmless.

Once you produce a specific antibody to defend against a particular antigen, your body is said to be immune, or protected against the harmful effects of that disease-causing substance. When this happens, you have an **immunity** to that antigen.

Antibodies help build immunities that defend against diseases in two ways, actively and passively. Active immunity occurs when your body makes its own antibodies in response to an antigen. Passive immunity occurs when antibodies produced by another source are introduced into your body.

■ Active Immunity

The child in **Figure 12-14** has chicken pox. Her body has been invaded by an antigen. You cannot see it, but her immune system has started to make antibodies. Once enough antibodies have formed to defeat the antigen, her health will be restored. These

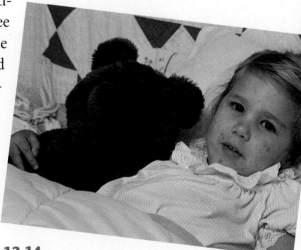

Figure 12-14

Antibodies produced to fight chicken pox leave the body with an active immunity against the disease.

antigens. Each kind of antibody recognizes and responds to only one kind of antigen. There are millions of different antigens in the world. How does your body know which antibodies to make? That is the work of B cells—a type of white blood cell.

B Cells

Each B cell contains a different antibody on its surface. There are about two trillion different B cells in your body at any one time, so the odds are very high that there is a B-cell antibody to match any antigen you might encounter. When the antibody on the surface of the B cell meets its matching antigen, it bonds to it. The two fit

together perfectly, and antibody production begins.

Plasma and Memory Cells

The B cell then forms either plasma cells or memory cells. A plasma cell can produce between 3000 and 30 000 antibodies per second and offers short-term protection. Memory cells give you lifelong immunity to certain diseases. Long after the infection is over and the plasma cells have died, memory cells continue to circulate. The next time the same antigen invades, the memory cells immediately start large-scale antibody production. There is no time for an infection to take hold.

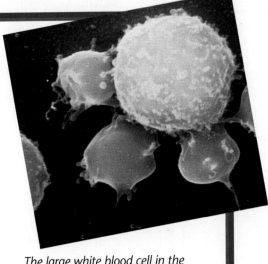

The large white blood cell in the photograph above is a B cell.

What Do You Think?

What memory cells might you have in your blood? Make a list of sicknesses that you have had that you are unlikely to get again. Compare lists with your classmates.

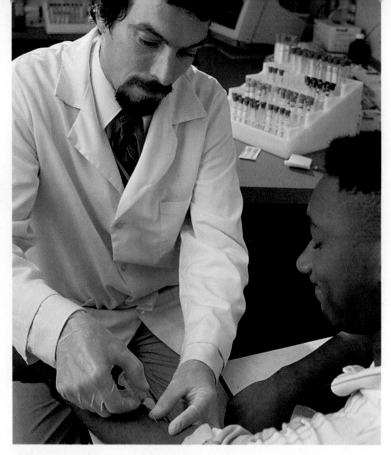

Figure 12-15

Children are given vaccines so that their bodies will have active immunity against certain diseases without having to get the disease first.

cine causes your body to form antibodies against the measles antigen. If the antigen later enters your body, antibodies that can destroy it are already available in your bloodstream. The antigens are destroyed before they have a chance to break down your body's immune system and cause illness.

However, a vaccine for measles will not protect you against the mumps. Even some diseases that are called by the same name, such as influenza (flu), change rapidly, and last year's flu antibodies will probably not protect you against this year's strain of the flu.

■ Passive Immunity

Passive immunity is similar to active immunity because both are the result of the work of antibodies in the body. However, in passive immunity, antibodies produced from another human or animal are injected into the body.

For example, when you were born, you were a bundle of passive immunity because you were born with all the antibodies that your mother had in her blood. These antibodies moved through the placenta from her blood to yours. However, they stayed with you only a few months. Passive immunity does not last as long as active immunity because the antibodies gradually disappear. Newborn babies lose their passive immunity in a few months. Then they are vaccinated to develop their own immunity, or they are injected with antibodies from another source.

antibodies will stay in her blood long after the antigen has been destroyed. If the antigen enters her body again, the cells making antibodies again become active. In this way, her body has developed an active immunity to a particular disease such as chicken pox.

■ Vaccines

Another way to develop active immunity to a certain disease is to introduce a dead or weakened form of the antigen to the body. This causes the body to produce antibodies. The introduction of an antigen into the body by inoculation or through the mouth is called a vaccination. **Figure 12-15** shows a vaccine being administered. A **vaccine** gives you active immunity against a specific disease without you having to get the disease first. For example, suppose you receive a vaccine for measles. The vac-

You probably were once injected by a doctor or nurse with antibodies to a disease called tetanus. If the antibodies are still present in your body, you have a passive immunity. Tetanus toxin is produced by a bacterium in soil and can enter your body through a cut or puncture wound. The toxin paralyzes muscles and can cause death by suffocation if the muscles that control breathing become paralyzed. Tetanus antitoxin is produced in horses when they respond to injections of the tetanus antigen.

When you receive a tetanus shot, antibodies made by horses are injected into your body. These antibodies provide you with limited immunity. Throughout your life, periodic booster shots keep you immune to the tetanus antigen. Unfortunately, you cannot be immunized against some of the most common diseases such as the cold.

Figure 12-16

Ⓐ When a horse is injected with the tetanus antigen, its body responds by producing antibodies to fight the antigen.

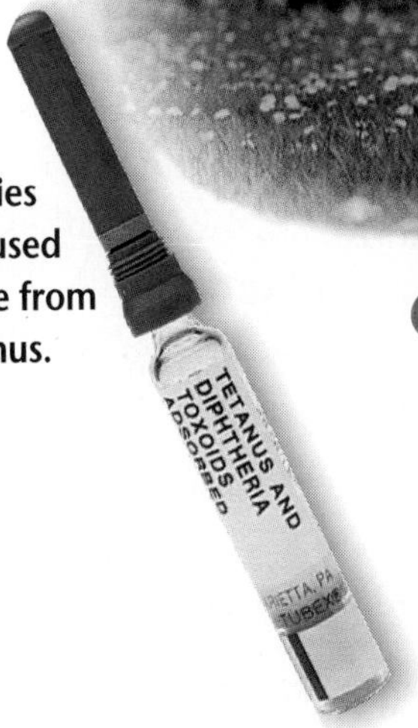

Ⓑ Tetanus antibodies are ready to be used to keep someone from developing tetanus.

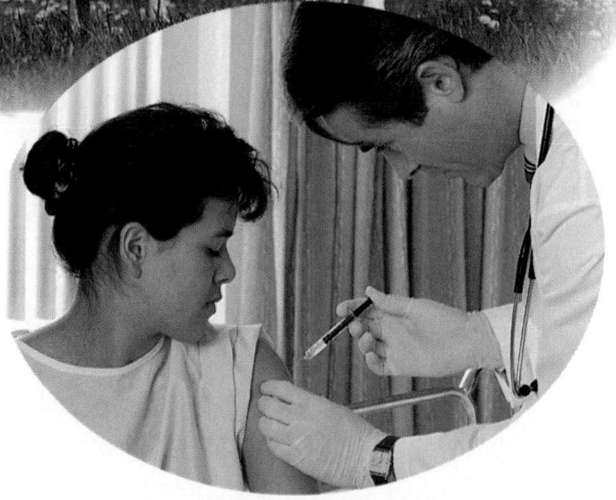

Ⓒ An injection of the antibodies made by a horse will give this person passive immunity against tetanus.

How Do We Know?

The First Vaccination

Edward Jenner, a British physician, was the first to realize that a person could be immunized against a disease. He observed that dairymaids in his home town who caught cowpox, a disease that resulted in sores on their hands, never caught smallpox, a much more serious disease that often resulted in death.

In 1796, Jenner took fluid from the sore of a dairymaid who had been infected with cowpox. He inserted the fluid into two small cuts on the arms of an eight-year-old boy, James Phipps. The boy developed cowpox. Forty-eight days later, Jenner inserted smallpox into the boy's arm. Phipps showed no signs of smallpox then, or over the rest of his life. Jenner had effectively vaccinated James Phipps against smallpox.

Communicable Diseases

The last time you had a cold or the flu, you probably felt miserable. Your symptoms very likely included body aches, watery eyes, congested lungs, and a runny nose. Eventually, after a few days of rest, your symptoms disappeared. Using what you have learned about antibodies and antigens, describe what was happening in your body the last time you got one of these diseases. Why did you get sick in the first place?

Find Out! ACTIVITY

How do agents that cause disease spread?

There are different ways that diseases are spread. Learn about one in this activity.

What To Do

1. Work with a partner. Place a drop of peppermint or lemon food flavoring on a cotton ball.
2. Rub the cotton ball in the shape of an X over the palm of your right hand and let it dry. Can you smell the flavoring?
3. Dry your hands on a towel. Now, shake hands with a classmate.

Conclude and Apply

1. How do you know if the flavoring has been passed to your classmate?
2. What does this tell you about how some diseases are spread?

As you found out in the Find Out activity, things in your environment can be picked up and passed very easily. Some of the more common things in your environment are viruses.

Colds are caused by viruses. Viruses are not bacteria. In fact there has been debate over whether they are alive or not. Viruses seem to be mostly DNA or RNA and must be inside a living cell to reproduce. When viruses reproduce, they produce thousands of copies of themselves and frequently destroy the host cell.

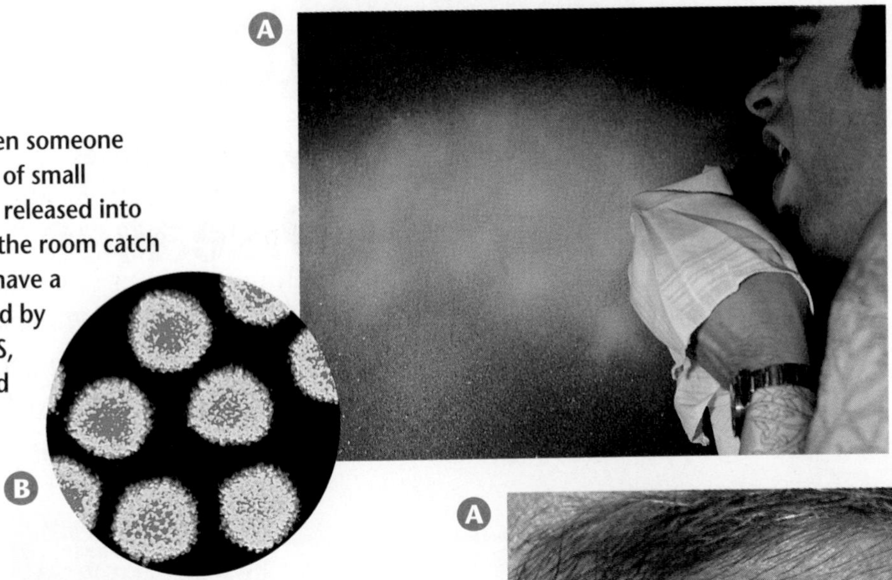

Figure 12-17

A cold is caused by a virus. When someone with a cold sneezes (A) a spray of small droplets containing the virus is released into the air. Could someone else in the room catch this person's cold? Viruses (B) have a core of DNA or RNA surrounded by protein. Viruses also cause AIDS, measles, mumps, influenza, and viral pneumonia.

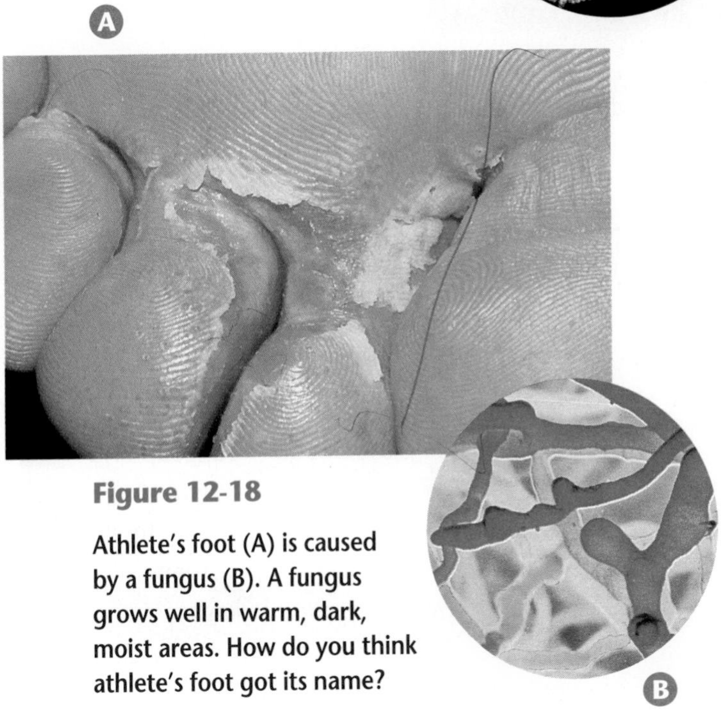

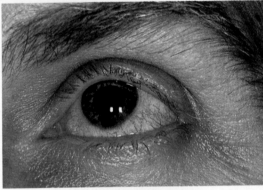

Figure 12-18

Athlete's foot (A) is caused by a fungus (B). A fungus grows well in warm, dark, moist areas. How do you think athlete's foot got its name?

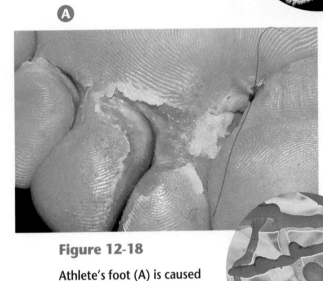

Figure 12-19

This person (A) is suffering from pinkeye, a disease that makes the eyeballs appear reddish-pink. Pinkeye is caused by bacteria (B) which are tiny living organisms. Is pinkeye communicable? Bacteria also cause tetanus, tuberculosis, typhoid fever, and bacterial pneumonia.

Viruses can be passed from person to person. When a person suffering with a cold coughs or sneezes, he or she releases small droplets containing the virus into the air.

If you don't wash your hands after they have come in contact with a contaminated object, you may also pick up the virus, which you can then pass with a handshake. Viruses can also be passed when sharing a drinking glass.

A cold is an example of a communicable disease, one that is spread, or transmitted, from one organism to another. Viruses are only one kind of agent that causes a communicable disease. Disease-causing bacteria, protists, and fungi also cause communicable diseases. To help prevent the spread of disease-causing organisms, however, water systems and swimming pools are treated with chlorine.

Stopping the Spread of Communicable Diseases

There are different types of communicable diseases. They can be caused by viruses, bacteria, protists, and fungi. You have likely been told more times than you care to remember to wash your hands before eating or after coming in contact with a possibly diseased item such as the rotting apple in this experiment. Does it really matter what you do?

Preparation

Problem
Is the spread of disease affected by washing or disinfecting?

Form a Hypothesis
How will the spread of disease be affected by different treatments of an infected object?

Objectives
- Determine the effect of different treatments of infected objects.
- Infer how this experiment is related to stopping the spread of communicable diseases.

Materials
6 fresh apples	sandpaper
rotting apple	cotton ball
6 sealable plastic bags	bar soap and
labels and pencil	water
surgical gloves	antibacterial
alcohol	soap
paper towels	knife

Safety

Plan the Experiment

1 Decide how you will treat each apple in the test.

2 How might the condition of the apple's skin affect the spread of disease? Does your test take this into account?

3 Will you clean several apples? With what types of cleaners? How will you know that your hands aren't reinfecting the clean apples?

4 Prepare your plan *in your Science Journal.* Prepare a way to record your observations after a week's time.

Check the Plan

1 Reread your plan and make any necessary modifications.

2 Have your teacher check your plan before you begin.

Analyze and Conclude

1. **Observe and Compare** Observe and compare any changes in the apples.

2. **Recognize Cause and Effect** Share your findings with other students. What was the purpose of each apple? What caused the effects you observed?

3. **Infer** Infer the effect that cleaning has on the spread of disease. Was your hypothesis accurate?

4. **Hypothesize** What situations might you be in where washing your hands might be important in fighting the spread of disease?

Going Further

Why is it important that people who work in restaurants wash their hands before leaving a restroom?

Sexually Transmitted Diseases

You've seen how diseases can be passed from person to person by contact with contaminated objects. Some of the most serious diseases are those transmitted by sexual contact. Diseases transmitted from one person to another person during sexual contact are called sexually transmitted diseases, or STDs.

Figure 12-20

This photograph shows the bacteria, magnified, that cause gonorrhea, a common sexually transmitted disease.

Genital herpes is an example of an STD. It causes small, painful blisters on the genitals. The herpes virus hides in the body for long periods and then reappears suddenly. There is no cure for herpes, and there is no vaccine to prevent it.

Gonorrhea and syphilis are two other common STDs. **Figure 12-20** shows the bacteria that cause gonorrhea. If the disease is not treated with antibiotic drugs, it can lead to sterility. It can also cause blindness in babies born to an infected mother. Syphilis is a more serious disease that can cause death in later stages if left untreated. It can be given to babies born to untreated women.

Sexually transmitted diseases are difficult to treat. Penicillin is used to treat syphilis and gonorrhea. However, there is one strain of gonorrhea that is resistant to penicillin.

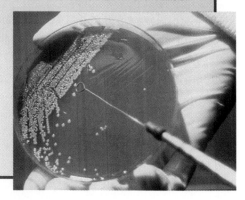

AIDS and Your Immune System

If you listen to the news or read newspapers or magazines, you've undoubtedly heard of AIDS. The word *AIDS* stands for Acquired Immune Deficiency Syndrome. It is a disease that was first identified in the early 1980s. Today, people around the world are suffering from AIDS.

AIDS is caused by a virus, (HIV) shown in **Figure 12-21**, that attacks a type of lymphocyte in the immune system. Lymphocytes are white blood cells that normally produce specific antibodies in the presence of antigens, thereby destroying invading antigens. Because HIV destroys lymphocytes, the body is left with no way to fight invading antigens that cause other diseases. For this reason, most people with AIDS die not from AIDS, but from diseases caused by other factors.

Your immune system is a complex group of defenses that your body possesses to fight diseases. It is made up of cells, tissues, organs, and body systems that fight bacteria, viruses, and harmful chemicals. When your immune system recognizes a foreign protein or chemical, it forms antibodies that help your body build defenses. While there are many diseases that can be prevented by vaccinations, there is, as yet, no vaccine for AIDS.

Recognizing Cause and Effect

How is not washing your hands, not covering your mouth when you cough, or not covering your nose when you sneeze related to the spread of disease? If you need help, refer to the **Skill Handbook** on page 684.

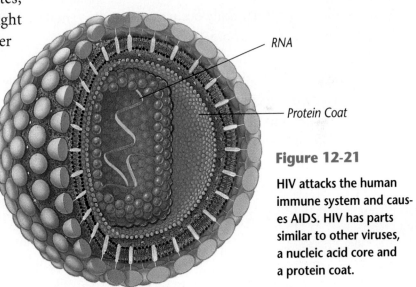

RNA

Protein Coat

Figure 12-21

HIV attacks the human immune system and causes AIDS. HIV has parts similar to other viruses, a nucleic acid core and a protein coat.

check your UNDERSTANDING

1. What is the platelets' role in healing skin?
2. Explain how skin and blood protect your body from disease-causing organisms.
3. How are active and passive immunity alike? How do they differ?
4. Why is it hard to avoid communicable diseases?
5. **Apply** Some vaccinations require booster shots. What would happen if you failed to get your booster shots for a particular disease?

HOW IT WORKS

How Do Antibiotics Fight Infections?

Suppose you wake up one morning with a sore throat, swollen glands, and a fever. You go to the doctor, who prepares a throat culture. The following day the results come back positive—you have strep throat. Your doctor then prescribes an antibiotic. It's not long before you are feeling better, and the infection is gone.

Antibiotics

Antibiotics are naturally occurring chemicals produced by microorganisms, like the Penicillium mold in the picture. They kill or limit the growth of other microorganisms. This activity occurs without affecting human cells or tissues and makes these chemicals lifesavers. Until antibiotics came into widespread use, bacterial diseases were a leading cause of death.

Use of Antibiotics

The widespread use of antibiotics in medicine was not established until 1927. That's when a British scientist accidentally discovered that a mold called Penicillium had killed some bacteria that was being studied in the lab. As you may have guessed, Penicillium is responsible for the antibiotic that you might take for a sore throat.

Because antibiotics are produced by microorganisms, scientists can produce these drugs in large quantities by simply encouraging the growth of these organisms.

How Antibiotics Work

Antibiotics work in different ways. Some, like penicillin, interfere with a bacterium's ability to repair its cell wall—a rigid, supporting structure. The bacterium then bursts and dies. Other antibiotics prevent proteins from being made in the bacterium. Proteins are important compounds in cell structures. They also act as enzymes that direct cell functions. A cell cannot survive if it is unable to make proteins.

What Do You Think?

You already know that penicillin was discovered accidentally, but did you know that some of the more important antibiotics have been found in rather strange places? For example, the antibiotic bacitracin was originally isolated from a patient's skinned knee. Another antibiotic, streptomycin, was isolated from bacteria found in the throat of a chicken. Given these examples, where do you think scientists could look in order to develop new antibiotics?

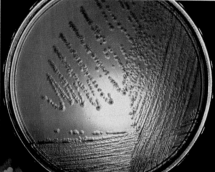

Bacterial throat culture

Penicillium mold

Science and Society

Health Workers with AIDS

What would you do if your family doctor had AIDS? Would you find another doctor?

According to the Centers for Disease Control (CDC) in Atlanta, 6436 health-care workers in the United States have developed AIDS since the early 1980s. More than 46 000 others are estimated to be HIV positive. HIV is the virus that causes AIDS. Yet this is just 0.1 percent of this country's 4.5 million health-care professionals.

Risk of Infection

Medical experts generally agree that the risks of infection are very small for patients. Many routine procedures, like checkups or blood pressure reading, pose no risk at all because there is no exchange of blood or other body fluids involved in these procedures. Even in surgery, the chances of infection are small when proper precautions are taken. Ordinary dental care is thought to be more of a concern because there is generally some bleeding in a patient's mouth.

HIV Testing

However, despite the small risks, many citizens are pressuring politicians at different levels of government to pass laws to require HIV testing for all health-care professionals.

Most medical experts oppose such testing. They say that required testing is impractical and expensive. To be reliable, workers would have to be tested every six months. Civil rights groups also oppose mandatory testing. Involuntary testing, they say, violates a person's right to privacy.

The American Medical Association and the American Dental Association have urged members to tell patients if they are HIV positive or if they have AIDS.

Science Journal

Consider the pros and cons of determining whether health-care workers are HIV infected. Should these workers be required to tell their patients? Their employers? Do patients have an obligation to tell their doctors whether they are HIV infected?

Health CONNECTION

Vaccines and the Developing World

Three-quarters of the world's people live in Latin America, the Caribbean, Africa, and Asia. About 86 percent of all births and 96 percent of all infant and child deaths occur in these parts of the world. Many of these deaths are the result of childhood diseases that could be prevented through immunization.

Immunization is a relatively simple and inexpensive process. In Latin America, the Caribbean, Africa, and Asia, it is one of the most effective and inexpensive ways to prevent disease. About 60 million children in these countries are now vaccinated each year against diphtheria, pertussis, tetanus, polio, tuberculosis, and measles. Yet millions more are not immunized. For example, measles alone still kills two million children in these countries each year.

Vaccines

Part of the problem is the nature of the vaccines themselves. Some vaccines must be kept refrigerated at all times, and refrigeration often is not available. Some vaccines require a series of booster shots spread over several weeks or months. Getting to a clinic can be extremely difficult, so many children do not get completely immunized.

Some experts have recommended that new or improved vaccines be developed. Such vaccines should not require refrigeration, should be given as close to birth as possible, and should be given in just one dose. Because of the spread of AIDS, vaccines should be simple to give in a way that does not require an injection.

Although it costs only about $10 per child for immunization, international agencies and health-care workers struggle to find funding for their programs.

You Try It!

Find out what vaccines you received as a child. Ask your doctor whether any new vaccines are given now that were not available when you were an infant.

Immunologists study diseases of the immune system. They attend college and graduate school or medical school. They work for hospitals, research institutions, and some are in private practice.

HISTORY CONNECTION

Charles Richard Drew: Blood Bank Pioneer

Many hospitals bear the name of Charles Richard Drew. As a medical student, Drew became interested in blood transfusion. His interest was sparked by the fact that there are four blood types in humans (A, B, AB, or O) and that a transfusion cannot be successful if the recipient and the donor have different blood types.

Drew saw many patients die from blood loss. Delay was caused by typing a patient's blood, finding donors, and drawing and administering the blood. Drew saw the need for blood to be preserved, stored, and ready for use in emergency situations.

Research and Discovery

After becoming a surgeon, Drew was given research money. He studied how blood and transfusion relate to shock. During shock, a patient's blood pressure drops dramatically and the pulse grows weak. Drew found that patients given adequate amounts of blood during shock had a chance for survival. There was one obstacle—blood was difficult to preserve.

Drew studied the factors that made blood unfit for transfusion and made a pioneering discovery. He found that plasma, the liquid part of the blood without the cells, could be stored for a long time and could be given to any patient, regardless of blood type!

Drew's discovery became very important during World War II when blood supplies were short. Furthermore, hospitals were using different procedures to collect and process blood. As a result, much of the blood became contaminated—and completely useless.

Blood Bank

Charles Drew organized the "Blood for Britain" project. His blood bank project was so successful that by the end of 1940, Britain no longer needed blood from the United States. In 1941 the American Red Cross goal was to set up a program to collect blood for American soldiers wounded in the war. Drew led the way!

Throughout his career, Drew was recognized as a pioneer in blood transfusion. He was the first African American to receive a Doctor of Science degree. In 1950, at the age of 46, Drew died in a tragic auto accident. His legacy continues, though, in every blood bank throughout the world—tributes to the brilliance of Dr. Charles Richard Drew.

What Do You Think?

How did Drew's discovery help the American armies during World War II?

Science Journal

Review the statements below about the big ideas presented in this chapter, and answer the questions. Then, re-read your answers to the Did You Ever Wonder questions at the beginning of the chapter. *In your Science Journal*, write a paragraph about how your understanding of the big ideas in the chapter has changed.

1 The cells and liquid in your blood carry oxygen and nutrients to all body cells and remove carbon dioxide and other wastes. *Describe how this occurs.*

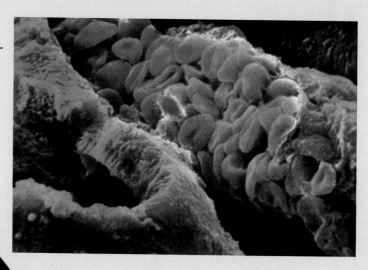

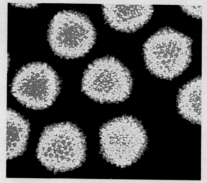

2 Your skin, blood, and organs work together in the immune system to defend your body from disease. Your body can have active or passive immunity to some diseases. *What is the difference between active and passive immunity?*

3 Disease-causing organisms can invade your body, but cleanliness and good health can help fight many communicable diseases. *Describe two means for reducing the chance of catching a communicable disease.*

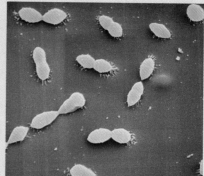

Using Key Science Terms

antibodies   plasma

antigens   platelets

clotting   red blood cells

hemoglobin   vaccine

immunity   white blood cells

For each set of terms below, explain the relationship that exists.

1. red blood cells, hemoglobin
2. antibodies, antigens
3. clotting, platelets
4. plasma, red blood cells
5. vaccine, antibodies
6. white blood cells, antibodies
7. immunity, antigens

Understanding Ideas

Answer the following questions in your Journal using complete sentences.

1. What is plasma and what are its components?
2. Does the number of white blood cells remain constant in your body? Why or why not?
3. What are platelets and what is their function?
4. If you have already had a tetanus shot, should you get another one if you step on a rusty nail? Why or why not?
5. Why is AIDS a fatal illness?

Developing Skills

Use your understanding of the concepts developed in this chapter to answer each of the following questions.

1. **Concept Mapping** Complete the concept map of blood.

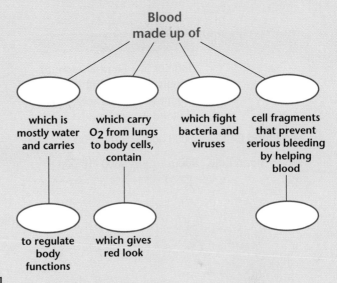

2. **Interpreting Data** Using your calculation of your body's mass of blood from the Explore activity on page 371, calculate how much of that mass is plasma.

3. **Observing and Inferring** To further see how diseases are spread as done in the Find Out activity on page 388, have four or five classmates moisten their hands and sprinkle their hands with glitter. Have the remaining students shake hands with at least one classmate with glittered hands. After noticing how easily the glitter was passed, continue to do the regular activities of the day. After 30 or more minutes have passed, notice where the glitter is now.

Critical Thinking

In your Journal, *answer each of the following questions.*

1. Look at the following chart. Would a patient with this blood cell count show any symptoms of illnesses? Explain your answer.

Blood Cell Counts		
	Number in 1 Cubic Millimeter of Blood	Normal Amount in 1 Cubic Millimeter of Blood
Red Blood Cells	5 000 000	5 000 000
White Blood Cells	9000	5000 -10 000

2. You had a cold last year. This year you got another cold. What does this indicate about your immune system?
3. If the number of white blood cells in your body increases, what might this mean?

Problem Solving

Read the following problem and discuss your answers in a brief paragraph.

You and your younger brother have been invited to a birthday cookout at a friend's house. Your friend's little sister has just come down with chicken pox. You had the disease four years ago but your younger brother has never had the disease.

1. Should you both attend the party?
2. What is likely to happen to you?
3. What is likely to happen to your brother?

CONNECTING IDEAS

Discuss each of the following in a brief paragraph.

1. **Theme—Systems and Interactions** You go to the doctor feeling very tired and run down. The doctor draws blood for tests and takes notes on your vital signs such as blood pressure, breathing, and pulse rates. Later, the doctor says you have a lung infection. What did the blood tests reveal about your white blood cells?
2. **Theme—Systems and Interactions** How is your diet important to the blood in your body?
3. **Theme—Systems and Interactions** Where in your body can you find bacteria that don't cause disease?
4. **Physics Connection** Briefly explain how the partial pressure of oxygen affects oxygen transport by red blood cells.
5. **Health Connection** Describe some of the reasons why measles kills two million children a year in some countries.

our fluid ENVIRONMENT

In this unit, you investigated how movements of air and water molecules are affected by differences in temperature and density, and by Earth's rotation.

You studied the chemistry of carbon compounds and the chemistry that occurs in your digestive system to break down some of these compounds. Finally, you saw how blood circulates these compounds to all other parts of your body.

Try the exercises and activity that follow—they will challenge you to use and apply some of the ideas you learned in this unit.

CONNECTING IDEAS

1. What is being measured when you obtain a reading of air pressure, water pressure, or blood pressure? How are these readings similar? In what way is a measurement of blood pressure different than the measurements of air or water pressure?

2. Organisms living in the oceans depend on sea water for certain things in order to survive. In a similar way, your cells depend on your blood for some of these same things. Make a list of those things that both sea water and blood provide.

Exploring Further ACTIVITY

How are people affected by changes in the weather?

Many people are affected by changes in the weather. Sometimes this is just the inconvenience of dealing with storms, but sometimes changes in weather affect their well being.

What To Do

1. Design a research project to study the effects of dark, dreary, rainy days on the moods that people project as related to the moods of these same people on bright, sunny days.

2. Conduct your research project and record your observations *in your Journal.*

3. Are your moods affected by changes in the weather?

UNIT 4

Changes in Life and Earth Over Time

Life on Earth may have begun billions of years ago in a place that looked like this. Bacteria and other simple organisms lived, reproduced, and died in springs and pools rich with chemical nutrients. Eventually, plants and animals evolved from these beginnings to fill available niches on Earth. Over time, many species became extinct, and new organisms evolved to take their place. Our world—and the life on it—slowly changed . . . as it continues to do to this day.

NATIONAL GEOGRAPHIC try it!

Try to imagine the passage of time covering billions of years. It's hard, even though we know that's how old Earth is. In that time, mountains formed and humans evolved. When did some of the events in Earth's history occur? How do the times at which those events took place compare?

What To Do

1. Draw a calendar for the year. Use boxes for each month, but don't bother with the exact dates. Just include four lines for each month to represent the weeks.

2. Give January, June, September, and December five weeks.

3. If the entire calendar represents the age of Earth, then each day is about 12.5 million years.

4. Today is December 31st. Mark and label when you think the following events took place on the calendar: when the Appalachian Mountains were formed; when dinosaurs first appeared; when the Grand Canyon started to form; and when the American Declaration of Independence was signed.

Reproduction

Science Journal

Before you begin to study about how organisms reproduce, think about these questions and answer them *in your Science Journal*. When you finish the chapter, compare your journal write-up with what you have learned.

A blur of buzzing yellow and black zips by Linda like a miniature B-52 bomber. Its destination? The zinnias beckoning with their bright red and yellow blooms from the Orozcos' flower garden.

Why do bees visit zinnias? They drink the nectar and collect the pollen that zinnias produce. Bees use nectar and pollen for food. While collecting pollen, bees also transfer pollen from one flower to another, helping flowers make seeds and reproduce. Both plants and animals, including human beings, need to reproduce if their species are to survive. Plants and animals don't reproduce in exactly the same way, of course. But for both, the process almost always begins with the union of a female egg and a male sperm. How does this union take place? How are the egg and the sperm produced? How do insects help plants reproduce? In this chapter, you'll discover the answers as you learn about the life process called reproduction.

▶ *In the activity on the next page, explore some of the characteristics of a chicken egg.*

Explore! ACTIVITY

What's an egg?

An egg may be just breakfast to you, but it is much more to a chicken.

What To Do

1. Your teacher will provide you with a chicken egg. Look at the physical traits of the egg, such as its size, color, and presence of a shell.

2. What do your observations indicate about the habitat of chickens?

3. Now examine the internal structure of the egg. Break open the chicken egg and pour the contents into a dish. What does the membrane just inside the shell look like?

4. Carefully examine the yolk and egg white. Based on what you can see, might this egg have grown into a chicken?

5 Make a drawing of the parts of the egg.

6. *In your Journal*, describe the appearance and possible functions of the parts of the chicken egg.

Sex Cells – A Different Story

13-1

Section Objectives

- Compare and contrast eggs and sperm.
- Contrast chromosome number in body cells and sex cells.

Key Terms

body cell, sex cells, sperm, eggs

Cell Types

Your body contains trillions and trillions of cells, the basic unit of structure in all living things. Just as whole organisms grow and die, individual cells grow and die. In the short time it takes you to read this paragraph, millions of the cells within your body will die.

■ Body Cells

How can your body continue to work properly even as millions of its cells are dying? Your body is constantly producing new cells. Even as cells are dying, new cells are being produced at a faster rate. Most of the cells that make up your body, your **body cells**, reproduce exact copies of themselves by mitosis. You may recall that in mitosis, one parent cell forms two identical new cells. The instructions that "tell" a cell how to develop, whether to be a blood cell or skin cell or some other kind of cell, are contained in the cell's chromosomes. All human body cells contain 46 chromosomes. Mitosis produces two new body cells, each with 46 chromosomes, just like the parent cell.

All species of organisms have a certain number of chromosomes in their body cells. This number is the same for all members of the species. For example, a body cell of a dog, whether it is a poodle or a collie, contains 78 chromosomes.

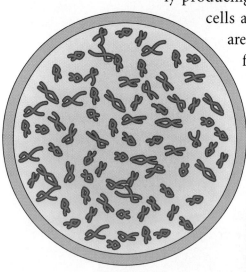

Figure 13-1

The 78 chromosomes in a puppy's body cells are what tells it to grow up to be a 0.5 kilogram chihuahua or a 66 kilogram wolfhound. How is this cell like a human body cell? How is it different?

Does a relationship exist between chromosome number and the complexity of an organism?

Are you more complex than a fruit fly? What about a goldfish? Does complexity of an organism depend on the number of chromosomes in its body cells?

What To Do

1. List the following organisms according to chromosome number, beginning with the smallest number of chromosomes: grasshopper—24, giant sequoia—22, fruit fly—8, tomato—24, guinea pig—64, goldfish—94, spider plant—24, dog—78, human—46.

2. Next to each organism, indicate the kingdom to which it belongs.

Conclude and Apply

1. Which organisms listed have the same chromosome number?

2. Are the organisms in Question 1 in the same kingdom?

3. *In your Journal*, state what you can conclude about a relationship between chromosome number and complexity of an organism.

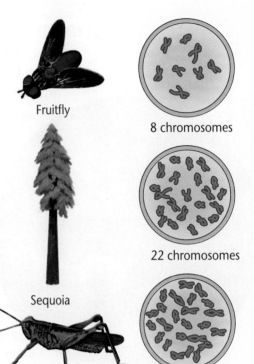

Fruitfly

8 chromosomes

Sequoia

22 chromosomes

Grasshopper

24 chromosomes

■ Sex Cells

Body cells are not the only kind of cell in your body, and mitosis is not the only kind of cell reproduction. In order for many organisms to produce offspring, they must produce **sex cells**. If you are a male, your body produces sex cells called **sperm**. If you are a female, your body produces sex cells called **eggs**. Offspring may be produced only when egg and sperm have united. Sex cells play an important role in reproduction. In the next section, you will learn how sex cells are produced.

Sperm and Eggs – Alike and Different

Figures 13-2 and **13-3** show a human sperm and a human egg. As you can see, sex cells are quite different from each other. Look closely at the

Figure 13-2

A SEM (scanning electron micrograph) makes possible this close-up of human sperm. A healthy adult human male normally produces about 200 million sperm each day.

physical traits of these cells. Sperm have tails and can swim, like tadpoles; eggs cannot. Sperm are very tiny and can be seen only under a microscope; eggs are one of the few human cells that can be seen with the naked eye. (Nerve cells are another.) A human egg is about the size of the point of a needle. Eggs contain a food supply in the form of a yolk. Tiny sperm do not.

■ Numbers Don't Lie

Another way that sperm and eggs differ is in the number produced. A bull can produce as many as five bil-

---

Which Came First— The Chicken or the Egg?

The first group of vertebrates able to lay its eggs on dry land appeared around 310 million years ago. Those eggs were encased in leathery shells, similar to the shells found on eggs laid by modern reptiles. The first land vertebrates were successful in the new environment because the shell protected the egg from predators and prevented it from drying out.

Parts of the Egg

In the Explore activity on page 405, you looked at the shelled egg of a chicken. In animals that lay shelled eggs, the

Bird eggs come in all colors and sizes, but they all have protective shells.

lion sperm at one time. But a cow usually produces only one egg at a time. This is the case with most mammals, including humans. Human males produce lots of sperm, while females produce relatively few eggs. Although the traits of sperm and eggs are quite different, the main job of these sex cells is the same; to join together to produce a new organism.

■ Chromosome Number

You have learned that a human body cell contains 46 chromosomes. You have also learned that body cells are produced through mitosis. Remember, through the process of mitosis, each new human body cell

Figure 13-3

Again using SEM, this human egg has been made large enough to see in detail. Why can't it produce a baby alone?

contains 46 chromosomes, just like the parent body cell. This ensures that the new cells look and function exactly like the parent cell. Sex cells are formed by a different process. Do you think that a human sex cell contains 46 chromosomes like a body cell? You will discover the answer to this question in the following activity.

Like birds, reptiles lay shelled eggs.

shell is deposited around the fertilized egg cell just before it leaves the animal's reproductive tract. Packaged along with the fertilized egg is a large food supply called the yolk. Albumen, a protein in the white of the egg, provides water and additional nutrients.

Shelled eggs have several protective membranes. The first membrane to form encloses the yolk. Another membrane surrounds the embryo and is liquid-filled. This liquid-filled space acts as a shock absorber, cushioning the developing embryo.

A third membrane lines the eggshell and allows the embryo to exchange oxygen and carbon dioxide with the air outside. The remaining membrane forms a sac into which the embryo excretes wastes.

Shelled eggs provide a developing embryo with everything it needs to survive. Why do you think they were such an important adaptation for the evolution of land vertebrates?

What Do You Think?

In most animals that lay unshelled eggs in water, fertilization is external. What kind of fertilization occurs in animals that lay shelled eggs? What is the advantage of this kind of fertilization?

Explore! ACTIVITY

How do the number of chromosomes in body cells and sex cells compare?

What do peas, tomatoes, rabbits, chickens, and crayfish have in common with one another? What do they have in common with you? You might think you have nothing in common with these organisms. But this activity will show you that you do, in fact, share certain characteristics with even a pea.

What To Do

1. Study the table. What relationship do you see between the number of chromosomes in body cells and sex cells of humans and peas?

2. *In your Journal*, predict the numbers that complete the table.

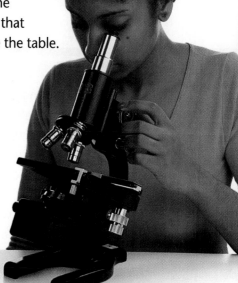

Cell Chart			
Organism	Body Cell Chromosomes	Egg Chromosomes	Sperm Chromosomes
Human	46	23	23
Pea	14	7	7
Tomato	24		
Corn	20		
Rabbit	44		
Chicken	78		
Mouse	40		
Crayfish	200		

There is a major difference between the number of chromosomes contained in a body cell and a sex cell. Sex cells, whether sperm or eggs, contain half the number of chromosomes contained in a body cell of the organism. In the next section, you will learn why these special cells contain half the number of chromosomes that body cells contain.

check your UNDERSTANDING

1. Tell which of the following phrases describe sperm, eggs, both, or neither: relatively large, relatively small, tail present, stored food present, formed by mitosis, body cell, sex cell, formed by meiosis.

2. The muscle cells in a housefly's leg contain 24 chromosomes. If each of the following cell types came from a housefly, how many chromosomes would each contain: sperm, body cell, egg, eye cell?

3. **Apply** What do the physical traits of a human sperm indicate about the environment in which the sperm cell lives and functions?

Meiosis Makes Sex Cells

The Process of Meiosis

Mitosis is a process of cell division in which a body cell makes an identical copy of itself. But as you learned in the last section, sex cells contain half the number of chromosomes found in body cells. Sex cells can't be formed by mitosis.

Sex cells are formed by a process called **meiosis**. In the following activity, you will make a model of meiosis.

Section Objectives
- Describe the process of meiosis.
- Determine the results of meiosis and why it is needed.
- Determine where and when meiosis occurs.

Key Terms
meiosis, testis, ovary

Explore! ACTIVITY

How are sex cells formed?

What To Do

1. Obtain a package of colored candies and five paper cups.

2. Place two pairs of candies in one cup. The candies of pair one should be the same color. The candies of pair two should be the same color, but a different color from the candies in pair one.

3. Add four more candies identical to the ones already in the cup.

4. Divide the eight candies evenly between two other cups, so that each cup contains the same number of each color of candy.

5. Finally, divide the contents of the two cups evenly so that the end product is four cups that each contain one of each color of candy.

6. *In your Journal*, explain the relationship between the number of candies first placed in the original cup (four candies) and those contained in the final four cups.

In the meiosis model you just made, candy represented chromosomes. The first cup represented a body cell, but the final four cups represented sex cells. What does this indicate about the relationship between the number of chromosomes in a body cell and the number of chromosomes in sex cells, which are cells that form by meiosis?

Meiosis – A Closer View

Now that you have a general idea of what occurs during meiosis, let's look at the process in detail. **Figure 13-4** shows the steps that make up this process. Meiosis begins in a cell in the reproductive organs of an organism. The number of chromosomes in the cell varies among different species of organisms. For this example, the cell in **Figure 13-4** has two pairs of chromosomes for a total of four chromosomes.

Figure 13-4

All reproductive cells reproduce the same way, through the process of meiosis. Meiosis involves two divisions of the chromosomes in the original cell.

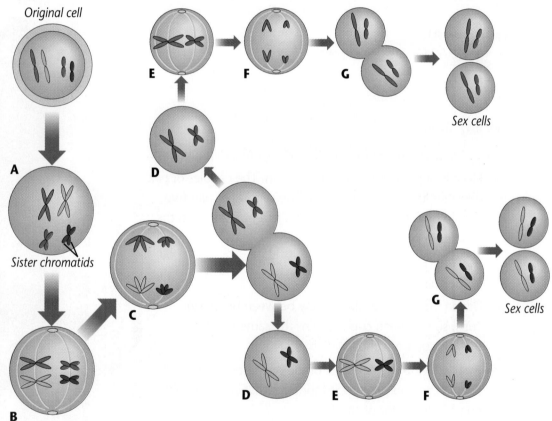

A Each chromosome doubles itself, forming two identical copies called sister chromatids. How many chromosomes are in the diagrams? How many chromatids?

B The doubled chromosomes come together in matching pairs. Where do they line up?

C The chromosomes now separate. Where are they pulled? Are the chromosomes that have been pulled to one end like one another, or are they different?

D The first division in meiosis has occurred as the cell divides, forming two new cells. What are the contents of these cells?

E The chromosomes again line up along the center of each new cell. How does this differ from step B?

F Now the sister chromatids separate and move to opposite ends of the cell. How is this stage of meiosis very similar to mitosis?

G The cells divide. How many new cells are formed? Compared to the original cell, how many chromosomes do the four new cells have?

Once you understand meiosis, study **Figure 13-5**, which shows a comparison of mitosis and meiosis. In the following Investigate, you will take a closer look at these two processes.

Figure 13-6

As in other sexually reproducing animals, meiosis produces egg and sperm in these two cats.

Figure 13-5

The end products of mitosis and meiosis are very different even though the two processes start out similarly.

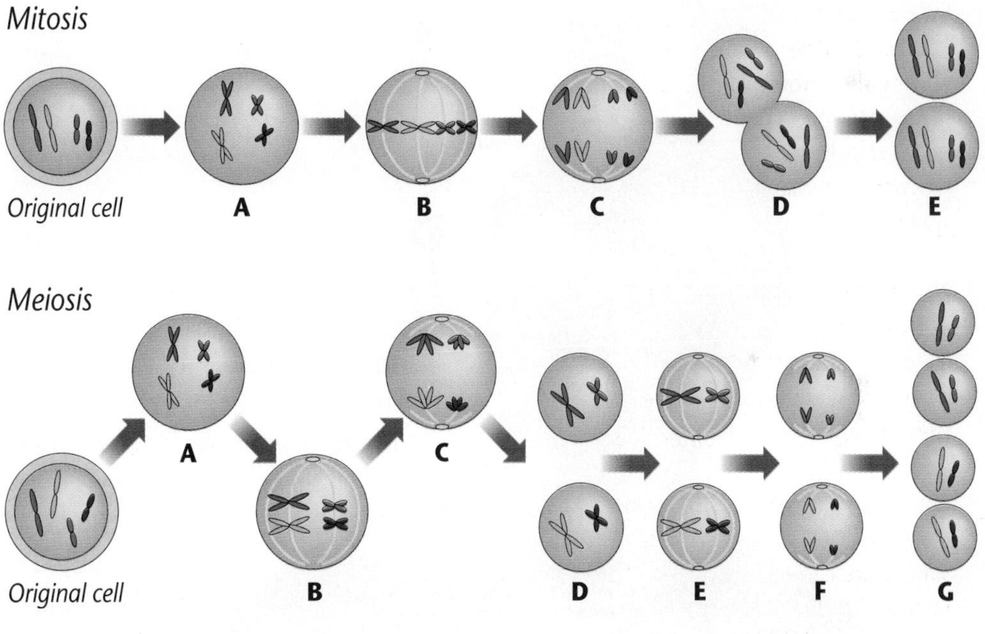

A The chromosomes double in both mitosis and meiosis.

Mitosis

Original cell   **A**   **B**   **C**   **D**   **E**

B The chromosomes line up in pairs in meiosis, but not in mitosis.

Meiosis

Original cell   **A**   **B**   **C**   **D**   **E**   **F**   **G**

C In meiosis, the chromosomes separate but chromatids remain joined. In mitosis, chromatids separate.

D Chromatids are still joined in meiosis, but not in mitosis.

E Mitosis is complete, but another division is about to take place in meiosis. The chromosomes line up along the center of the cell.

F The chromatids separate.

G Compare the end products of meiosis with the end products of mitosis. How do they differ?

INVESTIGATE!

Mitosis and Meiosis

You can make models of the steps of mitosis and meiosis.
Your model will allow you to compare the end results of
mitosis and meiosis.

Problem
How is meiosis different from mitosis?

Materials
yarn strands, four different colors
tape or glue
scissors
large sheets of paper

Safety Precautions

What To Do

1 Copy the data table *into your Journal*.

2 In your group, develop a plan for ***modeling*** the steps of mitosis and meiosis using the materials provided. Refer to the data table for the number of chromosomes to include in your model. You may also want to sketch diagrams of your plan to use as patterns. If you need additional help, the steps of mitosis and meiosis are shown in Figure 13-5 on page 413. (Note: A suggested way for drawing and modeling chromosomes is shown in photos B and C on page 415.)

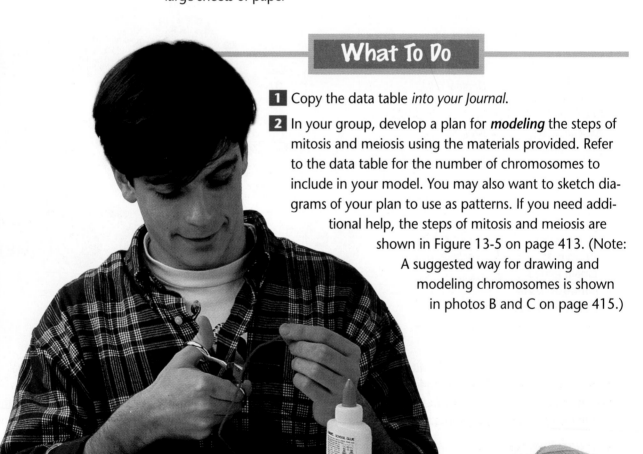

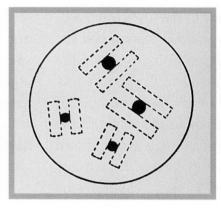

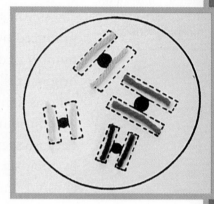

A   B   C

3 Before you make your model, have your teacher check your plan.

4 Make your model following the plan you have developed.

5 When you are finished with your model, complete your data table.

Data and Observations		
COMPARING MITOSIS AND MEIOSIS	MITOSIS	MEIOSIS
Type of cell undergoing reproduction		
Number of chromosomes before cell begins to reproduce	4	4
Chromosome pairs in the original cell		
Final number of chromosomes in each new cell at the end of reproduction		
Chromosome pairs in each new cell at conclusion of reproduction		

Analyzing

1. *Compare* the location and arrangement of chromosomes in the cell during Step B of mitosis and meiosis on page 413.

2. *Compare* the location and arrangement of chromosomes in the cell during Step C of mitosis and meiosis on page 413.

Concluding and Applying

3. How do the end results of mitosis and meiosis differ?

4. **Going Further** *Predict* what would occur if sex cells were produced by mitosis rather than by meiosis.

Where and When Meiosis Occurs

As you saw in the Investigate, cells produced by meiosis contain half the number of chromosomes found in the original cell, while cells produced by mitosis contain the same number of chromosomes as in the original cell. Because sperm and eggs are produced by meiosis, they have half as many chromosomes as body cells from the same organism.

Meiosis can occur only in the sex organ of a living thing. In humans, sperm are produced in a male sex organ called a **testis**. A male has two testes. Eggs are produced in a female sex organ called an **ovary**. Females have two ovaries. Where does meiosis occur in your body?

■ Sexual Maturity

From the time you were an embryo, mitosis has been occurring in most of your body cells. This is not true of meiosis. For males, meiosis begins when the organism reaches sexual maturity. For females, meiosis begins before birth. Chromosomes duplicate themselves, but cells remain in this stage until the female is sexually mature. Then the process of meiosis continues. Cells divide to form eggs, usually one at a time.

The time of your own sexual maturity is marked by the production of sex cells by your sex organs. If you are a male, your testes will be producing sperm for the rest of your life.

Figure 13-7

Although these family members are each unique, they display many similar characteristics.

How Do We Know?

How do scientists count chromosomes?

Various cell staining techniques help scientists examine and even count chromosomes within a cell. Counts can be made from a body cell and a sex cell of an organism and then compared. Scientists are also able to stop meiosis or mitosis at a particular stage to observe exactly what is occurring at that time in each process.

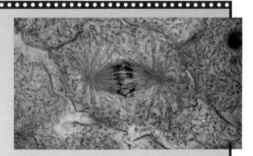

However, the number of sperm your body produces will decrease as you age. If you are a female, your ovaries will produce eggs until between the ages of 45 and 55.

The time of sexual maturity differs in all living things. For humans, sexual maturity usually occurs between the ages of 10 and 14. A mouse can reach sexual maturity at the age of 2 months. Sexual maturity in a corn plant occurs when the plant is between 3 and 4 months old, while most dandelion plants reach sexual maturity when 4 to 5 weeks old.

■ Why Meiosis Is Needed

Did you ever wonder why you resemble some members of your family more than others? You probably share physical traits with each of your parents because you inherited genetic material from each of them. Half of the 46 chromosomes in each of your body cells resemble half of the chromosomes in your mother's body cells. The other half of the chromosomes in your body cells resemble half of the chromosomes in your father's body cells.

In order to understand why this happens, think again about meiosis. Meiosis produces sex cells that contain half the number of chromosomes found in a body cell. Human eggs contain 23 chromosomes. Human sperm also contain 23 chromosomes. During fertilization, an egg and a sperm join. The cell that results contains 46 chromosomes. You should now understand why sex cells must divide by meiosis. If human sex cells formed by mitosis, each would contain 46 chromosomes. The cell produced by fertilization would contain 92 chromosomes!

In this section, you have compared two methods of cell division. You have learned why it is important that sex cells divide by meiosis rather than mitosis. In the next section, you will discover how sex cells meet during fertilization.

check your UNDERSTANDING

1. How many times in meiosis do chromosomes double themselves? How many times do matching pairs of chromosomes line up along the cell center in groups of four? How many times do sister chromatids separate?
2. Why must an egg and sperm have half the number of chromosomes as the fertilized egg?
3. Where does the process of meiosis occur in your body?
4. **Apply** Cells from the muscle of a cat's thigh contain 38 chromosomes each. Based on this information, how many chromosomes does a cat sperm contain? Explain how you arrived at your answer.

13-3 Plant Reproduction

Section Objectives
- Diagram the structure of a typical flower.
- Describe how flowering plants reproduce.

Key Terms

stamen
pistil

The Need for Fertilization

On its own, a single egg or sperm cannot form a new offspring. An egg and sperm must come together. But the joining of an egg and a sperm is no easy task. In most plants and animals, a sizeable distance lies between the male and female sex organs. Most organisms have structures that aid the fertilization process. In this section, you'll learn about fertilization in plants. In the next section, you'll read about fertilization in animals.

Figure 13-8
Flowers seem like pretty decorations, but they have important work to do.

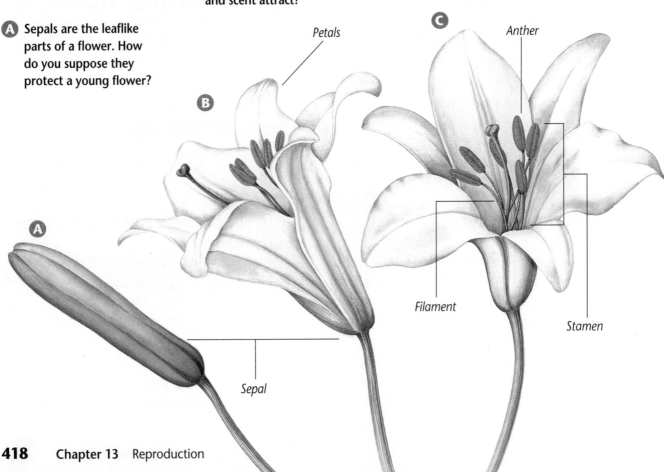

B Petals are the colored parts that protect the flower's sex organs. What do their color and scent attract?

C The stamen is the male reproductive organ. The saclike anther at the top is held up by a long filament. Anthers produce pollen. What reproductive cell is in this pollen?

A Sepals are the leaflike parts of a flower. How do you suppose they protect a young flower?

Petals

Anther

Filament

Stamen

Sepal

Plant Reproduction

Nearly all the plants you are familiar with are seed plants. Like animals, seed plants have both body cells and sex cells. A plant's body cells grow and divide by mitosis. The body cells develop into roots, stems, and leaves. A plant's sex cells are produced by meiosis in the reproductive organs of the plant. If a seed plant's male and female sex cells join, a new seed develops.

■ Flowering Plants

Have you ever stopped to admire a flower in bloom? **Figure 13-8** shows the anatomy of a flower. In this figure,

you will notice the male reproductive organ, the **stamen**. You'll also notice the female reproductive organ, the **pistil**. Study and read about these and other flower parts in the figure.

All of the structures shown in **Figure 13-8** are found in flowers. Some flowers contain both male and female structures, while others have only male or female parts. Whether an egg and sperm come from the same plant or different plants, pollen must be transferred from the male part to the female part for a new organism to develop. This process is called pollination.

Connect to...
Earth Science

Rhododendrons and azaleas prefer cool, moist soil that contains humus, and is acidic, with a pH between 4.5 and 6.5. Prepare a table that shows how soil, climate, and moisture conditions in your area compare with the requirements for Rhododendrons and azaleas.

D The pistil is the female reproductive organ. Its top end is called the stigma. How do you suppose the stigma's sticky surface helps ensure pollination?

E The pistil, like the stamen, has a long, stalk-like structure. It's called the style. The pistil's base is rounded. It is the flower's ovary. What reproductive cells are produced there? What reproductive cells will be deposited there?

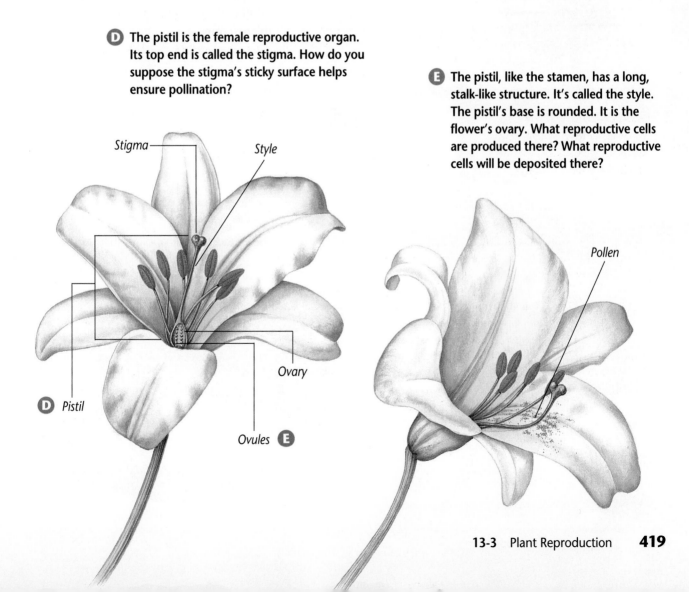

Stigma — Style

Ovary

D Pistil

Ovules **E**

Pollen

Parts of a Flower

Many plants are both male and female. Examining the parts of a flower will help you identify the male and female reproductive organs. Investigating these structures will help you understand how pollination occurs.

Preparation

Problem
How does pollination occur?

Form a Hypothesis
How do you think the characteristics of the parts of a flower ensure pollination?

Objectives
- Identify the parts of an actual flower.
- Give the function of each part of a flower and its role in pollination.

Materials
tulip, lily, or gladiola
scalpel
hand lens
microscope
microscope slide
water
eyedropper
coverslip
forceps

Safety

Use caution when handling sharp objects.

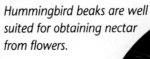

Hummingbird beaks are well suited for obtaining nectar from flowers.

DESIGN YOUR OWN
INVESTIGATION

Plan the Experiment

1 What parts of the flower will you examine? Use **Figure 13-8** to choose the parts to investigate. Will your choice cover the important organs?

2 What kind of observations will you make? What characteristics will you look at? Will color, number, or texture be important? How will you record your observations?

3 Will you observe these structures in more than one kind of flower?

4 What structure would you like to cut open and observe? What might you look at under a microscope?

5 Plan your experiment, taking into account the questions above.

Check the Plan

1 Will your plan be sufficient to allow you to test your hypothesis? Will you be able to answer the question stated in the problem?

2 Show your plan and your data table to your teacher. Include any suggestions and proceed with your investigation.

A

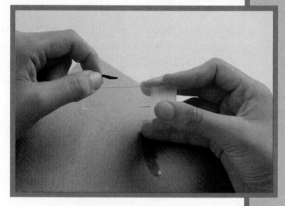

B

Analyze and Conclude

1. Explain Use your observations to explain how pollination occurs and what characteristics of the different plant structures are important to pollination.

2. Compare Compare your answer to question 1 with your hypothesis. What did this experiment show you?

3. Infer How is the stigma adapted for attracting pollen?

4. Using Computers Design a spreadsheet that could be used to compare the quantity of each structure in different types of flowers.

Going Further

You have probably seen bees travel among flowers in a garden. Hypothesize how the movement of a bee might aid in pollination.

Getting Sperm and Egg Together

Eggs are located inside the ovary of a flower. Sperm are found in pollen grains located in stamens. Usually, sperm from one flower fertilize the eggs of a different flower of the same species. How do sperm and egg get together?

Figure 13-9 shows the events that take place during pollination and fertilization. Keep in mind that pollination is the transfer of pollen from the male anther to the female stigma. Fertilization is the actual union of egg and sperm and takes place inside the pistil.

After fertilization, the ovary grows and develops into a fruit. The fertilized egg becomes an embryo within a future seed. This embryo will eventually develop into a new plant.

Figure 13-9

A The insect can't resist this flower's colorful petals and sweet scent. As the insect moves about, the flower's anther rubs pollen on the insect's body. The insect will deposit the pollen on a nearby flower. How else might this pollen reach the flower?

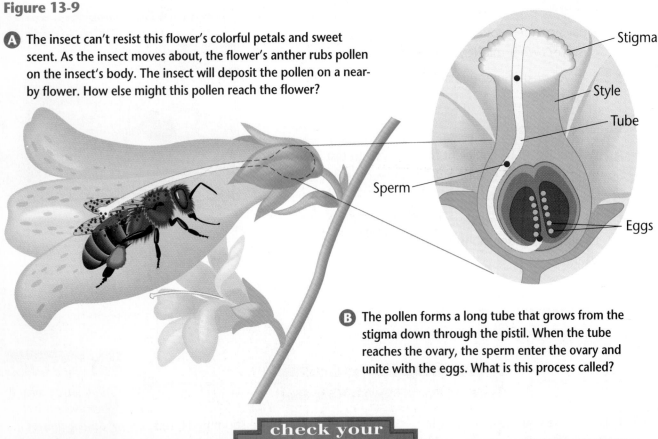

Stigma

Style

Tube

Sperm

Eggs

B The pollen forms a long tube that grows from the stigma down through the pistil. When the tube reaches the ovary, the sperm enter the ovary and unite with the eggs. What is this process called?

check your UNDERSTANDING

1. Diagram a typical flowering plant. Label all the parts of the flower, including the reproductive organs.
2. What are the roles of stamens and pistils in plant reproduction?
3. Describe the process of reproduction in a flowering plant.
4. **Apply** Could pollination occur in an ecosystem that didn't contain any insect populations? Explain your answer.

Animal Reproduction

Animal Reproduction

Unlike many plants, a frog does not have both male and female reproductive structures. A frog is either a male or a female. This is not the case, however, for all animals. Each earthworm, sponge, and flatworm contains both male and female parts in the same animal. But animals in most species are either male or female.

■ External Fertilization

Because a frog is either male or female, certain actions are necessary for fertilization to occur. The joining of a sperm and an egg occurs outside the bodies of the two frogs. This type of fertilization is called external fertilization. Follow the steps of fertilization in **Figure 13-10**.

Section Objectives
■ Compare and contrast external and internal fertilization in animals.
■ Demonstrate an understanding of how humans reproduce.

Key Terms
menstrual cycle, menstruation

Figure 13-10

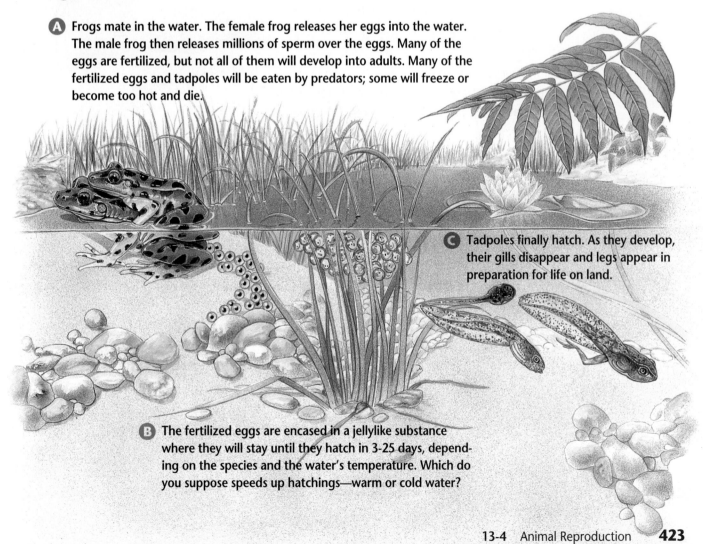

A Frogs mate in the water. The female frog releases her eggs into the water. The male frog then releases millions of sperm over the eggs. Many of the eggs are fertilized, but not all of them will develop into adults. Many of the fertilized eggs and tadpoles will be eaten by predators; some will freeze or become too hot and die.

C Tadpoles finally hatch. As they develop, their gills disappear and legs appear in preparation for life on land.

B The fertilized eggs are encased in a jellylike substance where they will stay until they hatch in 3-25 days, depending on the species and the water's temperature. Which do you suppose speeds up hatchings—warm or cold water?

Human Reproduction

■ Male Reproductive System

Like frogs, humans are either male or female. In humans, however, as in many other animals, fertilization occurs inside the body of the female. This is called internal fertilization because *internal* means "inside". The male reproductive system consists of organs and tissues that produce sperm and move them out of the body. **Figure 13-11** shows the parts of the male reproductive system. Study **Figure 13-11** and then do the Explore activity.

Explore! ACTIVITY

What is the pathway of sperm through the male reproductive system?

What To Do

1. Refer to the figure of the male reproductive system in Figure 13-11. Give the function of each part.

2. *In your Journal*, make an events chain concept map to illustrate the order of structures through which sperm pass in the male reproductive system.

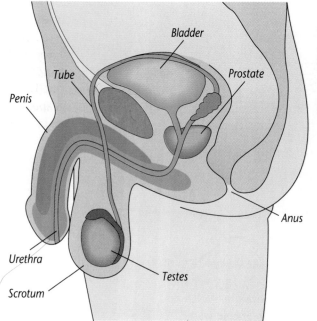

Figure 13-11

The testes are a pair of reproductive organs, which are covered and protected by the scrotum. The testes produce sperm, which are carried out of the body via the tube and urethra. The prostate produces fluids that enable the sperm to swim and keep them from drying out.

■ Female Reproductive System

The main job of the male reproductive system is to produce sex cells. The female reproductive system has two jobs—to produce sex cells and to provide a home to a developing embryo. **Figure 13-12** shows the parts of the female reproductive system that carry out these jobs. As you study **Figure 13-12**, think about the process of fertilization. Then, read the next section about where fertilization occurs.

■ Where Does Fertilization Occur?

You already know that fertilization in humans takes place internally. During mating, the male releases sperm directly into the female's vagina. Internal fertilization increases the chance that egg and sperm will meet. Millions of sperm are deposited into the female's reproductive system. A fertilized egg results only if a sperm joins with an egg and fertilizes it. It only takes one sperm to fertilize an egg. About every 28 days, the female reproductive system goes through a cycle that prepares an egg for fertilization.

Figure 13-12

A The female reproductive system includes the thick-walled uterus, two ovaries, two oviducts, and the vagina. Eggs develop within the ovaries, and are then released into the oviducts. From there, they travel to the uterus. Why do you suppose the uterus has thick, muscular walls?

B Eggs develop in the ovaries and are usually released one at a time. One egg is released about every 28 days. The large, bulging structure is an egg that is about to rupture from the ovary.

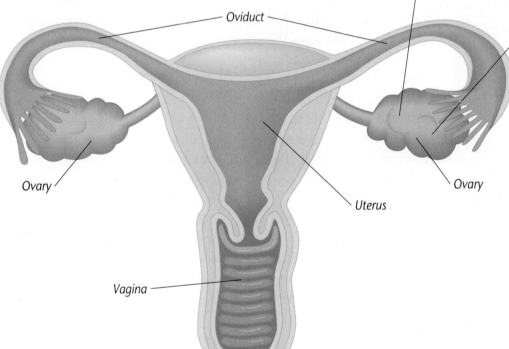

Immature eggs

Mature egg

Oviduct

Ovary

Ovary

Uterus

Vagina

Menstrual Cycle

When a human female is born, there are nearly half a million undeveloped eggs in her ovaries. Only about 500 of these eggs will ever develop. Beginning between the ages of 10 and 14, the ovaries begin to release an egg about once every 28 days. The egg is either fertilized, or it

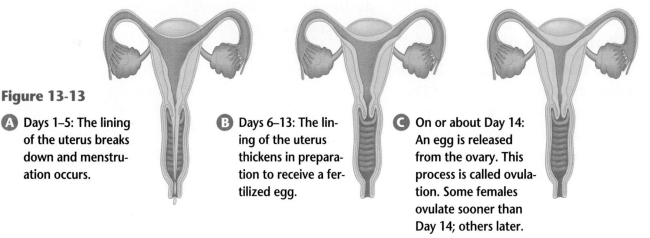

Figure 13-13

Ⓐ Days 1–5: The lining of the uterus breaks down and menstruation occurs.

Ⓑ Days 6–13: The lining of the uterus thickens in preparation to receive a fertilized egg.

Ⓒ On or about Day 14: An egg is released from the ovary. This process is called ovulation. Some females ovulate sooner than Day 14; others later.

Chemicals and Birth Defects

Although scientists do not know what causes the majority of birth defects in humans, they do know that certain chemicals and other substances pose risks to a developing fetus. How does a fetus come into contact with these substances?

Female Reproductive Health

Until recently, most attention to preventing birth defects focused on women while they were pregnant. Scientists had long assumed that most children born with birth defects had suffered some kind of damage while they were developing inside their mothers.

Male Reproductive Health

New research shows, however, that men's reproductive health also affects their children. For example, men exposed to lead may produce defective sperm. Defective sperm usually cannot fertilize an egg. If, however, fertilization does occur, the result may be a deformed fetus.

Men who smoke cigarettes or drink alcohol heavily may also have fertility problems or may have children with birth

is shed from the body in a monthly cycle called the menstrual cycle. The **menstrual cycle** is a cycle in which the ovary releases an egg and the uterus prepares to receive it, then discards it if the egg is not fertilized. The monthly discharge of egg, uterine lining, and blood through the vagina is called **menstruation**. This event and the other changes that take place during the menstrual cycle are shown in **Figure 13-13**.

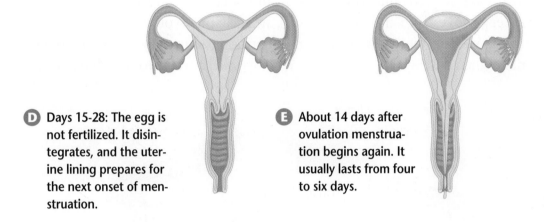

D Days 15-28: The egg is not fertilized. It disintegrates, and the uterine lining prepares for the next onset of menstruation.

E About 14 days after ovulation menstruation begins again. It usually lasts from four to six days.

defects that result from these habits. It has long been known, for example, that women who smoke during pregnancy risk having low birth weight babies. Research now indicates that low birth weight in babies can also result from fathers who smoke. Heavy drinking by men one month before fertilization can also cause low birth weight in babies.

Exactly how chemicals affect men's reproductive health is still mostly unknown. A toxin (poison) may directly damage sperm-producing cells in the testes, so not enough sperm are produced, and sterility results. Other times defective sperm are produced, which also may cause sterility. Or, the defective sperm might fertilize an egg and result in a damaged fetus. Men also might pass toxins in their semen to women. These toxins can then damage the egg.

*inter*NET
CONNECTION

Information on environmental health and birth defects is available from the Centers for Disease Control and Prevention on the World Wide Web. Use the information on the website to identify three toxins and their effects on reproductive health. How common are toxins? Do they affect men and women equally?

Healthy parents increase the likelihood of healthy babies.

Fertilization

If sperm are deposited in the vagina, they move up into the oviducts. If sperm are present as an egg leaves the ovary, fertilization can take place. When these sex cells unite, the fertilized egg moves into the uterus and attaches itself to the lining, where an embryo then develops.

You've learned that reproduction using sex cells and fertilization of an egg is called sexual reproduction. Seed plants and most animals—including humans—reproduce sexually. In the next chapter, you will learn how offspring produced by sexual reproduction inherit traits from both parents.

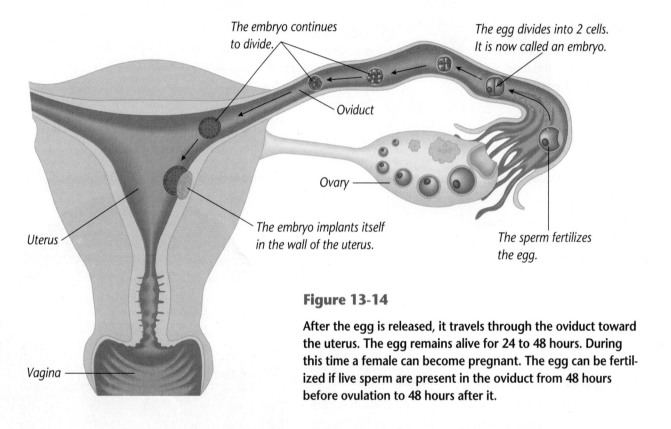

The embryo continues to divide.

The egg divides into 2 cells. It is now called an embryo.

Oviduct

Ovary

Uterus

The embryo implants itself in the wall of the uterus.

The sperm fertilizes the egg.

Vagina

Figure 13-14

After the egg is released, it travels through the oviduct toward the uterus. The egg remains alive for 24 to 48 hours. During this time a female can become pregnant. The egg can be fertilized if live sperm are present in the oviduct from 48 hours before ovulation to 48 hours after it.

check your UNDERSTANDING

1. What is the difference between internal and external fertilization?
2. Why can animals that reproduce through internal fertilization afford to produce so few eggs at a time?
3. **Apply** For each time period given, indicate whether fertilization can occur and briefly explain why it can or can't occur. Assume sperm are present.
   a. 24 hours after ovulation;
   b. 48 hours after menstruation has ended;
   c. during menstruation.

Science and Society

Curing Infertility

For a variety of reasons, one in twelve couples in the United States is experiencing infertility. They are unable to conceive a child. The number of people going to a doctor because of fertility problems recently exceeded one million.

Causes of Infertility

As the number of people dealing with infertility increases, new techniques are being developed for treatment. For example, one cause of infertility is that sperm are too weak to swim or don't have the right enzymes to break through the egg's outer membrane. To overcome this problem, doctors can now use a needle viewed under a powerful microscope to inject sperm directly into the egg.

Sometimes a woman fails to ovulate. When a woman does not release an egg through ovulation, she can be given hormones. Then she will produce many eggs, increasing her chances of getting pregnant.

Sometimes infertility occurs because the fertilized egg does not implant itself in the uterus. One-third of all pregnancies may end because implantation does not occur. To correct this problem, doctors pierce a tiny hole in the egg's protective outer layer. For some reason, eggs that are pierced attach better than those that aren't.

In Vitro Fertilization

The use of technology to assist in reproduction has increased dramatically since the first test tube baby was born over a decade ago. At that time, in vitro fertilization (IVF—fertilization in a glass dish) was revolutionary. Since then, more than 10 000 babies in the United States have been produced through IVF.

IVF is used when a woman is unable to conceive naturally. It can also be used when a man or woman is infertile but the woman is

still able to carry a developing child. Different combinations of egg and sperm are possible using IVF. The couple themselves may contribute eggs and sperm. Or the woman may give eggs that will be fertilized by sperm from a male donor. If the woman is infertile, her partner's sperm may be used to fertilize eggs donated by another woman.

Whose Embryo Is It?

As reproductive technology has become more complex and more widely used, it has raised many ethical questions. For example, more than one egg is fertilized during the

IVF procedure because not all fertilized eggs will survive. So several eggs are used to ensure that there will be at least one embryo that can be placed into the mother's uterus. The remaining embryos are frozen.

But questions have come up concerning what to do with these extra embryos. In one court case, a divorced couple fought about whether the woman can have custody of the embryos that were created while the couple was still married.

The High Cost of Having Children

Other questions relate to the cost of the treatment. IVF can cost from $6000 to $50,000 to produce one child. This means that only wealthy people or those with good health insurance have access to the procedure. Only nine states have laws that require insurance companies to pay for infertility treatments.

Still other concerns about the development of reproductive technology have to do with larger questions of world population growth. The world's population is currently 5.7 billion and is expected to double around the year 2050. There is growing concern that Earth cannot support such a large human population. Thus the use of scientific resources and millions of dollars to help certain people have children is seen by some as unwise.

Science Journal

In 1980, the federal government cut funding for research on IVF. Do you think that the government should support research in reproductive technology? To what extent is society responsible for helping couples who are infertile? Explain your point of view *in your Science Journal.*

Nurse-midwives study biology, chemistry, and medicine. They work at hospitals, clinics, and at birthing centers assisting women in childbirth.

CAREER connection

Technology Connection

Saving Endangered Species

Every year numerous animal species edge closer to extinction because of human activities. Loss of habitat is a major threat, as is illegal hunting. For example, the number of black rhinoceroses has fallen from 60 000 in 1970 to just 3500 today. The animal is slaughtered for its horn, which some people believe can cure diseases.

To increase the populations of some rare and endangered animals, scientists are using new methods in reproductive technology. One method is embryo transfer.

Harvesting the Embryos

For example, a female rhino is injected with hormones that will allow her to produce about 30 eggs at one time. The animal is then allowed to mate naturally or is fertilized by artificial insemination. In artificial insemination, sperm are collected from a male animal and are then deposited in the female's reproductive tract using a syringe. After fertilization, the embryos are collected and frozen in liquid nitrogen for later use.

An embryo from an endangered animal can be implanted into a substitute mother, also called a surrogate. There it will complete its development. The surrogate is usually a member of a related species. The advantage of this process is that it allows more offspring to be born than would otherwise occur naturally. A rhino, for example, undergoes a 15-month pregnancy and delivers just a single

calf. The rhino won't become pregnant again for at least four years.

Success Stories

Scientists have successfully used embryo transfer to produce Bengal tigers, African bongo antelope, and an endangered Indian desert cat. Producing the desert cat also involved the use of in vitro fertilization.

Some scientists expect that IVF and embryo transfer will replace more traditional breeding methods used by zoos. Live animals will no longer be shipped from one part of the world to another. Sperm, eggs, or embryos will be shipped to zoos trying to breed endangered species.

What Do You Think?

Why might embryo transfer and IVF be preferable to shipping live animals for zoo breeding programs?

HOW IT WORKS

Adaptations for Pollination

In one of the largest groups of plants, the adaptation that makes sexual reproduction possible is the flower. Flowers are reproductive organs. They produce eggs and pollen, which contain sperm. Pollen must be transferred from one flower to another for fertilization to occur.

Types of Pollinators

Each species of flowering plant generally depends on a particular kind of pollinator to carry out pollen transfer. In corn, for example, pollen is carried by the wind, while in roses, pollen is carried from one flower to another by bees.

If you examine a flower, you can determine how it is pollinated. Flowers pollinated by butterflies are usually long and narrow because these insects feed with a long, slender tongue. Because butterflies must land to feed, the flowers are upright and clustered to provide a landing platform. Butterflies seem to prefer white, cream, yellow, pink, and blue pastel-colored flowers.

Bees and wasps have short tongues, so the flowers they pollinate are usually open and shallow or have a broad tube shape with a landing platform. These insects are attracted to white, yellow, orange, blue, and violet flowers that have a sweet fragrance.

Birds also pollinate flowers. The most common bird pollinators are humming-

birds. Hummingbird flowers are often large and tube shaped to match the birds' long, thin beaks. These flowers contain abundant amounts of nectar deep within the flower that meet the birds' high metabolic needs. Anthers tend to stick out where they will brush against a hummingbird's head feathers and deposit pollen. Because hummingbirds see red and yellow well but have a poor sense of smell, they visit brightly colored flowers that are not very fragrant.

What Do You Think?

A plant has flowers that are dull-colored, unscented, and that produce little nectar. There are no petals and the anthers and stigmas hang out. How do you think this plant is pollinated? Considering how it is pollinated, do you think this plant would need to produce a little pollen or a lot for pollination to succeed? Why?

Science Journal

Review the statements below about the big ideas presented in this chapter, and answer the questions. Then, re-read your answers to the Did You Ever Wonder questions at the beginning of the chapter. *In your Science Journal*, write a paragraph about how your understanding of the big ideas in the chapter has changed.

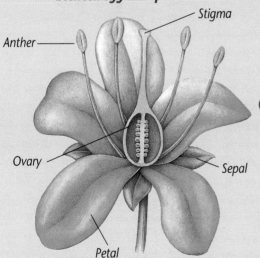

Mitosis

Meiosis

1 Mitosis produces body cells with the same number of chromosomes as the parent cell. Meiosis produces eggs and sperm that contain half the number of chromosomes as their parent cells. *How do the steps of mitosis and meiosis differ?*

2 In animals that reproduce sexually, eggs are produced in the ovaries of females, and sperm are produced in the testes of males. When united, egg and sperm produce a new organism containing the original chromosome number. *What are some differences between egg and sperm?*

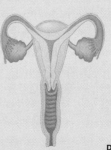

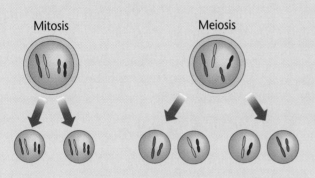

Stigma

Anther

Ovary

Sepal

Petal

3 Flowers are the reproductive organs of some sexually reproducing seed plants. *How does fertilization occur in a flowering plant?*

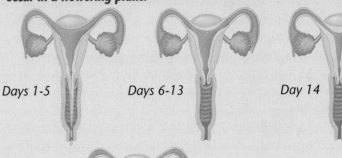

Days 1-5

Days 6-13

Day 14

Days 15-28

4 The menstrual cycle is the monthly cycle of changes in the human female reproductive system. The menstrual cycle prepares the reproductive system for fertilization. *What are the main changes that take place during the menstrual cycle?*

chapter 13
CHAPTER REVIEW

Using Key Science Terms

body cell	pistil
eggs	sex cell
meiosis	sperm
menstrual cycle	stamen
menstruation	testis
ovary	

An analogy is a relationship between two pairs of words generally written in the following manner: a:b::c:d. The symbol : is read "is to", and the symbol :: is read "as". For example, cat:animal::rose:plant is read "cat is to animal as rose is to plant." In the analogies that follow, a word is missing. Complete each analogy by providing the missing word from the list above.

1. sperm: testis: :_____: ovary
2. mitosis: body cells: :_____: sex cells
3. ovulation: egg: :_____: uterine lining and blood
4. vagina: human: :_____: flower
5. testis: male lion: :_____: male part of lily

Understanding Ideas

Answer the following questions in your Journal using complete sentences.

1. How are a human egg and sperm alike?
2. A muscle cell of a frog contains 26 chromosomes. How many chromosomes does a frog's egg contain? Explain your answer.
3. In what organ(s) of the human body does meiosis occur?
4. Mitosis has been occurring in your body since you were an embryo. Is this true of meiosis? Explain your answer.

5. What role do insects play in plant pollination?
6. Can fertilization occur without ovulation? Explain your answer.
7. How does internal fertilization increase the likelihood of fertilization occurring?
8. What is menstruation?
9. Why do offspring produced by sexual reproduction resemble their parents?

Developing Skills

Use your understanding of the concepts developed in each chapter to answer each of the following questions.

1. **Concept Mapping** Complete the concept map of the menstrual cycle.

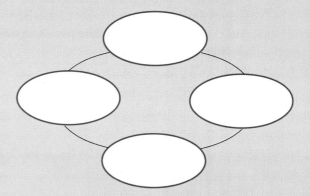

2. **Concept Mapping** Complete the concept map of plant reproduction.

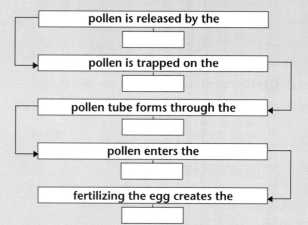

pollen is released by the

pollen is trapped on the

pollen tube forms through the

pollen enters the

fertilizing the egg creates the

3. Observing Repeat the Investigate activity on page 420 using another type of flower. Use the same data table to identify the flower parts and list the number and color of those parts of the new flower.

4. Compare and Contrast Repeat the Explore activity on page 411, but this time model the events of mitosis. How do the numbers of candies in the original cup and end cups compare with those for meiosis?

Critical Thinking

In your Journal, *answer each of the following questions.*

1. If just two fish can release millions of sperm and thousands of eggs, why aren't Earth's oceans choking with aquatic life?

2. Is fertilization likely to occur on day 1 of the menstrual cycle? Explain your answer.

3. Pollination can occur either between male and female parts of the same plant or between male and female parts of different plants of the same species. Which would likely produce nearly identical offspring?

4. Sperm are extremely active cells. Located behind the head of each sperm is a packet of mitochondria. What function do the mitochondria serve in sperm?

Problem Solving

Read the following problem and discuss your answers in a brief paragraph.

Gabriella's biology report was on a particular type of catfish. Gabriella chose this species of catfish because of some interesting facts about the fish's reproductive behavior. Interestingly enough, in this type of catfish, males are actively involved in the process of reproduction. Fertilized catfish eggs develop inside the mouth of the male parent. After reading more about the fish in general, Gabriella became puzzled. Gabriella found, in her research, that fish reproduce by external fertilization. What would you explain to Gabriella to help her understand the reproductive behavior of this catfish?

CONNECTING IDEAS

Discuss each of the following in a brief paragraph.

1. **Theme—Systems and Interactions** Use your knowledge of mitosis to explain how skin grows back after it has been scraped off during a fall.

2. **Theme—Systems and Interactions** Explain why a diet with the essential nutrients is necessary for growth and repair of the body.

3. **Theme—Scale and Structure** Sequence the events of fertilization in humans.

4. **How It Works** Describe three adaptations to pollination found in flowers.

5. **Technology Connection** Describe one method scientists use to increase the populations of rare and endangered animals.

CHAPTER 14

Heredity

When people go to their family reunion, they may notice that they share traits with some of their other relatives, not just brothers and sisters. They may even look like someone who is distantly related. Sometimes a trait, such as curly, red hair, won't appear for several generations. Is such an occurrence an accident, or is there a pattern that can be predicted? In this chapter you will use your knowledge of reproduction to discover patterns of heredity—a process important not only to your appearance but also to your health.

▶ **In the activity on the next page, explore some of your traits and determine if they are inherited.**

Did you ever wonder...

- ✓ Why certain features run in some families but not in others?
- ✓ How features are passed from one generation to the next?
- ✓ What your children could look like?

Science Journal

Before you begin to study heredity, think about these questions and answer them *in your Science Journal*. When you finish the chapter, compare your journal write-up with what you have learned.

Explore! ACTIVITY

Which of your features have you inherited?

Have you ever heard words similar to these: "You got your curly, red hair from Grandfather," or "You are tall, just like Aunt Nikki"? The very features that make you you first appeared in your parents or other ancestors, then were passed down to you. See what some of your traits are in this activity. If you prefer, you can observe a friend's traits.

What To Do

1. Look at yourself in a mirror. Identify at least five of your features.

2. What color are your eyes?

3. What color is your hair? Is it straight or curly?

4. What is the shape of your nose or mouth? For example, does your nose turn up at the end? Is one of your lips fuller than the other?

5. Who else in your family has each of your features? Write a paragraph *in your Journal* about which features you inherited.

How Organisms Get Their Traits

Section Objectives

- Define trait.
- Explain and draw pedigrees.
- Describe how pedigrees are used to trace patterns of inheritance.

Key Terms

traits
pedigree

What's a Trait?

We share certain features with more than 1 1/2 million different kinds of organisms on Earth. Humans, like all living things, are made up of cells that require energy to do their work, to grow, and to reproduce. Even so, each human being also has features that make him or her different from every other living thing, and even from every other human.

You may want to know where your features came from. Where did you get your long legs? Your high cheekbones? Your dark, curly hair? Each one of your features taken alone may be similar to that of someone else. However, your features and those of someone else will not be identical. In fact, every living thing has specific characteristics called **traits** that are unique.

Traits can be expressed in different ways. In humans, how many different hair colors are there? For each color, how many different shades exist? Can you think of other traits that are expressed in a variety of different ways? What about skin color or texture? What about the shape of your nose, ears, or mouth? Are all people the same height or weight?

Figure 14-1

Different generations of a family inherit traits that have been passed from one generation to the next. These traits may be nearly identical in expression–for example, nose shape may be nearly identical in a father and son. Or, traits may be similar, but not identical, as in the case of hair color. In this family, what traits have been passed to the children from the grandparents?

Family Pedigrees

Could you tell which people are closely related in a family just by looking at a photograph? Some of the family members would look very much alike. Others wouldn't resemble each other at all. It is difficult to believe that some people are closely related when they look so different from one another.

To find out how family members can have such different features, we can use a tool called a pedigree to trace each trait in a family. A **pedigree** is a diagram that shows the history of a trait from one generation to the next. Imagine three generations of the Giuliano family—a brother and sister, Joseph and Anna, with their parents,

Mr. and Mrs. Giuliano, and grandparents. To see how Anna could have straight hair, for example, while Joseph has curly hair like both his parents, we can draw a pedigree for the trait of hair condition in three generations of the Giuliano family.

Study **Figure 14-2**, which shows the Giuliano family pedigree. Does anyone in the family have straight hair besides Anna? If so, who? Do more members of the Giuliano family have straight hair or curly hair? What does this pedigree suggest about hair condition? Does Anna have straight hair purely by chance, or did she inherit it even though both her parents have curly hair?

Connect to...

Chemistry

Albinism, the lack of pigment in eyes, skin, hair, scales, or feathers, is an inherited trait that affects people and other animals. Albinos are unable to make the pigment melanin. Prepare a short report that explains why albinos cannot make melanin from the amino acid tyrosine.

 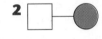

Figure 14-2

(A) In this pedigree, different family members are represented in different ways. Look at Figures 1, 2, and 3. Squares represent males, and circles represent females. Shaded shapes represent family members with curly hair, and shapes that are not shaded represent family members with straight hair. Two parents are connected with a horizontal line, and one or more lines connects the children of those parents.

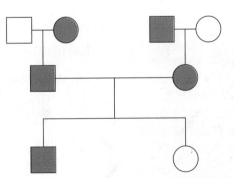

(B) The oldest children in a pedigree are placed on the left, and the youngest are placed on the right. Joseph and Anna are represented by the two shapes in the bottom row. Is Anna older than Joseph?

Find Out! ACTIVITY

What can a pedigree tell you about a family?

The inheritance of many traits in humans is not as simple and direct as the pedigree for hair condition might lead you to believe. Hair color, for example, is a much more complicated trait.

What To Do

1. Look back over the list of your features that you made at the beginning of this chapter. Choose one trait and draw a pedigree for your family. Be sure to select a trait that is observable in at least two generations, for example in your parents and their children.

2. Decide what shaded shapes will represent, for example, blue versus brown eyes, brown versus blond hair, curly versus straight hair.

3. Include as many generations and as many of your relatives as you can. If you prefer, you can use a friend's family rather than your own.

Conclude and Apply

1. Who else in the family has the trait expressed in the same way you do or your friend does?

2. Do more family members have the trait expressed in one way than the other? Write an explanation for this observation *in your Journal*.

SKILLBUILDER

Making and Using Tables

Choose five physical traits such as curly hair, freckles, dimples, left-handedness, and the space between the top front teeth. Arrange the traits in a table. Survey five of your family members for each of the traits and arrange the data in your table. If you prefer, you may survey a friend's family. If you need help, refer to the **Skill Handbook** on page 680.

■ Do Traits Appear Randomly?

Do you see a pattern in the appearance of traits such as curliness of hair, or do traits appear and disappear at random? Random means that nothing is causing one trait to appear more often than another. It's like the lottery. Each number in the lottery has an equal chance of coming up because of randomness. No one number is favored over another. If it were, everyone would be a winner because everyone could guess the winning numbers! In the case of two traits, if the traits are appearing randomly, there is an equal chance that either trait will appear. In a large group of people, that would mean that about one-half of the people could have one trait, and one-half would have the other trait. To find out if traits appear in patterns or randomly, try the following activity.

Do more students have attached or unattached earlobes?

Some people have earlobes that are attached like the one on the left in the illustration. Others have earlobes that hang free like the one on the right.

What To Do

1. Count the number of your classmates with each type of earlobe.

Conclude and Apply

1. How do the two numbers compare—are they nearly equal, or is one much larger than the other? If so, which?
2. What might your data suggest about the occurrence of this trait?

3. Do you think the trait occurs randomly? *In your Journal*, explain how you think traits are inherited—either randomly or in patterns.

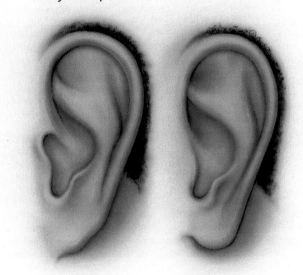

■ Mendel's Work with Peas

Gregor Mendel was an Austrian monk who did a series of experiments to show that traits do not occur purely at random. He recognized that traits occur in family pedigrees according to certain patterns of inheritance. Although Mendel's parents were rather poor, he was sent to a good school some distance from home. Mendel was a good student and loved nature and the out-of-doors. At the age of 20, he decided to enter a monastery. There he devoted a lot of time to his nature experiments.

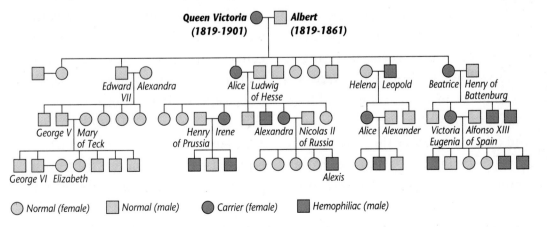

Figure 14-3

Hemophilia is a disease found in Queen Victoria's family. Blood of a hemophiliac has difficulty clotting. Does the disease appear to be present in a random fashion or does it appear to be inherited in a pattern? Explain your answer.

Figure 14-4

Each of the pea traits studied by Mendel has two different forms. Seeds can be round or wrinkled. The inheritance of one or the other form of a trait doesn't depend on any of the other traits inherited. A round seed; for example, may be green or yellow.

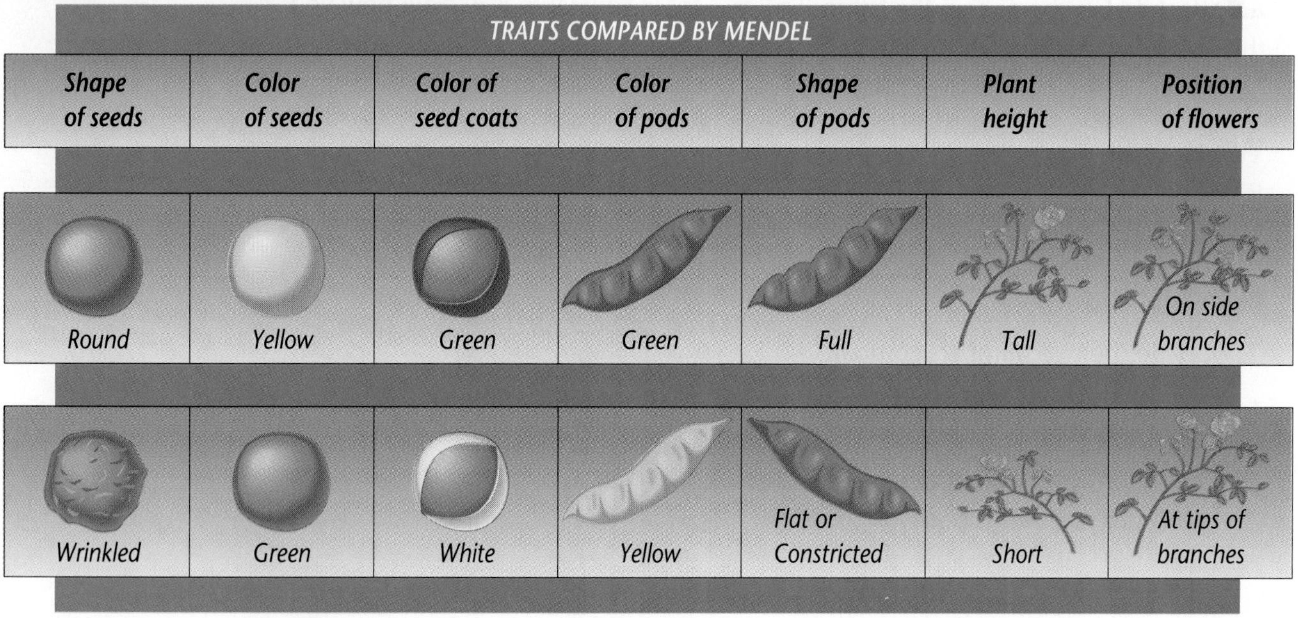

TRAITS COMPARED BY MENDEL						
Shape of seeds	Color of seeds	Color of seed coats	Color of pods	Shape of pods	Plant height	Position of flowers
Round	Yellow	Green	Green	Full	Tall	On side branches
Wrinkled	Green	White	Yellow	Flat or Constricted	Short	At tips of branches

■ Variation in Pea Plants

During his experiments, Mendel observed the variation in different plants. Variation is the occurrence of an inherited trait that makes a person or thing different from other members within the same species. He observed, for example, that pea plants varied in the shape and color of their seeds. Some seeds were smooth, and others were wrinkled. Some seeds were green, and others were yellow. Some pea plants were tall, others short. Mendel noticed that some pea plants produced red flowers and others white flowers. Some of the many variations that Mendel observed in pea plants are shown in **Figure 14-4**. Notice that for each trait–pea color or pea shape, for instance–there are two variations.

■ Mendel's Experiments with Pea Plants

Mendel hypothesized that the variation in the plants was controlled by something inherited from the parent plants because particular traits kept appearing across generations. He designed experiments in which he crossed pea plants with different variations of a trait. He then carefully recorded the results, generation after generation. He found that certain traits kept appearing again and again while others appeared only occasionally. For example, Mendel crossed pea plants that varied in height as in **Figure 14-5**. Was there a pattern in these results that supported Mendel's hypothesis that the traits of offspring come from their parents? Or were the results random?

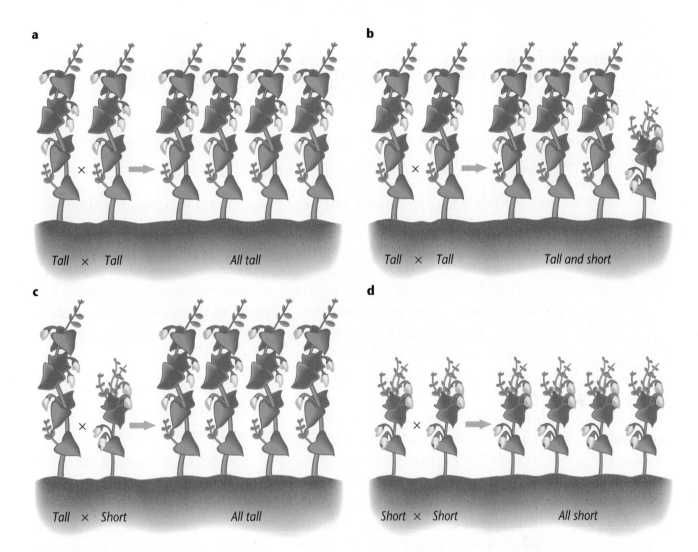

a Tall × Tall — All tall

b Tall × Tall — Tall and short

c Tall × Short — All tall

d Short × Short — All short

Figure 14-5

Mendel performed many crosses with pea plants and got many different kinds of results. Sometimes tall plants crossed with other tall plants produced all tall plants (a). But, sometimes tall plants crossed with tall plants produced one short plant for every three tall plants (b). Short plants crossed with other short plants always produced more short plants (d), but sometimes a short plant crossed with a tall plant produced all tall plants (c). Do you think Mendel's results led him to conclude that traits of pea plants appeared randomly?

check your UNDERSTANDING

1. What are traits, and how are they useful in understanding heredity?
2. Draw a pedigree for a family with two brown-eyed parents, a brown-eyed son, and a blue-eyed daughter, who is the oldest child. What is the significance of the shading in the shapes in your pedigree?
3. How did Gregor Mendel use pedigrees to form his hypothesis that the traits of off-spring come from their parents?
4. **Apply** If Joseph Giuliano grows up and marries a woman who has curly hair, can you say for sure that their children will have curly hair? Explain.

Mendel's Work Explained

14-2

Section Objectives

- Define gene and tell where genes are located.
- Explain how the sorting of genes during meiosis demonstrates inheritance of traits.
- Describe how dominant and recessive genes explain pedigrees and the results of Mendel's pea plant experiments.

Key Terms

dominant trait
recessive trait
gene
pure dominant
pure recessive
heterozygote

What Kinds of Traits Are There?

When Mendel crossed tall pea plants and collected and planted the seeds that were produced, the offspring always grew into tall pea plants. Likewise, short pea plants crossed with short pea plants produced short pea plants time after time. Because the results of these crosses were always the same, he referred to these traits as pure. These crosses were shown in **Figure 14-5(a)** and **(d)**, shown on page 443. As shown in **Figure 14-5(c)**, when Mendel crossed pure tall with pure short peas, the offspring were always tall. The short trait seemed to disappear. Mendel called tallness, which

was always expressed, a **dominant trait** because it seemed to dominate or cover up the short trait. He called shortness a **recessive trait** because it seemed to disappear. What really happened to the recessive trait of shortness? Mendel crossed more pea plants to find out.

■ Crossing Offspring That Both Have Tall and Short Parents

Mendel tried crossing tall plants with tall plants again as shown in **Figure 14-5(b)**. This time the parents of the crossed plants were tall and short. What happened? Shortness reappeared in the offspring of the crossed plants! Mendel counted the offspring and found about three tall pea plants for every short one. Mendel concluded that a trait must be controlled by factors inherited from both parents. These factors interact to determine how the trait is expressed in the offspring.

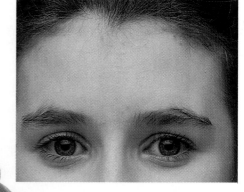

Figure 14-6

Dimples, hitchhiker's thumb, and a widow's peak hairline are examples of different traits that can be inherited by human beings. These traits follow the patterns of inheritance described by Mendel. For example, dimples are a dominant trait, and lack of dimples is a recessive trait. How many of these traits did you inherit?

Mendel's Factors Are Genes

We now know that the factors that Mendel used to explain his results are located on chromosomes within the cell. Each chromosome has many, many genes that are arranged along its length, like beads in a necklace. A **gene** is a specific location on a chromosome that controls a certain trait. Chromosomes usually occur in pairs; therefore, the genes they carry usually occur in pairs, too.

Gregor Mendel had been right. A trait is controlled by two factors, one from each parent. The interaction of these two factors, now called genes, determines how the trait is expressed.

■ How Genes Are Represented

How can we represent genes in a picture? Geneticists use letters to represent pairs of genes. A capital letter represents the gene for the dominant trait, *T* for tall. A small letter represents the gene for the recessive trait, *t* for short. But, let's step back for a moment and consider where the *T* gene and the *t* gene come from.

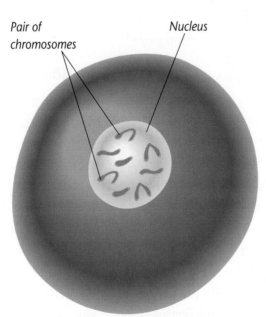

Pair of chromosomes

Nucleus

Figure 14-7

Traits are carried on chromosomes in the form of genes. Chromosomes and genes occur in pairs. In the kind of inheritance Mendel described, there are two genes for each trait. Either gene may be dominant or recessive so that you end up with two dominant genes, two recessive genes, or one of each.

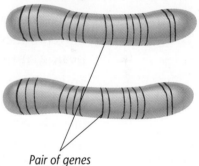

Pair of genes

How Do We Know?

Where are genes located on chromosomes?

Using a technique called gene splicing, scientists remove a section of a chromosome from one kind of organism and splice or insert it into a chrornosome of a different kind of organism. The trait controlled by the transferred gene now appears in the second organism. This demonstrates that the gene or genes that control the trait must be located on the section of transferred chromosome. Pictured here are chromosome pieces from a different organism being spliced into a bacterium's chromosome.

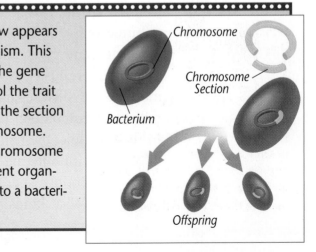

Chromosome

Chromosome Section

Bacterium

Offspring

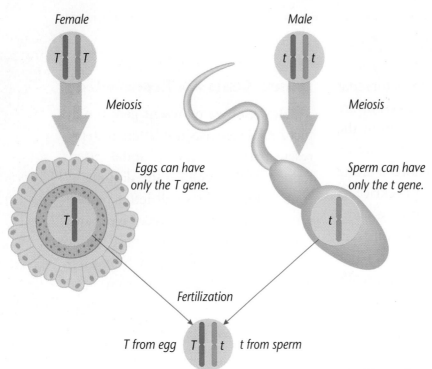

Female   Male

T   T   t   t

Meiosis   Meiosis

Eggs can have only the T gene.

Sperm can have only the t gene.

T   t

Fertilization

T from egg   T   t   t from sperm

All tall offspring

Figure 14-8

The reproductive cells of a tall female and a short male unite to produce offspring that are all tall. Since all of the offspring will be tall like the female parent, was the male parent's gene for shortness important? Explain.

■ Where Genes in Sex Cells Come From

As you learned in the last chapter on reproduction, when cells undergo meiosis, their chromosomes duplicate and pair up, then separate twice so that each egg or sperm has only one of each of the originally paired chromosomes. When a sperm fertilizes an egg, a chromosome from the egg pairs with the same kind of chromosome from the sperm. Each parent has contributed one chromosome per pair and one gene per trait in the offspring. **Figure 14-8** shows how chromosome pairs that separate in the sex cells can recombine in the offspring. In this example, the female can produce eggs with only the *T* gene. The male can produce sperm with only the *t* gene. What kinds of genes can the offspring have?

■ How Are Genes Expressed?

The previous example showed that females with only the *T* gene and males with only the *t* gene can produce one kind of offspring. This same example helps to explain Mendel's results. When Mendel crossed what he called pure-tall and pure-short pea plants, the offspring were all tall. Why did shortness disappear? The **pure dominant** trait of tallness is represented in **Figure 14-8** by a double capital *TT*, and the **pure recessive** trait of shortness is represented by a double small *tt*. Pea plants with the gene pair *Tt* will grow to be tall plants because they have a gene for tallness, which is dominant. However, their tallness is not a pure trait. They also have recessive genes for shortness, which are not expressed. An organism with one dominant gene and one recessive gene for a trait is called a **heterozygote**. The offspring in **Figure 14-8** are heterozygous for tallness.

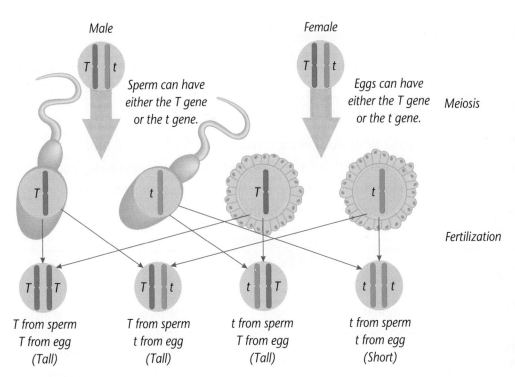

Male

Sperm can have either the T gene or the t gene.

Female

Eggs can have either the T gene or the t gene.

Meiosis

Fertilization

T from sperm
T from egg
(Tall)

T from sperm
t from egg
(Tall)

t from sperm
T from egg
(Tall)

t from sperm
t from egg
(Short)

Figure 14-9

The reproductive cells of both the male and female parent in this diagram contain one dominant tall gene and one recessive short gene for height. Examine the offspring produced by these parents. How many tall offspring are there? How many short offspring? How do the offspring shown here compare with those Mendel observed when he crossed tall plants?

Explore! ACTIVITY

Can you explain how Mendel got tall and short plants when he crossed tall heterozygotes?

What To Do

1. Make a diagram to show the possible offspring of two **Tt** parents (tall heterozygotes).
2. What genes do the sex cells of these two parents carry?
3. What gene pairs result in tall offspring?
4. What gene pairs produce short offspring?
5. What is the ratio of tall to short offspring?
6. *In your Journal*, explain how your ratio compares to Mendel's results.

Do you think Mendel could tell the difference between tall pea plants with **TT** genes and tall pea plants with **Tt** genes? It is impossible to tell by looking at a tall pea plant whether it is a pure dominant with **TT** genes or whether it is a heterozygote with **Tt** genes.

447

INVESTIGATION

Albino Offspring in Plants

Humans who have the albino trait have no skin pigment, which makes them more susceptible to skin cancer than people without the trait. Plants having the albino trait lack the green pigment called chlorophyll, and thus cannot carry out photosynthesis. In this activity, you'll investigate the albino trait in plants.

Preparation

Problem
What kind of inheritance patterns are associated with the albino trait?

Form a Hypothesis
As a group, discuss what you know about dominant traits and recessive traits. Then form a hypothesis about whether you would expect the albino trait to be a dominant or recessive trait.

Objectives
• Infer patterns of inheritance associated with a particular trait.
• Predict the occurrence of recessive and dominant traits in selected seedlings.

Materials
petri dishes with covers

scissors

water

labels

tobacco seeds A

paper towels

tobacco seeds B

Safety

Always use scissors with caution. Carry them with the pointed end downward.

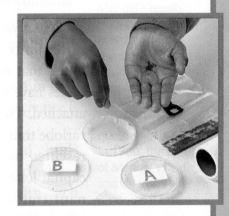

Plan the Experiment

1 As a group, agree upon a way to test your hypothesis. Write down what you will do at each step of your test.

2 Assign a task to each member of the group. Who will water the seeds? Who will record the data?

3 How will you summarize your observations? If you need a data table, design one now *in your Science Journal.*

Check the Plan

Discuss and decide upon the following points and write them down.

1 How will you ensure that the two sets of seeds do not become mixed?

2 How long will you conduct your test?

3 Make sure your teacher approves your experiment before you proceed.

4 Carry out your experiment. Record your observations.

This albino turtle is missing the colored pigment normally found in turtles.

Analyze and Conclude

1. Compare and Contrast Using your data, calculate the percentage of albino seedlings from both type A and type B seeds. How does this compare to the class totals? Did your results support your hypothesis?

2. Interpret Data If green pigment is the dominant trait and albinism is the recessive trait, use your own symbols to determine what different gene combinations the green seedlings could have.

3. Predict Predict whether a cross of heterozygous and pure recessive parents would give you the results you observed in the type B seedlings.

Going Further

Infer what different gene combinations the parents of the type B seeds must have had to produce the results you observed in their offspring.

Mendel's Work Refined

Section Objectives

- Describe sickle-cell anemia and explain how it illustrates a pattern of inheritance called incomplete dominance.
- Recognize the usefulness of genetic counseling.

Key Terms

sickle-cell anemia

Sickle-cell Anemia

When you studied circulation and blood, you learned that your red blood cells carry oxygen and nutrients to all of the other cells throughout your body. The red blood cells are normally shaped like a donut without a hole. In some people, however, the red blood cells may have a different shape. People who have a disease called **sickle-cell anemia** have misshapen red blood cells. Many of these red blood cells are shaped like curved sickles, as shown in **Figure 14-12**.

Red blood cell shape is an inherited trait. Most people have all round cells. Some people have some round and some sickle-cells. They have slightly less oxygen delivered to their

Looking at Color Blindness

Colors do not appear the same to everyone. If you're color-blind, green may look grayish. Red may appear yellowish. A person with normal color vision will see a number in the picture of the circle different from what a color-blind person will see. Color blindness is a sex-linked trait. This and other sex-linked traits occur more often in males than females.

Sex Chromosomes

To understand how sex-linked traits work, you have to learn about the chromosomes that determine sex. In humans, there are two types of sex chromosomes—*X* and *Y*. You

learned that chromosomes come in pairs. Females have two *X* chromosomes that are designated as *XX*. Males have one of each type that are designated as *XY*.

How Sex-Linked Traits Are Inherited

Sex-linked traits are usually controlled by genes on the *X* chromosome. A male can inherit a recessive sex-linked trait if the gene for the trait is present on only his *X* chromosome. That's because the *Y* chromosome often doesn't influence the inheritance of traits. The female, on the other hand, must have both affected

body tissues than normal. They have the sickle-cell trait. Fewer people have all sickle-cells, which prevent them from getting enough oxygen to their tissues. They have sickle-cell anemia.

■ Incomplete Dominance

Sickle-cell anemia is different from the inherited traits that Mendel studied because neither gene that determines red blood cell shape is dominant. The sickle-cell trait is not hidden when the gene for normal blood cell shape is present. The Investigate will help you understand how genetic counselors might predict this inherited condition in a child.

Figure 14-12

Ⓐ Sickle-shaped blood cells (right) often become stuck in capillaries. They also can't carry as much oxygen as normal cells (left). In severe cases, sickle-cell anemia can be fatal.

Ⓑ A represents the gene for normal red blood cells. A' represents the gene for sickled cells. When both genes are present, both blood cell types are present. The person has sickle cell trait. What happens when the genes are A'A'? AA?

	A	A'
A	AA	AA'
A'	AA'	A'A'

A = Normal
A' = Sickle

X chromosomes for the trait to show.

You Try It!

Interpret the different combination of genes present in a mother and father of three families to determine the traits of each parent. *N* stands for normal trait, while *C* stands for color-blind trait.

Family	Father	Mother
1	$X^N Y$	$X^N X^C$
2	$X^C Y$	$X^N X^N$
3	$X^C Y$	$X^C X^N$

What are the possibilities of a son or a daughter inheriting color blindness in each instance? Can you explain why males are color-blind more often than females?

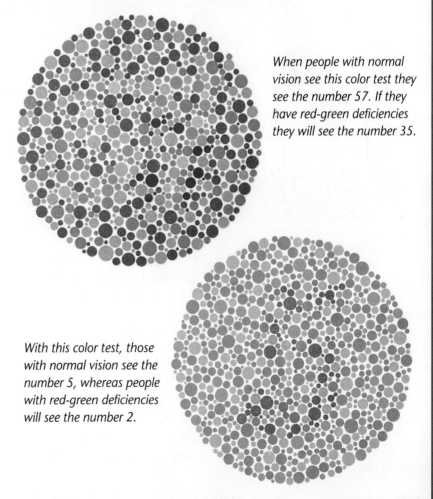

When people with normal vision see this color test they see the number 57. If they have red-green deficiencies they will see the number 35.

With this color test, those with normal vision see the number 5, whereas people with red-green deficiencies will see the number 2.

Genetic Counseling

A genetic counselor advises couples on how probable it is that their children will have an inherited disease like sickle-cell anemia. We call diseases that are inherited genetic diseases. Imagine that you are a genetic counselor and that a couple has come to you for advice.

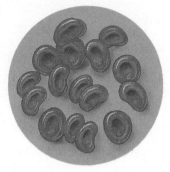
Mother

Father

Problem

What is the chance that the couple's children will inherit sickle-cell anemia?

What To Do

1 Copy the data table *into your Journal.*

2 Blood samples from the parents are illustrated. Study the cells in each sample as if you were observing them through a microscope. *Classify* the cells in your data table as all normal, half normal and half sickled, or all sickled.

3 What can you *infer* about the condition of each sample? Record your inferences in your table as normal, sickle-cell trait, or sickle-cell anemia.

4 What can you *infer* about the gene combination of each parent? Record your inferences in the table as *AA*, *AA'*, or *A'A'*.

A

B

Data and Observations			
BLOOD SAMPLE	BLOOD CELLS	BLOOD CONDITION	GENE COMBINATION
Father			
Mother			

Analyzing

1. Draw a Punnett square to show the possible gene combinations in the couple's children. Can you *predict* what the chance might be of each gene combination occurring?

2. How would the possible gene combinations change if both the father and mother had the sickle-cell trait? Draw a Punnett square to show your answer.

Concluding and Applying

3. What would you tell the couple about their chances of having a child with sickle-cell anemia? What are their chances of having a child with sickle-cell trait?

4. **Going Further** Two more parents come to you for advice. They both carry the sickle-cell trait. Because they already have one child with sickle-cell anemia, they are concerned that their next child is at increased risk of having sickle-cell anemia, too. What would you tell them?

Advances in Genetics

Knowledge in the field of genetics has grown tremendously since Mendel's time. Present-day geneticists have extended Mendel's rules of inheritance. They have also found that many health conditions are hereditary. Some, like sickle-cell anemia, are caused by specific genes. Others are caused by abnormal arrangements of chromo-somes. In a condition called Down syndrome, three chromosomes are present where only a pair should be. **Figure 14-13** shows this condition. In addition to genetic counseling, scientists have applied their knowledge of heredity in other useful ways. Breeding offspring with desired traits means better plant and animal varieties to improve the foods you eat.

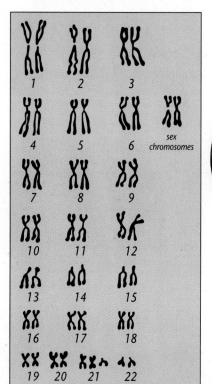

Figure 14-13

To detect Down syndrome, chromosomes from a tissue sample are photographed under the microscope, and then arranged in pairs. An extra chromosome in the 21st pair indicates Down syndrome. Traits include changes in physical appearance and mild to severe mental retardation. Many people with Down syndrome, however, live normal, productive lives.

check your UNDERSTANDING

1. How do normal red blood cells differ from the red blood cells of someone with sickle-cell trait? With sickle-cell anemia?

2. Is the presence of sickled red blood cells a dominant or a recessive trait? Explain.

3. What kind of advice do families receive from genetic counseling?

4. **Apply** What would you need to know to advise a couple on the likelihood that any one of their children will inherit cystic fibrosis? Cystic fibrosis is an inherited disease in which mucus clogs the lungs and digestive system, starving the body of both oxygen and nutrients.

 **14-4** ## How Do Genes Control Traits?

What Is DNA?

What do your chromosomes really look like? What are the genes that control your thousands of different traits actually made of? The chromosomes in the nucleus of each of your cells are made of long threads of a material called DNA. **DNA** contains the master code that instructs all your cells in their daily jobs. Genes are short pieces of this DNA that make up your chromosomes. Each piece of DNA that corresponds to a gene determines a trait. How? To understand how a gene actually determines a trait, you need to understand more about the material called DNA.

Section Objectives
- Explain what DNA is and where it's found.
- Model the structure of DNA.
- Relate genes to the model of DNA.

Key Terms
DNA

Explore! ACTIVITY

How are airport codes similar to the DNA code?

The airline industry uses three-letter codes for the names of airports all over the world.

What To Do

1. The photograph shows three examples of baggage tags used by airports. Which airports are the bags with these tags going to?

2. Why do you suppose airlines use these codes?

3. *In your Journal,* infer how airline codes and the DNA code are similar.

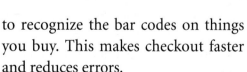

Have you ever sent a message to someone using a code? In order to read your message, the other person had to know or be able to figure out the meaning of the symbols in your code. Airline personnel quickly recognize the three-letter codes. Machines recognize codes, too. Supermarket scanning machines are programmed to recognize the bar codes on things you buy. This makes checkout faster and reduces errors.

Chromosomes contain codes embedded in the chemical structure of DNA. Before your body cells divide, the DNA code of the parent cell is duplicated, and the copied DNA is passed on to the daughter cells. The new cells recognize the code of instructions that dictates what proteins to make, which in turn determine how each trait is expressed. For example, certain proteins produce curly hair, and slightly different proteins produce straight hair.

■ The Structure of DNA

Let's look more closely at a DNA molecule, shown in **Figure 14-14**. The DNA molecule looks like a twisted ladder. The steps of the ladder are made of chemical compounds called bases. There are four bases in DNA – adenine, guanine, cytosine, and thymine. They fit together like pieces of a jigsaw puzzle.

Figure 14-14

DNA makes up the chromosomes within the nucleus of the cell. DNA itself is composed of four bases, adenine, guanine, cytosine, and thymine. They are represented by the letters A, G, C, and T. This drawing shows how the bases occur in certain pairs. Adenine always pairs with thymine, and guanine always pairs with cytosine. The code carried by DNA is determined by the order of the four bases.

Physics
CONNECTION

DNA Fingerprinting

It's almost as though each person has a specific product bar code. With the exception of identical twins, who have identical DNA, every person in the world has a different set of genes, and each person's DNA is unique. DNA is like a fingerprint.

The unique nature of DNA means that each person should be able to be identified by his or her DNA. This has an important application in crime solving.

Skin cells contain DNA. If a person is murdered, and the police find bits of the murderer's skin under the victim's fingernails, these bits can be used to identify the suspect. If the sus-

pect is guilty, the DNA of the skin left at the scene and the DNA of the suspected person will match exactly.

How DNA Fingerprinting Works

DNA fingerprinting helps identify criminals. Here is how it works: Scientists can remove the DNA from almost any kind of cell left behind by the criminal. The DNA is treated so that it produces an image of the chemicals that it contains, similar to those pictured on the next page. How is this done? First, the DNA is treated with enzymes that chop it up at specific places in the molecule.

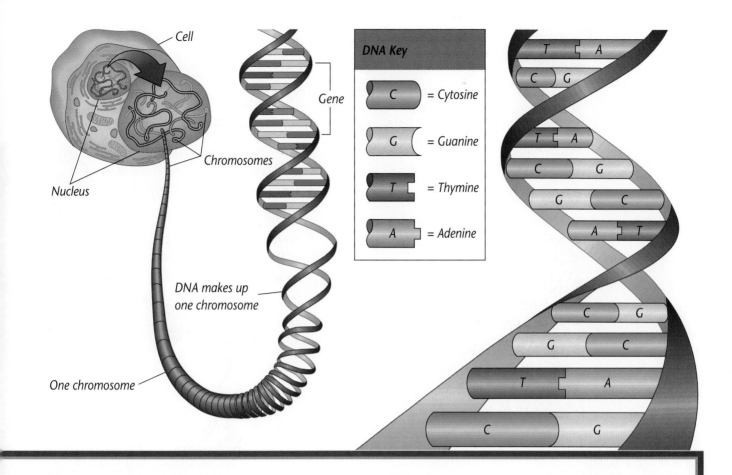

Cell

Nucleus

Chromosomes

DNA makes up one chromosome

One chromosome

Gene

DNA Key

C = Cytosine

G = Guanine

T = Thymine

A = Adenine

Then, the pieces of DNA are separated according to size by a technique known as electrophoresis. In this technique, the DNA pieces are applied to a slab of jellylike material. The slab of jellylike material is then exposed to an electric field. The DNA pieces move across the jellylike material in response to the electric field. Where a piece of DNA stops moving depends on its size. Larger molecules are slowed down more. Each DNA pattern produced by this technique is unique and can be used to identify an individual. The picture of the DNA collected at the crime scene is compared with DNA images from other cell samples of the murder suspect.

You Try It

Sample A in the figure is a DNA fingerprint taken from one strand of hair. The hair was found on the body of a murder victim at the crime scene. It does not belong to the victim. Samples B through G are DNA fingerprints from six suspects. To whom does the hair belong?

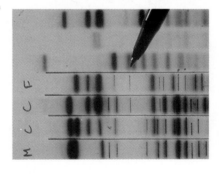

This photograph shows the DNA fingerprint that results when pieces of DNA are separated by electrophoresis. The dark bands represent pieces of the DNA molecule.

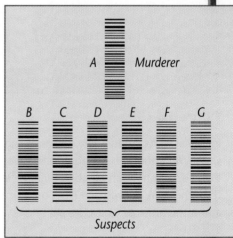

A Murderer

B C D E F G

Suspects

Can you make a candy model of DNA?

Scientists make models of DNA to help them visualize what DNA looks like. You can do this, too.

What To Do

1. Use two long pieces of licorice rope for the side rails of the ladder model of DNA.

2. To make the steps of the ladder, use four different colors of gumdrops for the bases.

3. Use toothpicks to connect the bases to each other and to the licorice.

4. When you've assembled your model, carefully twist it a little to visualize how the DNA molecule spirals.

Conclude and Apply

1. How many gumdrops form each step of the ladder?

2. What do your four colors of gumdrops represent?

3. Can base A form a step with base C? Explain why or why not *in your Journal.*

Figure 14-15

Identical twins are the only human beings who have identical DNA. What does this say about the order of their base pairs? If you do not have an identical twin, your DNA is different from the DNA of everyone else on Earth. What does this say about the order of your base pairs?

Different genes consist of different arrangements of A, G, C, and T bases. Just as four letters of the alphabet can be rearranged to make many different words, these four bases can be arranged in different ways to form different chemical messages. These messages control different traits. Some genes control the traits that determine how you look. Other genes control every way your body functions inside: how your blood cells carry oxygen, how you digest your food, how your reproductive organs produce eggs or sperm, and thousands of other details.

All of the characteristics that you have are affected by the DNA that you have in your cells. It controls the color of your eyes, the color of your hair, and whether or not you can digest certain foods. These characteristics are called traits, and the traits that appear in you depend on the kind of proteins your cells make.

Parents pass copies of their DNA on to their offspring. The way each individual develops depends on the instructions coded in the DNA an individual receives from both parents. You are like your parents in many ways, but different too. Because so many different combinations are possible, you are different from your brothers and sisters, from other relatives, from your classmates, and from everyone else on Earth. You are unique.

Figure 14-16

Have you ever heard the expression "Variety is the spice of life"? The expression means that life is full of excitement because much variety exists in the world around you. For example, the fact that these young people display variety by being different adds much excitement to their lives. Yet in spite of their differences, what similarities do these young people share?

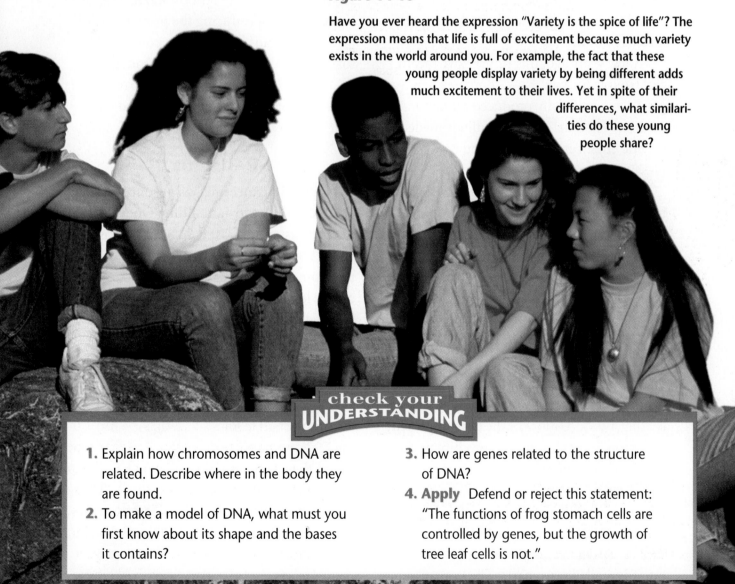

1. Explain how chromosomes and DNA are related. Describe where in the body they are found.
2. To make a model of DNA, what must you first know about its shape and the bases it contains?
3. How are genes related to the structure of DNA?
4. **Apply** Defend or reject this statement: "The functions of frog stomach cells are controlled by genes, but the growth of tree leaf cells is not."

Science and Society

Genetic Engineering: Pro and Con

You're a diabetic. You have to take insulin every single day. Recently, you've had bad news. The insulin you take is produced from pigs, and you have developed an allergy to it.

A few years ago, this would have meant real trouble for you. Now, though, a new product—artificially produced human insulin—is available. The insulin is made by genetic engineering, and for you it's a real lifesaver. Literally!

DNA is the material that passes on genetic information in the cells of almost all living things. Genetic engineering is a new technology that allows scientists to separate a short string of DNA from one species and insert it into the DNA of another species.

Often the new host species is a bacterium, and the DNA carries the code for a desirable protein, such as a hormone. After the DNA is inserted into the DNA of the bacteria, the bacteria are allowed to reproduce. As they do so, they produce more of the desired protein —a protein they would not produce under usual circumstances.

Products of Genetic Engineering—Medicines

Human insulin is produced in this way, but it is made in two parts. The human genes for the two different proteins that make up the insulin molecule are inserted into the DNA of two separate groups of bacteria. The bacteria grow, producing the proteins. The proteins are purified and then combined to form insulin. Other medicines produced by bacteria include human growth hormone for the treatment of dwarfism and a medicine that dissolves blood clots.

Frost-Resistant Plants

Genetic engineering has produced many products for use in agriculture. One makes plants resistant to frost damage. There is a species of bacterium that commonly grows on the leaves of plants. Normally, the bacteria produce a protein that enables ice to crystallize on the leaves. Scientists have removed the gene for this protein from the DNA of the bacteria, so the protein is no longer produced. If the altered bacteria are sprayed on plants, ice will not form on the plants' leaves.

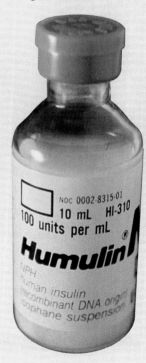

HUMAN GROWTH HORMONE GENE

MT
PROMOTER

pBR

Human Growth Hormone

Genes from other species have been introduced into the DNA of mammals. For instance, using a machine called a "gene gun," the gene for human growth hormone has been inserted into the DNA of mice. In the picture above, one mouse now has the gene that produces human growth hormone in its DNA. Can you tell which mouse it is?

Concerns About Genetic Engineering

At first glance, genetic engineering seems wonderful. However, some groups are concerned that there may be problems associated with it.

One of the main concerns is that genetically-engineered organisms

might accidentally escape from a laboratory. Scientists have developed guidelines to head off such accidents. Laboratories dealing with potentially harmful organisms have strict security procedures.

Another concern is that even beneficial organisms that are released intentionally may not be as good as we first thought. Bacteria released to help a crop could multiply and spread beyond the field where they're applied. They could harm the environment in ways that we can't even foresee. For example, if plants are engineered to be more resistant to weed killers, couldn't that eventually lead to more weed killers in the environment?

Science Journal

Some people think all genetic research should stop until we are able to see more clearly just what the risks are. Do you agree? Explain your point of view *in your Science Journal.*

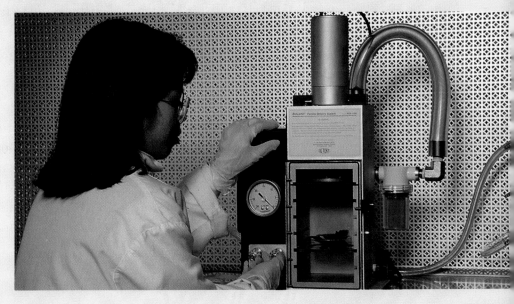

Art Connection

Craig Schaffer — Sculptor

ake the DNA ladder, twist it, and what do you get? If you are sculptor Craig Schaffer, you get six-sided stars that double as candlesticks. By looking at the structure of DNA in a different way, Schaffer turned the stuff of life itself into art for a Jewish house of worship. Interpreting the structure of DNA as art is only one of the ways in which Schaffer has been inspired by natural forms. He uses stone, wood, metal, and even plastic to explore the artistic possibilities of the natural world.

"People think that art and science are at opposite ends of the poles," says Schaffer, "but really they are very similar." The sculptor believes that artists and scientists share several traits—both are very curious about the world around them, and both perform experiments to test their ideas. Like a scientist, an artist often begins with a question, or hypothesis. How does shape influence function? Are there repeating patterns in seemingly disorganized structures? These are some of the questions artists may ask as they begin to explore new possibilities. Artists follow the scientific method, Schaffer explains, because they begin each new work with a different question. They try something new, then learn from the results. Often an artist may move along a different path as a result of one experiment, just as a scientist's experiments often lead to a new hypothesis.

Schaffer feels that you can learn how an artist evolves by viewing work from various times in the artist's life. At a retrospective show, you can see how an artist's perspective has changed over time. Why, for example, would an artist paint the same mountain over and over again throughout his or her life? Schaffer explains that, each time, the artist wanted to know what would happen if one variable was altered. Scientists operate in exactly the same way.

What Do You Think?

Schaffer believes that art and science share common traits. Do you agree with him? Explain why. Many artists are interested in natural forms. Find out what made the work of Frank Lloyd Wright so original, and how natural forms influenced his work.

Science Journal

Review the statements below about the big ideas presented in this chapter, and answer the questions. Then, reread your answers to the Did You Ever Wonder questions at the beginning of the chapter. *In your Science Journal*, write a paragraph about how your understanding of the big ideas in the chapter has changed.

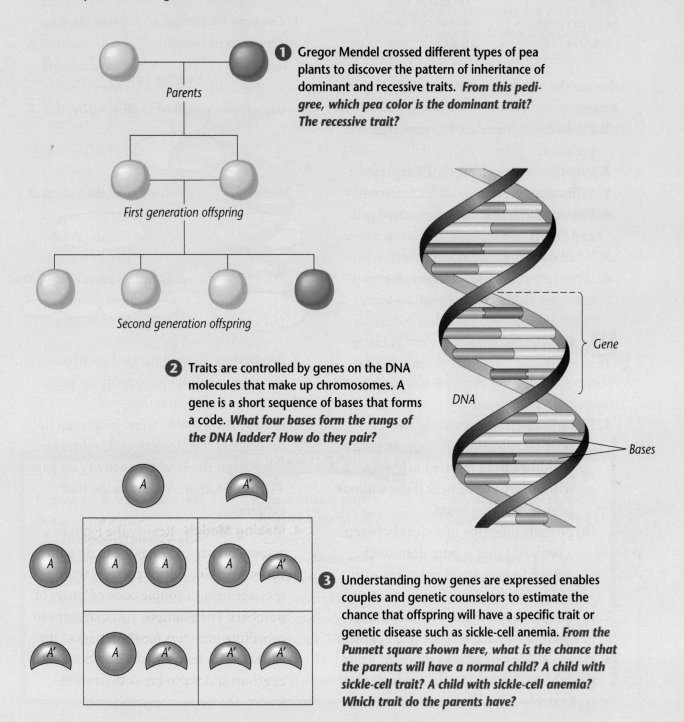

Parents

First generation offspring

Second generation offspring

1 Gregor Mendel crossed different types of pea plants to discover the pattern of inheritance of dominant and recessive traits. *From this pedigree, which pea color is the dominant trait? The recessive trait?*

Gene

DNA

Bases

2 Traits are controlled by genes on the DNA molecules that make up chromosomes. A gene is a short sequence of bases that forms a code. *What four bases form the rungs of the DNA ladder? How do they pair?*

A   A'

A   A   A   A   A'

A'   A   A'   A'   A'

3 Understanding how genes are expressed enables couples and genetic counselors to estimate the chance that offspring will have a specific trait or genetic disease such as sickle-cell anemia. *From the Punnett square shown here, what is the chance that the parents will have a normal child? A child with sickle-cell trait? A child with sickle-cell anemia? Which trait do the parents have?*

CHAPTER 15

Moving Continents

Did you ever wonder...

✓ **What the bottoms of the oceans look like?**

✓ **Why California has so many earthquakes?**

✓ **How a dormant volcano could suddenly erupt after 600 years?**

Science Journal

Before you begin to study about moving continents, think about these questions and answer them *in your Science Journal.* When you finish the chapter, compare your journal write-up with what you have learned.

You can hardly imagine how beautiful Earth must look from space. Then you see the satellite photo of Earth on the jigsaw puzzle you were given. The picture is spectacular! You can't wait to begin working on the puzzle.

For days, you fit pieces together, and ever so slowly the puzzle begins to take shape. You easily finish North America and Europe. They are now intact on the puzzle. You turn your attention to completing the African continent, and you make an interesting discovery. You notice that although the pieces you've placed all fit together well, the continent doesn't look like the picture on the puzzle box. You recheck your work and discover that some of the pieces you placed on the western coast of Africa actually belong on the eastern coast of South America. How could you have made this mistake? Is it possible that your puzzle pieces fit in two different places?

▶ *In the next activity, you'll explore the information you use to help you put together a puzzle.*

Explore! ACTIVITY

What clues are used to piece together puzzles?

What To Do

1. Cut a picture out of an old magazine and paste it on lightweight cardboard.

2. Then cut the picture into pieces of different sizes and shapes. Try to piece it back together again. *In your Journal*, record the clues you used to help you put the picture together.

469

The Moving Continents

Section Objectives
- Explain the hypothesis of continental drift.
- Identify and discuss four pieces of evidence used to support the hypothesis of continental drift.

Key Terms

continental drift

Continental Drift

Have you ever told your friends a true story that they did not believe? Maybe you gave them all kinds of specific details to support your story—and they still wouldn't believe you.

The same sort of thing happened to the people who first said that the continents move. No one would believe them.

Alfred Wegener observed the similarity in the shapes of continental coastlines. Wegener thought that the fit of the continents wasn't a coincidence. He hypothesized that all the continents were once joined as one large supercontinent called Pangaea, which means "all Earth." Wegener believed that Pangaea broke apart about 200 million years ago, and that the continents had since moved. In 1912, Wegener proposed his hypothesis known as **continental drift**.

Because of lack of proof, however, Wegener's hypothesis was not taken seriously by other scientists. One reason Wegener's ideas were scoffed at was because he was not a geologist. He had been trained as a meteorologist. After his hypothesis was rejected by other scientists, Wegener decided

Figure 15-1

A Fossils and fossil remains of the plants and animals shown here have been found on more than one continent. Mesosaurus fossils, for example, have been discovered in South America and in Africa.

B One explanation for the fact that some animal fossils have been found on more than one continent is that they swam from one continent to another. This hypothesis, however, is believed to be incorrect. Look at the animals pictured in the diagram. Why is it hard to believe they could swim across oceans?

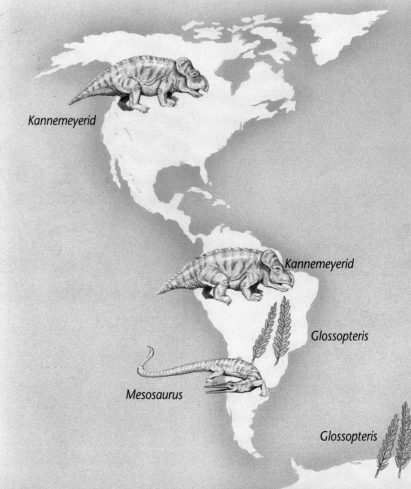

Kannemeyerid

Kannemeyerid

Glossopteris

Mesosaurus

Glossopteris

to gather more data to support his idea.

Fossil Evidence

To develop his supercontinent idea, Wegener also started with the puzzle-like fit of the continents, but then he gathered additional information to help in the reconstruction of Pangaea. One type of data he gathered was fossil information. Wegener discovered something unusual about two types of fossils, a reptile called Mesosaurus, and a fern called Glossopteris. What was so unusual is that Mesosaurus fossils are found in South America and Africa, and Glossopteris fossils are found in Africa, South America, India, Australia, and Antarctica. What could explain how these organisms got from one continent to another? And, how could Glossopteris live in climates as different as tropical Africa and polar Antarctica? **Figure 15-1** shows some of the fossil evidence Wegener had.

Glacier Evidence

Wegener believed these answers could be explained by his hypothesis of continental drift. But he needed more evidence. Wegener gathered evidence of deposits of glacial sediment and grooved bedrock in the southern parts of South America, Africa, India, and Australia. Although these areas are now located in middle and low latitudes, and their climates are quite different from one another, Wegener thought these areas must have been connected and covered by glaciers.

In the next Investigate, you will explore the fit of the continents using the evidence Wegener had.

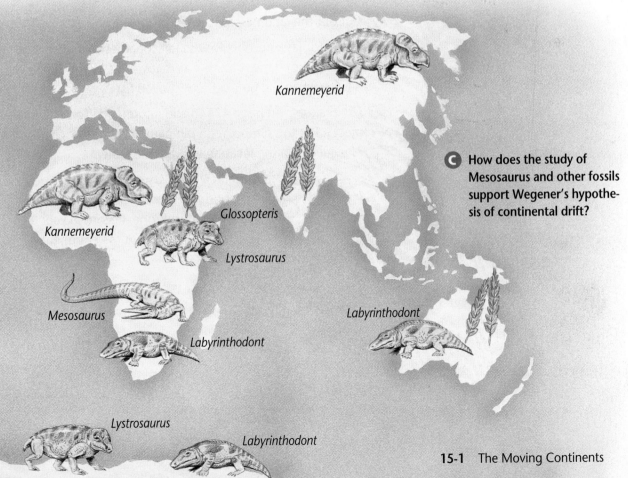

Kannemeyerid

Kannemeyerid

Glossopteris

Lystrosaurus

Mesosaurus

Labyrinthodont

Labyrinthodont

Lystrosaurus

Labyrinthodont

C How does the study of Mesosaurus and other fossils support Wegener's hypothesis of continental drift?

INVESTIGATE!

Reconstruct Pangaea

You know that a scientist must have evidence to support a hypothesis. In this activity, you will examine evidence that Pangaea existed.

Problem
What evidence is helpful in reconstructing Pangaea?

Materials
world map (Appendix H)	large sheet of paper
5 sheets unlined paper	scissors
	glue

What To Do

1 Trace the continents and Greenland from the world map onto the unlined paper. Label each landmass.

2 Cut out the landmasses.

3 The landmasses probably won't fit together exactly, but try to fit the shapes together as many ways as you can. Keep track of the number of ways you try.

4 *Use the table* on page 473 to add information to the pieces. Put the symbol found in parentheses for each type of evidence in the location listed in the table.

5 Using the new data, try again to fit the labeled landmasses together. *Compare* your first attempt with this one. Record *in your Journal* the number of ways the continents fit together.

A **B** **C**

6 When you have the best fit, glue the assembled pieces to the large piece of paper. This is your reconstruction of Pangaea.

Evidence of Pangaea		
TYPE OF EVIDENCE	**SYMBOL**	**LOCATION**
Type A mountains	(AAAA):	eastern North America, western Europe, southern tip of Greenland
Type C mountains	(CCCC):	southern end of South America, southern end of Africa
Evidence of glaciers	(XXXX):	western Australia, southern tip of India, southern Africa, southeastern South America, Antarctica
Type G fossils	(GGGG):	western Australia, southern tip of India, southern Africa, southeastern South America, Antarctia
Type M fossils	(MMMM):	southern tip of Africa, southern tip of South America

Analyzing

1. Using only the shapes of the landmasses as evidence, how many ways did they fit together?

2. Using the shapes plus the evidence from the data table, how many ways did the landmasses fit together?

Concluding and Applying

3. How did the additional evidence help you *construct a model* of Pangaea?

4. How does this reconstruction of Pangaea help explain the evidence of glaciers in Africa where no glaciers currently exist?

5. **Going Further** From what evidence can you *infer* that India may once have been separated from Asia?

■ Reconstructing Pangaea

Think back to the Explore activity at the beginning of this chapter. How did you fit the pieces of the magazine picture together? One clue you probably used was their shapes. What other clues did you use? Wegener also used the shapes of the continents to build his model of Pangaea. But just as you also used the picture on the pieces of each puzzle as clues, Wegener used the fossil and glacier evidence as "pictures" to put together Pangaea.

Look at the **Figure 15-2** below. Notice where the southern parts of South America, Africa, India, and Australia are located when the continents were joined. Is it possible that those parts could have been covered by glaciers?

Figure 15-2

A About 250 million years ago, the arrangement of the continents formed the supercontinent Pangaea. Modern day Europe, Asia, and North America can be found in the northern portion of Pangaea. What continents can be found in the southern portion of Pangaea?

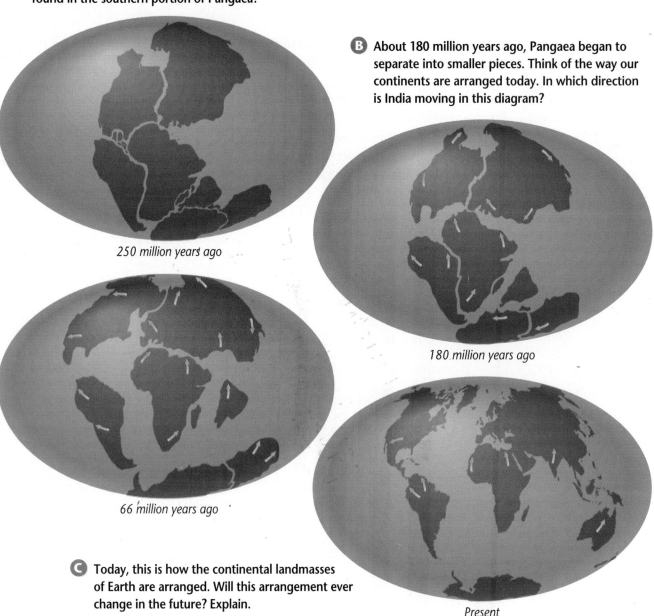

250 million years ago

B About 180 million years ago, Pangaea began to separate into smaller pieces. Think of the way our continents are arranged today. In which direction is India moving in this diagram?

180 million years ago

66 million years ago

C Today, this is how the continental landmasses of Earth are arranged. Will this arrangement ever change in the future? Explain.

Present

Clues From Rocks

If the continents were once all part of the same supercontinent, shouldn't the rock structures of continents that were once joined be similar along the place they split apart? **Figure 15-3** and **15-4** show some of the rock clues that supported Wegener's hypothesis. You would expect to find similar types, ages, and structures of rocks along the coastal areas of two continents that were once joined.

Unfortunately, Wegener was never able to explain how or why the continents move. However, additional evidence found in the 1950s and 1960s revived the hypothesis. Today, the idea of moving continents has been largely accepted. In the following section, you will read about the evidence that has helped support it.

North
Europe
Asia
Africa
South
America
Australia
Antarctica
Glacial deposits
Matching folded mountains
• Coal deposits

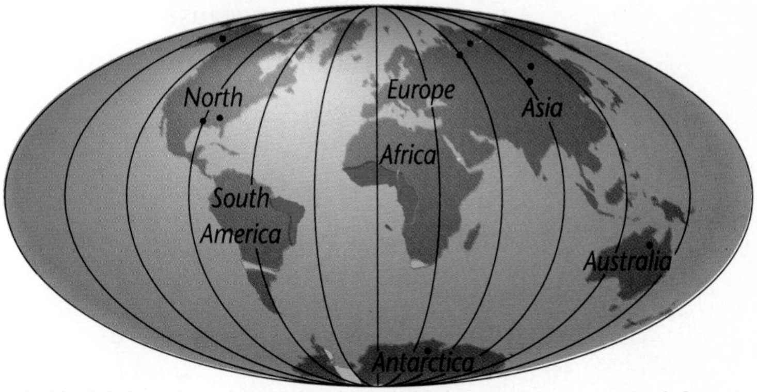

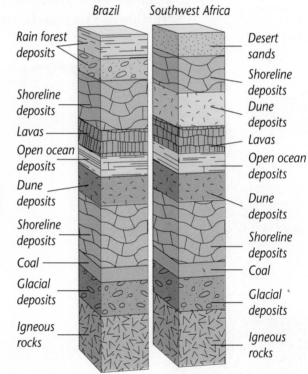

Figure 15-3

Similar rocks and rock formations can be found scattered throughout the world as shown in the map above.

Figure 15-4

A lot can be discovered about the geologic history of an area by studying its rock layers. What can you infer about continental movement by comparing the layers of these two rock columns from Brazil and Africa?

Brazil
Southwest Africa
Rain forest deposits
Shoreline deposits
Lavas
Open ocean deposits
Dune deposits
Shoreline deposits
Coal
Glacial deposits
Igneous rocks
Desert sands
Shoreline deposits
Dune deposits
Lavas
Open ocean deposits
Dune deposits
Shoreline deposits
Coal
Glacial deposits
Igneous rocks

check your UNDERSTANDING

1. How did Wegener use four types of evidence to help support his hypothesis of continental drift?
2. Fossils indicate that tropical plants once lived on what is now Antarctica. What two explanations can you give for this?
3. **Apply** Continental slopes are the steep edges of the continents that plunge deep to the ocean floor. If continental slopes, not shorelines, mark the true edges of continents, how would it change your reconstruction of Pangaea?

15-2 Sea-Floor Spreading

Section Objectives
- Explain how sea-floor spreading supports the hypothesis of continental drift.
- Explain how the age of rocks and magnetic clues confirm sea-floor spreading.

Key Terms
sea-floor spreading

The Layered Earth

If Wegener had possessed more information about what lay beneath the continents, he might have been better able to explain how continents can move. **Figure 15-5** shows a model of Earth's inner structure. The layered structure of Earth can be compared to the structure of a peach. Earth is made of many layers just as a peach seed is surrounded by the pit, the juicy flesh, and the skin.

The extremely dense inner core is made of mostly iron and nickel. While the surrounding outer core is made of the same material, it's liquid. The next layer, the mantle, has some unusual properties. While it is solid, it can flow like a liquid because of the tremendous heat and pressure. The outermost layer, the one we live on, is the crust. The crust is the thinnest of all of Earth's layers.

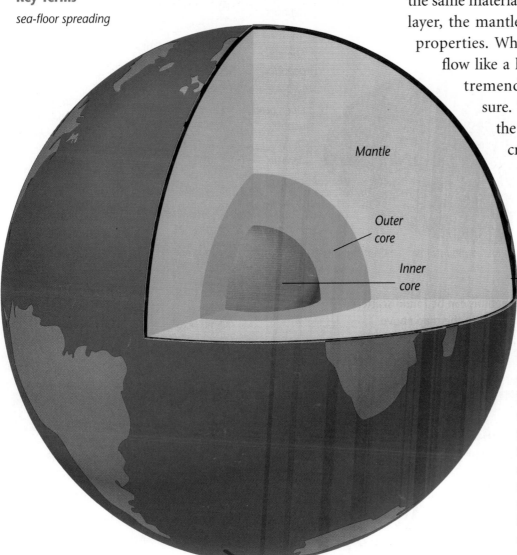

Mantle

Outer core

Inner core

Crust

Figure 15-5

Each of the layers of Earth has characteristics that make them different from each other. Even though they have never actually seen inside Earth, scientists have learned much about its different layers by studying how seismic waves travel through them.

Clues on the Ocean Floor

During Wegener's lifetime, little was known about the ocean floor. However, by the late 1950s, research vessels had crisscrossed Earth's oceans, taking thousands of echo soundings. Echo sounding was made possible by sound wave technology. Scientists would send a sound wave to the seafloor, and the sound would echo back up to the ship. Scientists could time the returning sound and determine how far from the surface the seafloor was. The resulting maps showed mountains and valleys just like those on the continents. The most amazing discovery was mountain chains thousands of kilometers long as shown in **Figure 15-6**. These mountain chains are called mid-ocean ridges. Along the middle of these ridges are narrow regions called rift valleys.

The seafloor maps also showed the location of deep trenches. The deepest trench, the Marianas Trench in the Western Pacific Ocean, is over 11 kilometers deep in some parts.

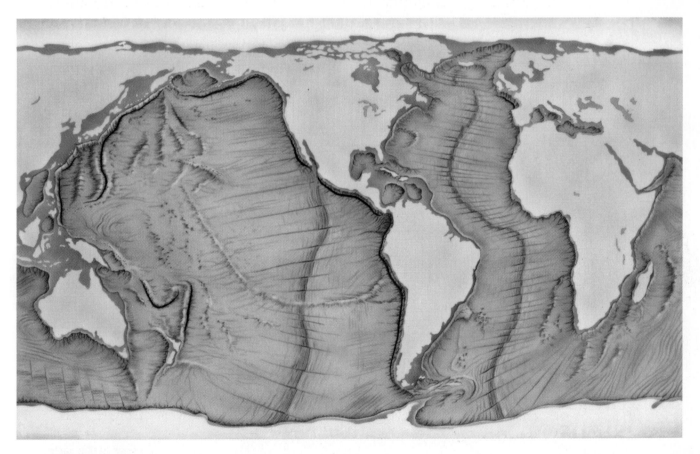

Figure 15-6

Many people think the ocean floor is smooth and flat. But if you drained the water from the oceans, it would look like the diagram above. Look at the features of the ocean floor. How are the features of the ocean floor similar to, and different from, the features of continents?

Connect to...

Life Science

Giant tube worms live by deep undersea vents that occur along mid-ocean ridges. Make a report that explains how the tube worms obtain nutrients, since there are no plants where they live.

Age Evidence

In the 1960s, scientists on board the research ship Glomar Challenger began gathering information about rocks in the ocean crust. The scientists used a hollow drill bit and drill pipe to drill into the seafloor and pull out samples, in the same way you could stick a straw into gelatin and pull out a sample. None of the ocean floor rock samples was older than 200 million years. This was surprising because some rocks have been found on the continents that are more than three billion years old! Rocks at the mid-ocean ridges were very young, but rocks became increasingly older farther away from the ridges. This was true in both directions from the mid-ocean ridges. Why were the rocks near the ridges younger than those further away?

In the 1960s, a hypothesis known as **sea-floor spreading** emerged. This hypothesis states that molten material from Earth's mantle is forced upward to the surface at mid-ocean ridges and cools to form new seafloor. Movement in Earth's mantle forces plates apart, allowing the magma to flow onto Earth's surface and form new seafloor. **Figure 15-7** shows how sea-floor spreading works.

Figure 15-7

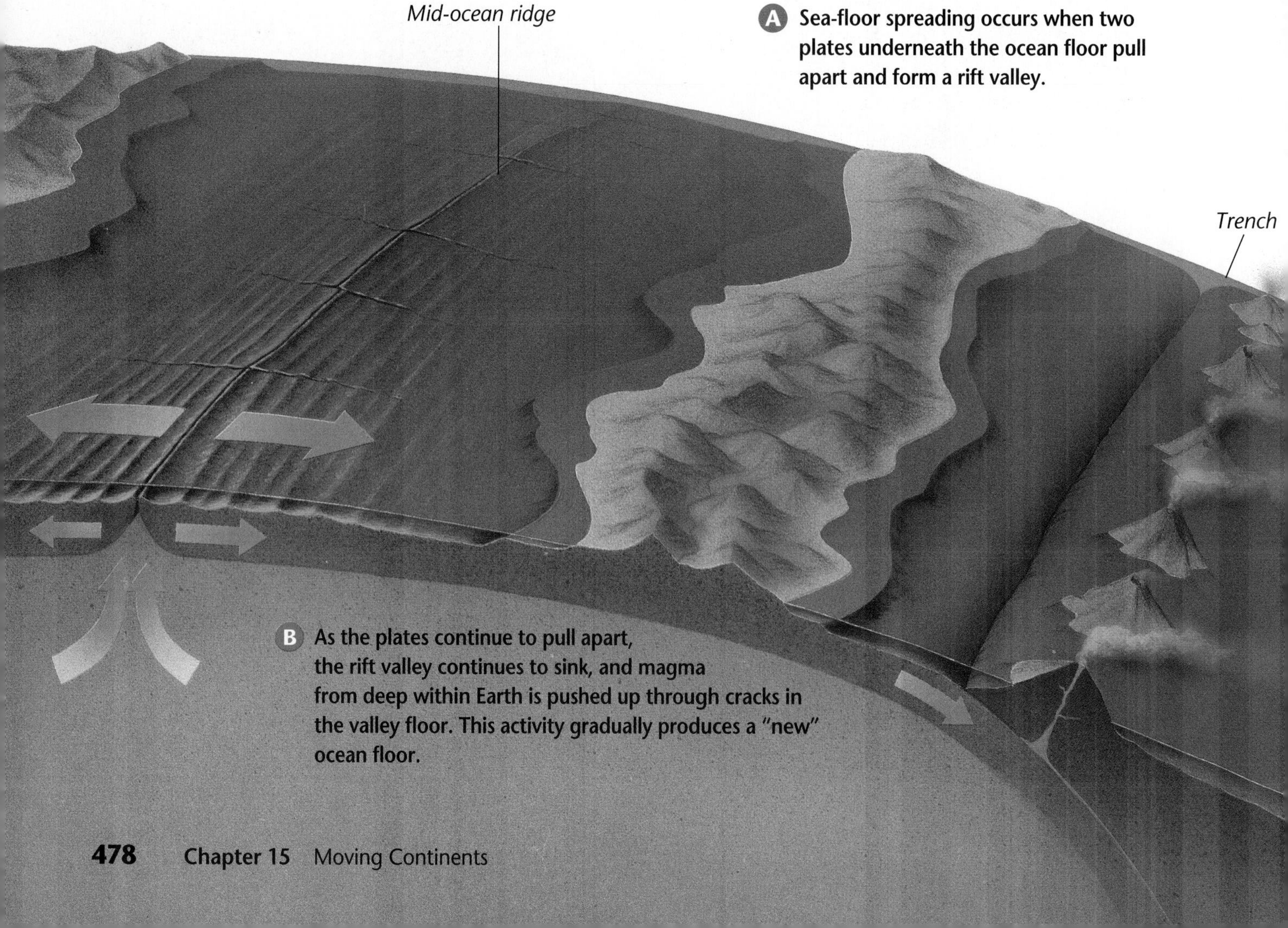

Ⓐ Sea-floor spreading occurs when two plates underneath the ocean floor pull apart and form a rift valley.

Mid-ocean ridge

Trench

Ⓑ As the plates continue to pull apart, the rift valley continues to sink, and magma from deep within Earth is pushed up through cracks in the valley floor. This activity gradually produces a "new" ocean floor.

Magnetic Clues

Like any hypothesis, sea-floor spreading had to be able to explain new information as it became available. The next information available, in this case, was magnetic information locked within the ocean floor rocks. But how can magnetic information become locked? The next Explore activity will help you understand the magnetic nature of rocks.

Explore! ACTIVITY

How does a magnet affect iron filings?

What To Do

1. Divide a stiff piece of cardboard into two sections. Carefully place a small amount of iron filings on one of the sections. Place a large bar magnet flat on a table.

2. Place the cardboard and filings on top of the magnet. Record *in your Journal* how the filings align themselves. Lightly spray the filings with clear lacquer in a well-ventilated area, covering the opposite side of the cardboard to keep it dry.

3. Change the position of the magnet by 90°. Spread a small amount of iron filings on the other section. Move this section on top of the magnet. *In your Journal,* describe what happens to the lacquered filings in the first section? To the filings you added?

Earth has a magnetic field much like that of a bar magnet. While lava is still liquid, the iron particles in it are free to move and align themselves with Earth's magnetic field. When the lava hardens into rock, the iron is no longer free to move. The hardened rock contains a record of how Earth's magnetic field was aligned at the time the lava cooled. In the Investigate, you will discover how magnetic evidence can support sea-floor spreading.

How Do We Know?

Earth's Magnetic Record

The iron particles in igneous rock align with Earth's magnetic field as the rock forms. This means that the iron exhibits its own magnetic field. By using a magnetometer—an instrument that detects and measures the presence of weak magnetic fields—scientists can tell in which direction Earth's north and south magnetic poles were located when a rock formed.

INVESTIGATION

Magnetic Data

Magnetic rock data provide an important clue to the theory of seafloor spreading. Iron particles in magma are free to move until the magma cools to form rock — then they are locked in place. The particles are aligned with the orientation of Earth's magnetic field at that time.

Preparation

Problem

How would you develop a model to show that magnetic data supports the theory of seafloor spreading?

Form a Hypothesis

State a hypothesis about how magnetic clues in the rocks indicate that the seafloor is spreading.

Objectives

- Develop a model showing how magnetic clues are used to indicate seafloor spreading.
- Infer how the ages of rocks on the seafloor are related to the study of magnetic clues.

Materials

metric ruler	tape
small magnetic compass	bar magnets
	pen or marker
2 student desks	paper

Plan the Experiment

1 As a group, agree upon and write out your hypothesis statement.

2 Examine the materials provided. Then determine how to make your model of seafloor spreading.

3 Discuss how your model will demonstrate magnetic clues from the ocean floor.

Check the Plan

1 Read over your entire experiment to make sure that all steps are in a logical order.

2 Study the photograph shown here. How will you use the small compasses to indicate how magnetic

clues, including alternating directions of magnetic north, indicate seafloor spreading?

3 How will you use the paper to demonstrate seafloor spreading?

4 Make sure your teacher approves your experiment before you proceed.

5 Carry out your experiment. Record your observations *in your Science Journal.*

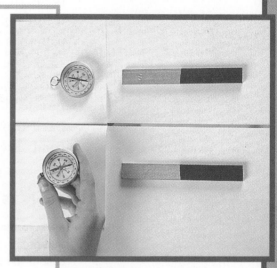

Analyze and Conclude

1. **Observe and Infer** Where are the "oldest" marks on your paper?

2. **Compare and Contrast** Compare your paper to the patterns in **Figure 15-8** shown on page 482. What are

the similarities? What are the differences?

3. **Draw a Conclusion** On the seafloor, is the youngest rock near to or far from the mid-ocean ridges? Explain.

Going Further

In your Science Journal, write a paragraph that explains the role of the bar magnets in your model. What do they represent? Also, explain how flipping the bar magnets models the behavior of Earth's magnetic field.

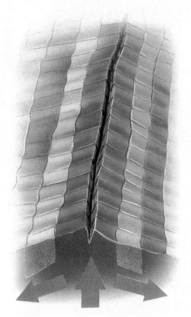

Just as you found a pattern to the stripes in the Investigate, scientists examining seafloor rocks found an interesting pattern in the magnetic records of the rocks. This pattern is shown in **Figure 15-8**. The rocks show that Earth's magnetic field has reversed itself many times. Each time the magnetic field switched, rocks

Figure 15-8

Rocks formed on both sides of mid-ocean ridges recorded the change in magnetic polarity each time the Earth's magnetic field reversed itself.

 Normal Polarity   *Reversed Polarity*

recorded the new field. The magnetic properties of rocks aligned with the magnetic orientation at the time that they formed.

Using magnetometers, research ships took magnetic readings on ocean floor igneous rocks and plotted the data on maps. The maps revealed that stripes of magnetically similar rock run parallel to a mid-ocean ridge. The pattern of stripes on one side of a mid-ocean ridge was very similar to the pattern on the other side. Radiometric dating revealed that the age of the rocks on either side of a rift is also very similar. What do these findings suggest about what happens at a mid-ocean ridge?

Sea-Floor Spreading

You have learned that changes in Earth's magnetic field help support the idea of sea-floor spreading. In this activity, you'll use data from the magnetic field profile of the Mid-Atlantic Ridge to measure

how fast the seafloor is spreading. You will work with six major peaks east and west of the Mid-Atlantic Ridge, for both normal and reversed polarity.

You Try It!

Materials
  paper
  pencil
  metric ruler
Procedure
1. Place the ruler through the first major peak west of the Mid-Atlantic Ridge. This peak shows reverse polarity and extends downward on the profile. Determine and record *in your Journal* the distance in kilo-

The discovery of similar magnetic records and ages of rock on both sides of a mid-ocean ridge helped support the hypothesis of sea-floor spreading. For one thing, the magnetic reversal showed that new rock was being formed at the mid-ocean ridges. For another, if the floor were not spreading, the ages and magnetic records of rocks on either side of a mid-ocean would probably not be the same.

While Wegener believed that the continents were moving, others believed that the seafloor was moving. Was it possible that both were correct? Like putting pieces of a puzzle together, scientists fit the two hypotheses together to show us the big picture of Earth in continual motion.

check your UNDERSTANDING

1. How are the ideas of continental drift and sea-floor spreading related?

2. Discuss two pieces of data used to support the idea of sea-floor spreading.

3. **Apply** Imagine a seafloor that is spreading. How could it be possible for the seafloor to spread, while the ocean remains the same width?

---

meters to the Mid-Atlantic Ridge using the distance scale.

2. Repeat Step 1 for each of the six major peaks east and west of the main ridge, for both normal and reversed polarity.

3. Find the average distance from the peak to the Mid-Atlantic for each pair of peaks on either side of the ridge. Record these values.

4. Place the ruler through each of the normal polarity peaks and find the age of the rocks.

5. Using the normal polarity readings, calculate the rate of movement in centimeters per year. You will need to convert kilometers to centimeters and then use this formula:

distance = rate x time.

6. Find the average rate of sea-floor spreading in both directions in one year, based on the rate of movement in one direction you determined in Step 5.

7. How many years would it take rock to move from the Mid-Atlantic Ridge to a trench 300 km away?

Underwater mountain chains like the Mid-Atlantic Ridge can be found on the floor of all of our oceans. Rift valleys extend the length of these mountain chains. What happens to the magma that erupts through the cracks of rift valleys?

Colliding Plates

15-3

Tectonic Plates

Section Objectives

■ Explain how plate tectonics accounts for the movement of continents.

■ Compare and contrast divergent, convergent, and transform plate boundaries.

■ Explain how convection currents inside Earth might be the cause of plate tectonics.

Key Terms

plate tectonics
lithosphere
divergent boundary
convergent
    boundary
transform fault
    boundary
asthenosphere

Do you enjoy reading mystery stories? Usually, the characters piece together clues or evidence. Think of the hypotheses of continental drift and sea-floor spreading as clues to a mystery. How can the two hypotheses be explained?

In the late 1960s, geologists developed a new theory to explain the apparent movement of the continents. The theory of **plate tectonics** suggests that Earth's crust and upper mantle are broken into sections called plates

that move. But what are the plates made of, and why do they move?

You already know that Earth's crust is a layer of solid rock. The uppermost portion of the mantle is also solid. Together, these two areas are the **lithosphere**.

How are these solid plates able to move around? As you can see in **Figure 15-9**, below the lithosphere is a portion of the mantle that is less solid. The material here behaves almost like putty; it's a solid that can flow. This putty-like layer is called the **asthenosphere**. The plates can be thought of as rafts that slide around on the asthenosphere. Because they cover the entire planet, there are always places where the plates are in contact with each other. The place where two plates meet is called a plate boundary. The directions of plate movement determine what occurs at a plate boundary. Let's look at the basic types of plate boundaries.

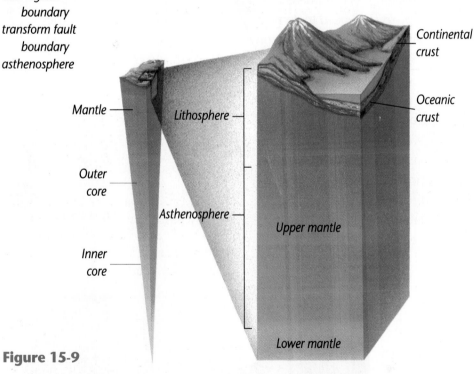

Figure 15-9

This diagram shows the different layers of the crust and the mantle of Earth. The rigid lithosphere moves around on top of the asthenosphere, which is capable of flowing gradually.

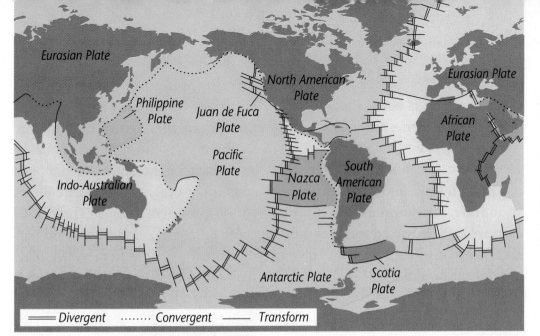

Figure 15-10

This map displays the lithospheric plates on which all of the oceans and continents of Earth move. Are all of the lithospheric plates of Earth the same size? On which plate do you live?

Eurasian Plate

Philippine Plate

Juan de Fuca Plate

North American Plate

Eurasian Plate

African Plate

Pacific Plate

Indo-Australian Plate

Nazca Plate

South American Plate

Antarctic Plate

Scotia Plate

═══ Divergent ······ Convergent ── Transform

■ Divergent Boundaries

The boundary between two plates that are moving away from each other and spreading apart is called a **divergent boundary**. Magma is forced upward to Earth's surface in the rift valley that forms between the two plates, creating new crust. Mid-ocean ridges are divergent boundaries. In the Atlantic Ocean, the North American Plate is moving away from the Eurasian and African plates. This divergent boundary is the Mid-Atlantic Ridge discussed earlier. This boundary is shown in **Figure 15-11.**

Figure 15-11

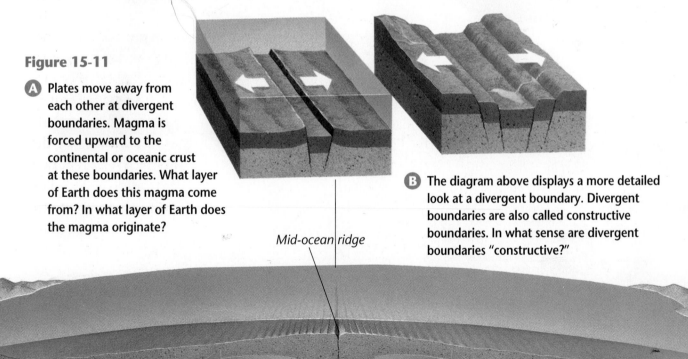

A Plates move away from each other at divergent boundaries. Magma is forced upward to the continental or oceanic crust at these boundaries. What layer of Earth does this magma come from? In what layer of Earth does the magma originate?

Mid-ocean ridge

B The diagram above displays a more detailed look at a divergent boundary. Divergent boundaries are also called constructive boundaries. In what sense are divergent boundaries "constructive?"

■ Convergent Boundaries

If new crust is being added at the divergent boundaries, why isn't Earth getting bigger? Earth doesn't get bigger because as new crust is added in one place, it sinks into Earth's interior at another. Crustal material can be destroyed where two plates meet head on. This type of boundary is called a **convergent boundary**. It is shown in **Figure 15-12**.

What do you think happens when two plates containing continental crust collide? The two plates crumple, forming mountain ranges. The Himalaya Mountains formed when the Indian Plate collided with the southern part of the Eurasian Plate.

Trenches are formed when a plate containing ocean floor crust collides with a continental plate. The denser ocean crust sinks under the continental crust, forming a trench. The plate that slides underneath melts under the tremendous heat and presssure. Trenches can also form when two plates of ocean floor crust collide.

Figure 15-12

At convergent boundaries, much of what happens when two plates collide depends on the type of crust at the leading edge of each plate. Continental crust is less dense than oceanic crust. How does this explain what's happening in these diagrams?

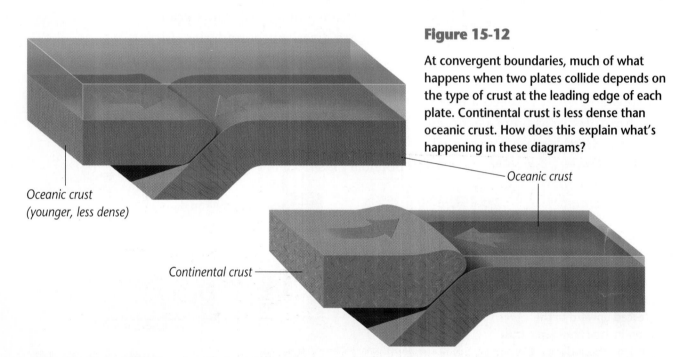

Oceanic crust
(younger, less dense)

Oceanic crust

Continental crust

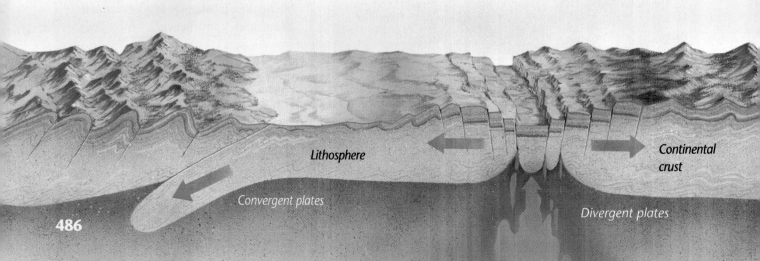

Lithosphere

Continental crust

Convergent plates

Divergent plates

■ Transform Fault Boundaries

A third type of plate boundary is shown in **Figure 15-13**. Called a **transform fault boundary**, it is formed when two plates slide past one another in opposite directions or in the same direction at different rates. Look back at **Figure 15-10**. Find where the North American and Pacific plates meet in California. This is the San Andreas Fault. The San Andreas is a transform fault boundary. Along this boundary, the Pacific Plate moves northwest compared with the North American Plate. The part of California that is on the Pacific Plate is actually moving northward in relation to the North American Plate at an average of two centimeters per year.

The formation of many landforms occurs as plates move around the surface of Earth, pulling apart from each other, colliding, and sliding past each other. **Figure 15-14** shows how boundaries can create landforms. From the majestic Himalayan Mountains, to the Great Rift Valley in Africa, plate movement shapes the land we live on. But what causes the plates to move? Next we will explore the driving force behind plate movements.

Figure 15-13

A fault is a line along which rocks or rock formations move. Faults can be so small that you have to look closely to see them, or they can be large enough to be seen from an airplane. How is the movement of material at a transform fault boundary different from the movement of material at convergent and divergent boundaries?

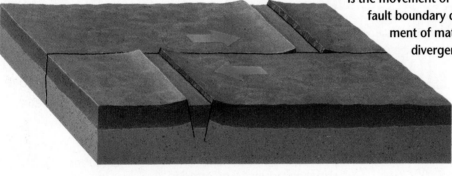

Figure 15-14

Convergent, divergent, and transform fault boundaries exist in various places along Earth's crust. Look at this diagram to find what kinds of landforms are typically created at such boundaries.

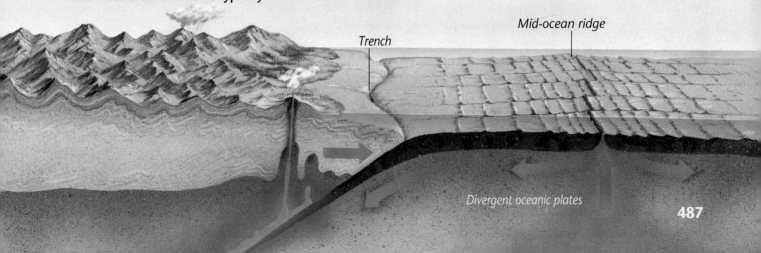

Trench

Mid-ocean ridge

Divergent oceanic plates

Causes of Plate Tectonics

How does the theory of plate tectonics explain the cause of plate movements? The driving force behind that movement is heat. A material that is hot is less dense than the same material that is cold. This is because the same mass takes up more volume when the material is heated. Remember that less dense material is forced up by more dense material. Think about how a room is heated. A radiator heats air in the room. The heated air is forced upward by cool, denser surrounding air. As it loses heat, the air becomes cooler and more dense.

The cooler air sinks to the floor, where it forces more warm air upward and the cycle is repeated. This cycle is called a convection current.

Figure 15-15 describes how this process occurs within Earth's asthenosphere. Remember that this layer can flow gradually like a thick liquid, even though it's more like a solid. Heat from the core warms the asthenosphere, causing convection currents to form. As these currents flow underneath the lithosphere, they pull on the plates, causing them to slowly move.

Moving Fluids and Moving Plates

Convection currents deep inside Earth provide energy that moves plates in Earth's lithosphere.

In the familiar environment of your home, convection is one of the main ways in which thermal energy is transferred in fluids. You've seen water move in a current as it boiled, and you've experienced that air is warmer near the ceiling and cooler near the floor. These are examples of the movement of fluids due to their different densities. Let's build a model of convection in action.

You Try It!

Materials
clear glass baking dish
immersion heater
plastic sandwich bag with
  wire tie or self-sealing bag
ice cubes
tape
2 eyedroppers
red and blue food coloring
water

Procedure
1. Fill the baking dish with cool water to about 2 cm from the top.
2. Put six ice cubes in the sandwich bag and close the bag with a wire tie.

Figure 15-15

Convection cells within the mantle cause the various plates in Earth's lithosphere to move around. As the plates bump into each other, boundaries form.

Trench

Mid-ocean ridge

Trench

Mantle

Convection cells

3. Put the bag in the water at one end of the pan. Tape the top of the bag to the outside of the pan to hold the bag in place.

4. Place the immersion heater in the water at the other end of the pan and plug it in. Wait about a minute for the water to heat. **CAUTION:** *Not all heaters can be used as immersion heaters. Use only approved*

immersion heaters. The heater is very hot. Do not touch it. Do not put any part of the heater in the water except the coil. Unplug the heater before you remove it from the water.

5. While you're waiting for the water to heat, fill one eyedropper with red food coloring and the other with blue food coloring.

6. Squeeze two drops of red food coloring into the water near the heater, about halfway from the bottom. Record your observations *in your Journal.*

7. Squeeze two drops of blue food coloring just under the surface of the water near the ice. Observe what happens.

What causes the movement of the red-colored water? What causes the movement of the blue-colored water? Ongoing convection currents are produced as liquids are heated, are pushed up by cooler, denser liquids, then cool and once again sink. Use your knowledge of Earth's mantle and lithosphere to explain how convection currents could produce plate movement.

Where Do Volcanoes Occur?

Volcanoes, like those shown in **Figure 15-19**, form in three kinds of places related to plate tectonics: divergent plate boundaries, convergent plate boundaries, and locations called hot spots.

■ Divergent Boundaries

Where the plates pull apart, magma is forced upward to Earth's surface and erupts as lava. Lava that flows from underwater rifts cools quickly in the cold ocean water. As eruptions continue over time, layers of cooled lava accumulate. Iceland was formed when the layers of lava accumulated to form an island.

■ Convergent Boundaries

Earth's most well-known volcanoes are found at convergent plate boundaries.

When one of the converging plates slides underneath the other, it's called a subduction zone. Melting of the subducted plate creates magma, which is forced upward to the surface. When the magma reaches the surface, it erupts as lava, forming volcanoes.

Today, plates continue to collide and subduct. Find Japan and the Philippines on your map of plate boundaries. Which plates are colliding? **Figure 15-20** shows how subduction can form an island chain.

■ Hot Spots

The Hawaiian Islands are actually the tips of volcanoes that have risen from the ocean floor. However, unlike Iceland, these islands did not form at a plate boundary. The Hawaiian Islands are in the middle of the Pacific Plate. How then are these islands related to plate tectonics?

Figure 15-19

A This is a new island forming off the coast of Iceland.

B In what ways can the eruption of Mount Saint Helens, or other volcanoes, be dangerous?

Some areas of Earth's mantle are hotter than others. In these areas, magma is forced up by surrounding denser material. The magma is forced up through cracks in the solid lithosphere and spills out as lava. These areas are known as **hot spots. Figure 15-20** also shows how hot spots can form islands. The Hawaiian Islands were formed as the Pacific plate moved over a hot spot in the middle of the Pacific Ocean. As the plate moved, island after island formed.

Plate tectonics is a story of energy transfer. The thermal energy from inside Earth is transferred to Earth's surface. Some is released as heat creating lava. Some is changed into energy of motion, causing the plates to move. Throughout geologic time, plate movements form and reform oceans, continents, and mountains.

Forming a Hypothesis

Mount Unzen in Japan and Mount Pinatubo in the Philippines both erupted in the spring of 1991. Use Figure 15-10 and the diagram in the Explore activity on page 491 to hypothesize how these volcanoes may have formed. If you need help, refer to the **Skill Handbook** on page 687.

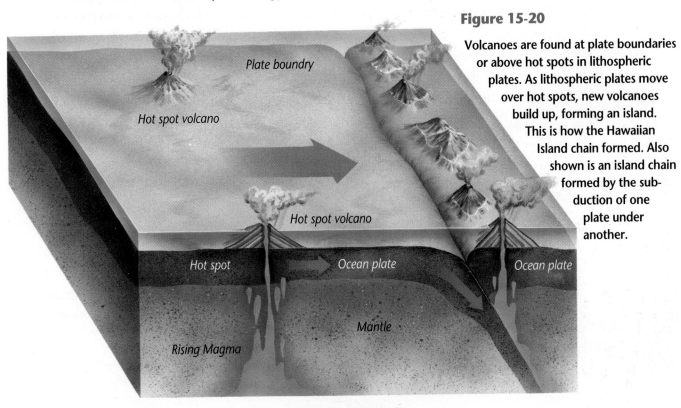

Figure 15-20

Volcanoes are found at plate boundaries or above hot spots in lithospheric plates. As lithospheric plates move over hot spots, new volcanoes build up, forming an island. This is how the Hawaiian Island chain formed. Also shown is an island chain formed by the subduction of one plate under another.

check your UNDERSTANDING

1. Both Japan and California are prone to earthquakes. Explain this fact using plate tectonics.

2. Where does lava come from that flows out of a rift? A convergent boundary?

3. **Apply** Today, a new Hawaiian volcano, Loihi Seamount, is forming. Look at a map of the Hawaiian islands. If Kauai is the oldest island of the chain, predict where Loihi Seamount is forming.

EXPAND *your view*

Science *and* Society

Volcanoes and Saving Lives

Barry Voigt adjusts a sensitive scientific instrument. He's in the midst of a landscape so alien that it could be on another planet. The rocks have edges as sharp as razors. He has to wear a mask for protection against poisonous fumes. It is truly hostile territory.

Voigt is on Merapi, a dangerous, active volcano in Indonesia. Here, 5890 meters above sea level, he risks his life carrying out research that may someday save thousands of lives.

A *Mt. Saint Helens, March, 1980– Earthquakes shook the mountain. The growing magma pocket produced a bulge on the north face of the mountain.*

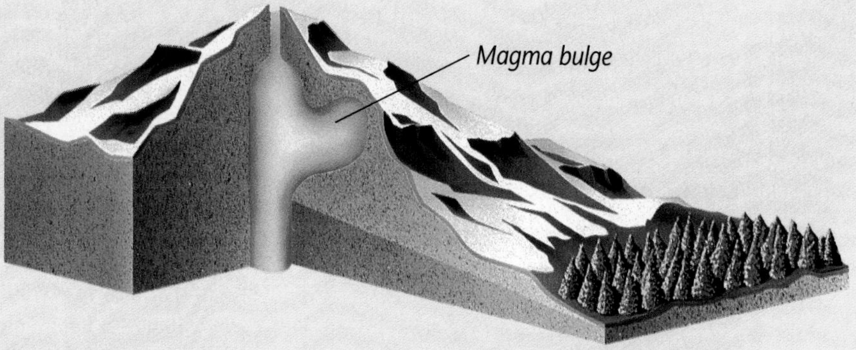

Magma bulge

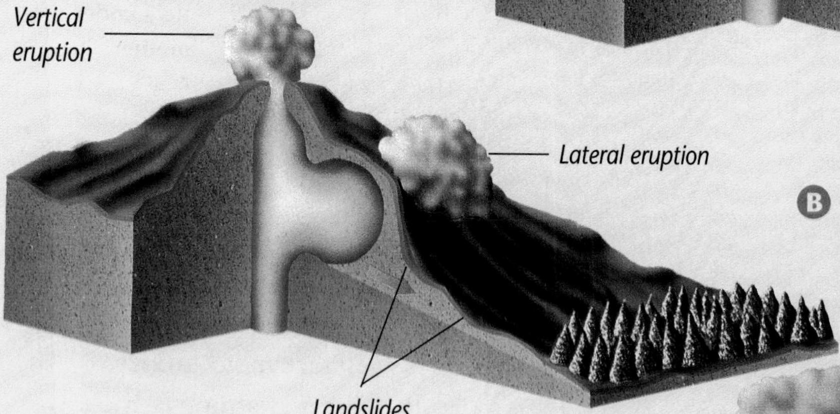

Vertical eruption

Lateral eruption

B *May 18, 1980– A new earthquake produced a landslide on the north face. The reduced pressure on the bulge caused steam to form inside the magma chamber. The steam exploded from the summit and near the bulge.*

Landslides

C *Freed from it's pocket, steam and ash then blasted horizontally. The entire chain of events from the landslide to the blast took less than 30 seconds!*

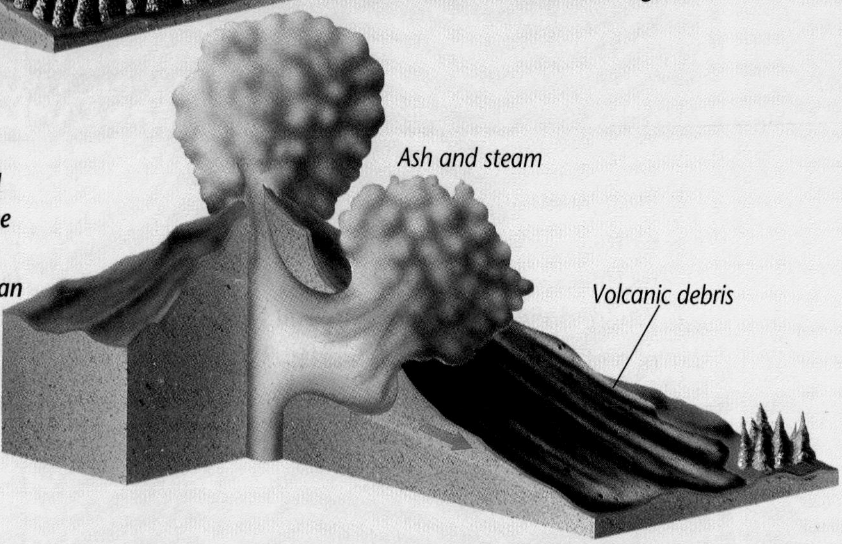

Ash and steam

Volcanic debris

Predicting Explosions

Voigt wants to reliably predict volcanic explosions weeks before they happen. That way, people in the path of a volcano's destruction would have plenty of time to get out of the way.

As recently as 1985, nearly 22 000 people died in the town of Armero in Colombia when a nearby volcano erupted. Authorities were hesitant to order an evacuation because they were not sure when the volcano would erupt. Reliable prediction could have prevented this and many similar tragedies.

An Unusual Eruption

Voigt began studying volcanoes in 1980, when earthquakes started to shake Mount Saint Helens in Washington. A specialist in rockslides and avalanches, Voigt predicted that rockslides caused by the earthquakes could make Mount Saint Helens erupt sideways. And that's what happened. The diagram on these two pages shows the sequence of the eruption.

Tools of the Trade

Voigt has developed new techniques for analyzing information from the special instruments he uses and for predicting when the rock in a volcano will give way and allow an eruption to take place.

To collect the data that he needs, Voigt uses an array of instruments such as laser measuring devices, seismographs, and instruments that measure tilt and movement of Earth.

*inter*NET CONNECTION

The Volcano World website has extensive information on all aspects of volcanoes. Visit the site to learn more about methods of predicting volcanic eruptions and about how volcanologists work.

If you had to protect a city within one kilometer of an active volcano, what prediction tools would you want to use? How would your prediction needs change if the city were 10 km away?

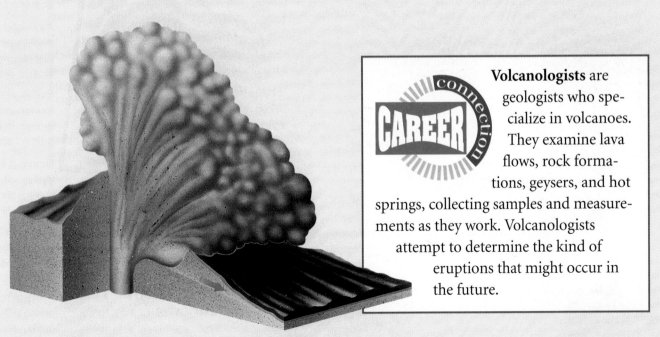

Volcanologists are geologists who specialize in volcanoes. They examine lava flows, rock formations, geysers, and hot springs, collecting samples and measurements as they work. Volcanologists attempt to determine the kind of eruptions that might occur in the future.

SciFacts

Where is the oldest thing on Earth?

Tiny crystals found in the heart of Western Australia appear to be the oldest known fragments of an ancient continent known as Gondwanaland. The crystals formed 4.3 billion years ago. Part of Earth's first crust as it cooled, these crystals existed when Australia was the easternmost part of Gondwanaland. About 130 million years ago, Gondwanaland began to break up into modern continents. Australia separated much later, about 65 million years ago.

The spectacular highlands of Australia's rust-colored Pilbara region, where the crystal-bearing rocks are found, are among the oldest and least-changed landscapes in the world. Fissured by deep gorges, which plunge into bedrock more than 2 billion years old, the Pilbara contains fossils 3.5 million years old. The rocks are among the oldest exposed rocks on Earth.

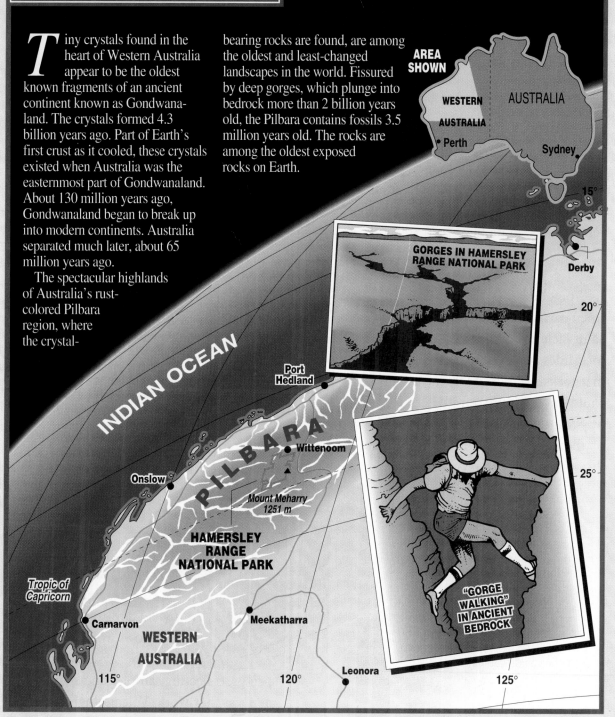

AREA SHOWN

AUSTRALIA

WESTERN AUSTRALIA

Perth

Sydney

15°

GORGES IN HAMERSLEY RANGE NATIONAL PARK

Derby

20°

INDIAN OCEAN

Port Hedland

PILBARA

Wittenoom

Onslow

Mount Meharry 1251 m

HAMERSLEY RANGE NATIONAL PARK

25°

"GORGE WALKING" IN ANCIENT BEDROCK

Tropic of Capricorn

Carnarvon

WESTERN AUSTRALIA

Meekatharra

Leonora

115°   120°   125°

Science Journal

In your Science Journal, explain what scientists might learn by studying crystals from Earth's first crust. Suggest why research like this is important.

Science Journal

Review the statements below about the big ideas presented in this chapter, and answer the questions. Then, reread your answers to the Did You Ever Wonder questions at the beginning of the chapter. *In your Science Journal*, write a paragraph about how your understanding of the big ideas in the chapter has changed.

1 The first evidence for continental drift was the obvious fit of some continents. *How does the fit of the continents suggest they have moved?*

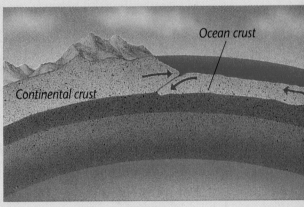

Ocean crust

Continental crust

2 A plate is a piece of lithosphere that usually contains both seafloor and part of a continent. *What causes the plates to move around?*

Lava

Magma

3 Horizontal movement of mantle material causes seafloor spreading. Magma is forced upward, pouring out of rift valleys and creating new seafloor. *Describe how crustal material is produced and consumed in plate interactions.*

4 In subduction, one plate slides under another, forcing the other plate upward. At a depth of 700 km, the subducted plate is mostly melted. *What can happen to the subducted plate after it has melted?*

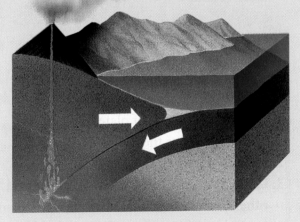

5 Most earthquakes and volcanoes occur near plate boundaries. *How can volcanoes occur in places other than plate boundaries?*

CHAPTER 16

GEOLOGIC TIME

Did you ever wonder...

- ✓ How old Earth is?
- ✓ How fossils are formed?
- ✓ How we know what dinosaurs looked like?

Science Journal

Before you begin to study geologic time, think about these questions and answer them *in your Science Journal*. When you finish the chapter, compare your journal write-up with what you have learned.

Imagine you've built a machine that can take you back in time. You strap yourself in, set the controls, and away you go. With each passing minute, you travel another million years back in time. Finally, after traveling for just over an hour, your time machine grinds to a halt. You've reached your time journey's end.

Outside your machine is lush green vegetation. Suddenly, you see a large, fierce-looking animal with long, sharp teeth eyeing you. A Tyrannosaurus! You've traveled back to the age of dinosaurs!

▶ **In this chapter, you'll see how scientists travel back in geologic time.**

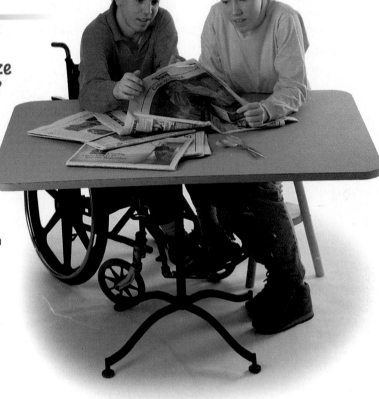

Explore! ACTIVITY

How can you discover and organize events that happened in the past?

Without knowing an exact date how can you figure out when one event occurred in relation to another?

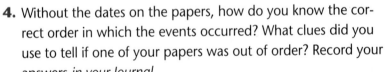

What To Do

1. Examine a stack of last week's newspapers with the dates cut off. The papers may be in the order in which they were read—oldest papers on the bottom, more recent toward the top. Some papers may be out of order.

2. Make a time line of all the front page stories during the past week.

3. *In your Journal* record the difficulties you had and the clues you used to organize your time line.

4. Without the dates on the papers, how do you know the correct order in which the events occurred? What clues did you use to tell if one of your papers was out of order? Record your answers *in your Journal.*

16-1 Fossils

Section Objectives

■ Explain the conditions necessary for fossils to form.

■ Describe two processes of fossil formation.

Key Terms

fossil

Traces from the Past

In the opening Explore activity, you used newspapers to model how scientists learn about events in Earth's past. You've probably read about dinosaurs and other previous inhabitants of Earth. You've also probably seen them depicted, not always accurately, in science fiction movies. But how do we know dinosaurs existed? What "newspaper stories" do scientists use as evidence of past life on Earth? The following Find Out activity will help you begin to answer these questions.

Find Out! ACTIVITY

What clues do organisms leave that they've been here?

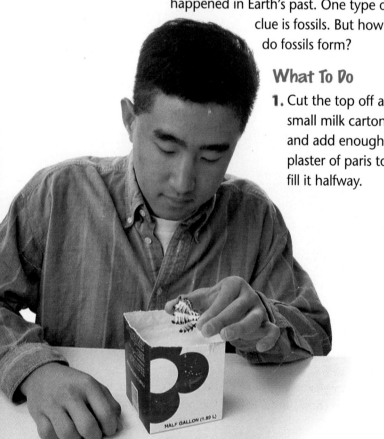

Earth scientists use many different types of clues to figure out what happened in Earth's past. One type of clue is fossils. But how do fossils form?

What To Do

1. Cut the top off a small milk carton and add enough plaster of paris to fill it halfway.

2. Mix in enough water to make the plaster smooth.

3. Coat a leaf, shell, bone, or other plant or animal part with petroleum jelly.

4. Press the coated object into the plaster of paris.

5. Allow the plaster to dry at least 24 hours before removing the object.

6. Examine and describe the plaster now. Record your observations *in your Journal.*

Conclude and Apply

1. How do the object and the plaster impression differ? How are they similar?

2. What kind of details can you see in the plaster impression?

3. What parts of the original object aren't preserved in the impression?

How Fossils Form

In the Find Out activity, you made plaster imprints of parts of organisms that were once alive. Such imprints in nature are one kind of fossil. A **fossil** is the remains or trace of an organism that was once alive. A fossil can show us what an organism looked like when it was alive. It also can tell us when, where, and how an organism once lived. In fact, fossils have helped geologists determine approximately when life on Earth began and what types of plants, animals, and other organisms lived in the past.

How are fossils formed? Study **Figure 16-1** to find out.

Connect to...

Life Science

Fossils are evidence of life of the past. Look on pages 520-521, choose one of the geologic periods and find out what kind of fossils are commonly found in rocks from that period.

Figure 16-1

Formation of a Dinosaur Fossil

When an animal dies, scavengers and bacteria eat away the soft tissues of the animal. What parts of its body will be left to fossilize?

The sediment collecting on the dinosaur's remains protect its bones and teeth. Slowly over time, the remains become encased in sediments, and minerals replace them.

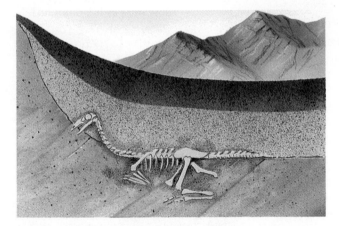

Layer on layer of sediment begin to compress deeper layers and rock forms. If shifts in the earth move and lift the rock, how might the dinosaur fossil be affected?

After tens of millions of years, the dinosaur fossil is near Earth's surface again. Erosion may expose the fossil by wearing away the rock in which it is buried. What factors on Earth's surface cause this erosion?

Types of Fossils

It takes more than a quick burial to make a fossil. Most of the fossils we see are remains or traces of the hard parts of organisms. Organisms have a better chance of being preserved if they have hard parts, such as bones, shells, teeth, or wood. Such hard parts are less likely to be disturbed or eaten by other organisms and are less likely to be broken. The replacement of minerals and the mold-and-cast process are two of the ways in which these hard parts of organisms eventually produce fossils.

Figure 16-2 shows how mold-and-cast fossils form.

■ Replacement of Minerals

Sometimes, water partially or completely dissolves the original material of the organism, depositing minerals such as quartz in its place. A mineral like quartz is harder than the original calcite in a shell, so the fossil of the shell becomes harder than the shell. Fossils formed in this way are harder than original materials because some or all of the original materials have been replaced by new, harder minerals.

Figure 16-2

Mold and Cast Fossilization Process

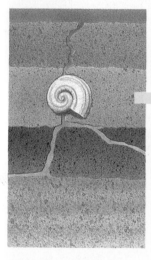  

D Fossils such as this ammonite can be formed either by replacement of minerals, or by mold-and-cast formation. Ammonites were shelled animals that were similar to squid. They lived during the same time as the dinosaurs.

A The shell of an animal becomes encased in sediment that is undergoing compaction and cementation to form rock.

B The shell is gradually dissolved by groundwater that flows through the sediment and rock. This leaves a hole in the rock shaped like the shell. This hole is a mold.

C Water carries dissolved minerals that recrystallize in the mold. The mold is filled by these new minerals and a fossil called a cast is formed.

Fossils and Geologic Time

In the opening Explore activity, you used clues from newspaper stories to put past events in order. One method scientists use to learn about events for which there is no written history is to study fossils. They use fossils and other clues to organize the events in Earth's past into a time line.

Figure 16-3 shows you examples of fossils from different times.

In the next section, you'll see how fossils can help you separate the millions of years of geologic time into time periods by giving you clues to determine the relative ages of the rock layers in which they are found.

Figure 16-3

Scientists use fossils to help divide geologic time. These fossils represent three different geologic eras.

Dunkleosteus

A *Dunkleosteus* was an armored fish that lived during the Devonian Period of the Paleozoic Era (about 375 million years ago). It grew more than 10 meters long and had a massive, armored skull.

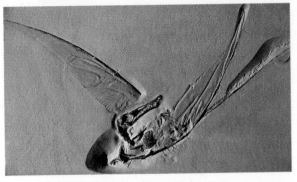
Pterosaur

B Pterosaurs lived in the Mesozoic Era. This one lived about 150-160 million years ago. How do you suppose this animal traveled?

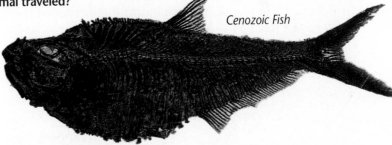
Cenozoic Fish

C This fish is the youngest fossil. It lived during the Oligocene Epoch of the Cenozoic Era (about 30 million years ago).

check your UNDERSTANDING

1. What conditions are necessary for fossils to form?
2. How can scavengers and bacteria make it difficult for fossils to form?
3. Compare and contrast fossil formation by replacement of minerals with mold-and-cast fossil formation.
4. How can water both help and hinder fossil formation?
5. **Apply** A shallow pond dries in the summer heat, and a fish dies for lack of water. Is a fossil of the fish likely to be formed? Why or why not?

16-2 Finding the Age of Rock Layers

Section Objectives

- Describe two methods used to date rock layers relative to one another.
- Explain how an unconformity may occur.

Key Terms

principle of superposition
unconformity

Using Fossils to Find the Age of Rock Layers

Think again about the Explore activity on page 503. Just as you used clues in newspaper stories to figure out the order of events, scientists use fossils to help them figure out which events in Earth's past occurred before others. In fact, fossils can show us which rock layers in Earth's crust formed before other rock layers. Do the activity below to find out how.

Find Out! ACTIVITY

How can fossils be used to date rock layers?

See how fossils can be used to help you find out when an event occurred.

What To Do

1. The next diagram below represents sedimentary rock layers containing fossils. Study the diagram carefully.

2. The organisms that produced the fossils lived during seven different divisions of time in Earth's history. These divisions are shown in the table.

3. *In your Journal*, construct a three-column table that shows rock layer numbers, fossil types found in each layer, and the range of possible ages for each rock layer. Use the illustration to help you complete columns 1 and 2.

4. Use the information in the table to identify the

Fossils in Rock Layers		
Ended Million Years Ago	Began Million Years Ago	Fossil Types of This Time
225	280	D
280	320	B D
320	345	B D
345	400	A B D
400	425	A B
425	500	A B C
500	544	A C

earliest time at which the fossils in each layer could have appeared together, then identify the most recent time the fossils could have appeared.

Conclude and Apply

1. You can date only two layers to one specific time. Which layers are they, and why is this so?

2. Why isn't it possible to determine during which specific period each of the other layers formed?

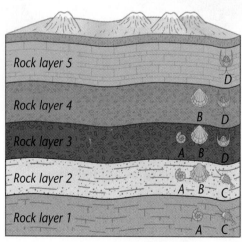

Rock layer 5
Rock layer 4 — B D
Rock layer 3 — A B D
Rock layer 2 — A B C
Rock layer 1 — A C

The Principle of Superposition

In the Find Out activity, you saw how fossils can be used to figure out the age of rocks. Now you'll learn about a geologic principle that helps you determine the age of rocks relative to one another.

You know that sediments are deposited in layers, which then form layers of sedimentary rock. New layers form on top of older layers.

The **principle of superposition** states that, in layers of rock, the oldest layers are at the bottom, and the youngest layers are at the top if the layers have not been disturbed.

What might disturb rock layers? In Chapter 15, you learned about plate tectonics and mountain building. Violent conditions in Earth can disturb rock layers, and produce rock layers that seem to oppose the principle of superposition.

Figure 16-4

Grand Canyon's Geologic Layers
The Grand Canyon in Arizona is a great gaping hole showing many of Earth's layers.

A The rocks near the Grand Canyon's cliff tops are only about 250 million years old. How do their fossils compare to today's animal and plant life?

B The limestones halfway up the Grand Canyon are about 400 million years old. They contain fossils of bony-plated fish.

C Bacteria were the only organisms living during the time 2-billion-year-old rock at the bottom of the Grand Canyon formed.

When Earth's plates collide and form mountains, the rock layers are no longer horizontal. Faults, earthquakes, and volcanic eruptions may also rearrange layers of rock. However, it's important to remember that younger sedimentary rocks always form on top of older sedimentary rocks.

■ Unconformities

Sometimes an entire layer or layers of sedimentary rock are completely missing from an area. Look at **Figure 16-5(a)**. How many layers of rock do you see? Now compare **16-5(a)** with **16-5(b)**. What's missing in **Figure 16-5(b)**? The record of plants and animals that existed during the time represented by the middle layer of rock of **Figure 16-5(a)** has not been preserved in the layers of **16-5(b)**. How might the missing layer of Earth's history change the interpretation of when the top and bottom rock layers were formed? How would it affect your knowledge of when certain organisms lived?

When layers of rock that formed in a place are missing, the gap in that area's geologic history is called an **unconformity**. Geologists can use unconformities to learn about Earth and its history. Unconformities have several causes. One cause is that a

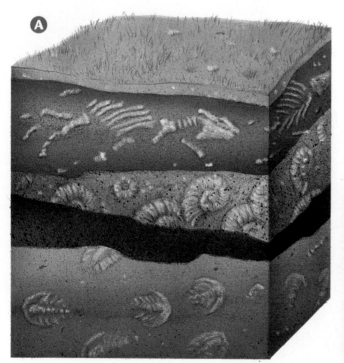

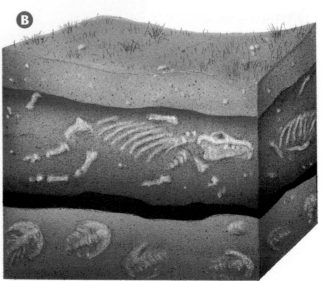

Figure 16-5

Plate tectonics, lack of deposition, erosion, and other processes cause unconformities like the one in the rock layers to the right in this figure. If you were a geologist, what would lead you to believe that an unconformity existed in these layers if you happened to come across them in an outcrop?

Figure 16-6

Formation of Unconformities

A Most sediments are deposited under water. They undergo compaction and cementation and eventually become sedimentary rocks.

B At any time during the deposition or formation of sedimentary rock Earth processes may force layers of sediment or rock above sea level. The layers are exposed to weathering and erosion, and part or all of a layer may be removed.

C New sediments accumulate on the eroded rock. The new sediments eventually become rock, and an unconformity is formed.

period of time went by when no new deposition occurred to form new layers of rock. In this case, a record of plants and animals of this time period would not have been preserved.

What else could cause an unconformity? Look at **Figure 16-6**. In (**a**), sediments have hardened to form layers beneath water. In (**b**), layers have been exposed to weathering and erosion. Layer 4 was completely eroded away and part of layer 3 was also removed. In (**c**), eroded layer 3 is again under water, and sediments have formed two new layers on top of it. But the upper surface of layer 3 now indicates an incomplete record of Earth's history in this area. This sur-

face is an unconformity.

An unconformity could be easily overlooked by an observer. At first glance, the rock layers may seem normal; they are all horizontal, and there is no sign of disturbance. But a closer look may show an uneven, eroded surface in one of the layers. An experienced geologist would realize that this layer contains an incomplete history of the time during which it was originally formed.

Now that you know about unconformities, the principle of superposition, and other ways of determining the relative ages of rocks, do the Investigate on the following pages to apply what you've learned.

Determining Relative Ages of Rock Layers

You've learned that clues in rock layers can be used to determine the relative ages of the rocks in those layers. In this activity, you will observe and infer the ages of rock layers.

Problem
How do you determine the relative ages of rock layers?

Materials
pen or pencil   paper

What To Do

1 Study the figure at the bottom of this page. The key will help you interpret the scientific illustration of the different types of rock layers.

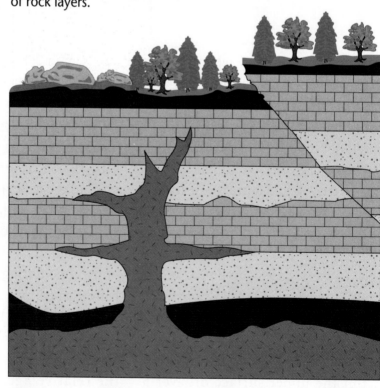

■ *Granite*   ▥ *Limestone*   ⸪ *Sandstone*   ■ *Shale*

A

B

2 *Infer* the relative ages of the rock layers, unconformities, and the fault in the figure.

3 *In your Journal,* write down the sequence of events that resulted in the cross-section you see here.

Volcanic eruptions can rearrange layers of rock, and the lava flow creates new landforms

Analyzing

1. Where can you observe an unconformity? What is your evidence?

2. Determine which layer is incomplete because of the unconformity. Explain your answer.

3. Is it possible that there were originally more layers of rock between the top and bottom of the figure than are now shown? Explain your answer.

Concluding and Applying

4. What can you *infer* caused the unconformity?

5. Assume that the layers have not been over-turned. Based on the figure alone, do you know whether the shale was deposited before or after the fault occurred? Explain.

6. **Going Further** *Predict* what may happen to the top limestone layer above the fault. Explain your prediction.

Rock Layers and Geologic Time

The Investigate gave you a chance to apply what you've learned about rock layers. It showed you how much you've already learned about rock layers and geologic time. The more people learn, however, the harder it becomes to keep information organized. Eventually, there are so many things we know and want to remember that we have to put all the pieces of information in some sort of order.

As scientists learned more and more about rock layers and geologic time, they too needed some way to organize the information they had gathered. In the next section, you'll learn about a system geologists use to organize the information they've learned about rock layers and geologic time. You'll also look at some of the discoveries they've made concerning these different spans of time.

Figure 16-7

Rocks in Bryce Canyon National Park show distinct layers that can be used to interpret the geologic history of the area.

check your UNDERSTANDING

1. Describe how fossils can be used to determine the ages of rock layers.
2. Describe how the principle of superposition is used to determine the relative ages of rock layers.
3. Give two examples of situations that can cause an unconformity.
4. **Apply** A geologist finds a series of rocks.

The sandstone contains a fossil that is 400 million years old. The shale contains some fossils that are between 540 and 500 million years old. The limestone contains fossils that are between 500 and 400 million years old. Which rock bed is oldest? Which rock bed is most likely below the others? Explain. Draw an illustration to help you.

16-3 Early Earth History

Time Brings Change

At one time, you may have thought that mountains existed forever. But based on what you learned in Chapter 15 and in Section 16-2 of this chapter, you now know that the geological features of Earth change constantly.

Not only the geologic features, but Earth's climates also change continually. At various times in the past, Earth has been both warmer and colder than it is now.

How did changes in Earth's geology and climate affect the plants and animals on Earth? What happened to the dinosaurs pictured in **Figure 16-8**.

We have a geologic record of Earth's past preserved in Earth's rocks. Geologists organized this record by developing a geologic time scale that is similar to a calendar. The following Explore activity will show you how you could organize events in your life by constructing a personal time scale.

Figure 16-8

Time brings change in the living things on Earth. For instance, you can see the differences in living things during two eras of Earth's history. This change in life forms and in the fossils found in rocks is one of the important pieces of evidence scientists use to help divide geologic time.

Boundary between two time spans

Life in the Age of Dinosaurs

Life in the Age of Mammals

Can you make a time scale of your life?

If you had to construct a time scale, how would you start? This activity will help you out.

What To Do

1. On 3 x 5 cards, write important events that have happened in your lifetime, one event per card.

2. Arrange the cards in the order in which the events happened. Then cut two blank cards in half to make the following labels: Preschool Years; Early Elementary Years; Late Elementary Years; Middle School Years.

3. Place each label before the group of events that occurred during its time description.

4. *In your Journal,* draw a time line that puts all of these events in order.

5. (Answer these questions *in your Journal.*) Did you know exact dates for some of the events? Was knowing exact dates helpful? What did they add to the time line?

Age of Rocks

How do geologists determine the age of rocks? You know that rock layers can be assigned ages relative to each other. But geologists do more than assign relative ages to rocks. They assign absolute ages, too. Where do they get them?

Radiometric Dating

Most materials contain some radioactive atoms— that is, atoms that decay, or give off

Fossils, like these trilobites, are useful in determining the relative age of rocks.

particles from their nuclei. Geologists use radioactive decay of atoms as a kind of atomic clock. To find the age of rocks, they must find minerals that undergo radioactive decay within rocks.

So what do geologists do when they want to find a numerical age for something like the boundary between two time periods? How do geologists calculate how long ago something occurred?

Geologists look for igneous rocks that are closely associated with the geologic event that they want to date. For instance, if they wanted to find the age of a bed of sedimentary rock, they might look for layers of

The Geologic Time Scale

In the Explore activity, you made a time scale based on the events in your life. Geologists organize events in Earth's past using another kind of time scale, a geologic time scale.

The geologic time scale is organized into lengths of time based on events such as extinctions and mountain-building events that happened during those times.

The geologic time scale is organized into four divisions. Three of the four major divisions in the geologic time scale are called **eras**.

In your life time scale, you divided your early life history into two "eras": Preschool Years and Early Elementary Years. The geologic time scale similarly divides early Earth history into two times: Precambrian Time and the Paleozoic Era. Precambrian Time is so huge an amount of time that it must be divided into eras itself.

These geologic labels help us organize information so we can better understand and discuss it. When we put all the information together, we end up with a sequence of events in Earth's history. Investigate the events scientists use to construct the geologic time scale.

volcanic ash or other igneous rocks that cover the sedimentary rocks. This way they would know that they were close to the right age. The actual matching up of rocks is done much more precisely. However, the result is that the igneous rocks are dated and geologists know the age of the event they are studying.

Rocks Help Tell Time

Geologists have found igneous rocks associated with a great many important events in geologic history. They have been able to calculate a fairly accurate date for the beginning of each geologic period, and often for individual beds of sedimentary rock. These dates help

place the geologic time scale, which is based on relative ages, into an absolute time scale, which is based on actual ages.

As Earth has changed over the eons, each change has left a record in the rocks. By using various atomic clocks in a process called radiometric dating, geologists have learned the absolute ages of different pieces of the planet. Putting all the information together lets them reconstruct an accurate record of the history of Earth.

Some minerals, such as micas, have radioactive atoms in their structure. These minerals can be used for absolute dating.

What Do You Think?

Suppose you are a geologist who has calculated the absolute age of a mineral sample that came from a sedimentary rock. Have you determined the age of the rock? Why or why not?

Geologic Time Scale

You can arrange your past into short periods of time by dating major events in your life, such as your first day of school. Earth's history is also arranged or subdivided in this way. Scientists use major events in Earth's past, such as the appearance and disappearance of organisms or important geologic events, to subdivide Earth's history into the geologic time scale.

Preparation

Problem
What kind of model can be used to show the subdivisions of Earth's geologic past?

Hypothesis
As a group, discuss what you know about Earth's geologic history and important events in its past. Then form a hypothesis about how you would model the subdivisions of geologic time.

Objectives
- Observe and infer how the ages of rocks and fossils and geologic events are used to subdivide Earth's history on the geologic time scale.
- Design a model for the subdivisions of geologic time.

Materials
adding machine tape
meterstick or metric ruler
set of colored pencils
pencil
scissors

Safety

Take care not to cut yourself while using the scissors.

Earth History Events	Approximate years before present
Oldest known rocks	3900 million
Oldest microfossils	3600 million
Early sponges	600 million
Beginning of the Cambrian period (Paleozoic Era) —animals evolve hard parts	545 million
First vertebrates	510 million
Beginning of the Ordovician	505 million
Beginning of the Silurian Period	438 million
First land plants	435 million
Beginning of Devonian Period	408 million
First amphibians	367 million
Beginning of the Mississippian Period	360 million
Appalachian Mountains rise	330 million
Beginning of Pennsylvanian Period	320 million
First reptiles	315 million
Beginning of Permian Period	286 million
Extinction of trilobites —largest mass Extinction in Earth's history	246 million
Beginning of Triassic Period (Mesozoic Era)	245 million
First dinosaurs and mammals	225 million
Beginning of Jurassic Period	208 million
First birds	150 million
Beginning of Cretaceous Period	144 million
Rocky Mountains begin to rise	80 million
Extinction of the dinosaurs	66 million
Beginning of Paleocene Epoch (Cenozoic Era)	66 million
First horses	50 million
First elephants	40 million
Early human ancestors	5 million
Beginning of the most recent ice age	1 million
First modern humans	500 000
Continental ice retreats from North America	10 000
Eratosthenes calculates Earth's circumference	2100
Pompeii destroyed	1900
Columbus lands in America	500
U.S. Civil War	135
Astronauts land on the moon	25
Today	0

DESIGN YOUR OWN
INVESTIGATION

Plan the Experiment

1 As a group, agree upon and write out your hypothesis statement.

2 Study **Figure 16-9** on pages 520-521 to review the table of Earth's major events. Then determine how you will construct your model of geologic time using the table and the materials listed on the opposite page.

3 Determine a scale to use for your model of Earth's history.

Check the Plan

1 Which of Earth's major events will you include in your model of geologic time? Will you include the dates that they occurred on as well?

2 Design a small version of the model you plan to construct. Is your scale reasonable?

3 How will you summarize your

data? If you need a data table, design one *in your Science Journal.*

4 Make sure your teacher approves your experiment before you proceed.

5 Carry out your experiment. Record your observations.

Crinoids, which are related to starfish, were common during the Paleozoic Era.

Analyze and Conclude

1. **Compare and Contrast** Compare events from your past or the existence of humans on Earth with the duration of geologic time.

2. **Sequence** Using the geologic time scale on pages 520-521, sequence the ages of the major divisions of

geologic time on your model.

3. **Estimate** Based on the geologic time scale, what percent of geologic time occurred during Precambrian time?

Going Further

Form a hypothesis about why more is known about geologic events during the era for which you were able to obtain the most information.

Precambrian Time

You've had a chance to get a feel for the vast length of time in Earth's history. Let's begin to explore it at the beginning. The geologic time scale begins with Earth's beginning—about 4.6 billion years ago. The first major division of geologic time was more than 4 billion years long. In fact, this first division, **Precambrian time,** makes up about 88 percent of Earth's history to date.

However, information about life and events in the Precambrian can be difficult to get. In the past, Precambrian rocks may have been buried deep within Earth where they were

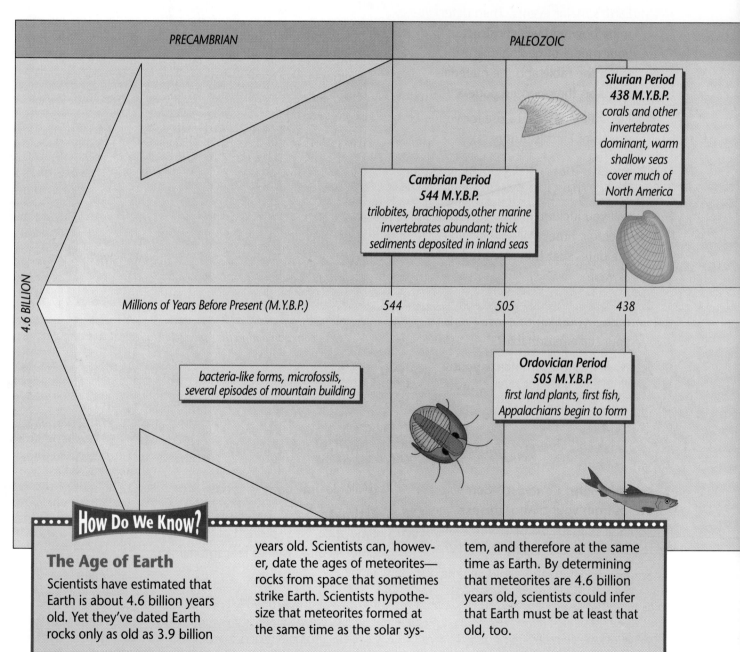

PRECAMBRIAN

PALEOZOIC

Silurian Period
438 M.Y.B.P.
corals and other invertebrates dominant, warm shallow seas cover much of North America

Cambrian Period
544 M.Y.B.P.
trilobites, brachiopods, other marine invertebrates abundant; thick sediments deposited in inland seas

4.6 BILLION

Millions of Years Before Present (M.Y.B.P.)   544   505   438

bacteria-like forms, microfossils, several episodes of mountain building

Ordovician Period
505 M.Y.B.P.
first land plants, first fish, Appalachians begin to form

How Do We Know?

The Age of Earth

Scientists have estimated that Earth is about 4.6 billion years old. Yet they've dated Earth rocks only as old as 3.9 billion years old. Scientists can, however, date the ages of meteorites—rocks from space that sometimes strike Earth. Scientists hypothesize that meteorites formed at the same time as the solar system, and therefore at the same time as Earth. By determining that meteorites are 4.6 billion years old, scientists could infer that Earth must be at least that old, too.

changed by heat and pressure so that information is lost, even if the rocks are eventually exposed by erosion. Precambrian rocks that were not buried have been exposed to water, wind, and ice longer than younger rocks, and so have been eroded significantly.

The Precambrian rocks we do find have fossils that show that through much of Precambrian Time the dominant form of life on Earth was cyanobacteria. These bacteria altered Earth's ancient atmosphere, which had little oxygen, by adding large amounts of oxygen through photosynthesis. Oxygen made it possible for the soft-bodied animals that evolved near the end of the Precambrian Time to live on Earth.

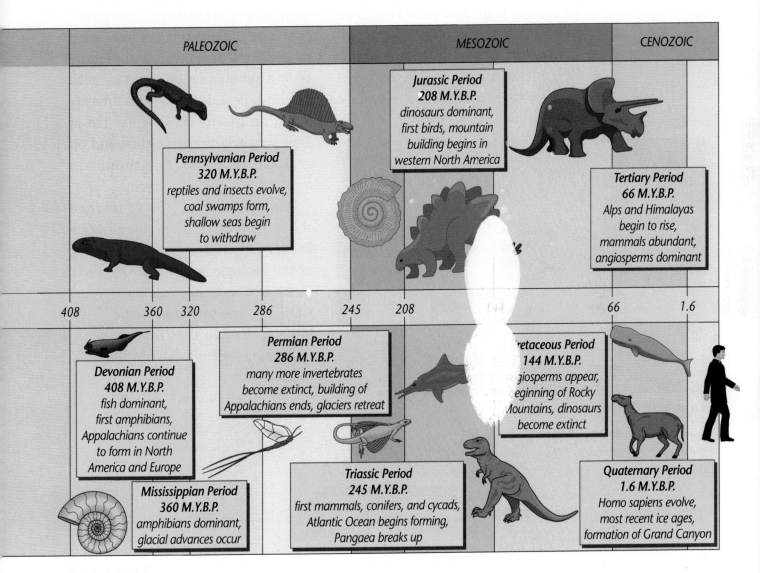

Figure 16-9

This geologic time scale has been adjusted to show all of Earth's history in a small space. Note how each of the eras is divided into periods. The Paleozoic Era has 7 periods:—what are they? The Mesozoic Era has 3 periods, and the Cenozoic Era has 2 periods. Using eras, periods, and smaller time divisions geologists are able to organize the geologic time scale.

The Paleozoic Era

When organisms have hard parts, fossil formation is easier. The appearance of fossils formed by organisms with hard parts marks the beginning of the second major geologic time scale division, the **Paleozoic Era.** The Paleozoic Era began about 544 million years ago. Examine **Figure 16-9,** or look at your time line. How long did the Paleozoic Era last?

Warm shallow seas covered much of Earth's surface during the early part of the Paleozoic Era. Therefore, most

life-forms were marine. Examples of Paleozoic life-forms include trilobites (distant relatives of the horseshoe crab), brachiopods (animals similar in shape to clams), and crinoids (relatives of starfish). The first fish evolved during the Paleozoic Era.

To better classify events and organisms of the Paleozoic Era, geologists have divided this era into seven subdivisions, as you can see in **Figure 16-9.** A subdivision of an era is called a **period.** Periods in geologic time are based on life-forms that existed at approximately the same time and on geologic events, such as mountain building and plate movements.

In this section, you've learned about the organisms that lived during Earth's early history and about some of the geologic events that occurred. In the next section, you'll journey forward in time to the present. You'll look at the two eras that make up middle and recent Earth history.

Figure 16-10

A variety of marine organisms existed during the Paleozoic Era.

check your UNDERSTANDING

1. What life-forms existed during the Paleozoic Era that did not exist during Precambrian Time?

2. What changes in Earth's geology during early Earth history can still be recognized now?

3. **Apply** When were trilobites abundant? What does the presence of trilobite fossils in a rock layer tell you about the age of the rock layer? What do they tell you about the geologic history of the area?

16-4 Middle and Recent Earth History

What Happened to Ancient Life-forms?

Look closely at the Permian Period in **Figure 16-9** on pages 520-521. You'll see that mass extinctions occurred near the end of the Paleozoic Era. Trilobites and other marine invertebrates died out.

What happened to these life-forms? Scientists hypothesize that changes in the environment caused their extinction. You may be aware that Earth was both warmer and colder at certain times in its history than it is today. Climate changes are one explanation for past mass extinctions.

But if you look again at **Figure 16-9**, you'll find that new life-forms appeared during the next era of geologic time. In fact, one life-form became so abundant that it dominated much of this era. It is the life-form you met on your imaginary time travel at the beginning of this chapter. Do the Explore activity that follows to begin your study of the Mesozoic Era.

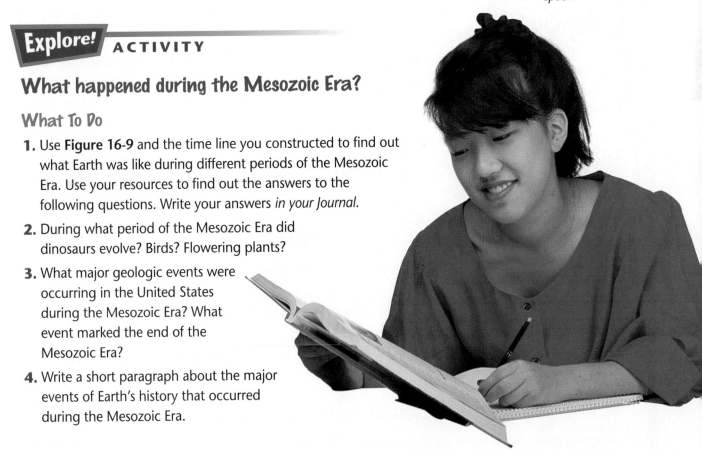

Explore! ACTIVITY

What happened during the Mesozoic Era?

What To Do

1. Use **Figure 16-9** and the time line you constructed to find out what Earth was like during different periods of the Mesozoic Era. Use your resources to find out the answers to the following questions. Write your answers *in your Journal.*

2. During what period of the Mesozoic Era did dinosaurs evolve? Birds? Flowering plants?

3. What major geologic events were occurring in the United States during the Mesozoic Era? What event marked the end of the Mesozoic Era?

4. Write a short paragraph about the major events of Earth's history that occurred during the Mesozoic Era.

Section Objectives
- Give examples of the different life-forms of the Mesozoic and Cenozoic Eras.
- Describe the major geologic changes of the Mesozoic and Cenozoic Eras.
- Explain the subdivisions of the Mesozoic and the Cenozoic Eras.

Key Terms
Mesozoic Era
Cenozoic Era
epoch

The Mesozoic Era

Figure 16-11

A timeline of dinosaurs that lived during the Mesozoic Era. You can see that not all dinosaurs lived at the same time. How long was the Reign of Dinosaurs?

The **Mesozoic Era** began after the Paleozoic Era ended. This time is often called "the age of dinosaurs" because dinosaurs were so abundant. However, dinosaurs were not the only organisms that appeared during the Mesozoic Era. Fossil evidence suggests that the first mammals appeared as well, along with the first birds and the first flowering plants.

Organisms weren't the only things changing during the Mesozoic Era. According to **Figure 16-12**, what kind of events that would result in changes to Earth's landforms occurred during this time?

As you learned in Chapter 15, Earth's plates are continually moving. These plates brought all of Earth's landmasses together into one large

Triassic Period

Jurassic Period

Life Science CONNECTION

A Lizard with the Bends!

Divers take care to avoid the bends, a potentially fatal condition that can develop if they rise too rapidly from deep water to the surface. As divers ascend from a dive, the water pressure decreases. If the divers ascend too quickly, bubbles can form in their tissues and blood. These bubbles can cause breathing difficulties or paralysis, or they can prevent blood from flowing to various body parts.

Old Wounds

Two University of Kansas scientists, Larry D. Martin and Bruce M. Rothschild, have discovered that these problems also existed for mosasaurs, which were

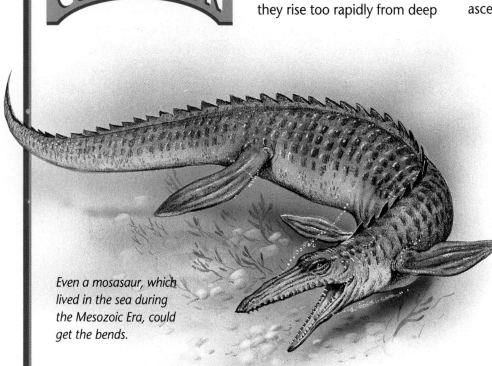

Even a mosasaur, which lived in the sea during the Mesozoic Era, could get the bends.

continent toward the end of the Paleozoic Era. This ancient continent is called Pangaea. **Figure 16-12** describes what happened to Pangaea during the Mesozoic Era.

Figure 16-12

Earth's surface has also changed through time. At the beginning of the Mesozoic Era the ancient supercontinent of Pangaea separated into two smaller land masses, which in turn began to break up and move apart to form the present day arrangement of the continents.

Cretaceous Period

sea reptiles that lived millions of years ago. Martin and Rothschild noticed that seven mosasaur vertebrae in a museum collection were fused together. Taking a closer look, they found a shark's tooth embedded in the bone, leading them to believe that infection caused by the shark bite had caused the vertebrae to fuse. Not only did this tell something about the dietary habits of sharks at the time, but it also showed that the mosasaur survived the attack.

Martin and Rothschild were fascinated by what they found and they wanted to compare the fused vertebrae with normal vertebrae from the mosasaur. When they looked at normal vertebrae, they discovered areas of dead bone, resulting, they believe, from a lack of blood flow to the affected bone. Based on their years of study, they speculated that the mosasaur they examined had developed the bends by a rapid ascent to the water's surface. The bends, in turn, caused blood to stop flowing to some part of the spinal column, resulting in areas of bone death.

Ancient Ailments

The studies of Martin and Rothschild, which are described in a scientific journal, are part of the growing field of paleopathology, the study of illnesses and injuries in ancient animals. Other paleopathologists have used modern medical techniques such as X rays and dental examination to diagnose illnesses and identify injuries of creatures that lived long ago.

As alien as mosasaurs and other ancient animals may seem to us, we know they suffered illnesses similar to those of modern animals. They probably responded to changes in their surroundings much as we would today. Sometimes the similarities between ancient and modern animals are more amazing than the differences.

You Try It!

Describe some ways that the jobs of physicians, paleopathologists, and detectives might be similar.

Although we know little about it, Precambrian Time spans some four billion years—seven times longer than the Paleozoic, Mesozoic, and Cenozoic Eras put together.

The Cenozoic Era

The mass extinctions and other physical and environmental changes at the end of the Mesozoic Era set the stage for the beginning of the **Cenozoic Era.** Look at **Figure 16-9** again. Into how many periods is the Cenozoic Era divided?

The periods of the Cenozoic Era are also subdivided. Why do you think this is so?

The geologic record is more complete in the Cenozoic Era than in previous eras because the rocks are younger. They've been exposed to less erosion and fewer destructive geologic processes. As a result, there's more information for geologists to organize. They need to use smaller periods of time. Thus, the periods of the Cenozoic Era are further subdivided into **epochs.**

Figure 16-13

Today's continents had not yet achieved their present positions at the beginning of the Cenozoic Era. In addition, while organisms looked more similar to plants and animals present on Earth today, there were still a great many differences. These animals were alive relatively late in the Cenozoic Era. To what living animals do they appear to be related?

Let's take a closer look at some of the geologic changes that occurred during the Cenozoic Era. During this time, the African Plate collided with the Eurasian Plate, forming the Alps. When the Indian Plate began to collide with the Eurasian Plate, the Himalaya Mountains started to form. Both mountain ranges are continuing to rise even now.

In the cooler climate of the Cenozoic Era, the number of flowering plants increased. Also, the number of insects, plant-eating mammals, and meat-eating mammals increased. Most scientists think the human species, *Homo sapiens*, first appeared about 500 000 years ago but didn't become a dominant animal until about 10 000 years ago.

A period of 10 000 years may seem like a long time, but it's short compared to Earth's history, as you've seen. You've just started to explore some of Earth's changes. In the next chapter, you'll explore in more detail how life-forms have changed through Earth's history.

check your UNDERSTANDING

1. Which life-forms existed in the Mesozoic Era that did not exist in the Paleozoic Era? Which life-forms existed in the Cenozoic Era that did not exist in the Mesozoic Era?

2. What changes did the movement of plates create in Earth's geology in the Mesozoic Era? What changes did this movement create in Earth's geology in the Cenozoic Era?

3. Why is the Cenozoic Era divided into epochs as well as periods?

4. **Apply** Mammals began to become abundant on Earth shortly before the dinosaurs became extinct. Suggest a way in which mammals may have contributed to the extinction of the dinosaurs.

Science and Society

The Mysterious End of the Dinosaur Age

The disappearance of the dinosaurs is a mystery as fascinating as the best of detective stories! Dinosaurs thrived on Earth for about 160 million years.

About 66 million years ago, the dinosaurs and many other animals disappeared. No one is certain why. Scientists have examined the evidence (fossils and rock layers) to find clues that led to some amazing hypotheses.

Evidence for an Impact

Among the several hypotheses is the idea that an enormous rock-like object called a meteorite collided with Earth.

Some of the effects of such a collision, if it were to occur today, are shown in the figure on page 529. Dust from the collision may have filled the upper atmosphere and blocked the sunlight from the ground below. Without sunlight, plants couldn't survive. Without plants, plant-eating dinosaurs would have starved. This, in turn, would have brought about the end of meat-eating dinosaurs that fed on plant-eating dinosaurs.

In support of the meteorite impact hypothesis, scientists have found an unusual clay layer that was deposited about the same time the dinosaurs became extinct. In the clay layer, scientists have found the element iridium, which usually is not common near Earth's surface but is found in greater amounts in meteorites.

Even though evidence exists for the impact hypothesis, some scientists interpret it differently. For example, some suggest that

the clay layer containing iridium can be explained by large numbers of volcanic eruptions. The eruptions brought iridium from deep within Earth to its surface. Volcanic ash could have blocked sunlight from Earth and led to the death of plant and animal species.

Extinction by Slow Changes

Another hypothesis suggests that there was nothing unusual about the extinction of dinosaurs. They disappeared gradually because of slow changes in their environment. Experts support this hypothesis by pointing out that many animals besides the dinosaurs have become extinct because of gradual changes on Earth. No single disaster was necessary to kill the dinosaurs, they say.

Changes in the Climate

Scientists may disagree about what caused the disappearance of dinosaurs. But they do agree that there were large changes in climate 66 million years ago that may have helped end the age of dinosaurs.

While some researchers try to determine what happened to the dinosaurs, others study the changes occurring right now on our planet. Could present-day changes eventually bring an end to the plant and animal species that currently inhabit Earth?

Scientists want to know how much and how quickly Earth's climate could be changed by human activities and how such changes could affect life on Earth. By examining climatic changes over millions of years, they can estimate how Earth's future climate may be affected by human activity.

*inter*NET CONNECTION

Visit the University of California Museum of Paleontology on the World Wide Web to learn about an organism that lived during the Cretaceous Period. What did it eat, for example? Did it live in water? Was the climate tropical or cold? Use what you learn to sketch the creature or sculpt it in clay.

This shows some of the immediate effects of a meteorite impact which can include surface destruction, earthquakes, tsunamis, and wildfires.

Technology Connection

Building a Dinosaur

Imagine yourself surrounded by hundreds of ancient bones. They were embedded in rock, retrieved by paleontologists, and carefully delivered to you for assembly. It's your responsibility to reconstruct the skeleton of a creature that lived millions of years ago.

The Bony Jigsaw Puzzle

It's like a giant, and very valuable, jigsaw puzzle—with an unknown number of pieces missing. The picture below gives you an idea of how big the pieces are. It's your job to put them together for museum visitors. But how?

You'd need to study diagrams drawn by other people who have already reconstructed similar skeletons. Then, by examining the skeletal parts, you could sort out the pieces and their relation to one another.

How to Fill in the Blanks

You'd also have to build a support to hold the bones together. And you'd have to replace missing pieces, combining your knowledge of prehistoric life with your sculpting ability. Sculpting tools used for this may include potter's clay, fiberglass, dental plaster, and sculpting knives.

For missing parts, you'd have to cast molds. If a rib is missing, you might make a mold of the matching rib. The plaster rib could then be placed opposite the prehistoric animal's original rib.

A missing part or parts may need to be sculpted. To do this accurately, you'd have to draw on all available knowledge about the creature or similar creatures.

You would have to be willing to put up with very slow progress because the reconstruction process can take years of work. So why do people spend their lives rebuilding such creatures? Many became fascinated with prehistoric animals as children and wanted to contribute to scientific knowledge about these animals as adults.

YOU TRY IT!

Find pictures of a dinosaur and its skeleton. Using the skeleton as a guide, write a description you could give an artist who could paint a detailed picture of the dinosaur.

Science Journal

Review the statements below about the big ideas presented in this chapter, and answer the questions. Then, reread your answers to the Did You Ever Wonder questions at the beginning of the chapter. *In your Science Journal*, write a paragraph about how your understanding of the big ideas in the chapter has changed.

1 Fossils are the remains or traces of organisms that were once alive. *What conditions favor the formation of fossils?*

2 Deposited sediments can be cemented or compacted into a layer of rock. Rock layers may be dated relative to each other, but erosion and other forces can create unconformities. *If you are looking at layers of rock in an area and find an unconformity, what does that tell you about the record of Earth history in that area?*

3 Earth's history can be divided into units of time called eras. *What kinds of events help us divide time into eras?*

Precambrian Time	Paleozoic Era								Mesozoic Era			Cenozoic Era						
Almost 4 billion years	Cambrian Period (40 million years)	Ordovician Period (70 million years)	Silurian Period (30 million years)	Devonian Period (50 million years)	Mississippian Period (40 million years)	Pennsylvanian Period (35 million years)	Permian Period (40 million years)		Triassic Period (35 million years)	Jurassic Period (65 million years)	Cretaceous Period (80 million years)	Paleocene Tertiary Period	Eocene Tertiary Period	Oligocene Tertiary Period	Miocene Tertiary Period	Pliocene Tertiary Period	Pleistocene Quaternary Period	Recent Quaternary Period

Using Key Science Terms

Cenozoic Era   Mesozoic Era

epoch   Paleozoic Era

era   period

fossil   Precambrian Time

principle of   unconformity
    superposition

For each set of terms below explain the relationship that exists.

1. fossil, unconformity, principle of superposition
2. epoch, era, period
3. Mesozoic Era, Paleozoic Era, Cenozoic Era, Precambrian Time

Understanding Ideas

Answer the following questions in your Journal using complete sentences.

1. What is an unconformity?
2. Explain the principle of superposition.
3. Why is information about Precambrian Time sparse?
4. Which would be more likely to be found as a fossil—a jellyfish or a clam?
5. Why do scientists use the geologic time scale?

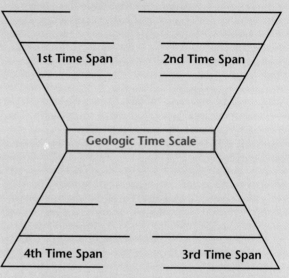

Developing Skills

Use your understanding of the concepts developed in each section to answer each of the following questions.

1. **Concept Mapping** Complete the concept map of Geologic Time.

1st Time Span	2nd Time Span

Geologic Time Scale

4th Time Span	3rd Time Span

2. **Forming a Hypothesis** Using the information from the Investigation activity on page 518, form a hypothesis as to why more is known about recent history than about the Precambrian Time. How could you test your hypothesis?

3. **Interpreting Scientific Illustrations** Using **Figure 16-9** as you did in the Explore activity on page 523, determine during what era and period the North American ice ages occurred.

Critical Thinking

In your Journal, *answer each of the following questions.*

1. What is the most significant difference between Precambrian and Paleozoic life-forms?
2. Compare and contrast a fossil cast and a fossil mold.
3. How does an unconformity affect our fossil record of life on Earth?
4. The pie graph represents geologic time. Determine which major division of geologic time is represented by each portion of the graph.

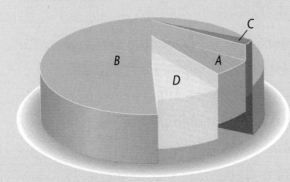

Problem Solving

Read the following problem and discuss your answers in a brief paragraph.

Neila enjoyed finding and collecting fossils. She had investigated many of the rock outcrops in her city and had begun an excellent collection of local fossil types. Her favorite fossil was a particular species of brachiopod known as *Mucrospirifer*. She identified her fossil using pictures and descriptions from a book on Paleozoic fossils.

While on a trip with her family to visit relatives in another state, Neila found what seemed like the same species of *Mucrospirifer* fossil in a rock formation on her aunt's farm.

1. What could Neila say about the rocks in which she found both fossils?
2. Could she say exactly how old the rocks were? Why or why not?

CONNECTING IDEAS

Discuss each of the following in a brief paragraph.

1. **Theme - Systems and Interactions** What relation does the ocean have to the development of life on Earth?
2. **Theme - Scale and Structure** Rock layers disturbed by a fault must be older than the fault itself. Explain.
3. **Theme - Stability and Change** How might a mass extinction be reflected in the fossil record?
4. **Life Science Connection** How can scientists determine why an animal died?
5. **Science and Society** Compare and contrast the "rock from space" hypothesis and the "volcanic eruption" hypothesis, that explain the extinction of dinosaurs.

CHAPTER 17

EVOLUTION OF LIFE

Did you ever wonder...

✓ **How a new species of animal evolves from a single ancestor?**

✓ **What you can learn from fossils about how and where an organism lived?**

✓ **How similar you might be to other animals or organisms?**

Science Journal

Before you begin to study how living things evolve, think about these questions and answer them *in your Science Journal*. When you finish the chapter, compare your journal write-up with what you have learned.

A sidewinder loops sideways over the desert sand. A camel munches noisily on a tall desert plant. A lizard perched atop a rock keeps watch like an armored guard. The sidewinder, lizard, camel, and even the desert plant are adapted to the hot, dry, desert climate. Many kinds of snakes exist besides the sidewinder—garter snakes, rattlesnakes, king snakes, and water snakes. These snakes display a variety of shapes, sizes, and colors, and they don't all live in the desert. What accounts for these differences in snakes? What accounts for the huge variety of plants and animals? In this chapter, you will examine a process that offers an explanation—evolution.

In the activity on the next page, explore the variation in the lengths of pine needles.

Can you find any differences?

A quick walk around your school or neighborhood can introduce you to the variety that exists in living things. In this activity, you will explore how much variety you find in pine needles.

What To Do

1. Collect about 20 pine needles from a single tree.

2. Measure the lengths of the pine needles to the nearest millimeter. Record your findings.

3. What was the length of the longest needle? What was the length of the shortest needle?

4. Write a summary of what you discovered about the lengths of pine needles *in your Journal*.

525

17-1 Raw Materials of Evolution

Section Objectives
- Explain how variation occurs in populations.
- Give examples of how adaptations help organisms survive.

Key Terms
variation

Variations and Adaptations

Have you ever gone into a pet store and watched the playful puppies? Even with puppies, you could find dogs of different sizes, colors, and shapes. Some had long, silky coats, and others had short, curly coats. Snakes and lizards, cacti and pine trees, poodles and cocker spaniels all have some differences in color, size, or shape that set them apart from other members of their own species.

Figure 17-1

The different colors of fur on these puppies are an example of variation within a species.

Variations

You discovered in the Explore activity that not all pine needles are the same size. The dogs in **Figure 17-1** are all the same breed but they have different colored coats. The sizes of the pine needles and the colors of the dogs' coats are examples of variation. A **variation** is an appearance of an inherited trait or a behavior that makes one organism different from others of the same species. Remember from Chapter 14 how traits are passed from generation to generation. If you were able to see the parents of the puppies shown in the photograph, you would find that they were not the same color as all of their offspring. Traits such as coat color show variation even when the parents are the same.

The different colored coats of the dogs really don't make any difference in whether these animals will survive, but coat color can make a difference to other animals in nature. How do some variations help organisms survive in their environments? Try the following activity to find out.

Which beans are easier to find?

Imagine you are a predator searching for food. What would make it easier for you to find your prey?

What To Do

1. Work with a partner. Place one large sheet of dark red construction paper and one large sheet of white construction paper next to each other on your desk.

2. Turn around. Then, have your partner scatter 25 white beans on the white paper.

3. Turn back and see how many beans you can pick up one at a time in 10 seconds. Record your results.

4. Then, turn your back again, and have your partner scatter the 25 white beans on the dark red paper.

5. Turn around and see how many beans you can pick up in 10 seconds. Record your results.

6. Use the dark red beans instead of the white beans and repeat this activity.

Conclude and Apply

1. When was it easier to find the white beans?

2. When was it easier to find the red beans?

3. *In your Journal,* write an explanation of what variation you were working with.

■ Adaptations

The color of the dogs and the color of the beans are both variations. Sometimes a variation will be advantageous, or helpful, to an organism. That organism has a better chance of surviving because of the variation. Sometimes, however, a variation can make it more difficult for an organism to survive. Didn't you find it easier to pick out the white beans when they were on the red construction paper than when they were on the white paper? This activity models what might happen in nature when an animal—say, a white squirrel—doesn't blend in with its surroundings. The squirrel would be a lot easier to see and capture, wouldn't it? The squirrel has a variation that makes it less able to survive. An organism that has a variation that makes it better able to survive is said to have an adaptation. What is an example of an adaptation?

DID YOU KNOW?

The *Kallima* butterfly is a striking example of protective coloring. The butterfly looks a lot like a leaf, with leaf veins, imitation holes (where insects might have dined), and leaf coloring.

A Matter of Survival

Read the How Do We Know on page 541. Remember that speckled moths blended with the lichens on tree trunks and black moths blended with the soot-blackened trees. In this Investigation, you will model a bird searching for moths against various backgrounds.

Preparation

Problem
How can the color and pattern of an organism affect its survival?

Form a Hypothesis
As a group, decide on a hypothesis that predicts how the color and pattern of a moth affects its survival from predators.

Objectives
- Model how successful a bird would be in finding and catching moths against different backgrounds.
- Compare how color factors affect the survival rate of moths.
- Infer which moths would survive most easily in certain environments.

Materials
20 moths cut from uniform small print newspaper
20 moths cut from black construc tion paper
scissors
tape
thin cardboard
forceps
stop watch
newspaper
black construction paper

Safety Precautions

Use care with scissors.

When it is at rest, the Indian Leaf butterfly looks very much like a decaying leaf, making it virtually invisible to predators.

Plan the Experiment

1 First cut out moths for your experiment by using the moth on page 546 to make a template from the thin cardboard.

2 Examine the materials. Use them to design an experiment to test your hypothesis.

3 How many possible combinations of moths and backgrounds will you test? How many trials will you run for each test?

4 Who will act as a bird? Will the same person do all the trials?

5 *In your Science Journal* or on a computer, construct a data table that can include all the test combinations and trials for each test.

Check the Plan

1 Do you know what your variable is in each test?

2 How are you measuring the differences in the tests? What data will you record?

Analyze and Conclude

1. **Analyze** Was your hypothesis supported? Explain using the data recorded in the table.

2. If the moths were red, blue, or green, how would this affect the results of this experiment?

3. **Infer** How did this investigation model a form of natural selection?

4. **Apply** Using the information from this investigation, explain how coloration helps turtles and toads survive. What about zebras? How do they survive?

Going Further

Predict what would happen if there were three different colors of moths with the third an intermediate between speckled and black. How would you test your prediction?

17-3 Evidence of Evolution

Section Objectives

- Determine how fossils are evidence of evolution.
- Compare the similarity in structure and chemical make-up of cells.
- Determine how homologous structures are evidence of evolution.

Key Terms

homologous structure
primate

Fossils

Suppose you suspected that two organisms were related but didn't know for sure if they were or how they were. Scientists can find evidence of evolution in many different places. They are like detectives in search of clues to solve a mystery. Some evidence of evolution comes from fossils.

You learned in Chapter 16 that fossils are remains of life from earlier times. While many fossils are imprints, some are petrified bone or wood, plants or animals frozen in ice, or organisms trapped in plant resin.

■ Patterns in the Fossil Record

Recall from Chapter 16 that fossils are usually found within rock layers. If you could cut away a section of Earth, you would see the rock layers, almost like the layers of a cake, as in **Figure 17-9**. If the layers have not been disturbed, the older layers are on the bottom. The younger layers are on top. Fossils found in the older layers are generally earlier forms of life.

Sometimes fossils provide evidence about the climate or landscape of an area during earlier periods. Fossils of marine organisms have been found hundreds of kilometers from the nearest ocean. How did marine animals move inland? The plates that make up Earth's crust are continuously moving. This movement causes mountains to rise up where valleys or even oceans may have existed.

Figure 17-9

Many fossils are found in rock layers. Over time, new layers of rock form on top of old layers. Thus, earlier life-forms like trilobites are found in the bottom layers, while later life-forms such as dinosaurs are found in layers closer to the top. Which fossils in the diagram are older, the human fossils or the fish fossils?

Cell Structure

Let's return to the analogy of a scientist being a detective. Suppose the detective was trying to prove that an unidentified accident victim was a member of a certain family. One possible method could be comparing the physical characteristics of the victim with the characteristics of members of the family. Height, weight, color of hair, and structure of the face are some of the characteristics that might be compared. If many of the characteristics are similar, then a case could be made that the victim and family members were related. Scientists use the same methods of comparing similarities among organisms for finding evidence of evolution. Try the following activity and see what similarities you can find in different cells.

Connect to...
Earth Science

Fossil ferns and coal deposits have been found in Antarctica. Prepare a map of Pangaea showing how Antarctica could have supported a temperate climate.

Explore! ACTIVITY

What is the basic structure of the cell?

What To Do

1. Your teacher will give you two slides to use for this activity.

2. Carefully study the slides under the microscope. Begin with the slide of the cyanobacterium *Oscillatoria*.

3. Make a sketch of the structure of this moneran.

4. Study the slide of the *Elodea* cells.

5. Make a simple sketch of the cell structure of this freshwater organism.

6. Compare the two drawings. *In your Journal*, write a description of how the two cells are similar.

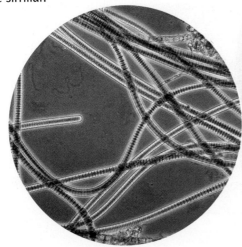

549

Your drawings from the Explore activity probably included structures such as cell walls, nuclei, and chloroplasts. In addition, you may remember that all cells have a cell membrane and contain a gel-like material called cytoplasm. Cells also have other structures such as mitochondria, endoplasmic reticulum, and vacuoles in common.

Figure 17-10

Bacteria (right) have a very simple cell structure, while protists (left) are more complex and have structures such as an eyespot, which can detect light.

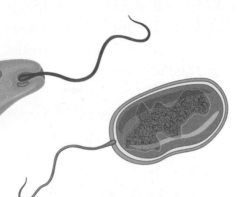

■ Comparing Cells of Modern Organisms with Cells of Ancient Organisms

Because cells from modern organisms have some similar structures, you might suggest that these cells are also similar to those of ancient organisms. But how could this idea be proven? The oldest fossils show organisms that lived about 3.5 billion years ago. These organisms resemble some very simple bacteria that live today. These organisms are found in salt ponds and hot sulfur springs—the same kind of environment scientists believe existed on Earth millions of years ago. The resemblance suggests a relatedness between ancient and modern organisms.

Chemistry CONNECTION

Hair cells are made of proteins, which the body uses to build and repair cells.

Chemical Building Blocks of Life

All living organisms share many of the same elements—oxygen, nitrogen, hydrogen, sulfur, phosphorus, and most importantly, carbon. Atoms of these six elements combine and bond in various ways to become the molecules of life.

DNA

In all living things, the basic molecule of life is DNA (deoxyribonucleic acid). The DNA molecule is formed from four smaller molecules. In every plant and animal on Earth, these four molecules are the chemical foundation of life. The four molecules combine in different ways. These combinations form a code containing thousands of messages. Some of these messages determine heredity. Others run the day-to-day operations of the body. For instance, they

Chemical Makeup of the Cell

Just as cells have many common structures, their contents are chemically similar. All organisms have the same molecules that are building blocks of their cells: proteins, fats, and carbohydrates.

■ Similarities in DNA

Recall from Chapter 14 that the chemical DNA controls the characteristics, or traits, of all organisms. When new cells are formed, they receive the same DNA code as the original cell. Scientists know that the DNA of each species has a specific sequence for the four kinds of bases. The more closely related one species is to another, the more similar their DNA codes are.

Figure 17-11

Ⓐ The DNA of each species has a specific sequence for the four types of nitrogen bases.

Ⓑ The sequences of the nitrogen bases in the DNA of humans and gorillas are very similar.

give cells the instructions for making protein molecules.

Proteins

Proteins are absolutely vital to all life. They serve many different functions. Some are part of skin, hair, horns, and feathers. Others are parts of the body's defense system. The blood protein, hemoglobin, carries oxygen from the lungs to the body tissues. Hormones, such as insulin (which controls sugar metabolism), are made of proteins. So are enzymes, which help chemical processes occur.

Amino Acids

Protein molecules are formed of many amino acids linked together in a long sequence, like beads on a string or railroad cars in a train. The DNA code instructs the cell where to place each amino acid in the sequence. Only 20 types of amino acids form into proteins. However, those 20 can combine in hundreds of millions of different ways. Proteins have complicated shapes that are folded and coiled.

What Do You Think?

Animals cannot manufacture many of their own amino acids. They must get them by eating plants. Because most plants contain small amounts of amino acids, animals must eat large quantities to get enough for

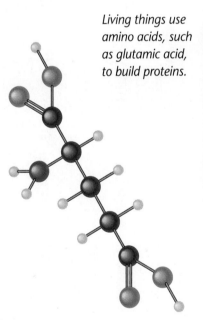

Living things use amino acids, such as glutamic acid, to build proteins.

their bodies' needs. Animals that eat other animals and animal products, such as milk and eggs, do not have this problem. Can you explain why?

Homologous Structures

You learned that comparing cell structure and comparing cell chemistry are ways to determine relatedness among organisms. The comparison of other body structures can also show relatedness. **Figure 17-12** shows body parts from different animals. The human arm, bird's wing, dolphin's flipper, and bat's wing all perform different functions. However, all of these body parts contain approximately the same number and types of bones and muscles. If you were able to trace the development of these animals from the embryo stage to adult, you would see that each limb developed from similar tissues in the embryos. Body parts of different organisms that are similar in origin and structure are called **homologous structures**. Homologous structures also provide evidence of evolution because they suggest that organisms evolve from a common ancestor.

Figure 17-12

Ⓐ The human arm, bird wing, bat wing, and dolphin flipper are all homologous structures. The structure of the bird wing is basically similar to that of the human arm, but the wrist and finger bones differ considerably.

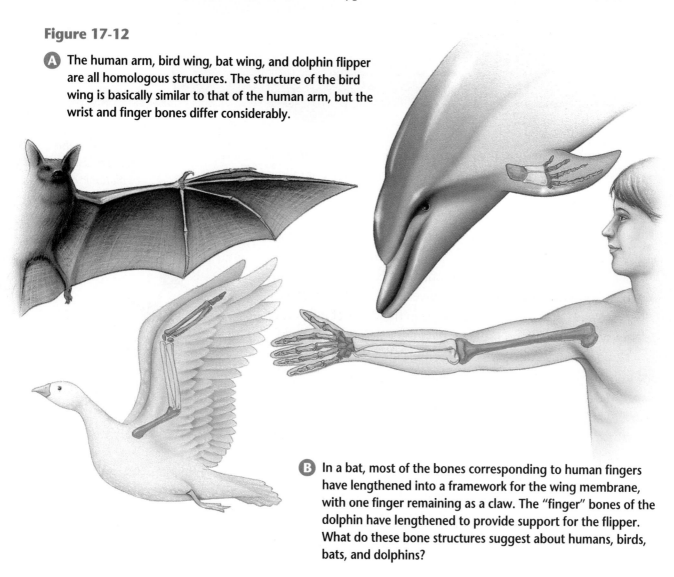

Ⓑ In a bat, most of the bones corresponding to human fingers have lengthened into a framework for the wing membrane, with one finger remaining as a claw. The "finger" bones of the dolphin have lengthened to provide support for the flipper. What do these bone structures suggest about humans, birds, bats, and dolphins?

Evidence from Embryos

Study the embryos in **Figure 17-13**. In the early stages of development, all of these animals look similar. They all have tails and gills or gill slits. Fish, and many aquatic amphibians, such as mudpuppies and sirens, are the only vertebrates to keep the gills as adults. All other vertebrates develop lungs. In humans, a tail-like stump disappears but fish, birds, and reptiles retain tails as adults. These similarities among vertebrate embryos suggest that there is a common ancestor for all of the vertebrates.

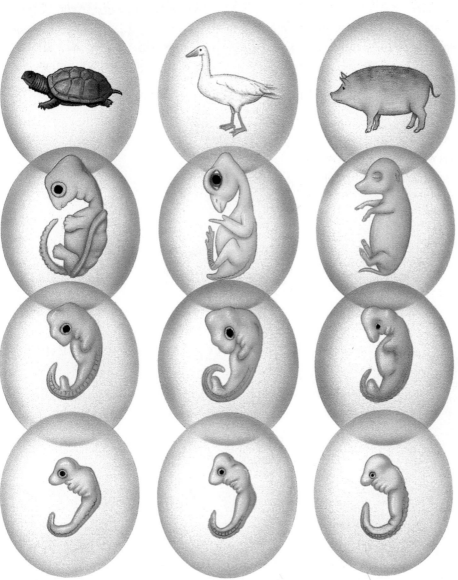

Figure 17-13

The embryos of turtles, chickens, and pigs all look very similar. All of these embryos have tails and gills or gill slits. As the embryos develop, the gills will be replaced by lungs.

INVESTIGATE!

How Are Your Arms Like Chicken Wings?

In this activity, you will find out if your arm and a chicken's wing are homologous structures.

Problem

What are the similarities and differences between human arms and chicken wings?

Materials

cooked chicken wing	paper towels
forceps	dissecting pan
scalpel	drawing paper
model of human arm and hand bones	pencil
	colored pencils

Safety Precautions

Use care with sharp instruments. Dispose of chicken wings as your teacher instructs you.

What To Do

1 Place a chicken wing in the dissecting pan. Use the scalpel to remove as much meat as possible from the wing (Photos A and B). **CAUTION:** *Care should be used to prevent cutting yourself.*

2 Wrap the meat in a paper towel and follow your teacher's instructions for discarding it. **CAUTION:** *Don't eat the meat.*

3 Examine the bones of the wing. Draw the bones separately and as they fit together (Photo C).

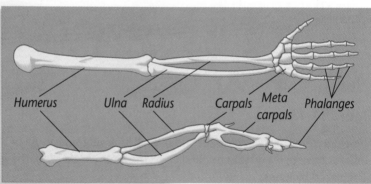

Humerus   Ulna   Radius   Carpals   Meta carpals   Phalanges

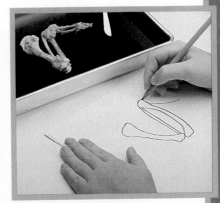

A   **B**   **C**

4 *Hypothesize* how the bones in your arm and hand might be similar to the bones in a chicken wing.

5 Study the bones of the human arm and hand. Draw how the bones fit together.

6 *Compare* the bones of the wing and the human arm and hand. Color any structures you think are homologous the same color.

7 Wrap the chicken bones in a paper towel and follow your teacher's instructions for discarding them. Clean your scalpel, forceps, and dissecting pan. Be sure to wash your hands thoroughly with soapy water after this activity.

The fossil of the archaeopteryx shows that the animal had scales and teeth like a reptile, but also had feathers like a bird, providing evidence that birds evolved from reptiles.

Analyzing

1. How do the bones in the human arm compare to the bones in the chicken wing? Consider size, shape, and number.

2. *Compare and contrast* the bones in the human hand to the bones in the chicken wing. Again consider size, shape, and number.

Concluding and Applying

3. Do your observations support your original hypothesis? If not, formulate a new hypothesis.

4. Based on information gained from this activity, could you *classify* your arm and a chicken wing as homologous structures? Why or why not?

5. Going Further *In your Journal*, write a plan for what you could do to make sure the structures are homologous.

Evidence of Human Evolution

You know that the DNA of chimpanzees and gorillas has been found to be very similar to the DNA of humans. **Primates**, the group of mammals that includes monkeys, apes, and humans, share many characteristics. Opposable thumbs allow you and other primates to grasp and hold objects. Flexible shoulders allow the gymnast to swing on the bars as other primates swing through trees. Binocular vision allows you to judge depth with your eyes just like chimps, monkeys, and lemurs. Each piece of evidence suggests that all of the primates evolved from a common ancestor.

You have learned that change is normal. It's not surprising then that life has changed and is continuing to change on Earth.

Figure 17-14

A A monkey is able to hold fruit because it has opposable thumbs.

B Flexible shoulders enable this gymnast to swing on the bars.

C Like other primates, humans have binocular vision, which gives us the ability to perceive depth.

check your UNDERSTANDING

1. If you were digging on the side of a cliff, how might fossils at the bottom differ from those at the top?
2. What are some structures common to all cells?
3. What do all primates have in common?
4. Why are homologous structures considered evidence of evolution?
5. **Apply** Suppose a scientist had the DNA sequence of four organisms. How could he or she determine which two organisms belong to the same species?

Science *and* Society

Evolution on the Farm

In nature, species that are well adapted to their environment have a better chance of surviving and passing their genes on to the next generation than those that aren't. This process is known as natural selection because conditions in nature have selected which organisms will survive and which will not.

Ancient Farming Methods

When people began to grow their own food, they developed a process called artificial selection, and thus influenced the evolution of many species of plants and animals. The earliest farmers saved seeds from their best plants—the biggest, strongest, or best tasting crops—to plant the next year. In this way, certain traits were nurtured while others were discouraged. People used this form of artificial selection for thousands of years.

Progress in the 20th Century

During the past 100 years, scientists have become very sophisticated at artificial selection. After learning the laws of genetic inheritance, agricultural scientists began to breed plants scientifically. Working with farmers, they experimented with different species, trying to develop plants that would mature more quickly and produce more food, that could withstand hot and cold weather, and

that could resist diseases and insects. Sometimes they even developed plants that were more nutritious than before.

Despite all the progress in plant breeding, farmers still must battle unwanted insect pests in their fields. Insect pests not only eat the plants, they carry the bacteria and viruses that cause plant diseases.

Insect Control

Some farmers spray their crops with insecticides to control harmful organisms. However, using the poisonous chemicals in insecticides has caused problems. First, chemicals that are dangerous to insects are often dangerous to humans, too. The chemical must be washed from harvested crops to prevent poisoning those who eat them. Second, insecticides can enter rivers and affect

other wildlife in the environment. Third, without realizing it, the scientists and farmers who developed and used insecticides were also interfering with natural selection.

Insecticide Resistance

Many species of insects are now resistant to the chemicals in certain insecticides. When farmers originally used these insecticides, insects that had insecticide-resistant genes survived. These insects reproduced, passing the gene for resistance to their offspring. The insects that weren't resistant died, leaving no offspring. Because of this artificial selection, many types of insects are now resistant. The insecticides no longer kill any of them. As a result, new and stronger insecticides have been developed.

Natural Pesticides

During the past decade or so, scientists have developed new techniques for fighting unwanted insects. Certain plants contain natural substances that repel insects. Using a new technology called genetic engineering, scientists can move genes from one organism to another. Many scientists feel that it may be possible to transfer genes that control the production of these insect-repelling substances from one kind of plant to another. The receiving plant would then have the genetic trait to repel insect pests. Natural plant chemicals would not endanger humans or harm the environment but only affect the insects that feed on that particular plant species.

Scientists have also been using artificial selection with insects, as well as the plants they eat. For example, scientists have used genetic engineering to give certain insects genetic diseases that will spread in the insect population. They also have developed new kinds of insecticides that do not poison the insects but instead affect their growth hormones. These insects cannot mature into adulthood, so they cannot reproduce.

What Do You Think?

Before any plants are genetically engineered to repel insect pests, should effects on insect species be considered? What if that insect species becomes extinct or a new insect species evolves?

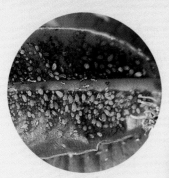

The milkweed aphid has developed resistance to pesticides.

Another type of insect that has developed resistance to pesticides is the spined stink bug.

The soybean pod worm is no longer killed by pesticides because it also has developed resistance.

Technology
Connection

When Were Rock Pictures Painted?

When scientists find a prehistoric site, they want to learn as much as they can about the people who lived there. They study the pots, spears, and other objects that are scattered around such places. They also study the paintings, called pictographs, on cave walls and other rocks.

Carbon-14 Dating

Carbon-14 dating helps scientists calculate just how long ago a basket was woven or a piece of horn was carved. However, until recently, they could not use carbon-14 dating to learn the age of pictographs. Carbon-14 dating was impossible because of the similarity between the carbon in the paint and the carbon in the limestone rock the paintings are on. Because of this problem, scientists had to use the carbon-14 dates of objects near the paintings and the style of the art to estimate the age of pictographs.

Rock Dating Updated

A few years ago, some scientists used a limestone chip from an ancient pictograph to invent a way to separate the two kinds of carbon. First, the scientists scraped paint from the rock and put it in a container. Next, they filled the container with a gas that changed the carbon from the paint into carbon dioxide but left the carbon from the rock alone. Finally, they measured the carbon-14 that originated from the carbon dioxide in the paint.

Using the earlier method, the scientists would have estimated the age of the pictograph to be from 2000 to 6000 years old.

Using their new method, the scientists calculated that the paint was 3865 years old, plus or minus 100 years.

Science Journal
What could scientists thousands of years from now learn about our society from studying murals painted on the sides of buildings? Explain your ideas *in your Science Journal.*

Radiocarbon dating uses isotopes of carbon to date rocks or fossils. Which isotope of carbon is used in carbon-14 dating?

Science Journal

Review the statements below about the big ideas presented in this chapter, and answer the questions. Then, reread your answers to the Did You Ever Wonder questions at the beginning of the chapter. *In your Science Journal,* write a paragraph about how your understanding of the big ideas in the chapter has changed.

1 Variations are differences in inherited traits among members of the same species. Variations that cause an organism to be better suited to its environment are adaptations. *What are some variations in the organisms shown in the photograph? Are these variations adaptations?*

2 Charles Darwin is credited with developing the theory of natural selection. This theory states that natural selection is a process in which living things that are better adapted to their environment are more likely to survive and reproduce. *How does natural selection lead to evolution?*

3 Scientists get evidence for evolution from fossils, the chemical structure of organisms, and the physical structure of cells and body parts. Evolution is an ongoing process. *What are some examples of scientific evidence of evolution?*

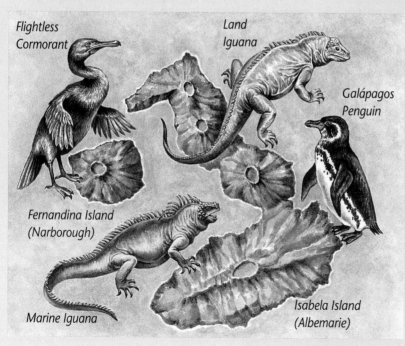

Flightless Cormorant

Land Iguana

Galápagos Penguin

Fernandina Island (Narborough)

Marine Iguana

Isabela Island (Albemarie)

Using Key Science Terms

evolution   natural selection
homologous structure   primate
mutation   variation

Explain the differences in the terms given below. Then, explain how the terms are related.
1. mutation, variation
2. natural selection, evolution
3. variation, homologous structure

Understanding Ideas

Answer the following questions in your Journal using complete sentences.
1. What does "survival of the fittest" mean?
2. Why is variation important?
3. How are humans adapted to their environment?
4. How are mutations important in the process of evolution?
5. How do wolves function as selecting agents?

Developing Skills

Use your understanding of the concepts developed in this chapter to answer each of the following questions.

1. **Observing and Inferring** To further examine how a trait can improve or decrease survival potential of a species as in the Find Out activity on page 537, use a large (22 × 28 cm) piece of green paper, green thread, 3 other colors of thread, tweezers (forceps), and a watch with a second hand. Cut 2-cm pieces of each color of thread and scatter them on the paper. Taking turns, use the tweezers and count how many pieces of thread can be picked up in 10 seconds. Which color of thread was picked up most often? Which color was picked up least often? Which is the most beneficial trait for the thread animals?

2. **Concept Mapping** Complete the concept map of evolution. Use the following terms: size, natural selection, adaptations, drought-resistant plant, type of feet, type of beak, variations, color.

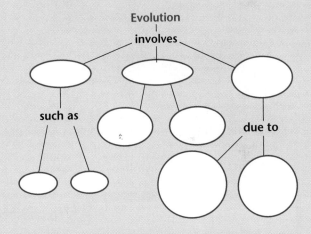

3. **Observing and Inferring** Find variations within a species as you did in the Explore activity on page 535. Collect 25 leaves from different trees of the same species. Measure the leaves and record the measurements. Note the shortest and longest measurements in addition to the most common length of the leaves. What other traits might vary within the species?

4. **Recognizing Cause and Effect** Recalling the findings from the Investigate on page 546, list other examples of animals that rely on color for survival.

Critical Thinking

In your Journal, *answer each of the following questions.*

1. Use what you've learned about evolution through natural selection to hypothesize how humans might evolve over time if our atmosphere keeps becoming more polluted.

2. Study the sketches of the Arctic fox (A), red fox (B), and desert fox (C). How might the variations you observe have evolved?

3. Animal A and animal B share 89 percent of the DNA code. Animal A and animal C share 91 percent of the DNA code. Which animals are more closely related?

4. Why were Darwin's observations of the Galápagos finches important to his theory of natural selection?

Problem Solving

Read the following problem and discuss your answers in a brief paragraph.

Rumors of a primitive human-like animal have circulated in a remote wilderness area for over 100 years. An individual finds the remains of what appears to be a human-like animal and claims that this is the mysterious beast. The remains consist of some long hairs and a partial skeleton. As a scientist, what could you do to prove that the beast was real or a hoax?

CONNECTING IDEAS

Discuss each of the following in a brief paragraph.

1. **Theme—Systems and Interactions** Fossils of two almost identical animals that lived millions of years ago were found in both Africa and South America. How do you explain this from what you have learned about evolution and plate tectonics?

2. **Theme—Scale and Structure** Farmers often breed domestic animals and plants to have certain characteristics. Give an example of this type of breeding and tell how it is different from natural selection.

3. **Theme—Systems and Interactions** How do the disciplines of life science, Earth science, and physical science all contribute evidence of evolution?

4. **Technology Connection** What can be learned when using carbon-14 dating techniques? How can carbon-14 dating help scientists learn about life in the past?

5. **Science and Society** Scientists have discovered ways to modify the genes of some living organisms. Do you think human evolution will be affected by these techniques?

CHANGES IN LIFE AND EARTH OVER TIME

In this unit, you learned that the face of Earth and the living things on it are very different today than they were in the distant past. In geologic time, measured in millions of years, continents have moved, mountains have appeared and disappeared, and many life forms have flourished and then become extinct. Also, you explored in depth the processes that produce the genetic diversity on which natural selection works.

Try the exercises and activity that follow—they will challenge you to use and apply some of the ideas you learned in this unit.

CONNECTING IDEAS

1. Coal deposits are located in some very cold regions of the world near the Arctic Circle. Relate the appearance of coal in these areas to the climate that must have existed when the coal beds started forming and why the coal appears in these areas today.

2. Suppose that conditions in an area change so much that certain easily chewed and digested plants died off over a short period of time. The only plants remaining as a supply of food had extremely tough cell walls that could not be easily chewed. What characteristics would better prepare one organism to survive this sudden change in the environment better than another?

Exploring Further ACTIVITY

What would you say to Darwin if he were alive today?

What To Do

1. *In your Journal*, write a letter to Charles Darwin. Provide him with evidence that he was not aware of that would support his ideas on evolution and natural selection.

2. Using what you know about heredity, evolution, and natural selection, how would you answer someone who claims that evolution could not occur because we have never found an organism that is half of one species and half of another?

Observing the World Around You

Look up! There's a whole universe beckoning. These giant antennas scan the sky in search of radio waves emitted by planets, stars, and galaxies. In this unit you'll discover the processes by which stars are born and burn out. You'll learn how energy and the movement of molecules support the structure of our universe and how it has changed over time.

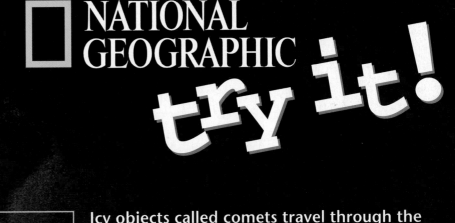

NATIONAL GEOGRAPHIC

try it!

Icy objects called comets travel through the solar system and around the sun. You can make a model to show how a comet moves around the sun. Use the diagram provided by your teacher.

What To Do

1. On a piece of cardboard, draw a circle about 8 inches in diameter and divide it into 16 equal pie-shaped sections.

2. Cut out small, rectangular sections from the outer portion of the disk between each section.

3. Now, draw a comet near the outer edge of one section.

4. In each of the other sections, draw a comet a little farther in its progression around the sun.

5. Push a tack through the center of the disk and into a stick.

6. While standing in front of a mirror, hold the disk in front of your face with the pictures facing the mirror.

7. While looking through the slits, slowly spin the disk. You should be able to see the comet moving around the sun.

CHAPTER 18

FISSION AND FUSION

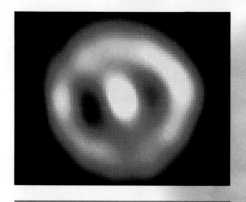

Did you ever wonder...

✓ How all the positive particles stay in an atom's nucleus even though they repel each other?

✓ What happens to naturally occurring radioactive elements?

✓ What happens in a nuclear reaction?

Science Journal

Before you begin your study of fission and fusion, think about these questions and answer them *in your Science Journal*. When you have finished the chapter, compare your journal write-up with what you have learned.

*Y*ou're outdoors. The sun is providing you with the light and warmth that makes life possible, thanks to nuclear reactions. On your way to school, you pass by a woman out jogging. She could have died a year ago from thyroid cancer, but she's alive today thanks to medical breakthroughs made possible by nuclear science.

Just what are nuclear reactions? How and why will they play an important role in your life and in the decisions you will be asked to make? In this chapter you'll learn about this important source of energy.

▶ *In the Explore activity on the next page, find out where you may have some radioactive material in your home.*

Explore! ACTIVITY

Is there a use for radioactive elements in your home?

Y ou have probably seen smoke detectors in your home and other buildings. Some contain radioactive material. Periodically, you have to replace the battery in a smoke detector, so it is possible to take one apart and see what makes it work.

What To Do

1. Watch while your teacher removes the outside cover of a smoke detector.

2. Look for a small metal cover or cage.
   CAUTION: *Don't take this metal cage apart!*

3. Most home smoke detectors contain information about the radioactive material as shown in the photo. The radioactive safety symbol indicates an area where radioactive materials are located. Look for this symbol inside the smoke detector.

4. Describe it *in your Journal.* What does it say?

18-1 Radioactivity, Natural and Artificial

Section Objectives

■ Describe an artificial transmutation.

■ Compare artificial and natural transmutations.

Key Terms

transmutation
artificial
  transmutation

Getting to the Source of Nuclear Energy

When you talk about nuclear energy, radioactivity, and nuclear reactions, you are talking about changes that are taking place in the nucleus of an atom. You are going to take a closer look at the forces inside the nucleus of an atom. You will see that changes may occur in the nucleus naturally, but that humans can also cause changes.

Explore! ACTIVITY

How do protons stick together in an atom's nucleus?

What To Do

1. Group ten BB pellets in a pile on a tray.

2. Roll one BB pellet along the tray toward the pile. What happens to the BBs in the pile when they are struck?

3. Now lightly coat the ten BB pellets with salad oil.

4. Regroup the BB pellets and roll a pellet towards the pile. Observe the behavior of the BBs when they are struck.

5. Did the pile of BBs in steps 2 and 4 break apart in the same way?

6. Why did they behave differently?

In the Explore activity, you observed a model for the behavior of nuclear particles. The uncoated BBs rolled apart. The BBs coated with oil behave in a similar manner to protons in the nuclei of atoms. A force, modeled by the oil, seems to be holding them together.

An atomic nucleus contains positively charged protons. Just like any objects with similar electric charge, the protons repel one another. Yet the protons in a nucleus are very close to each other. Some force must be holding the protons together.

There are neutrons in the nucleus as well. Neutrons aren't charged so they don't repel protons. Neutrons don't attract protons electrically either, but they do help to hold the nucleus together. Protons and neutrons share a force that holds the nucleus together. It's an extremely strong force that holds protons to protons, protons to neutrons, and neutrons to neutrons. Although this force is very strong it works only over extremely short distances. It's called the strong nuclear force. As shown in **Figure 18-2**, the protons and neutrons must be nearly touching or the strong force has no effect. As a result, this strong force can't hold every nucleus together.

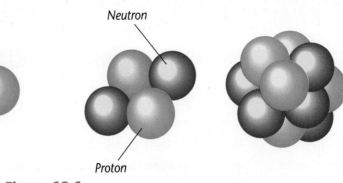

Figure 18-1

The atomic nucleus of hydrogen is the simplest and consists of one positively charged proton. The nucleus of helium contains two protons and two neutrons. The force that holds protons and neutrons together is called the strong nuclear force. A more massive element needs more neutrons so that the strong force can hold the nucleus together. If there are not enough neutrons, the nucleus will become unstable and decay. The heaviest elements are always unstable. Uranium has 92 protons. Is uranium stable or unstable?

The nucleus of a lighter element stays together if it has roughly equal numbers of protons and neutrons. For example, the most common isotopes of He, C, N, and O have exactly as many neutrons as protons. In a more massive element, more neutrons are needed so that the strong force can balance the repulsion between the protons. If there are too few or too many neutrons, the nucleus is unstable. The nucleus will expel a particle to become more stable. When this happens, we say that the element is radioactive and it decays. Some elements of light and medium mass are radioactive. Unlike the lighter elements, elements with more than 83 protons are always unstable, whatever the number of neutrons.

Figure 18-2

Because both of these protons have a positive charge, the electric force causes them to repel each other. However, when they are very close together, the strong nuclear force overcomes the force of repulsion. As a result, the protons and neutrons are held together in the nucleus. What would happen to the protons if the neutrons were removed from the nucleus?

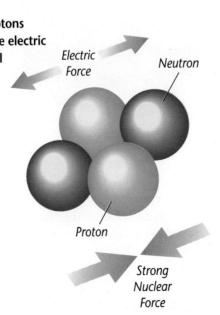

Decay Transmutes Elements

In the first Explore activity, you looked inside a smoke detector. The most common radioactive element used in smoke detectors is americium-241, element number 95.

■ Transmutation—Ejecting Alpha Particles

Americium decays by expelling an alpha particle. An alpha particle is a helium nucleus without its electrons. It contains two protons and two neutrons. An element is defined by its atomic number, the number of protons in its nucleus. Americium has 95. If an americium atom loses two protons, it's not americium anymore. As shown in **Figure 18-3**, it becomes an atom with 93 protons—an atom of the element neptunium. When a nucleus emits an alpha particle, it loses two protons, so it becomes a lighter element two numbers lower on the periodic table. Because the alpha particle has a mass number of 4, the nucleus must also lose two neutrons, and the new element has a mass number that is 4 smaller than the original. When an atom changes from one element to another by emitting particles, or decaying, it's called **transmutation**.

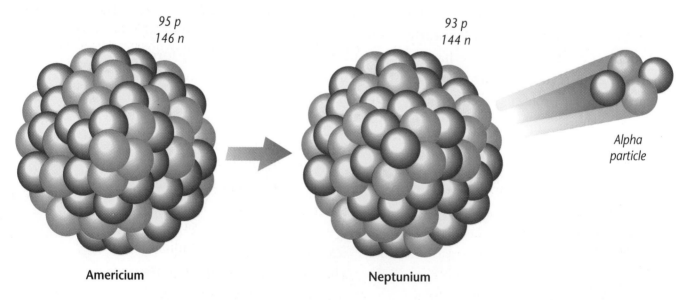

95 p
146 n

93 p
144 n

Alpha particle

Americium

Neptunium

Figure 18-3

Americium has 95 protons, so it is an unstable element. When an atom of americium decays, it ejects an alpha particle. An alpha particle is a helium nucleus, which consists of two protons and two neutrons. After emitting an alpha particle, an atom of americium is left with 93 protons. It has changed into an atom of the element neptunium. Will the atom of neptunium itself decay?

Figure 18-4

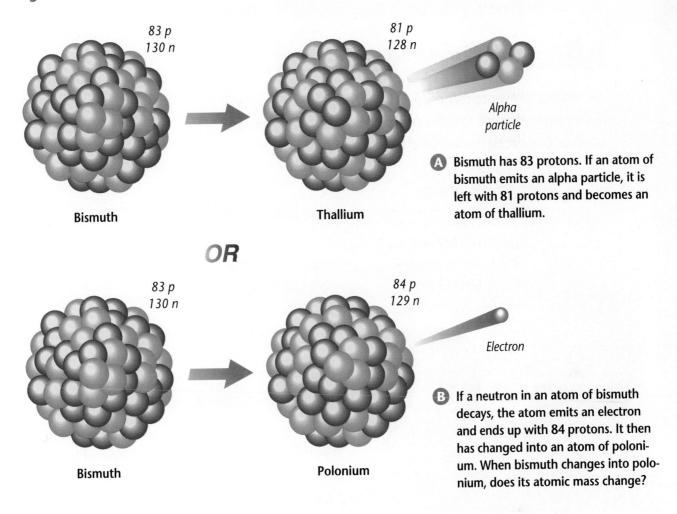

83 p
130 n

81 p
128 n

Alpha particle

Bismuth

Thallium

A Bismuth has 83 protons. If an atom of bismuth emits an alpha particle, it is left with 81 protons and becomes an atom of thallium.

OR

83 p
130 n

84 p
129 n

Electron

Bismuth

Polonium

B If a neutron in an atom of bismuth decays, the atom emits an electron and ends up with 84 protons. It then has changed into an atom of polonium. When bismuth changes into polonium, does its atomic mass change?

■ Transmutation—Ejecting Electrons

Transmutation also occurs when a nucleus emits an electron. But there are no electrons in a nucleus. How can a nucleus emit a particle it doesn't have? If there are too many neutrons in a nucleus, a neutron can become unstable. This neutron decays into an electron and a proton. The nucleus now has one more proton. The atom turns into an atom of an element one number higher on the periodic table. Because the mass of the electron is so small, the atomic mass of the element doesn't change much. For example,

an isotope of bismuth (83) can either emit an alpha particle to become thallium (81), or decay a neutron and emit an electron to become polonium (84). These alternatives are illustrated in **Figure 18-4**.

The spontaneous radioactive decay that occurs in certain isotopes of all elements is an example of natural transmutation. The time it takes for a given mass of an element to transmute can be determined. A time interval known as half-life measures this length or period of time. In the next Investigate you will make a model of half-life.

Measuring Half-Life

All radioactive materials decay at a steady rate. The rate differs from element to element and from isotope to isotope. Radioactive decay is measured in terms of half-life.

Problem
How can coin tossing simulate radioactive decay?

Materials
100 pennies	container with cover
graph paper	colored pencils

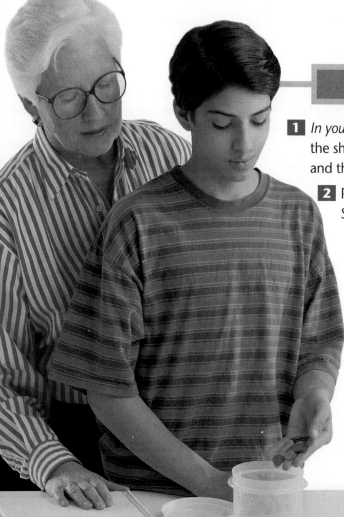

What To Do

1 *In your Science Journal*, prepare a data table to record the shake number, the predicted number of heads, and the actual number of heads.

2 Place the 100 coins in the container and cover it. Shake for several seconds.

3 *Predict* before each shake the number of coins that will be heads up. Record your prediction in your data table.

4 Gently pour the coins in a single layer on a desktop. Separate the coins into piles with heads up and tails up.

5 Count the coins with heads up and record the number in your data table.

A   B   C

6 Put only the coins with heads up back into the container. Shake the container.

7 Repeat steps 3, 4, 5, and 6 until no coins remain.

8 *Make a graph* of the shake number on the horizontal axis versus the number of heads on the vertical axis. With different colored pencils, plot your predicted results and your actual results.

9 Work with the other groups in your class to *calculate* the predicted and actual number of heads remaining for each shake for the entire class. Plot a graph of the predicted and actual class results as you plotted your own results.

Analyzing

1. Each penny represents one atom. Are the atoms represented stable or unstable?

2. How many shakes represent one half-life?

3. Are there still unstable atoms after one half-life? After two or more half-lives?

Concluding and Applying

4. *Compare* the number of heads actually remaining to the predicted numbers on your graphs for both your results and for the class results. For which set of data were the actual results closer to the predicted results? Why do you think this was so?

5. Going Further *Infer* whether a radioactive sample is safe once it is one half-life old. Justify your answer.

■ Half-Life

In the Investigate, you found that your class turned up heads at a rate rather than turning a certain number each time. It was a matter of dropping a certain fraction of heads each time you shook the container. From that, you figured out that your class would lose half the pennies every shake.

That's how radioactive materials decay. Half of their nuclei transmute in a certain amount of time. The period it takes for half of the nuclei to transmute is called the half-life of the element. If you had one gram of iodine-131 whose half-life is 8 days,

after eight days you would have one-half gram of iodine-131 and one-half gram of xenon, the element iodine transmutes to. After another eight days, you'd have one-quarter gram of iodine-131 and three-quarters gram of xenon. What particle does an iodine-131 nucleus eject?

Elements with relatively short half-lives are useful in medicine to help physicians diagnose ailments. But some half-lives are as long as billions of years. These elements help geologists determine the age of the rocks they find.

Life Science CONNECTION

Has Your Food Been Irradiated?

Irradiating this fruit has slowed the ripening process, thus keeping it fresh for a longer period of time.

There are a variety of techniques to keep food fresh and healthful for an extended time. One of these techniques is irradiation—a process that exposes the food to small amounts of radiation.

This weak radiation kills bacteria such as *Salmonella*. Salmonella poisoning is usually contracted by eating chicken contaminated with salmonella bacteria. In the United States, salmonella affects two million people yearly—two thousand of whom do not recover. The low-dose radiation also kills most of the insect pests that feed on fresh produce.

Irradiation can be used to extend the shelf life of fruits and vegetables by slowing the ripening process. In this case, the

Changing Stable Elements

In 1919, physicist Ernest Rutherford allowed alpha particles (helium nuclei) to move through nitrogen gas. As a result, some alpha particles collided with nitrogen nuclei. Rutherford was surprised to see that in some collisions, a particle left the nitrogen nuclei at a much higher speed than the incoming alpha. He identified the particle as a proton. Because the nitrogen nucleus gained two protons from the alpha particle and lost one, the result was that the nitrogen nucleus gained one proton. A nitrogen atom changed or transmuted from nitrogen (element number 7) to oxygen (element number 8).

When a transmutation doesn't happen spontaneously but is caused in any way, the reaction is an **artificial transmutation**.

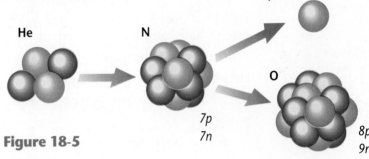

He   N   proton   O

7p
7n

8p
9n

Figure 18-5

Nitrogen is artificially transmuted to oxygen plus 1 proton.

---

radiation breaks down some of the substances that cause ripening.

Is Irradiation Safe?

The Food and Drug Administration, the government agency charged with making sure that our food is safe to eat, has approved the irradiation process. In fact, governments of 37 countries have approved the process. Although irradiated food is never radioactive, some people fear that irradiated food will spread radioactivity throughout the environment. Others argue that the process alters the molecular makeup of food.

Proper safeguards at processing plants should make the process less dangerous than using chemicals and pesticides.

For some people, the risk of reaction to sulfites and nitrates is a far greater concern than eating irradiated food.

Irradiated food is not radioactive. It can't spread radioactivity throughout the fruit stand or salad bar.

What Do You Think?

Find out if your state has banned the sale of irradiated food. Interview your family members and find out if they support or oppose irradiation of food. List the reasons they give. Are their reasons based on the risks involved with irradiated food or the fear of radiation? Decide if you support or oppose irradiation of food. Present your views to your class.

This fruit was not irradiated, so it has rotted more quickly.

Making New Elements

Artificial transmutation was big news and created a lot of excitement among scientists when it was first described. It opened the way to producing elements that didn't exist on Earth. Some of them may have been part of the planet once, but all their nuclei had long ago decayed, transmuting into other elements. Scientists could now make one element out of another by bombarding it with particles.

Alpha particles from radioactive elements were adequate to bombard such light elements as nitrogen, neon, and sodium. But heavier elements contain more protons in their nuclei. These protons repel the protons in alpha particles. Alpha particles would never reach the target nucleus. First, however, scientists had to find different ways to bombard nuclei.

One way to give a particle more energy is to increase the speed. For example, you could throw a BB at a piece of glass and the BB would bounce off the glass. If, however, you shot the BB from a BB gun, the BB would be moving fast enough to break the glass. To give particles more energy, particle accelerators were invented. Particle accelerators speed up, or accelerate, subatomic particles such as protons, alpha particles, and electrons until they have enough energy to penetrate a large nucleus.

Figure 18-6

Particle accelerators speed up subatomic particles until they have enough energy to penetrate the nuclei of heavier elements. This photograph of the particle accelerator at Fermilab in Illinois shows the outline of the underground tunnel, which is more than 6.3 kilometers, or almost 4 miles, long.

Adding to the Periodic Table

By 1930, nearly all the elements through uranium, element 92, had been studied. But four elements with numbers 43, 61, 85, and 87 eluded researchers. These elements had not been found in nature, so researchers were eager to produce them in the laboratory. The problem was that nuclei of elements close to that of the missing elements were large enough to repel alpha particles.

Particle accelerators allowed scientists to find missing elements by creating them in the laboratory. Element 43 is now known as technetium, 61 is promethium, 85 is astatine, and 87 is francium. These elements have half-lives ranging from less than a second for astatine to more than six hours for technetium. As shown in **Figure 18-8**, not only did the particle accelerator allow scientists to fill gaps in the periodic table, it also allowed them to expand it. Increasingly powerful particle accelerators have made it possible for scientists to create atoms of elements beyond uranium. More than a dozen elements beyond uranium have been created in the laboratory. They are all radioactive and have half-lives of only a few seconds or less.

| 55 Cs 132.91 | 56 Ba 137.33 |
| ? | 88 Ra (226) |

| 60 Nd 144.24 | ? | 62 Sm 150.36 |
| 92 U 238.03 | | |

Figure 18-7

By using a particle accelerator to bombard atoms of known elements with particles, scientists were able to produce the missing elements and fill in the gaps in the periodic table.

24 Cr Chromium 51.9961	25 Mn Manganese 54.9380	26 Fe Iron 55.847
42 Mo Molybdenum 95.94	?	44 Ru Ruthenium 101.07
74 W Tungsten 183.85	75 Re Rhenium 186.207	76 Os Osmium 190.2

| 52 Te Tellurium 127.60 | 53 I Iodine 126.9045 | 54 Xe Xenon 131.29 |
| 84 Po Polonium 208.9824* | ? | 86 Rn Radon 222.017* |

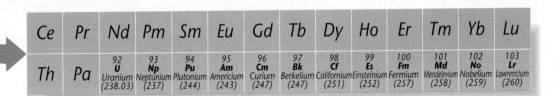

Na	Mg												Al	Si	P	S	Cl	Ar
K	Ca	Sc	Ti	V	Cr	Mn	Fe	Co	Ni	Cu	Zn	Ga	Ge	As	Se	Br	Kr
Rb	Sr	Y	Zr	Nb	Mo	Tc	Ru	Rh	Pd	Ag	Cd	In	Sn	Sb	Te	I	Xe
Cs	Ba	La	Hf	Ta	W	Re	Os	Ir	Pt	Au	Hg	Tl	Pb	Bi	Po	At	Rn
Fr	Ra	Ac	104 Rf Rutherfordium (261)	105 Ha Hahnium (262)	106 Sg Seaborgium (263)	107 Ns Nielsbohrium (262)	108 Hs Hassium (265)	109 Mt Meitnerium (266)	110 Uun (unnamed)	111 Uuu (unnamed)	112 Uub (unnamed)						

| Ce | Pr | Nd | Pm | Sm | Eu | Gd | Tb | Dy | Ho | Er | Tm | Yb | Lu |
| Th | Pa | 92 U Uranium (238.03) | 93 Np Neptunium (237) | 94 Pu Plutonium (244) | 95 Am Americium (243) | 96 Cm Curium (247) | 97 Bk Berkelium (247) | 98 Cf Californium (251) | 99 Es Einsteinium (252) | 100 Fm Fermium (257) | 101 Md Mendelevium (258) | 102 No Nobelium (259) | 103 Lr Lawrencium (260) |

Figure 18-8

More powerful particle accelerators have enabled scientists to create new elements beyond uranium with atomic numbers of 93 through 112.

Figure 18-9

In agricultural labs, small amounts of radioactive isotopes are mixed with fertilizers. By following the traces of the radioisotopes through plants, scientists can tell how well various fertilizers work. Do you think the radioactive isotopes harm the plants? Why or why not?

■ Tracer Elements

Artificial transmutation has also made it easy to manufacture radioactive isotopes of elements that are normally stable. You'll recall that isotopes are different forms of the same element. They're different only in the number of neutrons in their nuclei. Radioactive isotopes are especially useful because scientists can easily fol-

low their progress as they move through a biological system. Isotopes used in this way are called tracers. Also many of the artificial radioactive isotopes have extremely short half-lives. This allows them to be introduced into living things without the danger that is associated with long-term radioactivity. For years, physicians relied on iodine-131 as a radioactive tracer. Today, the majority of patients receive artificially-made technetium as a tracer.

Humans are not the only organisms studied with tracers. As shown in **Figure 18-9**, at an agricultural lab, small amounts of radioactive isotopes are mixed with various fertilizers. By seeing how the radioactivity moves into plants, scientists can tell how well each fertilizer works. The woman who was jogging is alive today because doctors could treat her thyroid cancer with a radioactive isotope of iodine. And thousands of lives have been saved from fires because of home smoke detectors with americium—a new element produced using artificial transmutation. In the next section, you'll discover other ways in which the atom and its nucleus are useful in everyday living.

check your UNDERSTANDING

1. What happens to cause a transmutation when an alpha particle hits an atom's nucleus?
2. How is artificial transmutation different from natural transmutation?
3. Name a particle that can cause an artificial transmutation.
4. **Apply** An atom of nitrogen (element number 7) absorbs an alpha particle containing two protons. What element does it become?

Fission

Splitting the Atom

In 1938, scientists in laboratories around the world were studying nuclear transmutations. Among them were German physicists Otto Hahn, and Fritz Strassman, who were bombarding uranium with neutrons. They expected to produce elements more massive than uranium. They were stunned to end up with atoms that acted as if they were atoms of barium. Could it possibly be barium, which was much lighter than uranium? Hahn wrote about the results to his former co-worker, Lise Meitner. She came up with an explanation.

Section Objectives

■ Describe nuclear fission.

■ Outline a nuclear fission reaction.

■ Model a chain reaction.

Key Terms

fission

chain reaction

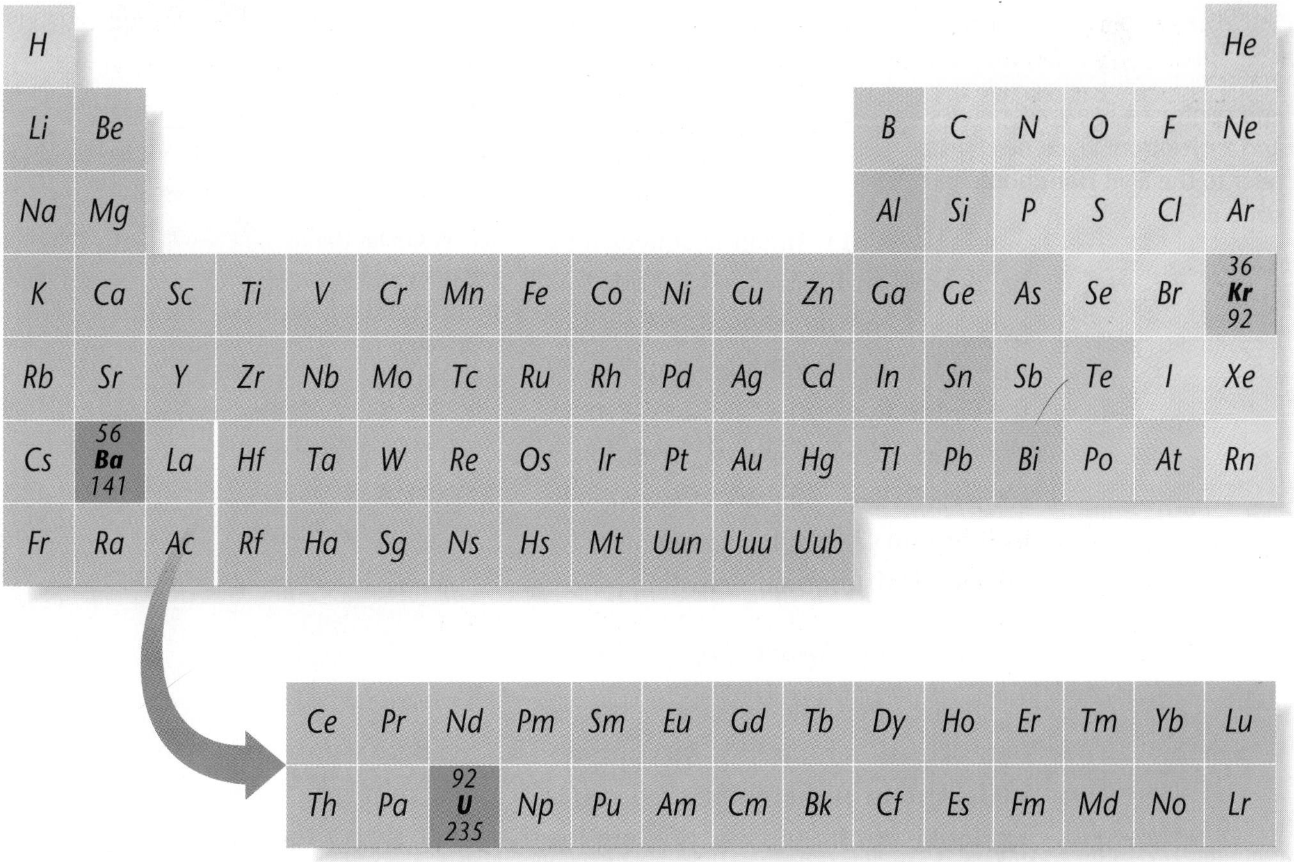

Figure 18-10

Firing a neutron at a uranium nucleus breaks it up into a barium nucleus and a krypton nucleus.

Figure 18-11

A neutron striking a nucleus of uranium does not have enough energy to split the nucleus apart. Instead, the neutron knocks the nucleus out of shape, causing it to bulge outward at the sides. What will eventually happen to the nucleus?

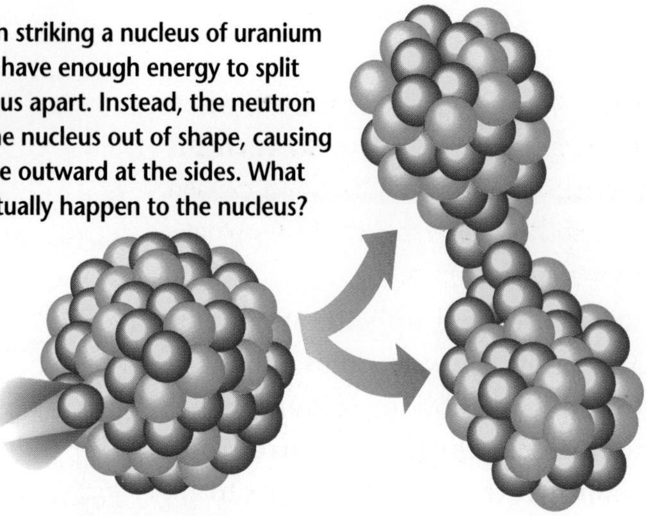

SKILLBUILDER

Comparing and Contrasting

Atomic particles can be accelerated by means of a linear accelerator or a cyclotron. Compare and contrast a linear accelerator and a cyclotron. If you need help, refer to the **Skill Handbook** on page 683.

A neutron hitting a uranium nucleus might not have the energy to split the nucleus in two, but it may have enough energy to knock it out of shape for an instant, as shown in **Figure 18-11**. Imagine squeezing a balloon, as in **Figure 18-12**. Your fingers don't cut the balloon in half, but they do press the middle in and make the ends bulge out.

If the impact of a neutron has a similar effect on a larger nucleus, such as uranium's, the nucleus might never go back to its original shape.

■ Breaking Apart the Nucleus

Remember that the electric forces between the protons in the nucleus make the protons repel each other while the strong force is holding the protons together. But the strong nuclear force works only over a very short distance. Where the sides of the nucleus are squeezed together, there might not be enough force to hold

the two bulges together anymore. The repelling force among the protons is stronger than the attraction of the strong force and the two bulges tear away from each other to form two smaller nuclei. Thinking of the way cells divide, Meitner named this process nuclear **fission**. A uranium-235 nucleus could therefore split into a barium-141 nucleus and a krypton-92 nucleus. Three neutrons and a large amount of energy are released. This fission reaction is shown in **Figure 18-14**.

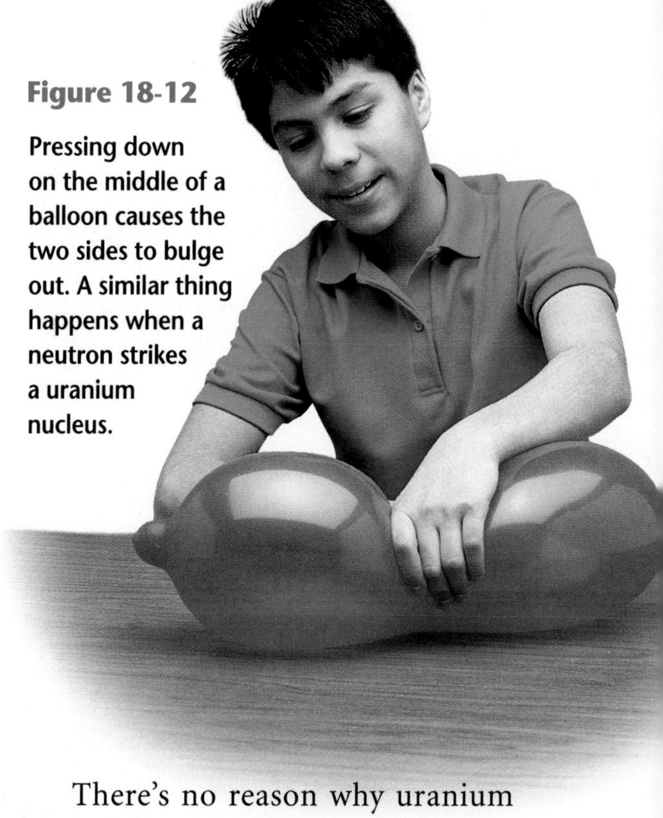

Figure 18-12

Pressing down on the middle of a balloon causes the two sides to bulge out. A similar thing happens when a neutron strikes a uranium nucleus.

There's no reason why uranium must split into barium and krypton rather than other elements. All that matters is that all the protons and neutrons are accounted for in the split. In fact, Hahn and Strassman found traces of lanthanum as well as barium in the products of their reaction.

The Power of Fission

However the nucleus splits, two important things happen. First, a great deal of energy is released. When you add up the mass of a barium-141 nucleus and a krypton-92 nucleus, you find there is not as much mass as was in the uranium-235 nucleus before it split. What happened to the missing mass? It turned into energy. How much energy? One uranium molecule splitting into barium and krypton puts out more energy than the chemical energy released in the explosion of 6 600 000 molecules of TNT.

The second important thing that happens is that neutrons are produced by the reaction. And each of these neutrons is available to bombard another uranium nucleus. What

if the three neutrons emitted when the uranium nucleus split each hit another uranium nucleus and caused it to split? The result could be what's known as a chain reaction.

Figure 18-13

These stamps were printed to honor Otto Hahn and Lise Meitner for their contributions to our knowledge of nuclear fission.

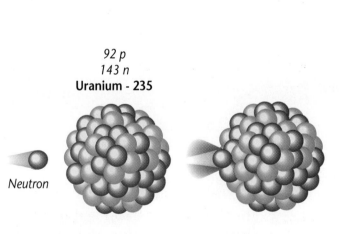

92 p
143 n
Uranium - 235

Neutron

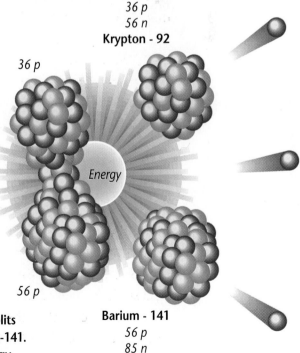

36 p
56 n
Krypton - 92

36 p

Energy

56 p

56 p
Barium - 141
56 p
85 n

Figure 18-14

One isotope of uranium has 92 protons and 143 neutrons, so its atomic mass is 235. This isotope is called uranium-235. When a neutron strikes a nucleus of uranium-235, the nucleus splits up. The result is a nucleus of krypton-92 and a nucleus of barium-141. This process releases three neutrons and a huge amount of energy.

What is a chain reaction?

What To Do

1. Select one classmate to be the first free neutron.

2. The rest of the class should divide into groups of three. Each group represents a radioactive nucleus.

3. In each group, two students will be neutrons. The third person represents both a proton and energy.

4. To start, the first free neutron will collide with any nucleus.

5. That nucleus then splits and the two neutrons rush off to collide with two other nuclei. The proton should indicate the energy accompanied with this split by raising both arms above his/her head. Each time a neutron hits a nucleus, the student representing that neutron stays with the third student in the nucleus, the proton. They'll represent the two nuclei and the energy from the collision.

6. Continue colliding and splitting until each nucleus has undergone fission. Be sure that you move in straight lines.

Conclude and Apply

1. How long were you able to keep track of who was going where?

2. How quickly did the process build?

Nuclear Reactors

You probably already know that a nuclear reactor is a device that produces electrical energy from a controlled nuclear chain reaction. A diagram of a reactor is shown in the figure.

The fission taking place in a nuclear reactor makes the reactor extremely hot. That thermal energy is used to heat water, causing it to boil. Steam from the boiling water turns the turbine. The turbine then turns the generator, which produces electricity.

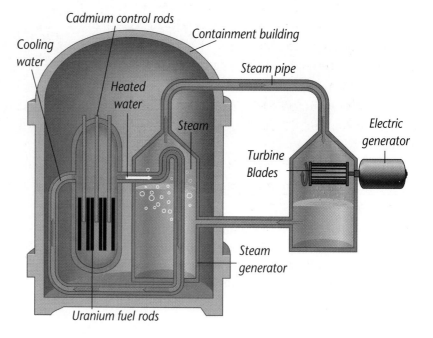

Cadmium control rods

Containment building

Cooling water

Steam pipe

Heated water

Steam

Electric generator

Turbine Blades

Steam generator

Uranium fuel rods

When each reaction causes more reactions, energy released can grow at a fantastic rate. When the neutron released by one reaction creates the next reaction, and that reaction creates the reaction after that, you have a **chain reaction. Figure 18-15** shows the special way that nuclei are pictured. As shown in **Figure 18-16**, a chain reaction can occur at a steady rate if each reaction creates just one more reaction. In the case of uranium fission, each reaction can create three more. The reactions multiply very rapidly.

You saw how quickly the energy increased in your classroom. Imagine, then, what it would be like on the atomic scale. If only two neutrons from one reaction caused another

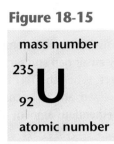

Figure 18-15

mass number

235
$_{92}$U

92

atomic number

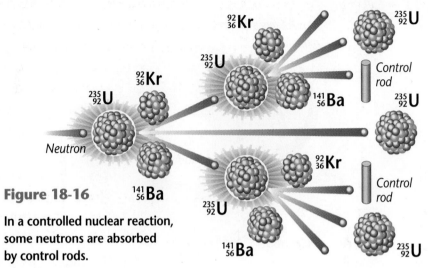

Figure 18-16

In a controlled nuclear reaction, some neutrons are absorbed by control rods.

Reactor Design

Modern nuclear reactors vary in design, but they all work on the same principle. In the core of the reactor is fuel, usually pellets of uranium oxide. The fuel pellets are surrounded by water, which slows down the neutrons produced by the fission reaction. Only slow neutrons can cause U-235 to undergo fission. As soon as one nucleus undergoes fission, a chain reaction can start. Cadmium rods absorb enough neutrons to keep the reaction from going out of control. But how do we use the energy that the reactions release?

Generating Electrical Energy

Most nuclear reactors make electricity. Look at the diagram again. The fission taking place in the reactor makes the reactor intensely hot. The thermal energy heats the water surrounding the fuel rods. Because the water is pressurized, it doesn't boil. The superheated water passes through a heat exchanger where it heats other water, causing it to boil. The reactor water, now much cooler, is then pumped back to the reactor. Steam from the boiling water in the heat exchanger turns the turbine that turns the

generator that makes the electricity. Trace the flow. See if you can tell where nuclear energy becomes thermal energy, where thermal energy becomes mechanical energy, and where mechanical energy becomes electrical energy.

What Do You Think?

Trace the path of the water that is used inside the reactor. Is this the same water that goes to the cooling towers? Is it the same water that turns the turbines? Why do you think the water from the reactor core is contained in the core and not pumped through the turbines?

Figure 18-17

A fission bomb is composed of a mass of uranium-235 separated by an air gap and surrounded by a conventional explosive such as TNT. When the TNT is detonated, the uranium-235 is suddenly compressed, and an uncontrolled chain reaction begins. This releases a tremendous amount of energy, resulting in a violent explosion.

After compression fission reaction

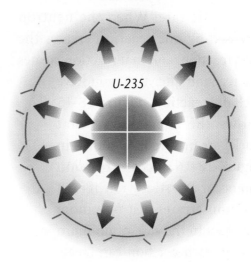

U-235

Before compression

Mass of reactive material U-235

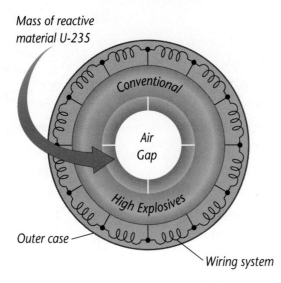

Conventional

Air Gap

High Explosives

Outer case

Wiring system

reaction, there would be about 1000 fission reactions after only one millisecond. After just two milliseconds, there would be a million reactions. After three there would be a billion. The reaction would be out of control. Remember, any single reaction releases tremendous amounts of energy. In a fraction of a second there would be an enormous amount of energy released—an explosion. The first atomic bombs worked by causing just

such a fission chain reaction. Fission chain reactions, however, can be controlled with neutron-absorbing material. By absorbing the neutrons before they can cause more fission, the rate of the reaction slows down. With the proper controls, a chain reaction can release as much energy as needed. The same reaction that is used to make atomic bombs is also used to generate electricity.

Understanding fission reactions is an important part of living in the twentieth century. In the next century, there will be other, more impressive nuclear reactions available. You'll read about one of these reactions in the next section.

check your UNDERSTANDING

1. What causes a fission reaction?
2. What is the sequence of events in fission reactions?
3. Where does the energy created by fission come from?

4. **Apply** If each uranium-235 releases three free neutrons in a nuclear fission chain reaction, how many free neutrons will exist after four reactions?

Fusion

Joining Nuclei Together

So far, we've seen that it's possible to both split nuclei and add particles to nuclei. Would it be possible to join two nuclei together? Yes, it's possible, but it's also very difficult. Two nuclei always repel each other because they're both positively charged. But if they are given enough energy, they come together close enough to let the strong force overcome the electric force. When that happens, the two nuclei can join into one. The joining of separate nuclei is called nuclear **fusion**.

Nuclear fusion is common in nature, but not on Earth. Fusion is what powers the stars, including our sun. Fusion occurs constantly inside the sun and provides an incredible amount of energy. Because of the extremely high temperatures involved, this process is known as thermonuclear fusion. The two original hydrogen nuclei contain more mass than the resulting helium nucleus.

Because the sun has more than one isotope of hydrogen, there are several fusion reactions that occur in the sun. One common reaction is illustrated in **Figure 18-18**. An ordinary atom of hydrogen has one particle in the nucleus, a proton. The symbol for ordinary hydrogen is $^{1}_{1}\text{H}$. The isotope of hydrogen that also has a neutron is called deuterium. It has two particles in its nucleus and its symbol is $^{2}_{1}\text{H}$. In a fusion reaction, two hydrogen nuclei fuse to produce deuterium. You can use a clay model to represent what happens as nuclear fusion occurs.

Figure 18-18

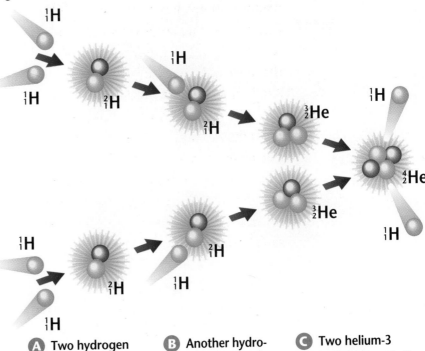

A Two hydrogen nuclei fuse to form deuterium and energy.

B Another hydrogen nucleus fuses with deuterium to form a helium-3 nucleus and energy.

C Two helium-3 nuclei form a helium-4 nucleus, 2 hydrogen nuclei, and more energy.

DESIGN YOUR OWN
INVESTIGATION

Nuclear Fusion

In a nuclear fusion reaction, atomic nuclei of small mass combine to form larger nuclei. This process releases a great amount of energy. In this experiment, you will use a model to visualize fusion.

Preparation

Problem
How can you model a fusion reaction?

Hypothesis
How will you use different materials to represent the steps in a fusion reaction?

Objectives
• Construct a model to simulate fusion.
• Explain fusion using the model.

Materials
small round objects of different colors such as clay balls, marbles, or grapes

Safety Precautions

Never eat food used in laboratory experiments. Dispose of food items after your experiment.

Fusion Reactions	
STEP 1	$^1_1H + ^1_1H \rightarrow ^2_1H + $ positron + energy
STEP 2	$^2_1H + ^1_1H \rightarrow ^3_2He + $ energy
STEP 3	$^3_2He + ^3_2He \rightarrow ^4_2He + 2^1_1H + $ energy

Plan the Experiment

1 Choose the objects that will represent the protons and neutrons for your model.

2 Determine how you will use your materials to show each step in the fusion reaction chart.

Check the Plan

1 Have you represented the energy in any way? The positron?

2 How will you identify each nucleus as hydrogen or helium?

3 Check your plan and model with your teacher.

Analyze and Conclude

1. **Analyze** What products do you have left over after making the helium nucleus? How many total nuclei of hydrogen does it take to make one helium nucleus?

2. **Predict** What would you predict the two hydrogen produced in the third step could be used for?

3. **Infer** Use the periodic table to compare the mass of one helium atom to the mass of four hydrogen atoms. What can you infer about the relationship between this difference in mass and the energy produced by the sun?

Going Further

Find out about the positron. Compare and contrast it with an electron.

As you saw in the second Investigate, the particles resulting from a fusion reaction have less mass than the original particles. The clay-ball model does not show what happens to that mass, but you already know. The difference in mass becomes the energy for the sun's light and heat. In fact, the energy released is more than enough to cause two other nuclei to fuse. This may sound similar to what happened during fission reactions —the makings of another chain reaction. That's exactly what a star is—a gigantic thermonuclear fusion chain reaction.

While fission releases energy by splitting larger nuclei into smaller ones, fusion does just the opposite. It fuses smaller nuclei into larger ones. Fusion of hydrogen into helium releases vast amounts of energy. It's the source of energy in stars. Researchers are working on peaceful uses of nuclear fusion. Many believe that fusion can be a clean, safe source of energy for the future. In the meantime, researchers also continue to study the thermonuclear fusion reactions that occur in the stars. In the last chapter of this book, you will learn more about the sun, the stars, and the other systems in outer space.

Figure 18-19

Nuclear fusion on the sun is a result of the extreme temperature and pressure conditions.

check your UNDERSTANDING

1. Compare and contrast nuclear fusion with nuclear fission.
2. What happens to extra mass when hydrogen is fused into helium?
3. What is the sequence of events that must occur for fusion to take place?
4. **Apply** Would thorium (element number 90) be better suited for a fission or fusion reaction?

HOW IT WORKS

Healing Radiation

Radiation and natural radioactive decay are useful for treating a variety of cancers. Cancers are a group of disorders involving cells that divide much more rapidly than normal cells. These abnormal cells form masses called tumors. Researchers have shown that cancer cells are more sensitive to radiation than are normal cells. This means that radiation can be used to kill cancer cells within a tumor and leave surrounding normal cells unharmed.

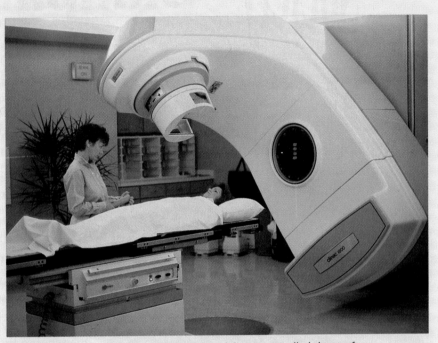

Special equiment that delivers controlled doses of radiation is used to treat certain forms of cancer.

Radioactive Beams

For instance, gamma radiation from cobalt-60 and cesium-137 are often directed at cancerous tumors. The beams of radiation are finely focused so that they are directed at only cancer cells and avoid healthy cells. This treatment requires expensive equipment, and the patient must go to the hospital every few days for another dose of radiation.

Radioactivity in a Tube

Another treatment uses the radioactive isotope sealed in a gold tube. The tube is implanted in the patient's tumor. The radiation kills the surrounding cancer cells, destroying the tumor from the inside out. This treatment is not dependent on expensive equipment and allows the patient some independence during treatment. Because the radioactive material is sealed in a capsule, materials with relatively long half-life may be used.

USING MATH

Manganese is a trace element needed by the body. Manganese-56 emits a beta particle and has a half-life of 2.6 hours. After 10.4 hours, what fraction of manganese would be in the patient's body? What other element would be in the patient's body as a result of treatment with manganese? Do you think manganese would be a good choice for radiation therapy?

Science and Society

No Nuclear Dumping

One of today's most hotly debated issues is the location of nuclear dump sites. As evidenced by a number of unpleasant incidents, nuclear waste is coming back to haunt us.

A startling example of the effects of nuclear waste occurred near Oak Ridge National Laboratory in Tennessee. In the 1940s, Oak Ridge was a research center for atomic weapons. The research produced several highly radioactive materials.

Protesters gather at the site of a new nuclear reactor.

The government and researchers in charge of the facility decided to sink the radioactive wastes under water. A 50-acre pond was created, and solid waste and drums of the liquid waste were placed at the bottom of the pond.

Radioactivity Spreads

In the 1960s, scientists working near Oak Ridge noticed turtles had traveled as far as five miles from the pond. More amazing was the realization that these animals had high concentrations of radioactive cesium in their tissues and organs.

Despite the intentions of the original researchers, the radioactivity had spread. Small plants and organisms beneath the water and at the facility's edge had absorbed some of the products of radiation. The plants were eaten by the small animals, such as turtles, that lived at the storage pond. The plants that carried radioactivity had entered the food chain.

The problem was one not only of the spread of radioactivity, but also of its concentration. As an animal, such as a small fish, repeatedly eats contaminated food, the radioactive elements concentrate in its tissues and organs. If a larger fish or bird feeds on the small fish, the radioactive elements are concentrated further. Animals feeding on plants and other animals from the storage pond had cesium concentration levels a thousand times higher than the cesium concentration levels of the storage pond. The increase in concentration as a result of the natural feeding process is called biomagnification.

Nuclear Reactors Produce Waste

Oak Ridge is a single example of the problems that accompany high-level nuclear waste. High-level waste is a by-product of the operation of nuclear reactors. Each reactor produces solid wastes, usually from the fuel rods of the reactors. Liquid waste is an acid-based substance produced during the treatment of the rods. For years, there were fewer than a dozen of these reactors. They were used for research and all were under the control of the government. But, as the nation's demand for electricity increased, the number of nuclear reactors also increased. Today's reactors are scattered across the country and are owned and operated by a number of widespread commercial interests.

Government scientists have suggested that high-level waste be buried two or three thousand feet beneath Earth's surface, in a geologically stable rock formation. They think this will be safe, but they cannot be sure.

In addition to the high-level waste, reactors also produce low-level waste. Hospitals, too, produce low-level waste. The half-life

of some of these materials is a few days, while other waste products have half-lives of 500 years.

Occasionally, metal drums filled with low-level radiation are dumped in shallow trenches. These sites are often affected by rainwater, and the containers may corrode, allowing the radioactive substances to leak into the ground and reach the groundwater supply. Drums stored in shuttered warehouses have leaked or corroded and contaminated the surrounding ground and water.

The federal government has authority over the disposal of high-level nuclear waste, while the states have control of low-level radiation sites. If waste is transported across state lines, the federal government can be asked to intercede.

Not in My Back Yard

Leaders across the country are meeting intense opposition to nuclear disposal sites. At every proposed site, the community protests. Voters promise to turn the political leaders out of office for approving the site. Yet every voter is, in some sense, responsible for creating nuclear waste. The nuclear reactors exist to supply an increased demand for electrical energy. Nuclear medicine has flourished, employing technology to cure illness or prolong life. Each of us benefits in some way from nuclear technology.

What Do You Think?

In 1982, the federal government ordered that construction of a solid nuclear waste depository site should be completed by 1998. What would you do if a proposed site were three miles from your home?

Nuclear waste is transported to storage facilities

Technology Connection

Fusion Reactors

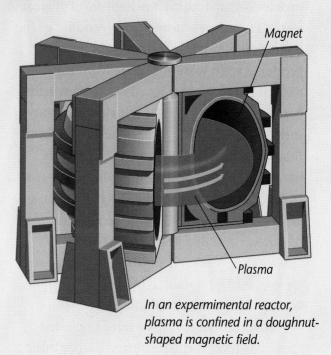

Magnet

Plasma

In an experimental reactor, plasma is confined in a doughnut-shaped magnetic field.

Nuclear fusion requires temperatures of more than 100 million degrees Celsius. No material can contain anything at such a temperature. However, scientists have been able to use a magnetic field to contain charged particles.

Magnetic Containment

When energy is added to hydrogen atoms, their electrons may be stripped away, forming a fluidlike material called a plasma that is comprised of electrons and ions. A design that might accomplish this is shown in the illustration.

A sudden increase in the magnetic field will compress the plasma, raising its temperature. This causes hydrogen nuclei to be fused into helium. The energy released by the reaction would be used to heat some other material, possibly liquefied lithium, at 186°C. The lithium, in turn, would boil water, producing steam to turn electric generators. Unfortunately, more energy is used by the equipment than is produced by the reaction.

Laser Fusion

A technique that doesn't require a sustained reaction uses pellets of frozen hydrogen-2 and hydrogen-3 dropped into a chamber. Here they are blasted by several high-powered laser beams. The concentrated laser light compresses the hydrogen and heats the pellets to fusion point.

Tritium

In late 1991, British researchers reported results of an experiment using tritium, an isotope of hydrogen that has two neutrons and one proton in its nucleus. They were able to produce a sustained fusion reaction for two seconds—a long time in nuclear circles. The reaction generated 2 million watts.

Science Journal

Expensive research is needed for a fusion reactor to become a reality. If a corporation funds a researcher who finds a solution, that corporation could make a huge profit from the discovery. If a government-funded researcher finds the solution, the government would share the development with all citizens. Do you think research should be funded by corporations or by the government? Why do you think as you do?

Science Journal

Review the statements below about the big ideas presented in this chapter, and answer the questions. Then, reread your answers to the Did You Ever Wonder questions at the beginning of the chapter. *In your Science Journal*, write a paragraph about how your understanding of the big ideas in the chapter has changed.

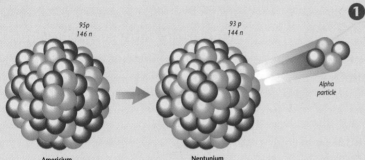

1 One element can change into another by emitting particles and changing its number of protons. This is called transmutation. You can force nuclei to transmute by bombarding them with alpha particles. *What is this process called?*

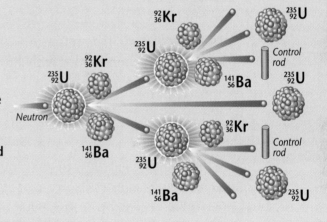

2 A collision with a neutron can cause a heavy nucleus to split into two lighter nuclei. This process is called nuclear fission. If the neutrons freed by one split can cause fission in other nuclei, a chain reaction can result. *What would happen if the chain reaction were uncontrolled? Why is fission a useful process?*

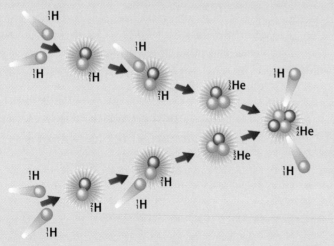

3 It's possible to fuse smaller nuclei into larger ones. Fusion of hydrogen into helium releases vast amounts of energy. *When does fusion take place in nature?*

Using Key Science Terms

artificial transmutation   fusion

chain reaction   transmutation

fission

Which science term describes each of the following processes?

1. Astatine-215 decays into bismuth-211.
2. Uranium-235 splits into lanthanum and rubidium.
3. Neutrons freed by the splitting of a plutonium nucleus cause other plutonium nuclei to split.
4. Two helium-3 nuclei combine to create helium-4 plus two free protons.
5. Molybdenum is bombarded with alpha particles to create technetium.

Understanding Ideas

Answer the following questions in your Journal using complete sentences.

1. What do electrical forces have to do with nuclear fission?
2. What causes a chain reaction?
3. How can a chain reaction be slowed?
4. What happens to the mass lost in a fission or fusion reaction?
5. Why is it necessary to fire alpha particles at extremely high energies to cause heavier elements to transmute?
6. How can a nucleus decay into an element with more protons?

Developing Skills

Use your understanding of the concepts developed in this chapter to answer each of the following questions.

1. **Concept Mapping** Create a spider concept map that describes nuclear reactions by summarizing the types, characteristics, and uses of the reactions described in the chapter. Use transmutation, artificial transmutation, fission, and fusion as the four main legs.

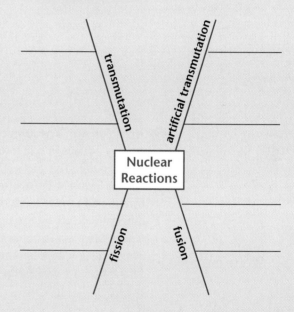

2. **Making and Using Graphs** Look closely at the table at the top of page 595. Do you see any relation between mass number and the half-life of the radioisotopes? Plot the mass numbers versus half-lives. Is it possible to predict the half-life of a radioisotope given its mass number?

Mass		
Radioisotope	Number	Half-Life
Radium	224	4 days
Thorium	234	24 days
Iodine	131	8 days
Bismuth	210	5 days
Polonium	210	138 days

3. Interpreting Data If you have a 10-gram sample of a radioactive element with a half-life of 91 days, how much of this element will remain after one year of radioactive decay?

Critical Thinking

In your Journal, *answer each of the following questions.*

1. How is a fire similar to a nuclear chain reaction?

2. Promethium-149 can transmute by the decay of a neutron and the ejection of an electron. What is the resulting element?

3. Write a nuclear reaction to show how radon-222 decays to give off an alpha particle and another element. What is the other element?

Problem Solving

Read the following problem and discuss your answers in a brief paragraph.

Kristine found an old alarm clock and put it next to her bed. During the night, Kristine was surprised by a greenish-white glow coming from the clock. Kristine did some research and found that the numerals and the hands of the clock were coated with a paint containing zinc sulfide and radium, a radioactive element with a half-life of 1600 years. The zinc sulfide emits little flashes of light when excited by radiation. These tiny flashes of light make the hands and numerals of the clock glow.

Will the glow of the hands change over time? Could uranium-238 have been used instead of radium? Explain your answer.

CONNECTING IDEAS

Discuss each of the following in a brief paragraph.

1. **Theme—Stability and Change** How can radioisotopes be used in the life and Earth sciences? Why are they such important tools?

2. **Theme—Energy** Compare and contrast the benefits and disadvantages of using nuclear reactions.

3. **A Closer Look** Design an events chain for the generation of electricity in a nuclear reactor. Begin with the bombarding neutrons and end with electric transmission lines.

4. **Life Science Connection** How can irradiation help combat the problem of starvation in third-world countries?

5. **Science and Society** Explain what effects biomagnification might have on society.

CHAPTER 19

THE solar SYSTEM

Did you ever wonder...

✓ **Where the solar system came from?**

✓ **What it's like on other planets?**

✓ **If there's life on other planets?**

Science Journal

Before you begin to study the solar system, think about these questions and answer them *in your Science Journal*. When you finish the chapter, compare your journal write-up with what you have learned.

Could it really happen to you? Probably not, but who doesn't like to dream about it? You suit up one day, board a spacecraft, and head out—way out. In a flash, you've left the atmosphere and entered the hushed, dark world of outer space.

After a while, you look back. There's the sun, shining steady and bright. Nine planets move around it. Some are huge, though not nearly as large as the sun. Others are tiny and pretty unimpressive. There's Earth, a small deep-blue globe with white, wispy clouds. Don't we Earthlings have a unique home in space? Yes, we do.

▶ *Once you read this chapter, you'll understand how special Earth is. Start your exploration with the activity on the next page.*

Uranus

Neptune

Jupiter

Explore! ACTIVITY

How do the different bodies that travel around the sun compare with one another?

Where can you start to make comparisons among objects that orbit the sun? You can start with careful observation and recording of observed differences.

What To Do

1. Using observable characteristics and the information in Appendix J on page 671, compare Earth with the other planets shown in the photographs on these two pages.

2. How does Earth compare in color? In shape? In size? Write your answers *in your Journal*.

Earth

Saturn

Venus

Images of the planets on these pages are not to scale.

The Solar System

19-1

Section Objectives

- Explain one hypothesis of how the solar system formed.
- Compare and contrast Earth with Mercury, Venus, and Mars.
- Relate studies of Venus and Mars to concerns about global warming and atmospheric ozone on Earth.

Key Terms

planet
solar system
terrestrial planets

A Star-Planet System

Have you ever looked past the treetops into the sky beyond the clouds and wondered what's out there? What have you observed in the sky? The first objects most people think of are the sun and the moon. Next, of course, are the stars—there are so many of them that it's easy to overlook other points of light in the night sky. These other points of light are planets. A **planet** is a body of matter that travels around a star in a fixed path called an orbit. Unlike stars, planets don't give off their own light. The planets we see in the night sky reflect sunlight.

The sun, the planets, and many smaller objects that travel around the sun make up the **solar system**. **Figure 19-1** will give you more information about the solar system and how the planets travel within it.

Figure 19-1

In a map of the solar system you can see the relative positions of planets and their relative distances from the sun. How many planets are there in our solar system? What seems to be unusual about the orbits of Neptune and Pluto?

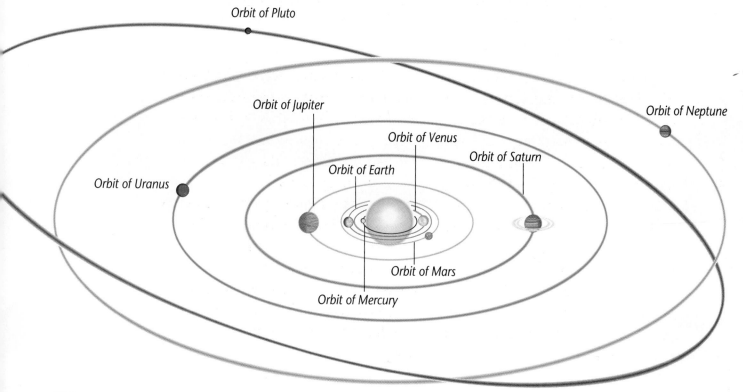

Orbit of Pluto

Orbit of Jupiter

Orbit of Venus

Orbit of Neptune

Orbit of Earth

Orbit of Saturn

Orbit of Uranus

Orbit of Mars

Orbit of Mercury

Formation of the Solar System

Throughout history, explanations have been offered to account for how the solar system was formed. According to one hypothesis today, shown in Figure 19-2, the solar system most likely formed more than 4.6 billion years ago from a slowly rotating cloud of dust and gas.

Figure 19-2

A About 5 billion years ago, the solar system was a slow, rotating cloud of dust particles and hydrogen and helium gases.

C Still later, some of the cloud material collapsed enough inward to form a newborn sun.

B Later, shock waves traveled through the cloud, causing it to shrink and spin more rapidly.

D Some time later, the solar system achieved its current arrangement.

The rotating cloud hypothesis helps explain why different types of planets are located where they are. For example, as planets near the sun formed, intense heat from the newly forming sun allowed only denser materials to condense and become solid. Icy materials would have been vaporized. The denser materials that remained behind were less abundant than the icy materials. This explains why the four planets nearest the sun are small and composed of dense, rocky material.

Materials vaporized by the thermal energy of the sun would have been pushed outward by solar winds. Huge gaseous planets formed farther from the sun, where the effect of the thermal energy and solar winds were less intense. Lighter gases and icy materials were able to condense along with some heavier materials.

You'll learn more about these two types of planets, their relative sizes, and their relative distances from the sun. Start by investigating the shape of a planet's orbit.

INVESTIGATE!

Orbits

You've learned that the planets travel around the sun along fixed paths called orbits. In this activity, you'll construct a model of a planetary orbit.

Problem
What's the shape of a planetary orbit?

Materials
thumbtacks or pins   metric ruler
string   pencil
cardboard   paper
    (21.5 cm x 28 cm)

Safety Precautions

Exercise care with thumbtacks or pins.

What To Do

1. Copy the data table *into your Journal*.

2. Place a blank sheet of paper on top of the cardboard and stick two thumbtacks or pins in the paper about 3 cm apart.

3. Tie a string into a circle with a circumference of about 15-20 cm. Loop the string around the tacks. As someone holds the tacks in place, place the pencil inside the loop and pull it taut.

Data and Observations			
Constructed Ellipse	d (cm)	L (cm)	e
1			
2			
3			
Earth's orbit			

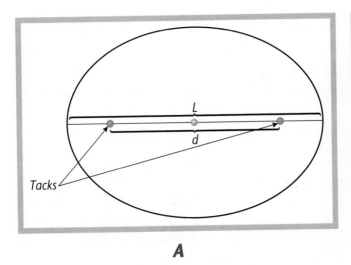

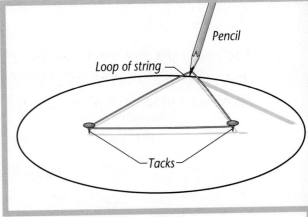

A

B

4 Keeping the string taut, move the pencil around the tacks until you have completed an elongated, closed curve, also known as an ellipse.

5 Repeat Steps 2 through 4 twice. First vary the distance between the tacks; then vary the circumference of the loop of string. Determine the effect of each change on the size and shape of the ellipse.

6 Planetary orbits are usually described in terms of eccentricity (e). You drew the ellipse around the two thumbtacks. The two points around which an ellipse is drawn are called the foci. The eccentricity of any ellipse is determined by dividing the distance between the foci (d) by the length of the major axis (L). See the diagram above.

7 Refer to Appendix J on page 671 to find the eccentricities of the planetary orbits.

8 Construct an ellipse with the same eccentricity as Earth's orbit.

Analyzing

1. What effect does a change in length of the string or distance between the tacks have on the ellipse?

2. Describe the shape of Earth's orbit. Where is the sun located within the orbit?

3. What are the eccentricities of the three ellipses you constructed?

Concluding and Applying

4. What must be done to the string or placement of tacks to decrease the eccentricity of an ellipse?

5. **Going Further** *Hypothesize* what might happen if Earth's orbit were more elliptical.

Motions of the Planets

In the Investigate you constructed a model of the path of planets around the sun. Planets move in a counter-clockwise direction around the sun.

For much of history, people thought that Earth was at the center of the universe. They were certain the sun, the moon, and planets were embedded in the surface of a large sphere that revolved around Earth. Ptolemy, an Egyptian astronomer, developed a different slant on this idea, as shown in **Figure 19-3**.

Copernicus, a Polish scientist, was the first to hypothesize that the planets, including Earth, orbit the sun. He published this revolutionary idea in 1543. As shown in **Figure 19-4**, Copernicus's model of the solar system had the planets traveling around the sun in circular orbits. Later observers discovered that certain planetary motions could not easily be explained by circular orbits. In the early 1600s, Johannes Kepler, a German mathematician, determined that planetary orbits were ellipses, and that the sun is offset from the exact center of an orbit. The orbit you constructed in the Investigate was in the shape of an ellipse.

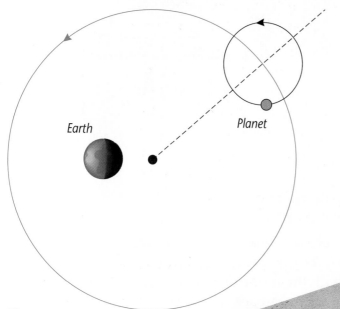

Figure 19-3

Ptolemy hypothesized that Earth was near the center of the universe and the planets moved around Earth in a complex orbit.

Figure 19-4

Copernicus changed people's view of the universe when he pointed out that Earth is not the center of the universe, but one of a number of planets that orbit the sun. This is a copy of Copernicus's original drawing of his theory.

Terrestrial Planets

Except for the fact that planets all orbit the sun, do they have much else in common? Let's compare Earth with its nearest planetary neighbors. Earth and its three nearest planetary neighbors have one thing in common: their surfaces are made up of solid rock. With the proper equipment, you could travel across their surfaces, collecting rock samples. Because of the size and composition of these planets, they are classified as Earth-like, or **terrestrial planets**.

■ Mercury

Mercury, Venus, Earth, and Mars make up the group of planets known as the terrestrial planets. Although Mercury is quite a bit smaller than the other members of this group, it is included because it has much more in common with Venus, Earth, and Mars than it does with the other planets of the solar system.

If you look back at **Figure 19-1** on page 598, you'll see that Mercury is the planet closest to the sun. It's the second smallest planet in diameter. Our first close look at Mercury came in 1974, when *Mariner 10* passed close to the planet and sent pictures back to Earth. As shown in **Figure 19-5**, the surface of Mercury looks much like the surface of Earth's moon.

Figure 19-5

Ⓐ Even from a great distance the craters on Mercury's surface are apparent.

Ⓑ Mercury's craters are similar to those of the moon. Because Mercury has a stronger gravitational pull than the moon, large walls do not form around the craters on Mercury. As a result, craters tend to be shallower on Mercury.

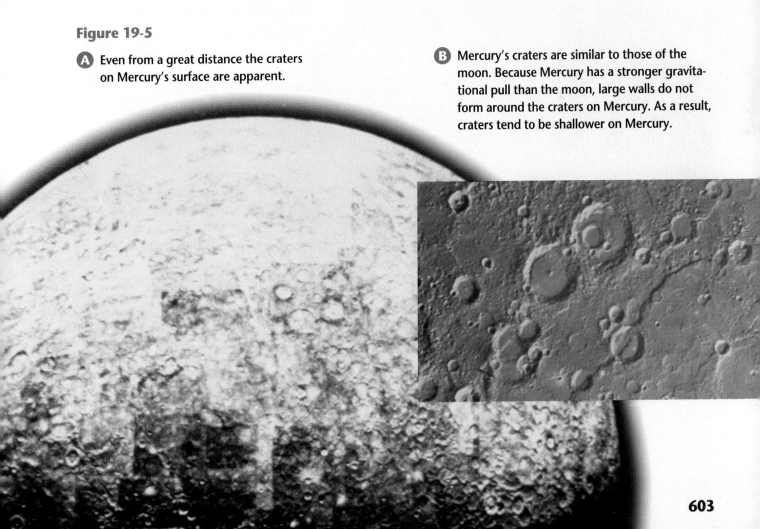

Because of its small mass, Mercury exerts a weak gravitational force compared to other planets. Thus, as you might expect, it has almost no atmosphere. And as you might also expect from its nearness to the sun, Mercury can get very hot. Daytime temperatures reach as high as 450°C. Mercury's thin atmosphere, however, allows thermal energy to radiate away from the planet; nighttime temperatures fall as low as -170°C.

Figure 19-6

Ⓐ Radar-imaging makes it possible for us to "see" through the clouds in Venus's atmosphere. The radar image below shows the surface of Venus.

■ Venus

Venus, which orbits the sun at an average distance of 108 million kilometers, is the second planet from the sun (See **Figure 19-1** on page 598). This planet is sometimes called Earth's twin because it is similar in diameter and mass to Earth. Venus has a thick blanket of dense clouds high up in the planet's atmosphere. These clouds contain sulfuric acid, which gives them a yellowish color.

Beneath this cloud layer lies an atmosphere made up mostly of carbon dioxide gas. This gas is much denser than the mixture of nitrogen and oxygen gases that makes up most of Earth's atmosphere. In fact, atmospheric pressure on the surface of Venus is 91 times greater than that exerted by Earth's atmosphere. You'd have to dive down nearly one kilometer in the ocean to experience pressure this great on Earth.

Ⓑ Radar images have shown us that Venus has landforms similar to those of Earth. This volcano is a good example.

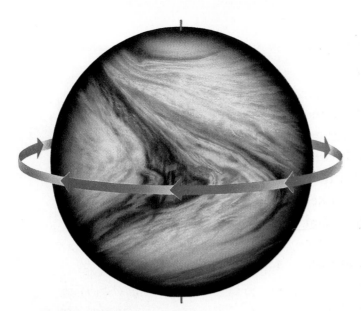

Figure 19-7

Venus rotates, or spins on its axis, from east to west. Most other planets in our solar system rotate from west to east.

The temperature on Venus's surface is 470°C! This temperature is high enough to melt lead. Compare this temperature with the highest temperature ever recorded on Earth, 58°C.

"Why is Venus so hot?" you ask. "Doesn't its cloud cover and dense atmosphere block out most of the sunlight?" You're right, clouds on Venus are so dense that only two percent of the sunlight that strikes the top of the clouds reaches Venus's surface. But don't forget the high percentage of carbon dioxide gas in the atmosphere. Carbon dioxide is one of the gases that contributes to the greenhouse effect. It acts something like the glass in a greenhouse. Like the glass, carbon dioxide traps the heat from solar radiation and holds it near the planet's surface. Hence, the temperature of the atmosphere rises higher and higher.

DID YOU KNOW?

Venus takes longer to rotate one complete turn than it does to complete one revolution around the sun. This means that a day on Venus is longer than its year.

Explore! ACTIVITY

How do the atmospheres of Venus, Earth, and Mars compare?

Venus, Earth, and Mars all have atmospheres that are quite different from one another. As you do this activity you'll find out how they differ.

What To Do

1. Study the data in this table.

2. Which planets have fairly similar atmospheres? Do all three planets have anything in common? Would you expect life as we know it to be present on Venus or Mars?

3. Answer the questions and explain your answers *in your Journal.*

Atmospheres of Terrestrial Planets					
Venus		**Earth**		**Mars**	
Gas	% of total	Gas	% of total	Gas	% of total
CO_2	96.5	CO_2	0.03	CO_2	95.0
N_2	3.5	N_2	78.1	N_2	2.7
O_2	0.002	O_2	20.9	O_2	0.15
H_2O	0.01	H_2O	0.05–4.0	H_2O	0.03

Mars

Mars is the fourth planet from the sun, orbiting the sun at an average distance of 228 million kilometers. Earth, which orbits the sun at an average distance of 150 million kilometers, is situated between Venus and Mars.

Much of the information we have about Mars came from the *Mariner 9* and *Viking* probes. In 1971, *Mariner 9* orbited Mars; in 1976, *Viking 1* and *2* landed on Mars. Knowledge gained from these probes changed our ideas about this planet completely.

Figure 19-8

The distinct red color of Mars is visible from Earth even without a telescope. This color comes from iron oxide in rocks on the surface of Mars.

Rehearsal for Mars

The first crewed landing on Mars will follow years of planning and practice. Astronauts will have to practice their roles and even their research activities many times before the launch. To do this, they will need to know exactly where they will be landing and what the area looks like.

This photograph of the surface of Mars was taken by a spacecraft that did not carry any astronauts.

■ Craggy, Barren Surface

The *Viking* probes sent back pictures of a reddish-colored, barren, rocky, windswept surface with many craters.

The *Viking* probes also revealed long channels on the surface of Mars. These channels look as if they were carved by flowing water at some time in Mars's past. Some of the information retrieved by the *Viking* missions is summarized in **Figure 19-9** on page 608.

■ Polar Ice Caps

Have you ever used dry ice? People place chunks of dry ice in water to make the foglike clouds that you see at concerts or plays. Dry ice is really frozen carbon dioxide. It's much colder than frozen water, and it's called dry ice because it doesn't melt to form

SKILLBUILDER

Interpreting Data

Use the information in Appendix J on page 671 to explain how Mars is like Earth. If you need help, refer to the **Skill Handbook** on page 690.

Exploring Mars by Robot

Robots with cameras and sensors will be sent to explore possible landing sites. These robots will be controlled by people on Earth and will send back pictures of the Martian surface along with information about its atmosphere.

Remote Sample Retrieval

A mission specialist and assistant will operate remote controls that will enable the robot surface probe to move around on the Martian surface. A second mission specialist will operate the Remote Sample Retrieval (RSR) System and collect samples for study. A successful mission is one in which the lander explores all parts of the Martian surface within range, without colliding with boulders or falling into craters. A successful mission also involves retrieving rock samples from the planet's surface and returning them to Earth for study.

After the mission is complete, scientists and astronauts will study the photos and rock samples. This information will be used to help prepare a crewed mission to Mars.

Robots will be useful in preparing for human exploration of Mars.

What Do You Think?

Discuss the difficulties of exploring another planet. Talk about the steps needed to make sure everything is successful.

a liquid. It just changes back to carbon dioxide gas. The northern polar ice cap on Mars is made up of frozen water and carbon dioxide. During the Martian summer, the carbon dioxide vaporizes, and the size of the polar cap decreases considerably. However, the southern polar cap of Mars changes little throughout the Martian year.

The surface of Mars is quite cold, mostly because the planet is so far from the sun. Actual temperatures range from a high of about -20°C to a low of -140°C.

■ Dead and Dusty

While some scientists have suggested that life may have existed on Mars long ago, today the surface of Mars is thought to be completely lifeless and lacks even the simplest organic molecules. Lack of ozone in Mars's atmosphere could be one reason for no life on the planet. Ozone absorbs harmful ultraviolet rays from the sun. Without this protection, organic molecules cannot survive.

By now, Earth looks pretty good. Earth is the only planet where the range of surface temperatures allows water to exist in all three of its physical states. The presence of liquid water is essential for life. Also, Earth has a great enough mass to hold an atmosphere, which is also essential to life.

Figure 19-9

Valles Marineris

A Valles Marineris is Mars's largest canyon. If placed on Earth, Valles Marineris would stretch from New York City to Los Angeles. How might this large canyon have been formed?

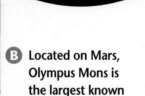

B Located on Mars, Olympus Mons is the largest known volcano in the solar system. It is about three times taller than the tallest mountain on Earth. If this volcano were on Earth, its base would stretch from Washington, D.C. to Boston.

check your UNDERSTANDING

1. Explain the current hypothesis of how the solar system formed.
2. In what ways are Venus, Earth, and Mars similar? In what ways are they different?
3. Why are temperatures higher on Venus than on Mercury, which is much closer to the sun?
4. **Apply** Make a table showing the important characteristics of the Earth-like planets.

19-2 The Outer Planets

The Gaseous Giants

Besides the four planets closest to the sun, there are five other planets in the solar system. These other planets are in orbits beyond that of Mars. How do these planets compare with the terrestrial planets?

Section Objectives

■ Compare the gaseous giant planets with the terrestrial planets.

■ Recognize that Pluto differs from the other planets and is therefore not classified with either group.

Key Terms

gaseous giant planets

Explore! ACTIVITY

Solar System Facts and Figures

O ne way to learn about planets is to analyze information collected by other scientists. Here's your chance to learn about planets.

What To Do

1. Use Appendix J on page 671 to compare each planet's size with Earth's. What is the largest planet in the solar system?

 2. Distances within the solar system are often measured in astronomical units, AU for short. Earth's average distance from the sun is 1 AU. How many AUs is Neptune from the sun?

3. Compare the periods of revolution and the periods of rotation for the planets. On which planet is a period of rotation longer than a period of revolution?

4. Record your answers *in your Journal*.

You've visited four planets so far. Now you'll leave the terrestrial planets and travel to the gaseous giants.

The **gaseous giant planets** are huge, low-density planets composed mainly of gases. Much of what we know about these planets was learned from the *Voyager* space probes. Launched in 1977, *Voyager 1* and *Voy-* *ager 2* provided a wealth of new information about Jupiter, Saturn, Uranus, and Neptune. Begin your travel out to the far planets by making a model in the Investigation on the following pages.

SKILLBUILDER

Recognizing Cause and Effect

Look at the figures for period of revolution and average distance to the sun for the planets in Appendix J on page 671. How are these two aspects of a planet related? If you need help, refer to the **Skill Handbook** on page 684.

DESIGN YOUR OWN
INVESTIGATION

Distances in the Solar System

The distances between planets — and between planets and the sun — vary considerably throughout the solar system. In this activity, make a scale model of the solar system and use it to discover how these distances are related.

Preparation

Problem

How are interplanetary distances related?

Form a Hypothesis

As a group, review the information in Appendix J on page 671. Then form a hypothesis about how you would model the solar system using scale dimensions and the materials listed below.

Objectives

- Make a table of scale distances that will represent planetary distances to be used in a model of the solar system.
- Make a model of the distances between the sun and the planets of the solar system
- Infer how interplanetary distances are related.

Materials

string
adding machine tape
meterstick
scissors
pencil
construction paper

Safety Precautions

Take care when using scissors.

Plan the Experiment

1 As a group, agree upon and write out your hypothesis statement.

2 Design a table of scale distances to be used in your model.

3 Write a description of how you will build your model, explaining how it will demonstrate relative distances between and among the sun and the planets of the solar system.

4 How will you summarize your data? If you need a data table, design one now *in your Science Journal*.

Check the Plan

1 Read over your model description to make sure that all steps are in a logical order.

2 Do any parts of your model need to be constructed before the overall model is produced?

3 How will you determine whether your model successfully demonstrates the large distances between and among the sun and planets in the solar system?

4 Make sure your teacher approves your experiment before you proceed.

5 Carry out your experiment. Record your observations.

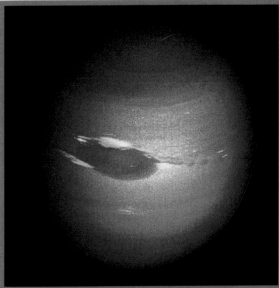

The planet Neptune as photographed by *Voyager 2.*

Analyze and Conclude

1. **Use Numbers** Explain how scale distance is determined.

2. **Compare and Contrast** Compare distances between the outer planets, then compare distances between the inner planets. Summarize how the distances within each group compares to the group's distance from the sun.

3. **Formulate Models** In addition to scale distances, what other information would you need to construct an exact scale model of the solar system?

Going Further

Proxima Centauri, the closest star to the solar system, is about 40 trillion (40 × 10¹²) km from the sun. Using a scale of 10 cm = 1 AU, calculate the length of tape you would need to include this star on your scale model.

Jupiter

Jupiter is larger than all the other planets put together and contains more than twice their total mass. The planet is surrounded by strong magnetic and gravitational fields.

Jupiter is composed mainly of gaseous and liquid hydrogen and helium, with smaller amounts of ammonia, methane, and water vapor. Because of its strong gravity, the atmosphere of hydrogen and helium gases may become a liquid ocean as you travel deeper into the planet. Below this ocean is a solid rocky core about the size of Earth. The only part of Jupiter that has been seen is its outer covering of clouds. The *Voyager* probes and later, the *Galileo* spacecraft provided vivid pictures of bands of red, white, tan, and brown clouds. Within these clouds are continuous storms of swirling gas. The most spectacular storm is the Great Red Spot, which was first seen through a telescope in 1664. Jupiter also has faint dust rings around it.

Sixteen moons revolve around Jupiter. Four of them are quite large. Io is the closest large moon to the surface of the planet. Ganymede, another moon, is the largest satellite in the solar system. It's larger than the planet Mercury. Examine **Figure 19-10** to learn more about these larger moons.

Figure 19-10

Moons of Jupiter

Europa
Rocky interior is covered by a 100 km thick ice crust, which has a network of cracks, indicating tectonic activity.

Callisto
Has a heavily cratered ice-rock crust several hundred km thick. Crust surrounds a water or ice mantle around a rocky core.

Ganymede

Io
The most volcanically active object in the solar system. Sulfur lava gives it its distinctive red and orange color.

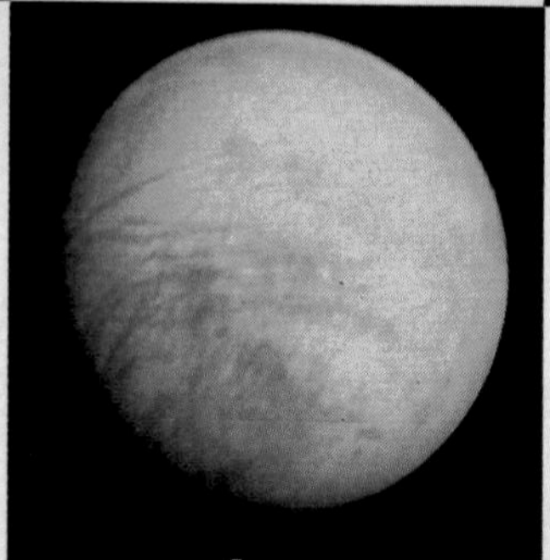

Io

Ganymede
Has an ice crust about 100 km thick, covered with grooves. Crust surrounds a 900 km thick slushy mantle of water and ice. Has a rocky core.

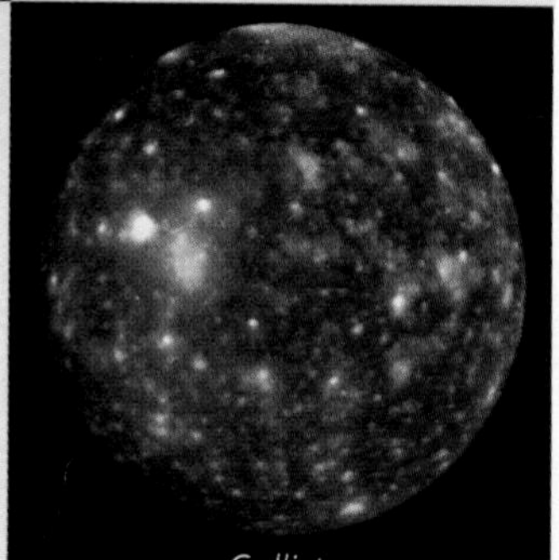

Europa

Callisto

Saturn

Saturn is the second largest planet in the solar system, but it has the lowest density. If Saturn were placed in water, it would float. Saturn's structure is similar to that of Jupiter. Its atmosphere contains the same gases. Below the atmosphere is an ocean of liquid helium and hydrogen that surrounds a small rocky core. Look at **Figure 19-11** to see what Saturn looks like.

Saturn is circled by several broad rings, each of which is made up of hundreds of smaller, narrower rings. Each ring is composed of millions of particles ranging in size from specks of dust to chunks of rock several meters in diameter. Saturn also has at least 20 moons orbiting it. The largest of these, Titan, is larger than the planet Mercury. Titan is surrounded by a dense atmosphere of nitrogen, argon, and methane, and it may have organic molecules on its surface.

Figure 19-11

A Saturn is the second largest planet in the solar system. In addition to its rings, it has at least 20 moons.

B Amateur astronomers and the Hubble Space Telescope photographed this rapidly growing "white spot" on Saturn in the early 1990s. What do you think this white spot might be?

How Do We Know?

Planetary Rings

Images sent back from space probes of Saturn have shown that we can see through the rings, indicating that they are made up of many individual particles.

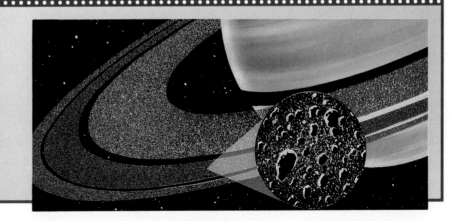

Uranus

The next stop on our space journey is Uranus, the seventh planet from the sun. Uranus is a large, gaseous planet with 15 moons and a system of thin, dark rings. Its atmosphere is composed of hydrogen, helium, and methane. Methane gives the planet its blue-green color. Beneath its atmosphere, Uranus probably has a liquid mantle surrounding a rocky core.

Uranus has a very high degree of tilt to its axis of rotation. **Figure 19-12** shows you this unusual feature.

98°

Figure 19-12

Ⓐ Uranus was first observed and described in 1781. Space probes have allowed us to collect much more information about the planet.

Ⓑ Uranus has an axial tilt of about 98°. Compare that with Earth's axial tilt of about 23.5°.

Physics
CONNECTION

Out Beyond Pluto

What do we know of the outer reaches of our solar system? What's out there beyond Pluto, the ninth planet? And how do we know?

Is There a Tenth Planet?

No, probably not. The best evidence of an unknown planet would be an unusual variation in the orbit of a known planet. In fact, that's how both Neptune and Pluto were found. After the seventh planet, Uranus, was located in 1781, astronomers who studied Uranus's orbit were puzzled. The orbit had a wobble in it that they couldn't explain. Was there an eighth planet whose gravitational force was affecting the orbit of Uranus? There was. In 1846 it was discovered and named Neptune. But the observed orbit of Uranus still didn't match its calculated orbit, even when Neptune was taken into account. Astronomers started looking for another unknown planet. In 1930 Pluto was discovered.

Is There Another Asteroid Belt?

Yes, there may be. Already one object orbiting beyond Pluto has been found and named 1992 QBI. Astronomers suggest that it's made mostly of ice and measures about 200

Neptune

The outermost of the gaseous giant planets is Neptune. Neptune's atmosphere and structure are much like those of Uranus. Neptune also has a system of rings that varies in thickness.

Neptune has at least eight moons, of which Triton is the most interesting. Triton has a thin atmosphere composed mainly of nitrogen gas; large geysers have been observed on its surface.

Neptune is normally the eighth planet from the sun. However, Pluto's orbit is so elliptical that it passes Neptune's orbit so that Pluto is sometimes closer to the sun than Neptune. In fact, Pluto is currently closer and will remain so until 1999.

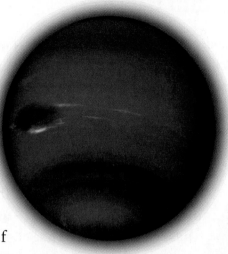

Figure 19-13

The "great dark spot" in the Southern Hemisphere of Neptune is interpreted as a storm, similar to the Great Red Spot of Jupiter.

kilometers across. Data from the Hubble Space Telescope indicate the presence of the Kuiper belt. This belt is thought to be a vast disk of icy comets near Neptune's orbit.

Where Does Our Solar System End?

Scientists have a name for the boundary between local space—space that contains our solar system—and interstellar space—the space between solar systems. They call the boundary the heliopause, and they call the space it encloses the heliosphere. Picture the heliosphere as an envelope of gas, dust, and radiation emitted by our sun. The heliopause is where this envelope ends. Thanks to data

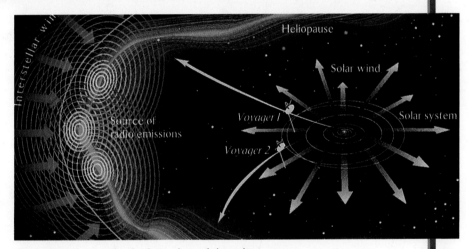

The heliopause marks the boundary of the solar system.

sent back from the two *Voyager* spacecraft, astronomers can now calculate approximately how big the envelope is. They expect the heliopause to be found about 11 billion miles from the sun.

What Do You Think?

If you were piloting a spacecraft through the solar system outward from our sun, how would you be able to tell when you had crossed the heliopause? Think of some ways the data from your instruments would change at that boundary.

Pluto and Charon

Figure 19-14

An image of Pluto and Charon from the Hubble Space Telescope.

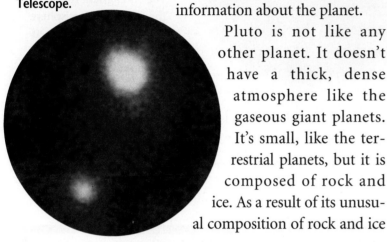

No space probes have passed near Pluto. Scientists used Neptune's gravity to deflect *Voyager* away from Pluto and toward Triton. However, photographs from the Hubble Space Telescope have provided us with some information about the planet.

Pluto is not like any other planet. It doesn't have a thick, dense atmosphere like the gaseous giant planets. It's small, like the terrestrial planets, but it is composed of rock and ice. As a result of its unusual composition of rock and ice and its small size Pluto is not considered either a gaseous giant or a terrestrial planet. The only thing Pluto has in common with some other planets is that it has a moon, Charon. Charon's diameter is one half of Pluto's, and its orbit is so close to Pluto that the two bodies can be thought of as a double planet. This leads to a very unusual pattern of rotation and revolution as shown in **Figure 19-15**.

So far, you've seen the terrestrial planets and the gaseous giants. That just about does it for the solar system, right? Well, think again as you move into the next section to study other objects in the solar system.

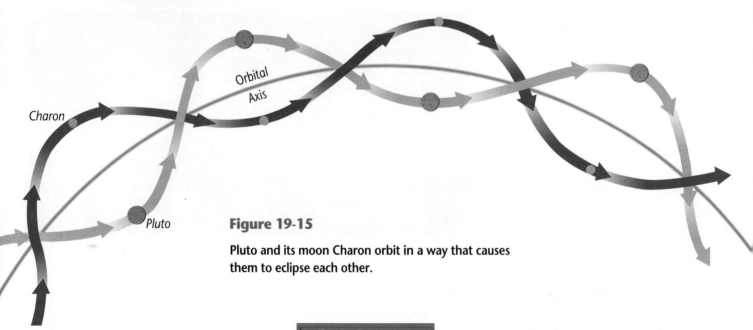

Figure 19-15

Pluto and its moon Charon orbit in a way that causes them to eclipse each other.

check your UNDERSTANDING

1. Compare and contrast the gaseous giant planets and the terrestrial planets.
2. How is Pluto different from other planets?
3. **Apply** If you had to stop during a space flight, which would make a better landing point, Saturn or its rings? Why?

Other Objects in the Solar System

Comets

Except for the planets and their satellites, perhaps the best known objects in the solar system are comets. A **comet** is a large chunk of ice, dust, frozen gases, and rock fragments that moves through space. **Figure 19-16** shows more about the structure and behavior of comets.

Where do comets come from? Most astronomers hypothesize that comets originate in an icy cloud that surrounds the solar system beyond the orbit of Pluto. This birthplace of comets is called the Oort cloud after the Dutch astronomer Jan Oort, who proposed the presence of this cloud. According to one hypothesis, a chunk of icy material is pulled from the cloud by a passing star. The material is captured by the sun's gravity and pulled toward it, producing a comet. Another belt of comets, the Kuiper belt, may exist near Neptune.

Figure 19-16

A Which way does the tail of a comet always point? When is the tail of a comet largest? When is it smallest?

Sun

Dust tail

Dust tail

Coma

Ion tail

Nucleus

B Halley's Comet orbits the sun every 75-79 years. When it appeared in 1910, it was spectacular. When it appeared in 1986, it was difficult to see.

C The comet's coma, a glowing cloud of gas that surrounds the comet's rock nucleus, forms as the comet approaches the sun. The tails form when particles from the sun push gases away from the coma. A comet has two tails—one dust tail, and one ion tail.

Asteroids

An **asteroid** is a large chunk of rock traveling through space. As shown in **Figure 19-17** most asteroids are located in an area between the orbits of Mars and Jupiter known as the asteroid belt. The asteroids in this belt may be material that might have combined into another planet were it not for the strong influence of Jupiter's gravity. Some of the larger asteroids have been thrown out of the belt and are now scattered throughout the solar system. It's likely that many asteroids have been captured by planetary gravity to become moons of the planets.

Most asteroids in the asteroid belt are about 1 kilometer or less in diameter. The largest asteroid, Ceres, is 940 kilometers in diameter.

Not all asteroids are found in the asteroid belt. Large asteroids pass close to Earth from time to time. In 1972, an asteroid estimated to be about 10 meters in diameter and weighing more than 1000 tons passed within 60 kilometers of Earth's surface.

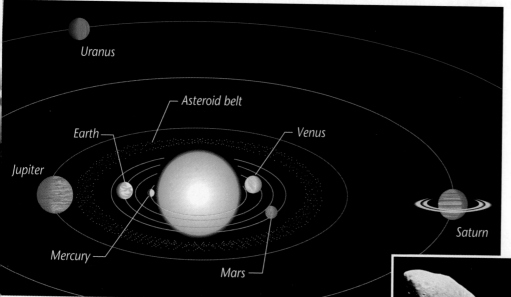

Figure 19-17

A Most asteroids orbit the sun in a belt between Jupiter and Mars. Do you think "runaway" asteroids could be responsible for some of the surface features that appear on many of our planets? Explain.

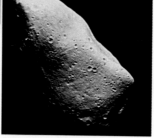

Gaspra

B Gaspra is one of the larger asteroids in the asteroid belt.

How Do We Know?

How large are asteroids?

Most of the asteroids in the solar system are too small and too distant to be observed and measured with conventional Earth-based telescopes. Astronomers can use the amount of thermal radiation given off by asteroids to determine their size, much in the same way as they use the same kind of radiation to measure the surface temperatures of planets.

Meteoroids, Meteors, and Meteorites

While the space between planets is mostly empty, space does contain millions of solid particles. Most of these particles come from comet nuclei that have broken up or collisions that have caused asteroids to break up. These small pieces of rock moving through space are then called meteoroids. Meteoroids range in size from grains of sand to huge fragments of rock.

Sometimes, a meteoroid enters Earth's gravitational field and is pulled toward Earth's surface. When a meteoroid enters the atmosphere, it becomes a **meteor**. Friction causes the meteor to glow as it streaks across the sky.

Most meteors burn up completely in Earth's atmosphere. However, occasionally a meteor survives and strikes Earth's surface. A meteor that strikes Earth's surface is called a **meteorite**. A few large meteorites have produced enormous craters on Earth's surface, such as the one shown in **Figure 19-18**.

Comets, meteoroids, and asteroids are probably all composed of material that formed early in the history of the solar system. Thus, a study of meteorites is also a study of the materials in comets and asteroids. Scientists study the structure and composition of these space objects in order to learn what the solar system was like long ago. Such knowledge could help us understand the formation and development of Earth and its relationship to other objects in the solar system.

Figure 19-18

This crater was formed when a meteorite struck the ground in Arizona. Impacts of this size are relatively rare. They happen only once in hundreds of thousands or millions of years.

check your UNDERSTANDING

1. How does a comet distant from the sun differ from one that is close to the sun?
2. Compare and contrast comets, meteoroids, and asteroids.
3. **Apply** Why are some asteroids no longer in the asteroid belt?

Science and Society

Will Humans or Robots Explore Mars?

Space scientists today are beginning to talk about sending astronauts to Mars. But talk of resuming piloted exploration has started a hot debate among those who believe humans should explore space and those who think space probes can do the job as well as humans.

Space Probes

Those in favor of using space probes say the cost of exploration would be much less than piloted exploration. They also point out that astronauts will not have to risk their lives if space probes are used.

Living In Space—Health Problems

Astronauts who survive a trip to another planet might suffer the health problems that have been suffered by astronauts in Earth orbit. For example, bones and muscles become weaker within a few days. Just imagine how weak they would be after a three-year trip to Mars!

Other health problems also result from prolonged weightlessness. The kidneys can eliminate too much fluid from the body. This could cause dehydration in an astronaut.

Being in Space on Earth

You may also wonder how a machine could explore as well on another planet as a human could.

In the future, scientists on Earth will be able to wear goggles and data gloves that will allow them to see what the probe sees and to control the probe. Earth-bound scientists would be able to experience the probe's visit almost as though they were there themselves.

Piloted Missions

Many people firmly believe humans, not robots, should be the space travelers. Dr. Carl Sagan, an astronomy professor, admits that robots could do the work of humans on Mars, but he feels that we should conduct piloted exploration if there is enough money to do so. One reason he favors this is because it would "provide an exciting, adventure-rich, and hopeful future for young people."

*inter*NET CONNECTION

NASA's Center for Mars Exploration website has current information on all aspects of Mars exploration. What are current plans for piloted and robotic missions to Mars? What are the technological and dollar limits that have been placed on such missions?

SCIFACTS

Did a fragmented comet strike Earth?

AREA SHOWN

10° 20° 30° Mediterranean Sea

AFRICA

Egypt

Red Sea

30°

Libya

Impact Area

20°

Chad

Sudan

Niger

0   500 km

0   500 mi.

Nigeria

10°N

Cameroon

Atlantic Ocean

10°W   0°

AREA SHOWN

NASA photo

Aorounga crater

Iowa

U N I T E D   S T A T E S

MISSOURI

ILLINOIS

Indiana

KANSAS

Hazel Green

Avon

Hicks

Weableau

Kentucky

Rose   Decaturville

Furnace Creek

Crooked Creek

0   100 km

0   100 mi.

Oklahoma   Arkansas

When remnants of comet Shoemaker-Levy crashed into Jupiter in 1994, pieces of the comet peppered Jupiter for more than a week. The event left a chain of disturbances visible from Earth. Astronomers were amazed at the time, but now they believe cascades of falling star stuff may not be so rare.

NASA geologists think they have found evidence of a similar episode here on Earth in the African nation of Chad. Scientists have known about the Aorounga crater for years, but radar images from orbiting satellites have uncovered two other features beneath desert sands nearby that also may be craters.

The two newest crater candidates were dubbed Aorounga Central and Aorounga North. Both are about 17 kilometers wide. If they are craters, they would have been caused by individual pieces of falling debris about 2 kilometers in diameter that hit Earth in rapid succession about 360 million years ago.

Scientists are also investigating what other satellite photos suggest may be another chain of impact craters running across Kansas, Missouri, and Illinois. Similar lines of craters also have been seen on the surface of Callisto, one of Jupiter's largest moons.

Science Journal

In your Science Journal, write about what might happen if a fragmented comet were to strike the Earth today.

Teens in SCIENCE

The Space Station Project

Candace Kendrick was still in high school when she began working on NASA's space station project at Johnson Space Center. Although she was just 17 years old, she had already put in years of hard work in math and science, her favorite subjects.

Apprentice Engineer

Candace was one of 17 students chosen to participate in the space center's eight-week summer program called SHARP (Summer High School Apprenticeship Program). The NASA program selects young people to work with engineers and scientists on projects at space research facilities in the United States.

In her NASA job, Candace studied ways of calibrating electrical instruments on the Space Station Freedom. "The calibration devices at NASA are great," she says. "But they're too big and generate too much heat to put on the already crowded space station."

Her project was to find ways to overcome heat and size problems. She also had to find ways to prevent electromagnetic interference among instruments aboard the station.

Calibration Problems

From day to day, she calibrated electrical instruments, such as voltmeters and ohmmeters. She spent her lunch hour studying at the library. She also learned from NASA electrical engineers and electricians.

The effort paid off for Candace, who wrote a research paper recommending use of a diode to calibrate space station equipment. Her report was well received by NASA personnel, and she hopes to participate in future NASA programs for college students.

Candace's friends describe her as serious and meticulous, and Candace agrees. "I really hate surface learning. That's one thing about physics and math. If you don't understand one thing, it's hard to go on to the next thing."

Her advice to those who want to follow in her footsteps? "Concentrate on math. If you really want to go into engineering, math is really important. It's probably important for anything you go into, but it's really important for engineering. And take the honors classes because they'll help you a lot, even if it's scary."

What Do You Think?

What specialized courses should you take to pursue the career of your dreams? In what ways can you use the courses you are taking now to help you in the future?

Science Journal

Review the statements below about the big ideas presented in this chapter, and answer the questions. Then, reread your answers to the Did You Ever Wonder questions at the beginning of the chapter. *In your Science Journal*, write a paragraph about how your understanding of the big ideas in the chapter has changed.

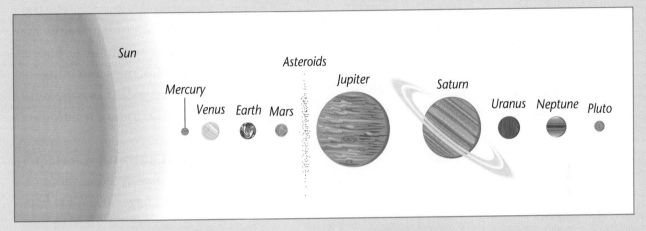

Sun   Asteroids   Jupiter   Saturn
Mercury   Venus Earth Mars   Uranus Neptune Pluto

1 The major components of the solar system are the sun and the nine planets that revolve around the sun. *What is the shape of the orbital path of planets?*

2 The planets are classified into two groups—Earth-like, or terrestrial, planets, and gaseous giant planets. *Why might gaseous giant planets have more moons than terrestrial planets?*

3 Scientists hypothesize that the solar system formed more than 4.6 billion years ago from a huge rotating cloud of gas and dust that condensed to form the sun and planets. *How does the formation of the solar system explain observed orbits of planets?*

4 Comets and asteroids are other important components of the solar system. *How might the position of the asteroid belt explain how it originated?*

Using Key Science Terms

asteroid   meteorite

comet   planet

gaseous giant planets   solar system

meteor   terrestrial planets

1. Distinguish between a meteor and a meteorite.
2. What are some similarities and differences between asteroids and comets?
3. What are the four terrestrial planets and what do they have in common?
4. What are the four gaseous planets and what do they have in common?
5. How is a planet related to a solar system?

Understanding Ideas

Answer the following questions in your Journal *using complete sentences.*

1. Why are surface probes or landings on Jupiter or Saturn unlikely events?
2. Why is the surface temperature on Venus so much higher than on Earth?
3. What is an asteroid belt?
4. Compare and contrast the characteristics of Neptune and Uranus.
5. Which planet is presently closer to the sun, Neptune or Pluto? Will this change? Why or why not?

Developing Skills

Use your understanding of the concepts developed in this chapter to answer each of the following questions.

1. **Concept Mapping** Develop an illustration that will help you organize information about the solar system including: relative position of planets and other objects, relative distances from the sun, relative sizes, and periods of rotation and revolution.
2. **Comparing and Contrasting** Refer to Appendix J again as you did in the Explore activity on page 609. What happens to the average orbital speed of the planets as they get farther away from the sun? Are these differences related to the sizes of the planets? Explain.
3. **Making Models** After making a model of distances in the solar system to scale in the Investigate on page 610, develop a scale to make a model of the planets (the scale will have to be different) and add the number of known satellites around each planet. Cut out the planets and satellites and attach them to the adding machine tape model of the distances between planets. Do any of the distances between planets or planet sizes surprise you? Is this an accurate scale model of the solar system? Explain.

Critical Thinking

In your Journal, *answer each of the following questions.*

1. Why are scientists concerned about the possible destruction of the ozone layer of Earth's atmosphere?

2. We are able to see Mercury and Venus only in the early morning or early evening sky. Study the diagram below. Then explain why we cannot see these two planets at midnight.

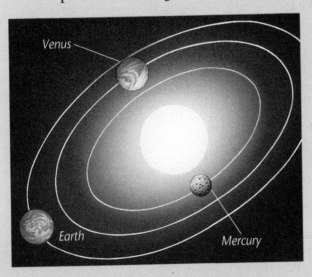

3. Why is the sun's gravitational acceleration so much stronger than that of any of the planets?

4. What might happen if an object the size of Io passed close to Earth?

Problem Solving

Read the following problem and discuss your answers in a brief paragraph.

A new planet has been discovered and you have been asked to calculate information on its speed and orbit.

1. What factors do you need to know in order to calculate the average speed of the planet along its orbit?

2. If you know the average orbital speed of the planet and its period of revolution, how could you calculate the length of its orbit?

CONNECTING IDEAS

Discuss each of the following in a brief paragraph.

1. **Theme—Systems and Interactions** Assuming the rotating cloud theory correctly describes the formation of the solar system, how might it relate to the Oort cloud?

2. **Theme—Scale and Structure** How is it possible for a day to be longer than a year?

3. **A Closer Look** Why might astronauts need to rehearse what they might do while on a planet?

4. **Science and Society** Do you think it will ever be possible to change the environment on Mars so that it can support a colony? Why or why not?

CHAPTER 20

STARS AND GALAXIES

Did you ever wonder...

✓ Why stars twinkle?
✓ How long the sun will last?
✓ Where you are in the universe?

Science Journal

Before you begin to study about stars and galaxies, think about these questions and answer them *in your Science Journal.* When you finish the chapter, compare your journal write-up with what you have learned.

When you look up at the sky at night, what do you see? Perhaps the blinking red lights on a jumbo jet, or the thin trail of a meteor as it streaks across the sky. How many stars can you see?

On a dark, clear night, away from street lamps, headlights, and house lights, you might see over 3000 stars. Many more can be seen with a telescope.

▶ *In the next activity, explore the night sky and find out how much you can see.*

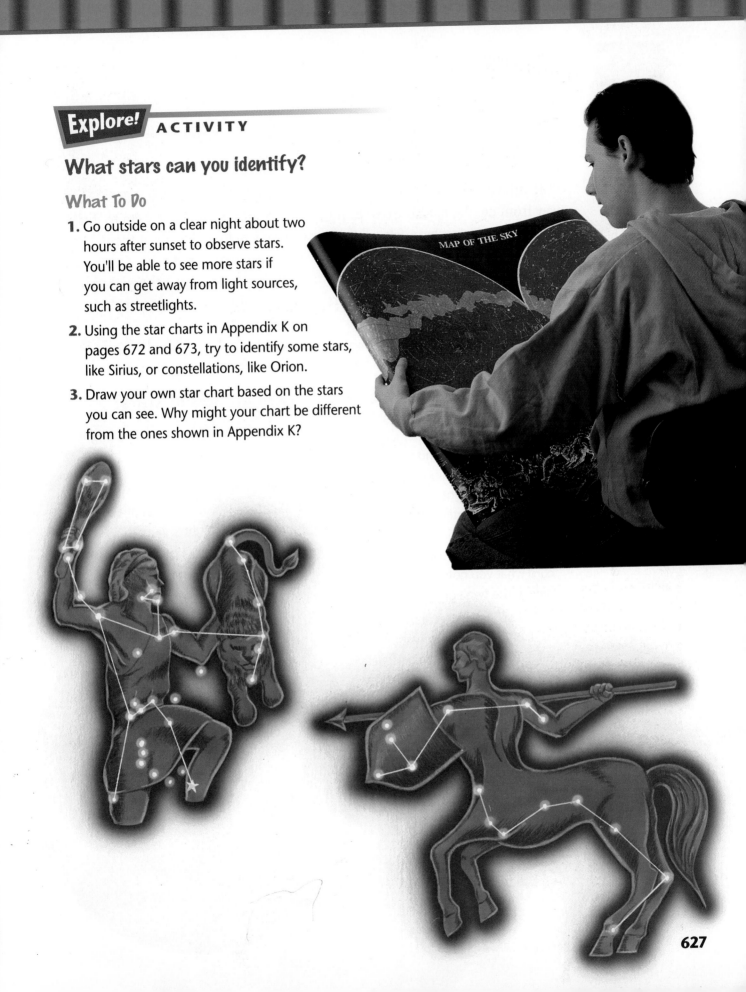

Explore! ACTIVITY

What stars can you identify?

What To Do

1. Go outside on a clear night about two hours after sunset to observe stars. You'll be able to see more stars if you can get away from light sources, such as streetlights.

2. Using the star charts in Appendix K on pages 672 and 673, try to identify some stars, like Sirius, or constellations, like Orion.

3. Draw your own star chart based on the stars you can see. Why might your chart be different from the ones shown in Appendix K?

MAP OF THE SKY

20-1 Stars

Section Objectives

- Compare and contrast a star's actual brightness with how bright it appears from Earth.
- Explain the process by which a star produces energy.
- Relate the temperature of a star to its color.

Key Terms

star
nebula
supernova
light-year

The Brightness of Stars

If you've ever lain down in a field away from city lights and gazed at the night sky, you may have felt what it's like to be covered with a blanket of stars. Above you lie thousands of twinkling points of light. Some stars are bright, like holiday lights, while others are so faint they seem to disappear if you look directly at them. Have you ever wondered why some stars look brighter than others? Explore this question in the next activity.

Find Out! ACTIVITY

What factors affect the observable brightness of stars?

What To Do

1. Have a classmate stand at the back of the classroom holding one small and one large flashlight (for example, a penlight and a utility flashlight). Turn off the overhead lights and have your classmate turn on the flashlights. Record what you notice about the brightness of the two lights *in your Journal*.

2. Have two classmates stand at the back of the classroom holding identical flashlights with new batteries. Have them turn on the flashlights. Turn off the overhead lights. Compare the brightness of the two flashlights. Next, have one of these classmates approach you with a lighted flashlight. What do you notice about the comparative brightness of the two lights now?

3. Ask the student closest to you to exchange his or her flashlight for the

penlight. Again, compare the brightness of the two lights.

Conclude and Apply

1. What are two factors that affect the brightness of light?

2. How might these factors relate to the brightness of stars?

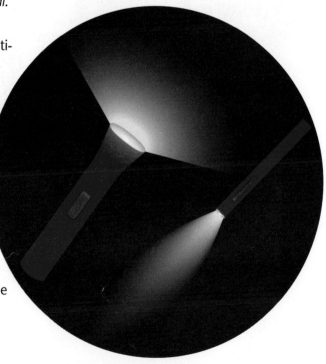

In the Find Out activity, you discovered how size and distance can affect how bright an object appears. The same is true of stars. One star can appear brighter than another simply because it is larger than the other star.

One star can also appear brighter than another because it is closer to Earth, just as in Step 2, when one of two identical flashlights looked brighter because it was moved closer to you. However, the closest stars aren't necessarily the brightest stars, as you observed in Step 3.

In order to understand the brightness of stars, you need to know what a star is. A **star** is a hot, glowing sphere of gas that produces energy by fusion, a process you learned about in Chapter 18. Some stars produce more energy and are therefore hotter than other stars of the same size. The hotter the star, the greater the energy, and therefore the greater the amount of light the star produces; just as the light from a flashlight with new batteries is brighter than the light from a flashlight with weak batteries.

■ Actual vs. Apparent Brightness

Because of the variables of star size, distance, and temperature, astronomers talk about the brightness of stars in two ways: actual brightness and apparent brightness.

The apparent brightness of a star is the amount of light received on Earth from the star. A star's apparent brightness is affected by its size and temperature as well as its distance from Earth. For example, a small, cool star can appear quite bright in the sky if it's close to Earth while a large, hot star can appear dim if it's far away. Apparent brightness can even be temporarily affected by conditions in Earth's atmosphere such as dust and moisture.

Look at **Figure 20-1**, for example. The apparent brightness of Sirius is greater than the apparent brightness of Rigel. In fact, Rigel is a much bigger and hotter star, but it's farther away from Earth. If the two stars were the same distance from Earth, Rigel would be much brighter.

Figure 20-1

Ⓐ Sirius appears as one of the brightest stars in the sky.

Ⓑ Although it's actually much bigger and brighter than Sirius, Rigel is almost 100 times farther away than Sirius, and so it does not appear as bright.

Connect to...

Physics

The stars closest to Earth are much farther away than the sun is. Nearby stars appear to change position throughout the year or exhibit parallax. Draw a diagram that helps define parallax.

The Origin of Stars

A star forms from a large cloud of gas and dust called a **nebula**. Look at the nebula in **Figure 20-2**. How would you describe its shape?

Even though gas and dust particles are very small, they exert a gravitational force on each other just as all matter does. As the gravitational force

Figure 20-2

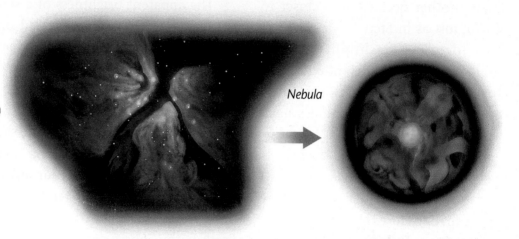

Ⓐ The particles of gas and dust in a nebula exert a gravitational force on each other causing the nebula to contract.

Nebula

Stellar Evolution

You learned that stars begin as nebulas and eventually evolve. A massive star uses up its hydrogen supply rapidly,

causing the star's core to contract. The temperature and pressure in the core rise, while the outer temperature slowly

The Hertzsprung-Russell diagram shows the relationships among a star's color, temperature, and brightness. Stars in the main sequence run from hot, bright stars in the upper left corner of the diagram to cool, faint stars in the lower right corner. What type of star listed in the diagram is the coolest, faintest type of star?

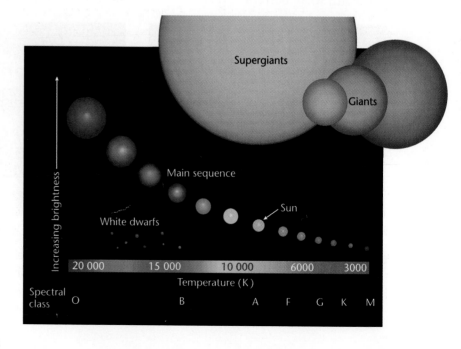

Supergiants

Giants

Main sequence

Sun

White dwarfs

Increasing brightness

| 20 000 | 15 000 | 10 000 | 6000 | 3000 |

Temperature (K)

Spectral class O   B   A   F   G K M

pulls the particles closer and closer together, the temperature inside the nebula increases. Once the temperature reaches 10 000 000°C, fusion begins to take place. The energy released from fusion radiates outward through the condensing ball of gas.

The release of energy into space signals the birth of the star.

After a new star is formed, it does not stay the same forever. Like organisms, stars have a type of life cycle. You'll learn more about the life of stars in the "A Closer Look" article below.

B As the particles move closer together, the temperature inside the nebula rises. When the temperature reaches 10 000 000°C, fusion begins, and a star is born.

Average star

falls. The star expands and becomes a red giant. In very large stars, the core heats up to very high temperatures, producing elements heavier than helium can form by fusion, and the star expands into a supergiant.

As the core of a star about the size of our sun uses up its supply of helium, the core contracts and the outer layers escape into space. The remaining core is white-hot and is called a white dwarf. White dwarfs were first observed in 1915. But it was 1939 before researchers, such as Subrahmanyan Chandrasekhar, an astrophysicist from India, offered an explanation of their evolution.

Chandrasekhar also hypothesized that stars much more massive than the sun have cores so dense that fusion continues even when the supplies of hydrogen and helium have been used up. Elements as heavy as iron are produced. Once iron is formed in the core, fusion stops. The core collapses violently, sending out shock waves. The outer portion of the star explodes into a **supernova**. What remains depends on the mass of the star. It may end up as a neutron star—a small, dense core of neutrons with an average radius of 15 kilometers.

The most massive stars, however, may collapse into black holes after the explosion. A black hole is so dense, not even light can escape its gravitational field. If a light shines at a black hole, the light simply disappears.

Classifying Stars

When you look up into the sky at night, you see stars that are in all different stages of their life cycles. Just as you can classify living things, you can classify stars. In the early 1900s, two scientists developed a system for classifying stars based on their surface temperatures and their absolute brightness. The Hertzsprung-Russell diagram shows that most stars fall along a line called the main sequence.

What Do You Think?

If black holes can't be seen using light telescopes, how do you think scientists could try to find them?

Determining a Star's Temperature

The stars you see from your backyard or bedroom window probably look white. But if you examined those stars with a powerful telescope, you would see that they range from bluish white to yellow, orange, and red.

Figure 20-3

As steel is heated and its temperature increases, it changes color. Here, the molten steel has turned yellow. If the steel continues to be heated, what color will it turn next?

Star color reveals the temperature of the star. Scientists have determined that very hot stars are bluish white. A relatively cool star looks orange or red. Stars the temperature of our sun have a yellow color.

The same is true of any object that gives off its own thermal energy. The difference in temperature shows up as a gradual change in color in the spectrum of light coming from the glowing object—whether that object is a nail or a star. **Figure 20-4** shows the color of stars that have different temperatures.

Figure 20-4

The temperature of a star determines the color of its light. The hottest stars have a bluish-white light, while cooler stars glow with a red light. Stars with a medium temperature, like the sun, have a yellow light. Which type of star is hotter, a red giant or a white dwarf?

Hydrogen Fusion: Energy of the Stars

All of the heat and light produced by stars requires an amazing amount of energy. But where does all of this energy come from?

Stars have large amounts of hydrogen gas. The extremely high temperature and pressure found in the core of a star causes four hydrogen atoms to fuse, forming helium, as shown in **Figure 18-18** on page 585. However, the mass of four hydrogens is slightly greater than the mass of one helium atom. What happens to the missing mass? It is converted to a tremendous amount of energy.

Fusion continues in a star's core until all of the hydrogen is used up. Then helium fuses to form carbon. This also releases an incredible amount of energy. Together, hydrogen fusion and helium fusion can power a star for billions of years, depending on how big the star is.

Figure 20-5

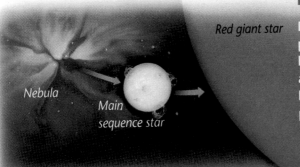

Nebula

Main sequence star

Red giant star

During stellar fusion, the net effect of the extreme heat and pressure inside a star fuses four hydrogen atoms into one helium atom. The process of fusion releases a tremendous amount of energy, which the star radiates into space as heat and light. Why do you think we don't use fusion power on Earth?

Orange star

■ Determining a Star's Composition

Starlight, like any other light, separates into bands of color called a spectrum when it passes through a prism. However, a star's spectrum has dark bands along the spectrum. This is caused by the absorption of certain wavelengths of light by gas in the star's atmosphere. Each element leaves a certain "fingerprint" of dark bands on a spectrum. By studying the bands in a star's spectrum, astronomers can tell what elements are in the star's atmosphere. Discover how this is done in the next Investigate.

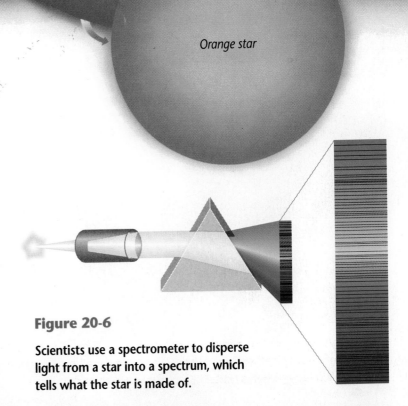

Figure 20-6

Scientists use a spectrometer to disperse light from a star into a spectrum, which tells what the star is made of.

Analyzing Spectra

By studying the bands in a star's spectrum, astronomers can discover what elements are present in the star. The same holds true for our sun. In this activity, observe a simplified spectra to determine the composition of the sun and several unknown objects.

Preparation

Problem
How would you use the spectrum of known substances in order to determine the elements present in the sun and other objects?

Form a Hypothesis
As a group, discuss what you know about the dark lines that are present in the spectrum of a star. Then form a hypothesis about how you would use the spectrum of known substances to determine the composition of the sun and other objects.

Objectives
- Determine the composition of a star using spectra.
- Conclude how the spectrum of a substance can be used to identify that substance.

Materials
ruler or straightedge
pencil
paper

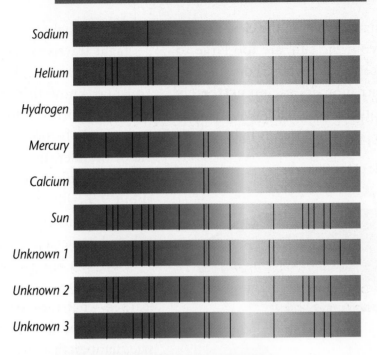

Sodium

Helium

Hydrogen

Mercury

Calcium

Sun

Unknown 1

Unknown 2

Unknown 3

Plan the Experiment

1 Study the spectra above. Determine how you will use the illustration in your experiment.

2 As a group, agree upon and write out your hypothesis statement.

3 Be specific, listing exactly what you will do at each step of your plan.

4 Design a data table *in your Science Journal* to summarize your observations.

Check the Plan

1 How will you determine if the elements in an unknown object match the spectrum of a known substance?

2 Make sure your teacher approves your experiment before you proceed.

3 Carry out your experiment. Record your observations.

Analyze and Conclude

1. **Interpret Scientific Illustrations** What process produces a dark line in the spectra?

2. **Interpret Data** What elements are contained in the sun? What ele-ments are contained in the unknown objects?

3. **Draw a Conclusion** How is a substance's spectrum similar to a fingerprint?

Going Further

Imagine that you and your group of scientists have just discovered a new galaxy. Write a short synopsis explaining how you plan to determine if the stars in the new galaxy are composed of the same elements as the stars within the Milky Way Galaxy.

Light-Years

Distances to even the closest stars, aside from the sun, are too large to measure in kilometers. For this reason, astronomers use an extremely large unit called a light-year to measure distances in space. A **light-year** is the distance light travels in one year.

Light travels faster than anything else in the universe, including sound. You may know this from watching lightning storms. Often, you see the flash of light before you hear the rumble of thunder. In space, light travels at 300 000 kilometers per second, or about 9.5 trillion kilometers in one year. One light-year, then, is about 9.5 trillion kilometers.

Now you know a lot more about the stars you see at night. You've learned what they are and how they form. You've discovered that their size, temperature, and distance from Earth affect how bright they appear. In the next section, you will explore the most important star in your life—the sun.

The Scale of the Universe

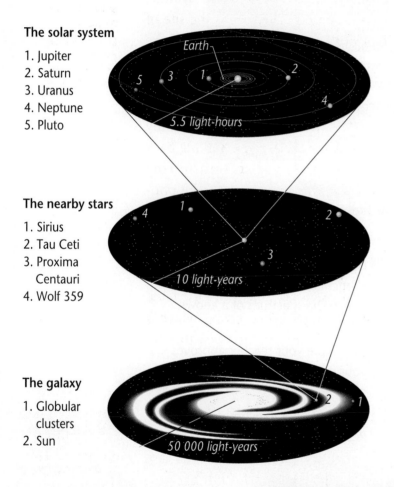

The solar system

1. Jupiter
2. Saturn
3. Uranus
4. Neptune
5. Pluto

Earth

5.5 light-hours

The nearby stars

1. Sirius
2. Tau Ceti
3. Proxima Centauri
4. Wolf 359

10 light-years

The galaxy

1. Globular clusters
2. Sun

50 000 light-years

Figure 20-7

This diagram shows how large the Milky Way Galaxy is. The top circle shows what is within 5.5 light-hours of Earth. However, as the bottom circle indicates, it's 50 000 light-years from the center to the edge of the Milky Way Galaxy. To compare these distances, calculate how many light-hours there are in a light-year.

check your UNDERSTANDING

1. How can two stars that have the same actual brightness look different to an observer on Earth?
2. Describe the process in which the sun produces energy.
3. What is true of the color of visible stars as you go from cooler to hotter?
4. **Apply** Suppose you observe an object explode that is 10 light-years away. When would the explosion have actually occurred?

Sun

The Sun and You

The sun supplies Earth and the entire solar system with energy. Energy from the sun warms air and water masses, causing global wind patterns, changes in weather, and ocean currents. We can harness the energy from the sun for use in heating and lighting our homes, schools, and businesses. What are some other positive ways in which the sun affects your life?

Although the sun is extremely beneficial to us, solar radiation can be harmful. If you've ever gotten a blistering sunburn, you've felt the harmful effects of the sun's radiation on your body. Prolonged exposure to ultraviolet rays from the sun can cause skin cancer. About 27 000 Americans develop skin cancer each year, and about 6000 die from it. Think of some ways that the sun has had a negative effect on you.

■ An Average Star

As you observed on the H-R diagram on page 630, most stars are known as main sequence stars. Our sun is just such a star. It is considered to be of average age and temperature. The actual brightness of our star is also about average for a star of its fairly average size, though it is a bit on the small side.

As you can see in **Figure 20-9** on page 638, the sun has many layers surrounding a dense core like a gigantic, gaseous onion. The core is the site of hydrogen fusion. Just outside of the core is a radiation zone in which energy bounces back and forth before it escapes to the convection zone. This is a cooler layer of gas that is constantly rising to the surface and sinking back to the radiation zone, transferring energy to the photosphere. The photosphere is the incredibly bright source of much of the light we see on Earth. The chromosphere is an active layer, which is home to magnificent solar displays that we'll discuss later. The outer layer is the corona, which is a gradual boundary between the sun and space.

Section Objectives
■ Describe phenomena on the sun's surface and recognize that sunspots, prominences, and solar flares are related.
■ Describe how phenomena on the sun's surface affect Earth.

Key Terms
sunspot

Figure 20-8

Using sunscreen when you are out in the sun can help prevent ultraviolet rays from damaging your skin.

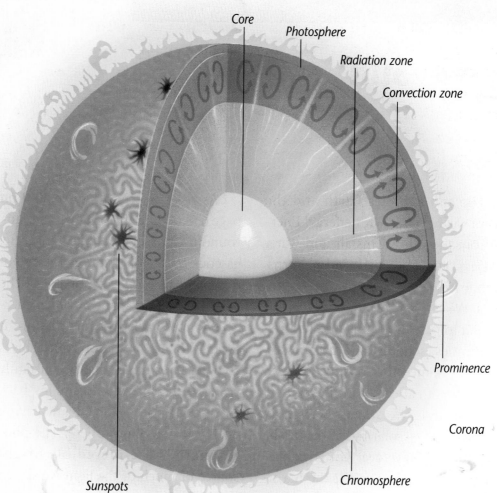

Figure 20-9

A When you look at a picture of the sun, what you're seeing is actually the lowest layer of the sun's atmosphere. This layer is the photosphere, which is about 300 kilometers, or about 187 miles, thick.

B The light from the corona is very faint, and it is clearly visible only when the moon moves between the sun and Earth and blocks out the photosphere. What is this event called?

Core
Photosphere
Radiation zone
Convection zone
Prominence
Corona
Chromosphere
Sunspots

■ Sunspots

Often, the sun is pictured as a perfectly smooth sphere. It's not. There are many features that can be studied, including dark areas of the sun's surface that are cooler than surrounding areas. Such a cool, dark area on the sun's surface is called a **sunspot**. You can see examples of sunspots in **Figure 20-10**.

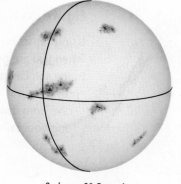
0 days, 0° Rotation

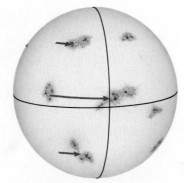
3.125 days, 45° Rotation

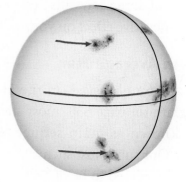
6.25 days, 90° Rotation

Figure 20-10

Because the sun is made up of gases, it does not rotate as a solid body, as Earth does. The sun rotates faster at its equator than at its poles. As a result, sunspots at the equator take about 25 days to go around the sun, while sunspots near the poles take up to 35 days.

638 Chapter 20 Stars and Galaxies

Galileo was the first to identify sunspots, and scientists have been fascinated by them ever since. One thing we've learned by studying sunspots is that the sun rotates. We can observe the movement of individual sunspots as they are carried by the sun's rotation.

Sunspots are not permanent features on the sun. They may appear and disappear over a period of several days or several months. Look at **Figure 20-11** and **Table 20-1**. The table shows the cycle of sunspot occurrences over a 27-year period.

Sometimes there are many large sunspots—a period called a sunspot maximum—while at other times there are only a few small sunspots or none at all—a sunspot minimum. Sunspot maximums occur about every 11 years. The next is expected in 2001. This 11-year cycle of sunspot occurrences is often called the cycle of solar activity.

SKILLBUILDER

Making and Using Graphs

Using the data presented in **Table 20-1**, make a bar graph showing the number of sunspots that have occurred on the sun over the past three decades. Plot years on the horizontal axis and number of sunspots on the vertical axis. If you need help, refer to the **Skill Handbook** on page 681.

Recent Sunspot Activity						Table 20-1
Date	Number of Sunspots	Date	Number of Sunspots	Date	Number of Sunspots	
1969	105	1978	93	1987	29	
1970	104	1979	155	1988	100	
1971	67	1980	155	1989	159	
1972	69	1981	140	1990	147	
1973	38	1982	116	1991	145	
1974	35	1983	67	1992	94	
1975	16	1984	46	1993	54	
1976	13	1985	18	1994	31	
1977	28	1986	14	1995	18	

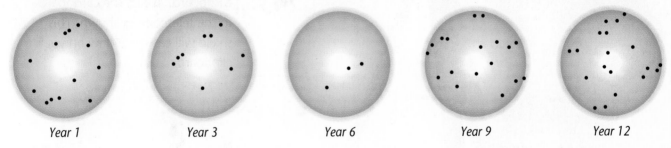

Year 1   Year 3   Year 6   Year 9   Year 12

Figure 20-11

As you can see from the pictures above, the number of sunspots changes from year to year. A year when there are a lot of large sunspots is called a sunspot maximum. Sunspot maximums occur about every 11 years. Based on the illustrations above, will there be many sunspots or few sunspots in year 21?

INVESTIGATE!

Tracking Sunspots

In the activity, you will measure the movement of sunspots and use your findings to determine the sun's period of rotation.

Problem

How can you trace the movement of sunspots?

Materials

several books   cardboard
clipboard   drawing paper
small tripod   scissors
small refracting
   telescope

Safety Precautions

Do not look through the telescope at the sun. Severe eye damage may result. Never look directly at the sun under any circumstances!

What To Do

CAUTION: *Never look directly at the sun. Do not look through the telescope at the sun. You could damage your eyes.*

1 Create a data table *in your Journal*. Find a spot where you can view the sun at the same time of day every day for 5 days.

2 Set up the telescope with the eyepiece facing away from the sun. Set up the clipboard with the drawing paper attached. Use the books to prop the clipboard upright. Point the eyepiece at the drawing paper.

3 Cut a hole out of the center of the cardboard. Attach the cardboard to the telescope as shown. This shield will cast a shadow on your clipboard.

A

B

C

4 Move the clipboard back and forth until you have the largest possible image of the sun on the paper. Adjust the telescope to form a clear image. Trace the outline of the sun on the paper.

5 Trace any sunspots that appear as dark areas on the sun's image. At the same time each day for a week, check the sun's image and trace the position of the sunspots.

6 The sun's diameter is approximately 1 400 000 kilometers. Using this SI measure, *calculate* the scale of your image. Estimate the size of the largest sunspots you observed.

7 *Calculate* and record how many kilometers any observed sunspots appear to move each day.

8 At the rate determined in Step 7, *predict* how many days it will take for the same sunspots to return to the same position in which you first saw them.

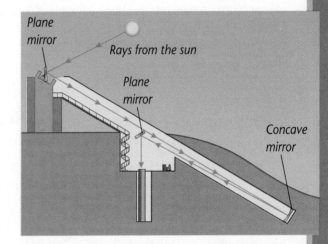

Solar telescopes use a series of mirrors to reflect light from the sun down into an underground observation room where the light can be studied.

Analyzing

1. Which part of the sun showed up in your image?

2. What was the average number of sunspots you observed each day?

Concluding and Applying

3. How can the movement of sunspots be *predicted*?

4. How can sunspots be used to prove that the sun is rotating?

5. Going Further How can sunspots be used to *infer* that the sun's surface is not solid like Earth's?

■ Prominences and Flares

Sunspots are related to other phenomena on the sun—prominences and solar flares. Some prominences look like huge arching columns of gas.

Gases near a sunspot sometimes brighten suddenly, shooting outward at high speed. These violent eruptions are called solar flares. **Figure 20-12A** is a photograph of a solar flare.

Solar flares can also interact with Earth's magnetic field, producing a beautiful, eerie light show. This spectacular display of lights is called the *aurora borealis*, or northern lights, in the Northern Hemisphere, and the *aurora australis* in the Southern Hemisphere. Next, you will observe some more spectacular light displays that can be seen only through the lens of a powerful telescope.

Figure 20-12

A Solar flares are typically a few thousand kilometers across. Most flares increase to their maximum brightness in a few seconds or minutes, and then fade out over several minutes or hours. A flare releases huge amounts of X rays and particles that stream towards Earth. What do you think that does to radio and television signals?

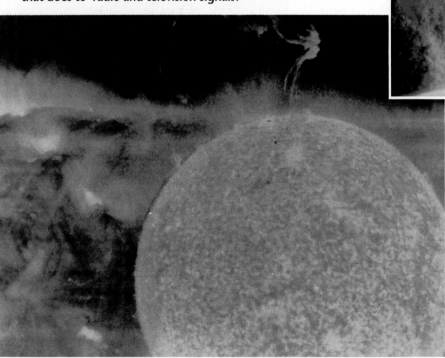

B Some prominences are so powerful that they eject matter from the sun out into space at speeds up to 1000 kilometers per second. Other prominences form huge loops over sunspot areas that can reach heights of hundreds of thousands of kilometers. Would there be more prominences during a sunspot maximum or a sunspot minimum?

check your UNDERSTANDING

1. In what ways are sunspots, prominences, and solar flares related?
2. What effect do solar phenomena have on Earth?

3. **Apply** How does our sun differ from most other stars? In what ways is our sun average? How would life be affected on Earth if the sun was larger or smaller?

Galaxies

Earth's Galaxy—and Others

One reason to study astronomy is to learn about your place in the universe. Through centuries of studying space, we know there's a lot more to the universe than the sun and planets in our solar system.

Suppose you need to give directions to your house to a distant cousin who lives in another country. You could probably do it. But suppose your cousin lives in a galaxy millions of light-years away. Look at **Figure 20-13**. What other information would you need to give your cousin?

You are living on a planet in a giant galaxy called the Milky Way. A **galaxy** is a large group of stars, gas, and dust held together by gravity. Our galaxy contains about 200 billion stars. The sun is just one of those stars, and Earth revolves around it.

Just as stars are grouped together within galaxies, galaxies are grouped into clusters. Even so, the galaxies in a cluster are separated by huge distances—often millions of light-years. The cluster the Milky Way belongs to is called the Local Group. It contains about 25 galaxies of various shapes and sizes. The three major types of galaxies are elliptical, spiral, and irregular.

Section Objectives
- Describe a galaxy and list three main types of galaxies.
- Identify several characteristics of the Milky Way Galaxy.

Key Terms
galaxy

Figure 20-13

A The Milky Way Galaxy contains about 200 billion stars, one of which is the sun. The Milky Way also contains many nebulas. Astronomers estimate that the Milky Way is about 100 000 light-years in diameter and about 15 000 light-years thick.

Milky Way

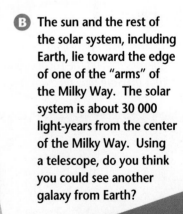

Earth

B The sun and the rest of the solar system, including Earth, lie toward the edge of one of the "arms" of the Milky Way. The solar system is about 30 000 light-years from the center of the Milky Way. Using a telescope, do you think you could see another galaxy from Earth?

Our solar system

■ Elliptical Galaxies

The most common type of galaxy is the elliptical galaxy. These galaxies are like large, three-dimensional ellipses. Many are football-shaped. Some elliptical galaxies are quite small, but others are so large that the entire Local Group of galaxies would fit inside them. **Figure 20-14A** shows an elliptical galaxy.

■ Spiral Galaxies

Spiral galaxies have arms that curve outward from a central hub, making them look something like a pinwheel. The spiral arms are made up of stars and dust. In between the arms are fewer stars. **Figure 20-14B** shows a typical spiral galaxy.

The fuzzy patch you can see on a clear night in the constellation of Andromeda is actually a spiral galaxy. It's so far away that you can't see its

Figure 20-14

Ⓐ Elliptical galaxies, like the one shown here, contain mostly older, dimmer stars.

Ⓑ Spiral galaxies, like the one shown here, contain a mixture of young and old stars.

Physics CONNECTION

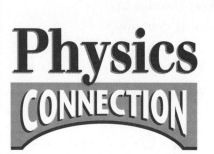

The red shift in the light from stars in galaxies beyond the Local Group means that they are moving away from Earth.

The Doppler Shift

Have you ever heard the horn of a train or car as it approached you and then passed? If you have, you know the sound becomes louder and louder as it approaches and then becomes fainter as it leaves. But the volume is not all that changes. The sound also changes, from lower to higher, then back to lower pitches as the train moves away. The change in pitch is called the Doppler shift. Scientists have been able to associate the Doppler shift with sound waves and with light waves.

Shifty Light

Astronomers understand that the change in wavelength on a light spectrum is similar to the change in pitch of the train's horn. The wavelength of light from an object becomes shorter as the object approaches, just as the sound waves did.

If a star were approaching, the dark lines of its spectrum would move toward the blue-violet part of the spectrum. But if the star were traveling away, the lines would move toward the red part of the spectrum.

individual stars. Instead, it appears as a hazy spot in the night sky. The Andromeda Galaxy is a member of the Local Group and is about 2 million light-years away from the Milky Way.

As you saw in **Figure 20-14B**, arms in a typical spiral galaxy start close to the center of the galaxy. Barred spiral galaxies have two spiral arms extending from a large bar that passes through the center of the galaxy. **Figure 20-15A** shows a barred spiral galaxy.

■ Irregular Galaxies

The third type of galaxy includes all those galaxies that don't fit into the other two categories. Irregular galaxies come in many different shapes and are smaller and less common than ellipticals or spirals. The Large Magellanic Cloud, shown in **Figure 20-15B**, is an irregular galaxy that orbits the Milky Way Galaxy at a mere distance of about 170 000 light-years.

Figure 20-15

Ⓐ The bar in a barred spiral galaxy contains gas and dust clouds and bright stars.

Ⓑ Irregular galaxies, like the one shown here, contain from 100 million to a few billion stars.

Observer
Red shift

Moving
light source

Observer
Blue shift

The Expanding Universe

In 1924, Edwin Hubble noticed that there is a red shift in the light from galaxies beyond the Local Group. What did this tell him about the universe? Because all galaxies beyond the Local Group show a red shift in their spectra, they must be moving away from Earth. Hubble then concluded that, for so many galaxies to be traveling away from Earth, the universe must be expanding.

You Try It!

You can get an idea of how distances between stars change by inflating a balloon slightly and then closing it with a clothespin. Use a felt-tipped pen to put dots in a number of places on the balloon. Next, inflate the balloon some more and watch how distances between dots change.

The dots move away from each other, just as galaxies in the universe are doing. Such

This diagram illustrates the Doppler shift of a moving object. An observer would note a red shift in the spectrum as an object moves away and a blue shift as it moves closer.

observations led scientists to the "big bang" theory, which states that our universe began with an incredibly large explosion. The explosion caused the universe to expand in all directions. Even today the universe continues to expand.

The Milky Way Galaxy

Our galaxy—the Milky Way—is about 100 000 light-years wide and contains more than 200 billion stars. These stars all orbit a central hub. You're familiar with one of these stars—the sun. The sun is located about 30 000 light-years from the center of the Milky Way galaxy. It orbits that center once every 240 million years.

The Milky Way is usually classified as a normal spiral galaxy. However, recent evidence suggests that it might be a barred spiral. It is difficult to know for sure because we have never seen our galaxy from the outside. We have an "insider's" view of the arrangement of the stars within the Milky Way. The next activity shows you why it is difficult to determine the shape of our galaxy while viewing it from inside.

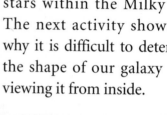

Figure 20-16

In addition to light and heat, stars also give off energy in other forms, such as radio waves. Astronomers study the radio energy from stars by using radio telescopes, like those shown here. Radio telescopes use a large dish to reflect and focus radio waves. Why do you think radio telescopes have to be much larger than optical telescopes?

How Do We Know?

The Position of the Solar System in the Galaxy

When plotting stars in the Milky Way, astronomers noted that there is a large concentration of stars about 30 000 light-years away. They hypothesize this concentration of stars is the center of the galaxy.

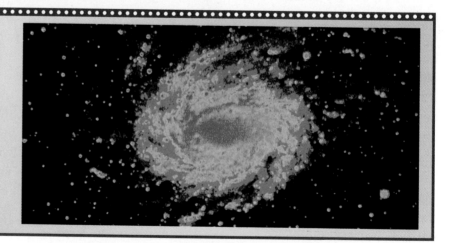

Explore! ACTIVITY

Why is determining the shape of the Milky Way so difficult?

What To Do

1. Place about 20 cups upside down on a table. Arrange them in the shape of a spiral galaxy. Look at the arrangement from above.

2. Next, kneel down so that you are at eye level with the cups. Look at the arrangement from this angle. From which view did the cups seem to be arranged in a pattern? Imagine that these cups are stars in the Milky Way galaxy. Which view represents what we see when we look at our galaxy from Earth?

As the activity showed, you can't see the normal spiral (or perhaps barred spiral) shape of the Milky Way because you are located within one of its spiral arms. What you can see of this galaxy is a faint band of light stretching across the sky.

Will we ever be able to travel into the center of the Milky Way and beyond? Probably not. It would take many generations of people to make a trip that long. What we can expect is to improve on the methods we now use to view it from Earth and from space. Astronomers are already doing this by using unique telescopes that examine the waves of radio and heat energy that come from the center of the Milky Way galaxy. And the more information that is gathered, the better you can understand your place in the universe.

check your UNDERSTANDING

1. List and describe the shapes of the three major types of galaxies. What do they all have in common?

2. Name and describe the shape of the galaxy that you live in. How do the stars in this galaxy move?

3. Why is the Large Magellanic Cloud classified as an irregular galaxy?

4. **Apply** Specify Earth's location as much as possible by identifying, in order of size from smallest to largest, the systems of planets and stars to which it belongs.

Science and Society

A Look at Light Pollution

Some people love to visit rural areas where many stars can be seen against a dark, moonless night sky. They may travel for miles to reach a mountaintop for clear viewing.

Other people love to watch city lights from a distance. In their eyes, the nighttime view of Los Angeles from nearby hills is beautiful—much like a galaxy on Earth.

Blinding Lights

But the sky and city lights don't always mix. Urbanites must have lights for reading, safety, and thousands of other needs. And while the lights serve their purpose in the city, they also obscure the night sky.

That's a problem for astronomers and other star watchers who refer to the city's glow as light pollution. You can see a good example of light pollution while watching a nighttime football game in an outdoor stadium. The stars in the sky seem to disappear because of the glow of the lights.

It's obvious that cities can't do without light, and that astronomers can't view the night sky through light pollution. Does this mean that scientific research must stop? Can compromise solve the problem for astronomers and city dwellers?

Environmentally Friendly Lighting

Some cities have taken measures to control light pollution. For example, one Arizona city near a mountaintop observatory has replaced its streetlights with lamps shining at wavelengths that can be filtered out by astronomers. The lamps are less expensive to operate, so the city is saving money while helping the pollution problem.

Light pollution might also be reduced by putting covers above some bright outdoor lights. This would allow the light to hit its target without illuminating the sky.

If such measures do not completely eliminate interference from light pollution, how can we solve the conflict between those who want to observe the stars and those who need

lights? Do you think the conflict could become as severe as disagreements over noise and air pollution?

Light vs. Night

To get a better idea of arguments that could be made about light pollution, pretend that your classroom is a courtroom. Some of your classmates are attorneys for a group of astronomers who say new lighting near their observatory has stopped their astronomy projects.

The attorneys also represent a neighborhood association that is upset over the new floodlights and neon lights near their homes. They say the lights keep them awake at night and make their neighborhood look cheap.

Defense attorneys should represent the businesses that added the new lighting. They say the businesses would lose business without all the bright signs. They also claim that the new lights have reduced the number of burglaries in the area.

Select classmates to serve as a judge and jury to hear the arguments. Other classmates can be witnesses for the neighborhood association, while others can be owners of the well-lit businesses. Reporters from newspapers and TV should be present.

Both teams of attorneys should talk to their clients (the astronomers, neighborhood association, and business owners) before the trial begins. The attorneys and judge should know the local zoning laws about lighting. After questioning their witnesses during the trial, the attorneys should make their closing arguments before the jury.

Remember that the news media should take notes for news coverage throughout the trial and when the jury announces its decision.

Remember also that some trials end when the plaintiffs and defendants finally reach an agreement outside of court.

interNET
CONNECTION

Visit the International Dark Sky Association's homepage on the World Wide Web. What other information do they offer that could have been used in the trial?

Technology *Connection*

Questions About Quasars

In the 1960s, radio telescopes detected starlike energy sources that were too small to be pinpointed by the best radio instruments of the time. Astronomers then began using optical instruments and searched photographs of suspected areas for objects that could be the source of the energy. Then, by using the best available instruments on large telescopes, scientists were able to identify starlike objects as the source of the energy emissions. The objects, however, did not behave like stars; their brightness was greater than that of an average star and appeared to vary rapidly from time to time. The spectra lines of the objects showed a Doppler red shift, indicating that the objects were moving away at great velocity and were at great distances from Earth. These objects were called quasars, which stands for quasi–stellar radio source. *Quasi* means "having a resemblance to," and *stellar* means "star."

Quasar Pioneer

Eleanor Margaret Burbidge, an English astronomer, has contributed greatly to current knowledge about quasars. Margaret Burbidge left England and took a research assignment at the California Institute of Technology. Later she served as research astronomer at Yerkes Observatory at Williams Bay, Wisconsin, and was elected a Fellow of the Royal Society of London in 1964. She then served as the first woman director of the Royal Greenwich Observatory at London, England.

Mighty Quasars

Quasars appear to be extremely luminous objects with relatively small sizes, great mass, and a great deal of energy. Quasars also appear to be traveling away from us at speeds up to nine-tenths of the speed of light, which is 300 000 km per sec. The light seen from quasars was given off many billions of years ago. Where they come from is still puzzling. However, observational evidence from the Hubble Space Telescope supports the idea that quasars are powered by enormous black holes in their cores, similar to active galaxies.

What Do You Think?

Do you think studying quasars is important? What could quasars tell us about the universe? Do you think the study is worth the time and money? Should money be spent in other ways?

Teens in SCIENCE

Space Camp

Would you be interested in training the way a real astronaut does? Thousands of fourth to twelfth graders who attend Space Camp/Space Academy in Huntsville, Alabama, receive five days of this type of training. They learn about the development of the space program.

3, 2, 1....

Space campers get to try many different kinds of simulators—devices that provide test conditions much like real experiences.

The primary activity at both Space Camp and Space Academy is the team mission. Campers get specific assignments during this two-hour simulation of an actual space shuttle flight.

...Ignition...

At the end of their five days, campers receive Space Camp diplomas and badges (a pair of wings) at a graduation ceremony. Many of them may return in future years for Space Academy I or II. One thing is sure—if any of them have dreams about becoming an astronaut like Mae Jemison, shown below, they have a much better idea of what it would be like after space camp!

Blast Off!

Dr. Mae Jemison made her childhood dreams come true on September 12, 1992, when the space shuttle Endeavour blasted off. She flew into space and orbited Earth for seven days. In addition to realizing her personal dreams, the flight marked a historical first. Dr. Jemison was the first African-American woman to travel in space.

Like all other astronauts, Jemison worked for the National Aeronautics and Space Administration (NASA). A strong back-

Dr. Mae Jemison, Space Shuttle Mission Specialist

ground in math, engineering, biology, or physics is required. Also, applicants must have three or more years of work-related experience. Mae Jemison was one of only 15 applicants selected from a pool of 2000. Dr. Jemison is proud to be a role model, speaking to students around the country. Her advice as a role model is "to do the best job you can and to be yourself."

What Do You Think?

Imagine that you are on a mission to explore the surface of the moon. What is your greatest thrill in doing this?

Science Journal

Review the statements below about the big ideas presented in this chapter, and answer the questions. Then, re-read your answers to the Did You Ever Wonder questions at the beginning of the chapter. *In your Science Journal*, write a paragraph about how your understanding of the big ideas in the chapter has changed.

1 There are more stars in the universe than you could count in a lifetime. Some are brighter than others, depending on how big, how hot, and how far away from Earth they are. The temperature and composition of a star can be determined by its color and by examining the dark-line spectrum of the light it emits. *How do most stars change as they go through their life cycle?*

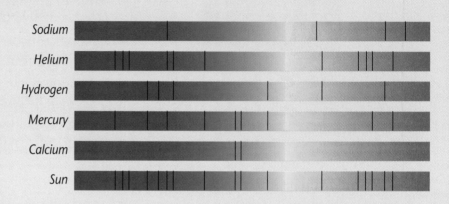

Sodium

Helium

Hydrogen

Mercury

Calcium

Sun

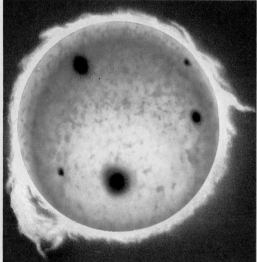

2 All life on Earth depends on one star—the sun. It is an average star in terms of its size and temperature. The surface of the sun contains sunspots, prominences, and solar flares. *How would things be different on Earth if the sun was much farther away?*

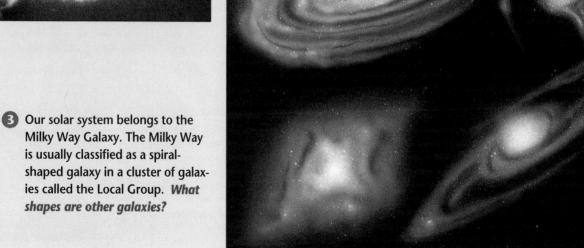

3 Our solar system belongs to the Milky Way Galaxy. The Milky Way is usually classified as a spiral-shaped galaxy in a cluster of galaxies called the Local Group. *What shapes are other galaxies?*

Using Key Science Terms

galaxy   star
light-year   sunspot
nebula   supernova

For each set of terms below, explain the relationship that exists.

1. nebula, star, supernova
2. star, sunspot
3. light-year, galaxy

Understanding Ideas

Answer the following questions in your Journal using complete sentences.

1. How does our sun compare in size and brightness to other stars?
2. Why would light from an explosion far out in space be "old news"?
3. How are galaxies classified? What are the three kinds of galaxies?

2. Concept Mapping Create an events chain concept map of the birth of a main sequence star.

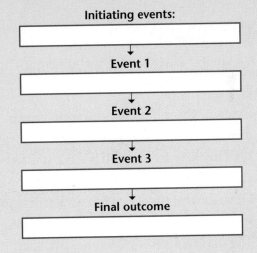

Initiating events:

↓

Event 1

↓

Event 2

↓

Event 3

↓

Final outcome

Developing Skills

Use your understanding of the concepts developed in this chapter to answer each of the following questions.

1. **Observing and Inferring** Observing the stars/constellations again as you did in the Explore activity on page 627, find a point of reference to stand near such as the edge of a building or a tree. Watch the star/constellation with respect to your point of reference for 30 minutes. What happens? Why?

3. **Recognizing Cause and Effect** Using the two flashlights from the Find Out activity on page 628, find a way to make the flashlights look the same brightness.

4. **Observing, Interpreting Data** To discover how objects can be identified by the substance's spectrum, a spectroscope can be made and used. Cover the ends of a cardboard or paper tube with paper. Make a small slit in the paper on one end of the tube and a small hole in the paper on the other end. Cover the hole with diffraction grating and tape it to the tube.

Looking through the diffraction grating, aim the slit at a light source. (Light sources should include a halogen light bulb, fluorescent light bulb, Bunsen burner or candle, but NOT the sun.) Move the spectroscope side-to-side slightly. Sketch the light patterns using colored pencils or crayons. What similarities did you see? Can light patterns be used for identification? How?

Critical Thinking

In your Journal, *answer each of the following questions.*

1. Explain why a hotter star might appear dimmer than a cooler star.
2. Explain why a small and a large star may appear to have the same brightness.
3. Describe the effects on life on Earth if the sun were to move one light-year away.
4. The diagram shows the forces that act within a star such as our sun. What do you think the overall effect of these forces is on the size of the star?

Problem Solving

Read the following problem and discuss your answers in a brief paragraph.

Suppose you had a rocket that could travel at the speed of light.

1. How long would it take you to complete a round-trip journey to a star that is 15 light-years from Earth?
2. Explain why it might be possible to take off for the star without realizing that it no longer exists.

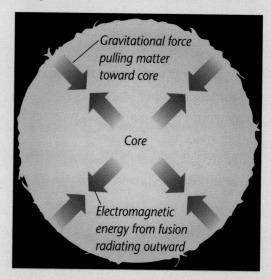
Gravitational force pulling matter toward core
Core
Electromagnetic energy from fusion radiating outward

CONNECTING IDEAS

Discuss each of the following in a brief paragraph.

1. **Theme—Energy** Recall from chapter 18 the difference between fusion and fission. How do we know fusion and not fission occurs in the sun?

2. **Theme—Systems and Interactions** How does Earth's closest star affect its ocean currents?

3. **Theme—Energy** How do we know that the sun contains hydrogen?

4. **A Closer Look** What kind of stars may become black holes? Why?

5. **Physics Connection** How is a red shift in light spectra evidence for the expansion of the universe?

observing
THE
WORLD
around you

In this unit, you investigated how transmutations of elements occur by fission and fusion. You learned that during fission, atoms split apart and during fusion, they are forced together. You explored the idea that the solar system began as a huge rotating cloud of gas and dust, and that the universe is composed of small particles and huge galaxies of stars. You have investigated how humans are attempting to artificially cause and control nuclear processes to produce energy for human use.

Try the exercises and activity that follow—they will challenge you to use and apply some of the ideas you learned in this unit.

CONNECTING IDEAS

1. Imagine you are planning a space mission to build a research base on another planet in our solar system. Pick the planet you would choose and describe the reasons for your choice and obstacles you would have to overcome to make your mission successful.

2. When four hydrogen nuclei undergo fusion to form a helium nucleus, mass is lost. Explain what happens to account for the loss of mass and how this demonstrates the conservation of mass and energy. How does this explain how stars produce so much energy?

Exploring Further ACTIVITY

How do the diameters of the planets in the solar system compare?

What To Do

1. Obtain charts or tables to provide information on the diameters of the planets.

2. Determine how many times bigger in diameter each planet is than Pluto, the smallest.

3. Mix up some cookie dough and cut out cookies having diameters based on this scale. Decorate your planet cookies and bake them. **CAUTION:** *Be sure to have an adult help you with this activity.*

Appendices

Table of Contents

International System of Units

The International System (SI) of Measurement is accepted as the standard for measurement throughout most of the world. Three base units in SI are the meter, kilogram, and second. Frequently used SI units are listed below.

Table A-1: Frequently used SI Units	
Length	1 millimeter (mm) = 1000 micrometers (µm)
	1 centimeter (cm) = 10 millimeters (mm)
	1 meter (m) = 100 centimeters (cm)
	1 kilometer (km) = 1000 meters (m)
	1 light-year = 9 460 000 000 000 kilometers (km)
Area	1 square meter (m^2) = 10 000 square centimeters (cm^2)
	1 square kilometer (km^2) = 1 000 000 square meters (m^2)
Volume	1 milliliter (mL) = 1 cubic centimeter (cm^3)
	1 liter (L) = 1000 milliliters (mL)
Mass	1 gram (g) = 1000 milligrams (mg)
	1 kilogram (kg) = 1000 grams (g)
	1 metric ton = 1000 kilograms (kg)
Time	1 s = 1 second

Temperature measurements in SI are often made in degrees Celsius. Celsius temperature is a supplementary unit derived from the base unit kelvin. The Celsius scale (°C) has 100 equal graduations between the freezing temperature (0°C) and the boiling temperature of water (100°C). The following relationship exists between the Celsius and kelvin temperature scales:

$$K = °C + 273$$

Several other supplementary SI units are listed below.

Table A-2: Supplementary SI Units			
Measurement	Unit	Symbol	Expressed in Base Units
Energy	Joule	J	$kg \cdot m^2/s^2$ or $N \cdot m$
Force	Newton	N	$kg \cdot m/s^2$
Power	Watt	W	$kg \cdot m^2/s^3$ or J/s
Pressure	Pascal	Pa	$kg/(m \cdot s^2)$ or N/m^2

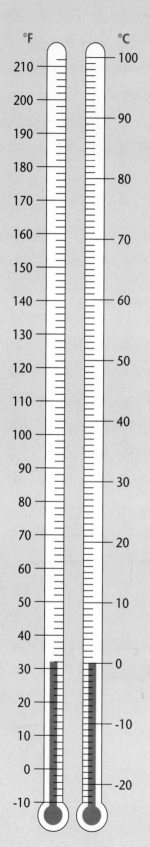

°F
210
200
190
180
170
160
150
140
130
120
110
100
90
80
70
60
50
40
30
20
10
0
-10

°C
100
90
80
70
60
50
40
30
20
10
0
-10
-20

Table B-1: SI/Metric to English Conversions

	When You Want to Convert:	Multiply By:	To Find:
Length	inches	2.54	centimeters
	centimeters	0.39	inches
	feet	0.30	meters
	meters	3.28	feet
	yards	0.91	meters
	meters	1.09	yards
	miles	1.61	kilometers
	kilometers	0.62	miles
Mass and Weight	ounces	28.35	grams
	grams	0.04	ounces
	pounds	0.45	kilograms
	kilograms	2.2	pounds
	tons	0.91	tonnes (metric tons)
	tonnes (metric tons)	1.10	tons
	pounds	4.45	newtons
	newtons	0.23	pounds
Volume	cubic inches	16.39	cubic centimeters
	cubic centimeters	0.06	cubic inches
	cubic feet	0.03	cubic meters
	cubic meters	35.3	cubic feet
	liters	1.06	quarts
	liters	0.26	gallons
	gallons	3.78	liters
Area	square inches	6.45	square centimeters
	square centimeters	0.16	square inches
	square feet	0.09	square meters
	square meters	10.76	square feet
	square miles	2.59	square kilometers
	square kilometers	0.39	miles
	hectares	2.47	acres
	acres	0.40	hectares
Temperature	Fahrenheit	5/9 (°F − 32)	Celsius
	Celsius	9/5 °C + 32	Fahrenheit

Safety in the Science Classroom

1. Always obtain your teacher's permission to begin an investigation.

2. Study the procedure. If you have questions, ask your teacher. Understand any safety symbols shown on the page.

3. Use the safety equipment provided for you. Goggles and a safety apron should be worn when any investigation calls for using chemicals.

4. Always slant test tubes away from yourself and others when heating them.

5. Never eat or drink in the lab, and never use lab glassware as food or drink containers. Never inhale chemicals. Do not taste any substances or draw any material into a tube with your mouth.

6. If you spill any chemical, wash it off immediately with water. Report the spill immediately to your teacher.

7. Know the location and proper use of the fire extinguisher, safety shower, fire blanket, first aid kit, and fire alarm.

8. Keep materials away from flames. Tie back hair and loose clothing.

9. If a fire should break out in the classroom, or if your clothing should catch fire, smother it with the fire blanket or a coat, or get under a safety shower. NEVER RUN.

10. Report any accident or injury, no matter how small, to your teacher.

Follow these procedures as you clean up your work area.

1. Turn off the water and gas. Disconnect electrical devices.

2. Return all materials to their proper places.

3. Dispose of chemicals and other materials as directed by your teacher. Place broken glass and solid substances in the proper containers. Never discard materials in the sink.

4. Clean your work area.

5. Wash your hands thoroughly after working in the laboratory.

Table C-1: First Aid

Injury	Safe Response
Burns	Apply cold water. Call your teacher immediately.
Cuts and bruises	Stop any bleeding by applying direct pressure. Cover cuts with a clean dressing. Apply cold compresses to bruises. Call your teacher immediately.
Fainting	Leave the person lying down. Loosen any tight clothing and keep crowds away. Call your teacher immediately.
Foreign matter in eye	Flush with plenty of water. Use eyewash bottle or fountain. Call your teacher immediately.
Poisoning	Note the suspected poisoning agent and call your teacher immediately.
Any spills on skin	Flush with large amounts of water or use safety shower. Call your teacher immediately.

APPENDIX D

Safety Symbols

These safety symbols are used to indicate possible hazards in the activities. Each activity has appropriate hazard indicators.

	DISPOSAL ALERT This symbol appears when care must be taken to dispose of materials properly.		**ANIMAL SAFETY** This symbol appears whenever live animals are studied and the safety of the animals and the students must be ensured.
	BIOLOGICAL HAZARD This symbol appears when there is danger involving bacteria, fungi, or protists.		**RADIOACTIVE SAFETY** This symbol appears when radioactive materials are used.
	OPEN FLAME ALERT This symbol appears when use of an open flame could cause a fire or an explosion.		**CLOTHING PROTECTION SAFETY** This symbol appears when substances used could stain or burn clothing.
	THERMAL SAFETY This symbol appears as a reminder to use caution when handling hot objects.		**FIRE SAFETY** This symbol appears when care should be taken around open flames.
	SHARP OBJECT SAFETY This symbol appears when a danger of cuts or punctures caused by the use of sharp objects exists.		**EXPLOSION SAFETY** This symbol appears when the misuse of chemicals could cause an explosion.
	FUME SAFETY This symbol appears when chemicals or chemical reactions could cause dangerous fumes.		**EYE SAFETY** This symbol appears when a danger to the eyes exists. Safety goggles should be worn when this symbol appears.
	ELECTRICAL SAFETY This symbol appears when care should be taken when using electrical equipment.		**POISON SAFETY** This symbol appears when poisonous substances are used.
	SKIN PROTECTION SAFETY This symbol appears when use of caustic chemicals might irritate the skin or when contact with microorganisms might transmit infection.		**CHEMICAL SAFETY** This symbol appears when chemicals used can cause burns or are poisonous if absorbed through the skin.

Care and Use of a Microscope

Coarse Adjustment *Focuses the image under low power*

Fine Adjustment *Sharpens the image under high and low magnification*

Arm *Supports the body tube*

Low-power objective *Contains the lens with low-power magnification*

Stage clips *Hold the microscope slide in place*

Base *Provides support for the microscope*

Eyepiece *Contains a magnifying lens you look through*

Body tube *Connects the eyepiece to the revolving nosepiece*

Revolving nosepiece *Holds and turns the objectives into viewing position*

High-power objective *Contains the lens with the highest magnification*

Stage *Platform used to support the microscope slide*

Diaphragm *Regulates the amount of light entering the body tube*

Light source *Allows light to reflect upward through the diaphragm, the specimen, and the lenses*

Care of a Microscope

1. Always carry the microscope holding the arm with one hand and supporting the base with the other hand.
2. Don't touch the lenses with your finger.
3. Never lower the coarse adjustment knob when looking through the eyepiece lens.
4. Always focus first with the low-power objective.
5. Don't use the coarse adjustment knob when the high-power objective is in place.
6. Store the microscope covered.

Using a Microscope

1. Place the microscope on a flat surface that is clear of objects. The arm should be toward you.
2. Look through the eyepiece. Adjust the diaphragm so that light comes through the opening in the stage.
3. Place a slide on the stage so that the specimen is in the field of view. Hold it firmly in place by using the stage clips.
4. Always focus first with the coarse adjustment and the low-power objective lens. Once the object is in focus on low power, turn the nosepiece until the high-power objective is in place. Use ONLY the fine adjustment to focus with the high-power objective lens.

Making a Wet Mount Slide

1. Carefully place the item you want to look at in the center of a clean glass slide. Make sure the sample is thin enough for light to pass through.
2. Use a dropper to place one or two drops of water on the sample.
3. Hold a clean coverslip by the edges and place it at one edge of the drop of water. Slowly lower the coverslip onto the drop of water until it lies flat.
4. If you have too much water or a lot of air bubbles, touch the edge of a paper towel to the edge of the coverslip to draw off extra water and force air out.

PERIODIC TABLE OF THE ELEMENTS

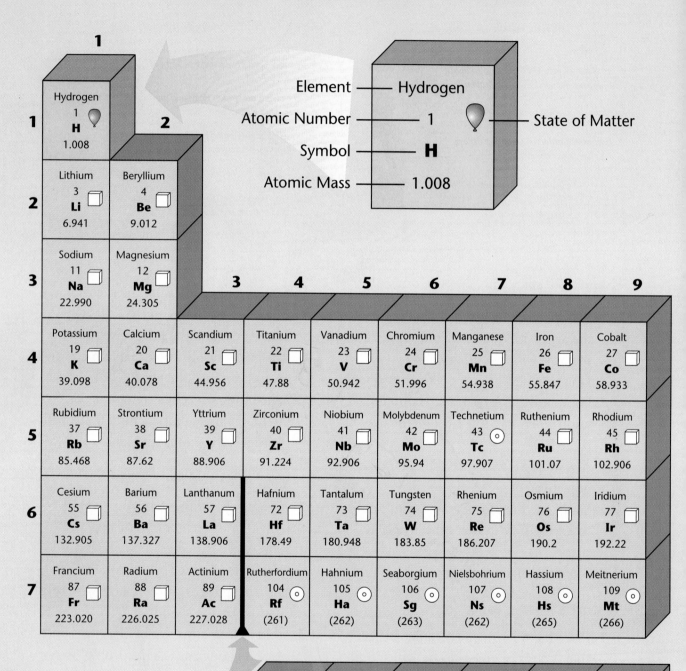

	1							
		2						
Element — Hydrogen								
Atomic Number — 1 — **State of Matter**								
Symbol — H								
Atomic Mass — 1.008								

	1	2	3	4	5	6	7	8	9
1	Hydrogen 1 **H** 1.008								
2	Lithium 3 **Li** 6.941	Beryllium 4 **Be** 9.012							
3	Sodium 11 **Na** 22.990	Magnesium 12 **Mg** 24.305							
4	Potassium 19 **K** 39.098	Calcium 20 **Ca** 40.078	Scandium 21 **Sc** 44.956	Titanium 22 **Ti** 47.88	Vanadium 23 **V** 50.942	Chromium 24 **Cr** 51.996	Manganese 25 **Mn** 54.938	Iron 26 **Fe** 55.847	Cobalt 27 **Co** 58.933
5	Rubidium 37 **Rb** 85.468	Strontium 38 **Sr** 87.62	Yttrium 39 **Y** 88.906	Zirconium 40 **Zr** 91.224	Niobium 41 **Nb** 92.906	Molybdenum 42 **Mo** 95.94	Technetium 43 **Tc** 97.907	Ruthenium 44 **Ru** 101.07	Rhodium 45 **Rh** 102.906
6	Cesium 55 **Cs** 132.905	Barium 56 **Ba** 137.327	Lanthanum 57 **La** 138.906	Hafnium 72 **Hf** 178.49	Tantalum 73 **Ta** 180.948	Tungsten 74 **W** 183.85	Rhenium 75 **Re** 186.207	Osmium 76 **Os** 190.2	Iridium 77 **Ir** 192.22
7	Francium 87 **Fr** 223.020	Radium 88 **Ra** 226.025	Actinium 89 **Ac** 227.028	Rutherfordium 104 **Rf** (261)	Hahnium 105 **Ha** (262)	Seaborgium 106 **Sg** (263)	Nielsbohrium 107 **Ns** (262)	Hassium 108 **Hs** (265)	Meitnerium 109 **Mt** (266)

Lanthanide Series

Cerium 58 **Ce** 140.115	Praseodymium 59 **Pr** 140.908	Neodymium 60 **Nd** 144.24	Promethium 61 **Pm** 144.913	Samarium 62 **Sm** 150.36	Europium 63 **Eu** 151.965

Actinide Series

Thorium 90 **Th** 232.038	Protactinium 91 **Pa** 231.036	Uranium 92 **U** 238.029	Neptunium 93 **Np** 237.048	Plutonium 94 **Pu** 244.064	Americium 95 **Am** 243.061

APPENDIX F

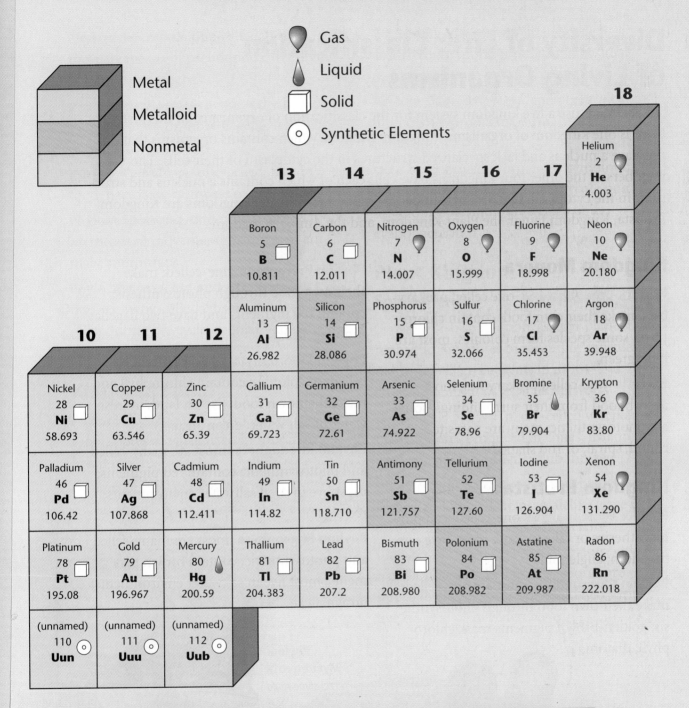

Gas

Liquid

Solid

Synthetic Elements

Metal

Metalloid

Nonmetal

18
Helium
2
He
4.003

13	14	15	16	17
Boron	Carbon	Nitrogen	Oxygen	Fluorine	Neon
5	6	7	8	9	10
B	C	N	O	F	Ne
10.811	12.011	14.007	15.999	18.998	20.180
Aluminum	Silicon	Phosphorus	Sulfur	Chlorine	Argon
13	14	15	16	17	18
Al	Si	P	S	Cl	Ar
26.982	28.086	30.974	32.066	35.453	39.948

10	11	12
Nickel	Copper	Zinc	Gallium	Germanium	Arsenic	Selenium	Bromine	Krypton
28	29	30	31	32	33	34	35	36
Ni	Cu	Zn	Ga	Ge	As	Se	Br	Kr
58.693	63.546	65.39	69.723	72.61	74.922	78.96	79.904	83.80
Palladium	Silver	Cadmium	Indium	Tin	Antimony	Tellurium	Iodine	Xenon
46	47	48	49	50	51	52	53	54
Pd	Ag	Cd	In	Sn	Sb	Te	I	Xe
106.42	107.868	112.411	114.82	118.710	121.757	127.60	126.904	131.290
Platinum	Gold	Mercury	Thallium	Lead	Bismuth	Polonium	Astatine	Radon
78	79	80	81	82	83	84	85	86
Pt	Au	Hg	Tl	Pb	Bi	Po	At	Rn
195.08	196.967	200.59	204.383	207.2	208.980	208.982	209.987	222.018
(unnamed)	(unnamed)	(unnamed)
110	111	112
Uun	Uuu	Uub

Gadolinium	Terbium	Dysprosium	Holmium	Erbium	Thulium	Ytterbium	Lutetium
64	65	66	67	68	69	70	71
Gd	Tb	Dy	Ho	Er	Tm	Yb	Lu
157.25	158.925	162.50	164.930	167.26	168.934	173.04	174.967
Curium	Berkelium	Californium	Einsteinium	Fermium	Mendelevium	Nobelium	Lawrencium
96	97	98	99	100	101	102	103
Cm	Bk	Cf	Es	Fm	Md	No	Lr
247.070	247.070	251.080	252.083	257.095	258.099	259.101	260.105

Seed Plants

Division Ginkgophyta deciduous gymnosperms; only one living species called the maiden hair tree; fan-shaped leaves with branching veins; reproduces with seeds; ginkgos

Division Cycadophyta palmlike gymnosperms; large compound leaves; produce seeds in cones; cycads

Division Coniferophyta deciduous or evergreen gymnosperms; trees or shrubs; needlelike or scalelike leaves; seeds produced in cones; conifers

Division Gnetophyta shrubs or woody vines; seeds produced in cones; division contains only three genera; gnetum

Division Anthophyta dominant group of plants; ovules protected at fertilization by an ovary; sperm carried to ovules by pollen tube; produce flowers and seeds in fruits; flowering plants

Animal Kingdom

Phylum Porifera aquatic organisms that lack true tissues and organs; they are asymmetrical and sessile; sponges

Phylum Cnidaria radially symmetrical organisms with a digestive cavity with one opening; most have tentacles armed with stinging cells; live in aquatic environments singly or in colonies; includes jellyfish, corals, hydra, and sea anemones

Phylum Platyhelminthes bilaterally symmetrical worms with flattened bodies; digestive system has one opening; parasitic and free-living species; flatworms

Phylum Cnidaria
Jellyfish

Phylum Arthropoda
Jumping spider

Phylum Arthropoda
Sally Light-foot crab

Division Coniferophyta
Slash Pine cones

Division Anthophyta
Fairyslipper

Division Anthophyta
Blackberries

Phylum Annelida
Christmas Tree worm

Phylum Nematoda round bilaterally symmetrical body; digestive system with two openings; some free-living forms but mostly parasitic; roundworms

Phylum Mollusca soft-bodied animals, many with a hard shell; a mantle covers the soft body; aquatic and terrestrial species; includes clams, snails, squid, and octopuses

Phylum Annelida bilaterally symmetrical worms with round segmented bodies; terrestrial and aquatic species; includes earthworms, leeches, and marine polychaetes

Phylum Arthropoda very large phylum of organisms that have segmented bodies with pairs of jointed appendages and a hard exoskeleton; terrestrial and aquatic species; includes insects, crustaceans, spiders, and horseshoe crabs

Phylum Echinodermata saltwater organisms with spiny or leathery skin; water-vascular system with tube feet; radial symmetry; includes starfish, sand dollars, and sea urchins

Phylum Chordata organisms with internal skeletons, specialized body systems, and paired appendages; all at some time have a notochord, dorsal nerve cord, gill slits, and a tail; includes fish, amphibians, reptiles, birds, and mammals

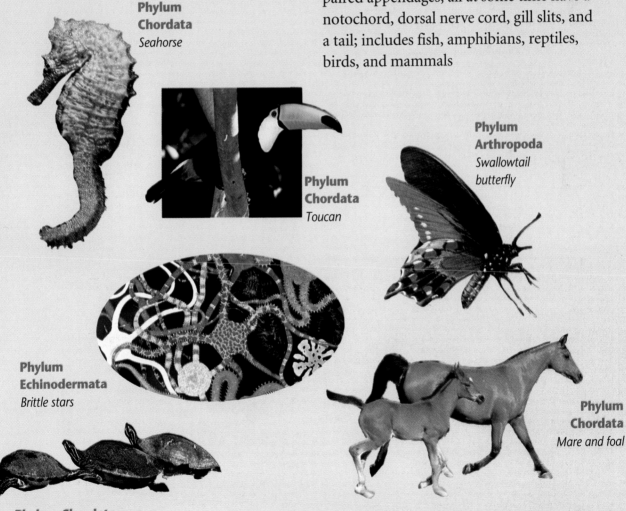

Phylum Chordata
Seahorse

Phylum Chordata
Toucan

Phylum Arthropoda
Swallowtail butterfly

Phylum Echinodermata
Brittle stars

Phylum Chordata
Mare and foal

Phylum Chordata
Peninsula turtles

APPENDIX H

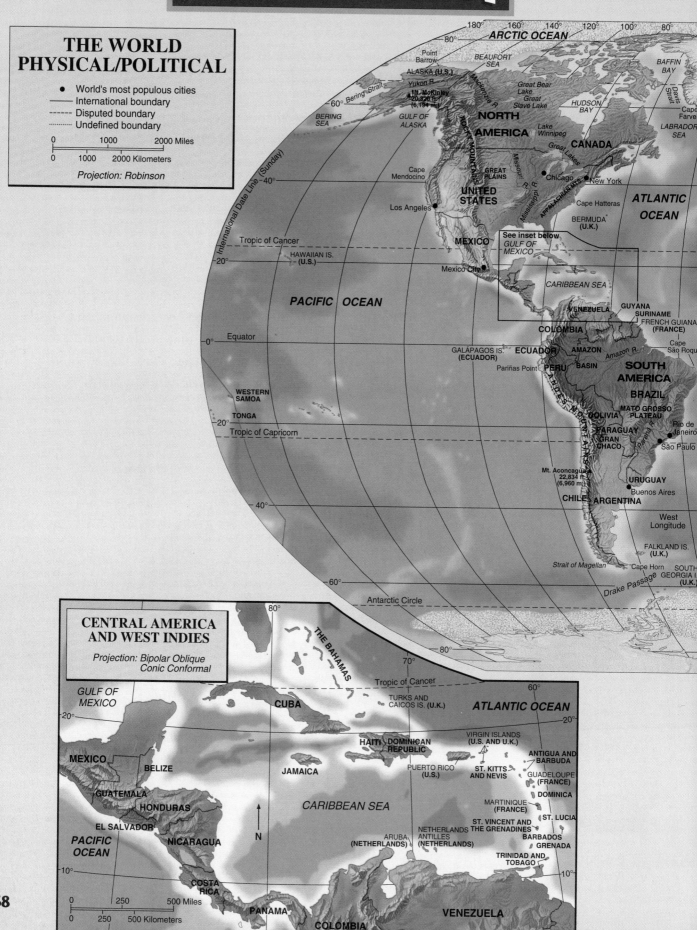

THE WORLD PHYSICAL/POLITICAL

- ● World's most populous cities
- —— International boundary
- ----- Disputed boundary
- ········· Undefined boundary

0   1000   2000 Miles
0   1000   2000 Kilometers

Projection: Robinson

CENTRAL AMERICA AND WEST INDIES

Projection: Bipolar Oblique Conic Conformal

0   250   500 Miles
0   250   500 Kilometers

APPENDIX H

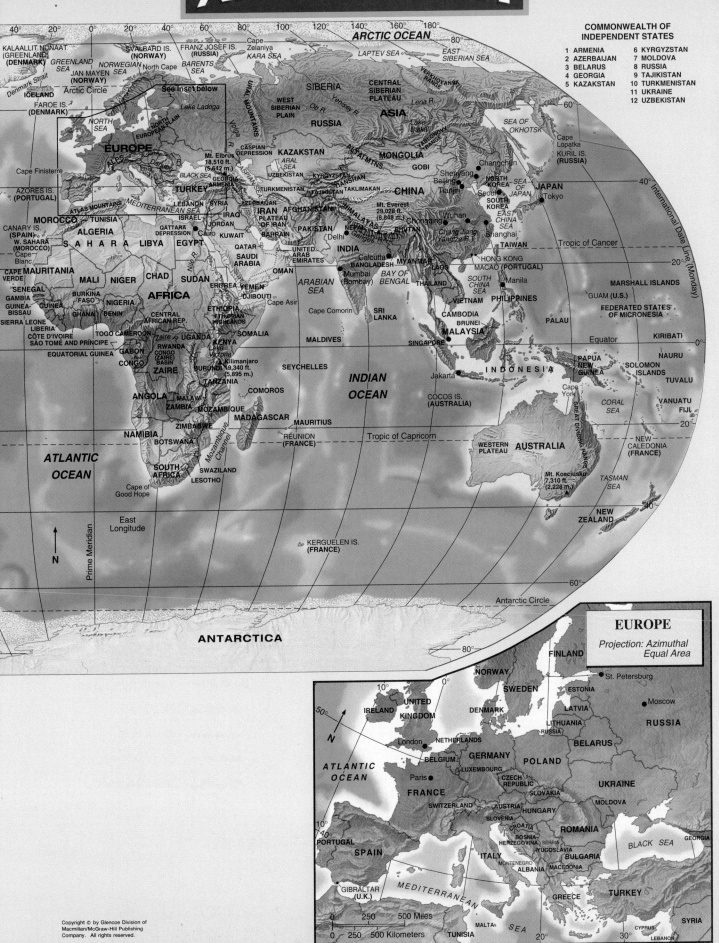

COMMONWEALTH OF INDEPENDENT STATES

1 ARMENIA	6 KYRGYZSTAN
2 AZERBAIJAN	7 MOLDOVA
3 BELARUS	8 RUSSIA
4 GEORGIA	9 TAJIKISTAN
5 KAZAKSTAN	10 TURKMENISTAN
	11 UKRAINE
	12 UZBEKISTAN

EUROPE

Projection: Azimuthal Equal Area

Weather Map Symbols

Sample Plotted Report at Each Station

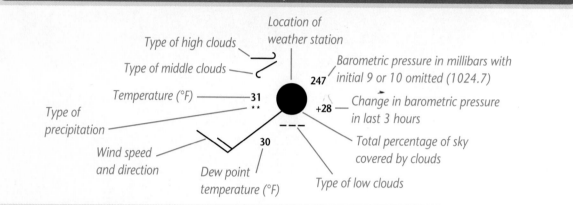

Symbols Used in Plotting Report

Precipitation

≡	Fog
٭	Snow
●	Rain
⊼	Thunder-storm
﹐	Drizzle
▽	Showers

Wind Speed and Direction

○	0 calm
/	1–2 knots
⟋	3–7 knots
⟍	8–12 knots
⟍⟍	13–17 knots
⟍⟍	18–22 knots
⟍⟍⟍	23–27 knots
⟍	48–52 knots

1 knot = 1.852 km/h

Sky Coverage

○	No cover
◔	1/10 or less
◔	2/10 or 3/10
◑	4/10
◑	1/2
◕	6/10
◕	7/10
◑	Overcast with openings
●	Complete overcast

Some Types of High Clouds

⌐⟩	Scattered cirrus
⌐⟩⟩	Dense cirrus in patches
⟩‿⊏	Veil of cirrus covering entire sky
‿⊏	Cirrus not covering entire sky

Some Types of Middle Clouds

∠	Thin altostratus layer
⫽	Thick altostratus layer
⟋	Thin altostratus in patches
⟋	Thin altostratus in bands

Some Types of Low Clouds

⌒	Cumulus of fair weather
⊔	Stratocumulus
- - -	Fractocumulus of bad weather
—	Stratus of fair weather

Fronts and Pressure Systems

(H) or High **(L) or Low**	Center of high or low pressure system
▲▲▲▲	Cold front
●●●●	Warm front
▲●▲●	Occluded front
●▲●▲	Stationary front

Solar System Information

Planet	Mercury	Venus	Earth	Mars	Jupiter	Saturn	Uranus	Neptune	Pluto
Diameter (km)	4878	12104	12756	6794	142796	120660	51118	49528	2290
Diameter (E = 1.0)*	0.38	0.95	1.00	0.53	11.19	9.46	4.01	3.88	0.18
Mass (E = 1.0)*	0.06	0.82	1.00	0.11	317.83	95.15	14.54	17.23	0.002
Density (g/cm^3)	5.42	5.24	5.50	3.94	1.31	0.70	1.30	1.66	2.03
Period of rotation days hours minutes R = retrograde	58 15 28	243 00 14$_R$	00 23 56	00 24 37	00 09 55	00 10 39	00 17 14$_R$	00 16 03	06 09 17
Surface gravity (E = 1.0)*	0.38	0.90	1.00	0.38	2.53	1.07	0.92	1.12	0.06
Average distance to sun (AU)	0.387	0.723	1.000	1.524	5.203	9.529	19.191	30.061	39.529
Period of revolution	87.97d	224.70d	365.26d	686.98d	11.86y	29.46y	84.04y	164.79y	248.53y
Eccentricity of orbit	0.206	0.007	0.017	0.093	0.048	0.056	0.046	0.010	0.248
Average orbital speed (km/s)	47.89	35.03	29.79	24.13	13.06	9.64	6.81	5.43	4.74
Number of known satellites	0	0	1	2	16	18	15	8	1
Known rings	0	0	0	0	1	thou-sands	11	4	0

Table J-1: Solar System Information

* Earth = 1.0

Star Charts

Shown here are star charts for viewing stars in the Northern Hemisphere during the four different seasons. These charts are drawn from the night sky at about 35° north latitude, but they can be used for most locations in the Northern Hemisphere. The lines on the charts outline major constellations. The dense band of stars is the Milky Way. To use, hold the chart vertically, with the direction you are facing at the bottom of the map.

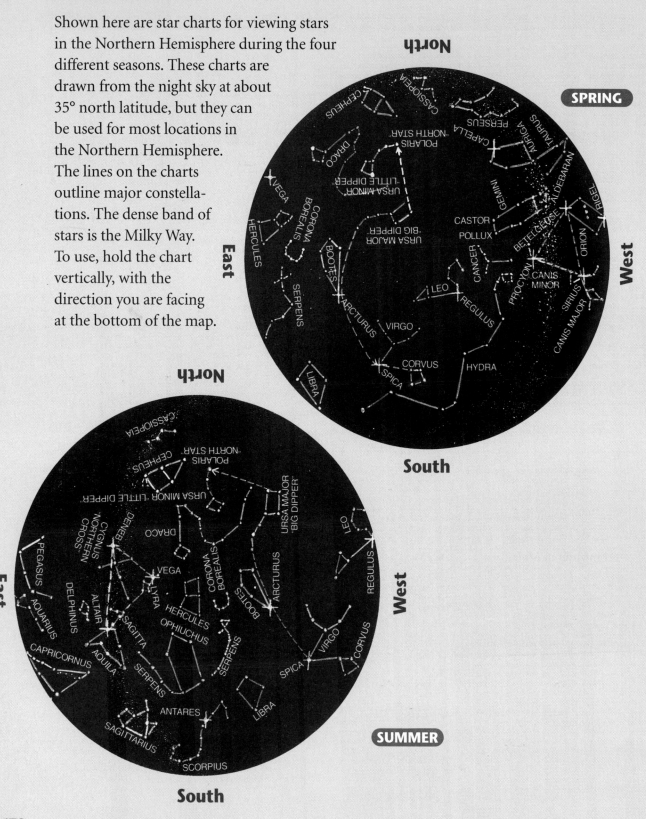

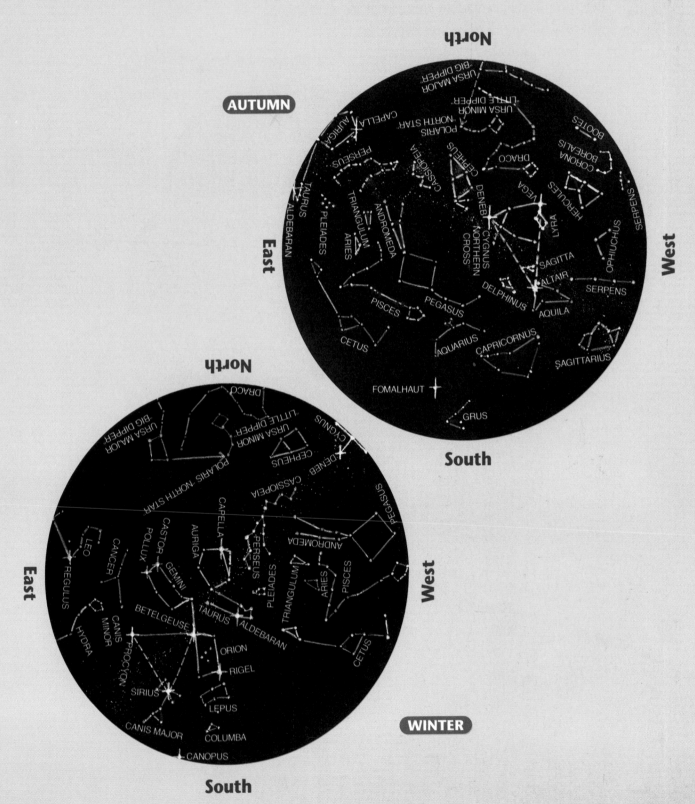

AUTUMN

North

East

West

South

WINTER

North

East

West

South

Animal Cell

Refer to this diagram of an animal cell as you read about cell parts and their jobs.

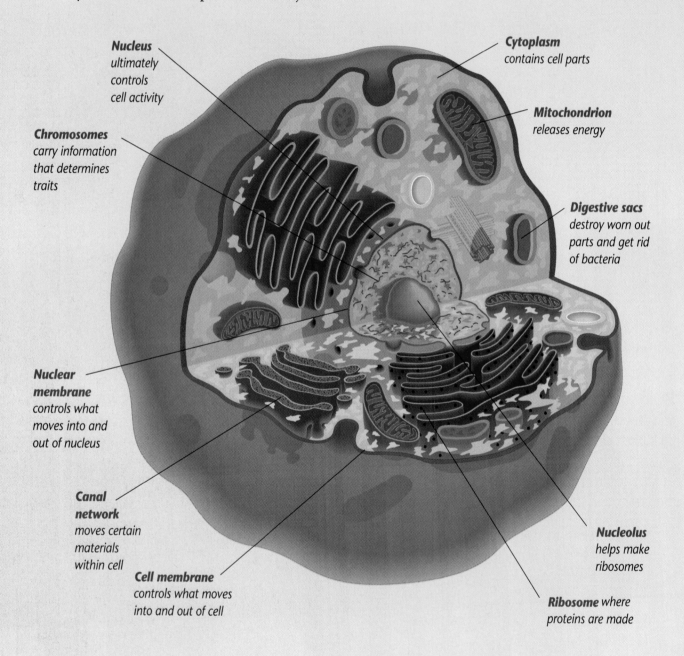

Nucleus
ultimately controls cell activity

Cytoplasm
contains cell parts

Mitochondrion
releases energy

Chromosomes
carry information that determines traits

Digestive sacs
destroy worn out parts and get rid of bacteria

Nuclear membrane
controls what moves into and out of nucleus

Canal network
moves certain materials within cell

Cell membrane
controls what moves into and out of cell

Nucleolus
helps make ribosomes

Ribosome *where proteins are made*

APPENDIX L

Plant Cell

Refer to this diagram of a plant cell as you read about cell parts and their jobs.

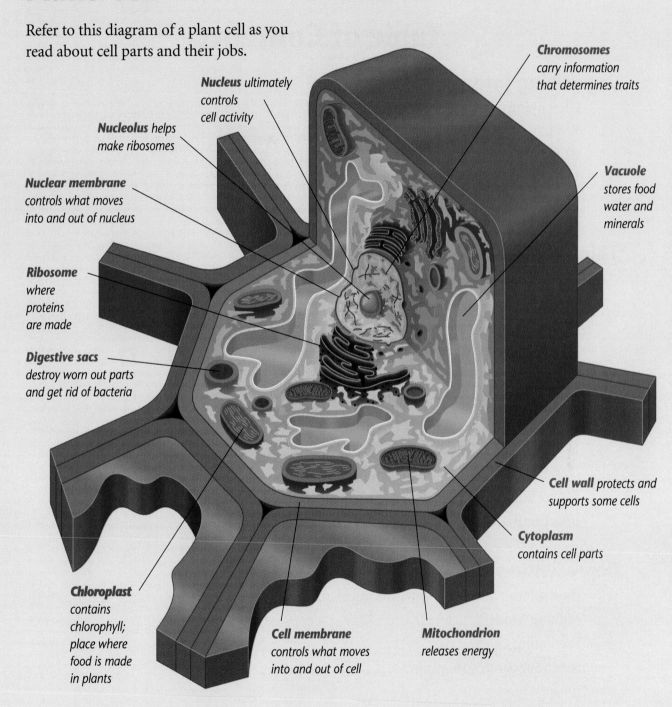

Nucleus *ultimately controls cell activity*

Nucleolus *helps make ribosomes*

Nuclear membrane *controls what moves into and out of nucleus*

Ribosome *where proteins are made*

Digestive sacs *destroy worn out parts and get rid of bacteria*

Chromosomes *carry information that determines traits*

Vacuole *stores food water and minerals*

Cell wall *protects and supports some cells*

Cytoplasm *contains cell parts*

Chloroplast *contains chlorophyll; place where food is made in plants*

Cell membrane *controls what moves into and out of cell*

Mitochondrion *releases energy*

Table of Contents

Organizing Information

Thinking Critically

Practicing Scientific Processes

Representing and Applying Data

Organizing Information

▶ Classifying

You may not realize it, but you make things orderly in the world around you. If you hang your shirts together in the closet, if your socks take up a particular corner of a dresser drawer, or if your favorite CDs are stacked together, you have used the skill of classifying.

Classifying is the process of sorting objects or events into groups based on common features. When classifying, first observe the objects or events to be classified. Then, select one feature that is shared by most members in the group but not by all. Place those members that share the feature into a subgroup. You can classify members into smaller and smaller subgroups based on characteristics.

How would you classify a collection of CDs? You might classify those you like to dance to in one subgroup and CDs you like to listen to in the next column, as in the diagram. The CDs you like to dance to could be subdivided into a rap subgroup and a rock subgroup. Note that for each feature selected, each CD only fits into one subgroup. Keep select-

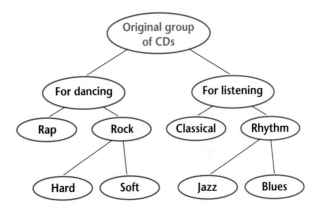

ing features until all the CDs are classified. The diagram above shows one possible classification.

Remember, when you classify, you are grouping objects or events for a purpose. Keep your purpose in mind as you select the features to form groups and subgroups.

▶ Sequencing

A sequence is an arrangement of things or events in a particular order. A sequence with which you are most familiar is the use of alphabetical order. Another example of sequence would be the steps in a recipe. Think about baking chocolate chip cookies. Steps in the recipe have to be followed in order for the cookies to turn out right.

When you are asked to sequence objects or events within a group, figure out what comes first, then think about what should come second. Continue to choose objects or events until all of the objects you started out with are in order. Then, go back over the sequence to make sure each thing or event in your sequence logically leads to the next.

▶ Concept Mapping

If you were taking an automobile trip, you would probably take along a road map. The road map shows your location, your destination, and other places along the way. By looking at the map and finding where you are, you can begin to understand where you are in relation to other locations on the map.

A concept map is similar to a road map. But, a concept map shows relationships among ideas (or concepts) rather than places. A concept map is a diagram that visually shows how concepts are related. Because the concept map shows relationships among ideas, it can make the meanings of ideas and terms clear, and help you understand better what you are studying.

Network Tree   Look at the concept map about Protists. This is called a network tree. Notice how some words are circled while others are written across connecting lines. The circled words are science concepts. The lines in the map show related concepts. The words written on the lines describe the relationships between concepts.

Network Tree

Protists

include

animal-like protists

plant-like protists

fungus-like protists

known as

known as

known as

protozoans

algae

water molds   slime molds

When you are asked to construct a network tree, write down the topic and list the major concepts related to that topic on a piece of paper. Then look at your list and begin to put them in order from general to specific. Branch the related concepts from the major concept and describe the relationships on the lines. Continue to write the more specific concepts. Write the relationships between the concepts on the lines until all concepts are mapped. Examine the concept map for relationships that cross branches, and add them to the concept map.

Events Chain   An events chain is another type of concept map. An events chain map, such as the one on the effects of gravity, is used to describe ideas in order. In science, an

Events Chain

Girl throws ball horizontally.

↓

Ball has a constant *horizontal* velocity.

↓

Gravity pulls on the ball.

↓

Ball *accelerates* downward.

↓

Ball moves both *forward* and *downward*.

↓

Ball hits the ground.

events chain can be used to describe a sequence of events, the steps in a procedure, or the stages of a process.

When making an events chain, first find the one event that starts the chain. This event is called the initiating event. Then, find the

next event in the chain and continue until you reach an outcome. Suppose you are asked to describe what happens when someone throws a ball horizontally. An events chain map describing the steps might look like the one on page 678. Notice that connecting words are not necessary in an events chain.

Cycle Map   A cycle concept map is a special type of events chain map. In a cycle concept map, the series of events does not produce a

Cycle Map

```
        Plants undergoing
        photosynthesis

which has been                    use
released by

   oxygen                         carbon
                                  dioxide

    in the                    which is
  presence of               released by

        respiration in
        animals and plants
```

final outcome. Instead, the last event in the chain relates back to the initiating event.

As in the events chain map, you first decide on an initiating event and then list each event in order. Since there is no outcome and the last event relates back to the initiating event, the cycle repeats itself. Look at the cycle map for photosynthesis shown above.

Spider Map   A fourth type of concept map is the spider map. This is a map that you can use for brainstorming. Once you have a central idea, you may find you have a jumble of ideas that relate to it, but are not necessarily clearly related to each other. By writing these

Spider Map

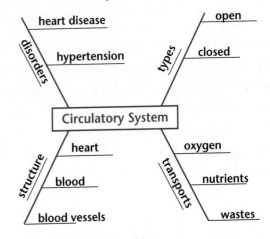

ideas outside the main concept, you may begin to separate and group unrelated terms so that they become more useful.

There is usually not one correct way to create a concept map. As you construct one type of map, you may discover other ways to construct the map that show the relationships between concepts in a better way. If you do discover what you think is a better way to create a concept map, go ahead and use the new way. Overall, concept maps are useful for breaking a big concept down into smaller parts, making learning easier.

▶ Making and Using Tables

Browse through your textbook, and you will notice tables in the text and in the activities. In a table, data or information is arranged in such a way that makes it easier for you to understand. Activity tables help organize the data you collect during an activity so that results can be interpreted more easily.

Parts of a Table   Most tables have a title. At a glance, the title tells you what the table is about. A table is divided into columns and rows. The first column lists items to be compared. In the table shown to the right, different magnitudes of force are being compared. The row across the top lists the specific characteristics being compared. Within the grid of the table, the collected data is recorded. Look at the features of the table in the next column.

What is the title of this table? The title is "Earthquake Magnitude." What is being compared? The distance away from the epicenter that tremors are felt and the average number of earthquakes expected per year are being compared for different magnitudes on the Richter scale.

Using Tables   What is the average number of earthquakes expected per year for an earthquake with a magnitude of 5.5 at the focus? Locate the column labeled "Average number expected per year" and the row "5.0 to 5.9." The data in the box where the column and row intersect is the answer. Did you answer "800"? What is the distance away from the epicenter for an earthquake with a

Earthquake Magnitude		
Magnitude at Focus	Distance from Epicenter that Tremors are Felt	Average Number Expected Per Year
1.0 to 3.9	24 km	>100 000
4.0 to 4.9	48 km	6200
5.0 to 5.9	112 km	800
6.0 to 6.9	200 km	120
7.0 to 7.9	400 km	20
8.0 to 8.9	720 km	<1

magnitude of 8.1? If you answered "720 km," you understand how to use the parts of a table.

Making Tables   To make a table, list the items to be compared down in columns and the characteristics to be compared across in rows. Make a table and record the data comparing the mass of recycled materials collected by a class. On Monday, students turned in 4 kg of paper, 2 kg of aluminum, and 0.5 kg of plastic. On Wednesday, they turned in 3.5 kg of paper, 1.5 kg of aluminum, and 0.5 kg of plastic. On Friday, the totals were 3 kg of paper, 1 kg of aluminum, and 1.5 kg of plastic. If your table looks like the one shown below, you are able to make tables to organize data.

Recycled Materials			
Day of Week	Paper (kg)	Aluminum (kg)	Plastic (kg)
Mon.	4	2	0.5
Wed.	3.5	1.5	0.5
Fri.	3	1	1.5

▶ Making and Using Graphs

After scientists organize data in tables, they may display the data in a graph. A graph is a diagram that shows how variables compare. A graph makes interpretation and analysis of data easier. There are three basic types of graphs used in science—the line graph, the bar graph, and the pie graph.

Line Graphs   A line graph is used to show the relationship between two variables. The variables being compared go on two axes of the graph. The independent variable always goes on the horizontal axis, called the *x*-axis. The dependent variable always goes on the vertical axis, called the *y*-axis.

Suppose a school started a peer study program with a class of students to see how science grades were affected.

Average Grades of Students in Study Program	
Grading Period	Average Science Grade
First	81
Second	85
Third	86
Fourth	89

You could make a graph of the grades of students in the program over the four grading periods of the school year. The grading period is the independent variable and is placed on the *x*-axis of your graph. The average grade of the students in the program is the dependent variable and would go on the *y*-axis.

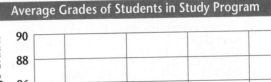
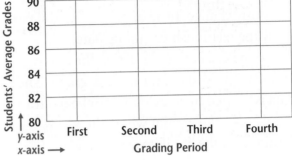

Average Grades of Students in Study Program

After drawing your axes, you would label each axis with a scale. The *x*-axis simply lists the four grading periods. To make a scale of grades on the *y*-axis, you must look at the data values. Since the lowest grade was 81 and the highest was 89, you know that you will have to start numbering at least at 81 and go through 89. You decide to start numbering at 80 and number by twos through 90.

Next, plot the data points. The first pair of data you want to plot is the first grading period and 81. Locate "First" on the *x*-axis and locate "81" on the *y*-axis. Where an imaginary vertical line from the *x*-axis and an imaginary horizontal line from the *y*-axis would meet, place the first data point. Place the other data points the same way. After all the points are plotted, connect them with straight lines.

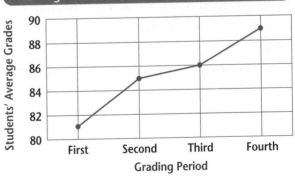

Average Grades of Students in Study Program

Bar Graphs   Bar graphs are similar to line graphs. They compare data that do not continuously change. In a bar graph, vertical bars show the relationships among data.

To make a bar graph, set up the *x*-axis and *y*-axis as you did for the line graph. The data is plotted by drawing vertical bars from the *x*-axis up to a point where the *y*-axis would meet the bar if it were extended.

Look at the bar graph comparing the masses lifted by an electromagnet with different numbers of dry cell batteries. The *x*-axis is the number of dry cell batteries, and the *y*-axis is the mass lifted.

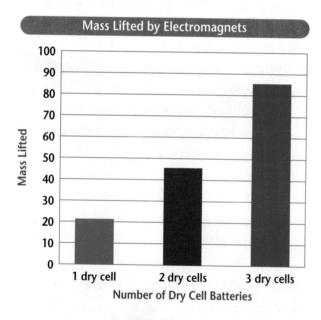

You find that there are 143 seeds in the package. This represents 100 percent, the whole pie.

You plant the seeds, and 129 seeds germinate. The seeds that germinated will make up one section of the pie graph, and the seeds that did not germinate will make up the remaining section.

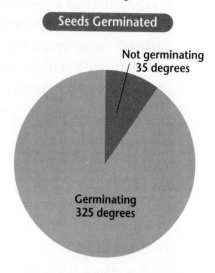

To find out how much of the pie each section should take, divide the number of seeds in each section by the total number of seeds. Then multiply your answer by 360, the number of degrees in a circle, and round to the nearest whole number. The section of the pie graph in degrees that represents the seeds germinated is figured below.

$$\frac{129}{143} \times 360 = 324.75 \text{ or } 325 \text{ degrees}$$

Plot this group on the pie graph using a compass and a protractor. Use the compass to draw a circle. Then, draw a straight line from the center to the edge of the circle. Place your protractor on this line and use it to mark a point on the edge of the circle at 325 degrees. Connect this point with a straight line to the center of the circle. This is the section for the group of seeds that germinated. The other section represents the group of 14 seeds that did not germinate. Label the sections of your graph and title the graph.

Pie Graphs   A pie graph uses a circle divided into sections to display data. Each section represents part of the whole. All the sections together equal 100 percent.

Suppose you wanted to make a pie graph to show the number of seeds that germinated in a package. You would have to count the total number of seeds and the number of seeds that germinated out of the total.

Thinking Critically

▶ Observing and Inferring

Imagine that you have just finished a volleyball game. At home, you open the refrigerator and see a jug of orange juice on the back of the top shelf. The jug feels cold as you grasp it. Then you drink the juice, smell the oranges, and enjoy the tart taste in your mouth.

As you imagined yourself in the story, you used your senses to make observations. You used your sense of sight to find the jug in the refrigerator, your sense of touch when you felt the coldness of the jug, your sense of hearing to listen as the liquid filled the glass, and your senses of smell and taste to enjoy the odor and tartness of the juice. The basis of all scientific investigation is observation.

Scientists try to make careful and accurate observations. When possible, they use instruments such as microscopes and thermometers or a pan balance to make observations. Measurements with a balance or thermometer provide numerical data that can be checked and repeated.

When you make observations in science, you'll find it helpful to examine the entire object or situation first. Then, look carefully for details. Write down everything you observe.

Scientists often make inferences based on their observations. An inference is an attempt to explain or interpret observations or to say what caused what you observed. For example, if you observed a CLOSED sign in a store window around noon, you might infer the owner is taking a lunch break. But, it's also possible that the owner has a doctor's appointment or has taken the day off to go fishing. The only way to be sure your inference is correct is to investigate further.

When making an inference, be certain to use accurate data and observations. Analyze all of the data that you've collected. Then, based on everything you know, explain or interpret what you've observed.

▶ Comparing and Contrasting

Observations can be analyzed by noting the similarities and differences between two or more objects or events that you observe. When you look at objects or events to see how they are similar, you are comparing them. Contrasting is looking for differences in similar objects or events.

Suppose you were asked to compare and contrast the planets Venus and Earth. You would start by looking at what is known about these planets. Arrange this information in a table, making two columns on a piece of paper and listing ways the planets are similar in one column and ways they are different in the other.

Comparison of Venus and Earth		
Properties	Earth	Venus
Diameter (km)	12 756	12 104
Average density (g/cm³)	5.5	5.3
Percentage of sunlight reflected	39	76
Daytime surface temperature (degrees)	300	750
Number of satellites	1	0

Similarities you might point out are that both planets are similar in size, shape, and mass. Differences include Venus having a hotter surface temperature that reflects more sunlight than Earth reflects. Also, Venus lacks a moon.

▶ Recognizing Cause and Effect

Have you ever watched something happen and then made suggestions as to why it happened? If so, you have observed an effect and inferred a cause. The event is an effect, and the reason for the event is the cause.

Suppose that every time your teacher fed the fish in a classroom aquarium, she or he tapped the food container on the edge of the aquarium. Then, one day your teacher just happened to tap the edge of the aquarium with a pencil while making a point about an ecology lesson. You observed the fish swim to the surface of the aquarium to feed. What is the effect, and what would you infer to be the cause? The effect is the fish swimming to the surface of the aquarium. You might infer the cause to be the teacher tapping on the edge of the aquarium. In determining cause and effect, you have made a logical inference based on your observations.

Perhaps the fish swam to the surface because they reacted to the teacher's waving hand or for some other reason. When scientists are unsure of the cause of a certain event, they design controlled experiments to determine what causes the event. Although you have made a logical conclusion about the behavior of the fish, you would have to perform an experiment to be certain that it was the tapping that caused the effect you observed.

▶ Measuring in SI

The metric system is a system of measurement developed by a group of scientists in 1795. It helps scientists avoid problems by providing standard measurements that all scientists around the world can understand. A modern form of the metric system, called the International System, or SI, was adopted for worldwide use in 1960.

Metric Prefixes			
Prefix	Symbol	Meaning	
kilo-	k	1000	thousand
hecto-	h	100	hundred
deka-	da	10	ten
deci-	d	0.1	tenth
centi-	c	0.01	hundreth
milli-	m	0.001	thousandth

The metric system is convenient because unit sizes vary by multiples of 10. When changing from smaller units to larger units, divide by 10. When changing from larger units to smaller, you multiply by 10. For example, to convert millimeters to centimeters, divide the millimeters by 10. To convert 30 millimeters to centimeters, divide 30 by 10 (30 millimeters equals 3 centimeters).

Prefixes are used to name units. Look at the table for some common metric prefixes and their meanings. Do you see how the prefix *kilo-* attached to the unit *gram* is *kilogram*, or 1000 grams? The prefix *deci-* attached to the unit *meter* is *decimeter*, or one-tenth (0.1) of a meter.

Length You have probably measured lengths or distances many times. The meter is the SI unit used to measure length. A baseball bat is about one meter long. When measuring smaller lengths, the meter is divided into smaller units called centimeters and millimeters. A centimeter is one-hundredth (0.01) of a meter, which is about the size of the width of the fingernail on your ring finger. A millimeter is one-thousandth of a meter (0.001), about the thickness of a dime.

Most metric rulers have lines indicating centimeters and millimeters. The centimeter lines are the longer, numbered lines, and the shorter lines are millimeter lines. When using a metric ruler, line up the 0 centimeter mark with the end of the object being measured, and read the number of the unit where the object ends.

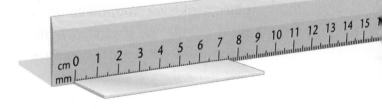

Surface Area Units of length are also used to measure surface area. The standard unit of area is the square meter (m^2). A square that's one meter long on each side has a surface area of one square meter. Similarly, a square centimeter (cm^2) is one centimeter long on each side. The surface area of an object is determined by multiplying the length times the width.

Volume The volume of a rectangular solid is also calculated using units of length. The cubic meter (m^3) is the standard SI unit of volume. A cubic meter is a cube one meter on each side. You can determine the volume of rectangular solids by multiplying length times width times height.

Liquid Volume During science activities, you will measure liquids using beakers and graduated cylinders marked in milliliters. A graduated cylinder is a cylindrical container marked with lines from bottom to top.

Liquid volume is measured using a unit called a liter. A liter has the volume of 1000 cubic centimeters. Since the prefix *milli-* means thousandth (0.001), a milliliter equals one cubic centimeter. One milliliter of liquid would completely fill a cube measuring one centimeter on each side.

Mass Scientists use balances to find the mass of objects in grams. You will use a beam balance similar to the one illustrated. Notice that on one side of the balance is a pan and on the other side is a set of beams. Each beam has an object of a known mass called a *rider* that slides on the beam.

Before you find the mass of an object, set the balance to zero by sliding all the riders back to the zero point. Check the pointer on the right to make sure it swings an equal distance above and below the zero point on the scale. If the swing is unequal, find and turn the adjusting screw until you have an equal swing.

Place an object on the pan. Slide the rider with the largest mass along its beam until the pointer drops below zero. Then move it back one notch. Repeat the process on each beam until the pointer swings an equal distance above and below the zero point. Add the masses on each beam to find the mass of the object.

You should never place a hot object or pour chemicals directly on the pan. Instead, find the mass of a clean beaker or a glass jar. Place the dry or liquid chemicals in the container. Then find the combined mass of the container and the chemicals. Calculate the mass of the chemicals by subtracting the mass of the empty container from the combined mass.

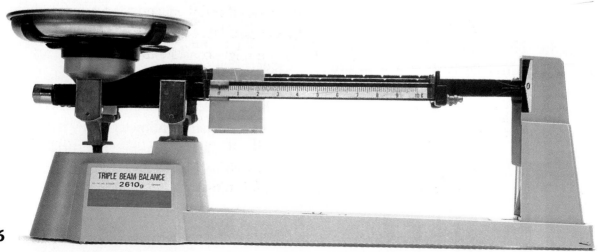

Practicing Scientific Processes

You might say that the work of a scientist is to solve problems. But when you decide how to dress on a particular day, you are doing problem solving, too. You may observe what the weather looks like through a window. You may go outside and see if what you are wearing is warm or cool enough.

Scientists use an orderly approach to learn new information and to solve problems. The methods scientists may use include observing, forming a hypothesis, testing a hypothesis, separating and controlling variables, and interpreting data.

▶ Observing

You observe all the time. Any time you smell wood burning, touch a pet, see

lightning, taste food, or hear your favorite music, you are observing. Observation gives you information about events or things. Scientists try to observe as much as possible about the things and events they study so that they can know that what they say about their observations is reliable.

Some observations describe something using only words. These observations are called qualitative observations. If you were making qualitative observations of a dog, you might use words such as furry, brown, short-haired, or short-eared.

Other observations describe how much of something there is. These are quantitative observations and use numbers as well as words in the description. Tools or equipment are used to measure the characteristic being described. Quantitative observations of a dog might include a mass of 45 kg, a height of 76 cm, ear length of 14 cm, and an age of 283 days.

▶ Using Observations to Form a Hypothesis

Suppose you want to make a perfect score on a spelling test. Begin by thinking of several ways to accomplish this. Base these possibilities on past observations. If you put each of these possibilities into sentence form, using the words if and then, you can form a hypothesis. All of the following are hypotheses you might consider to explain how you could score 100 percent on your test:

If the test is easy, then I will get a perfect score.

If I am intelligent, then I will get a perfect score.

If I study hard, then I will get a perfect score.

Scientists make hypotheses that they can test to explain the observations they have made. Perhaps a scientist has observed that plants that receive fertilizer grow taller than plants that do not. A scientist may form a hypothesis that says: If plants are fertilized, then their growth will increase.

▶ Designing an Experiment to Test a Hypothesis

Once you state a hypothesis, you probably want to find out if it explains an event or an observation or not. This requires a test. A hypothesis must be something you can test. To test a hypothesis, you design and carry out an experiment. Experiments involve planning and materials. Let's figure out how to conduct an experiment to test the hypothesis

stated before about the effects of fertilizer on plants.

First, you need to write out a procedure. A procedure is the plan that you follow in your experiment. A procedure tells you what materials to use and how to use them. In this experiment, your plan may involve using ten bean plants that are each 15-cm tall (to begin with) in two groups, Groups A and B. You will water the five bean plants in Group A with 200 mL of plain water and no fertilizer twice a week for three weeks. You will treat the five bean plants in Group B with 200 mL of fertilizer solution twice a week for three weeks.

You will need to measure all the plants in both groups at the beginning of the experiment and again at the end of the three-week period. These measurements will be the data that you record in a table. A sample table has been done for you. Look at the data in the table for this experiment. From the data, you can draw a conclusion and make a statement about your results. If the conclusion you draw from the data supports your hypothesis, then you can say that your hypothesis is

Growing Bean Plants		
Plants	Treatment	Height 3 Weeks Later
Group A	no fertilizer added to soil	17 cm
Group B	3 g fertilizer added to soil	31 cm

reliable. Reliable means that you can trust your conclusion. If it did not support your hypothesis, then you would have to make new observations and state a new hypothesis, one that you could also test.

▶ Separating and Controlling Variables

In the experiment with the bean plants, you made everything the same except for treating one group (Group B) with fertilizer. In any experiment, it is important to keep everything the same, except for the item you are testing. In the experiment, you kept the type of plants, their beginning heights, the soil, the frequency with which you watered them, and the amount of water or fertilizer all the same, or constant. By doing so, you made sure that at the end of three weeks any change you saw was the result of whether or not the plants had been fertilized. The only thing that you changed, or varied, was the use of fertilizer. In an experiment, the one factor that you change (in this case, the fertilizer), is called the independent variable. The factor that changes (in this case, growth) as a result of the independent variable is called the dependent variable. Always make sure that there is only one independent variable. If you allow more than one, you will not know what causes the changes you observe in the dependent variable.

Many experiments also have a control, a treatment that you can compare with the results of your test groups. In this case, Group A was the control because it was not treated with fertilizer. Group B was the test group. At the end of three weeks, you were able to compare Group A with Group B and draw a conclusion.

▶ Interpreting Data

The word *interpret* means to explain the meaning of something. Information, or data, needs to mean something. Look at the problem originally being explored and find out what the data shows. Perhaps you are looking at a table from an experiment designed to test the hypothesis: If plants are fertilized, then their growth will increase. Look back to the table showing the results of the bean plant experiment.

Identify the control group and the test group so you can see whether or not the variable has had an effect. In this example, Group A was the control and Group B was the test group. Now you need to check differences between the control and test groups. These differences may be qualitative or quantitative. A qualitative difference would be if the leaf colors of plants in Groups A and B were different. A quantitative difference would be the difference in numbers of centimeters of height among the plants in each group. Group B was in fact taller than Group A after three weeks.

If there are differences, the variable being tested may have had an effect. If there is no difference between the control and the test groups, the variable being tested apparently had no effect. From the data table in this experiment on page 688, it appears that fertilizer does have an effect on plant growth.

▶ What is Data?

In the experiment described on these pages, measurements have been taken so that at the end of the experiment, you had something concrete to interpret. You had numbers to work with. Not every experiment that you do will give you data in the form of numbers. Sometimes, data will be in the form of a description. At the end of a chemistry experiment, you might have noted that one solution turned yellow when treated with a particular chemical, and another remained clear, like water, when treated with the same chemical. Data therefore, is stated in different forms for different types of scientific experiments.

▶ Are All Experiments Alike?

Keep in mind as you perform experiments in science, that not every experiment makes use of all of the parts that have been described on these pages. For some, it may be difficult to design an experiment that will always have a control. Other experiments are complex enough that it may be hard to have only one dependent variable. Real scientists encounter many variations in the methods that they use when they perform experiments. The skills in this handbook are here for you to use and practice. In real situations, their uses will vary.

Representing and Applying Data

▶ Interpreting Scientific Illustrations

As you read this textbook, you will see many drawings, diagrams, and photographs. Illustrations help you to understand what you read. Some illustrations are included to help you understand an idea that you can't see easily by yourself. For instance, we can't see atoms, but we can look at a diagram of an atom and that helps us to understand some things about atoms. Seeing something often helps you remember more easily. The text may describe the surface of Jupiter in detail, but seeing a photograph of Jupiter may help you to remember that it has cloud bands. Illustrations also provide examples that clarify difficult concepts or give additional information about the topic you are studying. Maps, for example, help you to locate places that may be described in the text.

Captions and Labels   Most illustrations have captions. A caption is a comment that identifies or explains the illustration. Diagrams, such as the one of the feather, often have labels that identify parts of the item shown or the order of steps in a process.

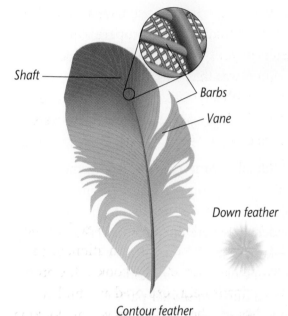

Shaft   Barbs
Vane
Down feather
Contour feather

Learning with Illustrations   An illustration of an organism shows that organism from a particular view or orientation. In order to understand the illustration, you may need to identify the front (anterior) end, tail (posterior) end, the underside (ventral), and the back (dorsal) side of the organism shown.

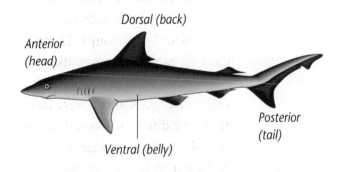

Dorsal (back)
Anterior (head)
Posterior (tail)
Ventral (belly)

You might also check for symmetry. Look at the illustration on the following page. A shark has bilateral symmetry. This means that drawing an imaginary line through the center of the animal from the anterior to posterior end forms two mirror images.

Bilateral symmetry

Two sides exactly alike

Radial symmetry is the arrangement of similar parts around a central point. An object or organism such as a hydra can be divided anywhere through the center into similar parts.

Some organisms and objects cannot be divided into two similar parts. If an organism or object cannot be divided, it is asymmetrical. Regardless of how you try to divide a natural sponge, you cannot divide it into two parts that look alike.

Some illustrations enable you to see the inside of an organism or object. These illustrations are called sections.

Look at all illustrations carefully. Read captions and labels so that you understand exactly what the illustration is showing you.

▶ Making Models

Have you ever worked on a model car or plane or rocket? These models look, and sometimes work, just like the real thing, but they are usually much smaller than the real thing. In science, models are used to help simplify large processes or structures that may be difficult to understand. Your understanding of a structure or process is enhanced when you work with materials to make a model that shows the basic features of the structure or process.

In order to make a model, you first have to get a basic idea about the structure or process involved. You decide to make a model to show the differences in size of arteries, veins, and capillaries. First, read about these structures. All three are hollow tubes. Arteries are round and thick. Veins are flat and have thinner walls than arteries. Capillaries are very small.

Now, decide what you can use for your model. Common materials are often best and cheapest to work with when making models. Different

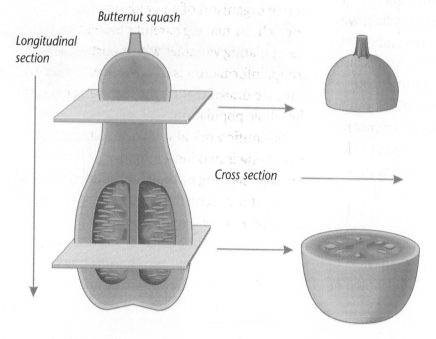

Butternut squash

Longitudinal section

Cross section

kinds and sizes of pasta might work for these models. Different sizes of rubber tubing might do just as well. Cut and glue the different noodles or tubing onto thick paper so the openings can be seen. Then label each. Now you have a simple, easy–to–understand model showing the differences in size of arteries, veins, and capillaries.

What other scientific ideas might a model help you to understand? A model of a molecule can be made from gumdrops (using different colors for the different elements present) and toothpicks (to show different chemical bonds). A working model of a volcano can be made from clay, a small amount of baking soda, vinegar, and a bottle cap. Other models can be devised on a computer.

▶ Predicting

When you apply a hypothesis, or general explanation, to a specific situation, you predict something about that situation. First, you must identify which hypothesis fits the situation you are considering. People use prediction to make everyday decisions. Based on previous observations and experiences, you may form a hypothesis that if it is wintertime, then temperatures will be lower. From past experience in your area, temperatures are lowest in February. You may then use this hypothesis to predict specific temperatures and weather for the month of February in advance. Someone could use these predictions to plan to set aside more money for heating bills during that month.

▶ Sampling and Estimating

When working with large populations of organisms, scientists usually cannot observe or study every organism in the population. Instead, they use a sample or a portion of the population. Sampling is taking a small portion of organisms of a population for research. By making careful observations or manipulating variables with a portion of a group, information is discovered and conclusions are drawn that might then be applied to the whole population.

Scientific work also involves estimating. Estimating is making a judgment about the size of something or the number of something without actually measuring or counting every member of a population.

Suppose you are trying to determine the effect of a specific nutrient on the growth of black-eyed Susans. It would be impossible to test the entire population of black-eyed Susans, so you would select part of the population for your experiment. Through careful experimentation and observation on a sample of the population, you could generalize the effect of the chemical on the entire population.

Here is a more familiar example. Have you ever tried to guess how many beans were in a sealed jar? If you did, you were estimating. What if you knew the jar of beans held one liter (1000 mL)? If you knew that 30 beans would fit in a 100-milliliter jar, how many beans would you estimate to be in the one-liter jar? If you said about 300 beans, your estimate would be close to the actual number of beans.

Scientists use a similar process to estimate populations of organisms from bacteria to buffalo. Scientists count the actual number of organisms in a small sample and then estimate the number of organisms in a larger area. For example, if a scientist wanted to count the number of microorganisms in a petri dish, a microscope could be used to count the number of organisms in a one square millimeter sample. To determine the total population of the culture, the number of organisms in the square millimeter sample is multiplied by the total number of millimeters in the culture.

GLOSSARY

This glossary defines each key term that appears in bold type in the text. It also indicates the chapter number and page number where you will find the word used.

absolute zero: coldness limit at which there can be no further cooling; at absolute zero, which is -273.15°C, the kinetic energy of molecules is decreased to zero; however, at absolute zero, matter still has a tiny amount of energy—representing the lowest possible energy that matter can have. (Chap. 7, p. 228)

air mass: large body of air whose temperature and amount of moisture result from the type of surface over which it developed; examples include cold and dry, hot and dry, or warm and moist air masses; day-to-day changes in the weather are caused by the movement and collision of air masses, which swirl over Earth's surface at different speeds and in various directions. (Chap. 8, p. 251)

alcohol: family of compounds that contain oxygen in the form of hydroxyl (—OH) groups; alcohols are formed when an —OH group replaces one or more hydrogen atoms in a hydrocarbon; examples are methanol, isopropyl alcohol, and ethanol; alcohols are used in fuel, disinfectants, and chemical manufacture. (Chap. 10, p. 315)

alkali metals: column 1 elements in the periodic table of elements; alkali metals are so reactive that they are never found uncombined in nature, can be cut with a knife, have a metallic lustre, conduct electricity and heat, are malleable, and in pure form must be stored in nonreactive liquids. (Chap. 5, p. 159)

alkaline earth metals: in the periodic table of elements, alkaline earth metals are column 2 elements such as magnesium, strontium, and barium and are not as reactive as alkali metals. (Chap. 5, p. 159)

alpha particle: positively charged particle—consisting of two protons and two neutrons—which is given off by a radioactive substance; alpha particles have more mass than beta particles and are unable to go through a thick sheet of paper. (Chap. 4, p. 117)

amines: organic compounds produced when an amine group (—NH$_2$) replaces one or more hydrogens in a hydrocarbon; amino acids, which are a type of amine-substituted hydrocarbon, form when both the —NH$_2$ and —COOH groups replace hydrogens on the same molecule. (Chap. 10, p. 316)

antibodies: specific substances produced by white blood cells in response to specific antigens; when the antibody on the surface of a B-cell, a type of white blood cell, meets its matching antigen, it bonds to it and produces antibodies to destroy it. (Chap. 12, p. 384)

antigens: proteins or chemicals or just about any large molecules— such molecules on the surface of bacteria and parasites—that are foreign to the body; when your body fights disease, it defends against antigens by producing a specific antibody to bind with a specific antigen, rendering it harmless. (Chap. 12, p. 384)

artificial transmutation: transmutation that does not happen spontaneously; scientists have forced nuclei to transmute by using particle accelerators, with the result that gaps in the periodic table have been filled in and more than a dozen new radioactive elements beyond uranium have been created. (Chap. 18, p. 575)

asteroids: traveling chunks of rock found mostly in the asteroid belt between the orbits of Mars and Jupiter; "runaway" asteroids may be captured by planetary gravity and become moons or may be responsible for some surface features of planets. (Chap. 19, p. 618)

asthenosphere: putty-like layer in Earth's crust on which plates slide around; capable of flow. (Chap 15, p. 484)

atomic mass: average mass of the isotope of an element found in nature; atomic mass of an element is calculated by determining the average mass of a sample of that element's atoms. (Chap. 5, p. 151)

atomic number: the number of protons in an atom of an element; atoms of the same element always have the same number of protons—for example, carbon always has an atomic number of 6 and strontium always has an atomic number of 38; elements appear in the periodic table of elements in order of increasing atomic number. (Chap. 5, p. 148)

balanced chemical equation: equation with the same number of atoms of each element on both sides of the equation; whole-number coefficients can be written to balance a chemical equation. (Chap. 6, p. 193)

beta particle: high-speed electron given off by a radioactive substance; these negatively charged particles have less mass than alpha particles and can penetrate paper but are stopped by a 1.5-mm sheet of aluminum. (Chap. 4, p. 117)

binary compound: compound made up of atoms of two elements; calcium fluoride, CaF$_2$, is an example of a binary compound. (Chap. 6, p. 187)

body cells: most numerous type of cell in your body—for example, bone cells, muscle cells, and brain cells are body cells; a body cell produces two identical copies of itself by mitosis; the number of chromosomes in a body cell varies among different species—for example, humans have 46, goldfish have 94, tomatoes have 24, and dogs have 78; body cells contain twice the number of chromosomes as sex cells. (Chap. 13, p. 406)

boiling: formation of bubbles rising to the surface of heated water that occurs when the pressure of water vapor escaping from the liquid's surface equals air pressure; boiling allows the water particles to gain enough kinetic energy to break away and become a gas. (Chap. 7, p. 220)

carbohydrates: organic compounds containing twice as many hydrogen atoms as oxygen atoms; carbohydrates provide energy for the body, and a balanced diet gets 50 percent of its calories from carbohydrate-rich foods such as pasta, rice, beans, and fruit. (Chap. 10, p. 323)

carboxylic acids: group of substituted hydrocarbons formed by displacement of a —CH₃ group by a carboxyl (—COOH) group; methanoic acid is the simplest carboxylic acid. (Chap. 10, p. 315)

Cenozoic Era: geologic division following the Mesozoic Era; the Alps formed and the Himalaya Mountains started to rise; life-forms included the first horses and elephants and the appearance of the first modern humans; because its geologic record is more complete, the periods of the Cenozoic are subdivided into epochs. (Chap. 16, p. 526)

chain reaction: reaction that can start if the neutrons freed by the split of one heavy nucleus into two lighter nuclei cause fission in other nuclei; in nuclear reactors, neutron-absorbing materials such as cadmium rods can be used so that fission chain reactions do not go out of control. (Chap. 18, p. 583)

circuit: any complete pathway through which electrical current flows; requires a source of potential difference, a conducting path, and resistance. (Chap. 1, p. 33)

clotting: process by which a broken blood vessel is sealed off by platelets, which release chemicals that react with substances in plasma and form sticky fibers that trap the blood cells—resulting in formation of a clot that seals the break and hardens into a scab. (Chap. 12, p. 381)

comet: large chunk of ice, dust, gases, and rock fragments that travels through space and is pulled into orbit by the sun's gravity. (Chap. 19, p. 617)

condensation: process in which a gas is changed into a liquid; for example, water droplets on a chilly window pane form as the result of water vapor molecules transferring energy to the cold surface of the glass and condensing. (Chap. 7, p. 221)

conductor: material that allows electrical charges to flow freely from place to place—examples include copper, gold, and silver; conductors are attracted to both positive and negative charges, and even very good conductors can offer some resistance to the flow of charges; power cables conduct electricity safely by wrapping conductors in such insulators as rubber. (Chap. 1, p. 28)

continental drift: hypothesis first proposed by Wegener that Earth's continents were once a single supercontinent called Pangaea, which broke into smaller landmasses about 200 million years ago and have since moved apart to form the present day arrangement of the continents. (Chap. 15, p. 470)

convergent boundary: boundary between two lithospheric plates colliding—for example, the head-on collision of plates with continental crust can form mountain ranges and plates with oceanic crust can form trenches; Earth's most famous volcanoes occur at convergent plate boundaries. (Chap. 15, p. 486)

covalent bond: type of bond formed between atoms when they share electrons; covalent bonds are strong and chemically stable—for example, when two atoms of Cl combine and share a pair of electrons, each atom, at some time, will have its outer energy level complete. (Chap. 6, p. 181)

current: rate at which electrical charges flow past a point in a circuit over a specific amount of time; the rate of current flowing through a bulb can be measured in amperes (A) by an instrument called an ammeter; current is equal to the potential difference divided by resistance, and can be found mathematically by V/R = I. (Chap. 1, p. 33)

density current: movement of ocean water produced when dense, more highly saline seawater sinks, pushing away less dense seawater at the ocean bottom; these vertical currents occur in water too deep to be affected by winds. (Chap. 9, p. 294)

dew point: temperature at which the water vapor in saturated air begins to condense; for example, clouds are formed when humid air cools to its dew point and condensed water clings to particles in the air. (Chap. 8, p. 245)

diffraction: bending of waves—such as light waves or water waves or sound waves—passing through openings, around obstacles, or by relatively sharp edges. (Chap. 3, p. 92)

digestion: mechanical and chemical breakdown of carbohydrates, fats, and proteins into smaller molecules that can be absorbed by the cells; the human digestive system includes the tongue, saliva glands, esophagus, liver, stomach, gall bladder, duodenum, pancreas, large and small intestines, rectum, and anus. (Chap. 11, p. 351)

divergent boundary: boundary between two lithospheric plates moving away from each other resulting in magma being forced upward to the continental or oceanic crust, where it erupts as lava and forms new crust; mid-ocean ridges are divergent boundaries; also called constructive boundaries. (Chap. 15, p. 485)

DNA: threadlike material making up the chromosomes within the cell nucleus; contains the master code that directs the cells in all their activities and passes on genetic information; the DNA of each species has a specific ladderlike sequence for the four types of paired bases—cytosine, guanine, thymine, and adenine. (Chap. 14, p. 457)

dominant trait: trait that seems to dominate, or cover up, a recessive trait; for example, when Mendel crossed pure tall with pure short pea plants, all plants in the first generation of offspring were tall, showing that the trait of tallness was dominant over shortness. (Chap. 14, p. 444)

E

eggs: female sex cells: a human egg can be seen with the unaided eye, contains a food supply, has 23 chromosomes, and develops in the ovaries in relatively small numbers; usually one human egg is released into the oviduct about every 28 days, and if fertilized by sperm, will implant into the uterine wall. (Chap. 13, p. 407)

electric generator: produces electricity for home and business use by inducing currents through rotating a coil within a magnetic field; in the United States, household alternating current changes direction 120 times/second. (Chap. 2, p. 72)

electric motor: motor that uses an electromagnet to change electric energy into mechanical energy, creating the ability of machines such as washers and vacuum cleaners to perform work. (Chap. 2, p. 70)

electrical charge: concentration of electricity; everything contains electrical charges, which can be either positive (+) or negative (-); electrical charges can be made to flow and do work in much the same way as water; can move easily through conductors but not through insulators. (Chap. 1, p. 23)

electromagnet: magnet produced by passing an electric current through a coil of wire wound around a core; for example, whenever you listen to a tape recording or ring an electric doorbell, you're using an electromagnet. (Chap. 2, p. 62)

electromagnetic spectrum: the entire range of electromagnetic waves as shown in both frequencies (10^3 to 10^{23} Hz) and wavelengths (10^5 to 10^{-15} m); for example, in the electromagnetic spectrum, gamma rays have the shortest wavelength and the highest frequency. (Chap. 3, p. 86)

electromagnetic waves: transverse waves that do not require a medium through which to travel and which are produced by an oscillating charge; an electromagnetic wave travels at a constant speed, so its wavelength is inversely proportional to its frequency; visible light, radio waves, and gamma waves are examples of electromagnetic waves. (Chap. 3, p. 82)

electron: negatively charged particle with a very small mass that orbits an atom's nucleus in an electron cloud; atoms contain an equal number of electrons and protons, resulting in an equal number of positive and negative charges. (Chap. 4, p. 113)

engineers: in the field of space exploration, engineers are individuals who work with scientists to help build and develop spacecraft to travel to other planets. (Chap. 19, p. 620)

environmental scientists: individuals working with environmental factors in a variety of ways—for example, monitoring air, water, and industry for pollutants. (Chap. 10, p. 332)

enzyme: protein molecule controlling the rate of different body processes; humans have over 700 enzymes—each with its own unique lock-and-key function—that are an essential part of chemical digestion and break nutrient molecules into smaller molecules; for example, an enzyme in saliva helps break down starch into sugar. (Chap. 11, p. 356)

epochs: subdivisions of the Tertiary and Quaternary Periods of the Cenozoic Era as the result of a more complete geologic record—the rocks are newer and have been exposed to fewer destructive geologic processes, so there is more information for geologists to organize. (Chap. 16, p. 526)

era: division of Earth's geologic time scale that is further divided into periods; the three major eras are the Paleozoic Era, the Mesozoic Era, and the Cenozoic Era; the fourth major division, Precambrian Time, covers such a huge time expanse that it is further divided into its own eras. (Chap. 16, p. 517)

evaporation: process of a liquid changing into a gas; molecules with the highest kinetic energy evaporate from the surface first, which lowers the average kinetic energy of the molecules still in the liquid. (Chap. 7, p. 219)

evolution: ongoing process of change in the inherited features of a population of organisms over time; evolutionary evidence can be drawn from such sources as fossil remains, the chemical structure of organisms, and the physical structure of cells. (Chap. 17, p. 544)

family of elements: organizational group in the periodic table of elements in which elements are listed in vertical columns based on their similar physical and chemical properties—for example, Family 17 (the halogens) is very reactive and often combines with other elements. (Chap. 5, p. 156)

fission: nuclear reaction in which a large nucleus is split and energy is released—for example, when a nucleus of uranium-235 is struck by a neutron, it splits into two lighter nuclei, and the process releases three neutrons and a huge amount of energy; nuclear reactors produce electrical energy from a controlled fission chain reaction. (Chap. 18, p. 580)

fossil: remains or traces of a once-living organism; can provide information about the organism's appearance, where and how it lived, and help divide geologic time; two methods of fossil formation are by replacement of minerals and mold-and-cast formation. (Chap. 16, p. 505)

front: boundary resulting from the collision between moving air masses, producing such weather events as rain, snow, or violent storms depending on the types of air masses that meet; fronts can be warm, cold, stationary, and occluded. (Chap. 8, p. 251)

fusion: joining of smaller nuclei into larger ones; fusion of hydrogen into helium releases vast amounts of energy and is the energy powering the stars, including the sun; nuclear fusion is common in nature but not on Earth. (Chap. 18, p. 585)

galaxy: elliptical, spiral, or irregular shaped group of stars, dust, and gas held together by gravity and grouped into clusters; Earth belongs to the Milky Way galaxy, which contains about 200 000 stars, is about 100 000 light-years in diameter and about 15 000 light-years thick. (Chap. 20, p. 643)

gamma rays: electromagnetic waves given off by a radioactive substance; gamma rays are highly penetrating and can go through paper and a 1-mm sheet of aluminum but are stopped by a 1.5-cm sheet of lead. (Chap. 4, p. 117)

gaseous giant planets: huge, low density planets made mainly of gases; these planets were formed farther from the sun, where the effects of solar winds and thermal energy were less intense; Jupiter, Saturn, Uranus, and Neptune are gaseous giant planets. (Chap. 19, p. 609)

gene: specific location on a chromosome; chromosomes and genes usually occur in pairs, and in Mendelian inheritance there are two genes for each trait, one contributed by each parent; genes can be either dominant or recessive. (Chap. 14, p. 445)

hemoglobin: iron-containing pigment that gives red blood cells their color; oxygen attaches to the iron in hemoglobin as red blood cells move through the lungs and is carried throughout your body for diffusion into body cells. (Chap. 12, p. 375)

heterozygote: individual with one dominant and one recessive gene for a specific trait—for example, if one parent contributes the dominant *T* gene for tallness and the other parent contributes the recessive *t* gene for shortness, then the offspring will be tall (*tT* or *Tt*) but will have recessive genes for shortness. (Chap. 14, p. 446)

homologous structure: similarity in structure and origin of the body parts of different organisms; for example, a bat's wing, a human's arm, and a dolphin's flipper are homologous structures and suggest that the organisms evolved from a common ancestor. (Chap. 17, p. 552)

hot spots: areas of Earth's mantle that are hotter than others; as lithospheric plates move over hot spots, magma is forced up through cracks in the lithosphere, where it erupts as lava and volcanoes build up; the movement of the Pacific plate over a hot spot in the Pacific Ocean resulted in the formation of the Hawaiian Islands. (Chap. 15, p. 495)

hurricane: intense, highly destructive storm formed from a swirling, low pressure system over a warm, moist tropical ocean; hurricanes are very large, have high winds that can be accompanied by torrential rain, and weaken as they strike land. (Chap. 8, p. 264)

hydrocarbon: compound that can be composed only of hydrogen and carbon or can form new compounds when other chemical groups are substituted for one or more hydrogen atoms; complex hydrocarbons can form biological compounds that make up living things; saturated hydrocarbons contain only a single covalent bond; unsaturated hydrocarbons contain double or triple covalent bonds. (Chap. 10, p. 308)

immunity: occurs once your body produces a specific antibody to defend against a specific antigen, which protects you against the disease; memory cells—which are formed by B-cells—can provide lifelong immunity to certain diseases; immunity can be acquired actively or passively. (Chap. 12, p. 385)

immunologists: individuals who study immune system diseases and work on the development of vaccines; college and medical school are required to become an immunologist. (Chap. 12, p. 396)

induced current: electric current produced by using a magnet; results when a magnetic field is changed in a coil—the field can be changed by moving either the coil or the magnet; our homes and businesses have electricity because of induced current produced by electric generators. (Chap. 2, p. 72)

induced magnetism: magnetism that occurs only in the presence of a magnetic field—when the magnetized object is removed from the magnetic field, its poles soon disappear. (Chap. 2, p. 57)

insulator: material that does not allow electrical charges to flow freely from place to place; examples include paper, rubber, plastic, wood, and glass; insulators help to transmit electricity safely from one location to another. (Chap. 1, p. 27)

intertidal zone: coastal ecosystem that is under water at high tide and exposed at low tide; supports a wide variety of highly adapted organisms such as mussels, oysters, chitons, and limpets. (Chap. 9, p. 281)

ion: positively or negatively charged atom whose charge results from the gain or loss of one or more electrons; the more electrons an atom gains or loses, the higher its charge. (Chap. 6, p. 177)

ionic bond: type of bond formed by the attraction of positively charged ions for negatively charged ions; ionic bonds hold ionic compounds together—for example, the positively charged sodium ion, Na^+, and the negatively charged chloride ion, Cl^-, are attracted to each other and form the neutral compound NaCl, which is held together by ionic bonds. (Chap. 6, p. 178)

isomers: compounds with identical chemical formulas but different molecular shapes, which seem to determine some of an isomer's properties; for example, butane (C_4H_{10}) has a straight carbon chain and melts at -138°C, whereas isobutane (C_4H_{10}) has a branched carbon chain and melts at -160°C. (Chap. 10, p. 311)

isotopes: atoms of the same element with different numbers of neutrons—examples of common isotopes are carbon-14, which has 6 protons and 8 neutrons in its nucleus and carbon-12, which has 6 protons and 6 neutrons in its nucleus; radioactive isotopes can be used to precisely determine levels of drugs, hormones, or viruses in a patient's body. (Chap. 5, p. 150)

kinetic-molecular theory: states that all ions, atoms, or molecules composing all forms of matter are in constant motion; the higher the temperature, the faster the particles move; explains familiar behaviors of matter such as boiling, evaporation, melting, condensation, and expansion. (Chap. 7, p. 210)

law of superposition: states that the oldest rock layers are at the bottom and the youngest rock layers are at the top if the layers have not been disturbed by such processes as earthquakes, volcanoes, and mountain building; younger sedimentary rocks always form on top of older sedimentary rocks and can help date rock layers relative to one another. (Chap. 16, p. 509)

light-year: distance light travels in one year; a light-year is the unit astronomers use to measure distances in space; 1 light-year is about 9.5 trillion kilometers. (Chap. 20, p. 636)

like charges: similar electrical charges that repel each other; for example, when two glass rods are charged by being rubbed with silk and then brought toward each other, they will repel one another. (Chap. 1, p. 23)

lipids: greasy-feeling organic compounds that contain twice as much energy per gram as carbohydrates; lipids include waxes, oils, and fats; a balanced diet gets 30 percent of its calories from fats, which are present in such foods as meats, nuts, and ice cream, which provide energy for the body. (Chap. 10, p. 324)

lithosphere: Earth's rocky crust and solid, uppermost part of the mantle; all the oceans and continents of Earth move slowly over the asthenosphere on lithospheric plates. (Chap. 15, p. 484)

loudspeaker: changes variations in electric current into sound waves in radios and speakers. (Chap. 2, p. 67)

magnetic field: three-dimensional region where magnetic forces act; Earth's huge magnetic field, which resembles a large bar magnet, extends far out into space and protects us from showers of high-energy charged particles. (Chap. 2, p. 54)

magnetic poles: in a bar magnet, the two ends that point north-south—the places where the magnetic field is strongest; two north-seeking poles repel each other, but a north-seeking pole and a south-seeking pole attract each other; compass needles point north and south because Earth has magnetic poles—much like a bar magnet—which may be produced by material deep in Earth's core. (Chap. 2, p. 51)

mass number: the total number of protons and neutrons in the nucleus of an atom; for example, if the nucleus of an atom has 6 protons and 6 neutrons, the mass of the atom is 12 atomic mass units, or 12 u. (Chap. 5, p. 148-149)

meiosis: process of cell division of all reproductive cells; meiosis involves two divisions of the chromosomes in the original cell, producing four new cells, each with half the number of chromosomes found in a body cell of that organism. (Chap. 13, p. 411)

menstrual cycle: in human females, the monthly cycle that prepares the reproductive system for fertilization, during which the uterine lining thickens, an egg is released, and if unfertilized is discarded in a process called menstruation. (Chap. 13, p. 427)

menstruation: in human females, the monthly discharge of the disintegrated, unfertilized egg along with the uterine lining and blood through the vagina; menstruation usually lasts four to six days. (Chap. 13, p. 427)

Mesozoic Era: geologic division following the Paleozoic Era; life-forms included the first dinosaurs, birds, mammals, and flowering plants; during the Mesozoic, Pangaea separated and the Rocky Mountains began to rise; dinosaurs were extinct at end of the Mesozoic. (Chap. 16, p. 524)

meteor: space object formed of rock fragments; meteors are called meteoroids until they enter Earth's atmosphere; meteors glow as they streak across the night sky and most burn up completely due to friction. (Chap. 19, p. 619)

meteorite: meteoroids that survive passing through Earth's atmosphere and hit Earth's surface, sometimes producing craters. (Chap. 19, p. 619)

minerals: inorganic compounds essential for good health; minerals are needed by the body to regulate its chemical reactions and include, for example, calcium for strong bone and tooth structure, iron to make red blood cells and carry oxygen, and magnesium for digestion of carbohydrates and proteins. (Chap. 11, p. 342)

molecules: neutral particles formed when electrons are shared by atoms rather than being gained or lost. (Chap. 6, p. 181)

mutation: permanent change in a chromosome or gene; most mutations have little effect on organisms but some mutations can be harmful or helpful; variations in color, size, and shape are often caused by mutations. (Chap. 17, p. 545)

natural selection: process in which organisms with variations better adapted to their environments are more likely to survive and reproduce; Darwin formed the theory of natural selection to explain evolution. (Chap. 17, p. 540)

nebula: large cloud of dust and gas whose particles exert a gravitational force on each other, causing the cloud to contract and its internal temperature to rise until fusion begins, resulting in a star being born. (Chap. 20, p. 630)

nekton: free-swimming marine animals; nekton move through various depths, reducing the effects that surface currents can have on them; fish, whales, and sea turtles are examples of nektonic life-forms. (Chap. 9, p. 292)

neutron: uncharged particle in the nucleus of an atom; a neutron has a mass about equal to that of a proton; neutrons and protons are made up of even smaller particles called quarks. (Chap. 4, p. 127)

nonpolar molecule: molecule with balanced charges whose electrons are shared equally; nonpolar molecules are not water soluble; oil is an example. (Chap. 6, p. 184)

nucleus: positively charged, dense center of an atom made up of protons and neutrons around which a cloud of electrons moves. (Chap. 4, p. 123)

nurse-midwives: individuals trained to provide both physical and emotional assistance to a woman giving birth; nurse-midwives study biology, chemistry, and medicine. (Chap. 13, p. 430)

nutrients: substances in food that are needed by the body for growth, development, and repair; proteins, fats, carbohydrates, vitamins, minerals, and water are nutrients; a lack of nutrients can produce disease. (Chap. 11, p. 339)

organic compound: carbon-containing substance; millions of organic compounds can be synthesized from raw materials containing carbon because carbon's atomic structure allows it to combine with so many other elements; chemicals made from organic compounds in petroleum or natural gas provide the world's major energy source. (Chap. 10, p. 306)

ovary: in human females, ovaries are the two sex organs in which eggs are produced by meiosis, which in females begins before birth and continues at sexual maturity, when an egg is released from an ovary about every 28 days until the individual is 45 to 55 years old. (Chap. 13, p. 416)

oxidation number: number of electrons that an atom gains, loses, or shares when bonding with another atom; for example, when Cl forms an ion, it gains an electron, has a charge of 1-, and an oxidation number of 1-; some elements have more than one oxidation number, such as Cr^{2+} and Cr^{3+}, or chromium(II) and chromium(III). (Chap. 6, p. 187)

Paleozoic Era: second major geologic time scale division; began about 545 million years ago and was characterized by warm, shallow seas covering much of Earth; life-forms included trilobites, the first fish, amphibians, land plants, and reptiles. (Chap. 16, p. 522)

pedigree: diagrammatic tool used to trace the existence of a specific trait among generations of a family; can show whether a trait has a pattern of appearance or is occurring randomly. (Chap. 14, p. 439)

period: geologic subdivision of an era based on the era's life-forms and geologic events; for example, the Mesozoic Era has three periods—Triassic, Jurassic, and Cretaceous—and the Cenozoic Era has two periods—Tertiary and Quaternary. (Chap. 16, p. 522; see also Chap. 5, p. 162)

period: one of the 7 horizontal rows in the periodic table of elements; each period starts as the pattern of chemical and physical properties of the elements begins to repeat itself; a period is made up of a series of elements with increasing atomic numbers. (Chap. 5, p. 162; see also Chap. 16, p. 522)

periodic table: organizes all the known elements into a table based on atomic mass and structure and helps you predict how elements will react with one another; the periodic table organizes elements into columns and rows and shows an element's atomic number, symbol, name, and atomic mass. (Chap. 5, p. 145)

peristalsis: smooth, muscular waves of contractions that move food through the esophagus, into the stomach, and through the entire digestive system. (Chap. 11, p. 357)

pistil: female reproductive organ of flowering plants composed of a sticky stigma, a stalk-like style, and a rounded base, which is its ovary; fertilization occurs when sperm-containing pollen grains deposited on the stigma forms a long tube that grows from the stigma through the pistil to the ovary, where the union of sperm and eggs takes place. (Chap. 13, p. 419)

planet: body of matter that moves around a star in a fixed, counterclockwise orbit; except for Pluto, which is small and formed of rock and ice, the planets of our solar system are classified as either Earth-like terrestrial planets or gaseous giant planets. (Chap. 19, p. 598)

plankton: microscopic life-forms that drift through the upper levels of the ocean and form the base of an extensive food web; plankton rely on currents to bring them nutrients and carry away wastes. (Chap. 9, p. 292)

plasma: liquid portion of your blood in which are suspended red and white blood cells and platelets; plasma is about 55 percent water and transports dissolved nutrients, minerals, and oxygen to all body cells and helps to carry away waste products to other organs for elimination; hormones are also transported by plasma. (Chap. 12, p. 373)

plate tectonics: geologic theory accounting for the movement of the continents, suggesting that the solid plates of the lithosphere are moved slowly by convection currents originating deep inside Earth. (Chap. 15, p. 484)

platelets: tiny, short-lived, non-nucleated, irregularly shaped cell fragments contained in blood; platelets help to prevent serious bleeding from broken blood vessels by the process of clotting. (Chap. 12, p. 381)

polar molecule: molecule with unbalanced charges as a result of electrons being shared unequally; for example, water is a polar molecule because its oxygen end has a slight negative charge and its hydrogen end has a slight positive charge. (Chap. 6, p. 184)

polyatomic ion: ammonium, nitrate, and phosphate are examples of polyatomic ions—all of which are made up of a group of positively or negatively charged covalently bonded atoms. (Chap. 6, p. 189)

polymer: large molecule composed of smaller organic molecules, called monomers, linked together, forming new bonds; some polymers are used in the manufacture of plastics; polymers are also found in biological compounds—mainly proteins, carbohydrates, and lipids. (Chap. 10, p. 321)

potential difference: change in total energy divided by the total electric charge; potential difference is measured in volts (V) or voltage; when potential difference stays the same, current decreases as resistance increases. (Chap. 1, p. 33)

Precambrian Time: first major division of geologic time that began more than 4 billion years ago and makes up about 90 percent of Earth's history to date; characterized by several episodes of mountain building and the altering of Earth's atmosphere by production of large amounts of oxygen by cyanobacteria, which were the dominant life-form during much of Precambrian Time. (Chap. 16, p. 520)

primates: mammalian group including apes, monkeys, and humans that shares many characteristics such as binocular vision, flexible shoulders, and opposable thumbs. (Chap. 17, p. 556)

proteins: organic compounds composed of long chains of amino acids; proteins are present in every living substance and are needed for growth and renewal of the body; a balanced diet gets 20 percent of its calories from such protein sources as milk, tofu, and fish. (Chap. 10, p. 322)

proton: positively charged particle in the nucleus of an atom; a proton's mass is about equal to that of a neutron; the number of protons in an element's nucleus determines the element's identity. (Chap. 4, p. 124)

pure dominant: trait resulting when the offspring receives the dominant form of a trait from each parent—for example, if both egg and sperm contain the dominant *T* gene for tallness, then the tallness of the offspring will be a pure dominant trait, or *TT*. (Chap. 14, p. 446)

pure recessive: trait resulting when the egg and sperm of each parent contains the recessive form of a trait—for example, if both parents pass on the recessive *e* gene for attached earlobes, then the attached earlobes of the offspring will be a pure recessive trait, or *ee*. (Chap. 14, p. 446)

R

radiation: transfer of energy by electromagnetic waves; for example, a lamp lights an area by radiating electromagnetic waves in the visible part of the spectrum. (Chap. 3, p. 87)

radioactivity: decay, or breaking apart, of unstable elements such as uranium and thorium, resulting in the release of high-energy particles; radiation from a radioactive source can be separated into alpha, beta, and gamma rays by using a magnetic field. (Chap. 4, p. 116)

recessive trait: trait that seems to disappear; for example, when Mendel crossed pure tall with pure short pea plants, the trait of shortness was recessive in the first generation of offspring but reappeared in about one-quarter of the second generation of offspring. (Chap. 14, p. 444)

red blood cells: tiny, most numerous type of blood cell in whole blood; your mature red blood cells lack a nucleus, are filled with iron-containing hemoglobin molecules, transport oxygen throughout the body, and return some carbon dioxide to the lungs for elimination; red blood cells are formed in the marrow of long bones. (Chap. 12, p. 375)

relative humidity: measure, expressed as a percentage, between the amount of water vapor in the air and the total amount of water vapor the air can hold at that specific temperature; an instrument called a psychrometer measures relative humidity. (Chap. 8, p. 244)

resistance: property of materials indicating how much energy is changed to thermal energy and light as an electrical charge passes through them; resistance depends on the material of the conductor in addition to the conductor's thickness and length. (Chap. 1, p. 34)

S

salinity: in the ocean, the measure of dissolved materials, primarily salts, resulting from the accumulation of elements and minerals from the atmosphere, volcanic eruptions, and runoff of water from land; the most common sea salts are sodium and chlorine. (Chap. 9, p. 283)

saturated: 100 percent relative humidity of air; occurs when air cannot hold additional moisture at a specific temperature. (Chap. 8, p. 245)

sea-floor spreading: occurs when plates beneath the ocean floor pull apart and magma from Earth's mantle is forced upward at mid-ocean ridges where it cools and forms a new seafloor; similar ages and magnetic records of rocks on both sides of a rift support the idea of sea-floor spreading. (Chap. 15, p. 478)

sex cells: reproductive cells formed through meiosis, a process that begins in an organism's reproductive organs and results in the formation of eggs or sperm—each of which contains half the number of chromosomes as a body cell of the parent organism; the job of sex cells is to unite and to produce offspring. (Chap. 13, p. 407)

sickle-cell anemia: potentially fatal genetic disease in which the red blood cells are misshapen, are unable to carry as much oxygen as normal cells, and can become stuck in capillaries. (Chap. 14, p. 452)

solar system: system formed about 5 billion years ago from a rotating cloud of hydrogen and helium gases and dust particles that condensed to form its major components—the sun and its nine planets. (Chap. 19, p. 598)

sperm: male sex cells; human sperm are microscopic, have tails, can swim, contain 23 chromosomes, and are produced in large numbers by the testes; fertilization in humans and many other animals takes place internally, with the male releasing millions of sperm into the female's reproductive system, where it takes only one sperm to fertilize an egg. (Chap. 13, p. 407)

stamen: in flowering plants, the male reproductive organ whose saclike anther is held up by a long filament; anthers produce sperm-containing pollen grains, which are transferred to the female's sticky stigma by various means including wind, birds, and insects. (Chap. 13, p. 419)

star: glowing, hot sphere of gas, such as the sun, whose brightness depends on how big and hot it is and its distance from Earth; stars form from nebulas and produce energy by fusion; types of stars include blue supergiants, brown dwarfs, red giants, and white stars. (Chap. 20, p. 629)

sublimation: process in which a solid is changed into a gas without first becoming a liquid; for example, solid carbon dioxide (dry ice) sublimates, and because it is much colder than regular ice, a water vapor fog forms as the air surrounding it cools. (Chap. 7, p. 220)

sunspots: cool, dark areas on the surface of the sun that may appear and disappear over days or months; years in which there are many large sunspots are called sunspot maximums, which occur about every 11 years. (Chap. 20, p. 638)

supernova: explosion of a massive, dense-cored star that occurs when no more material remains in the core to be transformed, resulting in the formation of a small neutron star. (Chap. 20, p. 631)

surface currents: movement of ocean water produced primarily by winds; affect the upper few hundred meters of seawater, influence climate by their warming or cooling effects, and provide a home for most marine organisms; the Gulf Stream is a surface current. (Chap. 9, p. 291)

T

terrestrial planets: the four small planets that were formed nearest the sun and whose surfaces are composed of dense, rocky material; Mercury, Venus, Earth, and Mars are terrestrial planets. (Chap. 19, p. 603)

testis: in human males, testes are the two sex organs that produce sperm by meiosis when the body reaches sexual maturity, usually at ages 10 to 14, with the amount of sperm decreasing gradually with age. (Chap. 13, p. 416)

GLOSSARY

thermal expansion: in a solid, the expansion that occurs as it is heated, resulting in its kinetic energy increasing and its particles moving farther apart; thermal expansion must be considered in designing such structures as railroad tracks, bridges, and highways. (Chap. 7, p. 214)

tornado: violent, funnel-shaped storm formed from a low pressure system; tornadoes are highly destructive, short-lasting, and move over land in a narrow path. (Chap. 8, p. 262)

traits: inherited characteristics of an organism; traits passed from one generation to another in a family may be nearly identical or similar and are controlled by genes carried on chromosomes; examples of traits are dimples, hitchhiker's thumb, and hair color. (Chap. 14, p. 438)

transform fault boundary: boundary formed when two plates slide past each other in the same direction at different speeds or slide past each other in opposite directions; the San Andreas Fault is a transform fault boundary. (Chap. 15, p. 487)

transformer: ensures that electricity produced by a power company has the correct voltage by raising (step-up transformer) or lowering (step-down transformer) the voltage to the needed level. (Chap. 2, p. 73)

transmutation: occurs when an atom of one element changes to an atom of another element by spontaneously emitting a particle, or by decaying—which changes its number of protons and its atomic number; the time it takes for a given mass of an element to transmute is known as its half-life. (Chap. 18, p. 570)

unconformity: occurs when layers of rock are missing, often because of such forces as plate tectonics, weathering and erosion, or lack of soil deposition, and results in an incomplete record of plants and animals that existed during that time. (Chap. 16, p. 510)

unlike charges: dissimilar electrical charges that attract one another; for example, rubbing a balloon with wool will enable the positively charged balloon to be stuck (attracted) to an uncharged wall. (Chap. 1, p. 23)

upwelling: interruption of the density current cycle resulting from the upward movement of cold water from deep in the ocean, replacing warmer surface water carried away by strong, wind-driven surface currents. (Chap. 9, p. 296)

vaccine: provides active immunity to a specific disease without having to get the disease first; vaccination introduces a dead or weakened form of the antigen to the body through inoculation or by mouth, and if the antigen later invades your body, it will be destroyed by antibodies already in your bloodstream. (Chap. 12, p. 386)

variations: differences in inherited traits or behaviors among members of the same species; advantageous variations help organisms survive in their environments and are called adaptations—examples are the webbed feet of ducks and the thick, white fur of polar bears. (Chap. 17, p. 536)

villi: tiny finger-like projections lining the folds of the small intestine; villi increase the surface area for absorption of nutrients into the bloodstream for delivery to individual cells. (Chap. 11, p. 360)

viscosity: resistance of a liquid to changing its shape; the stronger the attractive forces holding a liquid's molecules together, the higher its viscosity; different liquids have different viscosities—for example, water's low viscosity enables it to run down a grade quickly but honey has a high viscosity and runs down a grade slowly. (Chap. 7, p. 217)

vitamins: organic nutrients needed in small amounts by the body for good health; A, E, D, and K are fat-soluble vitamins and B and C are water-soluble vitamins; vitamins are found in such food sources as vegetables, meat, milk, fish, beans, and fruit; a deficiency in any one vitamin can sometimes result in a serious health problem. (Chap. 11, p. 347)

volcanologists: geologists who specialize in studying volcanoes in order to predict when and how a volcanic eruption will take place; volcanologists collect data using instruments such as laser measuring devices and seismographs. (Chap. 15, p. 497)

white blood cells: large, less numerous type of blood cell that fights bacteria, viruses, and other foreign substances—for example, when bacteria invade your body, blood carries white blood cells to the site, where they surround the bacteria and digest them. (Chap. 12, p. 376)

SPANISH GLOSSARY

This glossary defines each key term that appears in bold type in the text. It also indicates the chapter number and page number where you will find the word used.

absolute zero/cero absoluto: temperatura a la cual la energía cinética de las moléculas baja a cero; la temperatura más baja posible que puede tener la materia (Cap. 7, pág. 228)

agronomist/agrónomo: científico agrícola que estudia la biología (Cap. 11, pág. 364)

air mass/masa de aire: masa extensa de aire cuyas propiedades se determinan por la parte de la superficie terrestre sobre la cual se forma (Cap. 8, pág. 251)

alcohol/alcohol: nombre de una familia de compuestos que se forman cuando un grupo de hidroxilos reemplaza uno o más átomos de hidrógeno en un hidrocarburo (Cap. 10, pág. 315)

alkali metals/metales alcalinos: elementos en la columna 1 de la Tabla Periódica; son metales blandos que pueden cortarse fácilmente; poseen brillo metálico, son conductores del calor y de la electricidad y son maleables (Cap. 5, pág. 159)

alkaline earth metals/metales alcalinotérreos: metales en la segunda columna vertical de la Tabla Periódica; no son reactivos como los metales alcalinos (Cap. 5, pág. 159)

alpha particle/partícula alfa: partículas con carga positiva emitidas por sustancias radiactivas y con una masa mayor que las partículas beta (Cap. 4, pág. 117)

amine/amina: compuesto orgánico que se forma cuando el grupo de aminas, -NH₂, reemplaza el hidrógeno en un hidrocarburo (Cap. 10, pág 316)

antibodies/anticuerpos: sustancias que produce el cuerpo para responder a determinados antígenos (Cap. 12, pág. 384)

antigens/antígenos: proteínas y sustancias químicas que son agentes extraños para el cuerpo (Cap. 12, pág. 384)

artificial transmutation/transmutación artificial: reacción que se produce cuando una transmutación no ocurre espontáneamente, pero es causada por cualquier factor externo (Cap. 18, pág. 575)

asteroid/asteroide: trozo enorme de roca que viaja por el espacio (Cap. 19, pág. 618)

asthenosphere/astenosfera: capa menos sólida del manto terrestre en donde los materiales se comportan como masilla (Cap. 15, pág 484)

atomic mass/masa atómica: es la masa de un átomo medida en unidades de masa atómica (Cap. 5, pág. 151)

atomic number/número atómico: el número de protones en el átomo de un elemento (Cap. 5, pág. 148)

balanced chemical equation/ecuación química equilibrada: ecuación que posee el mismo número de átomos de cada elemento a ambos lados de la ecuación (Cap. 6, pág. 193)

beta particle/partícula beta: electrón de alta velocidad emitido por una sustancia radiactiva (Cap. 4, pág. 117)

binary compound/compuesto binario: compuesto formado por dos elementos (Cap. 6, pág. 187)

body cells/células corporales: células que forman el cuerpo, las cuales producen copias exactas de sí mismas por medio de la mitosis (Cap. 13, pág. 406)

boiling/ebullición: cambio del estado líquido al estado gaseoso, como por ejemplo, cuando hierve el agua (Cap. 7, pág. 220)

carbohydrates/carbohidratos: tipo de alimentos como azúcares y almidones que nos proporcionan energía (Cap. 10, pág. 323)

carboxylic acid/ácido carboxílico: ácido que se forma cuando un grupo -CH₃ es desplazado por un grupo carboxílico (-COOH) (Cap. 10, pág. 315)

Cenozoic Era/Era Cenozoica: era que comenzó después de terminar la Era Mesozoica (Cap. 16, pág. 526)

chain reaction/reacción en cadena: serie de reacciones que ocurren cuando el neutrón que libera una reacción desencadena la siguiente reacción y esa reacción desencadena la próxima reacción (Cap. 18, pág. 583)

circuit/circuito: trayectoria ininterrumpida por la cual fluye una corriente eléctrica (Cap. 1, pág. 33)

clotting/coagulación: proceso por el cual se cierra un vaso sanguíneo roto (Cap. 12, pág. 381)

comet/cometa: trozo enorme de hielo, polvo, gases congelados y fragmentos rocosos que se mueve por el espacio (Cap. 19, pág. 617)

condensation/condensación: proceso por el cual un gas se transforma en un líquido (Cap. 7, pág. 221)

conductor/conductor: material en el cual las cargas eléctricas pueden moverse libremente de un lugar a otro (Cap. 1, pág. 28)

continental drift/deriva continental: teoría de Alfred Wegener que dice que una vez todos los continentes estuvieron unidos en un solo supercontinente llamado Pangaea, el cual se separó hace cerca de 200 millones de años, provocando el movimiento de los continentes (Cap. 15, pág. 470)

convergent boundary/límite convergente: lugar donde chocan de frente dos placas (Cap. 15, pág. 486)

covalent bond/enlace covalente: enlace que se forma entre átomos que comparten electrones (Cap. 6, pág. 181)

current/corriente: la cantidad de carga eléctrica que se transmite a través de un punto de un circuito en un tiempo dado (Cap. 1, pág. 33)

density current/corriente de densidad: movimiento de agua que ocurre cuando el agua marina densa se mueve hacia un área de agua marina menos densa (Cap. 9, pág. 294)

dew point/punto de rocío: la temperatura a la cual el aire está saturado y se produce la condensación (Cap. 8, pág. 245)

diffraction/difracción: desviación de la luz alrededor de una barrera (Cap. 3, pág. 92)

digestion/digestión: proceso que descompone los carbohidratos, las grasas y las proteínas en moléculas más pequeñas y simples que pueden absorber y usar las células del cuerpo (Cap. 11, pág. 351)

divergent boundary/límite divergente: límite entre dos placas que se alejan y se separan una de la otra (Cap. 15, pág. 485)

DNA/DNA: siglas para el ácido ribonucleico; el DNA contiene el código maestro que imparte instrucciones a todas las células para sus funciones diarias (Cap. 14, pág. 457)

dominant trait/rasgo dominante: rasgo que parece dominar u ocultar por completo a otro rasgo (Cap. 14, pág. 444)

eggs/óvulos: células sexuales femeninas (Cap. 13, pág. 407)

electric generator/generador eléctrico: dispositivo que cambia la energía cinética de las rotaciones en energía eléctrica (Cap. 2, pág. 72)

electric motor/motor eléctrico: motor que usa un electroimán para cambiar la energía eléctrica en energía mecánica (Cap. 2, pág. 70)

electrical charge/carga eléctrica: concentración de electricidad (Cap. 1, pág. 23)

electromagnet/electroimán: imán fabricado con alambre conductor de corriente (Cap. 2, pág. 62)

electromagnetic spectrum/espectro electromagnético: la gama total de ondas electromagnéticas, desde las frecuencias extremadamente bajas hasta las frecuencias extremadamente altas (Cap. 3, pág. 86)

electromagnetic wave/onda electromagnética: combinación de un campo eléctrico y uno magnético que se forma de la oscilación de una corriente eléctrica (Cap. 3, pág. 82)

electron/electrón: partícula mucho más pequeña que el átomo (Cap. 4, pág. 113)

enzyme/enzima: molécula proteica que controla el ritmo de los diferentes procesos que se llevan a cabo en el cuerpo (Cap. 11, pág. 356)

epoch/época: subdivisión de los períodos de la Era Cenozoica (Cap. 16, pág. 526)

era/era: subdivisión principal de la escala del tiempo geológico (Cap. 16, pág. 517)

evaporation/evaporación: proceso por el cual un líquido cambia al estado gaseoso (Cap. 7, pág. 219)

evolution/evolución: cambio en los rasgos hereditarios de una población de organismos a través de cierto período de tiempo (Cap. 17, pág. 544)

family of elements/familia de elementos: elementos en la misma columna de la Tabla Periódica (Cap. 5, pág. 156)

fission/fisión: rompimiento del núcleo de un átomo acompañado de liberación de energía (Cap. 18, pág. 580)

fossil/fósil: restos de un organismo que una vez fue un ser vivo (Cap. 16, pág. 505)

front/frente: límite que se forma cuando una masa de aire en movimiento choca contra otra masa de aire (Cap. 8, pág. 251)

fusion/fusión: la unión de núcleos separados (Cap. 18, pág. 585)

galaxy/galaxia: gran agrupación de estrellas, gas, y polvo que se mantienen unidos debido a la gravedad (Cap. 20, pág. 643)

gamma ray/rayo gama: forma de radiación electromagnética (Cap. 4, pág. 117)

gaseous giant planets/planetas gigantes gaseosos: planetas inmensos de baja densidad compuestos principalmente de gases (Cap. 19, pág. 609)

gene/gene: ubicación específica en un cromosoma que controla un rasgo determinado (Cap. 14, pág. 445)

hemoglobin/hemoglobina: pigmento rojo que contiene hierro, el cual se encuentra en los glóbulos rojos (Cap. 12, pág. 375)

heterozygote/heterocigoto: organismo con un gene dominante y un gene recesivo para un rasgo (Cap. 14, pág. 446)

homologous structure/estructura homóloga: partes del cuerpo de organismos diferentes que tienen un origen y una estructura similares (Cap. 17, pág. 552)

hot spots/puntos críticos: zonas más calientes del manto terrestre, en las cuales el magma es forzado hacia la superficie por material más denso que se encuentra a su alrededor, a través de resquebrajaduras en la litosfera sólida (Cap. 15, pág. 495)

hurricane/huracán: sistema de baja presión, inmenso y turbulento, que se forma sobre los océanos tropicales (Cap. 8, pág. 264)

hydrocarbon/hidrocarburo: compuesto que contiene solamente carbono e hidrógeno (Cap. 10, pág. 308)

immunity/inmunidad: protección contra los efectos dañinos de sustancias causantes de enfermedades (Cap. 12, pág. 385)

induced current/corriente inducida: corriente eléctrica que se produce al usar un imán (Cap. 2, pág. 72)

induced magnetism/magnetismo inducido: magnetismo que ocurre solamente en presencia de un campo magnético (Cap. 2, pág. 57)

insulator/aislador: material en el cual las cargas eléctricas no se mueven libremente de un lugar a otro (Cap. 1, pág. 27)

intertidal zone/zona entre mareas: área del litoral entre la marea alta y la marea baja (Cap. 9, pág. 281)

ion/ion: partícula cargada formada por un átomo o por varios átomos que han ganado o perdido uno o más electrones (Cap. 6, pág. 177)

ionic bond/enlace iónico: la atracción entre iones positivos y negativos (Cap. 6, pág. 178)

isomers/isómeros: compuestos que poseen fórmulas químicas idénticas pero diferentes formas o estructuras moleculares (Cap. 10, pág. 311)

isotopes/isótopos: átomos del mismo elemento, pero con números diferentes de neutrones (Cap. 5, pág. 150)

kinetic-molecular theory/teoría molecular cinética: teoría que define, en parte, la energía térmica como un movimiento al azar de los átomos o las moléculas (Cap. 7, pág. 210)

law of superposition/ley de superposición: ley que asevera que, en las capas rocosas, las capas más antiguas se encuentran en la parte inferior y las capas más nuevas se encuentran en la parte superior, si las capas no han sido perturbadas (Cap. 16, pág. 509)

light-year/año luz: la distancia que viaja la luz en un año (Cap. 20, pág. 636)

like charges/cargas iguales: cargas que se repelen entre sí (Cap. 1, pág. 23)

lipids/lípidos: compuestos orgánicos que se sienten grasosos al tacto y que no se disuelven en agua (Cap. 10, pág. 324)

lithosphere/litosfera: parte de la superficie terrestre formada por la corteza y la parte superior del manto terrestres (Cap. 15, pág. 484)

loudspeaker/altoparlante: dispositivo en el cual las variaciones de la corriente eléctrica se transforman en energía sonora (Cap. 2, pág. 67)

magnetic field/campo magnético: región alrededor de un imán donde actúa la fuerza magnética (Cap. 2, pág. 54)

magnetic poles/polos magnéticos: los dos extremos de un imán que apuntan en dirección norte o sur (Cap. 2, pág. 51)

mass number/número de masa: el número total de protones y de neutrones en el núcleo de un átomo (Cap. 5, pág. 149)

meiosis/meiosis: proceso que forma las células sexuales (Cap. 13, pág. 411)

menstrual cycle/ciclo menstrual: ciclo en que el ovario libera un óvulo y el útero se prepara para recibirlo y luego lo desecha al no ser fecundado (Cap. 13, pág. 427)

menstruation/menstruación: descarga mensual del óvulo, del revestimiento uterino y de sangre a través de la vagina (Cap. 13, pág. 427)

Mesozoic Era/Era Mesozoica: llamada la "era de los dinosaurios", comenzó después de terminar la Era Paleozoica (Cap. 16, pág. 524)

meteor/meteoro: meteoroide que entra en la atmósfera terrestre (Cap. 19, pág. 619)

meteorite/meteorito: meteoroide que choca contra la superficie terrestre (Cap. 19, pág. 619)

minerals/minerales: compuestos inorgánicos que controlan muchas de las reacciones químicas que se llevan a cabo en el cuerpo (Cap. 11, pág. 342)

molecule/molécula: partícula neutra que se forma como resultado de átomos que comparten electrones (Cap. 6, pág. 181)

mutation/mutación: cambio permanente en un gene o en un cromosoma (Cap. 17, pág. 545)

natural selection/selección natural: proceso en el cual los organismos vivos mejor adaptados a su ambiente tienen mayores posibilidades de sobrevivir y producir progenie (Cap. 17, pág. 540)

nebula/nebulosa: nube inmensa de gas y polvo de la cual se forma una estrella (Cap. 20, pág. 630)

nekton/necton: organismos marinos que incluyen todas las formas de peces y otros animales que pueden nadar (Cap. 9, pág. 292)

neutron/neutrón: partícula sin carga, cuya masa es casi igual a la de un protón y que se encuentra en el núcleo de un átomo (Cap. 4, pág. 127)

nonpolar molecule/molécula no polar: molécula que no posee cargas desequilibradas como las de una molécula polar (Cap. 6, pág. 184)

nucleus/núcleo: centro denso de un átomo, el cual tiene carga positiva (Cap. 4, pág. 123)

nutrients/nutrimientos: sustancias en los alimentos que proporcionan energía y materiales para el desarrollo, crecimiento y reparación de las células (Cap. 11, pág. 339)

organic compound/compuesto orgánico: sustancia que contiene carbono (Cap. 10, pág. 306)

ovary/ovario: órgano sexual femenino donde se producen los óvulos (Cap. 13, pág. 416)

oxidation number/número de oxidación: número de electrones que un átomo gana o pierde o comparte con otro átomo (Cap. 6, pág. 187)

Paleozoic Era/Era Paleozoica: la segunda división principal del tiempo geológico que comenzó hace unos 545 millones de años (Cap. 16, pág. 522)

pedigree/pedigrí: diagrama que muestra la historia de un rasgo de una generación a la próxima (Cap. 14, pág. 439)

period/período: repetición de un patrón (Cap. 5, pág. 162); subdivisión de una era (Cap. 16, pág. 522)

periodic table/tabla periódica: diagrama organizado de los elementos que muestra un patrón repetitivo de sus propiedades (Cap. 5, pág. 145)

peristalsis/peristalsis: proceso durante el cual los músculos lisos del esófago se contraen en ondas llevando alimento al estómago (Cap. 11, pág. 357)

pistil/pistilo: órgano reproductor femenino de las plantas (Cap. 13, pág. 419)

planet/planeta: cuerpo celeste que viaja alrededor de una estrella en una trayectoria fija llamada órbita (Cap. 19, pág. 598)

plankton/plancton: organismos marinos que se mueven a la deriva (Cap. 9, pág. 292)

plasma/plasma: parte líquida de la sangre que consiste mayormente en agua (Cap. 12, pág. 373)

plate tectonics/tectónica de placas: teoría que sugiere que la corteza y el manto superior terrestres están separados en secciones llamadas placas, las cuales se encuentran en movimiento (Cap. 15, pág. 484)

platelets/plaquetas: fragmentos celulares que detienen el flujo de sangre que sale de un vaso sanguíneo roto (Cap. 12, pág. 381)

polar molecule/molécula polar: molécula que resulta de un enlace polar y que posee un polo ligeramente positivo y uno ligeramente negativo (Cap. 6, pág. 184)

polyatomic ion/ion poliatómico: grupo de átomos enlazados covalentemente ya sea que tengan una carga positiva o una negativa (Cap. 6, pág. 189)

polymers/polímeros: moléculas enormes formadas por muchas moléculas orgánicas más pequeñas que se unen para formar nuevos enlaces (Cap. 10, pág. 321)

potential difference/diferencia de potencial: cambio en la energía total dividido entre la carga total; llamada también voltaje (Cap. 1, pág. 33)

Precambrian Time/Tiempo Precámbrico: la primera división principal del tiempo geológico, la cual representa cerca del 90% de la historia de la Tierra hasta nuestros días (Cap. 16, pág. 520)

primate/primate: grupo de mamíferos que comprende a los monos, simios y seres humanos, quienes comparten características similares (Cap. 17, pág. 556)

proteins/proteínas: polímeros que se forman por la unión de varios aminoácidos (Cap. 10, pág. 322)

proton/protón: partícula con carga positiva en el núcleo de un átomo (Cap. 4, pág. 124)

pure dominant/dominante puro: rasgo que se produce al heredar la progenie dos genes dominantes (Cap. 14, pág. 446)

pure recessive/recesivo puro: rasgo que se produce al heredar la progenie dos genes recesivos (Cap. 14, pág. 446)

radiation/radiación: transferencia de energía por medio de ondas electromagnéticas (Cap. 3, pág. 87)

radioactivity/radiactividad: liberación de partículas de alta energía por elementos radiactivos (Cap. 4, pág. 116)

recessive trait/rasgo recesivo: rasgo que parece desaparecer en la progenie (Cap. 14, pág. 444)

red blood cells/glóbulos rojos: células sanguíneas cuya función principal es transportar oxígeno desde los pulmones hasta todas las demás células del cuerpo (Cap. 12, pág. 375)

relative humidity/humedad relativa: medida de la cantidad de vapor de agua en el aire en un momento determinado, comparada con la cantidad de vapor de agua que puede sostener el aire a esa temperatura (Cap. 8, pág. 244)

resistance/resistencia: propiedad de los materiales que indica la cantidad de energía que se transforma en energía térmica y en luz a medida que una carga eléctrica recorre los materiales (Cap. 1, pág. 34)

salinity/salinidad: medida de la cantidad de sólidos, especialmente sales, disueltos en el agua oceánica (Cap. 9, pág. 283)

saturated/saturado: aire que contiene toda la humedad que le es posible a una temperatura determinada (Cap. 8, pág. 245)

sea-floor spreading/expansión del suelo oceánico: hipótesis de Harry Hess que dice que la materia derretida del manto terrestre es forzada hacia la superficie en las dorsales oceánicas, donde se enfría para formar el nuevo suelo oceánico (Cap. 15, pág. 478)

sex cells/células sexuales: células que se producen por medio de la meiosis y cuya función es la de producir progenie (Cap. 13, pág. 407)

sickle-cell anemia/anemia drepanocítica: tipo de anemia en que los glóbulos rojos están deformados; muchos de estos glóbulos rojos tienen forma de hoz (Cap. 14, pág. 452)

solar system/sistema solar: sistema formado por el Sol, los planetas y muchos otros cuerpos más pequeños que viajan alrededor del Sol (Cap. 19, pág. 598)

sperm/espermatozoide: célula sexual masculina (Cap. 13, pág. 407)

stamen/estambre: órgano reproductor masculino de las plantas (Cap. 13, pág. 419)

star/estrella: esfera de gas brillante y caliente que produce energía por medio de la fusión (Cap. 20, pág. 629)

sublimation/sublimación: proceso por el cual un sólido se transforma directamente en un gas sin pasar por el estado de líquido (Cap. 7, pág. 220)

sunspot/mancha solar: área oscura en la superficie solar que es más fría que otras áreas a su alrededor (Cap. 20, pág. 638)

supernova/supernova: estrella masiva que explota después de agotar los materiales en su núcleo (Cap. 20, pág. 631)

surface current/corriente de superficie: movimiento de agua que afecta solamente unos cuantos metros de la parte superior del agua de mar (Cap. 9, pág. 291)

terrestrial planets/planetas terrestres: planetas cuyo tamaño y composición son parecidos a los de la Tierra (Cap. 19, pág. 603)

testis/testículos: órganos sexuales masculinos donde se producen los espermatozoides (Cap. 13, pág. 416)

thermal expansion/expansión térmica: expansión que ocurre a medida que se calienta un sólido (Cap. 7, pág. 214)

tornado/tornado: tormenta violenta en forma de embudo cuyos vientos arremolinados se mueven sobre la tierra en una trayectoria estrecha (Cap. 8, pág. 262)

traits/rasgos: características específicas de cada organismo vivo (Cap. 14, pág. 438)

transform fault boundary/límite de falla transformante: límite que se forma cuando dos placas se deslizan en direcciones opuestas o en la misma dirección, pero a velocidades diferentes (Cap. 15. pág. 487)

transformer/transformador: dispositivo que puede aumentar o disminuir el voltaje (Cap. 2, pág. 73)

transmutation/transmutación: cambio de un átomo de un elemento a otro al emitir partículas o al desintegrarse (Cap. 18, pág. 570)

unconformity/discordancia: brecha en la historia geológica de un área, en la cual faltan las capas rocosas que se formaron en ese lugar (Cap. 16, pág. 510)

unlike charges/cargas desiguales: cargas que se atraen entre sí (Cap. 1, pág. 23)

upwelling/corrientes ascendentes: movimiento ascendente de las aguas frías profundas que reemplazan las de la superficie (Cap. 9, pág. 296)

vaccine/vacuna: introducción en el cuerpo de un antígeno muerto o debilitado, ya sea por medio de inoculación o por vía oral, lo cual proporciona inmunidad activa contra una enfermedad específica (Cap. 12, pág. 386)

variation/variación: demostración de un rasgo o de un comportamiento heredado que hace que un organismo sea diferente a otros de la misma especie (Cap. 17, pág. 536)

villi/microvellosidades: pequeñísimas proyecciones en forma de dedos que cubren los pliegues del intestino delgado (Cap. 11, pág. 360)

viscosity/viscosidad: resistencia que presenta un líquido a cambiar de forma (Cap. 7, pág. 217)

vitamins/vitaminas: sustancias orgánicas que se necesitan para mantener la buena salud (Cap. 11, pág. 347)

white blood cells/glóbulos blancos: células sanguíneas que combaten las bacterias, los virus y otras materias extrañas que tratan de invadir el cuerpo constantemente (Cap. 12, pág. 376)

INDEX

The Index for *Science Interactions* will help you locate major topics in the book quickly and easily. Each entry in the Index is followed by the numbers of the pages on which the entry is discussed. A page number given in **boldface type** indicates the page on which that entry is defined. A page number given in *italic type* indicates a page on which the entry is used in an illustration or photograph. The abbreviation *act.* indicates a page on which the entry is used in an activity.

Illustrations

Bill Boyer/John Edwards 482, 493, 499; Cende Courtney-Hill/Morgan-Cain & Associates 542, 544, 560, 562; David De Gasperis/John Edwards 296, 483, 489, 509; John Edwards 243, 269, 540, 625, 632, 638, 643; Chris/Forsey Morgan-Cain & Associates (br) xx, 470-471, 478, 486, 495, 502-503, 505, 515, 524-525, 526-527, 528; David Fischer/John Edwards 485, 506, 511; David Fischer/ Morgan-Cain & Associates 486, 487, 499, 501; Tom Gagliano (t) xiii, xvi, (t) xxii, (r) xxvi, 112, 113, 117, 120, 121, 123, 124, 125, 131, (bl, br) 139, 141, 149, 151, 211, 216, 219, 220, 226, 227, 230, 232, (c) 234, 569, 570, 571, 575, 580, 581, 583, 585, 593; Henry Hill/John Edwards 282-283, 599, 605, 617, 630, 633, 638; Network Graphics xxi, 205, 260, 341-342, 351, 352, 353, 357, 359, 360, 366, 367, 372, 374, 375, 376, 381, 382, 383, 393, 539, 552, 553; Felipe Passalacqua 423; Stephanie Pershing/John Edwards 548, 613; BIll Pitzer, National Geographic Society 102, 232, 299, 498, 621; Pond & Giles/Morgan-Cain & Associates 418-419, 433, Precision Graphics xv, xxv, (l) xxvi, 1, 23, 26, 28, 29, 31, 33, 34, 36-37, 41, (t) 45, 50, 52-53, 54, (tl, tr) 56, 58, (tl) 63, (lc) 64, (bl) 66, (rc) 67, (tr) 68, 70, 72, 73, 76, (tr, bl) 77, 82, (bl) 83, 84, 85, 86-87, 94, 98, 104, 116, 130, (tr) 139, 148, 154, 157, 161, 164, 165, 167, 171, 172, 173, 176, 178, 180, 181, 184, 186, 187, 188, 189, 192, 193, 194, 195, 204, 207, 210, 216, 228, 229, (bc) 234, (tr) 243, 244, 245, 246, 250, 251, 252, 253, 255, 265, 266, (tr, bl) 269, 272, 275, 278, 280, 281, (bl) 283, 285, 287, 289, 290, 291, 292, 293, 295, 299, (tl) 301, 303, 307, 308, 309, 311, 315, 316, 321, 323, 329, 333, 339, 340, 343, 344, 346, 350, 356, 362, 363, 369, 384, 400, 406, 420, 422, 424, 425, 426, 427, 428, 433, 439, 441, 442, 443, 445, 446, 447, 450, 453, 456, 459, 465, 467, 473, 474, 475, 476, 482, 485, 486, 487, 490, 491, 492, 498, 508, 509, 512, 518, 520-521, 525, 533, 550, 551, 554, 556, 577, 579, 582, 584, 586, 592, 595, 598, 601, 602, 605, 614, 616, 617, 618, 623, 626, 628, 630, 633, 635, 636, 639, 641, 645, 652, 654; Max Ranft/John Walters & Associates 298; Chris Sahlin/John Edwards 282, 301, 496, 626, 652; Bill Singleton/John Edwards 484, 510; Charlie Thomas/ John Edwards 529; Sarah Woodward/Morgan-Cain & Associates 477.

Photographs

Richard Hutchings x (t), xi (b), xv, xvi, 2, 4, 6 (l), 8, 9, 12, 13, 14, 15 (l, r), 16 (tl, br), 23 (t), 24, 24-25, 25, 49, 53, 57, 59, 60, 61, 65, 66, 67, 68, 69, 71, 91, 96, 97, 99 (t), 111, 115 (b), 128, 129, 131 (b), 132, 133, 134, 143 (b), 144-145, 152, 153, 155, 179 (b)182185, 192195, 197 (b), 197 (c), 197 (t)198199, 200, 209, 212, 213 (l), 215 (br), 216, 217, 218, 219 (t), 220 (t), 222, 224, 225 (tl, tr), 236, 241, 274, 286, 287 (c, l), 294, 295, 305, 306, 312, 314, 318, 319, 322 (r), 324 (t), 326, 327, (c, l), 337, 343, 356, 358, 371, 373 (b), 378, 379 (r), 383, 388, 390, 391, 403, 411, 420, 421 (tl, tr), 437, 440, 447, 448, 449 (tc, tl, tr), 454, 455, 472, 473, 479, 480, 481, 489, 503, 512, 513 (tl, tr), 535, 554, 567, 568, 572, 573, 586, 587; Jose L. Pelaez xiii (r), xvii (t), 20-21, 21 (bl), 32, 45 (t), 48, 138, 142 (t), 208 (t), 246, 247, 250 (cl), 252, 258, 259, 261 (r), 320, 338, 340, 348, 349, 353 (t), 354, 355 (c, l), 361, 469 (tr, br), 600, 609, 627, 634, 635, 641 (r), 647; Peter Vadnai x (b), xxi, 21 (t, br), 22 (r), 27, 29, 35, 37, 38, 39, 40, 45 (b), 50 (r), 51 (t), 52, 55 (t), 58, 62 (t), 77 (br), 81, 88, 93 (t), 95 (b), 118, 119, 122, 131 (c), 179 (t, c), 230 (l), 245, 254, 276, 277 (tl, tr), 284, 287 (r), 304 (tc), 304-305, 321 (r), 325 (tl), 328 (l), 333 (b), 333 (t), 336 (t), 345, 387 (bl), 405, 410, 414, 414-415, 415 (c), 415 (l), 415 (r), 424, 444 (bl), 444 (r), 444 (tl), 457, 460 (r), 504, 516 (t), 518-519, 519 (c), 519 (l), 519 (r), 523, 537, 546, 547 (tl),

547 (tr), 549 (br), 555 (tc, tl, tr), 556 (r); Cover (bkgd)Dennis Hallinan/FPG, (tl)Nigel Dennis/Photo Researchers, (tr)Richard Small/Photo-Op, (b)Hank Morgan/Photo Researchers; title page (tl)Nigel Dennis/Photo Researchers, (tr)Richard Small/Photo-Op, (b)HankMorgan/Photo Researchers; xii (l)Alfred Pasieka/Peter Arnold, Inc., (r)Lillian Gee/Picture It; xiii (l)Craig Aurness/Woodfin Camp & Assoc.; xiv (t)Bard Martin/The Image Bank, (b)Michael Groen/Picture It; xvii (b)Manfred Kage/Peter Arnold, Inc.; xviii (l)David Phillips/Photo Researchers, (r)David Overcash/Bruce Coleman Inc.; xix (t)Jon Feingersh/The Stock Market, (b)Tom Van Sant/The Stock Market; xx (t)David Sumner/The Stock Market, (b)John Cancalosi/Okapia/Photo Researchers; xxii NASA; xxiii Doug Martin; xxiv (tl)Kristian Hilsen/Tony Stone Images, (tr)Joe McDonald/Bruce ColemanInc., (b)John Visser/Bruce Coleman Inc.; xxv (l)Stanley Schoenberger/Grant Heilman, (r)Wayne Eastep/The Stock Market; xxvi (l)Comstock/Russ Kinne, (r)Rosemary Weller/Tony Stone Images; 1 (t)courtesy U.S. Space Camp, (b)American Science & Engineering, Inc.; 3 Jay Freis/The Image Bank; 5 (t)courtesy Thermo King, (b)Dale Olson, courtesy Thermo King; 6 (r)Bettmann Archive; 7 RMIP/Richard Haynes; 11 (l)Gary Williams/Gamma Liaison, (r)National Center for Atmospheric Research Boulder CO; 16 (tr)Marvin E. Newman/The Image Bank, (bl)Mitchell Funk/The Image Bank; 17 Tom MartinPhotography/The Stock Market; 18-19, National Geographic Journeys (National Geographic Society/Roger Ressmeyer-CORBIS; 20 Hans Reinhard/BruceColeman Inc.; 22 (l)Bettmann Archive; 30 E.R. Degginger/Bruce Coleman Inc.; 33 Doug Martin; 42 David Nunuk/First Light Toronto; 43 Stock Montage, Inc.; 44 courtesy Sieu Ngo; 47 Aaron Haupt; 48-49 courtesy Ontario Science Center; 50 (l)M. Claye Jacana/Photo Researchers; 51 (bl)Bettmann Archive, (br)Diane Padys/FPG; 55 (b)Pekka Parviainen/Science Photo Library/Photo Researchers; 56 Doug Martin; 62 (b)David R. Frazier/Photolibrary; 63 (t)Comstock/Russ Kinne, (b)Kenji Kerins; 64 (l)Manfred Kage/Peter Arnold, Inc., (r)Kodansha; 74 (t)George Diebold/The Stock Market, (b)RogerTully/Tony Stone Images; 75 courtesy the DuSable Museum of African American History; 77 (t)courtesy GE Corporate R & D, (bl)Ken Ferguson; 78 KenFrick; 79 Kodansha; 80 Russell Ingram/The Stock Market; 80-81 Jan Cobb/The Image Bank; 83 Lillian Gee/Picture It; 86 (t)Robert Kristofik/The ImageBank, (c)Romilly Lockyer/The Image Bank, (b)Miguel Martin/The Image Bank; 087 (t)G.K. & Vikki Hart/The Image Bank, (b)Alfred Pasieka/Peter Arnold, Inc.; 89 Leonard Lessin/Peter Arnold Inc.; 90 NASA/Peter Arnold, Inc.; 92 (l)Runk/Schoenberger from Grant Heilman; 93 (b)Manfred Kage/Peter Arnold, Inc.; 94 Peter Steiner/The Stock Market; 95 (tl)Dr. Jeremy Burgess/Science Photo Library/Photo Researchers, (tc)Comstock/Bob Pizaro, (tr)N.Smythe/Photo Researchers; 99 (b)Telegraph Colour Library/FPG; 100 John Lamb/Tony Stone Images; 101 (tl)Michael Groen/Picture It, (bl)MichaelGroen/Picture It, (r)Stanley Schoenberger from Grant Heilman; 102 (t)Patricia Ann Tesman/The Image Bank, (b)Comstock/Russ Kinne; 103 courtesyAmerican Science and Engineering Inc. 104 David Parker/Science Photo Library/Photo Researchers; 106 Leonard Lessin/Peter Arnold, Inc.; 107 RoyMorsch/The Stock Market; 108-109 National Geographic Journeys (National Geographic Journeys/John Barton, R.G. Marsh Studios; 110 British TechnicalFilms/Science Photo Library/Photo Researchers; 110-111 George Diebold/The Stock Market; 113 Skip Comer; 114 Steve Dunwell/The Image Bank; 115 (t)Science Photo Library/Photo Researchers; 123 Jock Pottle/Esto Photographs; 125 (t)William E. Ferguson, (c)Doug Martin, (b)Ohio State UniversityArchive; 126 (t)courtesy Prof. C.M.